The Life and Times of the Thunderbolt Kid

The Life and Times of the Thunderbolt Kid

Bill Bryson

Doubleday

LONDON · TORONTO · SYDNEY · AUCKLAND · JOHANNESBURG

TRANSWORLD PUBLISHERS
61–63 Uxbridge Road, London W5 5SA
a division of The Random House Group Ltd

RANDOM HOUSE AUSTRALIA (PTY) LTD
20 Alfred Street, Milsons Point, Sydney,
New South Wales 2061, Australia

RANDOM HOUSE NEW ZEALAND LTD
18 Poland Road, Glenfield, Auckland 10, New Zealand

RANDOM HOUSE SOUTH AFRICA (PTY) LTD
Isle of Houghton, Corner of Boundary Road & Carse O'Gowrie,
Houghton 2198, South Africa

Published 2006 by Doubleday
a division of Transworld Publishers

Copyright © Bill Bryson 2006

The right of Bill Bryson to be identified as the author of this work has been asserted in
accordance with sections 77 and 78 of the Copyright, Designs and Patents Act 1988.

A catalogue record for this book is available from the British Library.
ISBN 9780385608268 (from Jan 2007)
ISBN 0385608268

Set in 11/16.25pt Giovanni Book by
Falcon Oast Graphic Art Ltd.

Printed and bound in Great Britain by
Clays Ltd, Bungay, Suffolk

1 3 5 7 9 10 8 6 4 2

Mixed Sources

Product group from well-managed
forests and other controlled sources
www.fsc.org   Cert no. TT-COC-2139
© 1996 Forest Stewardship Council

FSC

Contents

Preface and Acknowledgements

My kid days were pretty good ones, on the whole. My parents were patient and kind and approximately normal. They didn't chain me in the cellar. They didn't call me 'It'. I was born a boy and allowed to stay that way. My mother, as you'll see, sent me to school once in Capri pants, but otherwise there was little trauma in my upbringing.

Growing up was easy. It required no thought or effort on my part. It was going to happen anyway. So what follows isn't terribly eventful, I'm afraid. And yet it was by a very large margin the most fearful, thrilling, interesting, instructive, eye-popping, lustful, eager, troubled, untroubled, confused, serene and unnerving time of my life. Coincidentally, it was all those things for America, too.

Everything recorded here is true and really happened, more or less, but nearly all the names and a few of the details have been changed in the hope of sparing embarrassment. A small part of the story originally appeared in somewhat different form in the *New Yorker*.

As ever, I have received generous help from many quarters, and I would like to thank here, sincerely and alphabetically, Deborah Adams, Aosaf Afzal, Matthew Angerer, Charles Elliott, Larry Finlay, Will Francis, Carol Heaton, Jay Horning, Patrick Janson-Smith, Tom and Nancy Jones, Sheila Lee, Fred Morris,

Steve Rubin, Marianne Velmans, Daniel Wiles, and the staff of the Drake University and Des Moines Public Libraries in Iowa and Durham University Library in England.

I remain especially grateful to Gerry Howard, my astute and ever thoughtful American publisher, for a stack of *Boys' Life* magazines, one of the best and most useful gifts I have had in years, and to Jack Peverill of Sarasota, Florida, for the provision of copious amounts of helpful material. And of course I remain perpetually grateful to my family, not least my dear wife, Cynthia, for more help than I could begin to list, to my brother Michael, and to my incomparably wonderful, infinitely sporting mother, Mary McGuire Bryson, without whom, it goes without saying, nothing that follows would have been possible.

Chapter 1

HOMETOWN

SPRINGFIELD, ILL. (AP) – The State Senate of Illinois yesterday disbanded its Committee on Efficiency and Economy 'for reasons of efficiency and economy'.

– *Des Moines Tribune*, 6 February 1955

I N THE LATE 1950S, the Royal Canadian Air Force produced a booklet on isometrics, a form of exercise that enjoyed a short but devoted vogue with my father. The idea of isometrics was that you used any unyielding object, like a tree or wall, and pressed against it with all your might from various positions to tone and strengthen different groups of muscles. Since everybody already has access to trees and walls, you didn't need to invest in a lot of costly equipment, which I expect was what attracted my dad.

What made it unfortunate in my father's case was that he would do his isometrics on aeroplanes. At some point in every flight, he would stroll back to the galley area or the space by the emergency exit and, taking up the posture of someone trying to budge a very heavy piece of machinery, he would begin to push with his back or shoulder against the outer wall of the plane, pausing occasionally to take deep breaths before returning with quiet, determined grunts to the task.

Since it looked uncannily, if unfathomably, as if he were trying to force a hole in the side of the plane, this naturally drew attention. Businessmen in nearby seats would stare over the tops of their glasses. A stewardess would pop her head out of the galley and likewise stare, but with a certain hard caution, as if remembering some aspect of her training that she had not previously been called upon to implement.

Seeing that he had observers, my father would straighten up,

3

smile genially and begin to outline the engaging principles behind isometrics. Then he would give a demonstration to an audience that swiftly consisted of no one. He seemed curiously incapable of feeling embarrassment in such situations, but that was all right because I felt enough for both of us – indeed, enough for us and all the other passengers, the airline and its employees, and the whole of whatever state we were flying over.

Two things made these undertakings tolerable. The first was that back on solid ground my dad wasn't half as foolish most of the time. The second was that the purpose of these trips was always to go to a big city like Detroit or St Louis, stay in a large hotel and attend ballgames, and that excused a great deal – well, everything, in fact. My dad was a sportswriter for the *Des Moines Register*, which in those days was one of the country's best papers, and often took me along on trips through the Midwest. Sometimes these were car trips to smaller places like Sioux City or Burlington, but at least once a summer we boarded a silvery plane – a huge event in those days – and lumbered through the summery skies, up among the fleecy clouds, to a proper metropolis to watch Major League baseball, the pinnacle of the sport.

Like everything else in those days, baseball was part of a simpler world, and I was allowed to go with him into the changing rooms and dugout and on to the field before games. I have had my hair tousled by Stan Musial. I have handed Willie Mays a ball that had skittered past him as he played catch. I have lent my binoculars to Harvey Kuenn (or possibly it was Billy Hoeft) so that he could scope some busty blonde in the upper deck. Once on a hot July afternoon I sat in a nearly airless clubhouse under the left field grandstand at Wrigley Field in Chicago beside Ernie

Banks, the Cubs' great shortstop, as he autographed boxes of new white baseballs (which are, incidentally, the most pleasurably aromatic things on earth, and worth spending time around anyway). Unbidden, I took it upon myself to sit beside him and pass him each new ball. This slowed the process considerably, but he gave a little smile each time and said thank you as if I had done him quite a favour. He was the nicest human being I have ever met. It was like being friends with God.

I can't imagine there has ever been a more gratifying time or place to be alive than America in the 1950s. No country had ever known such prosperity. When the war ended the United States had $26 billion worth of factories that hadn't existed before the war, $140 billion in savings and war bonds just waiting to be spent, no bomb damage and practically no competition. All that American companies had to do was stop making tanks and battleships and start making Buicks and Frigidaires – and boy did they. By 1951, when I came sliding down the chute, almost 90 per cent of American families had refrigerators, and nearly three quarters had washing machines, telephones, vacuum cleaners and gas or electric stoves – things that most of the rest of the world could still only fantasize about. Americans owned 80 per cent of the world's electrical goods, controlled two-thirds of the world's productive capacity, produced over 40 per cent of its electricity, 60 per cent of its oil and 66 per cent of its steel. The 5 per cent of people on Earth who were Americans had more wealth than the other 95 per cent combined.

I don't know of anything that better conveys the happy bounty of the age than a photograph (reproduced in this volume as the endpapers at the front and back of the book) that ran in *Life* magazine two weeks before my birth. It shows the Czekalinski family of Cleveland, Ohio – Steve, Stephanie and two sons, Stephen and Henry – surrounded by the two and a half tons of food that a typical blue-collar family ate in a year. Among the items they were shown with were 450 pounds of flour, 72 pounds of shortening, 56 pounds of butter, 31 chickens, 300 pounds of beef, 25 pounds of carp, 144 pounds of ham, 39 pounds of coffee, 690 pounds of potatoes, 698 quarts of milk, 131 dozen eggs, 180 loaves of bread, and 8½ gallons of ice cream, all purchased on a budget of $25 a week. (Mr Czekalinski made $1.96 an hour as a shipping clerk in a Du Pont factory.) In 1951, the average American ate 50 per cent more than the average European.

No wonder people were happy. Suddenly they were able to have things they had never dreamed of having, and they couldn't believe their luck. There was, too, a wonderful simplicity of desire. It was the last time that people would be thrilled to own a toaster or waffle iron. If you bought a major appliance, you invited the neighbours round to have a look at it. When I was about four my parents bought an Amana Stor-Mor refrigerator and for at least six months it was like an honoured guest in our kitchen. I'm sure they'd have drawn it up to the table at dinner if it hadn't been so heavy. When visitors dropped by unexpectedly, my father would say: 'Oh, Mary, is there any iced tea in the Amana?' Then to the guests he'd add significantly: 'There usually is. It's a Stor-Mor.'

'Oh, a Stor-Mor,' the male visitor would say and raise his eyebrows in the manner of someone who appreciates quality cooling. 'We thought about getting a Stor-Mor ourselves, but in the end we went for a Philco Shur-Kool. Alice loved the E-Z Glide vegetable drawer and you can get a full quart of ice cream in the freezer box. *That* was a big selling point for Wendell Junior, as you can imagine!'

They'd all have a good laugh at that and then sit around drinking iced tea and talking appliances for an hour or so. No human beings had ever been quite this happy before.

People looked forward to the future, too, in ways they never would again. Soon, according to every magazine, we were going to have underwater cities off every coast, space colonies inside giant spheres of glass, atomic trains and airliners, personal jetpacks, a gyrocopter in every driveway, cars that turned into boats or even submarines, moving sidewalks to whisk us effortlessly to schools and offices, dome-roofed automobiles that drove themselves along sleek superhighways allowing Mom, Dad and the two boys (Chip and Bud or Skip and Scooter) to play a board game or wave to a neighbour in a passing gyrocopter or just sit back and enjoy saying some of those delightful words that existed in the Fifties and are no longer heard: *mimeograph, rotisserie, stenographer, ice box, rutabaga, panty raid, bobby sox, sputnik, beatnik, canasta, Cinerama, Moose Lodge, pinochle, daddy-o.*

For those who couldn't wait for underwater cities and self-driving cars, thousands of smaller enrichments were available right now. If you were to avail yourself of all that was on offer from advertisers in a single issue of, let's say, *Popular Science* magazine from, let's say, December 1956, you could, among much else, teach yourself ventriloquism, learn to cut meat (by correspondence or in person at the National School of Meat Cutting in Toledo, Ohio), embark on a lucrative career sharpening skates door to door, arrange to sell fire extinguishers from home, end rupture troubles once and for all, build radios, repair

7

radios, perform on radio, talk on radio to people in different countries and possibly different planets, improve your personality, get a personality, acquire a manly physique, learn to dance, create personalized stationery for profit, or 'make $$$$' in your spare time at home building lawn figures and other novelty ornaments.

My brother, who was normally quite an intelligent human being, once invested in a booklet that promised to teach him how to throw his voice. He would say something unintelligible through rigid lips, then quickly step aside and say, 'That sounded like it came from over there, didn't it?' He also saw an ad in *Mechanics Illustrated* that invited him to enjoy colour television at home for 65 cents plus postage, placed an order and four weeks later received in the mail a multi-coloured sheet of transparent plastic that he was instructed to tape over the television screen and watch the image through.

Having spent the money, my brother refused to concede that it was a touch disappointing. When a human face moved into the pinkish part of the screen or a section of lawn briefly coincided with the green portion, he would leap up in triumph. 'Look! Look! *That's* what colour television's gonna look like,' he would say. 'This is all just experimental, you see.'

In fact, colour television didn't come to our neighbourhood until nearly the end of the decade, when Mr Kiessler on St John's Road bought an enormous RCA Victor Consolette, the flagship of the RCA fleet, for a lot of money. For at least two years his was the only known colour television in private ownership, which made it a fantastic novelty. On Saturday evenings the children of the neighbourhood would steal into his yard and stand in his flowerbeds to watch a programme called *My Living Doll* through the double window behind his sofa. I am pretty certain that Mr Kiessler didn't realize that two dozen children of various ages and sizes were silently watching the TV with him or he wouldn't have played with himself quite so enthusiastically every time Julie Newmar bounded on to the screen. I assumed it was some sort of isometrics.

Every year for nearly forty years, from 1945 until his retirement, my father went to the baseball World Series for the *Register*. It was, by an immeasurably wide margin, the high point of his working year. Not only did he get to live it up for two weeks on expenses in some of the nation's most cosmopolitan and exciting cities – and from Des Moines all cities are cosmopolitan and exciting – but he also got to witness many of the most memorable moments of baseball history: Al Gionfriddo's miraculous one-handed catch of a Joe DiMaggio line drive, Don Larsen's perfect game in 1956, Bill Mazeroski's series-winning home run of 1960. These will mean nothing to you, I know – they would mean nothing to most people these days – but they were moments of near ecstasy that were shared by a nation.

In those days, World Series games were played during the day, so you had to bunk off school or develop a convenient chest infection ('Jeez, Mom, the teacher said there's a lot of TB going around') if you wanted to see a game. Crowds would lingeringly gather wherever a radio was on or a TV played. Getting to watch or listen to any part of a World Series game, even half an inning at lunchtime, became a kind of illicit thrill. And if you did happen to be there when something monumental occurred, you would remember it for the rest of your life. My father had an uncanny knack for being present at such moments – never more so than in the seminal (and what an apt word that can sometimes be) season of 1951 when our story begins.

In the National League (one of two principal divisions in Major League baseball, the other being the American League) the Brooklyn Dodgers had been cruising towards an easy championship when, in mid-August, their crosstown rivals the New York Giants stirred to life and began a highly improbable comeback. Suddenly the Giants could do no wrong. They won thirty-seven of forty-four games down the home stretch, cutting away at the Dodgers' once-unassailable lead in what began to seem a fateful manner. By mid-September people talked of little else but whether the Dodgers could hold on. Many dropped dead from the heat and excitement. The two teams finished the season in a perfect dead heat, so a three-game playoff series was hastily arranged to determine who would face the American League champions in the World Series. The *Register*, like nearly all distant papers, didn't dispatch a reporter to these impromptu playoffs, but elected to rely on wire services for its coverage until the Series proper got under way.

The playoffs added three days to the nation's exquisite torment. The two teams split the first two games, so it came down to a third, deciding game. At last the Dodgers appeared to recover their former poise and invincibility. They took a comfortable 4–1 lead into the final inning, and needed just three outs to win. But the Giants struck back, scoring a run and putting two more runners on base when Bobby Thomson (born in Glasgow, you may be proud to know) stepped to the plate. What Thomson did that afternoon in the gathering dusk of autumn has been many times voted the greatest moment in baseball history.

'Dodger reliever Ralph Branca threw a pitch that made

history yesterday,' one of those present wrote. 'Unfortunately it made history for someone else. Bobby Thomson, the "Flying Scotsman," swatted Branca's second offering over the left field wall for a game-winning home run so momentous, so startling, that it was greeted with a moment's stunned silence.

'Then, when realization of the miracle came, the double-decked stands of the Polo Grounds rocked on their 40-year-old foundations. The Giants had won the pennant, completing one of the unlikeliest comebacks baseball has ever seen.'

The author of those words was my father – who was abruptly, unexpectedly, present for Thomson's moment of majesty. Goodness knows how he had talked the notoriously frugal management of the *Register* into sending him the one thousand one hundred and thirty-two miles from Des Moines to New York for the crucial deciding game – an act of rash expenditure radically out of keeping with decades of careful precedent – or how he had managed to secure credentials and a place in the press box at such a late hour.

But then he had to be there. It was part of his fate, too. I am not *exactly* suggesting that Bobby Thomson hit that home run because my father was there or that he wouldn't have hit it if my father had not been there. All I am saying is that my father was there and Bobby Thomson was there and the home run was hit and these things couldn't have been otherwise.

My father stayed on for the World Series, in which the Yankees beat the Giants fairly easily in six games – there was only so much excitement the world could muster, or take, in a single autumn, I guess – then returned to his usual quiet life in Des Moines. Just over a month later, on a cold, snowy day in early December, his wife went into Mercy Hospital and with very little

fuss gave birth to a baby boy: their third child, second son, first
superhero. They named him William, after his father. They would
call him Billy until he was old enough to ask them not to.

Apart from baseball's greatest home run and the birth of the
Thunderbolt Kid, 1951 was not a hugely eventful year in America.
Harry Truman was President, but would shortly make way for
Dwight D. Eisenhower. The war in Korea was in full swing and not
going well. Julius and Ethel Rosenberg had just been notoriously
convicted of spying for the Soviet Union, but would sit in prison
for two years more before being taken to the electric chair. In
Topeka, Kansas, a mild-mannered black man named Oliver
Brown sued the local school board for requiring his daughter to
travel twenty-one blocks to an all-black school when a perfectly
good white one was just seven blocks away. The case, immortal-
ized as *Brown v. the Board of Education*, would be one of the most
far-reaching in modern American history, but wouldn't become
known outside jurisprudence circles for another three years when
it reached the Supreme Court.

America in 1951 had a population of one hundred and fifty
million, slightly more than half as much as today, and only about
a quarter as many cars. Men wore hats and ties almost everywhere
they went. Women prepared every meal more or less from scratch.
Milk came in bottles. The postman came on foot. Total government spending was $50 billion a year, compared with $2,500
billion now.

I Love Lucy made its television debut on 15 October, and Roy
Rogers, the singing cowboy, followed in December. In Oak Ridge,
Tennessee, that autumn police seized a youth on suspicion of
possessing narcotics when he was found with some peculiar

brown powder, but he was released when it was shown that it was a new product called instant coffee. Also new, or not quite yet invented, were ball-point pens, fast foods, TV dinners, electric can openers, shopping malls, freeways, supermarkets, suburban sprawl, domestic air conditioning, power steering, automatic transmissions, contact lenses, credit cards, tape recorders, garbage disposals, dishwashers, long-playing records, portable record players, Major League baseball teams west of St Louis, and the hydrogen bomb. Microwave ovens were available, but weighed seven hundred pounds. Jet travel, Velcro, transistor radios and computers smaller than a small building were all still some years off.

Nuclear war was much on people's minds. In New York on Wednesday 5 December, the streets became eerily empty for seven minutes as the city underwent 'the biggest air raid drill of the atomic age', according to *Life* magazine, when a thousand sirens blared and people scrambled (well, actually walked jovially, pausing upon request to pose for photographs) to designated shelters, which meant essentially the inside of any reasonably solid building. *Life*'s photos showed Santa Claus happily leading a group of children out of Macy's, half-lathered men and their barbers trooping out of barber shops, and curvy models from a swimwear shoot shivering and feigning good-natured dismay as they emerged from their studio, secure in the knowledge that a picture in *Life* would do their careers no harm at all. Only restaurant patrons were excused from taking part in the exercise on the grounds that New Yorkers sent from a restaurant without paying were unlikely to be seen again.

Closer to home, in the biggest raid of its type ever undertaken in Des Moines, police arrested nine women for prostitution

13

at the old Cargill Hotel at Seventh and Grand downtown. It was quite an operation. Eighty officers stormed the building just after midnight, but the hotel's resident ladies were nowhere to be found. Only by taking exacting measurements were the police able to discover, after six hours of searching, a cavity behind an upstairs wall. There they found nine goose-pimpled, mostly naked women. All were arrested for prostitution and fined $1,000 each. I can't help wondering if the police would have persevered quite so diligently if it had been naked men they were looking for.

The eighth of December 1951 marked the tenth anniversary of America's entry into the Second World War, and the tenth anniversary plus one day of the Japanese attack on Pearl Harbor. In central Iowa, it was a cold day with light snow and a high temperature of 28°F/–2°C but with the swollen clouds of a blizzard approaching from the west. Des Moines, a city of two hundred thousand people, gained ten new citizens that day – seven boys and three girls – and lost just two to death.

Christmas was in the air. Prosperity was evident everywhere in Christmas ads that year. Cartons of cigarettes bearing sprigs of holly and other seasonal decorations were very popular, as were electrical items of every type. Gadgets were much in vogue. My father bought my mother a hand-operated ice crusher, for creating shaved ice for cocktails, which converted perfectly good ice cubes into a small amount of cool water after twenty minutes of vigorous cranking. It was never used beyond New Year's Eve 1951, but it did grace a corner of the kitchen counter until well into the 1970s.

Tucked among the smiling ads and happy features were hints of deeper anxieties, however. *Reader's Digest* that autumn was asking 'Who Owns Your Child's Mind?' (Teachers with Communist sympathies apparently.) Polio was so rife that even *House Beautiful* ran an article on how to reduce risks for one's children. Among its tips (nearly all ineffective) were to keep all food covered, avoid sitting in cold water or wet bathing suits, get plenty of rest and, above all, be wary of 'admitting new people to the family circle'.

Harper's magazine in December struck a sombre economic note with an article by Nancy B. Mavity on an unsettling new phenomenon, the two-income family, in which husband and wife both went out to work to pay for a more ambitious lifestyle. Mavity's worry was not how women would cope with the demands of employment on top of child-rearing and housework, but rather what this would do to the man's traditional standing as breadwinner. 'I'd be ashamed to let my wife work,' one man told Mavity tartly, and it was clear from her tone that Mavity expected most readers to agree. Remarkably, until the war many women in America had been unable to work whether they wanted to or not. Up until Pearl Harbor, half of the forty-eight states had laws making it illegal to employ a married woman.

In this respect my father was commendably – I would even say enthusiastically – liberal, for there was nothing about my mother's earning capacity that didn't gladden his heart. She, too, worked for the *Des Moines Register*, as the Home Furnishings Editor, in which capacity she provided calm reassurance to two generations of homemakers who were anxious to know whether the time had come for paisley in the bedroom, whether they should have square sofa cushions or round, even whether their house itself passed muster. 'The one-story ranch house is here to stay,' she assured her readers, to presumed cries of relief in the western suburbs, in her last piece before disappearing to have me.

Because they both worked we were better off than most people of our socio-economic background (which in Des Moines in the 1950s was most people). We – that is to say, my parents, my brother Michael, my sister Mary Elizabeth (or Betty) and I – had a bigger house on a larger lot than most of my parents' colleagues. It was a white clapboard house with black shutters and a big screened porch atop a shady hill on the best side of town.

My sister and brother were considerably older than I – my sister by six years, my brother by nine – and so were effectively adults from my perspective. They were big enough to be seldom around for most of my childhood. For the first few years of my life, I shared a small bedroom with my brother. We got along fine. My brother had constant colds and allergies, and owned at least four hundred cotton handkerchiefs, which he devotedly filled with great honks and then pushed into any convenient resting place – under the mattress, between sofa cushions, behind the curtains. When I was nine he left for college and a life as a journalist in New York City, never to return permanently, and I had the room to myself after that. But I was still finding his handkerchiefs when I was in high school.

The only downside of my mother's working was that it put a little pressure on her with regard to running the home and particularly with regard to dinner, which frankly was not her strong suit anyway. My mother always ran late and was danger-ously forgetful into the bargain. You soon learned to stand aside about ten to six every evening, for it was then that she would fly in the back door, throw something in the oven, and disappear into some other quarter of the house to embark on the thousand other household tasks that greeted her each evening. In consequence she nearly always forgot about dinner until a point slightly beyond way too late. As a rule you knew it was time to eat when you could hear potatoes exploding in the oven.

We didn't call it the kitchen in our house. We called it the Burns Unit.

'It's a bit burned,' my mother would say apologetically at every meal, presenting you with a piece of meat that looked like something – a much-loved pet perhaps – salvaged from a tragic house fire. 'But I think I scraped off most of the burned part,' she would add, overlooking that this included every bit of it that had once been flesh.

Happily, all this suited my father. His palate only responded to two tastes – burned and ice cream – so everything was fine by him so long as it was sufficiently dark and not too startlingly flavourful. Theirs truly was a marriage made in heaven, for no one could burn food like my mother or eat it like my dad.

As part of her job, my mother bought stacks of housekeeping magazines – *House Beautiful, House and Garden, Better Homes and Gardens, Good Housekeeping* – and I read these with a certain avidity, partly because they were always lying around and in our house all idle moments were spent reading something, and partly because they depicted lives so absorbingly at variance with our own. The housewives in my mother's magazines were so collected, so organized, so calmly on top of things, and their food was perfect – their *lives* were perfect. They dressed up to take their food out of the oven! There were no black circles on the ceiling above their stoves, no mutating goo climbing over the sides of their forgotten saucepans. Children didn't have to be ordered to stand back every time they opened *their* oven doors. And their foods – baked Alaska, lobster Newburg, chicken cacciatore – why, these were dishes we didn't even dream of, much less encounter, in Iowa.

Like most people in Iowa in the 1950s, we were more cautious eaters in our house.* On the rare occasions when we were presented with food with which we were not comfortable or familiar – on planes or trains or when invited to a meal cooked by someone who was not herself from Iowa – we tended to tilt it up carefully with a knife and examine it from every angle as if determining whether it might need to be defused. Once on a trip to San Francisco my father was taken by friends to a Chinese restaurant and he described it to us afterwards in the sombre tones of someone recounting a near-death experience.

'And they eat it with sticks, you know,' he added knowledgeably.

'Goodness!' said my mother.

'I would rather have gas gangrene than go through that again,' my father added grimly.

In our house we didn't eat:

- pasta, rice, cream cheese, sour cream, garlic, mayonnaise, onions, corned beef, pastrami, salami or foreign food of any type, except French toast;
- bread that wasn't white and at least 65 per cent air;
- spices other than salt, pepper and maple syrup;

---

*In fact like most other people in America. The leading food writer of the age, Duncan Hines, author of the hugely successful *Adventures in Eating*, was himself a cautious eater and declared with pride that he never ate food with French names if he could possibly help it. Hines's other proud boast was that he did not venture out of America until he was seventy years old, when he made a trip to Europe. He disliked much of what he found there, especially the food.

- fish that was any shape other than rectangular and not coated in bright orange breadcrumbs, and then only on Fridays and only when my mother remembered it was Friday, which in fact was not often;
- soups not blessed by Campbell's and only a very few of those;
- anything with dubious regional names like 'pone' or 'gumbo' or foods that had at any time been an esteemed staple of slaves or peasants.

All other foods of all types – curries, enchiladas, tofu, bagels, sushi, couscous, yogurt, kale, rocket, Parma ham, any cheese that was not a vivid bright yellow and shiny enough to see your reflection in – had either not yet been invented or were still unknown to us. We really were radiantly unsophisticated. I remember being surprised to learn at quite an advanced age that a shrimp cocktail was not, as I had always imagined, a pre-dinner alcoholic drink with a shrimp in it.

All our meals consisted of leftovers. My mother had a seem-ingly inexhaustible supply of foods that had already been to the table, sometimes repeatedly. Apart from a few perishable dairy products, everything in the fridge was older than I was, sometimes by many years. (Her oldest food possession of all, it more or less goes without saying, was a fruit cake that was kept in a metal tin and dated from the colonial period.) I can only assume that my mother did all her cooking in the 1940s so that she could spend the rest of her life surprising herself with what she could find under cover at the back of the fridge. I never knew her to reject a food. The rule of thumb seemed to be that if you opened the lid and the stuff inside didn't make you actually recoil and take at least one staggered step backwards, it was deemed OK to eat.

Both my parents had grown up in the Great Depression and neither of them ever threw anything away if they could possibly avoid it. My mother routinely washed and dried paper plates, and smoothed out for reuse spare aluminium foil. If you left a pea on your plate, it became part of a future meal. All our sugar came in little packets spirited out of restaurants in deep coat pockets, as did our jams, jellies, crackers (oyster *and* saltine), tartare sauces, some of our ketchup and butter, all of our napkins, and a very occasional ashtray; anything that came with a restaurant table really. One of the happiest moments in my parents' life was when maple syrup started to be served in small disposable packets and they could add those to the household hoard.

Under the sink, my mother kept an enormous collection of jars, including one known as the toity jar. 'Toity' in our house was the term for a pee, and throughout my early years the toity jar was called into service whenever a need to leave the house inconveniently coincided with a sudden need by someone – and when I say 'someone', I mean of course the youngest child: me – to pee.

'Oh, you'll have to go in the toity jar then,' my mother would say with just a hint of exasperation and a worried glance at the kitchen clock. It took me a long time to realize that the toity jar was not always – or even often – the same jar twice. In so far as I thought about it at all, I suppose I guessed that the toity jar was routinely discarded and replaced with a fresh jar – we had hundreds after all.

So you may imagine my consternation, succeeded by varying degrees of dismay, when I went to the fridge one evening for a second helping of halved peaches and realized that we were all eating from a jar that had, only days before, held my urine. I recognized the jar at once because it had a Z-shaped strip of label adhering to it that uncannily recalled the mark of Zorro – a fact that I had cheerfully remarked upon as I had filled the jar with my precious bodily nectars, not that anyone had listened of course. Now here it was holding our dessert peaches. I couldn't have been more surprised if I had just been handed a packet of photos showing my mother *in flagrante* with, let's say, the guys at the gas station.

'Mom,' I said, coming to the dining-room doorway and holding up my find, 'this is the *toity* jar.'

'No, honey,' she replied smoothly without looking up. 'The toity jar's a *special* jar.'

'What's the toity jar?' asked my father with an amused air, spooning peach into his mouth.

'It's the jar I toity in,' I explained. 'And this is it.'

'Billy toities in a jar?' said my father, with very slight difficulty, as he was no longer eating the peach half he had just taken in, but resting it on his tongue pending receipt of further information concerning its recent history.

'Just occasionally,' my mother said.

My father's mystification was now nearly total, but his mouth was so full of unswallowed peach juice that he could not meaningfully speak. He asked, I believe, why I didn't just go upstairs to the bathroom like a normal person. It was a fair question in the circumstances.

'Well, sometimes we're in a hurry,' my mother went on, a touch uncomfortably. 'So I keep a jar under the sink – a special jar.'

21

I reappeared from the fridge, cradling more jars – as many as I could carry. 'I'm pretty sure I've used all these too,' I announced.

'That can't be right,' my mother said, but there was a kind of question mark hanging off the edge of it. Then she added, perhaps a touch self-destructively: 'Anyway, I always rinse all jars thoroughly before reuse.'

My father rose and walked to the kitchen, inclined over the waste bin and allowed the peach half to fall into it, along with about half a litre of goo. 'Perhaps a toity jar's not such a good idea,' he suggested.

So that was the end of the toity jar, though it all worked out for the best, as these things so often do. After that, all my mother had to do was mention that she had something good in a jar in the fridge and my father would get a sudden urge to take us to Bishop's, a cafeteria downtown, which was the best possible out-come, for Bishop's was the finest restaurant that ever existed.

Everything about it was divine – the food, the understated decor, the motherly waitresses in their grey uniforms who carried your tray to a table for you and gladly fetched you a new fork if you didn't like the look of the one provided. Each table had a little light on it that you could switch on if you needed service, so you never had to crane round and flag down passing waitresses. You just switched on your private beacon and after a moment a waitress would come along to see what she could help you with. Isn't that a wonderful idea?

The restrooms at Bishop's had the world's only atomic toilets – at least the only ones I have ever encountered. When you flushed, the seat automatically lifted and retreated into a seat-shaped recess in the wall, where it was bathed in a purple light that thrummed in a warm, hygienic, scientifically advanced fashion, then gently came down again impeccably sanitized, nicely warmed and practically pulsing with atomic thermo-luminescence. Goodness knows how many Iowans died from unexplained cases of buttock cancer throughout the 1950s and '60s, but it was worth every shrivelled cheek. We used to take visitors from out of town to the restrooms at Bishop's to show them the atomic toilets and they all agreed that they were the best they had ever seen.

But then most things in Des Moines in the 1950s were the best of their type. We had the smoothest, most mouth-pleasing banana cream pie at the Toddle House and I'm told the same could be said of the cheesecake at Johnny and Kay's, though my father was much too ill-at-ease with quality, and far too careful with his money, ever to take us to that outpost of fine dining on Fleur Drive. We had the most vividly delicious neon-coloured ice creams at Reed's, a parlour of cool opulence near Ashworth Swimming Pool (itself the handsomest, most elegant public swimming pool in the world, with the slimmest, tannest female lifeguards) in Greenwood Park (best tennis courts, most decorous lagoon, comeliest drives). Driving home from Ashworth Pool through Greenwood Park, under a flying canopy of green leaves, nicely basted in chlorine and knowing that you would shortly be plunging your face into three gooey scoops of Reed's ice cream is the finest feeling of well-being a person can have.

We had the tastiest baked goods at Barbara's Bake Shoppe, the meatiest, most face-smearing ribs and crispiest fried chicken at a restaurant called the Country Gentleman, the best junk food at a drive-in called George the Chilli King. (And the best farts afterwards; a George's chilli burger was gone in minutes, but the farts, it was said, went on for ever.) We had our own department stores, restaurants, clothing stores, supermarkets, drug stores, florist's, hardware stores, movie theatres, hamburger joints, you name it – every one of them the best of its kind.

Well, actually, who could say if they were the best of their kind? To know that, you'd have had to visit thousands of other towns and cities across the nation and taste all their ice cream and chocolate pie and so on because every place was different then. That was the glory of living in a world that was still largely free of global chains. Every community was special and nowhere was like everywhere else. If our commercial enterprises in Des Moines weren't the best, they were at least ours. At the very least, they all had things about them that made them interesting and different. (And they were the best.)

Dahl's, our neighbourhood supermarket, had a feature of inspired brilliance called the Kiddie Corral. This was a snug enclosure, built in the style of a cowboy corral and filled with comic books, where moms could park their kids while they shopped. Comics were produced in massive numbers in America in the 1950s – one billion of them in 1953 alone – and most of them ended up in the Kiddie Corral. It was *filled* with comic books. To enter the Kiddie Corral you climbed on to the top rail and dove in, then swam to the centre. You didn't care how long your mom took shopping because you had an infinite supply of comics to occupy you. I believe there were kids who lived in the Kiddie Corral. Sometimes when searching for the latest issue of *Rubber Man*, you would find a child buried under a foot or so of comics fast asleep or perhaps just enjoying their lovely papery smell. No institution has ever done a more thoughtful thing for children. Whoever dreamed up the Kiddie Corral is unquestionably in heaven now; he should have won a Nobel prize.

Dahl's had one other feature that was much admired. When your groceries were bagged (or 'sacked' in Iowa) and paid for, you didn't take them to your car with you, as in more mundane supermarkets, but rather you turned them over to a friendly man in a white apron who gave you a plastic card with a number on it and placed the groceries on a special sloping conveyor belt that carried them into the bowels of the earth and through a flap into a mysterious dark tunnel. You then collected your car and drove to a small brick building at the edge of the parking lot, a hundred or so feet away, where your groceries, nicely shaken and looking positively refreshed from their subterranean adventure, reappeared a minute or two later and were placed in your car by another helpful man in a white apron who took back the plastic card and wished you a happy day. It wasn't a particularly efficient system – there was often a line of cars at the little brick building if truth be told, and the juddering tunnel ride didn't really do anything except dangerously overexcite all carbonated beverages for at least two hours afterwards – but everyone loved and admired it anyway.

It was like that wherever you went in Des Moines in those days. Every commercial enterprise had something distinctive to commend it. The New Utica department store downtown had pneumatic tubes rising from each cash register. The cash from your purchase was placed in a cylinder, then inserted in the tubes and noisily fired – like a torpedo – to a central collection point, such was the urgency to get the money counted and back into the economy. A visit to the New Utica was like a trip to a future century.

Frankel's, a men's clothing store on Locust Street downtown, had a rather grand staircase leading up to a mezzanine level. A stroll around the mezzanine was a peculiarly satisfying experience, like a stroll around the deck of a ship, but more interesting because instead of looking down on empty water, you were taking in an active world of men's retailing. You could listen in on conversations and see the tops of people's heads. It had all the satisfactions of spying without any of the risks. If your dad was taking a long time being fitted for a jacket, or was busy demonstrating isometrics to the sales force, it didn't matter.

'Not a problem,' you'd call down generously from your lofty position. 'I'll do another circuit.'

Even better in terms of elevated pleasures was the Shops Building on Walnut Street. A lovely old office building some seven or eight storeys high and built in a faintly Moorish style, it housed a popular coffee shop in its lobby on the ground floor, above which rose, all the way to a distant ceiling, a central atrium, around which ran the building's staircase and galleried hallways. It was the dream of every young boy to get up that staircase to the top floor.

Attaining the staircase required cunning and a timely dash because you had to get past the coffee-shop manageress, a vicious, eagle-eyed stick of a woman named Mrs Musgrove who hated little boys (and for good reason, as we shall see). But if you selected the right moment when her attention was diverted, you could sprint to the stairs and on up to the dark eerie heights of the top floor, where you had a kind of gun-barrel view of the diners far below. If, further, you had some kind of hard candy with you – peanut M&Ms were especially favoured because of their smooth aerodynamic shape – you had a clear drop of seven or eight storeys. A peanut M&M that falls seventy feet into a bowl of tomato soup makes one *heck* of a splash, I can tell you.

You never got more than one shot because if the bomb missed the target and hit the table – as it nearly always did – it would explode spectacularly in a thousand candy-coated shards, wonderfully startling to the diners, but a call to arms to Mrs Musgrove, who would come flying up the stairs at about the speed that the M&M had gone down, giving you less than five seconds to scramble out a window and on to a fire escape and away to freedom.

Des Moines's greatest commercial institution was Younker Brothers, the principal department store downtown. Younkers was enormous. It occupied two buildings, separated at ground level by a public alley, making it the only department store I've ever known, possibly the only one in existence, where you could be run over while going from menswear to cosmetics. Younkers had an additional outpost across the street, known as the Store for Homes, which housed its furniture departments and which could be reached by means of an underground passageway beneath Eighth Street, via the white goods department. I've no idea why, but it was immensely satisfying to enter Younkers from the east side of Eighth and emerge a short while later, shopping completed, on the western side. People from out in the state used to come in specially to walk the passageway and to come out across the street and say, 'Hey. Whoa. Golly.'

Younkers was the most elegant, up to the minute, briskly efficient, satisfyingly urbane place in Iowa. It employed twelve hundred people. It had the state's first escalators – 'electric stairways' they were called in the early days – and first air conditioning. Everything about it – its silkily swift revolving

27

doors, its gliding stairs, its whispering elevators, each with its own white-gloved operator – seemed designed to pull you in and keep you happily, contentedly consuming. Younkers was so vast and wonderfully rambling that you seldom met anyone who really knew it all. The book department inhabited a shadowy, secretive balcony area, reached by a pokey set of stairs, that made it cosy and club-like – a place known only to aficionados. It was an outstanding book department, but you can meet people who grew up in Des Moines in the 1950s who had no idea that Younkers *had* a book department.

But its *sanctum sanctorum* was the Tea Room, a place where doting mothers took their daughters for a touch of elegance while shopping. Nothing about the Tea Room remotely interested me until I learned of a ritual that my sister mentioned in passing. It appeared that young visitors were invited to reach into a wooden box containing small gifts, each beautifully wrapped in white tissue and tied with ribbon, and select one to take away as a permanent memento of the occasion. Once my sister passed on to me a present she had acquired and didn't much care for – a die-cast coach and horses. It was only two and a half inches long, but exquisite in its detailing. The doors opened. The wheels turned. A tiny driver held thin metal reins. The whole thing had obviously been hand-painted by some devoted, underpaid person from the defeated side of the Pacific Ocean. I had never seen, much less owned, such a fine thing before.

From time to time after that for years I besought them to take me with them when they went to the Tea Room, but they always responded vaguely that they didn't like the Tea Room so much any more or that they had too much shopping to do to stop for lunch. (Only years later did I discover that in fact they went every week; it was one of those secret womanly things moms and daughters did together, like having periods and being fitted for bras.) But finally there came a day when I was perhaps eight or nine that I was shopping downtown with my mom, with my sister not there, and my mother said to me, 'Shall we go to the Tea Room?'

I don't believe I have ever been so eager to accept an invitation. We ascended in an elevator to a floor I didn't even know Younkers had. The Tea Room was the most elegant place I had ever been – like a state room from Buckingham Palace magically transported to the Middle West of America. Everything about it was starched and classy and calm. There was light music of a refined nature and the tink of cutlery on china and of ice water carefully poured. I cared nothing for the food, of course. I was waiting only for the moment when I was invited to step up to the toy box and make a selection.

When that moment came, it took me for ever to decide. Every little package looked so perfect and white, so ready to be enjoyed. Eventually, I chose an item of middling size and weight, which I dared to shake lightly. Something inside rattled and sounded as if it might be die cast. I took it to my seat and carefully unwrapped it. It was a miniature doll – an Indian baby in a papoose, beautifully made but patently for a girl. I returned with it and its disturbed packaging to the slightly backward-looking fellow who was in charge of the toy box.

'I seem to have got a *doll*,' I said, with something approaching an ironic chuckle.

He looked at it carefully. 'That's surely a shame because you only git one try at the gift box.'

'Yes, but it's a *doll*,' I said. 'For a girl.'

'Then you'll just have to git you a little girl friend to give it to, won'tcha?' he answered and gave me a toothy grin and an unfortunate wink.

Sadly, those were the last words the poor man ever spoke. A moment later he was just a small muffled shriek and a smouldering spot on the carpet.

Too late he had learned an important lesson. You really should never fuck with the Thunderbolt Kid.

Chapter 2
WELCOME TO KID WORLD

DETROIT, MICH. (AP) – Great news for boys! A prominent doctor has defended a boy's right to be dirty. Dr. Harvey Flack, director of the magazine *Family Doctor*, said in the September issue: 'Boys seem to know instinctively a profound dermatological truth – that an important element of skin health is the skin's own protective layer of grease. This should not be disturbed too frequently by washing.'

– *Des Moines Register*, 28 August 1958

S O THIS IS A BOOK about not very much: about being small and getting larger slowly. One of the great myths of life is that childhood passes quickly. In fact, because time moves more slowly in Kid World – five times more slowly in a classroom on a hot afternoon, eight times more slowly on any car journey of over five miles (rising to eighty-six times more slowly when driving across Nebraska or Pennsylvania lengthwise), and so slowly during the last week before birthdays, Christmases and summer vacations as to be functionally immeasurable – it goes on for decades when measured in adult terms. It is adult life that is over in a twinkling.

The slowest place of all in my corner of the youthful firmament was the large cracked leather dental chair of Dr D. K. Brewster, our spooky, cadaverous dentist, while waiting for him to assemble his instruments and get down to business. There time didn't move forward at all. It just hung.

Dr Brewster was the most unnerving dentist in America. He was, for one thing, about a hundred and eight years old and had more than a hint of Parkinsonism in his wobbly hands. Nothing about him inspired confidence. He was perennially surprised by the power of his own equipment. 'Whoa!' he'd say as he briefly enlivened some screaming device or other. 'You could do some damage with *that*, I bet!'

Worse still, he didn't believe in novocaine. He thought it

dangerous and unproven. When Dr Brewster, humming mind-lessly, drilled through rocky molar and found the pulpy mass of tender nerve within, it could make your toes burst out the front of your shoes.

We appeared to be his only patients. I used to wonder why my father put us through this seasonal nightmare, and then I heard Dr Brewster congratulating him one day on his courageous frugality and I understood at once, for my father was the twentieth century's cheapest man. 'There's no point in putting yourself to the danger and expense of novocaine for anything less than the whole or partial removal of a jaw,' Dr Brewster was saying.

'Absolutely,' my father agreed. Actually he said something more like 'Abmmffffmmfff,' as he had just stepped from Dr Brewster's chair and wouldn't be able to speak intelligibly for at least three days, but he nodded with feeling.

'I wish more people felt like you, Mr Bryson,' Dr Brewster added. 'That will be three dollars, please.'

Saturdays and Sundays were the longest days in Kid World. Sunday mornings alone could last for up to three months depending on season. In central Iowa for much of the 1950s there was no television at all on Sunday mornings, so generally you just sat with a bowl of soggy Cheerios watching a test pattern until WOI-TV sputtered to life some time between about 11.25 and noon – they were fairly relaxed about Sunday starts at WOI – with an episode of *Sky King*, starring the neatly kerchiefed Kirby Grant, 'America's favorite flying cowboy' (also its only flying cowboy; also the only one with reversible names). Sky was a rancher by trade, but spent most of his time cruising the Arizona skies in his beloved Cessna, *The Songbird*, spotting cattle rustlers and other earth-bound miscreants. He was assisted in these endeavours by his dimple-cheeked, pertly buttocked niece Penny, who provided many of us with our first tingly inkling that we were indeed on the road to robust heterosexuality.

Even at six years old, and even in an age as intellectually un-demanding as the 1950s, you didn't have to be hugely astute to see that a flying cowboy was a fairly flimsy premise for an action series. Sky could only capture villains who lingered at the edge of grassy landing strips and to whom it didn't occur to run for it until Sky had landed, taxied to a safe halt, climbed down from the cockpit, assumed an authoritative stance and shouted: 'OK, boys, freeze!' – a process that took a minute or two, for Kirby Grant was not, it must be said, in the first flush of youth. In consequence, the series was cancelled after just a year, so only about twenty episodes were made, all practically identical anyway. These WOI tirelessly (and, one presumes, economically) repeated for the first dozen years of my life and probably a good deal beyond. Almost the only thing that could be said in their favour was that they were more diverting than a test pattern.

The illimitable nature of weekends was both a good and a necessary thing because you always had such a lot to do in those days. A whole morning could be spent just getting the laces on your sneakers right since all sneakers in the 1950s had over seven dozen lace holes and the laces were fourteen feet long. Each morning you would jump out of bed to find that the laces had somehow become four feet longer on one side of the shoe than the other. Quite how sneakers did this just by being left on the floor overnight was a question that could not be answered – it was one of those things, like nuns and bad weather, that life threw at you periodically – but it took endless reserves of patience and scientific judgement to get them right, for no matter how painstakingly you shunted the laces around the holes, they always came out at unequal lengths. In fact, the more carefully you shunted, the more unequal they generally became. When by some miracle you finally got them exactly right, the second lace would always snap, leaving you to sigh and start again.

The makers of sneakers also thoughtfully pocked the soles with numberless crevices, craters, chevrons, mazes, crop circles and other rubbery hieroglyphs, so that when you stepped in a moist pile of dog shit, as you most assuredly did within three bounds of leaving the house, they provided additional absorbing hours of pastime while you cleaned them out with a stick, gagging quietly, but oddly content.

Hours more of weekend time needed to be devoted to picking burrs off socks, taking corks out of bottle caps, peeling frozen wrappers off Popsicles, prising apart Oreo cookies without breaking either chocolate disc half or disturbing the integrity of the filling, and carefully picking labels off jars and bottles for absolutely no reason.

In such a world, injuries and other physical setbacks were actually welcomed. If you got a splinter you could pass an afternoon, and attract a small devoted audience, seeing how far you could insert a needle under your skin – how close you could get to actual surgery. If you got sunburned you looked forward to the moment when you could peel off a sheet of translucent epidermis that was essentially the size of your body. Scabs in Kid World were cultivated the way older people cultivate orchids. I had knee scabs that I kept for up to four years, that were an inch and three quarters thick and into which you could press drawing pins without rousing my attention. Nosebleeds were much admired, needless to say, and anyone with a nosebleed was treated like a celebrity for as long as it ran.

Because days were so long and so little occurred, you were prepared to invest extended periods in just sitting and watching things on the off chance that something diverting might take place. For years, whenever my father announced that he was off to the lumberyard I dropped everything to accompany him in order to sit quietly on a stool in the wood-cutting room in the hope that Moe, the man who trimmed wood to order on a big buzzsaw, would send one of his few remaining digits flying. He had already lost most of six or seven fingers, so the chances of a lively accident always seemed good.

Buses in Des Moines in those days were electrically powered, and drew their energy from a complicated cat's cradle of overhead wires, to which each was attached by means of a metal arm. Especially in damp weather, the wires would spark like fireworks at a Mexican fiesta as the arm rubbed along them, vivdly underscoring the murderous potency of electricity. From time to time, the bus-arm would come free of the wires and the driver would have to get out with a long pole and push it back into place – an event that I always watched with the keenest interest because my sister assured me that there was every chance he would be electrocuted.

Other long periods of the day were devoted to just seeing what would happen – what would happen if you pinched a matchhead while it was still hot or made a vile drink and took a sip of it or focused a white-hot beam of sunlight with a magnifying glass on your Uncle Dick's bald spot while he was napping. (What happened was that you burned an amazingly swift, deep hole that would leave Dick and a team of specialists at Iowa Lutheran Hospital puzzled for weeks.)

Thanks to such investigations and the abundance of time that made them possible, I knew more things in the first ten years of my life than I believe I have known at any time since. I knew everything there was to know about our house for a start. I knew what was written on the undersides of tables and what the view was like from the tops of bookcases and wardrobes. I knew what was to be found at the back of every closet, which beds had the most dustballs beneath them, which ceilings the most interesting stains, and where exactly the patterns in wallpaper repeated. I knew how to cross every room in the house without touching the floor, where my father kept his spare change and how much you could safely take without his noticing (one-seventh of the quarters, one-fifth of the nickels and dimes, as many of the pennies as you could carry). I knew how to relax in an armchair in more than one hundred positions and on the floor in approximately seventy-five more. I knew what the world looked like when viewed through a Jell-O lens. I knew how things tasted – damp washcloths, pencil ferrules, coins and buttons, almost anything made of plastic that was smaller than, say, a clock radio, mucus of every variety of course – in a way that I have more or less forgotten now. I knew and could take you at once to any illustration of naked women anywhere in our house, from a Rubens painting of fleshy chubbos in *Masterpieces of World Painting* to a cartoon by Peter Arno in the latest issue of the *New Yorker* to my father's small private library of girlie magazines in a secret place, known only to him, me and one hundred and eleven of my closest friends, in his bedroom.

I knew how to get between any two properties in the

neighbourhood, however tall the fence or impenetrable the hedge that separated them. I knew the feel of linoleum on bare skin and what everything smelled like at floor level. I knew pain the way you know it when it is fresh and interesting – the pain, for example, of a toasted marshmallow in your mouth when its interior is roughly the temperature of magma. I knew exactly how clouds drifted on a July afternoon, what rain tasted like, how ladybirds preened and caterpillars rippled, what it felt like to sit inside a bush. I knew how to appreciate a really good fart, whether mine or someone else's.

The someone else was nearly always Buddy Doberman, who lived across the alley, a secretive lane that ran in a neighbourly fashion behind our houses. Buddy was my best friend for the first portion of my life. We were extremely close. He was the only human being whose anus I have ever looked at closely, or indeed at all, just to see what one looks like (reddish, tight and very slightly puckered, as I recall with a rather worrying clarity) and he was good tempered and had wonderful toys to play with, as his parents were both generous and well to do.

He was sweetly stupid, too, which was a bonus. When he and I were four his grandfather gave us a pair of wooden pirate swords that he had made in his workshop and we went with them more or less straight to Mrs Van Pelt's prized flower border, which ran for about thirty yards along the alley. In a whirl of frenzied motion that anticipated by several years the lively destructive actions of a strimmer, we decapitated and eviscerated every one of her beloved zinnias in a matter of seconds. Then, realizing the enormity of what we had just done – Mrs Van Pelt showed these flowers at the state fair; she talked to them; they were her children – I told Buddy that this was not a good time for me to be in trouble on account of my father had a fatal disease that no one knew about, so would he mind taking all the blame? And he did. So while he was sent to his room at three o'clock in the afternoon and spent the rest of the day as a weepy face at a high window, I was on our back porch with my feet up on the rail, gorging on fresh watermelon and listening to selected cool discs on my sister's portable phonograph. From this I learned an important lesson: lying is always an option worth trying. I spent the next six years blaming Buddy for everything bad that happened in my life. I believe he eventually even took the rap for burning the hole in my Uncle Dick's head even though he had never met my Uncle Dick.

Then, as now, Des Moines was a safe, wholesome city of two hundred thousand people. The streets were long, straight, leafy and clean and had solid Middle American names: Woodland, University, Pleasant, Grand. (There was a local joke, much retold, about a woman who was goosed on Grand and thought it was Pleasant.) It was a nice city – a comfortable city. Most businesses were close to the road and generally had lawns out front instead of parking lots. Public buildings – post offices, schools, hospitals – were always stately and imposing. Gas stations often looked like little cottages. Diners (or roadhouses) brought to mind the type of cabins you might find on a fishing trip. Nothing was designed to be particularly helpful or beneficial to cars. It was a greener, quieter, less intrusive world.

Grand Avenue was the main artery through the city, linking downtown, where everyone worked and did all serious shopping, with the residential areas beyond. The best houses in the city lay to the south of Grand on the west side of town, in a hilly, gorgeously wooded district that ran down to Waterworks Park and the Raccoon River. You could walk for hours along the wandering roads in there and never see anything but perfect lawns, old trees, freshly washed cars and lovely, happy homes. It was miles and miles of the American dream. This was my district. It was known as South of Grand.

The most striking difference between then and now was how many kids there were then. America had thirty-two million children aged twelve or under in the mid-1950s, and four million new babies were plopping on to the changing mats every year. So there were kids everywhere, all the time, in densities now unimaginable, but especially whenever anything interesting or unusual happened. Early every summer, at the start of the mosquito season, a city employee in an open jeep would come to the neighbourhood and drive madly all over the place – over lawns, through woods, bumping along culverts, jouncing into and out of vacant lots – with a fogging machine that pumped out dense, colourful clouds of insecticide through which at least eleven thousand children scampered joyously for most of the day. It was awful stuff – it tasted foul, it made your lungs chalky, it left you with a powdery saffron pallor that no amount of scrubbing could eradicate. For years afterwards whenever I coughed into a white handkerchief I brought up a little ring of coloured powder.

But nobody ever thought to stop us or suggest that it was perhaps unwise to be scampering through choking clouds of insecticide. Possibly it was thought that a generous dusting of DDT would do us good. It was that kind of age. Or maybe we were just considered expendable because there were so many of us.*

---

*Altogether the mothers of post-war America gave birth to 76.4 million kids between 1946 and 1964, when their poor old overworked wombs all gave out more or less at once, evidently.

41

The other difference from those days was that kids were always outdoors – I knew kids who were pushed out the back door at eight in the morning and not allowed back in until five unless they were on fire or actively bleeding – and they were always looking for something to do. If you stood on any corner with a bike – any corner anywhere – over a hundred children, many of whom you had never seen before, would appear and ask you where you were going.

'Might go down to the Trestle,' you would say thoughtfully. The Trestle was a railway bridge over the Raccoon River, from which you could jump in for a swim if you didn't mind paddling around among dead fish, old tyres, oil drums, algal slime, heavy metal effluents and uncategorized goo. It was one of ten recognized landmarks in our district. The others were the Woods, the Park, the Little League Park (or 'the Ballpark'), the Pond, the River, the Railroad Tracks (usually just 'the Tracks'), the Vacant Lot, Greenwood (our school), and the New House. The New House was any house under construction and so changed regularly.

'Can we come?' they'd say.

'Yeah, all right,' you would answer if they were your size or 'If you think you can keep up' if they were smaller. And when you got to the Trestle or the Vacant Lot or the Pond there would already be six hundred kids there. There were always six hundred kids everywhere except where two or more neighbourhoods met – at the Park, for instance – where the numbers would grow into the thousands. I once took part in an ice hockey game at the lagoon in Greenwood Park that involved four thousand kids, all slashing away violently with sticks, and went on for at least three quarters of an hour before anyone realized that we didn't have a puck.

Life in Kid World, wherever you went, was unsupervised, un-regulated and robustly – at times insanely – physical and yet it was a remarkably peaceable place. Kids' fights never went too far, which is extraordinary when you consider how ill-controlled children's tempers are. Once when I was about six, I saw a kid throw a rock at another kid, from quite a distance, and it bounced off the target's head (quite beautifully, I have to say) and made him bleed. This was talked about for years. Kids in the next county knew about it. The kid who did it was sent for about ten thousand hours of therapy.

We didn't otherwise engage in violence, other than accidentally, though we did sometimes (actually quite routinely) give a boy named Milton Milton knuckle rubs for having such a stupid name and also for spending his life pretending to be motorized. I never knew whether he was supposed to be a train or a robot or what, but he always moved his arms like pistons when he walked and made puffing noises, and so naturally we gave him knuckle rubs. We had to. He was born to be rubbed.

With respect to accidental bloodshed, it is my modest boast that I became the neighbourhood's most memorable contributor one tranquil September afternoon in my tenth year while playing football in Leo Collingwood's back yard. As always, the game involved about a hundred and fifty kids, so normally when you were tackled you fell into a soft, marshmallowy mass of bodies. If you were really lucky you landed on Mary O'Leary and got to rest on her for a moment while waiting for the others to get off. She smelled of vanilla – vanilla and fresh grass – and was soft and clean and painfully pretty. It was a lovely moment. But on this occasion I fell outside the pack and hit my head on a stone retaining wall. I remember feeling a sharp pain at the top of my head towards the back.

When I stood up, I saw that everyone was staring at me with a single rapt expression and inclined to give me some space. Lonny Brankovich looked over and instantly melted in a faint. In a candid tone his brother said: 'You're gonna die.' Naturally I couldn't see what absorbed them, but I gather from later descriptions that it looked as if I had a lawn sprinkler plugged into the top of my head, spraying blood in all directions in a rather festive manner. I reached up and found a mass of wetness. To the touch, it felt more like the kind of outflow you get when a truck crashes into a fire hydrant or oil is struck in Oklahoma. This felt like a job for Red Adair.

'I think I'd better go get this seen to,' I said soberly and with a fifty-foot stride left the yard. I bounded home in three steps and walked into the kitchen, fountaining lavishly, where I found my father standing by the window with a cup of coffee dreamily admiring Mrs Bukowski, the young housewife from next door. Mrs Bukowski had the first bikini in Iowa and wore it while hanging out her wash. My father looked at my spouting head, allowed himself a moment's mindless adjustment, then leaped instantly and adroitly into panic and disorder, moving in as many as six directions simultaneously, and calling in a strained voice to my mother to come at once and bring lots and lots of towels – 'old ones!' – because Billy was bleeding to death in the kitchen.

Everything after that went by in a blur. I remember my father seating me with my head pressed to the kitchen table as he endeavoured to staunch the flow of blood and at the same time get through on the phone to Dr Alzheimer, the family physician, for guidance. Meanwhile, my mother, ever imperturbable, searched methodically for old rags and pieces of cloth that could be safely sacrificed (or were red already) and dealt with the parade of children who were turning up at the back door with bone chips and bits of grey tissue that they had carefully lifted from the rock and thought might be part of my brain.

I couldn't see much, of course, with my head pressed to the table, but I did catch reflected glimpses in the toaster and my father seemed to be into my cranial cavity up to his elbows. At the same time he was speaking to Dr Alzheimer in words that failed to soothe. 'Jesus Christ, doc,' he was saying. 'You wouldn't *believe* the amount of blood. We're *swimming* in it.'

On the other end I could hear Dr Alzheimer's dementedly laid-back voice. 'Well, I *could* come over, I suppose,' he was saying. 'It's just that I'm watching an *awfully* good golf tournament. Ben Hogan is having a most marvellous round. Isn't it wonderful to see him doing well at his time of life? Now then, have you managed to stop the bleeding?'

'Well, I'm sure trying.'

'Good, good. That's excellent – that's excellent. Because he's probably lost quite a lot of blood already. Tell me, is the little fellow still breathing?'

'I think so,' my father replied.

I nodded swiftly and helpfully.

'Yes, he's still breathing, doc.'

'That's good, that's very good. OK, I tell you what. Give him two aspirin and nudge him once in a while to make sure he doesn't pass out – on no account let him lose consciousness, do you hear, because you might lose the poor little fellow – and I'll be over after the tournament. Oh, look at that – he's gone straight off the green into the rough.' There was the sound of Dr Alzheimer's

45

phone settling back into the cradle and the buzz of disconnection.

Happily, I didn't die and four hours later was to be found sitting up in bed, head extravagantly turbaned, well rested after a nap that came during one of those passing three-hour moments when my parents forgot to check on my wakefulness, eating tubs of chocolate ice cream, and regally receiving visitors from the neighbourhood, giving particular priority to those who came bearing gifts. Dr Alzheimer arrived later than promised, smelling lightly of bourbon. He spent most of the visit sitting on the edge of my bed and asking me if I was old enough to remember Bobby Jones. He never did look at my head. Dr Alzheimer's fees, I believe, were very reasonable, too.

Apart from medical practitioners, Iowa offered little in the way of natural dangers, though one year when I was about six we had an infestation of a type of giant insect called cicada killers. Cicada killers are not to be confused with cicadas, which are themselves horrible things – like small flying cigars, but with staring red eyes and grotesque pincers, if I recall correctly. Well, cicada killers were much worse. They only emerged from the ground every seventeen years, so nobody, even adults, knew much about them. There was great debate over whether the 'killer' in 'cicada killer' signified that they were killers of cicadas or that they were cicadas that killed. The consensus pointed to the latter.

Cicada killers were about the size of hummingbirds and had vicious stingers fore and aft, and they were awful. They lived in burrows and would come flying up unexpectedly from below, with a horrible whirring sound, rather like a chainsaw starting up, if you disturbed their nests. The greatest fear was that they would shoot up the leg of your shorts and become entangled in your underpants and start lashing out blindly. Castration, possibly by the side of the road, was the normal emergency procedure for cicada killer stings to the scrotal region – and they seldom stung anywhere else. You never really saw one because as soon as one whirred out of its burrow you pranced away like hell, pressing your shorts primly but prudently to your legs.

The worst chronic threat we had was poison sumac, though I never knew anyone, adult or child, who actually knew what it was or precisely how it would kill you. It was really just a kind of shrubby rumour. Even so, in any wooded situation you could always hold up a hand and announce gravely: 'We'd better not go any further. I think there might be sumac up ahead.'

'*Poison* sumac?' one of your younger companions would reply, eyes wide open.

'All sumac's poisonous, Jimmy,' someone else would say, putting a hand on his shoulder.

'Is it really bad?' Jimmy would ask.

'Put it this way,' you would answer sagely. 'My brother's friend Mickey Cox knew a guy who fell into a sumac patch once. Got it all over him, you know, and the doctors had to like amputate his whole body. He's just a head on a plate now. They carry him around in a hatbox.'

'Wow,' everyone would say except Arthur Bergen, who was annoyingly brainy and knew all the things in the world that couldn't possibly be so, which always exactly coincided with all the things you had heard about that were amazing.

'A head couldn't survive on its own in a box,' he would say.

'Well, they took it out sometimes. To give it air and let it watch TV and so on.'

'No, I mean it couldn't survive on its own, without a body.'

'Well, this one did.'

'Not possible. How are you going to keep a head oxygenated without a heart?'

'How should I know? What am I – Dr Kildare? I just know it's true.'

'It can't be, Bryson. You've misheard – or you're making it up.'

'Well, I'm not.'

'Must be.'

'Well, Arthur, I swear to God it's true.'

This would cause an immediate stunned silence.

'You'll go to hell for saying that if it's not true, you know,' Jimmy would point out, but quite unnecessarily for you knew this already. All kids knew this automatically, from birth.

Swearing to God was the ultimate act. If you swore to God and it turned out you were wrong, even by accident, even just a little, you still had to go to hell. That was just the rule and God didn't bend that rule for anybody. So the moment you said it, in any context, you began to feel uneasy in case some part of it turned out to be slightly incorrect.

'Well, that's what my brother said,' you would say, trying to modify your eternal liability.

'You can't change it now,' Bergen – who, not incidentally, would grow up to be a personal injury lawyer – would point out. 'You've already said it.'

You were all too well aware of this too. In the circumstances there was really only one thing to do: give Milton Milton a knuckle rub.

Only slightly less threatening than poison sumac were pulpy red berries that grew in clumps on bushes in almost everybody's back yard. These were also slightly vague in that neither bush nor berry seemed to have a name – they were just 'those red berries' or 'that bush with the red berries' – but they were universally agreed to be toxic. If you touched or held a berry even briefly and then later ate a cookie or sandwich and realized that you hadn't washed your hands, you spent an hour seriously wondering if you might drop dead at any moment.

Moms worried about the berries, too, and were forever shouting from the kitchen window not to eat them, which was actually unnecessary because children of the 1950s didn't eat anything that grew wild – in fact, didn't eat anything at all unless it was coated in sugar, endorsed by a celebrity athlete or TV star and came with a free prize. They might as well have told us not to eat any dead cats we found. We weren't about to.

Interestingly, the berries weren't poisonous at all. I can say this with some confidence because we made Lanny Kowalski's little brother, Lumpy,* eat about four pounds of them to see if they would kill him and they didn't. It was a controlled experiment, I hasten to add. We fed them to him one at a time and waited a decent interval to see if his eyes rolled up into his head or anything before passing him another. But apart from throwing up the middle two pounds, he showed no ill effects.

The only real danger in life was the Butter boys. The Butters were a family of large, inbred, indeterminately numerous individuals who lived seasonally in a collection of shanty homes in an area of perpetual wooded gloom known as the Bottoms along the swampy margins of the Raccoon River. Nearly every spring the Bottoms would flood and the Butters would all go

*So called because his pants always had a saggy lump of poo in them. I expect they still do.

back to Arkansas or Alabama or wherever it was they came from.

In between times they would menace us. Their speciality was to torment any children smaller than them, which was all children. The Butters were big to begin with but because they were held back year after year, they were much, much larger than any other child in their class. By sixth grade some of them were too big to pass through doors. They were ugly, too, and real dumb. They ate squirrels.

Generally the best option was to have some small child that you could offer as a sacrifice. Lumpy Kowalski was ideal for this as he was indifferent to pain and fear, and would never tell on you because he couldn't, or possibly just didn't, speak. (It was never clear which.) Also, the Butters were certain to be grossed out by his dirty pants, so they would merely paw him for a bit and then withdraw with pained, confused faces.

The worst outcome was to be caught on your own by one or more of the Butter boys. Once when I was about ten I was nabbed by Buddy Butters, who was in my grade but at least seven years older. He dragged me under a big pine tree and pinned me to the ground on my back and told me he was going to keep me there all night long.

I waited for what seemed a decent interval and then said: 'Why are you doing this to me?'

'Because I can,' he answered, but pronounced it 'kin'. Then he made a kind of glutinous, appreciative, snot-clearing noise, which was what passed in the Butter universe for laughter.

'But you'll have to stay here all night, too,' I pointed out. 'It'll be just as boring for you.'

'Don't care,' he replied, sharp as anything, and was quiet a long time before adding: 'Besides I can do this.' And he treated me to the hanging spit trick – the one where the person on top slowly suspends a gob of spit and lets it hang there by a thread, trembling gently, and either sucks it back in if the victim surrenders or lets it fall, sometimes inadvertently. It wasn't even like spit – at least not like human spit. It was more like the sort of thing a giant insect would regurgitate on to its forelimbs and rub on to its antennae. It was a mossy green with little streaks of red blood in it and, unless my memory is playing tricks, two very small grey feathers protruding at the sides. It was so big and shiny that I could see my reflection in it, distorted, as in an M. C. Escher drawing. I knew that if any part of it touched my face, it would sizzle hotly and leave a disfiguring scar.

In fact, he sucked the gob back in and got off me. 'Well, you let that be a lesson to you, you little skunk pussy poontang sissy,' he said.

Two days later the soaking spring rains came and put all the Butters on their tarpaper roofs, where they were rescued one by one by men in small boats. A thousand children stood on the banks above and cheered.

What they didn't realize was that the storm clouds that carried all that refreshing rain had been guided across the skies by the powerful X-ray vision of the modest superhero of the prairies, the small but perfectly proportioned Thunderbolt Kid.

Chapter 3

BIRTH OF A SUPERHERO

EAST HAMPTON, CONN. (AP) – A search of Lake Pocotopaug for a reported drowning victim was called off here Tuesday when it was realized that one of the volunteers helping the search, Robert Hausman, 23, of East Hampton, was the person being sought.

– *Des Moines Register*, 20 September 1957

A{\scriptsize T EVERY MEAL} she ever prepared throughout my upbringing (and no doubt far beyond), my mother placed a large dollop of cottage cheese on each plate. It appeared to be important to her to serve something coagulated and slightly runny at every meal. It would be understating things to say I disliked cottage cheese. To me cottage cheese looks like something you bring up, not take in. Indeed, that was the crux of my problem with it.

I had a distant uncle named Dee (who, now that I think of it, may not have actually been an uncle at all, but just a strange man who showed up at all large family gatherings) who had lost his voicebox and had a permanent hole in his throat as a result of some youthful injury or surgical trauma or something. Actually, I don't know why he had a hole in his throat. It was just a fact of life. A lot of rural people in Iowa in the Fifties had arresting physical features – wooden legs, stumpy arms, outstandingly dented heads, hands without fingers, mouths without tongues, sockets without eyes, scars that ran on for feet, sometimes going in one sleeve and out the other. Goodness knows what people got up to back then, but they suffered some mishaps, that's for sure.

Anyway, Uncle Dee had a throat hole, which he kept lightly covered with a square of cotton gauze. The gauze often came unstuck, particularly when Dee was in an impassioned mood, which was usually, and either hung open or fell off altogether. In either case, you could see the hole, which was jet black and

55

transfixing and about the size of a quarter. Dee talked through the hole in his neck – actually, belched a form of speech through it. Everyone agreed that he was very good at it – in terms of volume and steadiness of output, he was a wonder; many were reminded of an outboard motor running at full throttle – though in fact no one had the faintest idea what he was talking about, which was unfortunate as Dee was ferociously loquacious. He would burp away with feeling while those people standing beside him (who were, it must be said, nearly always newcomers to the family circle) watched his throat hole gamely but uncertainly. From time to time, they would say, 'Is that so?' and 'Well, I'll be,' and give a series of earnest, thoughtful nods, before saying, 'Well, I think I'll just go and get a little more lemonade,' and drift off, leaving Dee belching furiously at their backs.

All this was fine – or at least fine enough – so long as Uncle Dee wasn't eating. When Dee was eating you really didn't want to be in the same county, for Uncle Dee talked with his throat full. Whatever he ate turned into a light spray from his throat hole. It was like dining with a miniature flocking machine, or perhaps a very small snowblower. I've seen placid, kindly grown-ups, people of good Christian disposition – loving sisters, sons and fathers, and on one memorable occasion two Lutheran ministers from neighbouring congregations – engage in silent but prolonged and ferocious struggles for control of a chair that would spare them having to sit beside or, worse, across from Dee at lunch.

The feature of Dee's condition that particularly caught my attention was that whatever he put in his mouth – chocolate cream pie, chicken-fried steak, baked beans, spinach, rutabaga, Jell-O – by the time it reached the hole in his neck it had become cottage cheese. I don't know how but it did.

Which is precisely and obviously why I disdained the stuff. My mother could never grasp this. But then she was dazzlingly, good-naturedly forgetful about most things. We used to amuse ourselves by challenging her to supply our dates of birth or, if that proved too taxing, the seasons. She couldn't reliably tell you our middle names. At the supermarket she often reached the checkout and discovered that she had at some indeterminate point acquired someone else's shopping cart, and was now in possession of items – whole pineapples, suppositories, bags of food for a very large dog – that she didn't want or mean to have. She was seldom entirely clear on what clothes belonged to whom. She hadn't the faintest idea what our eating preferences were.

'Mom,' I would say each night, laying a piece of bread over the offending mound on my plate, rather as one covered a roadside accident victim with a blanket, 'you know I really do hate cottage cheese.'

'Do you, dear?' she would say with a look of sympathetic perplexity. 'Why?'

'It looks like the stuff that comes out of Uncle Dee's throat.'

Everyone present, including my father, would nod solemnly at this.

'Well, just eat a little bit, and leave what you don't like.'

'I don't like any of it, Mom. It's not like there's a part of it I like and a part that I don't. Mom, we have this conversation every night.'

'I bet you've never even tasted it.'

'I've never tasted pigeon droppings. I've never tasted ear wax. Some things you don't need to taste. We have this conversation every night, too.'

More solemn nods.

'Well, I had no idea you didn't like cottage cheese,' my mom would say in something like amazement and the next night there would be cottage cheese again.

Just occasionally her forgetfulness strayed into rather more dismaying territory, especially when she was pressed for time. I recall one particularly rushed and disorganized morning when I was still quite small – small enough, at any rate, to be mostly trusting and completely stupid – when she gave me my sister's old Capri pants to wear to school. They were a brilliant lime green, very tight, and had little slits at the bottom. They only came about three quarters of the way down my calves. I stared at myself in the back hall mirror in a kind of confused disbelief. I looked like Barbara Stanwyck in *Double Indemnity*.

'This can't be right, Mom,' I said. 'These are Betty's old Capri pants, aren't they?'

'No, honey,' my mom replied soothingly. 'They're *pirate* pants. They're very fashionable. I believe Kookie Byrnes wears them on *77 Sunset Strip*.'

Kookie Byrnes, a munificently coiffed star on this popular weekly television show, was a hero to me, and indeed to most people who liked interestingly arranged hair, and he *was* capable of endearingly strange things, that's for sure. That's why they called him Kookie. Even so, this didn't feel right.

'I don't think he can, Mom. Because these are girls' pants.'

'He does, honey.'

'Do you swear to God?'

'Oom,' she said distractedly. 'You watch this week. I'm sure he does.'

'But do you swear to God?'

'Oom,' she said again.

So I wore them to school and the laughter could be heard for miles. It went on for most of the day. The principal, Mrs Unnaturally Enormous Bosom, who in normal circumstances was the sort of person who wouldn't get off her ass if her chair was on fire, made a special visit to have a look at me and laughed so hard she popped a button on her blouse.

Kookie Byrnes, of course, never wore anything remotely like Capri pants. I asked my sister about this after school. 'Are you *kidding*?' she said. 'Kookie Byrnes is *not* homosexual.'

It was impossible to hold my mother's forgetfulness against her for long because it was so obviously and helplessly pathological, a quirk of her nature. We might as well have become exasperated with her for having a fondness for polka dots and two-tone shoes. It's what she was. Besides, she made up for it in a thousand ways – by being soft and kind, patient and generous, instantly and sincerely apologetic for every wrong, keen to make amends. Everybody in the world adored my mother. She was entirely without suspicion or malice. She never raised her voice or said no to any request, never said a word against any other human being. She liked everybody. She lived to make sandwiches. She wanted everyone to be happy. And she took me almost every week to dinner and the movies. It was the thing she and I did together.

Because of his work my father was gone most weekends, so every Friday, practically without fail, my mother would say to me, 'What do you say we go to Bishop's for dinner tonight and then take in a movie?' as if it were a rare treat, when in fact it was what we did regularly.

So at the conclusion of school on Fridays I would hasten

home, drop my books on the kitchen table, grab a handful of cookies and proceed downtown. Sometimes I caught a bus, but more often I saved the money and walked. It was only a couple of miles and the route was all diverting and agreeable if I went along Grand Avenue (where the buses didn't go; they were relegated to Ingersoll – the servants' entrance of the street world). I liked Grand Avenue very much. In those days it was adorned from downtown to the western suburbs with towering, interlaced elms, the handsomest streetside tree ever and a generous provider of drifts of golden leaves to shuffle through in autumn. But more than this, Grand felt the way a street should feel. Its office buildings and apartments were built close to the road, which gave the street a kind of neighbourliness, and it still had most of its old homes – mansions of exuberant splendour, nearly all with turrets and towers and porches like ships' decks – though these had now mostly found other uses as offices, funeral homes and the like. Interspersed at judicious intervals were a few grander institutional buildings: granite churches, a Catholic girls' high school, the stately Commodore Hotel (with an awninged walkway leading to the street – a welcome touch of Manhattan), a spooky orphanage where no children ever played or stood at a window, the official residence of the governor, a modest mansion with a white flagpole and the state flag. All seemed somehow exactly in proportion, precisely positioned, thoughtfully dressed and groomed. It was the perfect street.

Where it ceased being residential and entered the downtown, by the industrial-scale hulk of the Meredith Publishing Building (home of *Better Homes and Gardens* magazine), Grand made an abrupt dog leg to the left, as if it suddenly remembered an important appointment. Originally from this point it was intended to proceed

60

through the downtown as a kind of Midwestern Champs Elysées, running up to the steps of the state capitol building. The idea was that as you progressed along Grand you would behold before you, perfectly centred, the golden-domed glory of the capitol building (and it *is* quite a structure, one of the best in the country).

But when the road was being laid out some time in the second half of the 1800s there was a heavy rain in the night and the surveyors' sticks moved apparently – at least that was what we were always told – and the road deviated from the correct line, leaving the capitol oddly off centre, so that it looks today as if it has been caught in the act of trying to escape. It is a peculiarity that some people treasure and others would rather not talk about. I for one never tired of striding into the downtown from the west and being confronted with a view so gloriously not right, so cherishably out of kilter, and pondering the fact that whole teams of men could build an important road evidently without once looking up to see where they were going.

For its first couple of blocks, Des Moines's downtown had a slight but agreeably seedy air. Here there were dark bars, small hotels of doubtful repute, dingy offices and shops that sold odd things like rubber stamps and trusses. I liked this area very much. There was always a chance of hearing a bitter argument through an upstairs window and the hope that this would lead to gunfire and someone falling out the window on to an awning, as in the better Hollywood movies, or at least staggering out a door, hand on bloodied chest, and collapsing in the street.

Then fairly quickly downtown became more respectable and literally upstanding, more like a real downtown. This throbbing heart of the metropolis was of a fairly modest scale – only three or four blocks wide and four or five long – but it had a density of tallish brick buildings and it was full of people and life. The air was slightly dirty and blue. People walked with quicker steps and longer strides. It felt like a proper city.

Upon arriving downtown I had an unvarying routine. I would call first at Pinky's, a joke and novelty store in the Banker's Trust Building, which contained a large stock of dusty gag items – plastic ice cubes with a fly inside, chattering teeth, rubber turds for every occasion – that no one ever bought. Pinky's existed purely to give sailors, migrant workers and small boys a place to go when they were at a loose end downtown. I have no idea how it managed to stay in business. I can only assume that somehow in the 1950s you didn't have to sell much to remain solvent.*

When I had looked at everything there, I would do a circuit or two of the mezzanine at Frankel's, then check out any new Hardy Boys arrivals in the book department at Younkers. Generally I would call in at the long soda fountain at Woolworth's for one of their celebrated Green Rivers, a refreshing concoction of syrupy green fizz that was the schoolboy aperitif of the 1950s, and finally head over to the R&T (for *Register* and *Tribune*), at Eighth and Locust. There I would always take a minute to look through the large plate-glass windows that ran along the building at street level and gave views of the press room – a potentially excellent place to see a mangling, I always supposed – then proceed through the snappy revolving doors into the *Register's* lobby, where I would devote a few respectful minutes to a large, slowly revolving globe that was housed behind glass (always interestingly warm to the touch) in a side room.

The *Register* was proud of this globe. It was, as I recall, one of

*I have since learned from my more worldly informant Stephen Katz that Pinky's earned its keep by selling dirty magazines under the counter. I had no idea.

the largest globes in the world: big globes aren't easy to make apparently. This one was at least twice my size and beautifully manufactured and painted. It was tilted on its axis at a scientifically precise angle and spun at the same speed as Earth itself, completing one revolution in every twenty-four hours. It was, in short, a thing of wonder and grandeur – the finest technological marvel in Des Moines aside from the radioactive toilet seats at Bishop's cafeteria, which obviously were in a league of their own. Because it was so large and stately and real, it felt very much as if you were looking at the actual Earth, and I would walk around it imagining myself as God. Even now when I think of the nations of the Earth, I see them as they were on that big ball – as Tanganyika, Rhodesia, East and West Germany, the Friendly Islands. The globe may have had other fans besides me, but I never saw any passer-by give it so much as a glance.

At 5.30 precisely, I would proceed in an elevator up to the newsroom on the fourth floor – a place so quintessentially like a newsroom that it even had a swing gate through which you entered with a jaunty air, like Rosalind Russell in *His Girl Friday* – and passed through the Sports Department with a familiar 'Hey' to all the fellows there (they were my father's colleagues after all), past the chattering wire machines, and presented myself at my mother's desk in the Women's Department just beyond. I can see her perfectly now, sitting at a grey metal desk, hair slightly askew, hammering away on her typewriter, a venerable Smith Corona upright. I'd give anything – really almost anything at all – to pass just once more through that gate and see the guys in the Sports Department and beyond them my dear old mom at her desk typing away.

My arrival would always please and surprise her equally.

'Why, Billy, hello! My goodness, is it Friday?' she would say as if we hadn't met for weeks.

'Yes, Mom.'

'Well, what do you say we go to Bishop's and a movie?'

'That would be great.'

So we would dine quietly and contentedly at Bishop's and afterwards stroll to a movie at one of the three great and ancient downtown movie palaces – the Paramount, Des Moines and RKO-Orpheum – each a vast, spookily lit crypt done up in an elaborate style that recalled the heyday of ancient Egypt. The Paramount and Des Moines both held sixteen hundred people, the Orpheum slightly fewer, though by the late 1950s there were seldom more than thirty or forty at a showing. There has never been, will never again be, a better place to pass a Friday evening, sitting with a tub of buttered popcorn in a cubic acre of darkness facing a screen so enormous you could read the titles of books on bookcases, the dates on calendars, the licence plates of passing cars. It really was a kind of magic.

Movies of the Fifties were of unparalleled excellence. *The Brain That Wouldn't Die, The Blob, The Man from Planet X, Earth Versus the Flying Saucers, Zombies of the Stratosphere, The Amazing Colossal Man, Invasion of the Body Snatchers* and the *Incredible Shrinking Man* were just some of the inspired inventions of that endlessly imaginative decade. My mother and I never went to these, however. We saw melodramas instead, generally starring people from the lower-middle tiers of the star system – Richard Conte, Lizabeth Scott, Lana Turner, Dan Duryea, Jeff Chandler. I could never understand the appeal of these movies myself. It was all just talk, talk, talk in that gloomy, earnest, accusatory way that people in movies in the Fifties had. The characters nearly always turned away when speaking, so that they appeared inexplicably to be addressing a bookcase or floor lamp rather than the person standing behind them. At some point the music would swell and one of the characters would tell the other (by way of the curtains) that they couldn't take any more of this and were leaving.

'Me, too!' I would quip amiably to my mother and amble off to the men's room for a change of scene. The men's rooms in the downtown theatres were huge, and soothingly lit, and quite splendidly classy. They had good full-length mirrors, so you could practise gunslinger draws, and there were several machines – comb machines, condom machines – you could almost get your arm up. There was a long line of toilet cubicles and they all had those dividers that allowed you to see the feet of people in flanking cubicles, which I never understood, and indeed still don't. It's hard to think of a single circumstance in which seeing the feet of the person next door would be to anyone's advantage. As a kind of signature gesture, I would go into the far left-hand stall and lock the door, then crawl under the divider into the next stall and lock it, and so on down the line until I had locked them all. It always gave me a strange sense of achievement.

Goodness knows what I crawled through in order to accomplish this small feat, but then I *was* enormously stupid. I mean really quite enormously. I remember when I was about six passing almost a whole movie picking some interesting sweet-smelling stuff off the underside of my seat, thinking that it was something to do with the actual manufactured composition of the seat before realizing that it was gum that had been left there by previous users.

I was sick for about two years over what a grotesque and unhygienic activity I had been engaged in and the thought that I had then eaten greasy buttered popcorn and a large packet of Chuckles with the same fingers that had dabbled in other people's abandoned chewings. I had even – oh, yuk! yuk! – licked those fingers, eagerly transferring bucketloads of syphilitic dribblings and uncategorizable swill from their snapped-out Wrigley's and Juicy Fruits to my wholesome mouth and sleek digestive tract. It was only a matter of time – hours at most – before I would sink into a mumbling delirium and in slow, fevered anguish die.

After the movies we always stopped for pie at the Toddle House, a tiny, steamy diner of dancing grease fires, ill-tempered staff and cosy perfection on Grand Avenue. The Toddle House was little more than a brick hut consisting of a single counter with a few twirly stools, but never has a confined area produced more divine foods or offered a more delicious warmth on a cold night. The pies – flaky of crust, creamy of filling and always generously cut – were heaven on a plate. Normally this was the high point of the evening, but on this night I was distracted and inconsolable. I felt dirty and doomed. I would never have dreamed that worse still could possibly come my way, but in fact it was just about to. As I sat at the counter idly pronging my banana cream pie, feeling sorry for myself and my doomed intestinal tract, I drank from my glass of water and then realized that the old man sitting beside me was drinking from it, too. He was over two hundred years old and had a sort of grey drool at each corner of his mouth. When he put the glass down there were little white masticated bits adrift in the water.

'Akk, akk, akk,' I croaked in quiet horror as I took this in and clutched my throat with both hands. My fork fell noisily to the floor.

'Say, have I bin drinkin' yer water?' he said cheerfully.

'Yes!' I gasped in disbelief, and stared at his plate. 'And you were eating . . . *poached eggs*.'

Poached eggs were the second most obvious food-never-to-share-with-an-underwashed-old-man, exceeded only by cottage cheese – and only barely. As a sort of dribbly by-product of eating, the two were virtually indistinguishable. 'Oh, akk, akk,' I cried and made noises over my plate like a cat struggling to bring up a hairball.

'Well, I sure hope you ain't got no cooties!' he said and slapped me jovially on the back as he got up to pay his bill.

I stared at him dumbfounded. He settled his account, laid a toothpick on his tongue, and sauntered bowlegged out to his pickup truck.

He never made it. As he reached out to open the door, bolts of electricity flew from my wildly dilated eyes and played over his body. He shimmered for an instant, contorted in a brief, silent rictus of agony, and was gone.

It was the birth of ThunderVision. The world had just become a dangerous place for morons.

There are many versions of how the Thunderbolt Kid came to attain his fantastic powers – so many that I am not entirely sure myself, but I believe the first hints that I was not of Planet Earth, but rather from somewhere else (from, as I was later to learn, the Planet Electro in the Galaxy Zizz), lay embedded in the conversations that my parents had. I spent a lot of my childhood listening in on – monitoring really – their chats. They would have immensely long conversations that seemed always to be dancing about on the edge of a curious happy derangement. I remember one day my father came in, quite excitedly, with a word written down on a piece of paper.

'What's this word?' he said to my mother. The word was 'chaise longue'.

'*Shays lounge*,' she said, pronouncing it as all Iowans, perhaps all Americans, did. A chaise longue in those days exclusively signified a type of adjustable patio lounger that had lately become fashionable. They came with a padded cushion that you brought in every night if you thought someone might take it. Our cushion had a coach and four horses galloping across it. It didn't need to come in at night.

'Look again,' urged my father.

'*Shays lounge*,' repeated my mother, not to be bullied.

'No,' he said, 'look at the second word. Look closely.'

She looked. 'Oh,' she said, cottoning on. She tried it again. '*Shays lawn-gway*.'

'Well, it's just "long",' my father said gently, but gave it a gallic purr. '*Shays lohhhnggg*,' he repeated. 'Isn't that something? I must have looked at that word a hundred times and I've never noticed that it wasn't *lounge*.'

'*Lawngg*,' said my mother, marvelling slightly. 'That's going to take some getting used to.'

'It's French,' my father explained.

'Yes, I expect it is,' said my mother. 'I wonder what it means.'

'No idea. Oh, look, there's Bob coming home from work,' my father said, looking out the window. 'I'm going to try it out on him.' So he'd collar Bob in his driveway and they'd have an amazed ten-minute conversation. For the next hour, you would see my father striding up and down the alley, and sometimes into neighbouring streets, with his piece of paper, showing it to neighbours, and they would all have an amazed conversation. Later, Bob would come and ask if he could borrow the piece of paper to show his wife.

It was about this time I began to suspect that I didn't come from this planet and that these people weren't – couldn't be – my biological parents.

Then one day when I was not quite six years old I was in the basement, just poking around, seeing if there was anything sharp or combustible that I hadn't come across before, and hanging behind the furnace I found a woollen jersey of rare fineness. I slipped it on. It was many, many sizes too large for me – the sleeves all but touched the floor if I didn't repeatedly push them back – but it was the handsomest article of attire I had ever seen. It was made of a lustrous oiled wool, deep bottle green in colour, was extremely warm and heavy, rather scratchy and slightly moth-holed but still exceptionally splendid. Across the chest, in a satin material, now much faded, was a golden thunderbolt. Interestingly, no one knew where it came from. My father thought that it might be an old college football or ice hockey jersey, dating from some time before the First World War. But how it got into our house he had no idea. He guessed that the previous owners had hung it there and forgotten it when they moved.

But I knew better. It was, obviously, the Sacred Jersey of Zap, left to me by King Volton, my late natural father, who had brought me to Earth in a silver spaceship in Earth year 1951 (Electron year 21,000,047,002) shortly before our austere but architecturally exuberant planet exploded spectacularly in a billion pieces of rocky debris. He had placed me with this innocuous family in the middle of America and hypnotized them

69

into believing that I was a normal boy, so that I could perpetuate the Electron powers and creed.

This jersey then was the foundation garment of my super-powers. It transformed me. It gave me colossal strength, rippling muscles, X-ray vision, the ability to fly and to walk upside down across ceilings, invisibility on demand, cowboy skills like lassooing and shooting guns out of people's hands from a distance, a good voice for singing around campfires, and curious bluish-black hair with a teasing curl at the crown. It made me, in short, the kind of person that men want to be and women want to be with.

To the jersey I added a range of useful accoutrements from my existing stockpile – Zorro whip and sword, Sky King necker-chief and neckerchief ring (with secret whistle), Robin of Sherwood bow and arrow with quiver, Roy Rogers decorative cowboy vest and bejewelled boots with jingly tin spurs – which further fortified my strength and dazzle. From my belt hung a rattling aluminium army surplus canteen that made everything put into it taste curiously metallic; a compass and official Boy Scout Vitt-L-Kit, providing all the essential implements needed to prepare a square meal in the wilderness and to fight off wildcats, grizzlies and paedophile scoutmasters; a Batman flashlight with signalling attachment (for bouncing messages off clouds); and a rubber bowie knife.

I also sometimes carried an army surplus knapsack containing snack food and spare ammo, but I tended not to use it much as it smelled oddly and permanently of cat urine, and impeded the free flow of the red beach towel that I tied round my neck for flight. For a brief while I wore some underpants over my jeans in the manner of Superman (a sartorial quirk that one struggled to fathom) but this caused such widespread mirth in the Kiddie Corral that I soon gave up the practice.

On my head, according to season, I wore a green felt cowboy hat or Davy Crockett coonskin cap. For aerial work I donned a Johnny Unitas-approved football helmet with sturdy plastic face guard. The whole kit, fully assembled, weighed slightly over seventy pounds. I didn't so much wear it as drag it along with me. When fully dressed I was the Thunderbolt Kid (later Captain Thunderbolt), a name that my father bestowed on me in a moment of chuckling admiration as he unsnagged a caught sword and lifted me up the five wooden steps of our back porch, saving me perhaps ten minutes of heavy climb.

Happily, I didn't need a lot of mobility, for my superpowers were not actually about capturing bad people or doing good for the common man, but primarily about using my X-ray vision to peer beneath the clothes of attractive women and to carbonize and eliminate people – teachers, babysitters, old people who wanted a kiss – who were an impediment to my happiness. All heroes of the day had particular specialities. Superman fought for truth, justice and the American way. Roy Rogers went almost exclusively for Communist agents who were scheming to poison the water supply or otherwise disrupt and insult the American way of life. Zorro tormented an oafish fellow named Sergeant Garcia for obscure but apparently sound reasons. The Lone Ranger fought for law and order in the early west. I killed morons. Still do.

I used to give X-ray vision a lot of thought because I couldn't see how it could work. I mean, if you could see through people's clothing, then surely you would also see through their skin and right into their bodies. You would see blood vessels, pulsing

71

organs, food being digested and pushed through coils of bowel, and much else of a gross and undesirable nature. Even if you could somehow confine your X-rays to rosy epidermis, any body you gazed at wouldn't be in an appealing natural state, but would be compressed and distorted by unseen foundation garments. The breasts, for one thing, would be oddly constrained and hefted, basketed within an unseen bra, rather than relaxed and nicely jiggly. It wouldn't be satisfactory at all – or at least not nearly satisfactory enough. Which is why it was necessary to perfect ThunderVision™, a laser-like gaze that allowed me to strip away undergarments without damaging skin or outer clothing. That ThunderVision, stepped up a grade and focused more intensely, could also be used as a powerful weapon to vaporize irritating people was a pleasing but entirely incidental benefit.

Unlike Superman I had no one to explain to me the basis of my powers. I had to make my own way into the superworld, and find my own role models. This wasn't easy, for although the 1950s was a busy age for heroes, it was a strange one. Nearly all the heroic figures of the day were odd and just a touch unsettling. Most lived with another man, except Roy Rogers, the singing cowboy, who lived with a woman, Dale Evans, who dressed like a man. Batman and Robin looked unquestionably as if they were on their way to a gay mardi gras, and Superman was not a huge amount better. Confusingly, there were actually *two* Supermans. There was the comic-book Superman who had bluish hair, never laughed and didn't take any shit from anybody. And there was the television Superman, who was much more genial and a little bit flabby around the tits, and who actually got wimpier and softer as the years passed.

In similar fashion, the Lone Ranger, who was already not the kind of fellow you would want to share a pup tent with, was made odder still by the fact that the part was played on television by two different actors – by Clayton Moore from 1948 to 1951 and from 1954 to 1957, and by John Hart during the years in between – but the programmes were rerun randomly on local TV, giving the impression that the Lone Ranger not only wore a tiny mask that fooled no one, but changed bodies from time to time. He also had a catchphrase – 'A fiery horse with the speed of light, a cloud of dust and hearty "Hi-ho, Silver": the Lone Ranger' – that made absolutely no sense no matter how you looked at it.

Roy Rogers, my first true hero, was in many ways the most bewildering of all. For one thing, he was strangely anachronistic. He lived in a western town, Mineral City, that seemed comfortably bedded in the nineteenth century. It had wooden sidewalks and hitching posts, the houses used oil lamps, everyone rode horses and carried six-shooters, the marshal dressed like a cowboy and wore a badge – but when people ordered coffee in Dale's café it was brought to them in a glass pot off an electric hob. From time to time modern policemen or FBI men would turn up in cars or even light aeroplanes looking for fugitive Communists and when this happened I can clearly remember thinking, 'What the fuck?' or whatever was the equivalent expression for a five-year-old.

Except for Zorro – who really knew how to make a sword fly – the fights were always brief and bloodless, and never involved hospitalization, much less comas, extensive scarring or death. Mostly they consisted of somebody jumping off a boulder on to somebody passing on a horse, followed by a good deal of speeded-up wrestling. Then the two fighters would stand up and the good guy would knock the bad guy down. Roy and Dale both carried guns – everybody carried guns, including Magnolia, their comical black servant, and Pat Brady, the cook – but never shot to kill. They just shot the pistols out of bad people's hands and then knocked them down with a punch.

The other memorable thing about Roy Rogers – which I particularly recall because my father always remarked on it if he happened to be passing through the room – was that Roy's horse, Trigger, got higher billing than Dale Evans, his wife.

'But then Trigger *is* more talented,' my father would always say.

'And better looking, too!' we would faithfully and in unison rejoin.

Goodness me, but we were happy people in those days.

Chapter 4

THE AGE OF EXCITEMENT

**PRE-DINNER DRINKS WON'T
HARM HEART, STUDY SHOWS**

PHILADELPHIA, PENN. (AP) – A couple of cocktails before dinner,
and maybe a third for good measure, won't do your heart any
harm. In fact, they may even do some good. A research team at
Lankenau Hospital reached this conclusion after a study
supported in part by the Heart Association of Southeastern
Pennsylvania.

– Des Moines Register, 12 August 1958

I DON'T KNOW HOW they managed it, but the people responsible for the 1950s made a world in which pretty much everything was good for you. Drinks before dinner? The more the better! Smoke? You bet! Cigarettes actually made you healthier, by soothing jangly nerves and sharpening jaded minds, according to advertisements. 'Just what the doctor ordered!' read ads for L&M cigarettes, some of them in the *Journal of the American Medical Association* where cigarette ads were gladly accepted right up to the 1960s. X-rays were so benign that shoe stores installed special machines that used them to measure foot sizes, sending penetrating rays up through the soles of your feet and right out the top of your head. There wasn't a particle of tissue within you that wasn't bathed in their magical glow. No wonder you felt energized and ready for a new pair of Keds when you stepped down.

Happily, we were indestructible. We didn't need seat belts, airbags, smoke detectors, bottled water or the Heimlich manoeuvre. We didn't require child safety caps on our medicines. We didn't need helmets when we rode our bikes or pads for our knees and elbows when we went skating. We knew without written reminding that bleach was not a refreshing drink and that gasoline when exposed to a match had a tendency to combust. We didn't have to worry about what we ate because nearly all foods were good for us: sugar gave us energy, red meat made us strong, ice cream gave us healthy bones, coffee kept us alert and purring productively.

Every week brought exciting news of things becoming better, swifter, more convenient. Nothing was too preposterous to try. 'Mail Is Delivered by Guided Missile', the *Des Moines Register* reported with a clear touch of excitement and pride on the morning of 8 June 1959, after the US Postal Service launched a Regulus I rocket carrying three thousand first-class letters from a submarine in the Atlantic Ocean on to an airbase in Mayport, Florida, one hundred miles away. Soon, the article assured us, rockets loaded with mail would be streaking across the nation's skies. Special delivery letters, one supposed, would be thudding nosecone-first into our back yards practically hourly.

'I believe we will see missile mail developed to a significant degree,' promised Postmaster General Arthur Summerfield at the celebrations that followed. In fact nothing more was heard of missile mail. Perhaps it occurred to someone that incoming rockets might have an unfortunate tendency to miss their targets and crash through the roofs of factories or hospitals, or that they might blow up in flight, or take out passing aircraft, or that every launch would cost tens of thousands of dollars to deliver a payload worth a maximum of $120 at prevailing postal rates.

The fact was that rocket mail was not for one moment a realistic proposition, and that every penny of the million or so dollars spent on the experiment was wasted. No matter. The important thing was knowing that we could send mail by rocket if we *wanted* to. This was an age for dreaming, after all.

Looking back now, it's almost impossible to find anything that wasn't at least a little bit exciting at the time. Even haircuts could give unusual amounts of pleasure. In 1955, my father and brother went to the barber and came back with every hair on their heads standing to attention and sheared off in a perfect horizontal plane. This arresting style was known as a flat-top. They spent most of the rest of the decade looking as if they were prepared in emergencies to provide landing spots for some very small experimental aircraft, or perhaps special delivery messages sent by miniature missile. Never have people looked so ridiculous and so happy at the same time.

There was a certain endearing innocence about the age, too. On 3 April 1956, according to news reports, a Mrs Julia Chase of Hagerstown, Maryland, while on a tour of the White House, slipped away from her tour group and vanished into the heart of the building. For four and a half hours, Mrs Chase, who was described later as 'dishevelled, vague and not quite lucid', wandered through the White House, setting small fires – five in all. That's how tight security was in those days: a not-quite-lucid woman was able to roam unnoticed through the Executive Mansion for more than half a working day. You can imagine the response if anyone tried anything like that now: the instantaneous alarms, the scrambled Air Force jets, the SWAT teams dropping from panels in the ceiling, the tanks rolling across the lawns, the ninety minutes of sustained gunfire pouring into the target area, the lavish awarding of medals of bravery afterwards, including posthumously to the seventy-six people in Virginia and eastern Maryland killed by friendly fire. In 1956, Mrs Chase, when found, was taken to the staff kitchen, given a cup of tea and released into the custody of her family, and no one ever heard from her again.

Exciting things were happening in the kitchen too. 'A few years ago it took the housewife 5½ hours to prepare daily meals for a family of four,' *Time* magazine reported in a cover article in

1959, which I can guarantee my mother read with great avidity. 'Today she can do it in 90 minutes or less – and still produce meals fit for a king or a finicky husband.' *Time*'s anonymous tipsters went on to list all the fantastic new convenience foods that were just around the corner. Frozen salads. Spray-on mayonnaise. Cheese you could spread with a knife. Liquid instant coffee in a spray can. A complete pizza meal in a tube.

In tones of deepest approbation, the article noted how Charles Greenough Mortimer, chairman of General Foods and a culinary visionary of the first rank, had grown so exasperated with the dullness, the mushiness, the disheartening predictability of conventional vegetables that he had put his best men to work creating 'new' ones in the General Foods laboratories. Mortimer's kitchen wizards had just come up with a product called Rolletes in which they puréed multiple vegetables – peas, carrots and lima beans, for example – and combined the resulting mush into frozen sticks, which the busy homemaker could place on a baking tray and warm up in the oven.

Rolletes went the same way as rocket mail (as indeed did Charles Greenough Mortimer), but huge numbers of other food products won a place in our stomachs and hearts. By the end of the decade the American consumer could choose from nearly one hundred brands of ice cream, five hundred types of breakfast cereals and nearly as many makes of coffee. At the same time, the nation's food factories pumped their products full of delicious dyes and preservatives to heighten and sustain their appeal. By the end of the decade supermarket foods in the United States contained as many as two thousand different chemical additives, including (according to one survey) 'nine emulsifiers, thirty-one stabilizers and thickeners, eighty-five surfactants, seven anti-caking agents, twenty-eight anti-oxidants, and forty-four sequestrants'. Sometimes they contained some food as well, I believe.

Even death was kind of exciting, especially when being safely inflicted on others. In 1951 *Popular Science* magazine asked the nation's ten leading science reporters to forecast the most promising scientific breakthroughs that they expected the next twelve months to bring, and exactly half of them cited refinements to nuclear armaments – several with quite a lot of relish. Arthur J. Snider of the *Chicago Daily News*, for one, noted excitedly that American ground troops could soon be equipped with personal atomic warheads. 'With small atomic artillery capable of firing into concentrations of troops, the ways of tactical warfare are to be revolutionized!' Snider enthused. 'Areas that have in the past been able to withstand weeks and months of siege can now be obliterated in days or hours.' Hooray!

People were charmed and captivated – transfixed, really – by the broiling majesty and unnatural might of atomic bombs. When the military started testing nuclear weapons at a dried lake bed called Frenchman Flat in the Nevada desert outside Las Vegas it became the town's hottest tourist attraction. People came to Las Vegas not to gamble – or at least not exclusively to gamble – but to stand on the desert's edge, feel the ground shake beneath their feet and watch the air before them fill with billowing pillars of smoke and dust. Visitors could stay at the Atomic View Motel, order an Atomic Cocktail ('equal parts vodka, brandy, and champagne, with a splash of sherry') in local cocktail lounges, eat an Atomic Hamburger, get an Atomic Hairdo, watch the annual crowning of Miss Atom Bomb or the nightly rhythmic gyrations of a stripper named Candyce King who called herself 'the Atomic Blast'.

As many as four nuclear detonations a month were

conducted in Nevada in the peak years. The mushroom clouds were visible from any parking lot in the city,* but most visitors went to the edge of the blast zone itself, often with picnic lunches, to watch the tests and enjoy the fallout afterwards. And these were big blasts. Some were seen by airline pilots hundreds of miles out over the Pacific Ocean. Radioactive dust often drifted across Las Vegas, leaving a visible coating on every horizontal surface. After some of the early tests, government technicians in white lab coats went through the city running Geiger counters over everything. People lined up to see how radioactive they were. It was all part of the fun. What a joy it was to be indestructible.

Pleasurable as it was to watch nuclear blasts and take on a warm glow of radioactivity, the real joy of the decade – better than flat-tops, rocket mail, spray-on mayonnaise and the atomic bomb combined – was television. It is almost not possible now to appreciate just how welcome TV was.

In 1950, not many private homes in America had televisions. Forty per cent of people still hadn't seen even a single programme. Then I was born and the country went crazy (though the two events were not precisely connected). By late 1952, one third of American households – twenty million homes or thereabouts – had purchased TVs. The number would have been even higher except that large parts of rural America still didn't have coverage (or even, often, electricity). In cities, the saturation was much swifter. In May 1953, United Press reported that Boston now had

*Though Las Vegas was not in those days the throbbing city we know today. Throughout most of the 1950s it remained a small resort town way out in a baking void. It didn't get its first traffic light until 1952 or its first elevator (in the Riviera Hotel) until 1955.

more television sets (780,000) than bathtubs (720,000), and people admitted in an opinion poll that they would rather go hungry than go without their televisions. Many probably did. In the early 1950s, when the average factory worker's after-tax pay was well under $100 a week, a new television cost up to $500.*

TV was so exciting that McGregor, the clothing company, produced a range of clothing in its honour. 'With the spectacular growth of television, millions of Americans are staying indoors,' the company noted in its ads. 'Now, for this revolutionary way of life, McGregor works a sportswear revolution. Whether viewing – or on view – here's sportswear with the new point of view.'

The range was called Videos and to promote it the company produced an illustration, done in the wholesome and meticulous style of a Norman Rockwell painting, showing four athletic-looking young men lounging in a comfortable den before a glowing TV, each sporting a sharp new item from the Videos range – reversible Glen Plaid Visa-Versa Jacket, all-weather Host Tri-Threat Jacket, Durosheen Host Casual Jacket with matching lounge slacks, and, for the one feeling just a touch gay, an Arabian Knights sport shirt in a paisley gabardine, neatly paired with another all-weather jacket. The young men in the illustration look immensely pleased – with the TV, with their outfits, with their good teeth and clear complexions, with everything – and never mind that their clothes are patently designed to be worn out of doors. Perhaps McGregor expected them to stand in neighbours' flowerbeds and watch TV through windows as we did at Mr Kiessler's house. In any case, the McGregor range was not a great success.

*As late as 1959, earnings after tax for a factory worker heading a family of four were $81.03 a week, $73.49 for a single factory worker, though the cost of TVs had fallen significantly.

People, it turned out, didn't want special clothes for watching television. They wanted special food, and C. A. Swanson and Sons of Omaha came up with the perfect product in 1954: TV dinners (formally TV Brand Dinners), possibly the best bad food ever produced, and I mean that as the sincerest of compliments. TV dinners gave you a whole meal on a compartmentalized aluminium tray. All you had to add was a knife and fork and a dab of butter on the mashed potatoes and you had a complete meal that generally managed (at least in our house) to offer an interesting range of temperature experiences across the compartments, from tepid and soggy (fried chicken) to leap-up-in-astonishment scalding (soup or vegetable) to still partly frozen (mashed potatoes), and all curiously metallic tasting, yet somehow quite satisfying, perhaps simply because it was new and there was nothing else like it. Then some other innovative genius produced special folding trays that you could eat from while watching television, and that was the last time any child – indeed, any male human being – sat at a dining room table voluntarily.

Of course it wasn't TV as we know it now. For one thing, commercials were often built right into the programmes, which gave them an endearing and guileless charm. On *Burns and Allen*, my favourite programme, an announcer named Harry Von Zell would show up halfway through and stroll into George and Gracie's kitchen and do a commercial for Carnation Evaporated Milk ('the milk from contented cows') at the kitchen table while George and Gracie obligingly waited till he was finished to continue that week's amusing story.

Just to make sure that no one forgot that TV was a commercial enterprise, programme titles often generously incorporated the sponsor's name: *The Colgate Comedy Hour*, the

Lux-Schlitz Playhouse, *The Dinah Shore Chevy Show*, *G.E. Theater*, *Gillette Cavalcade of Sports* and the generously repetitive *Your Kaiser-Fraser Dealer Presents Kaiser-Fraser Adventures in Mystery*. Advertisers dominated every aspect of production. Writers working on shows sponsored by Camel cigarettes were forbidden to show villains smoking cigarettes, to make any mention in any context of fires or arson or anything bad to do with smoke and flames, or to have anyone cough for any reason. When a competitor on the game show *Do You Trust Your Wife?* replied that his wife's astrological sign was Cancer, writes J. Ronald Oakley in the excellent *God's Country: America in the Fifties*, 'the tobacco company sponsoring the show ordered it to be refilmed and the wife's sign changed to Aries.' Even more memorably, for a broadcast of *Judgment at Nuremberg* on a series called Playhouse 90, the sponsor, the American Gas Association, managed to have all references to gas ovens and the gassing of Jews removed from the script.

Only one thing exceeded America's infatuation with television and that was its love of the automobile. Never has a country gone more car-giddy than America did in the 1950s.

When the war ended, there were only thirty million cars on America's roads, roughly the same number as had existed in the 1920s, but then things took off in a big way. Over the next four decades, as a writer for the *New York Times* put it, the country 'paved 42,798 miles of Interstate highway, bought three hundred million cars, and went for a ride'. The number of new cars bought by Americans went from just sixty-nine thousand in 1945 to over five million four years later. By the mid-Fifties Americans were buying eight million new cars a year (this in a nation of approximately forty million households).

They not only wanted to, they *had* to. Under President Eisenhower, America spent three quarters of federal transport-ation dollars on building highways, and less than 1 per cent on mass transit. If you wanted to get anywhere at all, increasingly you had to do so in your own car. By the middle of the 1950s America was already becoming a two-car nation. As a Chevrolet ad of 1956 exulted: 'The family with two cars gets twice as many chores com-pleted, so there's more leisure to enjoy together!'

And what cars they were. They looked, in the words of one observer, as if they should light up and play. Many boasted features that suggested they might almost get airborne. Pontiacs came with Strato-Streak V8 engines and Strato-Flight Hydra-Matic transmissions. Chryslers offered PowerFlite Range Selector and Torsion-Aire Suspension, while the Chevrolet Bel-Air had a hold-on-to-your-hat feature called Triple-Turbine TurboGlide. In 1958, Ford produced a Lincoln that was over nineteen feet long. By 1961, the American car-buyer had over three hundred and fifty models to choose from.

People were so enamoured of their cars that they more or less tried to live in them. They dined at drive-in restaurants, passed their evenings at drive-in movies, did their banking at drive-in banks, dropped their clothes at drive-in dry cleaners. My father wouldn't have anything to do with any of this. He thought it was somehow unseemly. He wouldn't eat in any restaurant that didn't have booths and a place mat at each setting. (Nor, come to that, would he eat in any place that had anything better than booths and placemats.) So my drive-in experiences came when I went out with Ricky Ramone, who didn't have a dad but whose mom had a red Pontiac Star Chief convertible and *loved* driving fast with the top down and the music way up and going to the

A&W drive-in way out by the state fairgrounds on the east side of town, and so I loved her. I'm sure Ricky was conceived in a car, probably between bites at an A&W.

By the end of the decade, America had almost seventy-four million cars on its roads, nearly double the number of ten years before. Los Angeles had more cars than Asia, and General Motors was a bigger economic entity than Belgium, and more exciting, too.

TV and cars went together perfectly. TV showed you a world of alluring things – atomic bombs in Las Vegas, babes on water skis in Cypress Gardens, Florida, Thanksgiving Day parades in New York City – and cars made it possible to get there.

No one understood this better than Walt Disney. When he opened Disneyland on sixty acres of land near the nowhere town of Anaheim, twenty-three miles south of Los Angeles, in 1955, people thought he was out of his mind. Amusement parks were dying in America in the 1950s. They were a refuge of poor people, immigrants, sailors on shore leave and other people of low tone and light pockets. But Disneyland was of course different from the start. First, there was no way to reach it by any form of public transportation, so people of modest means couldn't get there. And if they did somehow contrive to reach the gates, they couldn't afford to get in anyway.*

But Disney's masterstroke was to exploit television for all that it was worth. A year before the park even opened, Disney launched a television series that was essentially a weekly

---

*It says much, I think, that the parking lot at Disneyland, covering one hundred acres, was larger than the park itself, at sixty acres. It could hold 12,175 cars – coincidentally almost exactly the number of orange trees that had been grubbed up during construction.

hour-long commercial for Disney enterprises. The programme was actually called *Disneyland* for its first four years and many of the episodes in the series, including the very first, were devoted to celebrating and drumming up interest in that paradise of fantasy and excitement that was swiftly rising from the orange groves at the smoggy end of California.

By the time the park opened, people couldn't wait to get there. Within two years it was attracting four and a half million visitors a year. The average customer, according to *Time* magazine, spent $4.90 on a day out at Disneyland – $2.72 for rides and admission, $2 for food and 18 cents for souvenirs. That seems pretty reasonable to me now – it is awfully hard to believe it wasn't reasonable then – but evidently these were shocking prices. The biggest complaint of Disney customers in the park's first two years, *Time* reported, was the cost.

From our neighbourhood you only went to Disneyland if your father was a brain surgeon or orthodontist. For everyone else, it was too far and too expensive. It was entirely out of the question in our case. My father was a fiend for piling us all in the car and going to distant places, but only if the trips were cheap, educational, and celebrated some forgotten aspect of America's glorious past, generally involving slaughter, uncommon hardship or the delivery of mail at a gallop. Riding in spinning teacups at 15 cents a pop didn't fit into any of that.

The low point of the year in our house came every midwinter when my father retired to his room and vanished into an enormous heap of roadmaps, guidebooks, musty volumes of American history, and brochures from communities surprised and grateful for his interest, to select the destination for our next summer vacation.

'Well, everybody,' he would announce when he emerged after perhaps two evenings' study, 'this year I think we'll tour battle-fields of the little-known War of the Filipino Houseboys.' He would fix us with a look that invited cries of rapturous approval.

'Oh, I've never heard of that,' my mom would say cautiously.

'Well, it was actually more of a slaughter than a war,' he would concede. 'It was over in three hours. But it's quite con-venient for the National Museum of Agricultural Implements at Haystacks. They have over seven hundred hoes apparently.'

As he spoke he would spread out a map of the western United States, and point to some parched corner of Kansas or the Dakotas that no outsider had ever willingly visited before. We nearly always went west, but never as far as Disneyland and California, or even the Rockies. There were too many Nebraska sodhouses to look at first.

'There's also a steam engine museum at West Windsock,' he would go on happily, and offer a brochure that no one reached for. 'They do a special two-day ticket for families, which looks to be very reasonable. Have you ever seen a steam piano, Billy? No? I'm not surprised. Not many people have!'

The worst thing about going west was that it meant stopping in Omaha on the way home to visit my mother's quizzical relatives. Omaha was an ordeal for everyone, including those we were visiting, so I never understood why we went there, but we always stopped off. It may be that my father was attracted by the idea of free coffee.

My mother grew up remarkably poor, in a tiny house that was really a shack, on the edge of Omaha's vast and famous stock-yards. The house had a small back yard, which ended in a sudden cliff, below which, spread out as far as the eye could see (or so it seems in memory), lay the hazy stockyards. Every cow for a thousand miles was brought there to moo hysterically and have a few runny shits before being taken away to become hamburger. You've never smelled such a smell as rose from the stockyards, especially on a hot day, or heard such an unhappy clamour. It was ceaseless and deafening – the sound all but bounced off the clouds – and it made you look twice at all meat products for about a month afterwards.

My mother's father, a good-hearted Irish Catholic named Michael McGuire, had worked the whole of his adult life as a hand in the stockyards on a paltry salary. His wife, my mother's mother, had died when my mother was very small, and he had raised five children more or less single-handed, with my mother and her younger sister Frances doing most of the housework. In her senior year of high school, my mother won a city-wide oration contest which carried as its reward a scholarship to Drake University in Des Moines. There she studied journalism and spent her summers working at the *Register* (where she met my father, a young sportswriter with a broad smile and a weakness for spectacular ties, if old photographs are any guide) and never really came back, something about which I think she always felt a little guilty. Frances eventually went off and became a nun of a timid and twittering disposition. Their father died quite young himself, long before I was born, leaving the house to my mother's three curiously inert brothers, Joey, Johnny and Leo.

It was an astonishment to me even when quite young to think that my mother and her siblings had come from the same genetic stock. I believe she may have felt a little that way herself. My father called her brothers the Three Stooges, though this perhaps suggests a liveliness and joie de vivre, not to mention an entertaining tendency to poke each other in the eyes with forked fingers, that was entirely lacking. They were the three most un-interesting human beings that I have ever met. They had spent their whole lives in this one tiny house, even though they must practically have had to share a bed. I don't know that any of them ever worked or even went outdoors much. The youngest, Leo, had an electric guitar and a small amplifier. If he was asked to play – and he loved nothing better – he would disappear into the bed-room for twenty minutes and emerge, startlingly, in a green sequinned cowboy suit. He knew only two songs, both employ-ing the same chords played in the same order, so fortunately his recitals didn't last long. Johnny spent his whole life sitting at a bare table quietly drinking – he had a fantastic red nose; I mean just fantastic – and Joey had no redeeming qualities at all. When he died, I don't believe anyone was much bothered. I think they may just have rolled his body over the cliff edge. Anyway, when you visited there was nothing to do. I don't recall that they even had a TV. There certainly weren't toys to play with or footballs to kick around. There weren't even enough chairs for everybody to sit down at the same time.

Years later, when Johnny died, my mother discovered he had a common-law wife that he had never told my mother about. I think this wife may actually have been in the closet or under the floor-boards or something when we were there. So it is perhaps not surprising that they always seemed kind of keen for us to leave.

Then in 1960, just before my ninth birthday, a really un-expected thing happened. My father announced that we were going to go on a *winter* vacation, over the Christmas holidays, but he wouldn't say where.

It had been an odd fall, but a good one, especially for my

dad. My father, you see, was the best baseball writer of his generation – he really was – and in the fall of 1960 I believe he proved it. At a time when most sportswriting was leaden or read as if written by enthusiastic but minimally gifted fourteen-year-olds, he wrote prose that was thoughtful, literate and comparatively sophisticated. 'Neat but not gaudy,' he would always say, with a certain flourish of satisfaction, as he pulled the last sheet out of the typewriter. No one could touch him at writing against a deadline, and on 13 October 1960, at the World Series in Pittsburgh, he put the matter beyond possible dispute.

The Series ended with one of those dramatic moments that baseball seemed to specialize in in those days: Bill Mazeroski of Pittsburgh hit a home run in the ninth inning that snatched triumph from the Yankees and handed it miraculously and un-expectedly to the lowly Pirates. Virtually all the papers in the country reported the news in the same dull, worthy, bewilderingly uninspired tones. Here, for instance, is the opening paragraph of the story that ran on page one of the *New York Times* the next morning:

The Pirates today brought Pittsburgh its first world series baseball championship in thirty-five years when Bill Mazeroski slammed a ninth-inning home run high over the left-field wall of historic Forbes Field.

And here is what people in Iowa read:

The most hallowed piece of property in Pittsburgh baseball history left Forbes Field late Thursday afternoon under a dirty gray sports jacket and with a police escort. That, of course, was home plate, where Bill Mazeroski completed his electrifying home run while Umpire Bill Jackowski, broad back braced and arms spread, held off the mob long enough for Bill to make it legal.

Pittsburgh's steel mills couldn't have made more noise than the crowd in this ancient park did when Mazeroski smashed Yankee Ralph Terry's second pitch of the ninth inning. By the time the ball sailed over the ivy-covered brick wall, the rush from the stands had begun and these sudden madmen threatened to keep Maz from touching the plate with the run that beat the lordly Yankees, 10–9, for the title.

Bear in mind that the story was written not at leisure but amid the din and distraction of a crowded press box in the immediate whooping aftermath of the game. Nor could a single thought or neat phrase (like 'broad back braced and arms spread') have been prepared in advance and casually dropped into the text. Since Mazeroski's home run rudely upended a nation's confident expectations of a victory by 'the lordly Yankees', every sportswriter present had to discard whatever he'd had in mind to say, even one batter earlier, and start afresh. Search as you will, you won't find a better World Series game report on file anywhere, unless it was another of my dad's.*

But I had no idea of this at the time. All I knew was that my father returned home from the Series in unusually high spirits, and revealed his startling plans to take us away on a trip over Christmas to some mysterious locale.

*Of course it's possible I overstate things – this is my father, after all – but if so it is not an entirely private opinion. In 2000, writing in the *Columbia Journalism Review*, Michael Gartner, a former president of NBC News who grew up in Des Moines, wrote that my father, the original Bill Bryson, 'may have been the best baseball writer ever, anywhere'.

'You wait. You'll like it. You'll see,' was all he would say, to whoever asked. The whole idea of it was unspeakably exciting – we weren't the type of people to do something so rash, so sudden, so *unseasonal* – but unnerving too, for exactly the same reasons. So on the afternoon of 16 December, when Greenwood, my elementary school, dispatched its happy hordes into the snowy streets to begin three glorious weeks of yuletide relaxation (and school holidays in those days, let me say, were of a proper and generous duration), the family Rambler was waiting out front, steaming extravagantly, even keenly, and ready to cut a trail across the snowy prairies. We headed west as usual, crossed the mighty Missouri River at Council Bluffs and made our way past Omaha. Then we just kept on going. We drove for what seemed like (in fact was) days across the endless, stubbly, snow-blown plains. We passed one enticing diversion after another – Pony Express stations, buffalo licks, a pretty big rock – without so much as a sideways glance from my father. My mother began to look faintly worried.

On the third morning, we caught our first sight of the Rockies – the first time in my life I had seen something on the horizon other than a horizon. And still we kept going, up and through the ragged mountains and out the other side. We emerged in California, into warmth and sunshine, and spent a week experiencing its wonders – its mighty groves of redwoods, the lush Imperial Valley, Big Sur, Los Angeles – and the delicious, odd feel of warm sunlight on your face and bare arms in December: a winter without winter.

I had seldom – what am I saying? I had never – seen my father so generous and care-free. At a lunch counter in San Luis Obispo he invited me – *urged* me – to have a large hot fudge sundae, and when I said, 'Dad, are you *sure*?' he said, 'Go on, you only live once' – a sentiment that had never passed his teeth before, certainly not in a commercial setting.

We spent Christmas Day walking on a beach in Santa Monica, and the next day we got in the car and drove south on a snaking freeway through the hazy, warm, endless nowhereness of Los Angeles. At length we parked in an enormous parking lot that was almost comically empty – we were one of only half a dozen cars, all from out of state – and strode a few paces to a grand entrance, where we stood with hands in pockets looking up at a fabulous display of wrought iron.

'Well, Billy, do you know where this is?' my father asked, unnecessarily. There wasn't a child in the world that didn't know these fabled gates.

'It's Disneyland,' I said.

'It certainly is,' he agreed and stared appreciatively at the gates as if they were something he had privately commissioned.

For a minute I wondered if this was all we had come for – to admire the gates – and if in a moment we would get back in the car and drive on to somewhere else. But instead he told us to wait where we were, and strode purposefully to a ticket booth where he conducted a brief but remarkably cheerful transaction. It was the only time in my life that I saw two $20 bills leave my father's wallet simultaneously. As he waited at the window, he gave us a broad smile and a little wave.

'Have I got leukaemia or something?' I asked my mother.

'No, honey,' she replied.

'Has Dad got leukaemia?'

'No, honey, everybody's fine. Your father's just got the Christmas spirit.'

At no point in all my life before or since have I been more astounded, more gratified, more happy than I was for the whole of that day. We had the park practically to ourselves. We did it all – spun gaily in people-sized teacups, climbed aboard flying Dumbos, marvelled at the exciting conveniences in the Monsanto All-Plastic House of the Future in Tomorrowland, enjoyed a submarine ride and riverboat safari, took a rocket to the moon. (The seats actually trembled. 'Whoa!' we all said in delighted alarm.) Disneyland in those days was a considerably less slick and manicured wonder than it would later become, but it was still the finest thing I had ever seen – possibly the finest thing that existed in America at the time. My father was positively enchanted with the place, with its tidiness and wholesomeness and imaginative picture-set charm, and kept asking rhetorically why all the world couldn't be like this. 'But cheaper, of course,' he added, comfortingly returning to character and steering us deftly past a souvenir stand.

The next morning we got in the car and began the thousand-mile trip across desert, mountain and prairie to Des Moines. It was a long drive, but everyone was very happy. At Omaha, we didn't stop – didn't even slow down – but just kept on going. And if there is a better way to conclude a vacation than by not stopping in Omaha, then I don't know it.

Chapter 5
THE PURSUIT OF PLEASURE

In Detroit, Mrs Dorothy Van Dorn, suing for divorce, complained that her husband 1) put all their food in a freezer, 2) kept the freezer locked, 3) made her pay for any food she ate, and 4) charged her the 3% Michigan sales tax.

– *Time* magazine, 10 December 1951

FUN WAS A DIFFERENT KIND OF THING in the 1950s, mostly because there wasn't so much of it. That is not, let me say, a bad thing. Not a great thing perhaps, but not a bad one either. You learned to wait for your pleasures, and to appreciate them when they came.

My most pleasurable experience of these years occurred on a hot day in August 1959 shortly after my mother informed me that she had accepted an invitation on my behalf to go to Lake Ahquabi for the day with Milton Milton and his family. This rash acceptance most assuredly was *not* part of my happiness, believe me, for Milton Milton was the most annoying, the most repellent, the *moistest* drip the world had yet produced, and his parents and sister were even worse. They were noisy, moronically argument-ative, told stupid jokes, and ate with their mouths so wide open you could see all the way to their uvulas and some distance beyond. Mr Milton had an Adam's apple the size of a champagne cork and bore as uncanny a resemblance to the Disney character Goofy as was possible without actually being a cartoon dog. His wife was just like him but hairier.

Their idea of a treat was to pass around a plate of Fig Newtons, the only truly dreadful cookie ever made. They actually yukked when they laughed – an event that gave them a chance to show you just what a well-masticated Fig Newton looks like in its final moments before oblivion (black, sticky, horrible). An hour with the Miltons was like a visit to the second circle of hell. Needless to say, I torched them repeatedly with ThunderVision, but they were strangely ineradicable.

On the one previous occasion on which I had experienced their hospitality, a slumber party at which it turned out I was the only guest, or possibly the only invitee who showed up, Mrs Milton had made me – I'll just repeat that: made me – eat chipped beef on toast, a dish closely modelled on vomit, and then sent us to bed at 8.30 after Milton passed out halfway through *I've Got a Secret*, exhausted after sixteen hours of pretending to be a steam shovel.

So when my mother informed me that she had, in her amiable dementia, committed me to yet another period in their company, my dismay was practically boundless.

'Tell me this isn't happening,' I said and began walking in small, disturbed circles around the carpet. 'Tell me this is just a bad, bad dream.'

'I thought you liked Milton,' said my mother. 'You went to his house for a slumber party.'

'Mom, it was the worst night of my *life*. Don't you remember? Mrs Milton made me eat baked throw-up. Then she made me share Milton's toothbrush because you forgot to pack one for me.'

'Did I?' said my mother.

I nodded with a kind of strained stoicism. She had packed my sister's toilet bag by mistake. It contained two paper-wrapped tampons and a shower cap, but not my toothbrush or the secret midnight feast that I had been faithfully promised. I spent the rest of the evening playing drums with the tampons on Milton's comatose head.

'I've never been so bored in my life. I *told* you all this before.'

'Did you? I honestly don't recall.'

'Mom, I had to share a toothbrush with Milton Milton after he'd been eating Fig Newtons.'

She received this with a compassionate wince.

'Please don't make me go to Lake Ahquabi with them.'

She considered briefly. 'Well, all right,' she said. 'But I'm afraid you'll have to come with us to visit Sister Gonzaga then.'

Sister Gonzaga was a great-aunt of formidable mien and yet another of the family's many nuns from my mother's side. She was six feet tall and very scary. There was a long-running suspicion in the family that she was actually a man. You always felt that underneath all that starch there was a lot of chest hair. In the summer of 1959, Sister Gonzaga was dying in a local hospital, though not nearly fast enough, if you asked me. Spending an afternoon in Sister Gonzaga's room at the Home for Dying Nuns (I'm not sure that that was its actual name) was possibly the only thing worse than a day out with the Miltons.

So I went to Lake Ahquabi, in a mood of gloomy submission, crammed into the Miltons' ancient, dinky Nash, a car with the comfort and stylish zip of a chest freezer, expecting the worst and receiving it. We got heatedly lost for an hour in the immediate vicinity of the state capitol building – something that was almost impossible for any normal family to do in Des Moines – and when we finally reached Ahquabi spent ninety minutes more, with much additional disputation, unloading the car and setting up a base camp on the shady lawn beside the small artificial beach. Mrs Milton distributed sandwiches, which were made of some kind of pink paste that looked like, and for all I know was, the stuff my grandmother used to secure her dentures to her gums. I went for a little walk with my sandwich and left it with a dog that would have nothing to do with it. Even a procession of ants, I noticed later, had detoured three feet to avoid it.

Having eaten, we had to sit quietly for forty-five minutes before swimming lest we get cramps and die horribly in six inches of water, which was as far in as young males ever ventured on account of perennial rumours that the coffee-coloured depths of Ahquabi harboured vicious snapping turtles that mistook small boys' pizzles for tasty food. Mrs Milton timed this quiet period with an egg timer, and encouraged us to close our eyes and have a little sleep until it was time to swim.

Far out in the lake there was moored a large wooden platform on which stood an improbably high diving board – a kind of wooden Eiffel Tower. It was, I'm sure, the tallest wooden structure in Iowa, if not the Midwest. The platform was so far out from shore that hardly anyone ever visited it. Just occasionally some teenaged daredevils would swim out to have a look around. Sometimes they would climb the many ladders to the high board, and even cautiously creep out on to it, but they always retreated when they saw just how suicidally far the water was below them. No human being had ever been known to jump from it.

So it was quite a surprise when, as the egg timer dinged our liberation, Mr Milton jumped up and began doing neck rolls and arm stretches and announced that he intended to have a dive off the high board. Mr Milton had been a bit of a diving star at Lincoln High School, as he never failed to inform anyone who spent more than three minutes in his company, but that was on a ten-foot board at an indoor pool. Ahquabi was of another order of magnitude altogether. Clearly, he was out of his mind, but Mrs Milton was remarkably untroubled. 'OK, hon,' she replied lazily from beneath a preposterous hat. 'I'll have a Fig Newton for you when you get back.'

Word of the insane intention of the man who looked like Goofy was already spreading along the beach when Mr Milton jogged into the water and swam with even strokes out to the platform. He was just a tiny, remote stick figure when he got there but even from such a distance the high board seemed to loom hundreds of feet above him – indeed, seemed almost to scrape the clouds. It took him at least twenty minutes to make his way up the zigzag of ladders to the top. Once at the summit, he strode up and down the board, which was enormously long – it had to be to extend beyond the edge of the platform far below – bounced on it experimentally two or three times, then took some deep breaths and finally assumed a position at the fixed end of the board with his arms at his sides. It was clear from his posture and poised manner that he was going to go for it.

By now all the people on the beach and in the water – several hundred altogether – had stopped whatever they were doing and were silently watching. Mr Milton stood for quite a long time, then with a nice touch of theatricality he raised his arms, ran like hell down the long board – imagine an Olympic gymnast sprinting at full tilt towards a distant springboard and you've got something of the spirit of it – took one enormous bounce and launched himself high and outwards in a perfect swan dive. It was a beautiful thing to behold, I must say. He fell with flawless grace for what seemed whole minutes. Such was the beauty of the moment, and the breathless silence of the watching multitudes, that the only sound to be heard across the lake was the faint whistle of his body tearing through the air towards the water far, far below. It may only be my imagination, but he seemed after a

103

time to start to glow red, like an incoming meteor. He was *really* moving.

I don't know what happened – whether he lost his nerve or realized that he was approaching the water at a murderous velocity or what – but about three quarters of the way down he seemed to have second thoughts about the whole business and began suddenly to flail, like someone entangled in bedding in a bad dream, or whose chute hasn't opened. When he was perhaps thirty feet above the water, he gave up on flailing and tried a new tack. He spread his arms and legs wide, in the shape of an X, evidently hoping that exposing a maximum amount of surface area would somehow slow his fall.

It didn't.

He hit the water – *impacted* really is the word for it – at over six hundred miles an hour, with a report so loud that it made birds fly out of trees up to three miles away. At such a speed water effectively becomes a solid. I don't believe Mr Milton penetrated it at all, but just bounced off it about fifteen feet, limbs suddenly very loose, and then lay on top of it, still, like an autumn leaf, spinning gently. He was towed to shore by two passing fishermen in a rowboat, and carried to a grassy area by half a dozen on-lookers who carefully set him down on an old blanket. There he spent the rest of the afternoon on his back, arms and legs bent slightly and elevated. Every bit of frontal surface area, from his thinning hairline to his toenails, had a raw, abraded look, as if he had suffered some unimaginable misfortune involving an industrial sander. Occasionally he accepted small sips of water, but otherwise was too traumatized to speak.

Later that same afternoon Milton Junior cut himself with a hatchet that he had been told on no account to touch, so that he ended up in pain and in trouble all at the same time. It was the best day of my life.

Of course, that isn't saying a huge amount when you consider that the previous best day in my life at this point was when Mr Sipkowicz, a teacher we didn't like much, licked a Lincoln Log.

Lincoln Logs were toy wooden logs with which you could build forts, ranchhouses, stockades, bunkhouses, corrals and many other structures of interest and utility to cowboys, according to the imaginative illustrations on the cylindrical box, though in fact the supplied materials were actually just barely enough to make one small rectangular cabin with one door and one window (though you could put the window to the right or left of the door, as you wished).

What Buddy Doberman and I discovered was that if you peed on Lincoln Logs you bleached them white. As a result we created, over a period of weeks, the world's first albino Lincoln Log cabin, which we took to school as part of a project on Abraham Lincoln's early years. Naturally we declined to say how we had made the logs white, prompting pupils and teachers alike to examine them keenly for clues.

'I bet you did it with lemon juice,' said Mr Sipkowicz, who was youthful, brash and odious and had an unfortunate taste for flashy ties, and who for a single semester had the distinction of being Greenwood's only male teacher. Before we could stop him – not that we had any intention or desire to, of course – he shot out a long, reptilian tongue and ran it delicately and experimentally – lingeringly, eye-flutteringly – over the longest log in the back wall, which by chance we had prepared only that morning, so that it was still very slightly moist.

'I can taste lemon, can't I?' he said with a pleased, knowing look.

'Not exactly!!!' we cried and he tried again.

'No, it's lemon,' he insisted. 'I can taste the tartness.' He gave another lick, savouring the flavour with such a deep, concentrated, twitchy intensity that for a moment we thought he had gone into shock and was about to topple over, but it was just his way of relishing the moment. 'Definitely lemon,' he said, brightening, and handed it back to us with great satisfaction all round.

Mr Sipkowicz's unbidden licking gave pleasure, of course, but the real joy of the experience was in knowing that we were the first boys in history to get genuine entertainment out of Lincoln Logs, for Lincoln Logs were inescapably pointless and dull – a characteristic they shared with nearly all other toys of the day.

It would be difficult to say which was the most stupid or disappointing toy of the 1950s since most of them were one or the other, except for those that were both. The one that always leaps to mind for me as most incontestably unsatisfactory was Silly Putty, an oily pink plastic material that did nothing but bounce erratically a dozen or so times before disappearing down a storm drain. (That was actually the best thing about it.) Others, however, might opt for the majestically unamusing Mr Potato Head, a box of plastic parts that allowed children to confirm the fundamental truth that even with ears, limbs and a goofy smile a lifeless tuber is a lifeless tuber.

Also notable for negative ecstasy was Slinky, a coil of metal that could be made to go head over heels down a flight of steps but otherwise did nothing at all, though it did redeem itself slightly from the fact that if you got someone to hold one end – Lumpy Kowalski was always very good for this – and stretched the other end all the way across the street and halfway up a facing slope and then let go, it hit them like a cannon ball. In much the same way, Hula Hoops, those otherwise supremely pointless rings, took on a certain value when used as oversized quoits to ensnare and trip up passing toddlers.

Perhaps nothing says more about the modest range of pleasures of the age than that the most popular candies of my childhood were made of wax. You could choose among wax teeth, wax pop bottles, wax barrels and wax skulls, each filled with a small amount of coloured liquid that tasted very like a small dose of cough syrup. You swallowed this with interest if not exactly gratification, then chewed the wax for the next ten or eleven hours. Now you might think there is something wrong with your concept of pleasure when you find yourself paying real money to chew colourless wax, and you would be right of course. But we did it and enjoyed it because we knew no better. And there was, it must be said, something good, something healthily restrained, about eating a product that had neither flavour nor nutritive value.

You could also get small artificial ice cream cones made of some crumbly chalk-like material, straws containing a gritty sugar so ferociously sour that your whole face would actually be sucked into your mouth like sand collapsing into a hole, root beer barrels, red hot cinnamon balls, liquorice wheels and whips, greasy candy worms, rubbery dense gelatin-like candies that tasted of unfamiliar (and indeed unlikeable) fruits but were good value as it took over three hours to eat each one (and three hours more to pick the gluey remnants out of your molars, sometimes with fillings attached), and jawbreakers the size and density of billiard balls, which were the best value of all as they would last for up to three months and had different-coloured strata that turned your tongue interesting new shades as you doggedly dissolved away one squamous layer after another.

At Bishop's, where they had a large and highly regarded assortment of penny candies by the cash register, you could also get a comparatively delicious liquorice treat known, with exquisite sensitivity, as nigger babies – though no one actually used that term any more except my grandmother. Occasionally, when visiting from her hometown of Winfield and dining with us at Bishop's, she would slip me a quarter and tell me to go and get some candy for the two of us to share later.

'And don't forget to get some **NIGGER BABIES**!' she would shout, to my intense mortification, across half an acre of crowded dining room, causing a hundred or so diners to look up.

Five minutes later as I returned with the purchase, pressed furtively to outside walls in a vain attempt to escape detection, she would spy me and cry out: 'Oh, there you are, Billy. Did you remember to get some **NIGGER BABIES**? Because I sure do love those . . . **NIGGER BABIES**!'

'Grandma,' I would whisper fiercely, 'you shouldn't say that.'

'Shouldn't say what – **NIGGER BABIES**?'

'Yes. They're called "*liquorice* babies".'

' "Nigger baby" is a bit offensive,' my mom would explain.

'Oh, sorry,' my grandmother would say, marvelling at the delicacy of city people. Then the next time we went to Bishop's, she would say, 'Billy, here's a quarter. Go and get us some of those – whaddaya call 'em – **LIQUORICE NIGGERS**!'

The other place to get penny candies was Grund's, a small grocery store on Ingersoll Avenue. Grund's was one of the last mom and pop grocers left in the city and certainly the last in our neighbour-hood. It was run by a doddering couple of adorable minuteness and incalculable antiquity named Mr and Mrs Grund. None of the stock had been renewed, or come to that sold, since about 1929. There were things in there that hadn't been seen in the wider retail world since Gloria Swanson was attractive – Othine skin bleach, Fels-Naptha soap, boxes of Wild Root hair tonic with a photograph of Joe E. Brown on the front. Everything was covered in a thick coating of dust, including Mrs Grund. I believe she may have been dead for some years. Mr Grund, however, was very much alive and delighted when the bell above his door tinklingly sounded the arrival of new customers, even though it was always children and even though they were there for a single nefarious purpose: to steal from his enormous aged stock of penny candies.

This is possibly the most shameful episode of my childhood, but it is one I share with over twelve thousand other former children. Everyone knew you could steal from the Grunds and never be caught. On Saturdays kids turned up from all over the Midwest, some of them arriving in charter buses, if I recall correctly, to stock up for the weekend. Mr Grund was serenely blind to misconduct. You could remove his glasses, undo his bow tie, gently ease him out of his trousers, and he wouldn't suspect a thing. Sometimes we made small purchases, but this was just to get him to turn round and engage his ancient cash register so that a hundred flying hands could dip into his outsized jars and help themselves to more. Some of the bigger kids just took the jars. Still, it has to be said we brightened his day, until we finally put him out of business.

At least candy gave actual pleasure. Most things that were

supposed to be fun turned out not to be fun at all. Model making, for instance. Making models was reputed to be hugely enjoyable but it was really just a mysterious ordeal that you had to go through from time to time as part of the boyhood process. The model kits always *looked* fun, to be sure. The illustrations on the boxes portrayed beautifully detailed fighter planes belching red and yellow flames from their wing guns and engaged in lively dogfights. In the background there was always a stricken Messerschmitt spiralling to earth with a dismayed German in the cockpit, shouting bitter epithets through the windscreen. You couldn't wait to recreate such lively scenes in three dimensions.

But when you got the kit home and opened the box the contents turned out to be of a uniform leaden grey or olive green, consisting of perhaps sixty thousand tiny parts, some no larger than a proton, all attached in some organic, inseparable way to plastic stalks like swizzle sticks. The tubes of glue by contrast were the size of large pastry tubes. No matter how gently you depressed them they would blurp out a pint or so of a clear viscous goo whose one instinct was to attach itself to some foreign object – a human finger, the living-room drapes, the fur of a passing animal – and become an infinitely long string.

Any attempt to break the string resulted in the creation of more strings. Within moments you would be attached to hundreds of sagging strands, all connected to something that had nothing to do with model aeroplanes or the Second World War. The only thing the glue wouldn't stick to, interestingly, was a piece of plastic model; then it just became a slippery lubricant that allowed any two pieces of model to glide endlessly over each other, never drying. The upshot was that after about forty minutes of intensive but troubled endeavour you and your immediate surroundings were covered in a glistening spider's web of glue at the heart of which was a grey fuselage with one wing on upside down and a pilot accidentally but irremediably attached by his flying cap to the cockpit ceiling. Happily by this point you were so high on the glue that you didn't give a shit about the pilot, the model or anything else.

The really interesting thing about playtime disappointment in the Fifties was that you never saw any of the disappointments coming. This was because the ads were so brilliant. Advertisers have never been so cunning. They could make any little meretricious piece of crap sound fantastic. Never before or since have commercial blandishments been so silken of tone, so capable of insinuating orgasmic happiness from a few simple materials. Even now in my mind's eye I can see a series of ads in *Boys' Life* from the A. C. Gilbert Company of New Haven, Connecticut, promising the most wholesome joy from their ingenious chemistry sets, microscope kits and world-famous Erector Sets. These last were bolt-together toys from which you could make all manner of engineering marvels – bridges, industrial hoists, fairground rides, motorized robots – from little steel girders and other manly components. These weren't things that you built on tabletops and put in a drawer when you were finished playing. These were items that needed a solid foundation and *lots* of space. I am almost certain that one of the ads showed a boy on a twenty-foot ladder topping out a Ferris wheel on which his younger brother was already enjoying a test ride.

What the ads didn't tell you was that only six people on the planet – A. C. Gilbert's grandsons presumably – had sufficient wealth and roomy enough mansions to enjoy the illustrated sets. I remember my father took one look at the price tag of a giant erection on display in Younkers toy department one Christmas and cried, 'Why, you could practically get a *Buick* for that!' Then he began randomly stopping other male passers-by and soon had a little club of amazed men. So I knew pretty early on that I was never going to get an Erector Set.

Instead I lobbied for a chemistry set, which I had seen in a fetching two-colour double-page spread in *Boys' Life*. According to the ad, this nifty and scientifically advanced kit would allow me to do exciting atomic energy experiments, confound the adult world with invisible writing, become a master of FBI fingerprinting techniques, and make the most satisfyingly enormous stinks. (It didn't actually promise the stinks, but that was implicit in every chemistry set ever sold.)

The set, when opened on Christmas morning, was only about the size of a cigar box – the one portrayed in the magazine had the approximate dimensions of a steamer trunk – but it was ingeniously packed, I must say, with promising stuff: test tubes and a nifty rack in which to set them, a funnel, tweezers, corks, twenty or so little glass pots of colourful chemicals, several of which were promisingly foul smelling, and a plump instruction booklet. Needless to say, I went straight for the atomic energy page, expecting to have a small, private mushroom cloud rising above my workbench by suppertime. In fact, what the instruction book told me, if I recall, was that all materials are made of atoms and that all atoms have energy, so therefore *everything* has atomic energy. Put any two things in a beaker together – any two things at all – give them a shake and, hey presto, you've got an atomic reaction.

All the experiments proved to be more or less like this. The only one that worked even slightly was one of my own devising, which involved mixing together all the chemicals in the set with Babbo cleaning powder, turpentine, some baking soda, two spoonfuls of white pepper, a dab of horseradish of a good age, and a generous splash of Electric-Shave shaving lotion. These when combined instantly expanded about a thousandfold in volume, and ran over the sides of the beaker and on to our brand new kitchen counter, where they began at once to hiss and crinkle and smoke, leaving a pinkish-red welt along the Formica join that would for ever after be a matter of pain and mystification to my father. 'I can't understand it,' he would say, peering along the edge of the counter. 'I must have mixed the adhesive wrong.'

However, the worst toy of the decade, possibly the worst toy ever built, was electric football. Electric football was a game that all boys were compelled to accept as a Christmas present at some point in the 1950s. It consisted of a box with the usual exciting and totally misleading illustrations containing a tinny metal board, about the size of a breakfast tray, painted to look like an American football pitch. This vibrated intensely when switched on, making twenty-two little men move around in a curiously stiff and frantic fashion. It took ages to set up each play because the men were so fiddly and kept falling over, and because you argued continuously with your opponent about what formations were legal and who got to position the last man, since clearly there was an advantage in waiting till the last possible instant and then abruptly moving your running back out to the sidelines where there were no defenders to trouble him. All this always ended in bitter arguments, punctuated by reaching across and knocking over your opponent's favourite players, sometimes repeatedly, with a flicked finger.

It hardly mattered how they were set up because electric

football players never went in the direction intended. In practice what happened was that half the players instantly fell over and lay twitching violently as if suffering from some extreme gastric disorder, while the others streamed off in as many different directions as there were upright players, before eventually clumping together in a corner, where they pushed against the unyielding sides like victims of a nightclub fire at a locked exit. The one exception to this was the running back who just trembled in place for five or six minutes, then slowly turned and went on an unopposed glide towards the wrong end zone until knocked over with a finger on the two-yard line by his distressed manager, occasioning more bickering.

At this point you switched off the power, righted all the fallen men, and painstakingly repeated the setting-up process. After three plays like this, one of you would say, 'Hey, do you wanna go and hit Lumpy Kowalski with a stretched Slinky?' and you would push the game out of the way under the bed where it would never be touched again.

The one place where there was real excitement was comic books. This really was the golden age of comics. Nearly one hundred million of them were being produced every month by the middle of the decade. It is almost impossible to imagine how central a place they played in the lives of the nation's youth – and indeed more than a few beyond youth. A survey of that time revealed that no fewer than 12 per cent of the nation's teachers were devoted readers of comic books. (And that's the ones that admitted it, of course.)

As the Thunderbolt Kid, I read comic books the way doctors read the *New England Journal of Medicine* – to stay abreast of developments in the field. But I was a devoted follower anyway and would have devoured them even without the professional need to keep my supernatural skills honed and productive.

But just as we were getting into comic books, a crisis came. Sales began to falter, pinched between rising production costs and the competition of television. Quite a number of kids now felt that if you could watch Superman and Zorro on TV, why tax yourself with reading words on a page? We in the Kiddie Corral were happy to see such fickle supporters go, frankly, but it was a near-mortal blow for the industry. In two years, the number of comic book titles fell from six hundred and fifty to just two hundred and fifty.

The producers of comic books took some desperate steps to try to rekindle interest. Heroines suddenly became unashamedly sexy. I remember feeling an unexpected but entirely agreeable hormonal warming at the first sight of Asbestos Lady, whose cannonball breasts and powerful loins were barely contained within the wisps of satin fabric with which some artistic genius portrayed her.

There was no space for sentiment in this new age. Captain America's teenaged companion Bucky was dispatched to the hospital with a gunshot wound in one issue and that was the last we ever heard of him. Whether he died or recovered weakly, passing his remaining years in a wheelchair, we didn't know and didn't care. Instead thereafter Captain America was helped by a leggy sylph named Golden Girl, soon augmented by Sun Girl, Lady Lotus, the raven-haired Phantom Lady and other femmes of sleek allure.

Nothing so good could last. Dr Fredric Wertham, a German-born psychiatrist in New York, began an outspoken campaign to rid the world of the baleful influence of comics. In an extremely popular, dismayingly influential book called *Seduction of the Innocent*, he argued that comics promoted violence, torture, criminality, drug-taking and rampant masturbation, though not presumably all at once. Grimly he noted how one boy he interviewed confessed that after reading comic books he 'wanted to be a sex maniac', overlooking that for most boys 'sex', 'mania' and 'want' were words that went together very comfortably with or without comic books.

Wertham saw sex literally in every shadow. He pointed out how in one frame of an action comic the shading on a man's shoulder, when turned at an angle and viewed with an imaginative squint, looked exactly like a woman's pudenda. (In fact it did. There was no arguing the point.) Wertham also announced what most of us knew in our hearts but were reluctant to concede – that many of the superheroes were not fully men in the red-blooded, girl-kissing sense of the term. Batman and Robin in particular he singled out as 'a wish dream of two homosexuals living together'. It was an unanswerable charge. You had only to look at their tights.

Wertham consolidated his fame and influence when he testified before a Senate committee that was looking into the scourge of juvenile delinquency. Just that year Robert Linder, a Baltimore psychologist, had suggested that modern teenagers were suffering from 'a form of collective mental illness' because of rock and roll. Now here was Wertham blaming comics for their sad, zitty failings.

'By 1955,' according to James T. Patterson in the book *Grand Expectations*, 'thirteen states had passed laws regulating the publication, distribution, and sale of comic books.' Alarmed and fearing further regulatory crackdown, the comic book industry abandoned its infatuations with curvy babes, bloody carnage, squint-worthy shadows and everything else that was thrilling. It was a savage blow.

To the dismay of purists, the Kiddie Corral began to fill with anodyne comic books featuring Archie and Jughead or Disney characters like Donald Duck and his nephews Huey, Dewey and Louie, who wore shirts and hats, but nothing at all below the waist, which didn't seem quite right or terribly healthy either. The Kiddie Corral began to attract little girls, who sat chattering away over the latest issues of Little Lulu and Casper the Friendly Ghost as if they were at a tea party. Some perfect fool even put Classic Comic Books in there – the ones that recast famous works of literature in comic book form. These were thrown straight out again, of course.

I vaporized Wertham, needless to say, but it was too late. The damage had been done. Pleasure was going to be harder to get than ever, and the kind we needed most was the hardest of all to get. I refer of course to lust. But that is another story and another chapter.

Chapter 6

SEX AND OTHER DISTRACTIONS

LONDON, ENGLAND (AP) – A high court jury awarded entertainer Liberace 8,000 pounds ($22,400) damages Wednesday in a libel suit against the London Daily Mirror. The jurors decided after 31/2 hours of deliberation that a story in 1956 by Mirror journalist William N. Connor implied that the pianist was a homosexual. Among the phrases Liberace cited in his suit was Connor's description of him as 'everything he, she or it can want.' He also described the entertainer as 'fruit-flavored.'

– *Des Moines Tribune*, 18 June 1959

*I dreamed
I went
to work
in my
maidenform* bra*

CHANSONETTE* with famous 'circular-spoke' stitching

Notice <u>two</u> patterns of stitching on the cups of this bra? Circles that uplift and support, spokes that discreetly emphasize your curves. This fine detailing shapes your figure <u>naturally</u>—keeps the bra shapely, even after machine-washing. The triangular cut-out between the cups gives you extra "breathing room" as the lower elastic insert expands. In white or black: A, B, C cups. **2.00**

Other styles: Broadcloth; Cotton; "Dacron"* Polyester 2.50; Lace, 3.50; with all-elastic back, 3.00; Contour, 3.00; Full-length, 3.50.
*REG. U.S. PAT. OFF. ©1964 BY **Maidenform, Inc.**, makers of bras, girdles, swimwear, and active sportswear.

In 1957, THE MOVIE *Peyton Place*, the steamiest motion picture in years, or so the trailers candidly invited us to suppose, was released to a waiting nation and my sister decided that she and I were going to go. Why I was deemed a necessary part of the enterprise I have no idea. Perhaps I provided some sort of alibi. Perhaps the only time she could slip away from the house unnoticed was when she was babysitting me. All I know is that I was told that we were going to walk to the Ingersoll Theater after lunch on Saturday and that I was to tell no one. It was very exciting.

On the way there my sister told me that many of the characters in the movie – probably most of them – would be having sex. My sister at this time was the world's foremost authority on sexual matters, at least as far as I was concerned. Her particular speciality was spotting celebrity homosexuals. Sal Mineo, Anthony Perkins, Sherlock Holmes and Dr Watson, Batman and Robin, Charles Laughton, Randolph Scott, Liberace, of course, and a man in the third row of the Lawrence Welk Orchestra who looked quite normal to me – all were unmasked by her penetrating gaze. She told me Rock Hudson was gay in 1959, long before anyone would have guessed it. She knew that Richard Chamberlain was gay before he did, I believe. She was uncanny.

'Do you know what sex is?' she asked me once we were in the privacy of the woods, walking in single file along the narrow path

121

through the trees. It was a wintry day and I clearly remember that she had on a smart new red woollen coat and a fluffy white hat that tied under her chin. She looked very smart and grown up to me.

'No, I don't believe I do,' I said or words to that effect.

So she told me, in a grave tone and with the kind of careful phrasing that made it clear that this was privileged information, all there was to know about sex, though as she was only eleven at this time her knowledge was perhaps slightly less encyclopaedic than it seemed to me. Anyway, the essence of the business, as I understood it, was that the man put his thing inside her thing, left it there for a bit, and then they had a baby. I remember wondering vaguely what these unspecified things were – his finger in her ear? his hat in her hatbox? Who could say? Anyway, they did this private thing, naked, and the next thing you knew they were parents.

I didn't really care how babies were made, to tell you the truth. I was far more excited that we were on a secret adventure that our parents didn't know about and that we were walking through The Woods – the more or less boundless *Schwarzwald* that lay between Elmwood Drive and Grand Avenue. At six, one ventured into the woods very slightly from time to time, played army a bit within sight of the street and then came out again (usually after Bobby Stimson got poison ivy and burst into tears) with a sense of gladness – of relief, frankly – to be stepping into clear air and sunshine. The woods were unnerving. The air was thicker in there, more stifling, the noises different. You could go into the woods and not come out again. One certainly never considered using them as a thoroughfare. They were far too vast for that. So to be conducted through them by a confident, smart-stepping person, while being given privy information, even if largely meaningless to me, was almost too thrilling for words. I spent most of the long hike admiring the woods' dark majesty and keeping half an eye peeled for gingerbread cottages and wolves.

As if that weren't excitement enough, when we reached Grand Avenue my sister took me down a secret path between two apartment buildings and past the back of Bauder's Drugstore on Ingersoll – it had never occurred to me that Bauder's Drugstore *had* a back – from which we emerged almost opposite the theatre. This was so impossibly nifty I could hardly stand it. Because Ingersoll was a busy road my sister took my hand and guided us expertly to the other side – another seemingly impossible task. I don't believe I have ever been so proud to be associated with another human being.

At the ticket window, when the ticket lady hesitated, my sister told her that we had a cousin in California who had a role in the movie and that we had promised our mother, a busy woman of some importance ('she's a columnist for the *Register*, you know'), that we would watch the film on her behalf and provide a full report afterwards. As stories go, it was not perhaps the most convincing, but my sister had the face of an angel, a keen manner and that fluffy, innocent hat; it was a combination impossible to disbelieve. So the ticket seller, after a moment's fluttery uncertainty, let us in. I was very proud of my sister for this, too.

After such an adventure, the movie itself was a bit of an anticlimax, especially when my sister told me that we didn't actually have a cousin in the film, or indeed in California. No one got naked and there were no fingers in ears or toes in hatboxes or anything. It was just lots of unhappy people talking to lampshades and curtains. I went off and locked the stalls in the men's room, though as there were only two of them at the Ingersoll even that was a bit disappointing.

By chance, soon afterwards I had an additional experience that shed a little more light on the matter of sex. Coming in from play one Saturday and finding my mother missing from her usual haunts, I decided impulsively to call on my father. He had just returned that day from a long trip to the West Coast – the World Series between the White Sox and Dodgers, as I recall – and we had a lot of catching up to do. So I rushed into his bedroom, expecting to find him unpacking. To my surprise, the shades were drawn and my parents were in bed wrestling under the sheets. More astonishing still, my mother was winning. My father was obviously in some distress. He was making a noise like a small trapped animal.

'What are you doing?' I asked.

'Ah, Billy, your mother is just checking my teeth,' my father replied quickly if not altogether convincingly.

We were all quiet a moment.

'Are you bare under there?' I asked.

'Why, yes we are.'

'Why?'

'*Well,*' my father said as if that was a story that would take some telling, 'we got a bit warm. It's warm work, teeth and gums and so on. Look, Billy, we're nearly finished here. Why don't you go downstairs and we'll be down shortly.'

I believe you are supposed to be traumatized by these things. I can't remember being troubled at all, though it was some years before I let my mother look in my mouth again.

It came as a surprise, when I eventually cottoned on, to

realize that my parents had sex – sex between one's parents always seems slightly unbelievable, of course – but also something of a comfort because having sex wasn't easy in the 1950s. Within marriage, with the man on top and woman gritting her teeth, it was just about legal, but almost anything else was forbidden in America in those days. Nearly every state had laws prohibiting any form of sex that was deemed remotely deviant: oral and anal sex of course; homosexuality obviously; even normal, polite sex between consenting but unmarried couples. In Indiana you could be sent to prison for fourteen years for aiding or instigating any person under twenty-one years of age to 'commit masturbation'. The Roman Catholic Archdiocese of the same state declared at about the same time that sex outside marriage was not only sinful, messy and reproductively chancy, but also promoted Communism. Quite how a shag in the haymow helped the relentless march of Marxism was never specified, but it hardly mattered. The point was that once an action was deemed to promote Communism, you knew you were never going to get anywhere near it.

Because lawmakers could not bring themselves to discuss these matters openly, it was often not possible to tell what exactly was being banned. Kansas had (and for all I know still has) a statute vowing to punish, and severely, anyone 'convicted of the detestable and abominable crime against nature committed with mankind or with beast', without indicating even vaguely what a detestable and abominable crime against nature might be. Bulldozing a rainforest? Whipping your mule? There was simply no telling.

Nearly as bad as having sex was thinking about sex. When Lucille Ball on *I Love Lucy* was pregnant for nearly the whole of the 1952–53 season, the show was not allowed to use the word 'pregnant', lest it provoke susceptible viewers to engage in sofa isometrics in the manner of our neighbour Mr Kiessler on St John's Road. Instead, Lucy was described as 'expecting' – a less emotive word apparently. Closer to home, in Des Moines in 1953 police raided Ruthie's Lounge at 1311 Locust Street, and charged the owner, Ruthie Lucille Fontanini, with engaging in an obscene act. It was an act so disturbing that two vice officers and a police captain, Louis Volz, made a special trip to see it – as indeed did most of the men in Des Moines at one time or another, or so it would appear. The act, it turned out, was that Ruthie, with sufficient coaxing from a roomful of happy topers, would balance two glasses on her tightly sweatered chest, fill them with beer and convey them without a spill to an appreciative waiting table.

Ruthie in her prime was a bit of a handful, it would seem. 'She was married sixteen times to nine men,' according to former *Des Moines Register* reporter George Mills in a wonderful book of memoirs, *Looking in Windows*. One of Ruthie's marriages, Mills reported, ended after just sixteen hours when Ruthie woke up to find her new husband going through her purse looking for her safe deposit key. Her custom of using her bosom as a tray would seem a minor talent in an age in which mail was delivered by rocket, but it made her nationally famous. A pair of mountains in Korea were named 'the Ruthies' in her honour and the Hollywood director Cecil B. De Mille visited Ruthie's Lounge twice to watch her in action.

The story has a happy ending. Judge Harry Grund threw the obscenity charges out of court and Ruthie eventually married a nice man named Frank Bisignano and settled down to a quiet life as a housewife. At last report they had been happily married for over thirty years. I'd like to imagine her bringing him ketchup, mustard and other condiments on her chest every evening, but of course I am only guessing.*

For those of us who had an interest in seeing naked women, there were pictures of course in *Playboy* and other manly periodicals of lesser repute, but these were nearly impossible to acquire legally, even if you cycled over to one of the more desperate-looking grocery shacks on the near-east side, lowered your voice two octaves, and swore to God to the impassive clerk that you were born in 1939.

Sometimes in the drugstore if your dad was busy with the pharmacist (and this was the one time I gave sincere thanks for the complex mechanics of isometrics) you could have a rapid shuffle through the pages, but it was a nerve-racking operation as the magazine stand was exposed to view from many distant corners of the store. Moreover, it was right by the entrance and visible from the street through a large plate-glass window, so you were vulnerable on all fronts. One of your mom's friends could walk past and see you and raise the alarm – there was a police call box on a telephone pole right out front, possibly put there for that purpose – or a pimply stock boy could clamp you on the shoulder from behind and denounce you in a loud voice, or your dad himself could fetch up unexpectedly while you were frantically distracted with trying to locate the pages in which Kim Novak was to be seen relaxing on a fleecy rug, airing her comely epidermis – so there was practically no pleasure and very little illumination in the exercise. This was an age, don't forget, in which you could be arrested for carrying beer on your bosom or

*Ruthie was often described in print as a former stripper. She protested that she had never been a stripper since she had never removed clothes in public. On the other hand, she had often gone onstage without many on.

committing an unspecified crime against nature, so what the consequences would be if you were caught holding photographs of
naked women in a family drugstore was almost inconceivable,
but you could be certain they would involve popping flashbulbs,
the WHO-TV mobile crime scene unit, banner headlines in the
paper, and many thousands of hours of community service.

On the whole therefore you had to make do with underwear
spreads in mail order catalogues or ads in glossy magazines,
which was desperate to be sure, but at least safely within the law.
Maidenform, a maker of brassieres, ran a well-known series of
print ads in the 1950s in which women imagined themselves half
dressed in public places. 'I dreamed I was in a jewelry store in my
Maidenform bra' ran the headline in one, accompanied by a
photo showing a woman wearing a hat, skirt, shoes, jewellery and
a Maidenform bra – everything, in short, but a blouse – standing
at a glass case in Tiffany's or some place like it. There was something deeply – and I expect unhealthily – erotic in these pictures.
Unfortunately, Maidenform had an unerring instinct for choosing
models of slightly advanced years who were not terribly attractive
to begin with and in any case the bras of that period were more
like surgical appliances than enticements to fantasy. One
despaired at the waste of such a promising erogenous concept.

Despite its shortcomings, the approach was widely copied.
Sarong, a manufacturer of girdles so heavy-duty that they looked
bulletproof, took a similar line with a series of ads showing
women caught by unexpected gusts of wind, revealing their
girdles *in situ*, to their own horrified dismay but to the leering
delight of all males within fifty yards. I have before me an ad from
1956 showing a woman who has just alighted from a Northwest
Airlines flight whose fur coat has inopportunely gusted open (as

a result of an extremely localized sirocco occurring somewhere just below and between her legs) to reveal her wearing a Model 124 embroidered nylon marquisette Sarong-brand girdle (available at fine girdlers everywhere for $13.95). But – and here's the thing that has been troubling me since 1956 – the woman is clearly not wearing a skirt or anything else between girdle and coat, raising urgent questions as to how she was dressed when she boarded the plane. Did she fly skirtless the whole way from (let's say for the sake of argument) Tulsa to Minneapolis or did she remove the skirt en route – and why?

Sarong ads had a certain following in my circle – my friend Doug Willoughby was a great admirer – but I always found them strange, illogical and slightly pervy. 'The woman can't have travelled halfway across the country without a skirt on surely,' I would observe repeatedly, even a little heatedly. Willoughby conceded the point without demur, but insisted that that was precisely what made Sarong ads so engaging. Anyway, it's a sad age, you'll agree, when the most titillating thing you can find is a shot of a horrified woman in a half-glimpsed girdle in your mother's magazines.

By chance, we did have the most erotic statue in the nation in Des Moines. It was part of the state's large civil war monument on the capitol grounds. Called 'Iowa', it depicts a seated woman who is holding her bare breasts in her hands, cupped from beneath in a startlingly provocative manner. The pose, we are told, was intended to represent a symbolic offering of nourishment, but really she is inviting every man who goes by to think hard about clambering up and clamping on. We used sometimes to ride our bikes there on Saturdays to stare at it from below. 'Erected in 1890' said a plaque on the statue. 'And causing them ever since,' we used to quip. But it was a long way to cycle just to see some copper tits.

The only other option was to spy on people. A boy named Rocky Koppell, whose family had been transferred to Des Moines from Columbus, lived for a time in an apartment in the basement of the Commodore Hotel and discovered a hole in the wall at the back of his bedroom closet through which he could watch the maid next door dressing and occasionally taking part in an earnest exchange of fluids with one of the janitors. Koppell charged 25 cents to peep through the hole, but lost most of his business when word got around that the maid looked like Adlai Stevenson, but with less hair.

The one place you knew you were never going to see naked female flesh was at the movies. Women undressed in the movies from time to time, of course, but they always stepped behind a screen to do so, or wandered into another room after taking off their earrings and absent-mindedly undoing the top button of their blouse. Even if the camera stayed with the woman, it always shyly dropped its gaze at the critical moment, so that all you saw was a dressing gown falling around the ankles and a foot stepping into the bath. It can't even be described as disappointing because you had no expectations to disappoint. Nudity was just never going to happen.

Those of us who had older brothers knew about a movie called *Mau Mau* that was released in 1955. In its initial manifestation it was a respectable documentary about the Mau Mau uprising in Kenya, soberly narrated by the television newscaster Chet Huntley. But the distributor, a man named Dan Sonney, decided the film wasn't commercial enough. So he hired a local crew of actors and technicians and filmed additional scenes in an orange grove in southern California. These showed topless 'native' women fleeing before men with machetes. These extra scenes he spliced more or less randomly into the existing footage to give the film a little extra pep. The result was a commercial sensation, particularly among boys aged twelve to fifteen. Unfortunately, I was only four in 1955, and so missed out on the only naked celluloid jiggling of the decade.

One year when I was about nine we built a treehouse in the woods – quite a good treehouse, using some first-rate materials appropriated from a construction site on River Oaks Drive – and immediately, and more or less automatically, used it as a place to strip off in front of each other. This was not terribly exciting as the group consisted of about twenty-four little boys and just one girl, Patty Hefferman, who already at the age of seven weighed more than a large piece of earth-moving equipment (she would eventually become known as All-Beef Patty), and was not, with the best will in the world, anyone's idea of Madame Eros. Still, for a couple of Oreo cookies she was willing to be examined from any angle for as long as anyone cared to, which gave her a certain anthropological value.

The only girl in the neighbourhood anybody really wanted to see naked was Mary O'Leary. She was the prettiest child within a million million galaxies, but she wouldn't take her clothes off. She would play in the treehouse happily with us when it was wholesome fun, but the moment things got fruity she would depart by way of the ladder and stand below and tell us with a clenched fury that was nearly tearful that we were gross and loathsome. This made me admire her very much, very much indeed, and often I would depart too (for in truth there was only so much of Patty Hefferman you could take and still eat my mom's

131

cooking) and accompany her to her house, praising her effusively for her virtue and modesty.

'Those guys really are disgusting,' I would say, conveniently overlooking that generally I was one of those guys myself.

Her refusal to take part was in an odd way the most titillating thing about the whole experience. I adored and worshipped Mary O'Leary. I used to sit beside her on her sofa when she watched TV and secretly stare at her face. It was the most perfect thing I had ever seen – so soft, so clean, so ready to smile, so full of rosy light. And there was nothing more perfect and joyous in nature than that face in the micro-instant before she laughed.

In July of that summer, my family went to my grandparents' house for the Fourth of July, where I had the usual dispiriting experience of watching Uncle Dee turn wholesome food into flying stucco. Worse still, my grandparents' television was out of commission and waiting for a new part – the cheerfully moronic local television repairman was unable to see the logic of keeping a supply of spare vacuum tubes in stock, an oversight that earned him a carbonizing dose of ThunderVision, needless to say – and so I had to spend the long weekend reading from my grandparents' modest library, which consisted mostly of Reader's Digest condensed books, some novels by Warwick Deeping, and a large cardboard box filled with *Ladies' Home Journals* going back to 1942. It was a trying weekend.

When I returned, Buddy Doberman and Arthur Bergen were waiting by my house. They barely acknowledged my parents, so eager were they to get me round the corner to have a private word. There they breathlessly told me that in my absence Mary O'Leary had come into the treehouse and taken her clothes off – every last stitch. She had done so freely, indeed with a kind of dreamy abandon.

'It was like she was in a trance,' said Bergen fondly.

'A *happy* trance,' added Buddy.

'It was really nice,' said Bergen, his stock of fond remembrance nowhere near exhausted.

Naturally I refused to believe a word of this. They had to swear to God a dozen times and hope for their mothers' deaths on a stack of bibles and much else in a grave vein before I was prepared to suspend my natural disbelief even slightly. Above all, they had to describe every moment of the occasion, something that Bergen was able to do with remarkable clarity. (He had, as he would boast in later years, a pornographic memory.)

'Well,' I said, keen as you would expect, 'let's get her and do it again.'

'Oh, no,' Buddy explained. 'She said she wasn't going to do it any more. We had to swear we'd never ask her again. That was the deal.'

'But,' I said, sputtering and appalled, 'that's not fair.'

'The funny thing is,' Bergen went on, 'she said she's been thinking about doing it for a long time, but waited until you weren't there because she didn't want to upset you.'

'Upset me? Upset me? Are you kidding? Upset me? Are you kidding? Are you kidding?'

You can still see the dent in the sidewalk where I beat my head against it for the next fourteen hours. True to her word, Mary O'Leary never came near the treehouse again.

Shortly afterwards, in an inspired moment, I took all the drawers out of my father's closet chest to see what, if anything, was underneath them. I used to strip down his bedroom twice a year, in spring and autumn, when he went to spring training and the World Series, looking for lost cigarettes, stray money and evidence that I was indeed from the planet Electro – perhaps a letter from King Volton or the Electro Congress promising some munificent reward for raising me safely and making sure that my slightest whims were met.

On this occasion, because I had more time than usual on my hands, I took the drawers all the way out to see if anything was behind or beneath them, and so found my father's modest girlie stash, comprising two thin magazines, one called *Dude*, the other *Nugget*. They were extremely cheesy. The women in them looked like Pat Nixon or Mamie Eisenhower – the sort of women you would pay *not* to see naked. I was appalled and astonished, not because my father had men's magazines – this was an entirely welcome development, of course; one to be encouraged by any means possible – but because he had chosen so poorly. It seemed tragically typical of my father that his crippling cheapness extended even to his choice of men's magazines.

Still, they were better than nothing and they did feature unclad women. I took them to the treehouse where they were much prized in the absence of Mary O'Leary. When I returned them to their place ten days or so later, just before he came home from spring training, they were conspicuously well thumbed. Indeed, it was hard not to notice that they had been enjoyed by a wider audience. One was missing its cover and nearly all the pictorials now bore marginal comments and balloon captions, many of a candid nature, in a variety of young hands. Often in the years that followed I wondered what my father made of these spirited emendations, but somehow the moment never seemed right to ask.

Chapter 7

BOOM!

MOBILE, ALA. (AP)– The Alabama Supreme Court yesterday upheld a death sentence imposed on a Negro handyman, Jimmy Wilson, 55, for robbing Mrs. Esteele Barker of $1.95 at her home last year. Mrs. Barker is white.

Although robbery is a capital offense in Alabama, no one has been executed in the state before for a theft of less than $5. A court official suggested that the jury had been influenced by the fact that Mrs. Barker told the jury that Wilson had spoken to her in a disrespectful tone.

A spokesman for the National Association for the Advancement of Colored People called the death sentence 'a sad blot on the nation,' but said the organization is unable to aid the condemned man because it is barred in Alabama.

– *Des Moines Register*, 23 August 1958

A T 7.15 IN THE MORNING local time on 1 November 1952, the United States exploded the first hydrogen bomb in the Eniwetok (or Enewetak or many other variants) Atoll in the Marshall Islands of the South Pacific, though it wasn't really a bomb as it wasn't in any sense portable. Unless an enemy would considerately stand by while we built an 80-ton refrigeration unit to cool large volumes of liquid deuterium and tritium, ran in several miles of cabling and attached scores of electric detonators, we didn't have any way of blowing anyone up with it. Eleven thousand soldiers and civilians were needed to get the device to go off at Eniwetok, so this was hardly the sort of thing you could set up in Red Square without arousing suspicions. Properly, it was a 'thermonuclear device'. Still, it was enormously potent.

Since nothing like this had ever been tried before, nobody knew how big a bang it would make. Even the most conservative estimates, for a blast of five megatons, represented more destructive might than all the firepower used by all sides in the Second World War, and some nuclear physicists thought the explosion might go as high as one hundred megatons – a blast so off the scale that scientists could only guess the chain of consequences. One possibility was that it might ignite all the oxygen in the atmosphere. Still, nothing ventured, nothing annihilated, as the Pentagon might have put it, and on the morning of 1 November somebody lit the fuse and, as I like to picture it, ran like hell.

The blast came in at a little over ten megatons, comparatively manageable but still enough to wipe out a city a thousand times the size of Hiroshima, though of course Earth has no cities that big. A fireball five miles high and four miles across rose above Eniwetok within seconds, billowing into a mushroom cloud that hit the stratospheric ceiling thirty miles above the Earth and spread outwards for over a thousand miles in every direction, disgorging a darkening snowfall of dusty ash as it went, before slowly dissipating. It was the biggest thing of any type ever created by humans. Nine months later the Soviets surprised the western powers by exploding a thermonuclear device of their own. The race to obliterate life was on – and how. Now we truly were become Death, the shatterer of worlds.

So it is perhaps not surprising that as this happened I sat in Des Moines, Iowa, quietly shitting myself. I had little choice. I was ten months old.

What was scary about the growth of the bomb wasn't so much the growth of the bomb as the people in charge of the growth of the bomb. Within weeks of the Eniwetok test the big hats at the Pentagon were actively thinking of ways to put this baby to use. One idea, seriously considered, was to build a device somewhere near the front lines in Korea, induce large numbers of North Korean and Chinese troops to wander over to have a look, and then set it off.

Representative James E. Van Zandt of Pennsylvania, a leading proponent of devastation, promised that soon we would have a device of at least a hundred megatons – the one that might consume all our breathable air. At the same time, Edward Teller, the semi-crazed Hungarian-born physicist who was one of the presiding geniuses behind the development of the H-bomb, was dreaming up exciting peacetime uses for nuclear devices. Teller and his acolytes at the Atomic Energy Commission envisioned using H-bombs to enable massive civil engineering projects on a scale never before conceived – to create open-pit mines where mountains had once stood, to alter the courses of rivers in our favour (ensuring that the Danube, for instance, served only capitalist countries), to blow away irksome impediments to commerce and shipping like the Great Barrier Reef of Australia. Excitedly they reported that just twenty-six bombs placed in a chain across the Isthmus of Panama would excavate a bigger, better Panama Canal more or less at once, and provide a lovely show into the bargain. They even suggested that nuclear devices could be used to alter the Earth's weather by adjusting the amount of dust in the atmosphere, for ever banishing winters from the northern US and sending them permanently to the Soviet Union instead. Almost in passing, Teller proposed that we might use the Moon as a giant target for testing warheads. The blasts would be visible through binoculars from Earth and would provide wholesome entertainment for millions. In short, the creators of the hydrogen bomb wished to wrap the world in unpredictable levels of radiation, obliterate whole ecosystems, despoil the face of the planet, and provoke and antagonize our enemies at every opportunity – and these were their *peacetime* dreams.

But of course the real ambition was to make a gigantically ferocious transportable bomb that we could drop on the heads of Russians and other like-minded irritants whenever it pleased us to do so. That dream became enchanting reality on 1 March 1954, when America detonated fifteen megatons of experimental bang over the Bikini atoll (a place so delightful that we named a lady's swimsuit after it) in the Marshall Islands. The blast exceeded all hopes by a considerable margin. The flash was seen in Okinawa, twenty-six hundred miles away. It threw visible fallout over an area of some seven thousand square miles – all of it drifting in exactly the opposite direction to what was forecast. We were getting good not only at making really huge explosions but at creating consequences that were beyond our capabilities to deal with.

One soldier, based on the island of Kwajalein, described in a letter home how he thought the blast would blow his barracks away. 'All of a sudden the sky lighted up a bright orange and remained that way for what seemed like a couple of minutes . . . We heard very loud rumblings that sounded like thunder. Then the whole barracks began shaking, as if there had been an earthquake. This was followed by a very high wind,' which caused everyone present to grab on to something solid and hold on tight. And this was at a place nearly two hundred miles from the blast site, so goodness knows what the experience was like for those who were even closer – and there were many, among them the unassuming native residents of the nearby island of Rongelap, who had been told to expect a bright flash and a loud bang just before 7 a.m., but had been given no other warnings, no hint that the bang itself might knock down their houses and leave them permanently deafened, and no instructions about dealing with the after-effects. As radioactive ash rained down on them, the puzzled islanders tasted it to see what it was made of – salt, apparently – and brushed it out of their hair.

Within minutes they found they weren't feeling terribly well. No one exposed to the fallout had any appetite for breakfast that morning. Within hours many were severely nauseated and blistering prolifically wherever ash had touched bare skin. Over the next few days, their hair came out in clumps and some started haemorrhaging internally.

Also caught in the fallout were twenty-three puzzled fishermen on a Japanese boat called, with a touch of irony that escaped no one, the Lucky Dragon. By the time they got back to Japan most of the crewmen were deeply unwell. The haul from their trip was unloaded by other hands and sent to market, where it vanished among the thousands of other catches landed in Japanese ports that day. Unable to tell which fish was contaminated and which not, Japanese consumers shunned fish altogether for weeks, nearly wrecking the industry.

As a nation, the Japanese were none too happy about any of this. In less than ten years they had achieved the unwelcome distinction of being the first victims of both the atom and hydrogen bombs, and naturally they were a touch upset and sought an apology. We declined to oblige. Instead Lewis Strauss, a former shoe salesman who had risen to become chairman of the Atomic Energy Commission (it was that kind of age), responded by suggesting that the Japanese fishermen were in fact Soviet agents.

Increasingly, the United States moved its tests to Nevada, where, as we have seen, people were a good deal more appreciative, though it wasn't just the Marshall Islands and Nevada where we tested. We also set off nuclear bombs on Christmas Island and the Johnston Atoll in the Pacific, above and below water in the South Atlantic Ocean, and in New Mexico, Colorado, Alaska and Hattiesburg, Mississippi (of all places), in the early years of testing. Altogether between 1946 and 1962, the United States detonated just over a thousand nuclear warheads, including some three hundred in the open air, hurling numberless tons of radioactive dust into the atmosphere. The USSR, China, Britain and France detonated scores more.

It turned out that children, with their trim little bodies and love of milk, were particularly adept at absorbing and holding on to strontium 90 – the chief radioactive product of fallout. Such was our affinity for strontium that in 1958 the average child – which is to say me and thirty million other small people – was carrying ten times more strontium than he had only the year before. We were positively aglow with the stuff.

So the tests were moved underground, but that didn't always work terribly well either. In the summer of 1962, defence officials detonated a hydrogen bomb buried deep beneath the desert of Frenchman Flat, Nevada. The blast was so robust that the land around it rose by some three hundred feet and burst open like a very bad boil, leaving a crater eight hundred feet across. Blast debris went everywhere. 'By four in the afternoon,' the historian Peter Goodchild has written, 'the radioactive dust cloud was so thick in Ely, Nevada, two hundred miles from Ground Zero, that the street lights had to be turned on.' Visible fallout drifted down on six western states and two Canadian provinces – though no one officially acknowledged the fiasco and no public warnings were issued advising people not to touch fresh ash or let their children roll around in it. Indeed, all details of the incident remained secret for two decades until a curious journalist filed suit under the Freedom of Information Act to find out what had happened that day.*

*Nuclear testing came to a noisy peak in October 1961 when the Soviets exploded a fifty-megaton device in the Arctic north of the country. (Fifty megatons is equivalent to fifty million tons of TNT – more than three thousand times the force of the Hiroshima blast of 1945, which ultimately killed two hundred thousand people.) The number of nuclear weapons at the peak of the

While we waited for the politicians and military to give us an actual Third World War, the comic books were pleased to provide an imaginary one. Monthly offerings with titles like *Atomic War!* and *Atom-Age Combat* began to appear and were avidly sought out by connoisseurs in the Kiddie Corral. Ingeniously, the visionary minds behind these comics took atomic weapons away from the generals and other top brass and put them in the hands of ordinary foot soldiers, allowing them to blow away inexhaustible hordes of advancing Chinese and Russian troops with atomic rockets, atomic cannons, atomic grenades and even atomic rifles loaded with atomic bullets. Atomic bullets! What a concept! The carnage was thrilling. Until Asbestos Lady stole into my life, capturing my young heart and twitchy loins, atomic war comics were the most satisfying form of distraction there was.

Anyway, people had many other far worse things to worry about in the 1950s than nuclear annihilation. They had to worry about polio. They had to worry about keeping up with the Joneses. They had to worry that Negroes might move into the neighbourhood. They had to worry about UFOs. Above all, they had to worry about teenagers. That's right. Teenagers became the number-one fear of American citizens in the 1950s.

There had of course been obnoxious, partly grown human beings with bad complexions since time immemorial, but as a social phenomenon teenagehood was a brand new thing. (The word *teenager* had only been coined in 1941.) So when teens began to appear visibly on the scene, rather like mutant creatures

Cold War was sixty-five thousand. Today there are about twenty-seven thousand, all vastly more powerful than those dropped on Japan in 1945, divided between possibly as many as nine countries. More than fifty years after the first atomic tests there, Bikini remains uninhabitable.

in one of the decade's many outstanding science fiction movies, grown-ups grew uneasy. Teenagers smoked and talked back and petted in the backs of cars. They used disrespectful terms to their elders like 'pops' and 'daddy-o'. They smirked. They drove in endless circuits around any convenient business district. They spent up to fourteen hours a day combing their hair. They listened to rock 'n' roll, a type of charged music clearly designed to get youngsters in the mood to fornicate and smoke hemp. 'We know that many platter-spinners are hop-heads,' wrote the authors of the popular book *USA Confidential*, showing a proud grasp of street patois. 'Many others are Reds, left-wingers or hecklers of social convention.'

Movies like *The Wild One, Rebel without a Cause, Blackboard Jungle, High School Confidential, Teenage Crime Wave, Reform School Girl* and (if I may be allowed a personal favourite) *Teenagers from Outer Space* made it seem that the youth of the nation was everywhere on some kind of dark, disturbed rampage. The *Saturday Evening Post* called juvenile crime 'the Shame of America'. *Time* and *Newsweek* both ran cover stories on the country's new young hoodlums. Under Estes Kefauver the Senate Subcommittee on Juvenile Delinquency launched a series of emotive hearings on the rise of street gangs and associated misbehaviour.

In point of fact, young people had never been so good or so devotedly conservative. More than half of them, according to J. Ronald Oakley in *God's Country: America in the Fifties*, were shown by surveys to believe that masturbation was sinful, that women should stay at home and that the theory of evolution was not to be trusted – views that many of their elders would have warmly applauded. Teenagers also worked hard, and contributed significantly to the nation's well-being with weekend and after-school jobs. By 1955, the typical American teenager had as much disposable income as the average family of four had enjoyed fifteen years earlier. Collectively they were worth $10 billion a year to the national balance sheet. So teenagers weren't bad by any measure. Still it's true, when you look at them now, there's no question that they should have been put down.

Only one thing came close to matching the fearfulness of teenagers in the 1950s and that was of course Communism. Worrying about Communism was an exhaustingly demanding business in the 1950s. Red danger lurked everywhere – in books and magazines, in government departments, in the teachings of schools, at every place of work. The film industry was especially suspect.

'Large numbers of moving pictures that come out of Hollywood carry the Communist line,' Congressman J. Parnell Thomas of New Jersey, chairman of the House Un-American Activities Committee, gravely intoned to approving nods in 1947, though on reflection no one could actually think of any Hollywood movie that seemed even slightly sympathetic to Marxist thought. Parnell never did specify which movies he had in mind, but then he didn't have much chance to for soon afterwards he was convicted of embezzling large sums from the government in the form of salaries for imaginary employees. He was sentenced to eighteen months in a prison in Connecticut where he had the unexpected pleasure of serving alongside two of the people, Lester Cole and Ring Lardner Junior, whom his committee had put away for refusing to testify.

Not to be outdone, Walt Disney claimed in testimony to HUAC that the cartoonists' guild in Hollywood – run by committed reds and their fellow travellers, he reported – tried to take over his studio during a strike in 1941 with the intention of making Mickey Mouse a Communist. He never produced any evidence either, though he did identify one of his former employees as a Communist because he didn't go to church and had once studied art in Moscow.

It was an especially wonderful time to be a noisy moron. Billy James Hargis, a chubby, kick-ass evangelist from Sapulpa, Oklahoma, warned the nation in weekly sweat-spattered sermons that Communists had insinuated themselves into, and effectively taken over, the Federal Reserve, the Department of Education, the National Council of Churches and nearly every other organization of national standing one could name. His pronouncements were carried on five hundred radio stations and two hundred and fifty television stations and attracted a huge following, as did his many books, which had titles like *Communism: The Total Lie* and *Is the Schoolhouse the Proper Place to Teach Raw Sex?*

Although he had no qualifications (he had flunked out of Ozark Bible College – a rare distinction, one would suppose), Hargis founded several educational establishments, including the Christian Crusade Anti-Communist Youth University. (I would love to have heard the school song.) When asked what was taught at his schools, he replied, 'anti-Communism, anti-Socialism, anti-welfare state, anti-Russia, anti-China, a literal interpretation of the Bible and states' rights'. Hargis eventually came undone when it was revealed that he had had sex with several of his students, male and female alike, during moments of lordly fervour. One couple, according to *The Economist*, made the discovery when they blushingly confessed the misdeed to each other on their wedding night.

At the peak of the Red Scare, thirty-two of the forty-eight states had loyalty oaths of one kind or another. In New York, Oakley notes, it was necessary to swear a loyalty oath to gain a fishing permit. In Indiana loyalty oaths were administered to professional wrestlers. The Communist Control Act of 1954 made it a federal offence to communicate any Communist thoughts by any means, including by semaphore. In Connecticut it became illegal to criticize the government, or to speak ill of the army or the American flag. In Texas you could be sent to prison for twenty years for being a Communist. In Birmingham, Alabama, it was illegal merely to be seen conversing with a Communist.

HUAC issued millions of leaflets entitled 'One Hundred Things You Should Know About Communism', detailing what to look out for in the behaviour of neighbours, friends and family. Billy Graham, the esteemed evangelist, declared that over one thousand decent-sounding American organizations were in fact fronts for Communist enterprises. Rudolf Flesch, author of the best-selling *Why Johnny Can't Read*, insisted that a failure to teach phonics in schools was undermining democracy and paving the way for Communism. Westbrook Pegler, a syndicated columnist, suggested that anyone found to have been a Communist at any time in his life should simply be put to death. Such was the sensitivity, according to David Halberstam, that when General Motors hired a Russian automotive designer named Zora Arkus-Duntov, it described him in press releases, wholly fictitiously, as being 'of Belgian extraction'.

No one exploited the fear to better effect than Joseph R. McCarthy, Republican senator from Wisconsin. In 1950, in a speech in Wheeling, West Virginia, he claimed to have in his pocket a list of two hundred and five Communists working in the

State Department. The next day he claimed to have another list with fifty-seven names on it. Over the next four years McCarthy waved many lists, each claiming to show a different number of Communist operatives. In the course of his spirited ramblings he helped to ruin many lives without ever producing a single promised list. Not producing evidence was becoming something of a trend.

Others brought additional prejudices into play. John Rankin, a senior congressman from Mississippi, sagely observed: 'Remember, Communism is Yiddish. I understand that every member of the Politburo around Stalin is either Yiddish or married to one, and that includes Stalin himself.' Against such men, McCarthy looked almost moderate and fairly sane.

Such was the hysteria that it wasn't actually necessary to have done anything wrong to get in trouble. In 1950, three former FBI agents published a book called *Red Channels: The Report of Communist Influence in Radio and Television*, accusing 151 celebrities – among them Leonard Bernstein, Lee J. Cobb, Burgess Meredith, Orson Welles, Edward G. Robinson and the stripper Gypsy Rose Lee – of various seditious acts. Among the shocking misdeeds of which the performers stood accused were speaking out against religious intolerance, opposing fascism and supporting world peace and the United Nations. None had any connection with the Communist Party or had ever shown any Communist sympathies. Even so, many of them couldn't find work for years afterwards unless (like Edward G. Robinson) they agreed to appear before HUAC as a friendly witness and name names.

Doing anything at all to help Communists became essentially illegal. In 1951, Dr Ernest Chain, a naturalized Briton who had won a Nobel Prize six years earlier for helping to develop penicillin, was barred from entering the United States because he had recently travelled to Czechoslovakia, under the auspices of the World Health Organization, to help start a penicillin plant there. Humanitarian aid was only permissible, it seems, so long as those being saved believed in free markets. Americans likewise found themselves barred from travel. Linus Pauling, who would eventually win two Nobel prizes, was stopped at Idlewild Airport in New York while boarding a plane to Britain, where he was to be honoured by the Royal Society, and had his passport confiscated on the grounds that he had once or twice publicly expressed a liberal thought.

It was even harder for those who were not American by birth. After learning that a Finnish-born citizen named William Heikkilin had in his youth briefly belonged to the Communist Party, Immigration Service employees tracked him down to San Francisco, arrested him on his way home from work, and bundled him on to an aeroplane bound for Europe, with nothing but about a dollar in change and the clothes he was wearing. Not until his plane touched down the following day did officials inform his frantic wife that her husband had been deported. They refused to tell her where he had been sent.

In perhaps the most surreal moment of all, Arthur Miller, the playwright, while facing congressional rebuke and the possibility of prison for refusing to betray friends and theatrical associates, was told that the charges against him would be dropped if he would allow the chairman of HUAC, Francis E. Walter, to be photographed with Miller's famous and dishy wife, Marilyn Monroe. Miller declined.

In 1954, McCarthy finally undid himself. He accused

General George Marshall, the man behind the Marshall Plan and a person of unquestioned rectitude, of treason, a charge quickly shown to be preposterous. Then he took on the whole of the United States Army, threatening to expose scores of subversive senior staff that he claimed the Army knowingly shielded within its ranks. In a series of televised hearings lasting thirty-six days in the spring of 1954 and known as the Army–McCarthy hearings, he showed himself to be a bullying, blustering buffoon of the first rank without a shred of evidence against anyone – though in fact he had always shown that. It just took this long for most of the nation to realize it.

Later that year McCarthy was severely censured by the Senate – a signal humiliation. He died three years later in disgrace. But the fact is that had he been just a tiny bit smarter or more likeable, he might well have become President. In any case, McCarthy's downfall didn't slow the assault on Communism. As late as 1959, the New York office of the FBI still had four hundred agents working full time on rooting out Communists in American life, according to Kenneth O'Reilly in *Hoover and the Un-Americans*.

Thanks to our overweening preoccupation with Communism at home and abroad America became the first nation in modern history to build a war economy in peacetime. Defence spending in the Fifties ranged between $40 billion and $53 billion a year – or more than *total* government spending on everything at the dawn of the decade. Altogether the US would lay out $350 billion on defence during the eight years of the Eisenhower Presidency. More than this, 90 per cent of our foreign aid was for military expenditures. We didn't just want to arm ourselves; we wanted to make sure that everybody else was armed, too.

Often, all that was necessary to earn America's enmity, and

land yourself in a lot of trouble, was to get in the way of our economic interests. In 1950, Guatemala elected a reformist government – 'the most democratic Guatemala ever had', according to the historian Howard Zinn – under Jacobo Arbenz, an educated landowner of good intentions. Arbenz's election was a blow for the American company United Fruit, which had run Guatemala as a private fiefdom since the nineteenth century. The company owned nearly everything of importance in the country – the ports, the railways, the communications networks, banks, stores and some 550,000 acres of farmland – paid little taxes and could count confidently on the support of a string of repressive dictators.

Some 85 per cent of United Fruit's land was left more or less permanently idle. This kept fruit prices high, but Guatemalans poor. Arbenz, who was the son of Swiss immigrants and something of an idealist, thought this was unfair and decided to remake the country along more democratic lines. He established free elections, ended racial discrimination, encouraged a free press, introduced a forty-hour week, legalized unions and ended government corruption.

Needless to say, most people loved him. In an attempt to reduce poverty, he devised a plan to nationalize, at a fair price, much of the idle farmland – including 1,700 acres of his own – and redistribute it in the form of smallholdings to a hundred thousand landless peasants. To that end Arbenz's government expropriated 400,000 acres of land from United Fruit, and offered as compensation the sum that the company had claimed the land was worth for tax purposes – $1,185,000.

United Fruit now decided the land was worth $16 million actually – a sum the Guatemalan government couldn't afford to pay. When Arbenz turned down United Fruit's demand for the higher level of compensation, the company complained to the United States government, which responded by underwriting a coup.

Arbenz fled his homeland in 1954 and a new, more compliant leader named Carlos Castillo was installed. To help him on his way, the CIA gave him a list of seventy thousand 'questionable individuals' – teachers, doctors, government employees, union organizers, priests – who had supported the reforms in the belief that democracy in Guatemala was a good thing. Thousands of them were never seen again.

And on that sobering note, let us return to Kid World, where the denizens may be small and often immensely stupid, but are at least comparatively civilized.

Chapter 8
SCHOOLDAYS

In Pasadena, California, student Edward Mulrooney was arrested after he tossed a bomb at his psychology teacher's house and left a note that said: 'If you don't want your home bombed or your windows shot out, then grade fairly and put your assignments on the board – or is this asking too much?'

– *Time* magazine, 16 April 1956

G REENWOOD, MY ELEMENTARY SCHOOL, was a wonderful old building, enormous to a small child, like a castle made of brick. Built in 1901, it stood off Grand Avenue at the far end of a street of outstandingly vast and elegant homes. The whole neighbourhood smelled lushly of old money.

Stepping into Greenwood for the first time was both the scariest and most exciting event of the first five years of my life. The front doors appeared to be about twenty times taller than normal doors, and everything inside was built to a similar imposing scale, including the teachers. Everything about it was intimidating and thrilling at once.

It was, I believe, the handsomest elementary school I have ever seen. Nearly everything in it – the cool ceramic water fountains, the polished corridors, the cloakrooms with their ancient, neatly spaced coat hooks, the giant clanking radiators with their intricate embossed patterns like iron veins, the glass-fronted cupboards, everything – had an agreeable creak of solid, classy, utilitarian venerability. This was a building made by craftsmen at a time when quality counted, and generations of devoted childhood learning suffused the air. If I hadn't had to spend so much of my time vaporizing teachers I would have adored the place.

Still, I was very fond of the building. One of the glories of life in that ancient lost world of the mid-twentieth century was that facilities designed for kids often were just smaller versions of

155

things in the adult world. You can't imagine how much more splendid this made them. Our Little League baseball field, for instance, was a proper ballpark, with a grandstand and a concession stand and press box, and real dugouts that were, as the name demands, partly subterranean (and never mind that they filled with puddles every time it rained and that the shorter players couldn't see over the edge and so tended to cheer at the wrong moments). When you ran up those three sagging steps and out on to the field you could seriously imagine that you were in Yankee Stadium. Superior infrastructure makes for richer fantasies, believe me. Greenwood contained all that in spades.

It had, for one thing, an auditorium that was just like a real theatre, with a stage with curtains and spotlights and dressing rooms behind. So however bad your school productions were – and ours were always extremely bad, partly because we had no talent and partly because Mrs De Voto, the music teacher, was a bit ancient and often nodded off at the piano – it felt like you were part of a well-ordered professional undertaking (even when you were standing there holding a long note, waiting for Mrs De Voto's chin to touch the keyboard, an event that always jerked her back into action with rousing gusto at exactly the spot where she had left off a minute or two before).

Greenwood also had the world's finest gymnasium. It was upstairs at the back of the school, which gave it a nicely unexpected air. When you opened the door, you expected to find an ordinary classroom and instead you had – hey! whoa! – a gigantic cubic vault of polished wood. It was a space to savour: it had cathedral-sized windows, a ceiling that no ball could ever reach, acres of varnished wood that had been mellowed into a honeyed glow by decades of squeaky sneakers and gentle drops of childish perspiration, and smartly echoing acoustics that made every bouncing ball sound deftly handled and seriously athletic. When the weather was good and we were sent outdoors to play, the route to the playground took us out on to a rickety metal fire escape that was unnervingly but grandly lofty. The view from the summit took in miles of rooftops and sunny countryside reaching practically to Missouri, or so it seemed.

Mostly we played indoors, however, because it was nearly always winter outside. Of course winters in those days, as with all winters of childhood, were much longer, snowier and more frigid than now. We used to get up to eleven feet of snow at a time – we seldom got less, in fact – and weeks of arctic weather so bitter you could pee icicles.

In consequence, they used to keep the school heated to roughly the temperature of the inside of a pottery kiln, so pupils and teachers alike existed in a state of permanent, helpless drowsiness. But at the same time the close warmth made everything deliciously cheery and cosy. Even Lumpy Kowalski's daily plop in his pants smelled oven-baked and kind of strangely lovely. (For six months of the year, his pants actually steamed.) On the other hand, the radiators were so hot that if you carelessly leaned an elbow on them you could leave flesh behind. The most infamous radiator-based activity was of course to pee on a radiator in one of the boys' bathrooms. This created an enormous sour stink that permeated whole wings of the school for days on end and could not be got rid of through any amount of scrubbing or airing. For this reason, anyone caught peeing on a radiator was summarily executed.

The school day was largely taken up with putting on or taking off clothing. It was an exhaustingly tedious process. It took most of the morning to take off your outdoor wear and most of the afternoon to get it back on, assuming you could find any of it among the jumbled, shifting heap of garments that carpeted the cloakroom floor to a depth of about three feet. Changing time was always like a scene at a refugee camp, with at least three kids wandering around weeping copiously because they had only one boot or no mittens. Teachers were never to be seen at such moments.

Boots in those days had strange, uncooperative clasps that managed to pinch and lacerate at the same time, producing some really interesting injuries, especially when your hands were numb with cold. The manufacturers might just as well have fashioned the clasps out of razor blades. Because they were so lethal, you ended up leaving the clasps undone, which was more macho but also let in large volumes of snow, so that you spent much of the day in sopping wet socks, which then became three times longer than your feet. In consequence of being constantly damp and hyperthermic, all children had running noses from October to April, which most of them treated as a kind of drip feeder.

Greenwood had no cafeteria, so everybody had to go home for lunch, which meant that we had to dress and undress four times in every school day – six if the teacher was foolish enough to include an outdoor recess at some point. My dear, dim friend Buddy Doberman spent so much of his life changing that he often lost track and would have to ask me whether we were putting hats on or off now. He was always most grateful for guidance.

Among the many thousands of things moms never quite understand – the manliness implicit in grass stains, the satisfaction of a really good burp or other gaseous eructation, the need from time to time to blow into straws as well as suck out of them – winter dressing has always been perhaps the most tragically conspicuous. All moms in the Fifties lived in dread of cold fronts slipping in from Canada, and therefore insisted that their children wear enormous quantities of insulating clothes for at least seven months of the year. This came mostly in the form of underwear – cotton underwear, flannel underwear, long underwear, thermal underwear, quilted underwear, ribbed underwear, underwear with padded shoulders, and possibly more; there was a *lot* of underwear in America in the 1950s – so that you couldn't possibly perish during any of the ten minutes you spent outdoors each day.

What they failed to take into account was that you were so mummified by extra clothing that you had no limb flexion whatever, and if you fell over you would never get up again unless someone helped you, which was not a thing you could count on. Layered underwear also made going to the bathroom an unnerving challenge. The manufacturers did put an angled vent in every item, but these never quite matched up, and anyway if your penis is only the size of a newly budded acorn it's asking a lot to thread it through seven or eight layers of underwear and still maintain a competent handhold. In any visit to the restroom, you would hear at least one cry of anguish from someone who had lost purchase in mid-flow and was now delving frantically for the missing appendage.

Mothers also failed to realize that certain clothes at certain periods of your life would get you beaten up. If, for instance, you wore snowpants beyond the age of six, you got beaten up for it. If you wore a hat with ear flaps or, worse, a chin strap, you could be sure of a beating, or at the very least a couple of scoops of snow down your back. The wimpiest, most foolish thing of all was to wear galoshes. Galoshes were unstylish and ineffective and even the name just sounded stupid and inescapably humiliating. If your mom made you wear galoshes at any point in the year, it was a death sentence. I knew kids who couldn't get prom dates in high school because every girl they asked remembered that they had worn galoshes in third grade.

I was not a popular pupil with the teachers. Only Mrs De Voto liked me, and she liked all the children, largely because she didn't know who any of them were. She wrote 'Billy sings with enthusiasm' on all my report cards, except once or twice when she wrote 'Bobby sings with enthusiasm.' But I excused her for that because she was kind and well meaning and smelled nice.

The other teachers – all women, all spinsters – were large, lumpy, suspicious, frustrated, dictatorial and unkind. They smelled peculiar, too – a mixture of camphor, mentholated mints and the curious belief (which may well have contributed to their spinsterhood) that a generous dusting of powder was as good as a bath. Some of these women had been powdering up for years and believe me it didn't work.

They insisted on knowing strange things, which I found bewildering. If you asked to go to the restroom, they wanted to know whether you intended to do Number 1 or Number 2, a curiosity that didn't strike me as entirely healthy. Besides, these were not terms used in our house. In our house, you either went toity or had a BM (for bowel movement), but mostly you just went 'to the bathroom' and made no public declarations with regard to intent. So I hadn't the faintest idea, the first time I requested permission to go, what the teacher meant when she asked me if I was going to do Number 1 or Number 2.

'Well, I don't know,' I replied frankly and in a clear voice. 'I need to do a big BM. It could be as much as a three or a four.'

I got sent to the cloakroom for that. I got sent to the cloakroom a lot, often for reasons that I didn't entirely understand, but I never really minded. It was a curious punishment, after all, to be put in a place where you were alone with all your classmates' snack foods and personal effects and no one could see what you were getting into. It was also a very good time to get some private reading done.

As a scholar, I made little impact. My very first report card, for the first semester of first grade, had just one comment from the teacher: 'Billy talks in a low tone.' That was it. Nothing about my character or deportment, my sure touch with phonics, my winning smile or can-do attitude, just a terse and enigmatic 'Billy talks in a low tone.' It wasn't even possible to tell whether it was a complaint or just an observation. After the second semester, the report said: 'Billy still talks in a low tone.' All my other report cards – every last one, apart from Mrs De Voto's faithful recording of my enthusiastic noise-making – had blanks in the comment section. It was as if I wasn't there. In fact, often I wasn't.

Kindergarten, my debut experience at Greenwood, ran for just half a day. You attended either the morning session or the afternoon session. I was assigned to the afternoon group, which was a lucky thing because I didn't get up much before noon in those days. (We were night owls in our house.) One of my very first experiences of kindergarten was arriving for the afternoon, keen to get cracking with the fingerpaints, and being instructed to lie down on a little rug for a nap. Resting was something we had to do a lot of in the Fifties; I presume that it was somehow attached to the belief that it would thwart polio. But as I had only just risen to come to school, it seemed a little eccentric to be lying down again. The next year was even worse because we were expected to turn up at 8.45 in the morning, which was not a time I chose to be active.

My best period was the late evening. I liked to watch the ten o'clock news with Russ Van Dyke, the world's best television newsman (better even than Walter Cronkite), and then *Sea Hunt* starring Lloyd Bridges (some genius at KRNT-TV decided 10.30 at night was a good time to run a show enjoyed by children, which was correct) before settling down with a largish stack of comic books. I was seldom asleep much before midnight, so when my mother called me in the morning, I usually found it inconvenient to rise. So I didn't go to school if I could help it.

I probably wouldn't have gone at all if it hadn't been for mimeograph paper. Of all the tragic losses since the 1950s, mimeograph paper may be the greatest. With its rapturously fragrant, sweetly aromatic pale blue ink, mimeograph paper was literally intoxicating. Two deep drafts of a freshly run-off mimeograph worksheet and I would be the education system's willing slave for up to seven hours. Go to any crack house and ask the people where their dependency problems started and they will tell you, I'm certain, that it was with mimeograph paper in second grade. I used to bound out of bed on a Monday morning because that was the day that fresh mimeographed worksheets were handed out. I draped them over my face and drifted off to a private place where fields were green, everyone went barefoot and the soft trill of pan pipes floated on the air. But most of the rest of the week I either straggled in around mid-morning, or didn't come in at all. I'm afraid the teachers took this personally.

They were never going to like me anyway. There was something about me – my dreaminess and hopeless forgetfulness, my lack of button-cuteness, my permanent default expression of pained dubiousness – that rubbed them the wrong way. They disliked all children, of course, particularly little boys, but of the children they didn't like I believe they especially favoured me. I always did everything wrong. I forgot to bring official forms back on time. I forgot to bring cookies for class parties and Christmas cards and valentines on the appropriate festive days. I always turned up empty-handed for show and tell. I remember once in kindergarten, in a kind of desperation, I just showed my fingers.

If we were going on a school trip, I never remembered to bring a permission note from home, even after being reminded daily for weeks. So on the day of the trip everybody would have to sit moodily on the bus for an interminable period while the principal's secretary tried to track my mother down to get her consent over the phone. But my mother was always out to coffee. The whole fucking women's department was always out to coffee. If they weren't out to coffee, they were out to lunch. It's a miracle they ever got a section out, frankly. The secretary would eventually look at me with a sad smile and we would have to face the fact together that I wasn't going to go.

So the bus would depart without me and I would spend the day in the school library, which I actually didn't mind at all. It's not as if I were missing a trip to the Grand Canyon or Cape Canaveral. This was Des Moines. There were only two places schools went on trips in Des Moines – to the Wonder Bread factory on Second Avenue and University, where you could watch freshly made bread products travelling round an enormous room on conveyor belts under the very light supervision of listless drones in paper hats (and you could be excused for thinking that the purpose of school visits was to give the drones something to stare at), and the museum of the Iowa State Historical Society, the world's quietest and most uneventful building, where you discovered that not a great deal had ever happened in Iowa; nothing at all if you excluded ice ages.

A more regular humiliation was forgetting to bring money for savings stamps. Savings stamps were like savings bonds, but bought a little at a time. You gave the teacher twenty or thirty cents (two dollars if your dad was a lawyer, surgeon or orthodontist) and she gave you a commensurate number of patriotic-looking stamps – one for each dime spent – which you then licked and placed over stamp-sized squares in a savings stamp book. When you had filled a book, you had $10 worth of savings and America was that much closer to licking Communism. I can still see the stamps now: they were a pinkish red with a picture of a minuteman with a three-cornered hat, a musket and a look of resolve. It was a sacred patriotic duty to buy savings stamps.

One day each week – I couldn't tell you which one now; I couldn't tell you which one then – Miss Grumpy or Miss Lesbos or Miss Squat Little Fat Thing would announce that it was time to collect money for US Saving Stamps and every child in the classroom but me would immediately reach into their desk or schoolbag and extract a white envelope containing money and join a line at the teacher's desk. It was a weekly miracle to me that all these other pupils *knew* on which day they were supposed to bring money and then actually *remembered* to do so. That was at least one step of sharpness too many for a Bryson.

One year I had four stamps in my book (two of them pasted

in upside down); in all the other years I had zero. My mother and I between us had not remembered once. The Butter boys all had more stamps than I did. Each year the teacher held up my pathetically barren book as an example for all the other pupils of how not to support your country and they would all laugh – that peculiar braying laugh that exists only when children are invited by adults to enjoy themselves at the expense of another child. It is the cruellest laugh in the world.

Despite these self-inflicted hardships, I quite enjoyed school, especially reading. We were taught to read from Dick and Jane books, solid hardbacks bound in a heavy-duty red or blue fabric. They had short sentences in large type and lots of handsome watercolour illustrations featuring a happy, prosperous, good-looking, law-abiding but interestingly strange family. In the Dick and Jane books, Father is always called Father, never Dad or Daddy, and always wears a suit, even for Sunday lunch – even, indeed, to drive to Grandfather and Grandmother's farm for a weekend visit. Mother is always Mother. She is always on top of things, always nicely groomed in a clean frilly apron. The family have no last name. They live in a pretty house with a picket fence on a pleasant street, but they have no radio or TV and their bathroom has no toilet (so no problems deciding between Number 1 and Number 2 in *their* household). The children – Dick, Jane and little Sally – have only the simplest and most timeless of toys: a ball, a wagon, a kite, a wooden sailboat.

No one ever shouts or bleeds or weeps helplessly. No meals ever burn, no drinks ever spill (or intoxicate). No dust accumulates. The sun always shines. The dog never shits on the lawn. There are no atomic bombs, no Butter boys, no cicada killers.

Everyone is at all times clean, healthy, strong, reliable, hard-working, American and white.

Every Dick and Jane story provided some simple but important lesson – respect your parents, share your possessions, be polite, be honest, be helpful, and above all work hard. Work, according to *Growing Up with Dick and Jane*, was the eighteenth new word we learned. I'm amazed it took them that long. Work was what you did in our world.

I was captivated by the Dick and Jane family. They were so wonderfully, fascinatingly different from my own family. I particularly recall one illustration in which all the members of the Dick and Jane family, for entertainment, stand on one leg, hold the other out straight and try to grab a toe on the extended foot without losing balance and falling over. They are having the most wonderful time doing this. I stared and stared at that picture and realized that there were no circumstances, including at gunpoint, in which you could get all the members of my family to try to do that together.

Because our Dick and Jane books at Greenwood were ten or fifteen years old, they depicted a world that was already gone. The cars were old-fashioned, the buses too. The shops the family frequented were of a type that no longer existed – pet shops with puppies in the window, toy stores with wooden toys, grocers where items were fetched for you by a cheerful man in a white apron. I found everything about this enchanting. There was no dirt or pain in their world. They could even go into Grandfather's hen house to collect eggs and not gag from the stink or become frantically attached to a blob of chicken shit. It was a wonderful world, a perfect world, friendly, hygienic, safe, better than real. There was just one very odd thing about the Dick and Jane books.

Whenever any of the characters spoke, they didn't sound like humans.

'Here we are at the farm,' says Father in a typical passage as he bounds from the car (dressed, not incidentally, in a brown suit), then adds a touch robotically: 'Hello, Grandmother. Here we are at the farm.'

'Hello,' responds Grandmother. 'See who is here. It is my family. Look, look! Here is my family.'

'Oh, look! Here we are at the farm,' adds Dick, equally amazed to find himself in a rural setting inhabited by loved ones. He, too, seems to have a kind of mental stuck needle. 'Here we are at the farm,' he goes on. 'Here is Grandfather, too! Here we are at the farm.'

It was like this on every page. Every character talked exactly like people whose brains had been taken away. This troubled me for a long while. One of the great influences of my life in this period was the movie *Invasion of the Body Snatchers*, which I found so convincingly scary that I took it as more or less real, and for about three years I watched my parents extremely closely for tell-tale signs that they had been taken over by alien life forms themselves, before eventually realizing that it would be impossible to tell if they had been; that indeed the first clue that they were turning into pod people would be their becoming *more normal* – and I wondered for a long time if the Dick and Jane family (or actually, for I wasn't completely stupid, the creators of the Dick and Jane family) had been snatched and were now trying to soften us up for a podding of our own. It made sense to me.

I loved the Dick and Jane books so much that I took them home and kept them. (There were stacks of spares in the cloakroom.) I still have them and still look at them from time to time.

And I am still looking for a family that would all try to touch their toes together.

Once I had the Dick and Jane books at home and could read them at my leisure, over a bowl of ice cream or while keeping half an eye on the television, I didn't see much need to go to school. So I didn't much go. By second grade I was pretty routinely declining my mother's daily entreaties to rise. It exasperated her to the point of two heavy sighs and some speechless clucking – as close to furious as she ever got – but I realized quite early on that if I just went completely limp and unresponsive and assumed a posture of sacklike uncooperativeness, stirring only very slightly from time to time to mumble that I was really quite seriously unwell and needed rest, she would eventually give up and go away, saying, 'Your dad would be *furious* if he was here now.'

But the thing was he wasn't there. He was in Iowa City or Columbus or San Francisco or Sarasota. He was always some-where. As a consequence he only learned of these matters twice a year when he was given my report card to review and sign. These always became occasions in which my mother was in as much trouble as I was.

'How can he have 26¼ absences in one semester?' he would say in pained dismay. 'And how, come to that, do you get a quarter of an absence?' He would look at my mother in further pained dismay. 'Do you just send part of him to school some-times? Do you keep his legs at home?'

My mother would make small fretful noises that didn't really amount to speech.

'I just don't get it,' my father would go on, staring at the report card as if it were a bill for damages unfairly rendered. 'It's gotten beyond a joke. I really think the only solution is a military academy.'

My father had a strange, deep attraction to military academies. The idea of permanent, systematized punishment appealed to a certain dark side of his character. Large numbers of these institutions advertised at the back of the *National Geographic* – why there I don't know – and I would often find those pages bookmarked by him. The ads always showed a worried-looking boy in grey military dress, a rifle many times too big for him at his shoulder, above a message saying something like:

Camp Hardship Military Academy
TEACHING BOYS TO KILL SINCE 1867
We specialize in building character and
eliminating pansy traits.
Write for details at PO Box 1,
Chicken Gizzard, Tenn.

It never came to anything. He would write off for a leaflet – my father was a fiend for leaflets of all types, and catalogues too if they were free – and find out that the fees were as much as for an Austin Healey sports car or a trip to Europe and drop the whole notion, as one might drop a very hot platter. Anyway, I wasn't convinced that military academies were such a bad thing. The idea of being at a place where rifles, bayonets and explosives were at the core of the curriculum had a distinct appeal.

Once a month we had a civil defence drill at school. A siren would sound – a special urgent siren that denoted that this was not a fire drill or storm alert but a nuclear attack by agents of the dark forces of Communism – and everyone would scramble out of their seats and get under their desks with hands folded over heads in the nuclear attack brace position. I must have missed a few of these, for the first time one occurred in my presence I had no idea what was going on and sat fascinated as everyone around me dropped to the floor and parked themselves like little cars under their desks.

'What is this?' I asked Buddy Doberman's butt, for that was the only part of him still visible.

'Atomic bomb attack,' came his voice, slightly muffled. 'But it's OK. It's only a practice, I think.'

I remember being profoundly amazed that anyone would suppose that a little wooden desk would provide a safe haven in the event of an atomic bomb being dropped on Des Moines. But evidently they all took the matter seriously for even the teacher, Miss Squat Little Fat Thing, was inserted under her desk, too – or at least as much of her as she could get under, which was perhaps 40 per cent. Once I realized that no one was watching, I elected not to take part. I already knew how to get under a desk and was confident that this was not a skill that would ever need refreshing. Anyway, what were the chances that the Soviets would bomb Des Moines? I mean, come on.

Some weeks later I aired this point conversationally to my father while we were dining together in the Jefferson Hotel in Iowa City on one of our occasional weekends away, and he responded with a strange chuckle that Omaha, just eighty miles to the west of Des Moines, was the headquarters of Strategic Air Command, from which all American operations would be directed in the event of war. SAC would be hit by everything the Soviets could throw at it, which of course was a great deal. We in

Des Moines would be up to our backsides in fallout within ninety minutes if the wind was blowing to the east, my father told me. 'You'd be dead before bedtime,' he added brightly. 'We all would.'

I don't know which I found more disturbing – that I was at grave risk in a way that I hadn't known about or that my father found the prospect of our annihilation so amusing – but either way it confirmed me in the conviction that nuclear drills were pointless. Life was too short and we'd all be dead anyway. The time would be better spent apologetically but insistently touching Mary O'Leary's budding chest. In any case, I ceased to take part in the drills.

So it was perhaps a little unfortunate that on the morning of my third or fourth drill, Mrs Unnaturally Enormous Bosom, the principal, accompanied by a man in a military uniform from the Iowa Air National Guard, made an inspection tour of the school and espied me sitting alone at my desk reading a comic adventure featuring the Human Torch and that shapely minx Asbestos Lady, surrounded by a roomful of abandoned desks, each sprouting a pair of backward-facing feet and a child's ass.

Boy, was I in trouble. In fact, it was worse than just being straightforwardly in trouble. For one thing, Miss Squat Little Fat Thing was also in trouble for having failed in her supervisory responsibilities and so became deeply, irremediably pissed off at me, and would for ever remain so.

My own disgrace was practically incalculable. I had embarrassed the school. I had embarrassed the principal. I had shamed myself. I had insulted my nation. To be cavalier about nuclear preparedness was only half a step away from treason. I was beyond hope really. Not only did I talk in a low tone, miss

171

lots of school, fail to buy savings stamps and occasionally turn up wearing girlie Capri pants, but clearly I came from a Bolshevik household. I spent more or less the rest of my elementary school career in the cloakroom.

Chapter 9

MAN AT WORK

In Washington, DC, gunman John A. Kendrick testified that he was offered $2,500 to murder Michael Lee, but declined the job because 'when I got done paying taxes out of that, what would I have left?'

– *Time* magazine, 7 January 1953

MARY McGUIRE

Typewriters rampant on field of editorship,
deadlines and print . . . D club's own little
sweetheart . . . tiny, crinkly-smiled
. . . Mr. McGuire's gift to journalism.

O NCE YOU STRIP OUT all those jobs where people have to look at, touch or otherwise deal with faeces and vomit – sewage workers and hospital bedpan cleaners and so on – being an after-noon newspaper boy in the 1950s and 1960s was possibly the worst job in history. For a start, you had to deliver the afternoon papers six days a week, from Monday through Saturday, and then get up on Sundays before dawn and deliver the Sunday papers too. This was so the regular morning paperboys could enjoy a day off each week. Why they deserved a day of rest and we didn't was a question that appears never to have occurred to anyone except evening newspaper boys.

Anyway, being a seven-day-a-week serf meant that you couldn't go away for an overnight trip or anything fun like that without finding somebody to do the route for you, and that was always infinitely more trouble than it was worth because the stand-in invariably delivered to the wrong houses or forgot to show up or just lost interest halfway through and stuffed the last thirty papers in the big US mailbox at the corner of Thirty-seventh Street and St John's Road, so that you ended up in trouble with the customers, the *Register* and *Tribune*'s circulation manager and the United States postal authorities – and all so that you could have your first day off in one hundred and sixty days. It really wasn't fair at all.

I started as a paperboy when I was eleven. You weren't

supposed to be allowed a route until you had passed your twelfth birthday, but my father, keen to see me making my own way in the world and herniated before puberty, pulled some strings at the paper and got me a route early. The route covered the richest neighbourhood in town, around Greenwood School, a district studded with mansions of rambling grandeur.* This sounded like a plum posting, and so it was presented to me by the route manager, Mr McTivity, a man of low ethics and high body odour, but of course mansions have the longest driveways and widest lawns, so it took whole minutes – in some cases, many, many whole minutes – to deliver each paper. And evening papers weighed a ton back then.

Plus I was absent-minded. In those days my hold on the real world was always slight at best, but the combination of long walks, fresh air and lack of distraction left me helplessly vulnerable to any stray wisp of fantasy or conjecture that chose to carry me off. I might, for instance, spend a little while thinking about Bizarro World. Bizarro World was a planet that featured in some issues of *Superman* comics. The inhabitants of Bizarro World did everything in reverse – walked backwards, drove backwards, switched televisions off when they wanted to watch and on when they didn't, drove through red lights but stopped at green ones, and so on. Bizarro World bothered me enormously because it was so impossibly inconsistent. The people didn't actually speak

---

*And these were grand houses. The house known as the Wallace home, an enormous brick heap at the corner of Thirty-seventh Street and John Lynde Road, had been the home of Henry A. Wallace, Vice-President from 1941 to 1945. Among the many worthies who had slept there were two sitting Presidents, Theodore Roosevelt and William Howard Taft, and the world's richest man, John D. Rockefeller. At the time, I knew it only as the home of people who gave very, very small Christmas tips.

backwards, but just talked in a kind of primitive cave man 'me no like him' type of English, which was not the same thing at all. Anyway, living backwards simply couldn't be made to work. At the gas station they would have to take fuel out of their cars rather than put it in, so how would they make their cars go? Eating would mean sucking poo up through their anus, sending it through the body and ejecting it in mouth-sized lumps on to forks and spoons. It wouldn't be satisfactory at all.

When I had exhausted that topic, I would generally devote a good stretch of time to 'what if' questions – what I would do if I could make myself invisible (go to Mary O'Leary's house about bath time), or if time stopped and I was the only thing on earth left moving (take a lot of money from a bank and then go to Mary O'Leary's house) or if I could hypnotize everyone in the world (ditto) or found a magic lamp and was granted two wishes (ditto) or anything at all really. All fantasies led ultimately to Mary O'Leary.

Then I might move on to imponderables. How could we be sure that we all saw the same colours? Maybe what I see as green you see as blue. Who could actually say? And when scientists say that dogs and cats are colour-blind (or not – I could never remember which it was), how do they *know*? What dog is going to tell them? How do migrating birds know which one to follow? What if the lead bird just wants to be alone? And when you see two ants going in opposite directions pause to check each other out, what information exactly are they exchanging? – 'Hey, nice feelers!', 'Don't panic, but that kid that's watching us has got matches and lighter fluid' – and how do they know to do whatever they are doing? *Something* is telling them to go off and bring home a leaf or a granule of sand – but who and how?

And then suddenly I would realize that I couldn't remember, hadn't actually consciously experienced, any of the last forty-seven properties I had visited, and didn't know if I had left a paper or just walked up to the door, stood for a moment like an under-functioning automaton and turned round and walked away again.

It is not easy to describe the sense of self-disappointment that comes with reaching the end of your route and finding that there are sixteen undelivered papers in your bag and you don't have the least idea – not the least idea – to whom they should have gone. I spent much of my prepubescent years first walking an enormous newspaper route, then revisiting large parts of it. Sometimes twice.

As if delivering papers seven days a week weren't enough, you also had to collect the subscription money. So at least three evenings a week, when you might instead have had your feet up and been watching *Combat* or *The Outer Limits*, you had to turn out again and try to coax some money out of your ungrateful customers. That was easily the worst part. And the worst part of the worst part was collecting from Mrs Vandermeister.

Mrs Vandermeister was seven hundred years old, possibly eight hundred, and permanently attached to an aluminium walker. She was stooped, very small, forgetful, glacially slow, interestingly malodorous, practically deaf. She emerged from her house once a day to drive to the supermarket, in a car about the size of an aircraft carrier. It took her two hours to get out of her house and into the car and then another two hours to get the car out of the driveway and up the alley. Partly this was because Mrs Vandermeister could never find a gear she liked and partly because when shunting she never moved forward or backward more than a quarter of an inch at a time, and seemed only barely in touch with the necessity of occasionally turning the wheel. Everyone on the alley knew not to try to go anywhere between 10 a.m. and noon because Mrs Vandermeister would be getting her car out.

Once on the open road, Mrs Vandermeister was famous over a much wider area. Though her trip to Dahl's was only about three quarters of a mile, her progress created scenes reminiscent of the streets of Pamplona when the bulls are running. Motorists and pedestrians alike fled in terror before her. And it was, it must be said, an unnerving sight when Mrs Vandermeister's car came towards you down the street. For a start, it looked as if it was driverless, such was her exceeding diminutiveness, and indeed it drove as if driverless, for it was seldom entirely on the road, particularly when bumping round corners. Generally there were sparks coming off the undercarriage from some substantial object – a motorcycle, a garbage can, her own walking frame – that she had collected en route and was now taking with her wherever she went.

Getting money from Mrs Vandermeister was a perennial nightmare. Her front door had a small window in it that provided a clear view down her hallway to her living room. If you rang the doorbell at fifteen-second intervals for an hour and ten minutes, you knew that eventually she would realize someone was at the door – 'Now who the heck is *that*!' she would shout to herself – and begin the evening-long process of getting from her chair to the front door, twenty-five feet away, bumping and shoving her walker before her. After about twenty minutes, she would reach the hallway and start coming towards the door at about the speed that ice melts. Sometimes she would forget where she was going and start to detour into the kitchen or bathroom, and you would have to ring the doorbell like fury to get her back on course. When eventually she came to the door, you would have an extra half-hour of convincing her that you were not a murderer.

'I'm the paperboy, Mrs Vandermeister!' you would shout at her through the little glass pane.

'Billy Bryson's my paperboy!' she would shout back at the doorknob.

'I *am* Billy Bryson! Look at me through the window, Mrs Vandermeister! Look up here! You can see me if you look up here, Mrs Vandermeister!'

'Billy Bryson lives three doors down!' Mrs Vandermeister would shout. 'You've come to the wrong house! I don't know why you've come here!'

'Mrs Vandermeister, I'm collecting for the paper! You owe me three dollars and sixty cents!'

When finally you persuaded her to haul open the door, she was always surprised to find you there – 'Oh, Billy, you gave me a start!' she'd say – and then there would be another small eternity while she went off, shuffling and wobbling and humming the Alzheimer theme tune, to find her purse, a half-hour more while she came back to ask how much again, another forgetful detour to toilet or kitchen, and finally the announcement that she didn't have that much cash and I'd have to call again on a future occasion.

'You shouldn't leave it so long,' she'd shout. 'It's only supposed to be a dollar twenty every two weeks. You tell Billy when you see him.'

At least Mrs Vandermeister had the excuse of being ancient and demented. What really maddened was being sent away by normal people, usually because they couldn't be bothered to get their purses out. The richer the people were the more likely they were to send you away – always with a fey can-you-ever-forgive-me smile and an apology.

'No, it's all right, lady. I'm very happy to hike a mile and a quarter here through three feet of snow on the coldest night of the year and leave empty-handed because you've got some muffins in the fucking oven and your nails are drying. No problem!'

Of course I never said anything like that, but I did start levying fines. I would add fifty or sixty cents to rich people's bills and tell them that it was because the month started on a Wednesday so there was an extra half-week to account for. You could show them on their kitchen calendar how there were an extra few days at the beginning or end of the month. This always worked, especially with men if they'd had a cocktail or two, and they always had.

'Son of a gun,' they'd say, shaking their head in wonder, while you pocketed their extra money.

'You know, maybe your boss isn't paying you the right amount each month,' I would sometimes pleasantly add.

'Yeah – hey, *yeah*,' they'd say and look really unsettled.

The other danger of rich people was their dogs. Poor people in my experience have mean dogs and know it. Rich people have mean dogs and refuse to believe it. There were thousands of dogs in those days, too, inhabiting every property – big dogs, grumpy dogs, stupid dogs, tiny nippy irritating little dogs that you positively ached to turn into a kind of living hacky-sack, dogs that wanted to smell you, dogs that wanted to sit on you, dogs that barked at everything that moved. And then there was Dewey. Dewey was a black Labrador, owned by a family on Terrace Drive called the Haldemans. Dewey was about the size of a black bear and hated me. With any other human being he was just a big slobbery bundle of softness. But Dewey wanted me dead for reasons he declined to make clear and I don't believe actually knew himself. He just took against me. The Haldemans laughingly dismissed the idea that Dewey had a mean streak and serenely ignored any suggestions that he ought to be kept tied up, as the law actually demanded. They were Republicans – Nixon Republicans – and so didn't subscribe to the notion that laws are supposed to apply to all people equally.

I particularly dreaded Sunday mornings when it was dark because Dewey was black and invisible, apart from his teeth, and it was just him and me in a sleeping world. Dewey slept wherever unconsciousness overtook him – sometimes on the front porch, sometimes on the back porch, sometimes in an old kennel by the garage, sometimes on the path, but always outside – so he was always there, and always no more than a millimetre away from wakefulness and attack. It took me ages to creep, breath held, up the Haldemans' front walk and up the five wide wooden creak-ready steps of their front porch and very, very gently set the paper down on the mat, knowing that at the moment of contact I would hear from some place close by but unseen a low, dark, threatening growl that would continue until I had withdrawn with respectful backward bows. Occasionally – just often enough to leave me permanently scarred and unnerved – Dewey would lunge, barking viciously, and I had to fly across the yard whimpering, hands held protectively over my butt, leap on my bike and pedal wildly away, crashing into fire hydrants and lamp posts and generally sustaining far worse injuries than if I had just let Dewey hold me down and gnaw on me a bit.

The whole business was terrible beyond words. The only

aspect worse than suffering an attack was waiting for the next one. The lone redeeming feature of life with Dewey was the rush of relief when it was all over, of knowing that I wouldn't have to encounter Dewey again for twenty-four hours. Airmen returning home from dangerous bombing runs will recognize the feeling.

It was in such a state of exultation one crisp and twinkly March morning that I was delivering a paper to a house half a block further on when Dewey – suddenly twice his normal size and with truly unwarranted ferocity – came for me at speed from round the side of the McManuses' house. I remember thinking, in the microsecond for reflection that was available to me, that this was very unfair. It wasn't supposed to happen like this. This was my time of bliss.

Before I could meaningfully react, Dewey bit me hard on the leg just below the left buttock, knocking me to the ground. He then dragged me around for a bit – I remember my fingers scraping through grass – and then abruptly he released me and gave a confused, playful, woofy bark and bounded back into the border shrubbery whence he had come. Irate and comprehensively dishevelled, I waddled to the road to the nearest street light and took down my pants to see the damage. My jeans were torn, and on the fleshy part of my thigh there was a small puncture and a very little blood. It didn't actually hurt very much, but it came up the next day in a wonderful purply bruise, which I showed off in the boys' bathroom at school to many appreciative viewers, including Mr Groober, the strange, mute school janitor who was almost certainly an escapee from *some* place with high walls and who had never appeared quite this ecstatic about anything before, and I had to go to the doctor after school and get a tetanus shot, which I didn't appreciate a whole lot, as you can imagine.

Despite the evidence of my wound, the Haldemans refused to believe that their dog had gone for me. '*Dewey?*' they laughed. 'Dewey wouldn't harm *any*one, honey. He wouldn't leave the property after dark. Why, he's afraid of his own shadow.' And then they laughed again. The dog that attacked me, they assured me, was some *other* dog.

Just over a week later, Dewey attacked Mrs Haldeman's mother, who was visiting from California. It had her down on the ground and was about to strip her face from her skull, which would have helped my case no end frankly. Fortunately for her, Mrs Haldeman came out just in time to save her mother and realize the shocking truth about her beloved pet. Dewey was taken away in a van and never seen again. I don't think anything has ever given me more satisfaction. I never did get an apology. However, I used to stick a secret booger in their paper every day.

At least rich people didn't move without telling you. My friend Doug Willoughby had a newspaper route at the more déclassé end of Grand Avenue, made up mostly of funny-smelling apartment buildings filled with deadbeats, shut-ins and people talking to each other through walls, not always pleasantly. All his buildings were gloomy and uncarpeted and all his corridors were so long and underlit that you couldn't see to the end of them, and so didn't know what was down there. It took resolution and nerve just to go in them. Routinely Willoughby would discover that a customer had moved away (or been led off in handcuffs) without paying him, and Willoughby would have to make up the difference, for that's the way it worked. The *Register* never ended up out of pocket; only the paperboy did. Willoughby told me once that in his best week as a newspaper boy he made $4, and that included Christmas tips.

I, on the other hand, was steadily prospering, particularly when my bonus fines were factored in. Shortly before my twelfth birthday I was able to pay $102.12 in cash – a literally enormous sum; it took whole minutes to count it out at the cash register as it was mostly in small change – for a portable black and white RCA television with foldaway antenna. It was a new slimline model in whitish grey plastic, with the control knobs on top – an exciting innovation – and so extremely stylish. I carried it up to my room, plugged it in, switched it on and was seldom seen again around the house.

I took my dinner on a tray in my room each evening and scarcely ever saw my parents after that except on special occasions like birthdays and Thanksgiving. We bumped into each other in the hallway from time to time, of course, and occasionally on hot summer evenings I joined them on the screened porch for a glass of iced tea, but mostly we went our separate ways. So from that point our house was much more like a boarding house – a nice boarding house where the people got along well but respected and valued each other's privacy – than a family home.

All this seemed perfectly normal to me. We were never a terribly close family when I think back on it. At least we weren't terribly close in the conventional sense. My parents were always friendly, even affectionate, but in a slightly vague and distracted way. My mother was forever busy attacking collar stains or scraping potatoes off the oven walls – she was always attacking something – and my father was either away covering a sporting event for the paper or in his room reading. Very occasionally they went to a movie at the Varsity Theater – it showed Peter Sellers comedies from time to time, on which they quietly doted – or to the library, but mostly they stayed at home happily occupying different rooms.

Every night about eleven o'clock or a little after I would hear my father going downstairs to the kitchen to make a snack. My father's snacks were legendary. They took at least thirty minutes to prepare and required the most particular and methodical laying out of components – Ritz crackers, a large jar of mustard, wheat germ, radishes, ten Hydrox cookies, an enormous bowl of chocolate ice cream, several slices of luncheon meat, freshly washed lettuce, Cheez Whiz, peanut butter, peanut brittle, a hard-boiled egg or two, a small bowl of nuts, watermelon in season, possibly a banana – all neatly peeled, trimmed, sliced, cubed, stacked or layered as appropriate, and attractively arrayed on a large brown tray and taken away to be consumed over a period of hours. None of these snacks could have contained less than twelve thousand calories, at least 80 per cent of it in the form of cholesterol and saturated fats, and yet my father never gained an ounce of weight.

There was one other notable thing about my father's making of snacks. He was bare-assed when he made them. It wasn't, let me quickly add, that he thought being bare-assed somehow made for a better snack; it was just that he was bare-assed already. One of his small quirks was sleeping naked from the waist down. He believed that it was more comfortable, and healthful, to leave the bottom half of the body unencumbered at night, and so when in bed wore only a sleeveless T-shirt. And when he went downstairs late at night to concoct a snack he always went so attired (or un-attired). Goodness knows what Mr and Mrs Bukowski next door must have thought as they drew their curtains and saw across the way (as surely they must) my father, bare-assed, padding about his kitchen, reaching into high cupboards and assembling the raw materials for his nightly feast.

Whatever dismay it may have caused next door, none of this was of any consequence in our house as everyone was in bed fast asleep (or in my case lying in the dark watching TV very quietly). But it happened that one night in about 1963, my father descended on a Friday night when my sister, unbeknown to him, was entertaining. Specifically, she and her good friends Nancy Ricotta and Wendy Spurgin were encamped in the living room with their boyfriends, watching television in the dark and swabbing each other's airways with their tongues (or so I have always imagined), when they were startled by a light coming on in the hallway above and the sound of my father descending the stairs.

As in most American homes, the living room in our house communicated with the rooms beyond by way of a doorless opening, in this case an arch about six feet wide, which meant that it offered virtually no privacy, so the sound of an approaching adult footfall was taken seriously. Instantly assuming positions of propriety, the six young people looked towards the entranceway just in time to see my father's lightly wobbling cheeks, faintly illumined by the ghostly flicker of television, passing through the hallway and proceeding onwards to the kitchen.

For twenty-five minutes they sat in silence, too mortified to speak, knowing that my father must return by the same route and that this time the encounter would be frontal.

Fortunately (insofar as such a word can apply here) my father must have peripherally noted them as he passed or heard voices or gasps or something, for when he returned with his tray he was snugly attired in my mother's beige raincoat, creating the impression that he was not only oddly depraved but a nocturnal cross-dresser as well. As he passed he mouthed a shy but pleasant good evening to the assembled party and disappeared back up the stairs.

It was about six months, I believe, before my sister spoke to him again.

Interestingly, at just about the time I acquired my television I realized that I didn't really like TV very much – or, to put it more accurately, didn't much like what was *on* TV, though I did like having the TV on. I liked the chatter and mindless laugh tracks. So mostly I left it babbling in the corner like a demented relative and read. I was at an age now where I read a lot, all the time. Once or twice a week I would descend to the living room, where there were two enormous (or so it seemed to me) built-in bookcases flanking the back window. These were filled with my parents' books, mostly hardback, mostly from the Book-of-the-Month Club, mostly from the 1930s and 1940s, and I would select three or four and take them up to my room.

I was happily indiscriminate in my selections because I had little idea which of the books were critically esteemed and which were popular tosh. I read, among much else, *Trader Horn*, *The Bridge of San Luis Rey*, *Our Hearts Were Young and Gay*, *Manhattan Transfer*, *You Know Me, Al*, *The Constant Nymph*, *Lost Horizon*, the short stories of Saki, several joky anthologies from Bennett Cerf, a thrilling account of life on Devil's Island called *Dry Guillotine*, and more or less the complete oeuvres of P. G. Wodehouse, S. S. Van Dine and Philo Vance. I had a particular soft spot for – and I believe may have been the last human being to read – *The Green Hat* by Michael Arlen with its wonderfully peerless names: Lady Pynte, Venice Pollen, Hugh Cypress, Colonel Victor Duck and the unsurpassable Trehawke Tush.

On one of these collecting trips, I came across, on a lower shelf, a Drake University Yearbook for 1936. Flipping through it, I discovered to my astonishment – complete and utter – that my mother had been homecoming queen that year. There was a picture of her on a float, radiant, beaming, slender, youthful, wearing a glittery tiara. I went with the book to the kitchen, where I found my father making coffee. 'Did you know Mom was home-coming queen at Drake?' I said.

'Of course.'

'How did *that* happen?'

'She was elected by her peers, of course. Your mom was quite a looker, you know.'

'Really?' It had never occurred to me that my mother looked anything except motherly.

'Still is, of course,' he added chivalrously.

I found it astounding, perhaps even a little out of order, that other people might find my mother attractive or desirable. Then I quite warmed to the idea. My mother had been a beauty. Imagine.

I put the book back. On the same section of shelf were eight or nine books entitled *Best Sports Stories of 1950* and so on for nearly every year up to the present, each consisting of thirty or forty of the best sports articles of that year as chosen by somebody well known like Red Barber. Each of these volumes contained a piece of work – in some cases two pieces – by my dad. Often he was the only provincial journalist included. I sat down on the window seat between the bookcases and read several of them right there. They were wonderful. They really were. It was just one bright line after another. One I recall recorded how University of Iowa football coach Jerry Burns ranged up and down the sidelines in dismay as his defensive team haplessly allowed Ohio State to score touchdowns at

189

will. 'It was a case of the defence fiddling while Burns roamed,' he wrote, and I was amazed to realize that the bare-assed old fool was capable of such flights of verbal scintillation.

In light of these heartening discoveries, I amended the Thunderbolt Kid story at once. I *was* their biological offspring after all – and pleased to be so. Their genetic material was my genetic material and no mistake. It turned out, on further consideration, that it must have been my father, not I, who had been dispatched to Earth from Planet Electro to preserve and propagate the interests of King Volton and his doomed race. That made vastly more sense when I thought about it. What better-sounding place, after all, for a superhero to grow up in than Winfield, Iowa? *That*, surely, was where the Thunderbolt Kid was intended to come from.

Unfortunately, I realized now, my father's space capsule had suffered a hard landing, and my father had received a concussive bump, which had wiped his memory clean and left him with one or two slightly strange habits – a crippling cheapness and a disinclination to wear underpants after dark being the principal ones – and spent his whole life tragically unaware that he had the innate capacity to summon up superpowers. Instead, it was left to his youngest son to make that discovery. That was why I needed special clothes to assume my Electron powers. I was an Earthling by birth, so I didn't come by these super-gifts naturally. I required the Sacred Jersey of Zap for that.

Of course. It all made sense now. This story just got better and better, in my view.

Chapter 10
DOWN ON THE FARM

MASON CITY, IOWA – A pretty blonde bride's playful tickling of her husband to get him out of bed to milk the cows led swiftly to tragedy early Tuesday. Mrs. Jennie Becker Brunner, 22, said through her tears in Cerro Gordo County jail cell here late in the day that she shot and killed her husband, Sam Brunner, 26, with his .45 caliber U.S. Army Colt pistol. Mrs. Brunner said she and her husband quarreled after she tickled him under the arm to get him out of bed.

– *Des Moines Register*, 19 November 1953

G IVE OR TAKE the occasional ticklish murder, Iowa has always been a peaceful and refreshingly unassertive place. In the one hundred and sixty years or so that it has been a state, only one shot has been officially fired in anger on Iowa soil, and even that wasn't very angry. During the Civil War, a group of Union soldiers, for reasons that I believe are now pretty well forgotten, discharged a cannonball across the state line into Missouri. It landed in a field on the other side and dribbled harmlessly to a halt. I shouldn't be surprised if the Missourians put it on a wagon and brought it back. In any case, nobody was hurt. This was not simply the high point in Iowa's military history, it was the only point in it.

Iowa has always been proudly middling in all its affairs. It stands in the middle of the continent, between the two mighty central rivers, the Missouri and Mississippi, and throughout my childhood always ranked bang in the middle of everything – size, population, voting preferences, order of entry into the Union. We were slightly wealthier, a whole lot more law-abiding, and more literate and better educated than the national average, and ate more Jell-O (a lot more – in fact, to be completely honest, we ate all of it), but otherwise have never been too showy at all. While other states of the Midwest churned out a more or less continuous stream of world-class worthies – Mark Twain, Abraham Lincoln, Ernest Hemingway, Thomas Edison, Henry Ford, F. Scott

Fitzgerald, Charles Lindbergh – Iowa gave the world Donna Reed, Wyatt Earp, Herbert Hoover and the guy who played Fred Mertz on *I Love Lucy*.

Iowa's main preoccupations have always been farming and being friendly, both of which we do better than almost anyone else, if I say so myself. It is the quintessential farm state. Everything about it is perfect for growing things. It occupies just 1.6 per cent of the country's land area, but contains 25 per cent of its Grade A topsoil. That topsoil is three feet deep in most places, which is apparently pretty deep. Stride across an Iowa farm field and you feel as if you could sink in up to your waist. You will certainly sink in up to your ankles. It is like walking around on a very large pan of brownies. The climate is ideal, too, if you don't mind shovelling tons of snow in the winter and dodging tornadoes all summer. By the standards of the rest of the world, droughts are essentially unknown and rainfall is distributed with an almost uncanny beneficence – heavy enough to give a healthful soaking when needed but not so much as to pummel seedlings or wash away nutrients. Summers are long and agreeably sunny, but seldom scorching. Plants love to grow in Iowa.

It is in consequence one of the most maximally farmed landscapes on earth. Someone once calculated that if Iowa contained nothing but farms, each of one hundred and sixty acres (presumably the optimal size for a farm), there would be room for 225,000 of them. In 1930, the peak year for farm numbers, there were 215,361 farms in the state – not far off the absolute maximum. The number is very much smaller these days because of the relentless push of amalgamation, but 95 per cent of Iowa's landscape is still farmed. The remaining small fraction is taken up by highways, woods, a scattering of lakes and rivers, loads of little towns and a few smallish cities, and about twelve million Wal-Mart parking lots.

I remember reading once at the State Fair that Iowa's farms produced more in value each year than all the diamond mines in the world put together – a fact that fills me with pride still. It remains number one in the nation for the production of corn, eggs, hogs and soybeans, and is second in the nation in total agricultural wealth, exceeded only by California, which is three times the size. Iowa produces one tenth of all America's food and one tenth of all the world's maize. Hooray.

And when I was growing up all this was as good as it has ever been. The 1950s has often been called the last golden age of the family farm in America, and no place was more golden than Iowa, and no spot had a lovelier glint than Winfield, the trim and cheerful little town in the southeast corner of the state, not far from the Mississippi River, where my father had grown up and my grandparents lived.

I loved everything about Winfield – its handsome Main Street, its imperturbable tranquillity, its lapping cornfields, the healthful smell of farming all around. Even the name was solid and right. Lots of towns in Iowa have names that sound slightly remote and lonesome and perhaps just a little inbred – Mingo, Pisgah, Tingley, Diagonal, Elwood, Coon Rapids, Ricketts – but in this green and golden corner of the state the town names were dependably worthy and good: Winfield, Mount Union, Columbus Junction, Olds, Mount Pleasant, the unbeatably radiant Morning Sun.

My grandfather was a rural route mailman by trade, but he owned a small farm on the edge of town. He rented out the land to other farmers, except for three or four acres that he kept for orchards and vegetables. The property included a big red barn and what seemed to me like huge lawns on all sides. The back of the house was dominated by an immense oak tree with a white bench encircling it. It seemed always to have a private breeze running through its upper branches. It was the coolest spot in a hundred miles. This was where you sat to shuck peas or trim green beans or turn a handle to make ice cream at the tranquil, suppertime end of the day.

My grandparents' house was very neat and small – it had just two bedrooms, one upstairs and one down – but was exceedingly comfortable and always seemed spacious to me. Years later I went back to Winfield and was astounded at how tiny it actually was.

From a safe distance, the barn looked like the most fun place in the world to play. It hadn't been used for years except to store old furniture and odds and ends that would never be used again. It was full of doors you could swing on and secret storerooms and ladders leading up to dark haymows. But it was actually awful because it was filthy and dark and lethal and every inch of it smelled. You couldn't spend five minutes in my grandfather's barn without banging your shins on some piece of unyielding machinery, cutting your arm on an old blade, coming into contact with at least three different types of ancient animal shit (all years old but still soft in the middle), banging your head on a nail-studded beam and recoiling into a mass of sticky cobwebs, getting snagged from the nape of your neck to the top of your buttocks on a strand of barbed wire, quilling yourself all over with splinters the size of toothpicks. The barn was like a whole-body workout for your immune system.

The worst fear of all was that one of the heavy doors would swing shut behind you and you would be trapped for ever in a foul smelly darkness, too far from the house for your plaintive cries to be heard. I used to imagine my family sitting round the dinner table saying, 'Well, I wonder whatever became of old Billy. How long has it been now? Five weeks? Six? He'd sure love this pie, wouldn't he? I'll certainly have another piece if I may.'

Even scarier were the fields of corn that pressed in on all sides. Corn doesn't grow as tall as it used to because it's been hybridized into a more compact perfection, but it shot up like bamboo when I was young, reaching heights of eight feet or more and filling 56,290 square miles of Iowa countryside with a spooky, threatening rustle by the dryish late end of summer. There is no more anonymous, mazelike, unsettling environment, especially to a dim, smallish human, than a field of infinitely identical rows of tall corn, each – including the diagonals – presenting a prospect of endless vegetative hostility. Just standing on the edge and peering in, you knew that if you ventured more than a few feet into a cornfield you would never come out. If a ball you were playing with dropped into a cornfield, you just left it, wrote it off, and went inside to watch TV.

So I didn't play alone much at Winfield. Instead I spent a lot of time following my grandfather around. He seemed to like the company. We got along very well. My grandfather was a quiet man, but always happy to explain what he was doing and glad to have someone who could pass him an oil can or a screwdriver. His name was Pitt Foss Bryson, which I thought was the best name ever. He was the nicest man in the world after Ernie Banks.

He was always rebuilding something – a lawnmower or washing machine; something with fan belts and blades and lots of swiftly whirring parts – and always cutting himself fairly spectacularly. At some point, he would fire the thing up, reach in to make an adjustment and almost immediately go, 'Dang!' and pull out a bloody, slightly shredded hand. He would hold it up before him for some time, wiggling the fingers, as if he didn't quite recognize it.

'I can't see without my glasses,' he would say to me at length. 'How many fingers have I got here?'

'Five, Grandpa.'

'Well, *that's* good,' he'd say. 'Thought I might have lost one.' Then he'd go off to find a bandage or piece of rag.

At some point in the afternoon, my grandmother would put her head out the back door and say, 'Dad, I need you to go uptown and get me some rutabaga.' She always called him Dad, even though he had a wonderful name and he wasn't her father. I could never understand that. She always needed him to get rutabaga. I never understood that either since I don't remember any of us ever being served it. Maybe it was a code word for prophylactics or something.

Going uptown was a treat. It was only a quarter of a mile or so, but we always drove, sitting on the high bench seat of my grandfather's Chevy, which made you feel slightly regal. Uptown in Winfield meant Main Street, a two-block stretch of retail tranquillity sporting a post office, two banks, a couple of filling stations, a tavern, a newspaper office, two small grocer's, a pool hall and a variety store.

The last stop on every shopping trip was a corner grocer's called Benteco's, where they had a screen door that *kerboinged* and *bammed* in a deeply satisfying manner, and made every entrance a kind of occasion. At Benteco's I was always allowed to select two bottles of NeHi brand pop – one for dinner, one for afterwards when we were playing cards or watching Bilko* or Jack Benny on TV. NeHi was the pop of small towns – I don't know why – and it had the intensest flavour and most vivid colours of any products yet cleared by the Food and Drug Administration for human consumption. It came in six select flavours – grape, strawberry, orange, cherry, lime-lemon (never 'lemon-lime') and root beer – but each was so potently flavourful that it made your eyes water like an untended sprinkler, and so sharply carbonated that it was like swallowing a thousand tiny razor blades. It was wonderful.

The NeHi at Benteco's was kept in a large, blue, very chilly cooler, like a chest freezer, in which the bottles hung by their necks in rows. To get to a particular bottle usually required a great deal of complicated manoeuvring, transferring bottles out of one row and into another in order to get the last bottle of grape, say. (Grape was the one flavour that could actually make you hallucinate; I once saw to the edge of the universe while drinking grape NeHi.) The process was great fun if it was you that was doing the selecting (especially on a hot day when you could bask in the cooler's moist chilled air) and a torment if you had to wait on some other kid.

The other thing I did a lot in Winfield was watch TV. My grandparents had the best chair for watching television – a beige leatherette recliner that was part fairground ride, part captain's seat from a spaceship, and all comfort. It was a thing of supreme beauty and utility. When you pulled the lever you were thrust – flung – into a deep recline mode. It was nearly impossible to get

---

*I know it was never actually called *Bilko*. It was *You'll Never Get Rich* and then later *The Phil Silvers Show*. But we called it *Bilko*. Everybody did. It was only on for four years.

up again, but it didn't matter because you were so sublimely comfortable that you didn't want to move. You just lay there and watched the TV through splayed feet.

My grandparents could get seven stations on their set – we could only get three in Des Moines – but only by turning the roof aerial, which was manipulated by means of a crank on the outside back wall of the house. So if you wanted to watch, say, KTVO from Ottumwa, my grandfather had to go out and turn the crank slightly one way, and if you wanted WOC from the Quad Cities he turned it another, and KWWI in Waterloo another way still, in each case responding to instructions shouted through a window. If it was windy or there was a lot of solar activity, he sometimes had to go out eight or nine times during a programme. If it was one of my grandmother's treasured shows, like *As the World Turns* or *Queen for a Day*, he generally just stayed out there in case an aeroplane flew over and made everything lapse into distressing waviness at a critical moment. He was the most patient man that ever lived.

I watched a lot of television in those days. We all did. By 1955, the average American child had watched five thousand hours of television, up from zero hours five years earlier. My favourite programmes were, in no particular order, *Zorro, Bilko, Jack Benny, Dobie Gillis, Love That Bob, Sea Hunt, I Led Three Lives, Circus Boy, Sugarfoot, M Squad, Dragnet, Father Knows Best, The Millionaire, Gunsmoke, Robin Hood, The Untouchables, What's My Line?, I've Got a Secret, Route 66, Topper* and *77 Sunset Strip*, but really I would watch anything.

My favourite of all was the *Burns and Allen Show* starring George Burns and Gracie Allen. I was completely enchanted with it because I loved the characters and their names – Blanche

Morton, Harry Von Zell – and because George Burns and Gracie Allen were, in my view, the funniest double act ever. George had a deadpan manner and Gracie always got the wrong end of every stick. George had a television in his den on which he could watch what his neighbours were up to without their knowing it, which I thought was just a brilliant notion and one that fed many a private fantasy, and he often stepped out of the production to talk directly to the audience about what was going on. The whole thing was years ahead of its time. I've never met another human being who even remembers it, much less doted on it.

Nearly every summer evening just before six o'clock we would walk uptown (all movement towards the centre was known as going uptown) to some shady church lawn and take part in a vast potluck supper, presided over by armies of immense, chuckling women who had arms and necks that sagged in an impossible manner, like really wet clothes. They were all named Mabel and they all suffered greatly from the heat, though they never complained and never stopped chuckling and being happy. They spent their lives shooing flies from food with spatulas (setting their old arms a-wobbling in a hypnotizing manner), blowing wisps of stray hair out of their faces, and making sure that no human being within fifty yards failed to have a heaped paper plate of hearty but deeply odd food – and dinners in the 1950s, let me say, were odd indeed. The main courses at these potluck events nearly always consisted of a range of meatloafs, each about the size of a V8 engine, all of them glazed and studded with a breathtaking array of improbable ingredients from which they drew their names – Peanut Brittle 'n' Cheez Whiz Upside Down Spam Loaf and that sort of thing. Nearly all of them had at least one ''n'' and an 'upside down' in their names somewhere. There would be perhaps twenty of these. The driving notion seemed to be that no dish could be too sweet or too strange and that all foods automatically became superior when upended.

'Hey, Dwayne, come over here and try some of this Spiced Liver 'n' Candy Corn Upside Down Casserole,' one of the Mabels would say. 'Mabel made it. It's delicious.'

'Upside *down?*' Dwayne would remark with a dry look that indicated a quip was coming. 'What happened – she drop it?'

'Well, I don't know. Maybe she did,' Mabel would reply, chuckling. 'You want chocolate gravy with that or biscuit gravy or peanut butter 'n' niblets gravy?'

'Hey, how about a little of all three?'

'You got it!'

The main dishes were complemented by a table of brightly coloured Jell-Os, the state fruit, each containing further imaginative components – marshmallows, pretzels, fruit chunks, Rice Krispies, Fritos corn chips, whatever would maintain its integrity in suspension – and you had to take some of each of these, too, though of course you wanted to because it all looked so tasty. Then came at least two big tables carrying tubs and platters of buttery mashed potatoes, bacon swimming in baked beans, creamed vegetables, devilled eggs, cornbreads, muffins, heavy-duty biscuits and a dozen types of cole slaw. By the time all these were loaded on to your paper plate, it weighed twelve pounds and looked, as my father once described it, distinctly post-operative. But there was no resisting the insistent blandishments of the many Mabels.

Everyone for miles came to the suppers. It didn't matter what the denomination of the church was. Everybody came. Everyone in town was practically Methodist anyway, even the Catholics. (My grandparents, for the record, were Lutherans.) It wasn't about religion; it was about sociable eating in bulk.

'Now don't forget to leave room for dessert,' one of the Mabels would say as you staggered off with your plate, but you didn't have to be reminded of that for the desserts were fabulous and celebrated, the best part of all. They were essentially the same dishes, but with the meat removed.

On the few nights when we weren't at a church social, we had enormous meals at my grandparents' house, often on a table carried out to the lawn. (It seemed important to people in those days to share dinner with as many insects as possible.) Uncle Dee would be there, of course, burping away, and Uncle Jack from Wapello, who was notable for never managing to finish a sentence.

'I tell you what they ought to do,' he would say in the midst of a lively discussion, and someone else more assertive would interject a comment and nobody would ever hear what Jack thought. 'Well, if you ask me,' he'd say, but nobody ever did. Mostly they sat around talking about surgical removals and medical conditions – goitres and gallstones, lumbago, sciatica, water on the knee – that don't seem to exist much any more. They always seemed so old to me, and slow, so glad to sit down.

But they sure were good natured. If we had a guest from beyond the usual family circle somebody would always bring out the dribble glass and offer the guest a drink. The dribble glass was the funniest thing I had ever seen. It was a fancy-looking, many-faceted drinking glass – exactly the sort of glass that you would give to an honoured guest – that appeared to be perfectly normal, and indeed was perfectly normal so long as you didn't tilt it. But cut into the facets were tiny, undetectable slits, ingeniously angled so that each time the glass was inclined to the mouth a good portion of the contents dribbled out in a steady run on to the victim's chest.

There was something indescribably joyous about watching an innocent, unaware person repeatedly staining him- or herself with cranberry juice or cherry Kool-Aid (it was always something vividly coloured) while twelve people looked on with soberly composed expressions. Eventually, feeling the seepage, the victim would look down and cry, 'Oh, my golly!' and everyone would burst out laughing.

I never knew a single victim to get angry or dismayed when they discovered the prank. Their best white shirt would be ruined, they would look as if they had been knifed in the chest, and they would laugh till their eyes streamed. God, but Iowans were happy souls.

Winfield always had more interesting weather than elsewhere. It was always hotter, colder, windier, noisier, sultrier, more punishing and emphatic than weather elsewhere. Even when the weather wasn't actually doing anything, when it was just muggy and limp and still on an August afternoon, it was more muggy and limp than anywhere else you have ever been, and so still that you could hear a clock ticking in a house across the street.

Because Iowa is flat and my grandparents lived on the very edge of town, you could see everything meteorological long before it got there. Storms of towering majesty often lit the western skies for two or three hours before the first drops of rain fell in Winfield. They talk about big skies in the western US, and they may indeed have them, but you have never seen such lofty clouds, such towering anvils, as in Iowa in July.

The greatest fury in Iowa – in the Midwest – is tornadoes. Tornadoes are not often seen because they tend to be fleeting and localized and often they come at night, so you lie in bed listening to a wild frenzy outside knowing that a tornado's tail could dip down at any moment and blow you and your cosy tranquillity to pieces. Once my grandparents were in bed when they heard a great roaring, like a billion hornets as my grandfather described it, going right past their house. My grandfather got up and peered out the bedroom window but couldn't see a thing and went back to bed. Almost at once the noise receded.

In the morning, he stepped outside to fetch in the newspaper and was surprised to find his car standing in the open air. He was sure he *had* put it away as usual the night before. Then he realized he had put the car away, but the garage was gone. The car was standing on its concrete floor. It didn't have a scratch on it. Nothing of the garage was ever seen again. Looking closer, he discovered a track of destruction running along one side of the house. A bed of shrubs that had stood against the house, in front of the bedroom window, had been obliterated utterly, and he realized that the blackness he had peered into the night before was a wall of tornado passing on the other side of the glass just an inch or two beyond his nose.

Just once I saw a tornado when I was growing up. It was moving across the distant horizon from right to left, like a killer apostrophe. It was about ten miles off and therefore comparatively safe. Even so it was unimaginably powerful. The sky everywhere was wildly, unnaturally dark and heavy and low, and every wisp of cloud in it, from every point in the compass, was being sucked into the central vortex as if being pulled into a black hole. It was like being present for the end of the world. The wind, steady and intense, felt oddly as if it was not pushing from behind, but pulling from the front, like the insistent draw of a magnet. You had to fight not to be pulled forward. All that energy was being focused on a single finger of whirring destruction. We didn't know it at the time, but it was killing people as it went.

For a minute or two the tornado paused in its progress and seemed to stand on one spot.

'That could mean it's coming towards us,' my father remarked to my grandfather.

I took this to mean that we would all now get in our cars and drive like hell in a contrary direction. That was the option I planned to vote for if anyone asked for a show of hands.

But my grandfather merely said, 'Yup. Could be,' and looked completely undisturbed.

'Ever seen a tornado up close, Billy?' my father said to me, smiling weirdly.

I stared at him in amazement. Of course not and I didn't want to. This business of not ever being frightened of anything was easily the most frightening thing about adults in the Fifties.

'What do we do if it's coming this way?' I asked in a pained manner, knowing I was not going to enjoy the answer.

'Well, that's a good question, Billy, because it's very easy to flee from one tornado and drive straight into another. Do you know, more people die trying to get out of the way of tornadoes than from any other cause?' He turned to my grandfather. 'Do you remember Bud and Mabel Weidermeyer?'

My grandfather nodded with a touch of vigour, as if to say, *Who could forget it?* 'They should have known better than to try to outrun a tornado on foot,' my grandfather said. 'Especially with Bud's wooden leg.'

'Did they ever find that leg?'

'Nope. Never found Mabel either. You know, I think it's moving again.'

He indicated the tornado and we all watched closely. After a few moments it became apparent that it had indeed resumed its stately march to the east. It wasn't coming towards us after all. Very soon after that, it lifted from the ground and returned into the black clouds above it, as if being withdrawn. Almost at once the wind dropped. My father and grandfather went back in the house looking slightly disappointed.

The next day we drove over and had a look at where it had gone and there was devastation everywhere – trees and power lines down, barns blown to splinters, houses half vanished. Six people died in the neighbouring county. I expect none of them were worried about the tornado either.

What I particularly remember of Winfield is the coldness of the winters. My grandparents were very frugal with the heat in their house and tended to turn it all but off at night, so that the house never warmed up except in the kitchen when a big meal was being cooked, like at Thanksgiving or Christmas, when it took on a wonderful steamy warmth. But otherwise it was like living in an Arctic hut. The upstairs of their house was a single long room, which could be divided into two by a pull-across curtain. It had no heating at all and the coldest linoleum floor in history.

But there was one place even colder: the sleeping porch. The sleeping porch was a slightly rickety, loosely enclosed porch on the back of the house that was only notionally separate from the outside world. It contained an ancient sagging bed that my grandfather slept in in the summer when the weather was unbearably hot. But sometimes in the winter when the house was full of guests it was pressed into service, too.

The only heat the sleeping porch contained was that of any human being who happened to be out there. It couldn't have been more than one or two degrees warmer than the world outside – and outside was perishing. So to sleep on the sleeping porch required preparation. First, you put on long underwear, pyjamas, jeans, a sweatshirt, your grandfather's old cardigan and bathrobe, two pairs of woollen socks on your feet and another on your hands, and a hat with ear flaps tied beneath the chin. Then you climbed into bed and were immediately covered with a dozen bed blankets, three horse blankets, all the household overcoats, a canvas tarpaulin and a piece of old carpet. I'm not sure that they didn't lay an old wardrobe on top of that, just to hold everything down. It was like sleeping under a dead horse. For the first minute or so it was unimaginably cold, shockingly cold, but gradually your body heat seeped in and you became warm and happy in a way you would not have believed possible only a minute or two before. It was bliss.

Or at least it was until you moved a muscle. The warmth, you discovered, extended only to the edge of your skin and not a micron further. There wasn't any possibility of shifting positions. If you so much as flexed a finger or bent a knee, it was like plunging them into liquid nitrogen. You had no choice but to stay totally immobilized. It was a strange and oddly wonderful experience – to be poised so delicately between rapture and torment.

It was the serenest, most peaceful place on earth. The view from the sleeping porch through the big broad window at the foot of the bed was across empty dark fields to a town called

Swedesburg, named for the nationality of its founders, and known more informally as Snooseville from the pinches of tobacco that the locals used to pack into their mouths as they went about their business. Snoose was a homemade mixture of tobacco and salt which was kept embedded between cheek and gum where the nicotine could be slowly and steadily absorbed. It was topped up hourly and kept in permanently. Some people, my father told me, even put in a fresh wad at bedtime.

I had never been to Swedesburg. There was no reason to go – it was just a small collection of houses – but at night in winter with its distant lights it was like a ship far out at sea. I found it peaceful and somehow comforting to see their lights, to think that all the citizens of Snooseville were snug in their homes and perhaps looking over at us in Winfield and deriving comfort in turn. My father told me that when he was a boy the people of Snooseville still spoke Swedish at home. Some of them could barely speak English at all. I loved that, too – the idea that it was a little outpost of Sweden over there, that they were all sitting around eating herring and black bread and saying, 'Oh, ja!' and just being happily Swedish in the middle of the American continent. When my dad was young if you drove across Iowa you would regularly come across towns or villages where all the inhabitants spoke German or Dutch or Czech or Danish or almost any other tongue from northern and central Europe.

But those days had long since passed. In 1916, as the shadow of the Great War made English-speaking people suspicious of loyalties, a governor of Iowa named William L. Harding decreed that henceforth it would be a crime to speak any foreign language in schools, at church, or even over the telephone in the great state of Iowa. There were howls that people would have to give up church services in their own languages, but Harding was not to be moved. 'There is no use in anyone wasting his time praying in other languages than English,' he responded. 'God is listening only to the English tongue.'

One by one the little linguistic outposts faded away. By the 1950s they were pretty much gone altogether. No one would have guessed it at the time, but the small towns and family farms were soon to become likewise imperilled.

In 1950, America had nearly six million farms. In half a century almost two thirds of them vanished. More than half the American landscape was farmed when I was a boy; today, thanks to the spread of concrete, only 40 per cent is – a severe decline in a single lifetime.

I was born into a state that had two hundred thousand farms. Today the number is much less than half that and falling. Of the seven hundred and fifty thousand people who lived on farms in the state in my boyhood, half a million – two in every three – have gone. The process has been relentless. Iowa's farm population fell by 25 per cent in the 1970s and by 35 per cent more in the 1980s. Another hundred thousand people were skimmed away in the 1990s. And the people left behind are old. In 1988, Iowa had more people who were seventy-five or older than five or younger. Thirty-seven counties out of ninety-nine – getting on for half – recorded more deaths than births.

It's an inevitable consequence of greater efficiency and con-tinuous amalgamation. Increasingly the old farms clump together into superfarms of three thousand acres or more. By the middle of this century, it is thought, the number of farms in Iowa could drop to as low as ten thousand. That's not much of a rural population in a space the size of England.

Without a critical mass of farmers, most small towns in Iowa have pretty well died. Drive anywhere in the state these days and what you see are empty towns, empty roads, collapsing barns, boarded farmhouses. Everywhere you go it looks as if you have just missed a terrible contagion, which in a sense I suppose you have. It's the same story in Illinois, Kansas and Missouri, and even worse in Nebraska and the Dakotas. Wherever there were once small towns, there are now empty main streets.

Winfield is barely alive. All the businesses on Main Street – the dime store, the pool hall, the newspaper office, the banks, the grocery stores – long ago disappeared. There is nowhere to buy NeHi pop even if it still existed. You can't purchase a single item of food within the town limits. My grandparents' house is still there – at least it was the last time I passed – but its barn is gone and its porch swing and the shade tree out back and the orchard and everything else that made it what it was.

The best I can say is that I saw the last of something really special. It's something I seem to say a lot these days.

Chapter 11

WHAT, ME WORRY?

LIES IN MORGUE 17 HOURS – ALIVE

ATLANTA, GA. (UP) – An elderly woman taken to a funeral home for embalming opened her eyes 17 hours after arriving and announced: 'I'm not dead.'

W. L. Murdaugh of Murdaugh Brothers funeral home here said two of his employees were made almost speechless.

The woman, listed as Julia Stallings, 70, seemed dazed after her long coma ended Sunday night, but otherwise appeared in good condition, Murdaugh said.

– Des Moines Tribune, 11 May 1953

Collier's

15c

August 5, 1950

HIROSHIMA, U.S.A.

Can Anything Be Done About It?

THE ONLY TIME I HAVE EVER broken a bone was also the first time I noticed that adults are not entirely to be counted on. I was four years old and playing on Arthur Bergen's jungle gym when I fell off and broke my leg.

Arthur Bergen lived up the street, but was at the dentist or something when I called, so I decided to have a twirl on his new jungle gym before heading back home.

I don't remember anything at all about the fall, but I do remember very clearly lying on damp earth, the jungle gym now above and around me and seeming awfully large and menacing all of a sudden, and not being able to move my right leg. I remember also lifting my head and looking down my body to my leg which was bent at an unusual – indeed, an entirely novel – angle. I began to call steadily for help, in a variety of tones, but no one heard. Eventually I gave up and dozed a little.

At some point I opened my eyes and a man with a uniform and a peaked cap was looking down at me. The sun was directly behind him so I couldn't see his face; it was just a hatted darkness inside a halo of intense light.

'You all right, kid?' he said.

'I've hurt my leg.'

He considered this for a minute. 'You wanna get your mom to put some ice on it. Do you know some people named . . .' – he consulted a clipboard – '. . . Maholovich?'

'No!'

He glanced at the clipboard again. 'A. J. Maholovich. 3725 Elmwood Drive.'

'No.'

'Doesn't ring a bell at all?'

'No.'

'This is Elmwood Drive?'

'Yes.'

'OK, kid, thanks.'

'It really hurts,' I said. But he was gone.

I slept a little more. After a while Mrs Bergen pulled into their driveway and came up the back steps with bags of groceries.

'You'll catch a chill down there,' she said brightly as she skipped past.

'I've hurt my leg.'

She stopped and considered for a moment. 'Better get up and walk around on it. That's the best thing. Oh, there's the phone.' She hurried into the house.

I waited for her to come back but she didn't. 'Hello,' I croaked weakly now. 'Help.'

Bergen's little sister, who was small and therefore stupid and unreliable, came and had a critical look at me.

'Go and get your mom,' I said. 'I'm hurt.'

She looked at my leg with comprehension if not compassion. 'Owie,' she said.

'Yes, owie. It really hurts.'

She wandered off, saying, 'Owie, owie,' but evidently took my case no further.

Mrs Bergen came out after some time with a load of washing to hang.

'You must really like it down there,' she chuckled.

'Mrs Bergen, I think I've really hurt my leg.'

'On that little jungle gym?' she said, with good-natured scepticism, but came closer to look at me. 'I don't think so, honey.' And then abruptly: 'Christamighty! Your leg! It's backwards!'

'It hurts.'

'I bet it does, I bet it does. You wait right there.'

She went off.

Eventually, after quite some time, Mr Bergen and my parents pulled up in their respective cars at more or less the same moment. Mr Bergen was a lawyer. I could hear him talking to them about liability as they came up the steps. Mr Bergen was the first to reach me.

'Now you do understand, Billy, that technically you were trespassing . . .'

They took me to a young Cuban doctor on Woodland Avenue and *he* was in a panic. He started making exactly the kind of noises Desi Arnaz made in *I Love Lucy* when Lucy did something really bone-headed – only he was doing this over my leg. 'I don' thin' I can do this,' he said, and looked at them beseechingly. 'It's a really bad break. I mean look at it. Wow.'

I expect he was afraid he would be sent back to Cuba. Eventually he was prevailed upon to set the break. For the next six weeks my leg remained more or less backwards. The moment they cut off the cast, the leg spun back into position and everyone was pleasantly surprised. The doctor beamed. 'Tha's a bit of luck!' he said happily.

Then I stood up and fell over.

'Oh,' the doctor said and looked troubled again. 'Tha's not good, is it?'

He thought for a minute and told my parents to take me home and to keep me off the leg for the rest of the day and overnight and see how it was in the morning.

'Do you think it will be all right then?' asked my father.

'I've no idea,' said the doctor.

The next morning I got up and stepped gingerly on to my wounded leg. It felt OK. It felt good. I walked around. It was fine. I walked a little more. Yes, it was definitely fine.

I went downstairs to report this good news and found my mother bent over in the laundry room sorting through clothes.

'Hey, Mom, my leg's fine,' I announced. 'I can walk.'

'Oh, that's good, honey,' she said, head in the dryer. 'Now where's that other sock?'

It wasn't that my mother and father were indifferent to their children's physical well-being by any means. It was just that they seemed to believe that everything would be fine in the end and they were always right. No one ever got lastingly hurt in our family. No one died. Nothing ever went seriously wrong – and not much went wrong in our town or state either, come to that. Danger was something that happened far away in places like Matsu and Quemoy, and the Belgian Congo, places so distant that nobody was really quite sure where they were.

It's hard for people now to remember just how enormous the world was back then for everybody, and how far away even fairly nearby places were. When we called my grandparents long distance on the telephone in Winfield, something we hardly ever did, it sounded as if they were speaking to us from a distant star. We had to shout to be heard and plug a finger in an ear to catch their faint, tinny voices in return. They were only about a hundred miles away, but that was a pretty considerable distance even well into the 1950s. Anything further – beyond Chicago or Kansas City, say – quickly became almost foreign. It wasn't just that Iowa was far from everywhere. Everywhere was far from everywhere.

America was especially blessed in this regard. We had big buffering oceans to left and right and no neighbours to worry us above or below, so there wasn't any need to be fearful about anything ever. Even world wars barely affected our home lives. During the Second World War, when the film mogul Jack Warner realized that from the air his Hollywood studio was indistinguishable from a nearby aircraft factory, he had a giant arrow painted on the roof above the legend 'Lockheed That-Away!' to steer Japanese bombers safely away from some of the valuable stars who didn't go to war (and that included Gary Cooper, Bob Hope, Fred MacMurray, Frank Sinatra, John Garfield, Gene Kelly, Alan Ladd, Danny Kaye, Cary Grant, Bing Crosby, Van Johnson, Dana Andrews, Ronald Reagan and John Wayne, among many other valiant heroes who helped America to act its way to victory) and towards the correct target.

No one ever knew whether Warner was in earnest with his sign or not, but it didn't really matter because no one seriously expected (at least not after the first jittery days of the war) that the Japanese would attack the US mainland. At the same time, on the other side of the country, when a Congressman grew concerned for the welfare of rooftop sentries at the Capitol Building who didn't ever seem to stir from their positions or enjoy a moment's relief, he was quietly informed that they were in fact dummies and that their anti-aircraft guns were wooden models. There was no point in wasting men and munitions on a target that was never going to be hit, even if it was the headquarters of the United States government.

For the record there was one manned attack on the American mainland. In 1942, a pilot named Nobuo Fujita took to the air from coastal waters off Oregon in a specially modified seaplane that was brought there aboard a submarine. Fujita's devious goal was to drop incendiary bombs on Oregon's forests, starting large-scale fires that would, if all went to plan, rage out of control and engulf much of the West Coast, killing hundreds and leaving Americans weeping and demoralized at the thought of all that damage caused by one little squinty-eyed man in a plane. In the event, the bombs either puttered out or caused only localized fires of no consequence.

The Japanese also, over a period of months, launched into the prevailing winds across the Pacific some nine thousand large paper balloons, each bearing a thirty-pound bomb timed to go off forty hours after launch – the length of time calculated that it would take to cross the Pacific to America. These managed to blow up a small number of curious souls whose last earthly utterance was something along the lines of 'Now what the heck do you suppose this is?', but otherwise did almost no damage, though one made it as far as Maryland.

Then in the Cold War years all this comfortable security abruptly vanished as the Soviet Union developed long-range ballistic missiles to match our own. Suddenly we were in a world where something horribly destructive could drop on us at any moment without warning wherever we were. This was a startling and unsettling notion, and we responded to it in a quintessentially 1950s way. We got excited about it.

For a number of years you could hardly open a magazine without learning of some new destructive marvel that could wipe us all out in a twinkle. An artist named Chesley Bonestell specialized in producing sumptuously lifelike illustrations of manmade carnage, showing warhead-laden rockets streaking gorgeously (excitingly!) across American skies or taking off from giant space stations on a beautifully lit, wondrously imagined Moon en route to an explosive attack on planet Earth.

The thing about Bonestell's paintings was that they seemed so real, so informed, so photographically exact. It was like looking at something as it happened, rather than imagining it as it one day might be. I can remember studying with boundless fascination, and more than a touch of misplaced longing, a Bonestell illustration in *Life* magazine showing New York City at the moment of nuclear detonation, a giant mushroom cloud rising from the familiar landscape of central Manhattan, a second cloud spreading itself across the outlying sprawl of Queens. These illustrations were meant to frighten, but really they excited.*

I'm not suggesting that we actually wanted New York to be blown up – at least not exactly. I'm just saying that if it *did* ever happen you could see a plus side to it. We would all die, sure, but our last word would be a sincere and appreciative '*Wow.*'

Then in the late 1950s the Soviets briefly developed a clear

---

*Bonestell was an interesting person. For most of his working life he was an architect, and ran a practice of national distinction in California until 1938 when, at the age of fifty, he abruptly quit his job and began working as a Hollywood film-set artist, creating background mattes for many popular movies. As a sideline he also began to illustrate magazine articles on space travel, creating imaginative views of moons and planets as they would appear to someone visiting from Earth. So when magazines in the Fifties needed lifelike illustrations of space stations and lunar launch pads, he was a natural and inspired choice. He died in 1986 aged ninety-eight.

lead in the space race and the excitement took on a real edge. The fear became that they would install giant space platforms in geostationary orbit directly above us, far beyond the reach of our gnat-like planes and weakly puffing guns, and that from this comfortable perch they would drop bombs on us whenever we peeved them.

In fact, that was never going to happen. Because of Earth's spin, you can't just drop bombs from space like water balloons. For one thing, they wouldn't drop; they would go into orbit. So you would have to fire them in some fashion, which required a level of delivery control the 1950s simply didn't command. And anyway because the Earth is spinning at a thousand kilometres an hour (give or take), you would have to master extremely precise trajectories to hit a given target. Any bomb fired from space was in fact far more likely to fall in a Kansas wheat field, or almost anywhere else on Earth, than through the roof of the White House. If bombarding each other from space had ever been a realistic option, we would have space stations up there in the hundreds now, believe me.

However, the only people who knew this in the 1950s were space scientists, and they weren't going to tell anybody because then we wouldn't give them money to develop their ambitious programmes. So magazines and Sunday supplements ran these breathless accounts of peril from above, because their reporters didn't know any better, or didn't wish to know any better, and because they had all these fantastic drawings by Chesley Bonestell that were such a pleasure to look at and just had to be seen.

So earthly devastation became both a constant threat and a happy preoccupation of that curiously bifurcated decade. Public service films showed us how private fallout shelters could be not only protective but *fun*, with Mom and Dad and Chip and Skip bunking down together underground, possibly for years on end. And why not? They had lots of dehydrated food and a whole stack of board games. 'And Mom and Dad need never worry about the lights running low with this handy pedal generator and two strong young volunteers to provide plenty of muscle power!' And no school! This was a lifestyle worth thinking about.

For those who didn't care to retreat underground, the Portland Cement Association offered a range of heavy-duty 'Houses for the Atomic Age!' – special 'all-concrete blast-resistant houses' designed to let the owners survive 'blast pressures expected at distances as close as 3,600 feet from ground zero of a bomb with an explosive force equivalent to 20,000 tons of TNT'. So the Russians could drop a bomb right in your own neighbour-hood and you could sit in comfort at home reading the evening newspaper and hardly know there was a war on. Can you imagine erecting such a house and *not* wanting to see how well it with-stood a nuclear challenge? Of course not. Let those suckers drop! We're *ready*!

And it wasn't just nuclear devastation that enthralled and excited us. The film world reminded us that we might equally be attacked by flying saucers or stiff-limbed aliens with metallic voices and deathly ray guns, and introduced us to the stimulating possibilities for mayhem inherent in giant mutated insects, blundering mega-crabs, bestirred dinosaurs, monsters from the deep, and one seriously pissed-off 50-foot woman. I don't imagine that many people, even those who now faithfully vote Republican, believed that any of that would actually happen, but certain parts of it – the UFOs and flying saucers, for instance – were far more plausible then than now. This was an age, don't forget, in which it was still widely believed that there might be civilizations on Mars or Venus. Almost anything was possible.

And even the more serious magazines like *Life* and *Look*, the *Saturday Evening Post*, *Time* and *Newsweek* found ample space for articles on interesting ways the world might end. There was almost no limit to what might go wrong, according to various theories. The Sun could blow up or abruptly wink out. We might be bathed in murderous radiation as Earth passed through the twinkly glitter of a comet's tail. We might have a new ice age. Or Earth might somehow become detached from its faithful orbit and drift out of the solar system, like a lost balloon, moving ever deeper into some cold, lightless corner of the universe. Much of the notion behind space travel was to get away from these irremediable risks and start up new lives with more interestingly padded shoulders inside some distant galactic dome.

Were people seriously worried about any of this? Who knows? Who knows what anyone in the 1950s was thinking about anything, or even if they were thinking at all. All I know is that any perusal of magazines from the period produces a curious blend of undiluted optimism and a kind of eager despair. Over 40 per cent of people in 1955 thought there would be a global disaster, probably in the form of world war, within five years and half of those were certain it would be the end of humanity. Yet the very people who claimed to expect death at any moment were at the same time busily buying new homes, digging swimming pools, investing in stocks and bonds and pension plans, and generally behaving like people who expect to live a long time. It was an impossible age to figure.

But even by the strange, elastic standards of the time, my parents were singularly unfathomable when it came to worry. As far as I can tell, they didn't fear a thing, even the things that other people really did worry about. Take polio. Polio had been a periodic feature of American life since the late 1800s (why it suddenly appeared then is a question that appears to have no answer) but it became particularly virulent in the early 1940s and remained at epidemic proportions well into the following decade, with between thirty thousand and forty thousand cases reported nationally every year. In Iowa, the worst year was 1952, which happened to be the first full year of my life, when there were over three thousand five hundred cases – roughly 10 per cent of the national total, or nearly three times Iowa's normal allotment – and one hundred and sixty-three deaths. A famous picture of the time from the *Des Moines Register* shows assorted families, including one man on a tall ladder, standing outside Blank Children's Hospital in Des Moines shouting greetings and encouragement to their quarantined children through the windows. Even after half a century it is a haunting picture, particularly for those who can remember just how unnerving polio was.

Several things made it so. First, nobody knew where it came from or how it spread. Epidemics mostly happened in the summer, so people associated polio with summer activities like picnics and swimming. That was why you weren't supposed to sit around in wet clothes or swallow pool water. (Polio was in fact spread through contaminated food and water, but swimming-pool water, being chlorinated, was actually one of the safer environments.) Second, it disproportionately affected young people, with symptoms that were vague and variable and always a worry to interpret. The best doctor in the world couldn't tell in the initial stages whether a child had polio or just flu or a summer cold. For those who did get polio, the outcome was frighteningly

225

unpredictable. Two-thirds of victims recovered fully after three or four days with no permanent ill effects at all. But others were partly or wholly paralysed. Some couldn't even breathe unaided. In the United States roughly 3 per cent of victims died; in outbreaks elsewhere it was as high as 30 per cent. Most of those poor parents calling through the windows at Blank Hospital didn't know which group their children would end up in. There wasn't a thing about it that wasn't a source of deepest anxiety.

Not surprisingly, a kind of panic came over communities when polio was reported. According to *Growing Up with Dick and Jane*, a history of the Fifties, at the first sign of a new outbreak, 'Children were kept away from crowded swimming pools, pulled out of movie theaters and whisked home from summer camps in the middle of the night. In newspapers and newsreels, images of children doomed to death, paralysis or years in an iron lung haunted the fearful nation. Children were terrified at the sight of flies and mosquitoes thought to carry the virus. Parents dreaded fevers and complaints of sore throats or stiff necks.'

Well, that's all news to me. I was completely unaware of any anxiety about polio. I knew that it existed – we had to line up from time to time after the mid-Fifties to get vaccinated against it – but I didn't know that we were supposed to be frightened. I didn't know about any dangers of any type anywhere. It was quite a wonderful position to be in really. I grew up in possibly the scariest period in American history and had no idea of it.

When I was seven and my sister was twelve, my dad bought a blue Rambler station wagon, a car so cruddy and styleless that even Edsel owners would slow down to laugh at you, and decided to break it in with a drive to New York. The car had no air conditioning, but my sister and I got the idea that if we laid the tailgate flat and stood on it, and held on to the roof rack, we could essentially get out of the car and catch a nice cooling breeze. In fact, it was like standing in the face of a typhoon. It couldn't have been more dangerous. If we relaxed our grip for an instant – to sneeze or satisfy an itch – we risked being whipped off our little platform and lofted into the face of a following Mack truck.

Conversely, if my father braked suddenly for any reason – and at least three or four times a day he provided us with sudden hold-on-to-your-hat swerves and a kind of bronco effect, braking when he dropped a lighted cigarette on to the seat between his legs and he and my mother jointly engaged in a frantic and generally entertaining search for it – there was a very good chance that we would be tossed sideways into a neighbouring field or launched – fired really – in a forward direction into the path of another mighty Mack.

It was, in short, insanely risky – a thought that evidently occurred to a highway patrolman near Ashtabula, Ohio, who set his red light spinning and pulled my dad over and chewed him out ferociously for twenty minutes for being so monumentally bone-headed with respect to his children's safety. My father took all this meekly. When the patrolman at last departed, my father told us in a quiet voice that we would have to stop riding like that until we crossed the state line into Pennsylvania in another hour or two.

It wasn't a terribly good trip for my dad. He had booked a hotel in New York from a classified ad in the *Saturday Review* because it was such a good deal, and then discovered that it was in Harlem. On the first night there, while my parents lay on the bed, exhausted from the ordeal of finding their way from Iowa to

227

1,252nd Street in upper Manhattan – a route not highlighted in any American Automobile Association guide – my sister and I decided to get something to eat. We strolled around the district for a while and found a corner diner about two blocks away. While we were sitting enjoying our hamburgers and chocolate sodas, and chatting amiably to several black people, a police car slid by, paused, backed up and pulled over. Two officers came in, looked around suspiciously, then came over to us. One of them asked us where we had come from.

'Des Moines, Iowa,' my sister replied.

'*Des Moines, Iowa!*' said the policeman, astounded. 'How did you get here from Des Moines, Iowa?'

'My parents drove us.'

'Your parents *drove* you here from Des Moines?'

My sister nodded.

'*Why?*'

'My dad thought it would be educational.'

'To come to Harlem?' The policemen looked at each other. 'Where are your parents now, honey?'

My sister told them that they were in the Hotel W. E. B. DuBois or Chateau Cotton Club or whatever it was.

'Your parents are staying *there*?'

My sister nodded.

'You really *are* from Iowa, aren'tcha, honey?'

The policemen took us back to the hotel and escorted us to our room. They banged on the door and my father answered. The policemen didn't know whether to be firm with my dad or gentle, to arrest him or give him some money or what. In the end they just strongly urged him to check out of the hotel first thing in the morning and to find a more appropriate hotel in a safer neighbourhood much lower down in Manhattan.

My father wasn't in a strong position to argue. For one thing, he was naked from the waist down. He was standing half behind the door so the police were unaware of his awkward position, but for those of us sitting on the bed the view was a memorably surreal one of my father, bare-buttocked, talking respectfully and in a grave tone of voice to two large New York policemen. It was a sight that I won't forget in a hurry.

My father was quite pale when the policemen left, and talked to my mother at length about what we were going to do. They decided to sleep on it. In the end, we stayed. Well, it was such a good rate, you see.

The *second* time I noticed that adults are not entirely to be trusted was also the first time I was genuinely made fearful by events in the wider world. It was in the autumn of 1962, just before my eleventh birthday, when I was home alone watching television and the programme was interrupted for a special announcement from the White House. President Kennedy came on looking grave and tired and indicated that things were not going terribly well with regard to the Cuban missile crisis – something about which at that point I knew practically nothing.

The background, if you need it, is that America had discovered that the Russians were preparing (or so we thought) to install nuclear weapons in Cuba, just ninety miles from American soil. Never mind that we had plenty of missiles aimed at Russia from similar distances in Europe. We were not used to being threatened in our own hemisphere and weren't going to stand for it now. Kennedy ordered Khrushchev to cease building launch pads in Cuba or else.

The Presidential address I saw was telling us that we were now at the 'or else' part of the scenario. I remember this as clearly as anything, largely because Kennedy looked worried and grey, not a look you wish to see in a President when you are ten years old. We had installed a naval blockade around Cuba to express our displeasure and Kennedy announced now that a Soviet ship was on its way to challenge it. He said that he had given the order that if the Soviet ship tried to pass through the blockade, American destroyers were to fire in front of its bow as a warning. If it still proceeded, they were to sink it. Such an act would, of course, be the start of the Third World War. Even I could see that. This was the first time that my blood ever ran cold.

It was evident from Kennedy's tone that all this was pretty imminent. So I went and ate the last piece of a Toddle House chocolate pie that had been promised to my sister, then hung around on the back porch, wishing to be the first to tell my parents the news that we were all about to die. When they arrived home they told me not to worry, that everything would be all right, and they were right of course as always. We didn't die – though I came closer than anybody when my sister discovered that I had eaten her piece of pie.

In fact, we all came closer to dying than we realized. According to the memoirs of Robert McNamara, the then Secretary of Defense, the Joint Chiefs of Staff at that time suggested – indeed, eagerly urged – that we drop a couple of nuclear bombs on Cuba to show our earnest and to let the Soviets know that they had better not even think about putting nuclear weapons in our back yard. President Kennedy, according to McNamara, came very close to authorizing such a strike.

Twenty-nine years later, after the break-up of the Soviet

Union, we learned that the CIA's evidence about Cuba was completely wrong (now there's a surprise) and that the Soviets in fact already had about one hundred and seventy nuclear missiles positioned on Cuban soil, all trained on us of course, and all of which would have been launched in immediate retaliation for an American attack. Imagine an America with one hundred and seventy of its largest cities – which, just for the record, would include Des Moines – wiped out. And of course it wouldn't have stopped there. That's how close we all came to dying.

I haven't trusted grown-ups for a single moment since.

Chapter 12
OUT AND ABOUT

JACKSON, MICH. (AP) – A teenaged girl and her 12-year-old brother were accused by police Saturday of trying to kill their parents by pouring gasoline on their bed and setting it alight while they were sleeping. The children told police their parents were 'too strict and were always nagging.' Mr. and Mrs. Sterling Baker were burned over 50 percent of their bodies and were listed in fair condition in a hospital.

– *Des Moines Tribune*, 13 June 1959

EVERY SUMMER, when school had been out for a while and your parents had had about as much of you as they cared to take in one season, there came a widely dreaded moment when they sent you to Riverview, a small, peeling amusement park in a dreary commercial district on the north side of town, with $2 in your pocket and instructions to enjoy yourself for at least eight hours, more if possible.

Riverview was an unnerving institution. The rollercoaster, a Himalayan massif of ageing wood, was the most rickety, confidence-sapping construction ever. The wagons were flocked inside and out with thirty-five years of spilled popcorn and hysterical vomit. It had been built in 1920, and you could feel its age in every groaning joint and cracked cross-brace. It was enormous – about four miles long, I believe, and some twelve thousand feet high. It was easily the scariest ride ever built. People didn't even scream on it; they were much too petrified to emit any kind of noise. As it passed, the ground would tremble with increasing intensity and it would shake loose a shower – actually a kind of avalanche – of dust and ancient birdshit from its filthy rafters. A moment later, there would be a passing rainshower of vomit.

The guys in charge of the rides were all closely modelled on Richard Speck, the Chicago murderer. They spent their working lives massaging zits and talking to groups of bouncy young women in bobby socks who unfathomably flocked to them. The rides weren't on timers of any kind, so if the attendants went off into their little booths to have sex, or fled over the fence and across the large expanse of open ground beyond at the appearance of two men with a warrant, the riders could be left on for indefinite periods – days if the employee had bolted with a vital key or crank. I knew a kid named Gus Mahoney who was kept on the Mad Mouse so long, and endured so many g-forces, that for three months afterwards he couldn't comb his hair forward and his ears almost touched at the back of his head.

Even the dodgem cars were insanely lively. From a distance the dodgem palace looked like a welder's yard because of all the sparks raining down from the ceiling, which always threatened to fall in the car with you, enlivening the ride further. The dodgem attendants didn't just permit head-on crashes, they actively encouraged them. The cars were so souped up that the instant you touched the accelerator, however lightly or tentatively, it would shoot off at such a speed that your head would become just a howling sphere on the end of a whip-like stalk. There was no controlling the cars once they were set in motion. They just flew around wildly, barely in contact with the floor, until they slammed into something solid, giving you the sudden opportunity to examine the steering wheel very closely with your face.

The worst outcome was to be caught in a car that turned out to be temperamental and sluggish or broke down altogether because forty other drivers, many of them small children who had never before had an opportunity to exact revenge on anything larger than a nervous toad, would fly into you with unbridled joy from every possible angle. I once saw a boy in a broken-down car bale out while the ride was still running – this was the one thing

you *knew* you were never supposed to do – and stagger dazedly
through the heavy traffic for the periphery. As he set foot on the
metal floor, over two thousand crackling bluish strands of
electricity leaped on to him from every direction, lighting him up
like a paper lantern and turning him into a kind of living X-ray.
You could see every bone in his body and most of his larger
organs. Miraculously he managed to sidestep every car that came
hurtling at him – and that was all of them, of course – and
collapsed on the stubbly grass outside, where he lay smoking
lightly from the top of his head and asked for someone to get
word to his mom that he loved her. But apart from a permanent
ringing in his ears, he suffered no major damage, though the
hands on his Zorro watch were for ever frozen at ten past two.

There wasn't anything at Riverview that wasn't horrible. Even
the Tunnel of Love was an ordeal. There was always a joker in the
leading boat who would dredge up a viscous ball of phlegm and
with a mighty *phwop* shoot it on to the low ceiling – an action that
was known as hanging a louie. There it would dangle, a saliva
stalactite, before draping itself over the face of a following boater.
The trick of successful louie-hanging – and I speak here with some
authority – had nothing to do with spit, but with how fast you
could run when the boat stopped.

Riverview was where you also discovered that kids from the
other side of town wanted you dead and were prepared to seize
any opportunity in any dark corner to get you that way. Kids from
the Riverview district went to a high school so forlorn and
characterless that it didn't have a proper name, but just a
geographical designation: North High. They detested kids from
Theodore Roosevelt High School, the outpost of privilege, comfort and quality footwear for which we were destined. Wherever

you went at Riverview, but particularly if you strayed from your group (or in the case of Milton Milton had no group), there was always a good chance that you would be pulled into the shadows and briskly drubbed and relieved of wallet, shoes, tickets and pants. There was always some kid – actually it was always Milton Milton now that I think of it – wandering in dismay in sagging undershorts or standing at the foot of the rollercoaster wailing helplessly at his jeans, now dangling from a rafter four hundred feet above the ground.

I knew kids who begged their parents not to leave them at Riverview, whose fingers had to be prised off car door handles and torn from any passing pair of adult legs, who left six-inch-deep grooves in the dust with their heels from where they were dragged from the car to the entrance gate and pushed through the turnstile, and told to have fun. It was like being put in a lion's cage.

The one amusement of the year that everyone did get genuinely excited about was the Iowa State Fair, which was held at enormous fairgrounds way out on the eastern edge of town late every August. It was one of the biggest fairs in the nation; the movie *State Fair* was filmed at and based on the Iowa State Fair, a fact that filled us all with a curious pride, even though no one to our knowledge had ever seen the movie or knew a thing about it.

The State Fair happened during the muggiest, steamiest period of the year. You spent all your time there soaked in perspiration and eating sickly foods – Sno Cones, cotton candy, ice cream bars, ice cream sandwiches, foot-long hot dogs swimming in gooey relish, bucketloads of the world's most sugary lemonade – until you had become essentially an ambulatory sheet of fly-paper and were covered from head to toe with vivid stains and stuck, half-dead insects.

The State Fair was mostly a celebration of the farming way of life. It had vast halls filled with quilts and jams and tasselled ears of corn and tables spread with dome-roofed pies the size of automobile tyres. Everything that could be grown, cooked, canned or sewn was carefully conveyed to Des Moines from every corner of the state and ardently competed over. There were also displays of shiny new tractors and other commercial manufactures in a hall of wonders known as the Varied Industries Building and every year there was something called the Butter Cow, which was a life-sized cow carved from an enormous (well, cow-sized) block of butter. It was considered one of the wonders of Iowa, and some way beyond, and always had an appreciative crowd around it.

Beyond the display buildings were ranks of enormous stinking pavilions, each several acres in size, filled with animal pens, mostly inhabited by hogs, and the amazing sight of hundreds of keen young men buffing, shampooing and grooming their beloved porkers in the hope of winning a coloured satin ribbon and bringing glory home to Grundy Center or Pisgah. It seemed an odd way to court fame.

For most people the real attraction of the fair was the midway with its noisy rides and games of chance and enticing sideshows. But there was one place that all boys dreamed of visiting above all others: the strippers' tent.

The strippers' tent had the brightest lights and most pulsating music. From time to time the barker would bring out some of the girls, chastely robed, and parade them around a little open-air stage while suggesting – and looking each of us straight in the eye

– that these girls could conceive of no greater satisfaction in life than to share their natural bounties with an audience of appreciative, red-blooded young men. They all seemed to be amazingly good looking – but then I *was* running a temperature of over 113 degrees just from the thought of being on the same planet as young women of such miraculously obliging virtue, so I might have been a touch delirious.

The trouble was that we were twelve years old when we became seriously interested in the strippers' tent and you had to be thirteen to go in. A dangling sign on the ticket booth made that explicitly clear. Doug Willoughby's older brother, Joe, who was thirteen, went in and came out walking on air. He wouldn't say much other than that it was the best thirty-five cents he had ever spent. He was so taken that he went in three times more and pronounced it better on each occasion.

Naturally we circumnavigated the strippers' tent repeatedly looking for a breach of any kind, but it was the Fort Knox of canvas. Every millimetre of hem was staked to the ground, every metal eyelet sealed solid. You could hear music, you could hear voices, you could even see the shadowy outlines of the audience, but you couldn't discern the tiniest hint of a female form. Even Doug Willoughby, the most ingenious person I knew, was completely flummoxed. It was a torment to know that there was nothing but this rippling wall of canvas between us and living, breathing, unadorned female epidermis, but if Willoughby couldn't find a way through there wasn't a way through.

The following year I assembled every piece of ID I could find – school reports, birth certificate, library card, faded membership card from the Sky King Fan Club, anything that indicated my age even vaguely – and went directly to the tent with Buddy Doberman. It was newly painted with life-sized images of curvy pin-ups in the style of Alberto Vargas, and looked *very* promising.

'Two for the front row, please,' I said.

'Scram,' said the grizzled man who was selling tickets. 'No kids allowed.'

'Ah, but I'm thirteen,' I said, and began to extract affidavits from my folders.

'Not old enough,' said the man. 'You gotta be fourteen.' He hit the dangling sign. The '13' on it had been covered over with a square of card saying '14'.

'Since when?'

'Since this year.'

'But why?'

'New rules.'

'But that's not fair.'

'Kid, if you got a gripe, write to your congressman. I just take the money.'

'Yes, but . . .'

'You're holding up the line.'

'Yes, but . . .'

'Scram!'

So Buddy Doberman and I sloped off while a line of young men leered at us. 'Come back when you've all growed up,' yukked a young man from a place called, I would guess, Moronville, then vanished under a withering glance of ThunderGaze.

Getting into the strippers' tent would become the principal preoccupation of my pubescent years.

*

241

Most of the year we didn't have Riverview or the State Fair to divert us, so we went downtown and just fooled around. We were extremely good at just fooling around. Saturday mornings were primarily devoted to attaining an elevated position – the roofs of office buildings, the windows at the ends of long corridors in the big hotels – and dropping soft or wet things on shoppers below. We spent many happy hours too roaming through the behind-the-scenes parts of department stores and office buildings, looking in broom cupboards and stationery cabinets, experimenting with steamy valves in boiler rooms, poking through boxes in storerooms.

The trick was never to behave furtively, but to act as if you didn't realize you were in the wrong place. If you encountered an adult, you could escape arrest or detention by immediately asking a dumb question: 'Excuse me, mister, is this the way to Dr Mackenzie's office?' or 'Can you tell me where the men's room is, please?' This approach never failed. With a happy chuckle the apprehending custodian would guide us back to daylight and set us on our way with a pat on the head, unaware that under our jackets were thirteen rolls of duct tape, two small fire extinguishers, an adding machine, one semi-pornographic calendar from his office wall and a really lethal staple gun.

On Saturdays there were usually matinees to go to, generally involving a double feature of all the movies that my mother didn't take me to – *The Man from Planet X*, *Revenge of Godzilla*, *Zombies from the Stratosphere*, something with the slogan 'Half-man, half-beast, but ALL MONSTER' – plus a handful of cartoons and a couple of Three Stooges shorts just to make sure we were maximally fired up. The main features usually involved some fractious, jerkily animated dinosaurs, a swarm of giant mutated insects and several thousand severely worried Japanese people racing through city streets just ahead of a large wave or trampling foot.

These movies were nearly always cheaply made, badly acted and largely incoherent, but that didn't matter because Saturday matinees weren't about watching movies. They were about racing around wildly, making noise, having pitched battles involving thrown candy and making sure that every horizontal surface was buried at least three inches deep in spilled popcorn and empty containers. Essentially matinees were an invitation to four thousand children to riot for four hours in a large darkened space.

Before every performance, the manager – who was nearly always a bad-tempered bald guy with a bow tie and a very red face – would take to the stage to announce in a threatening manner that if *any* child – any child at all – was caught throwing candy, or seemed to be about to throw candy, he would be seized by the collar and frogmarched into the waiting arms of the police. 'I'm watching you all, and I know where you live,' the manager would say and fix us with a final threatening scowl. Then the lights would dim and up to twenty thousand pieces of flying candy would rain down on him and the stage around him.

Sometimes the movies would be so popular or the manager so unseasoned and naive that the balcony would be opened, giving a thousand or so kids the joyous privilege of being able to tip wet and sticky substances on to the helpless swarms below. The running of the Paramount Theater was once entrusted to a tragically pleasant young man who had never dealt with children in a professional capacity before. He introduced an intermission in which children with birthdays who had filled out a card were

243

called up on stage and allowed to reach into a big box from which they could extract a toy, box of candy or gift certificate. By the second week eleven thousand children had filled out birthday cards. Many were making seven or eight extra trips to the stage under lightly assumed identities. Both the manager and the free gifts were gone by the third week.

But even when properly run, matinees made no economic sense. Every kid spent 35 cents to get in and another 35 cents on pop and candy, but left behind $4.25 in costs for repairs, cleaning and gum removal. In consequence matinees tended to move around from theatre to theatre – from the Varsity to the Orpheum to the Holiday to the Hiland – as managers abandoned the practice, had nervous breakdowns or left town.

Very occasionally the film studios or a sponsor would give out door prizes. These were nearly always ill-advised. For the premiere of *The Birds*, the Orpheum handed out one-pound bags of birdseed to the first five hundred customers. Can you imagine giving birdseed to five hundred unsupervised children who are about to go into a darkened auditorium? A little-known fact about birdseed is that when soaked in Coca-Cola and expelled through a straw it can travel up to two hundred feet at speeds approaching Mach 1 and will stick like glue to anything – walls, ceilings, cinema screens, soft fabrics, screaming usherettes, the back of the manager's suit and head, anything.

Because the movies were so bad, and the real action was out in the lobbies, nobody ever sat still for long. Once every half-hour or so, or sooner if nobody on the screen was staggering around with a stake through the eye or an axe in the back of his head, you would get up and go off to see if there was anything worth investigating in the theatre's public areas. In addition to the concession stands in the lobby, most theatres also had vending machines in dark, unsupervised corners, and these were always worth a look. There was a general conviction that just above where the cups dropped down or the candy bars slid out – slightly out of reach but tantalizingly close by – were various small levers and switches that would, if activated, dispense all the candy at once or possibly excite the change-release mechanism into setting loose a cascade of silvery coins. Doug Willoughby once brought a small flashlight and one of those angled mirrors that dentists use, and had a good look around the insides of a vending machine at the Orpheum, and became convinced that if he found someone with sufficiently long arms he could make the machine his servant.

So you may imagine the delight on his face on the day that someone brought him a kid who was about seven feet tall and weighed forty pounds. He had arms like garden hoses. Best of all, he was dim and pliant. Encouraged by a clutch of onlookers that quickly grew to a crowd of about two hundred, the kid dutifully knelt down and stuck his arm up the machine, probing around as Willoughby directed. 'Now go left a little,' Willoughby would say, 'past the capacitor, under the solenoid and see if you can't find a hinged lid. That'll be the change box. Do you feel it?'

'No,' the kid responded, so Willoughby fed in a little more arm.

'Do you feel it now?' Willoughby asked.

'No, but— ow!' the kid said suddenly. 'I just got a big shock.'

'That'll be the earthing clamp,' said Willoughby. 'Don't touch that again. I mean, really, don't touch that again. Try going around it.' He fed in a little more arm. 'Now do you feel it?'

'I can't feel anything, my arm's asleep,' said the kid after a

245

time, and then added: 'I'm stuck. I think my sleeve's caught on something.' He grimaced and manoeuvred his arm, but it wouldn't come free. 'No, I'm really stuck,' he announced at last.

Somebody went and got the manager. He came bustling up a minute or so later accompanied by one of his oafish assistants.

'What the hell,' he growled, forcing his way through the crowd. 'Move aside, move aside. Goddam it all. What the hell. What the hell's going on? Goddam kids. *Move*, boy! Goddam it to hell. God damn. God damn. What the hell.' He reached the front of the crowd and saw, to his astonishment and disgust, a boy obscenely violating the innards of one of his vending machines. 'The hell you *doing*, buster? Get your arm out of there.'

'I can't. I'm stuck.'

The manager yanked on the kid's arm. The kid wailed in pain.

'Who put you up to this?'

'They all did.'

'Are you aware that it is a federal offence to tamper with the insides of a Food-O-Mat machine?' the manager said as he yanked more and the kid wailed. 'You are in a *world* of trouble, young man. I am going to personally escort you to the police station. I don't even want to *think* about how long you'll be in reform school, but you'll be shaving by the time of your next matinee, buster.'

The kid's arm would not come free, though it was now several inches longer than it had been earlier. Clucking, the manager produced an enormous ring of keys – the kind of ring that, once seen, made a man like him decide to drop all other plans and go straight into movie theatre management – unlocked the machine and hauled open the door, dragging the protesting kid along with it. For the first time in history the inside of a vending machine was exposed to children's view. Willoughby whipped out a pencil and notebook and began sketching. It was an entrancing sight – two hundred candy bars stacked in columns, each inhabiting a little tilted slot.

As the manager bent over to try to disentangle the kid's arm and shirt from the door, two hundred hands reached past him and deftly emptied the machine of its contents.

'Hey!' said the manager when he realized what was happening. Furious and sputtering, he snatched a large box of Milk Duds from a small boy walking past.

'Hey! That's mine!' protested the boy, grabbing back and holding on to the box with both hands. 'It's mine! I paid for it!' he shouted, feet flailing six inches off the floor. As they struggled, the box ripped apart and all the contents spilled out. At this, the boy covered his face with his hands and began weeping. Two hundred voices shrilly berated the manager, pointing out that the Food-O-Mat machine didn't dispense Milk Duds. During this momentary distraction the kid with the long arms slid out of his shirt and fled topless back into the theatre – an act of startling initiative that left everyone gaping in admiration.

The manager turned to his oafish assistant. 'Go get that kid and bring him to my office.'

The assistant hesitated. 'But I don't know what he looks like,' he said.

'Pardon?'

'I didn't see his face.'

'He's got no shirt on, you moron. He's bare-chested.'

'Yeah, but I still don't know what he looks like,' the assistant muttered, and stalked into the theatre, flashlight darting.

The boy with the long arms was never seen again. Two

hundred kids had free candy. Willoughby got to study the inside of the vending machine and work out how it functioned. It was a rare victory for the inhabitants of Kid World over the dark, repressive forces of Adult World. It was also the last time the Orpheum ever had a children's matinee.

Willoughby was the smartest person I ever met, particularly with regard to anything mechanical or scientific. Afterwards he showed me the sketch he'd made when the door was open. 'It's astoundingly simple,' he said. 'I could hardly believe the lack of complexity. Do you know, it doesn't have an internal baffle or backflow gate or anything. Can you believe that?'

I indicated that I was prepared to be as amazed as the next man.

'There's nothing to stop reverse entry – nothing,' he said, shaking his head in wonder, and slid the plans into his back pocket.

The following week there was no matinee but we went to see *How the West Was Won*. About half an hour into the movie, he took me to the Food-O-Mat machine, reached into his jacket and pulled out two telescopic car aerials. Extending them, he inserted them into the machine, briefly manipulated them and down came a box of Dots.

'What would you like?' he said.

'Could I have some Red Hots?' I asked. I loved Red Hots.

He wriggled again and a box of Red Hots came down. And with that Willoughby became my best friend.

Willoughby was amazingly brainy. He was the first person I knew who agreed with me about Bizarro World, the place where things went backwards, though for rather more refined reasons than mine.

'It's preposterous,' he would agree. 'Think what it would do to mathematics. You couldn't have prime numbers any more.'

I'd nod cautiously. 'And when they got sick they'd have to suck puke back into their mouths,' I'd add, trying to get the conversation back to more comfortable territory.

'Geometry would be right out the window,' Willoughby would go on, and begin listing all the theorems that would fall apart in a world running in reverse.

We often had conversations like that, where we were both talking about the same thing, but from perspectives miles apart. Still it was better than trying to discuss Bizarro World with Buddy Doberman, who was surprised to learn it wasn't a real place.

Willoughby had an absolute genius for figuring out how to get fun out of unpromising circumstances. Once his dad came to give us a ride home from the movies, but told us that he had to stop at City Hall to pay his property taxes or something, so we were left sitting in the car at a meter outside an office building on Cherry Street for twenty minutes. Now normally this would be about as unpromising a circumstance as one could find oneself in, but as soon as his dad was round the corner, Willoughby bobbed out of the car and rotated the windscreen washer – I didn't even know you could do such a thing – so that it pointed towards the sidewalk, then got into the driver's seat and told me on no account to make eye contact with or seem to notice anyone passing by. Then each time someone walked past he would squirt them – and car windscreen washers put out a *lot* of water, a surprising amount, believe me.

The victims would stop in dumbfounded puzzlement on the spot where they had been drenched and look suspiciously in our direction – but we had the windows up and seemed completely oblivious of them. So they would turn to study the building behind them, and Willoughby would drill them in the back with another soaking blast. It was wonderful, the most fun I had ever had. I would be there still if it were up to me. Who would ever think to investigate a car windscreen washer for purposes of amusement?

Like me, Willoughby was a devotee of Bishop's, but he was a more daring and imaginative diner than I could ever be. He liked to turn on the table light and send the waitresses off on strange quests.

'Could I have some Angostura bitters, please?' he would say with a look of choirboy sweetness. Or: 'Please could I have some fresh ice cubes; these are rather misshapen.' Or: 'Would you by any chance have a spare ladle and some tongs?' And the waitresses would go clumping off to see what they could find for him. There was something about his cheery face that inspired an eagerness to please.

On another occasion he pulled from his pocket, with a certain theatrical flourish, a neatly folded white handkerchief from which he produced a perfectly preserved large, black, flat, ugly, pincered stag beetle – what was known in Iowa as a June bug – and set it adrift on his tomato soup. It floated beautifully. One might almost have supposed it had been designed for the purpose.

Then he put the table light on. An approaching waitress, spying the beetle, shrieked and dropped an empty tray, and got the manager, who came hastening over. The manager was one of those people who are so permanently and comprehensively

stressed that even their hair and clothes appear to be at their wits'
end. He looked as if he had just stepped from a wind tunnel.
Seeing the floating insect, he immediately embarked on a nervous
breakdown.

'Oh my goodness,' he said. 'Oh my goodness, my goodness.
I don't know how this has happened. This has never happened
before. Oh my goodness, I am so sorry.' He whisked the offending
bowl off the table, holding it at arm's length, as if it were actively
infectious. To the waitress he said, 'Mildred, get these young men
whatever they want – what*ever* they want.' To us he said: 'How
about a couple of hot fudge sundaes? Would that help to fix
matters for you?'

'Yes, please!' we replied.

He snapped his fingers and sent Mildred off to get us
sundaes. 'With plenty of nuts and extra cherries,' he called. 'And
don't forget the whipped cream.' He turned to us more con-
fidentially. 'Now you won't tell anyone about this, will you, boys?'
he said.

We promised not to.

'What do your parents do?'

'My father's a health inspector,' Willoughby said brightly.

'Oh my God,' said the manager, draining of blood, and
rushed off to make sure our sundaes were the largest and most
elaborate ever served at Bishop's.

The following Saturday, Willoughby led me into Bishop's
again. This time he drank half his water, then pulled from his
jacket a jar filled with pondwater, which he used to top up
his glass. When he held the glass up to the light there were about
sixteen tadpoles swimming in it.

'Excuse me, should my water be like this?' he called to a

251

passing waitress, who stared at the water with a transfixed look, then went off to get back-up. Within a minute we had half a dozen waitresses examining the water with consternation, but no shrieking. A moment later our friend the manager turned up.

He held the glass up. 'Oh my *good*ness,' he said and went pale. 'I am so sorry. I don't know how this could have happened. Nothing like this has ever happened before.' He looked at Willoughby more closely. 'Say, weren't you here last week?'

Willoughby nodded apologetically.

I assumed we were about to be heaved out on our ears, but the manager said: 'Well, I am so sorry again, son. I cannot apologize enough.' He turned to the waitresses. 'This young man seems to be jinxed.' To us, he said, 'I'll get your sundaes,' and went off to the kitchen, pausing here and there en route to crouch down and look discreetly at the water of other diners.

The one thing Willoughby always lacked was a sense of proportion. I begged him not to push his luck, but the following week he insisted on going to Bishop's again. I refused to sit with him, but took a table across the way and watched as he hummingly pulled from his pocket a brown paper bag and carefully tipped into his soup about two pounds of dead flies and moths that he had retrieved from the overhead light fitting in his bedroom. They formed a mound about four inches high. It was a magnificent sight, but perhaps just a touch deficient in terms of plausibility.

By chance the manager was passing as Willoughby put on his light. The manager looked at the offending bowl in horror and utter dismay and then at Willoughby. I thought for a moment that he was going to faint or perhaps even die. 'This is just not poss—' he said and then a giant light bulb went on over his head as he realized that indeed it wasn't possible for anyone to be served a bowl of soup with two pounds of dead insects in it.

With commendable restraint he escorted Willoughby to the street door, and asked him – not demanded, but just asked him quietly, politely, sincerely – never to return. It was a terrible banishment.

All the Willoughbys – mother, father, four boys – were touched with brilliance. I used to think we had a lot of books in our house because of our two big bookcases in the living room. Then I went to the Willoughbys' house. They had books and bookcases *everywhere* – in the hallways and stairwells, in the bathroom, the kitchen, around all the walls of the living room. Moreover, theirs were works of real weight – Russian novels, books of history and philosophy, books in French. I realized then we were hopelessly outclassed.

And their books were read. I remember once Willoughby showed me a paragraph about farmboy bestiality he had come across in a long article about something else altogether in the *Encyclopaedia Britannica*. I don't remember the details now – it's not the sort of thing one retains for forty years – but the gist of the passage was that 32 per cent of farmboys in Indiana (or something like that: I'm pretty sure it was Indiana; it was certainly a high number) at one time or another had enjoyed sexual congress with livestock.

This amazed me in every possible way. It had never occurred to me that any farmboy or other human being, in Indiana or elsewhere, would ever willingly have sex with an animal, and yet here was printed evidence in a respectable publication that a significant proportion of them had at least given it a try. (The article was a touch coy on how enduring these relationships were.) But even more amazing than the fact itself was the finding of it. The *Encyclopaedia Britannica* ran to twenty-three volumes spread over eighteen thousand pages – some fifty million words in all, I would estimate – and Willoughby had found the only riveting paragraph in the whole lot. How did he do it? Who *reads* the *Encyclopaedia Britannica*?

Willoughby and his brothers opened new worlds, un-suspected levels of possibility, for me. It was as if I had wasted every moment of existence up to then. In their house anything could be fascinating and entertaining. Willoughby shared a bed-room with his brother Joe, who was one year older and no less brilliant at science. Their room was more laboratory than bed-room. There was apparatus everywhere – beakers, vials, retorts, Bunsen burners, jars of chemicals of every description – and books on every subject imaginable, all well-thumbed: applied mechanics, wave mechanics, electrical engineering, mathematics, pathology, military history. The Willoughby boys were always doing something large scale and ambitious. They made their own helium balloons. They made their own rockets. They made their own gunpowder. One day I arrived to find that they had built a rudimentary cannon – a test model – out of a piece of metal pipe into which they stuffed gunpowder, wadding and a silver ball-bearing about the size of a marble. This they laid on an old tree stump in their back yard, aimed at a sheet of plywood about fifteen feet away. Then they lit the fuse and we all retired to a safe position behind a picnic table turned on its side (in case the whole thing blew up). As we watched, the burning fuse somehow unbalanced the pipe and it began to roll slowly across the stump, taking up a new angle. Before we could react, it went off with a stupendous bang and blew out an upstairs bathroom window of a house three doors away. No one was hurt, but Willoughby was grounded for a month – he was commonly grounded – and had to pay $65 restitution.

The Willoughby boys really were able to make fun out of nothing at all. On my first visit, they introduced me to the exciting sport of match fighting. In this game, the competitors arm themselves with boxes of kitchen matches, retire to the basement, turn off all the lights and spend the rest of the evening throwing lighted matches at each other in the dark.

In those days kitchen matches were heavy-duty implements – more like signal flares than the weedy sticks we get today. You could strike them on any hard surface and fling them at least fifteen feet and they wouldn't go out. Indeed, even when being beaten vigorously with two hands, as when lodged on the front of one's sweater, they seemed positively determined not to fail. The idea, in any case, was to get matches to land on your opponents and create small, alarming bush fires on some part of their person; the hair was an especially favoured target. The drawback was that each time you launched a lighted match you betrayed your own position to anyone skulking in the dark nearby, so that after an attack on others you were more or less certain to discover that your own shoulder was robustly ablaze or that the centre of your head was a beacon of flame fuelled from a swiftly diminishing stock of hair.

We played for three hours one evening, then turned on the lights and discovered that we had all acquired several amusing bald patches. Then we walked in high spirits down to the Dairy Queen on Ingersoll Avenue for refreshment and a breath of air, and came back to discover two fire engines out front and Mr

Willoughby in an extremely animated state. Apparently we had left a match burning in a laundry basket and it had erupted in flames, climbed up the back wall and scorched a few rafters, filling much of the house above with smoke. To all of this a team of firemen had enthusiastically added a great deal of water, much of which was now running out the back door.

'What were you *doing* down there?' Mr Willoughby asked in amazement and despair. 'There must have been eight hundred spent matches on the floor. The fire marshal is threatening to arrest me for arson. In my own house. What were you *doing*?'

Willoughby was grounded for six weeks after that, and so we had to suspend our friendship temporarily. But that was OK because by chance I had also become friends at this time with another schoolmate named Jed Mattes, who offered a complete contrast to Willoughby. For one thing, Jed was gay, or at least soon would be.

Jed had charm and taste and impeccable manners, and thanks to him I was exposed to a more refined side of life – to travel, quality food, literary fiction, interior design. It was unexpectedly refreshing. Jed's grandmother lived in the Commodore Hotel on Grand Avenue, which was rather an exotic thing to do. She was over a thousand years old and weighed thirty-seven pounds, which included sixteen pounds of make-up. She used to give us money to go to the movies, sometimes quite enormous sums, like $40 or $50, which would buy you a very nice day out in the early 1960s. Jed never wanted to go to movies like *Attack of the 50-Foot Woman*. He favoured musicals like *The Unsinkable Molly Brown* or *My Fair Lady*. I can't say these were my absolute first choices, but I went with him in a spirit of friendship and they did lend me a certain sheen of cosmopolitanism. Afterwards, he would take us in a cab – to me a form of conveyance of impossible elegance and splendour – to Noah's Ark, an esteemed Italian eatery on Ingersoll. There he introduced me to spaghetti and meatballs, garlic bread, and other worldly dishes of a most sophisticated nature. It was the first time I had ever been presented with a linen napkin or been confronted with a menu that wasn't laminated and slightly sticky and didn't have photographs of the food in it.

Jed could talk his way into anything. We used often to go and look in the windows of rich people's houses. Occasionally he would ring the front door bell.

'Excuse me for intruding,' he would say when the lady of the house arrived, 'but I was just admiring your living room curtains and I simply have to ask, where did you find that velour? It's *won*derful.'

The next thing you knew we'd be in the house, getting a full tour, with Jed cooing in admiration at the owner's inspired improvements and suggesting modest additional touches that might make it better still. By such means we became welcome in all the finest homes. Jed struck up a particular friendship with an aged philanthropist named A. H. Blank, founder of Blank Children's Hospital, who lived with his tottering, blue-haired wife in a penthouse apartment in the ritziest and most fashionable new address in Iowa, a building called The Towers, on Grand Avenue. Mr and Mrs Blank owned the whole of the tenth floor. It was the highest apartment between Chicago and Denver, or at the very least Grinnell and Council Bluffs, they told us. On Friday nights we would often stop by for cocoa and coffee cake and a view of the city – indeed of most of the Midwest, it seemed – from the Blanks' extensive balconies. It was in every sense the high point of all our weeks. I waited years for Mr Blank to die in the hope that he would leave me something, but it all went to charity.

One Saturday after going to the movies (*Midnight Lace* starring Doris Day, which we immediately agreed was OK but by no means one of her best), we were walking home along High Street – an unusual route; a route for people of an adventurous disposition – when we passed a small brick office building with a plaque that said 'Mid-America Film Distribution' or something like that, and Jed suggested we go in.

Inside, a small, elderly man in a lively suit was sitting at a desk doing nothing.

'Hello,' said Jed, 'I hope I'm not intruding, but do you have any old film posters you don't require any longer?'

'You like movies?' said the man.

'Like them? Sir, no, I *love* them.'

'No kidding,' said the man, pleased as anything. 'That's great, that's great. Tell me, son, what's your favourite movie?'

'I think that would have to be *All About Eve*.'

'You like that?' said the man. 'I've got that here somewhere. Hold on.' He took us into a storeroom that was packed from floor to ceiling with rolled posters and began searching through them. 'It's here somewhere. What else you like?'

'Oh, gosh,' said Jed, '*Sunset Boulevard, Rebecca, An Affair to Remember, Lost Horizon, Blithe Spirit, Adam's Rib, Mrs Miniver, Mildred Pierce, The Philadelphia Story, The Man Who Came to Dinner, Now Voyager, A Tree Grows in Brooklyn, Storm Warning, The Pajama Game, This Property Is Condemned, The Asphalt Jungle, The Seven-Year Itch, From This Day Forward* and *How Green Was My Valley*, but not necessarily in that order.'

'I got those!' said the man excitedly. 'I got all those.' He started passing posters to Jed in a manic fashion. He turned to me. 'What about you?' he said politely.

'*The Brain That Wouldn't Die*,' I answered hopefully.

He grimaced and shook his head. 'I don't handle B stuff,' he said.

'*Zombies on Broadway*?'

He shook his head.

'*Island of the Undead*?'

He gave up on me and turned back to Jed. 'You like Lana Turner movies?'

'Of course. Who doesn't?'

'I've got 'em all – every one since *Dancing Co-Ed*. Here, I want you to have them.' And he began piling them on to Jed's arms.

In the end, he gave us more or less everything he had – posters dating back to the late 1930s, all in mint condition. Goodness knows what they would be worth now. We took them in a cab back to Jed's house and divided them up on his bedroom floor. Jed took all the ones for movies starring Doris Day and Debbie Reynolds. I got the ones with men running along in a crouch with guns blazing. We were both extremely happy.

Some years later, I went away to Europe for a summer and ended up staying two years. While I was away my parents cleared out my bedroom. The posters went on a bonfire.

There were certain things I couldn't comfortably share with Jed and the one that stuck out most was my lustful wish to see a naked woman. I don't think an hour passed in the 364 days following my rejection at the State Fairgrounds that I didn't think at least twice about the strippers' tent. It was the only possible place to see naked female flesh *in* the flesh, and my need was growing urgent.

By the March following my fourteenth birthday, I was crossing off on a calendar the number of days till the State Fair. By late June I was frequently short of breath. On 20 July I laid out the clothes I was going to wear the following month. It took me three hours to choose. I considered taking opera glasses, but decided against it on the grounds that they would probably steam up.

The official opening of the fair was 20 August. Normally no sane person went to the State Fair on its opening day because the crowds were so vast and suffocating, but Doug Willoughby and I went. We had to. We just had to. We met soon after dawn and took a bus all the way out to the east side. There we joined the cheerful throngs and waited three hours in line to be among the first in.

At 10 a.m. the gates swung open and twenty thousand people went whooping across the landscape, like the attacking hordes in *Braveheart*. You may be surprised to hear that Willoughby and I didn't go straight to the strippers' tent but rather bided our time. It was our considered intention to savour the occasion, so we had a good look round the exhibition halls. Possibly this was the first time in history that anyone has treated quilts and a butter cow as a form of foreplay, but we knew what we were doing. We wanted to let the girls have a chance to limber up, get into their stride. We didn't wish to attend an inferior show on our first visit.

At 11 a.m. we fortified ourselves with a popular ice cream confection known as a Wonder Bar, then proceeded to the strippers' tent and took our place in the line, pleased to be taking up one of the privileges of our seniority. But shortly before reaching the ticket booth, Willoughby nudged me in the ribs and indicated the dangling sign. It was new and it said: 'Absolutely NO MINORS! You must be SIXTEEN and have GENUINE I.D.'

I was speechless. At this rate, I would be getting a senior citizen discount by the time I saw my first naked woman.

At the window the man asked how old we were.

'Sixteen,' said Willoughby briskly, as if he would say anything else.

'You don't look sixteen to me, kid,' said the man.

'Well, I have a slight hormone deficiency.'

'You got I.D.?'

'No, but my friend here will vouch for me.'

'Fuck off.'

'But we were rather counting on attending one of the shows, you see.'

'Fuck off.'

'We've been waiting for this day for a year. We've been here since six a.m.'

'Fuck off.'

And so we slunk away. It was the cruellest blow I had suffered in my life.

The following week I went to the fair with Jed. It was an interesting contrast since he spent hours in the farmwives' section chatting to ladies in frilly-edged aprons about their jams and quilts. There wasn't a thing in the world of domestic science that didn't fascinate him and not a single obstacle or potential setback that didn't awake his immediate compassion. At one point he had a dozen women, all looking like Aunt Bea on the *Andy Griffith Show*, gathered round, all enjoying themselves immensely.

'Well, wasn't that just *wonderful*?' he said to me afterwards and gave an enormous happy sigh. 'Thank you so much for indulging me. Now let's take you to the strippers' tent.'

I had told him about my disappointment the previous week, and reminded him now that we were too young to gain admission.

'Age is but a technicality,' he said breezily.

At the tent, I held back while Jed went up to the ticket window. He talked to the man for some time. Occasionally they both looked at me, nodding gravely, as if in agreement about some notable deficiency on my part. Eventually Jed came back smiling and handed me a ticket.

'There you go,' he said cheerfully. 'I hope you don't mind if I don't join you.'

I was quite unable to speak. I looked at him in wonder and with difficulty stammered: 'But how?'

'I told him you had an inoperable brain tumour, which he didn't quite buy, and then I gave him ten bucks,' Jed explained. 'Enjoy!'

Well, what can I say other than that it was the highlight of my life? The stripper – there was only one per show, it turned out, something Willoughby's brother had neglected to tell us – was majestically bored, sensationally bored, but there was something unexpectedly erotic in her pouty indifference and glazed stare, and she really wasn't bad looking. She didn't strip off completely. She retained a sequined blue G-string and had nipple caps and tassels on her breasts, but it was still a divine experience, and when, as a kind of climax – a term I use advisedly but with a certain scientific precision – she leaned out over the audience, not six feet from my adoring gaze, and gave a ten-second twirl of the tassels, propelling them briefly but expertly in *opposite* directions – what a talent was this! – I thought I had died and that this was heaven.

I still firmly believe it will be much like that if I ever get there. And knowing that, there has scarcely been a moment in all the years since that I have not been extremely good.

Chapter 13

THE PUBIC YEARS

In Coeur D'Alene, Idaho, after householders reported that a car was tearing around the neighborhood in reverse, Assistant Police Chief Robert Schmidt investigated and found behind the wheel a teen-age girl who explained: 'My folks let me have the car, and I ran up too much mileage. I was just unwinding some of it.'

– *Time* magazine, 9 July 1956

ACCORDING TO THE Gallup organization 1957 was the happiest
year ever recorded in the United States of America. I don't
know that anyone has ever worked out why that largely uneventful year should have marked the giddy peak of American bliss, but
I suspect it is more than coincidental that the very next year was
the year that the New York Giants and the Brooklyn Dodgers
dumped their hometown fans and decamped to California.

Goodness knows it was time for baseball to expand westward
– it was ridiculous to have teams crammed into the old cities of
the East and Midwest but not in any of the newer municipal
colossi of the Western states – but the owners of the Dodgers and
Giants weren't doing it for the good of baseball. They were doing
it out of greed. We were entering a world where things were done
because they offered a better return, not a better world.

People were wealthier than ever before, but life somehow
didn't seem as much fun. The economy had become an unstoppable machine: gross national product rose by 40 per cent in
the decade, from about $350 billion in 1950 to nearly $500
billion ten years later, then rose by another third to $658 billion
in the next six years. But what had once been utterly delightful
was now becoming very slightly, rather strangely unfulfilling.
People were beginning to discover that joyous consumerism is a
world of diminishing returns.

By the closing years of the 1950s most people – certainly

most middle-class people – had pretty much everything they had ever dreamed of, so increasingly there was nothing much to do with their wealth but buy more and bigger versions of things they didn't truly require: second cars, lawn tractors, double-width fridges, hi-fis with bigger speakers and more knobs to twiddle, extra phones and televisions, room intercoms, gas grills, kitchen gadgets, snowblowers, you name it. Having more things of course also meant having more complexity in one's life, more running costs, more things to look after, more things to clean, more things to break down. Women increasingly went out to work to help keep the whole enterprise afloat. Soon millions of people were caught in a spiral in which they worked harder and harder to buy labour-saving devices that they wouldn't have needed if they hadn't been working so hard in the first place.

By the 1960s, the average American was producing twice as much as only fifteen years before. In theory at least, people could now afford to work a four-hour day, or two-and-a-half-day week, or six-month year and still maintain a standard of living equivalent to that enjoyed by people in 1950 when life was already pretty good – and arguably, in terms of stress and distraction and sense of urgency, in many respects much better. Instead, and almost uniquely among developed nations, Americans took none of the productivity gains in additional leisure. We decided to work and buy and have instead.

Of course not everyone shared equally in the good times. Black people who tried to improve their lot, particularly in the Deep South, particularly in Mississippi, were often subjected to the most outrageous and shocking abuse (made all the more so by the fact that most people at the time didn't seem shocked or outraged at all). Clyde Kennard, a former Army sergeant and paratrooper and a person of wholly good character, tried to enrol at Mississippi Southern College in Hattiesburg in 1955. He was sent away, but thought it over and came back and asked again. For this repetitive wilful uppitiness, university officials – I'll just make that quite clear: not students, not under-educated townspeople in white sheets, but university officials – planted illicit liquor and a bag of stolen chicken feed in his car and had him charged with grand theft. Kennard was tried and sent to prison for seven years for crimes he didn't commit. He died there before his term was completed.

Elsewhere in Mississippi at that time the Reverend George Lee and a man named Lamar Smith tried, in separate incidents, to exercise their right to vote. Smith actually succeeded in casting a ballot – in itself something of a miracle – but was shot dead on the courthouse steps five minutes later as he emerged with a dangerously triumphant smile. Although the killing was in broad daylight in a public place, no witnesses came forward and no assailant was ever charged. The Reverend Lee, meanwhile, was turned away at his polling station, but shot dead anyway, with a shotgun from a passing car as he drove home that night. The Humphreys County sheriff ruled the death a traffic accident; the county coroner recorded it as being of unknown causes. There were no convictions in that case either.

Perhaps the most shocking episode of all occurred in Money, Mississippi, when a young visitor from Chicago named Emmett Till rashly whistled at a white woman outside a country store. That evening Till was hauled from his relatives' house by white men, driven to a lonesome spot, beaten to a pulp, shot dead and dumped in the Tallahatchie River. He was fourteen years old.

Because Till was so young and because his mother in

Chicago insisted on leaving the coffin open so that the world could see what her son had suffered, there was, finally, a national outcry. In consequence, two men – the husband of the woman who had been whistled at and his half-brother – were arrested and a trial was duly held. The evidence against the two was pretty overwhelming. They hadn't done much to cover their tracks, but then they didn't need to. After less than an hour's deliberation, the jury – all local people, all white of course – found them not guilty. The verdict would have been quicker, remarked the grinning foreman, if the jurors hadn't taken a break to drink a bottle of pop. The next year, knowing that they could never be retried, the two accused men happily admitted in an interview in *Look* magazine that they had indeed beaten and killed young Till.

Meanwhile, things weren't going terribly well for America in the wider world. In the autumn of 1957, the Soviets successfully tested their first intercontinental ballistic missile, which meant that now they could kill us without leaving home, and within weeks of that they launched the world's first satellite into space. Called Sputnik, it was a small metal sphere about the size of a beachball that didn't do much but orbit the Earth and go 'ping' from time to time, but that was very considerably more than we could do. The following month the Soviets launched Sputnik II, which was much larger at eleven hundred pounds and carried a little dog (a little *Communist* dog) called Laika. Our vanity stung, we responded by announcing a satellite launch of our own, and on 6 December 1957, at Cape Canaveral in Florida, the burners were fired on a giant Viking rocket carrying a fancy new Vanguard satellite. As the world watched, the rocket slowly rose two feet, toppled over and exploded. It was a humiliating setback. The papers referred to the incident variously as 'Kaputnik',

'Stayputnik', 'Sputternik' or 'Flopnik', depending on how comfortable they were with wit. President Eisenhower's normally steady popularity ratings dropped twenty-two points in a week.

America didn't get its first satellite into space until 1958 and that wasn't awfully impressive: it weighed just thirty-one pounds and was not much larger than an orange. All four other major launches by the US that year crashed spectacularly or refused to take to the air. As late as 1961, over a third of US launches failed.

The Soviets meanwhile went from strength to strength. In 1959 they landed a rocket on the Moon and took the first pictures of its backside, and in 1961 successfully put the first astronaut, Yuri Gagarin, into space and safely brought him home again. One week after the Gagarin space trip came the disastrous American-led Bay of Pigs invasion in Cuba, bringing extra layers of embarrassment and worry to national life. We were beginning to look hopeless and outclassed at whatever we did.

News from the world of popular culture was generally dis-couraging as well. Research showed that cigarettes really did cause cancer, as many people had long suspected. Tareyton, my father's brand, quickly rushed out a series of ads calmly reassuring smokers that 'All the tars and nicotine trapped in the filter are guaranteed not to reach your throat' without mentioning that all the lethal goos *not* trapped in the filter would. But consumers weren't so easily taken in by fatuous and misleading claims any longer, particularly after news came out that advertisers had been engaged in secret trials of devious subliminal advertising. During a test at a movie house in Fort Lee, New Jersey, patrons were shown a film in which two clipped phrases – 'Drink Coca-Cola' and 'Hungry? Eat Popcorn' – were flashed on the screen for 1/3000 of a second every five seconds – much too fast to be consciously noted, but subconsciously influential, or so it seemed, for sales of Coke went up 57.7 per cent and popcorn by nearly 20 per cent during the period of the experiment, according to *Life* magazine. Soon, *Life* warned us, all movies and television programmes would be instructing us hundreds of times an hour what to eat, drink, smoke, wear and think, making consumer zombies of us all. (In fact, subliminal advertising didn't work and was soon abandoned.)

Elsewhere on the home front, juvenile crime continued to rise and the education system seemed to be falling apart. The most popular non-fiction book of 1957 was an attack on American education standards called *Why Johnny Can't Read*, warning us that we were falling dangerously behind the rest of the world, and linking the success of Communism to a decline in American reading. Television got itself into a terrible scandal when it was revealed that many of the game shows were rigged. Charles Van Doren, boyish, modest, good-looking scion of a family of distinguished academics and intellectuals (his father and uncle had both won Pulitzer prizes), became a national hero, held up as a model to youngsters for his good manners and lack of swagger, while winning almost $130,000 on the programme *Twenty-One*, but then had to admit that he had been fed the answers. So had many other contestants on other shows, including a Protestant minister named Charles Jackson. Wherever you looked, it was just one bad thing after another. And nearly all this disturbed tranquillity occurred in the space of just over a year. People have never gone from happy to not happy more quickly.

In Des Moines as the decade came to an end the change was mostly physical. Chain stores and restaurants began to come in, causing flurries of excitement wherever they arose. Now we would be able to dine at the same restaurants, eat the same fast foods, wear the same clothes, direct visitors to the same motel beds as people in California and New York and Florida. Des Moines would be exactly like everywhere else, a prospect that most people found rather thrilling.

The city lost its elm trees to Dutch elm disease, leaving the main thoroughfares looking starkly naked. Often now along streets like Grand and University avenues the old houses were bulldozed to splinters, and in no time at all there would rise in their place a bright new gas station, a glassy restaurant, an apartment complex in a sleek modern style, or just a roomy new parking lot for a neighbouring business. I remember going away one year on vacation (a tour of Pony Express routes of the Plains States) and coming home to find that two stately Victorian houses across from Tech High School on Grand had become sudden vague memories. In their place, in what now seemed an enormous clearing, stood a sun-catching, concrete-white, multi-storey Travelodge motel. My father was apoplectic, but most people were pleased and proud – the Travelodge was more than just a motel, you see: it was a *motor lodge*, something far finer; Des Moines was coming up in the world – and I was both amazed and impressed that such a dramatic change could be effected so quickly.

At about the same time, a Holiday Inn opened on Fleur Drive, a park-like boulevard, mostly residential, leading from the city to the airport. It was a comparatively discreet building, but it had an enormous, exceedingly lively sign by the roadside – a thrumming angular tower of starbursts and garish cascades and manic patterns made by light bulbs chasing after each other in tireless circles – that exercised my father greatly. 'How could they let them put up a sign like that?' he would despair every time we drove past it from 1959 to his death twenty-five years later. 'Have you ever seen anything more ugly in your life?' he would ask no one in particular.

I thought it was wonderful. I couldn't wait for more signs like it everywhere, and I quickly got my wish as newer, more insistent, more car-friendly businesses popped up all over. In 1959, Des Moines got its first shopping mall, way out on Merle Hay Road, a part of town so remote, so out in the fields, that many people had to ask where it was. The new mall had a parking lot the size of a New England state. No one had ever seen so much asphalt in one place. Even my father got excited by this.

'Wow, look at all the places you can *park*,' he said, as if for all these years he had been cruising endlessly, unable to terminate a journey. For about a year the most dangerous place to drive in Des Moines was the parking lot of Merle Hay Mall because of all the cars speeding at joyous random angles across its boundless black-top without reflecting that other happy souls might be doing likewise.

My father never shopped anywhere else after that. Neither did most people. By the early 1960s, people exchanged boasts about how long it had been since they had been downtown. They had found a new kind of happiness at the malls. At just the point where I was finally growing up, Des Moines stopped feeling like the place I had grown up in.

After Greenwood I moved on to Callanan Junior High School for grades seven to nine – the early teen years. Callanan was a much worldlier school. Its catchment area covered a broader cross-section of the city so that its enrolment was roughly half black and half white. For many of us this was our first close-up experience of black kids. Suddenly there were six hundred fellow students who were stronger, fleeter, tougher, braver, hipper and cannier than we were. This was when you realized for certain something that you had always privately suspected – that you were never going to take Bob Cousy's place on the Boston Celtics, never going to break Lou Brock's base-stealing records for the St Louis Cardinals, never going to be invited to Olympic trials in any sport. You weren't even going to make the junior varsity softball team now.

This was evident from the very first day when Mr Schlubb, the pear-shaped PE teacher, sent us all out to run half a dozen laps round a preposterously enormous cinder track. For the Greenwood kids – all of us white, marshmallowy, innately unphysical, squinting unfamiliarly in the bright sunshine – it was a shock to the system of an unprecedented order. Most of us ran as if slogging through quicksand and were gasping for air by the first bend. On the second lap a boy named Willis Pomerantz burst into tears because he had never perspired before and thought he was leaking vital fluids, and three others petitioned to be sent to the nurse. The black kids without exception sailed past us in a jog, including a three-hundred-pound spheroid named Tubby Brown. These kids weren't just slightly better than us, they were better by another order of magnitude altogether, and it was like this, we would find, in all sports.

Winters at Callanan were spent playing basketball in a dim-lit gymnasium – we seemed to spend hours at it every day – and no white kid I know ever even *saw* the ball. Honestly. You would just see a sequence of effortless blurs moving about between two

275

or three lanky black kids and then the net would go swish, and you would know to turn round and lope down to the other end of the court. Mostly you just tried to stay out of the way, and never ever raised your hands above your waist, for that might be taken as a sign that you wanted a pass, which was in fact the last thing you wanted. A boy named Walter Haskins once unthinkingly scratched the side of his head near the basket, and the next instant was hit square in the face so hard with a ball that the front of his head went completely concave. They had to use a bathroom plunger to get it back to normal, or so I was told.

The black kids were all immensely tough, too. I once saw an overfed white lummox named Dwayne Durdle foolishly and remorselessly pick on a little black kid named Tyrone Morris in the serving line in the cafeteria, and when Tyrone could take no more, he turned with a look of weariness and sad exasperation and threw a flurry of punches into Durdle's absorbent face so fast that you didn't actually see his hands move. All you heard was a kind of rubbery *flubba-da-dubba* sound and the *ping* of teeth ricocheting off walls and radiators. As Durdle sank to his knees, glassy-eyed and gurgling, Tyrone thrust an arm far down his throat, grabbed hold of something deep inside and turned him inside out.

'Goddam *fool* muthah-fuckah,' Tyrone said in amazed dismay as he retrieved his tray and continued on to the dessert section.

There were, however, almost no overt bad feelings between blacks and whites at Callanan. The black kids were poorer than the rest of us almost without exception, but otherwise were just the same in nearly all respects. They came from solid, hard-working homes. They spoke with identical voices, shopped at the same stores, wore the same clothes, went to the same movies. We were all just kids. Apart from my grandmother asking for nigger babies at Bishop's, I don't remember hearing a single racist remark in the whole of my upbringing.

I wouldn't pretend that we didn't notice that black kids were black, but it was as close to not noticing as you could get. It was much the same with other ethnic groups. Some years ago when I came to apply a pseudonym to one of my boyhood friends, I chose the name Stephen Katz partly in honour of a Des Moines drugstore called Katz's, which was something of a local institution in my childhood, and partly because I wanted a short name that was easy to type. Never did it occur to me that the name was Semitic. I never thought of *anybody* in Des Moines as being Jewish. I don't believe anyone did. Even when they had names like Wasserstein and Liebowitz, it was always a surprise to learn they were Jewish. Des Moines wasn't a very ethnic place.

Anyway, Katz wasn't Jewish. He was Catholic. And it was at Callanan that I met him when he was recruited by Doug Willoughby to join in an organized takeover of the Audio-Visual Club – a cunning but unusual move and a lasting testament to Willoughby's genius. Club members were put in charge of maintaining and showing the school's enormous cache of educational films. Whenever a teacher wanted to show a movie – and some teachers did little else because it meant they didn't have to teach or even spend much time in the classroom – a member of the elite AV team would wheel a projector to the room in question, expertly thread and loop the film through half a dozen sprockets and show the desired educational offering.

Historically, the AV Club was the domain of the school's geekiest students, as you would expect, but Willoughby at once saw the advantages the club offered to normal people. For one thing, it provided a key to the only locked space in the building to which students had access and where we could almost certainly smoke once he had cracked the ventilation problem (which he quickly did). Further, it gave access to an enormous supply of movies, including all the sex education films made between roughly 1938 and 1958. Finally, and above all, it provided a legitimate excuse to be at large in the empty hallways of Callanan during class time. If challenged by a teacher while roaming through the shiny corridors (and what a delightful, relaxing, privileged place school corridors are when empty) you could simply say: 'I'm just going up to the AV room to do some essential maintenance on a Bell and Howell 1040-Z,' which was in fact more or less true. What you didn't say was that you would also be smoking half a pack of Chesterfields while there.

So at Willoughby's behest, fifteen of us joined the club, and as our first order of business voted all the existing members out. Only Milton Milton was allowed to stay as a sort of token geek and because he gave us half a bottle of crème de menthe he'd stolen from his dad's liquor cabinet and because he threatened to report us to his parents, the principal, the school board and the county sheriff, whom he dubiously claimed as a close family friend, if we didn't allow him to remain in the club.

The AV room was tucked away in an obscure corner of the building, upstairs and at the back. It was like the school attic. It contained a large assortment of old stage props, costumes, scripts, yearbooks from the 1920s and 1930s and dusty shelves of old films – hygiene movies, newsreels, sex education films, marijuana-will-melt-your-brain films and much else. We spent many happy hours showing the sex education films on the walls.

Willoughby discovered a film splicing kit and spent hours

editing the films for his own amusement, putting goose-stepping Nazis into movies about the Oregon Trail and so on. His finest moment was in a sex education film when the narrative line 'Johnny had just experienced his first nocturnal emission' was immediately followed by a shot of Naval Academy cadets throwing their hats in the air.

It was in the AV Club, as I say, that I met a transfer student from the Catholic school system named Stephen Katz. I have never come close to doing the real Stephen Katz justice on any of the occasions I have put him in my books – no mortal author could – and I'm afraid I won't now except to say that he is the most extraordinary human being I have ever met, and in many ways the best. In those days he was the chipperest, friendliest, most party-ready human being the earth had ever known when sober and even more so when drunk, which he was much of the time even at the age of fourteen. I have never known anyone so drawn to, so amiably at home with, intoxicants. It was evident from the first moment that he was an engaging danger.

Often Katz and Willoughby and I skipped school and spent long days trying to get into Willoughby's older brother Ronald's chest of drawers. Ronald had an enormous collection of men's magazines, which he kept securely locked in a large chest in his bedroom. Ronald was the oldest, smartest and by far best behaved of the Willoughby boys – he was an altar boy, Explorer Scout, member of the student council, hall monitor, permanent asshole – and more cunning than his three brothers put together. Not only was every drawer in the chest locked with ingenuity, but each drawer when opened had been given an impenetrable lid that seemed to offer no way in at all. On top of all this, much of the room, from the doorknob to certain of the floorboards, was lethally booby-trapped. Depending on what the intruder touched or tampered with, he might receive a bracing electric shock or come under multiple attacks from flying missiles, falling weights, swinging hammers, lunging mousetraps or generous effusions of homemade pepper spray.

I particularly remember a moment of brief-lived delight when Willoughby, after hours of forensic examination, finally figured out how to open the second drawer of the chest – it had something to do with rotating a piece of carved filigree on the chest moulding – and in the same instant there came a whistling sound, and a slender homemade dart, about six inches long and beautifully made, embedded itself with a resonant *thwoing* in the chest not two inches to the left of Willoughby's fortuitously inclined head. Attached to the shaft of the dart was a slip of paper on which was neatly written: 'WARNING: I SHOOT TO KILL.'

'He's fucking crazy,' we agreed in unison.

After that Willoughby shrouded himself in every defensive item of apparel he could think of – welder's goggles, hockey mitts, heavy overcoat, catcher's chest protector, motorcycle helmet, and whatever else came to hand – while Katz and I hovered in the hallway urging him on and asking for updates on progress.

There was a particular urgency to the task because *Playboy* had lately taken to showing pubic hair. It is hard to believe that until the 1960s such an important erogenous zone remained undiscovered, but it is so. Prior to this, women in men's magazines had no reproductive apparatus at all – at least none that they were prepared to show to strangers. They seemed to suffer from an odd reflex medical condition – *vaginis timiditus*, Willoughby called it – that for some reason compelled them, whenever a camera was produced, to wrench their hips and fling one leg over another as if trying to get their lower half to face backwards. For years I thought that was the position women naturally adopted when they were naked and at ease. When *Playboy* first showed pubic hair, for at least seventy-two hours it featured in every male conversation in America. ('Check your oil for you, mister? Seen the new *Playboy* yet?') Woolworth's sold out its entire stock of magnifying glasses in twenty-four hours.

We longed with all our hearts to enter that privileged inner circle, as it were. But in over two years of trying, Willoughby never did get into his brother's private stock, until one day in frustration he broke open the bottom drawer with a fireman's axe, and a cornucopia of men's magazines – my goodness, but his brother was a collector – came sliding out. I have seldom passed a more agreeable or instructive afternoon. Willoughby was grounded for two months for that, but we all agreed it was a noble sacrifice, and he did have the satisfaction of getting his brother in trouble too, for some of these magazines were frankly quite disturbing.

As always, my timing with regard to actual female flesh remained impeccably abysmal. In the summer between eighth and ninth grades, I went away to visit my grandparents, where I had the usual delightful interludes with my Uncle Dee, the human flocking machine, and came back to find that in my absence a girl of radiant prettiness and good cheer named Kathy Wilcox had come to Willoughby's house to borrow some tracing paper and ended up teaching him and Katz a new game she had learned at Bible camp – at Bible camp!!!!! – in which you blindfolded a volunteer, spun the volunteer round for a couple of minutes, and then pressed firmly on his or her chest thirty or so times, at which point the victim would amusingly faint.

'Happens every time,' they said.

281

'I'm sorry, did you just say "her chest" – "pressed on *her* chest"?' I said.

Kathy Wilcox was a young woman with a chest worth pressing. The mere mention of her name was enough to make every corpuscle of blood in my body rush to the pelvic region and swell up in huge pointless readiness. They nodded happily. I couldn't believe this was happening to me again.

'Kathy Wilcox's chest? You were pressing on Kathy Wilcox's chest? With your hands?'

'Repeatedly,' said Willoughby, beaming.

Katz confirmed it with many happy nods.

My despair cannot be described. I had missed out on the only genuinely erotic, hands-on experience that there would ever be involving boys aged fourteen and instead had passed forty-eight hours watching a man turn assorted foods into flying whey.

Smoking was the big discovery of the age. Boy, did I love smoking and boy did it love me. For a dozen or so years I did little in life but sit at desks hunched over books French inhaling (which is to say drawing ropes of smoke up into the nostrils from the mouth, which gives a double hit of nicotine with every heady inhalation as well as projecting an air of cerebral savoir faire, even at the cost of having a nicotine-stained upper lip and permanent yellowy-brown circlets about the nostrils) or lounge back with hands behind head blowing languorous smoke rings, at which I grew so proficient that I could bounce them off pictures on distant walls or fire one smoke ring through another – skills that marked me out as a Grand Master of smoking before I was quite fifteen.

We used to smoke in Willoughby's bedroom, sitting beside a window fan that was set up to blow outwards, so that all the smoke was pulled into the whirring blades and dispatched into the open air beyond. There was a prevailing theory in those days (of which my father was a devoted, and eventually solitary, advocate) that if the fan blew outwards it drew all the hot air from the room and pulled cool air in through any other open window. It was somehow supposed to be much more economical, which is where the appeal lay for my father. In fact, it didn't work at all – all it did was make the outside a little cooler – and pretty soon everyone abandoned it, except my father who continued to cool the air outside his window till his dying day.

Anyway, the one benefit of having a fan blow outwards was that it allowed you to finish each smoke with a flourish: you flicked the butt into the humming blades, which diced it into a shower of outward-flying sparks that was rather pleasing to behold and neatly obliterated the cigarette in the process, leaving no visible evidence below. It all worked very well until one August evening when Willoughby and I had a smoke, then went out for air, unaware that a solitary wayward ember had been flung back into the room and lodged in a fold of curtain, where it smouldered for an hour or so and then burst into a low but cheerful flame. When we returned to Willoughby's house, there were three fire trucks out front; fire hoses were snaked across the lawn, through the front door and up the stairs; Willoughby's bedroom curtains and several pieces of furniture were on the front lawn soaked through and still smoking lightly; and Mr Willoughby was on the front porch in a state of high emotion waiting to interview his son.

Mr Willoughby's troubles did not end there, however. The

following spring, to celebrate the last day of the school year, Willoughby and his brother Joseph decided to make a bomb that they would pack in confetti and bury the night before in the centre of the Callanan lawn, a handsome sward of never-walked-upon grass enclosed by a formal semi-circular driveway. At 3.01 p.m., just as a thousand chattering students were pouring from the school's four exits, the bomb, activated by an alarm clock timer, would go off with an enormous bang that would fill the air with dirt and drifting smoke and a pleasing shower of twirling coloured paper.

The Willoughby brothers spent weeks mixing up dangerous batches of gunpowder in their bedroom and testing various con-coctions, each more robust than the previous one, in the woods down by the railroad tracks near Waterworks Park. The last one left a smoking crater almost four feet across, threw strips of confetti twenty-five feet into the air and made such a reverberat-ing, city-wide bang that squad cars hastened to the scene from eight different directions and cruised slowly around the area in a suspicious, squinty-eyed manner for almost forty minutes (making it the longest spell that Des Moines cops had ever been known to go without doughnuts and coffee).

It promised to be a fantastic show – the most memorable letting-out day in the history of Des Moines schools. The plan was that Willoughby and his brother would rise at four, walk to the school grounds under cover of darkness, plant the bomb and withdraw to await the end of the school day. To that end they assembled the necessary materials – spade, dark clothes, ski masks – and carefully prepared the bomb, which they left ticking away on the bedroom desk. Why they set the timer is a question that would be asked many times in the coming days. Each brother would vigorously blame the other. What is certain is that they retired to bed without its occurring to either of them that 3.01 *a.m.* comes before 3.01 *p.m.*

So it was at that dark hour, fifty-nine minutes before their own alarm went off, that the peaceful night was rent by an enormous explosion in Doug and Joseph Willoughby's bedroom. No one in Des Moines was out at that hour, of course, but anyone passing who chanced to glance up at the Willoughbys' house at the moment of detonation would have seen first an intense yellow light upstairs, followed an instant later by two bedroom windows blowing spectacularly outwards, followed a second after that by a large puff of smoke and a cheery flutter of confetti.

But of course the truly memorable feature of the event was the bang, which was almost unimaginably robust and startling. It knocked people out of bed up to fourteen blocks away. Automatic alarms sounded all over the city, and the ceiling sprinklers came on in at least two office buildings. A community air raid siren was briefly activated, though whether by accident or as a precaution was never established. Within moments two hundred thousand groggy, bed-flung people were peering out their bedroom windows in the direction of one extremely well-lit, smoke-filled house on the west side of town, through which Mr Willoughby, confused, wild of hair, at the end of an extremely stretched tether, was stumbling, shouting: 'What the fuck? What the fuck?'

Doug and his brother, though comically soot-blackened and unable to hear anything not shouted directly into their ears for the next forty-eight hours, were miraculously unharmed. The only casualty was a small laboratory rat that lived in a cage on the desk-top and was now just a lot of disassociated fur. The blast knocked the Willoughby home half an inch off its foundations and generated tens of thousands of dollars in repair bills. The police, fire department, sheriff's office and FBI all took a keen interest in prosecuting the family, though no one could ever quite agree on what charges to bring. Mr Willoughby became involved in protracted litigation with his insurers and embarked on a long programme of psychotherapy. In the end, the whole family was let off with a warning. Doug Willoughby and his brother were not allowed off the property except to go to school or attend confession for the next six months. Technically, they are still grounded.

And so we proceeded to high school.

Drinking became the preoccupation of these tall and festively pimpled years. All drinking was led by Katz, for whom alcohol was not so much a pastime as a kind of oxygen. It was a golden age for misbehaviour. You could buy a six-pack of Old Milwaukee beer for 59 cents (69 cents if chilled) and a pack of cigarettes (Old Gold was the brand of choice for students of my high school, Roosevelt, for no logical or historic reason that I am aware of) for 35 cents, and so have a full evening of pleasure for less than a dollar, even after taking into account sales tax. Unfortunately it was impossible to buy beer, and nearly as difficult to buy cigarettes, if you were a minor.

Katz solved this problem by becoming Des Moines's most accomplished beer thief. His career of crime began in seventh grade when he hit on a scheme that was simplicity itself. Dahl's, as part of its endless innovative efficiency, had coolers that opened from the back as well as the front so that they could be stocked from behind from the storeroom. Also inside the storeroom was a wooden pen filled with empty cardboard boxes waiting to be flattened and taken away for disposal. Katz's trick was to approach a member of staff by the stock-room door and say, 'Excuse me, mister. My sister's moving to a new apartment. Can I take some empty boxes?'

'Sure, kid,' the person would always say. 'Help yourself.'

So Katz would go into the stock room, select a big box, load it quickly with delicious frosty beer from the neighbouring beer cooler, put a couple of other boxes on top as cover, and stroll out with a case of free beer. Often the same employee would hold the door open for him. The hardest part, Katz once told me, was acting as if the boxes were empty and didn't weigh anything at all.

Of course you could ask for boxes on only so many occasions without raising suspicion, but fortunately there were Dahl's stores all over Des Moines with the same help-yourself coolers, so it was just a matter of moving around from store to store. Katz got away with it for over two years and would be getting away with it still, I daresay, except that the bottom gave way on a box once at the Dahl's in Beaverdale as Katz was egressing the building, and sixteen quart bottles of Falstaff smashed on to the floor in a foamy mess. Katz was not built for running, and so he just stood grinning until a member of staff strolled over and took him unresisting to the manager's office. He spent two weeks at Meyer Hall, the local juvenile detention centre, for that.

I had nothing to do with store thefts. I was far too cowardly and prudent to so conspicuously break the law. My contribution was to forge drivers' licences. These were, if I say it myself, small masterpieces – albeit bearing in mind that state drivers' licences were not terribly sophisticated in those days. They were really just pieces of heavy blue paper, the size of a credit card, with a kind of wavy watermark. My stroke of brilliance was to realize that the back of my father's cheques had almost exactly the same wavy pattern. If you cut one of his cheques to the right size, turned it over and, with the aid of a T-square, covered the blank side with appropriate-sized boxes for the bearer's name and address and so on, then carefully inked the words 'Iowa Department of Motor Vehicles' across the top with a fine pen and a straight edge, and produced a few other small flourishes, you had a pretty serviceable fake driver's licence.

If you then put the thing through an upright office typewriter such as my father's, entering false details in the little boxes, and in particular giving the bearer a suitably early date of birth, you had a product that could be taken to any small grocery store in town and used to acquire limitless quantities of beer.

What I didn't think of until much too late was that the obverse side of these homemade licences sometimes bore selected details of my father's account – bank name, account number, telltale computer coding and so on – depending on which part of the cheque I had cut to size with scissors.

The first time this occurred to me was about 9.30 a.m. on a weekday when I was summoned to the office of the Roosevelt principal. I had never visited the principal's office before. Katz was there already, in the outer waiting room. He was often there.

'What's up?' I said.

But before he could speak I was called into the inner sanctum. The principal was sitting with a plainclothes detective who introduced himself as Sergeant Rotisserie or something like that. He had the last flat-top in America.

'We've uncovered a ring of counterfeit driver's licences,' the sergeant told me gravely and held up one of my creations.

'A *ring*?' I said and tried not to beam. My very first foray into crime and already I was, single-handedly, a 'ring'. I couldn't have been more proud. On the other hand, I didn't particularly want to be sent to the state reform school at Clarinda and spend the next three years having involuntary soapy sex in the showers with guys named Billy Bob and Cletus Leroy.

He passed the licence to me to examine. It was one I had done for Katz (or 'Mr B. Bopp', as he had rather rakishly restyled himself). He had been picked up while having a beer-induced nap on the grassy central reservation of Polk Boulevard the night before and a search of his personal effects at the station house had turned up the artificial licence, which I examined with polite interest now. On the back it said 'Banker's Trust' and beneath that was my father's name and address – something of a giveaway to be sure.

'That's your father, isn't it?' said the detective.

'Why, yes it is,' I answered and gave what I hoped was a very nice frown of mystification.

'Like to tell me how that happened?'

'I can't imagine,' I said, looking earnest, and then added: 'Oh, wait. I bet I know. I had some friends over last week to listen to records, you know, and some fellows we'd never seen before crashed in on us, even though it wasn't even a party.' I lowered my voice slightly. 'They'd been drinking.'

The detective nodded grimly, knowledgeably. He'd been to this slippery slope before.

'We asked them to leave, of course, and eventually they did when they realized we didn't have any beer or other intoxicants, but I just bet you while we weren't looking one of them went through my dad's desk and stole some cheques.'

'Any idea who they were?'

'I'm pretty sure they were from North High. One of them looked like Richard Speck.'

The detective nodded. 'It starts to make sense, doesn't it? Do you have any witnesses?'

'Oom,' I said, a touch noncommittally, but nodded as if it might be many.

'Was Stephen Katz present?'

'I think so. Yes, I believe he was.'

'Would you go out and wait in the outer room and tell Mr Katz to come in?'

I went out and Katz was sitting there. I leaned over to him and said quickly: 'North High. Crashed party. Stole cheques. Richard Speck.'

He nodded, instantly understanding. This is one of the reasons why I say Katz is the finest human being in the world. Ten minutes later I was called back in.

'Mr Katz here has corroborated your story. It appears these boys from North High stole the cheques and ran them through a printing press. Mr Katz here was one of their customers.'

He looked at Katz without much sympathy.

'Great! Case solved!' I said brightly. 'So, can we go?'

'You can go,' said the sergeant. 'I'm afraid Mr Katz will be coming downtown with me.'

So Katz took the rap, allowing me to keep a clean sheet, God bless him and keep him. He spent a month in juvenile detention.

The thing about Katz was that he didn't do bad things with alcohol because he wanted to; he did them because he needed to. Casting around for a new source of supply, he set his sights higher. Des Moines had four beer distribution companies, all in brick depots in a quiet quarter at the edge of downtown where the railroad tracks ran through. Katz watched these depots closely for a couple of weeks and realized that they had practically no security and never worked on Saturdays or Sundays. He also noticed that railroad boxcars often stood in sidings beside the depots, particularly at weekends.

So one Sunday morning Katz and a kid named Jake Bekins drove downtown, parked beside a boxcar and knocked off its padlock with a sledgehammer. They slid open the boxcar door and discovered that it was filled solid with cases of beer. Wordlessly they filled Bekins's car with boxes of beer, shut the boxcar door and drove to the house of a third party, Art Froelich, whose parents were known to be out of town at a funeral. There, with Froelich's help, they carried the beer down to the basement. Then the three of them went back to the boxcar and repeated the process. They spent the whole of Sunday transferring beer from the boxcar to Froelich's basement until they had emptied the one and filled the other.

Froelich's parents were due home on Tuesday, so on Monday Katz and Bekins got twenty-five friends to put up $5 each and they rented a furnished apartment in an easygoing area of town known as Dogtown near Drake University. Then they transferred all the beer by car from Froelich's basement to the new apartment. There Katz and Bekins drank seven evenings a week and the rest of us dropped in for a Schlitz cocktail after school and for more prolonged sessions at weekends.

Three months later all the beer was gone and Katz and a small corps of henchmen returned downtown and spent another Sunday emptying out another boxcar from another distributor. When, three months after that, they ran out of beer again, they

291

ventured downtown once more, but more cautiously this time because they were certain that after two big robberies somebody would be keeping a closer watch on the beer warehouses.

Remarkably, this seemed not to be so. This time there were no boxcars, so they knocked a panel out of one of the warehouse delivery-bay doors, and slipped through the hole. Inside was more beer than they had ever seen at once – stacks and stacks of it standing on pallets and ready to be delivered to bars and stores all over central Iowa on Monday.

Working nonstop, and drafting in many willing assistants, they spent the weekend loading cars one after another with beer and slowly emptying the warehouse. Froelich expertly worked a forklift and Katz directed traffic. For a whole miraculous weekend, a couple of dozen high school kids could be seen – if anyone had bothered to look – moving loads of beer out of the warehouse, driving it across town and carrying it in relays into a slightly sagging and decrepit apartment house on Twenty-third Street and Forest Avenue. As word got around, other kids from other high schools began turning up, asking if they could take a couple of cases.

'Sure,' Katz said generously. 'There's plenty for all. Just pull your car up over there and try not to leave any fingerprints.'

It was the biggest heist in Des Moines in years, possibly ever. Unfortunately so many people became involved that everyone in town under the age of twenty knew who was responsible for it. No one knows who tipped off the police, but they arrested twelve principal conspirators in a dawn raid three days after the theft and took them all downtown in handcuffs for questioning. Katz was of course among them.

These were good kids from good homes. Their parents were

mortified that their offspring could be so wilfully unlawful. They called in expensive lawyers, who swiftly cut deals with the prosecutor to drop charges if they named names. Only Katz's parents wouldn't come to an arrangement. They couldn't comfortably afford to and anyway they didn't believe it was right. Besides, *somebody* had to take the rap – you can't just let every guilty person go or what kind of criminal justice system would you have, for goodness' sake? – so it was necessary to elect a fall guy and everyone agreed that Katz should be that person. He was charged with grand theft, a felony, and sent to reform school for two years. It was the last we saw of him till college.

I got through high school by the skin of my teeth. It was my slightly proud boast that I led the school in absences all three years and in my junior year achieved the distinction of missing more days than a boy with a fatal illness, as Mrs Smolting, my careers counsellor, never tired of reminding me. Mrs Smolting hated me with a loathing that was slightly beyond bottomless.

'Well, frankly, William,' she said with a look of undisguised disdain one day after we had worked our way through a long list of possible careers, including vacuum cleaner repair and selling things door to door, and established to her absolute satisfaction that I lacked the moral fibre, academic credentials, intellectual rigour and basic grooming skills for any of them, 'it doesn't appear that you are qualified to do much of anything.'

'I guess I'll have to be a high school careers counsellor then!' I quipped lightly, but I'm afraid Mrs Smolting did not take it well. She marched me to the principal's office – my second visit in a season! – and lodged a formal complaint.

I had to write a letter of abject apology, expressing respect for Mrs Smolting and her skilled and caring profession, before they would allow me to continue to my senior year, which was a serious business indeed because at this time, 1968, the only thing that stood between one's soft tissue and a Vietcong bullet was the American education system and its automatic deferment from the draft. A quarter of young American males were in the armed forces in 1968. Nearly all the rest were in school, in prison or were George W. Bush. For most people, school was the only realistic option for avoiding military service.

In one of his last official acts, but also one of his most acclaimed ones, the Thunderbolt Kid turned Mrs Smolting into a small hard carbonized lump of a type known to people in the coal-burning industry as a clinker. Then he handed in a letter of carefully phrased apology, engaged in a few months of light buckling down, and graduated, unshowily, near the bottom of his class.

The following autumn he enrolled at Drake, the local university. But after a year or so of desultory performance there, he went to Europe, settled in England and was scarcely ever heard from again.

Chapter 14
FAREWELL

In Milwaukee, uninjured when his auto swerved off the high-way, Eugene Cromwell stepped out to survey the damage and fell into a 50-foot limestone quarry. He suffered a broken arm.

– *Time* magazine, 23 April 1956

FROM TIME TO TIME when I was growing up, my father would call us into the living room to ask how we felt about moving to St Louis or San Francisco or some other big-league city. The *Chronicle* or *Examiner* or *Post-Dispatch*, he would inform us sombrely, had just lost its baseball writer – he always made it sound as if the person had not returned from a mission, like a Second World War airman – and the position was being offered to him.

'Money's pretty good, too,' he would say with a look of frank consternation, as if surprised that one could be paid for routinely attending Major League baseball games.

I was always for it. When I was small, I was taken with the idea of having a dad working in a field where people evidently went missing from time to time. Then later it was more a desire to pass what remained of my youth in a place – any place at all – where daily hog prices were not regarded as breaking news and corn yields were never mentioned.

But it never happened. In the end he and my mother always decided that they were content in Des Moines. They had good jobs at the *Register* and a better house than we could afford in a big city like San Francisco. Our friends were there. We were settled. Des Moines felt like, Des Moines was, home.

Now that I am older I am glad we didn't leave. I have a life-long attachment to the place myself, after all. Every bit of formal education I have ever had, every formative experience, every inch of vertical growth on my body took place within this wholesome, friendly, nurturing community.

Of course much of the Des Moines I grew up in is no longer there. It was already changing by the time I reached adolescence. The old downtown movie palaces were among the first to go. The Des Moines Theater, that wonderful heap of splendour, was torn down in 1966 to make way for an office building. I didn't realize it until I read a history of the city for this book, but the Des Moines was not just the finest theatre in the city, but possibly the finest surviving theatre of any type between Chicago and the West Coast. I was further delighted to discover that it had been built by none other than A. H. Blank, the philanthropist with the penthouse apartment that Jed Mattes and I used to visit. He had spent the exceptionally lavish sum of $750,000 on the building in 1918. It is extraordinary to think that it didn't even survive for half a century. The other principal theatres of my childhood – the Paramount, Orpheum (later called the Galaxy), Ingersoll, Hiland, Holiday and Capri – followed one by one. Nowadays if you want to see a movie you have to drive out to a shopping mall, where you can choose between a dozen pictures, but just one very small size of screen, each inhabiting a kind of cinematic shoebox. Not much magic in that.

Riverview Park closed in 1978. Today it's just a large vacant lot with nothing to show that it ever existed. Bishop's, our beloved cafeteria, closed about the same time, taking its atomic toilets, its little table lights, its glorious foods and kindly waitresses with it. Many other locally owned restaurants – Johnny and Kay's, Country Gentleman, Babe's, Bolton and Hay's, Vic's Tally-Ho, the beloved Toddle House – went around the same time. Katz helped the Toddle House on its way by introducing to it a new concept called 'dine and dash', in which he and whoever he had been drinking with would consume a hearty late-night supper and then make a hasty exit without paying, calling over their shoulder if challenged, 'Short of cash – gotta dash!' I wouldn't say that Katz single-handedly put the Toddle House out of business, but he didn't help.

The *Tribune*, the evening paper which I lugged thanklessly from house to house for so many years, closed in 1982 after it was realized that no one had actually been reading it since about 1938. The *Register*, its big sister, which once truly was the pride of Iowa, got taken over by the Gannett organization three years later. Today it is, well, not what it was. It no longer sends a reporter to baseball spring training or even always to the World Series, so it is perhaps as well my father is no longer around.

Greenwood, my old elementary school, still commands its handsome lawn, still looks splendid from the street, but they tore out the wonderful old gym and auditorium, its two most cherishable features, to make way for a glassy new extension out back, and the other distinguishing touches – the cloakrooms, the clanking radiators, the elegant water fountains, the smell of mimeograph – are long gone, too, so it's no longer really the place I knew.

My peerless Little League park, with its grandstand and press box, was torn down so that somebody could build an enormous apartment building in its place. A new, cheaper park was built down by the river bottoms near where the Butters used to live, but the last time I went down there it was overgrown and appeared to be abandoned. There was no one to ask what happened because there are no people outdoors any more – no kids on bikes, no neighbours talking over fences, no old men sitting on porches. Everyone is indoors.

Dahl's supermarket is still there, and still held in some

affection, but it lost the Kiddie Corral and grocery tunnel years ago during one of its periodic, and generally dismaying, renovations. Nearly all the other neighbourhood stores – Grund's Groceries, Barbara's Bake Shoppe, Reed's ice cream parlour, Pope's barbershop, the Sherwin-Williams paint store, Mitcham's TV and Electrical, the little shoe repair shop (run by Jimmy the Italian – a beloved local figure), Henry's Hamburgers, Reppert's Drugstore – are long gone. Where several of them stood there is now a big Walgreen's drugstore, so you can buy everything under one roof in a large, anonymous, brightly lit space from people who have never seen you before and wouldn't remember you if they had. It stocks men's magazines, I was glad to note on my last visit, though these are sealed in plastic bags, so it is actually harder now to see pictures of naked women than it was in my day, which I would never have believed possible, but there you are.

All the downtown stores went one by one. Ginsberg's and the New Utica department stores closed. Kresge's and Woolworth's closed. Frankel's closed. Pinkie's closed. J. C. Penney bravely opened a new downtown store and that closed. The Shops Building lost its restaurant. Then somebody got mugged or saw a disturbed homeless person or something, and nobody went downtown after dark at all ever, and all the rest of the restaurants and night spots closed. In the ultimate indignity, even the bus station moved out.

Younkers, the great ocean liner of a department store, became practically the last surviving relic of the glory days of my childhood. For years it heroically held on in its old brown building downtown, though it closed whole floors and retreated into ever tinier corners of the building to survive. In the end it had only sixty employees, compared with over a thousand in its heyday. In the summer of 2005, after one hundred and thirty-one years in business, it closed for the last time.

When I was a kid, the Register and Tribune had an enormous photo library, in a room perhaps eighty feet by sixty feet, where I would often pass an agreeable half-hour if I had to wait for my mom. There must have been half a million pictures in there, maybe more. You could look in any drawer of any filing cabinet and find real interest and excitement from the city's past – five-alarm fires, train derailments, a lady balancing beer glasses on her bosom, parents standing on ladders at hospital windows talking to their polio-stricken children. The library was the complete visual history of Des Moines in the twentieth century.

Recently I returned to the R & T looking for illustrations for this book, and discovered to my astonishment that the picture library today occupies a small room at the back of the building and that nearly all the old pictures were thrown out some years ago.

'They needed the space,' Jo Ann Donaldson, the present librarian, told me with a slightly apologetic look.

I found this a little hard to take in. 'They didn't give them to the state historical society?' I asked.

She shook her head.

'Or the city library? Or a university?'

She shook her head twice more. 'They were recycled for the silver in the paper,' she told me.

So now not only are the places mostly gone, but there is no record of them either.

Life moved on for people, too – or in some unfortunate cases stopped altogether. My father slipped quietly into the latter category in 1986 when he went to bed one night and didn't wake up, which is a pretty good way to go if you have to go. He was just shy of his seventy-first birthday when he died. Had he worked for a bigger newspaper, I have no doubt my father would have been one of the great baseball writers of his day. Because we stayed, the world never got a chance to see what he could do. Nor, of course, did he. In both cases, I can't help feeling that they didn't know what they were missing.

My mother stayed on in the family home for as long as she could manage, but eventually sold up and moved to a nice old apartment building on Grand. Now in her nineties, she remains gloriously cheerful, healthy and perky, keen as ever to spring up and make a sandwich from some Tupperwared memento at the back of her fridge. She still keeps an enormous stock of jars under the sink (though none has ever experienced a drop of toity, she assures me) and retains one of the Midwest's most outstanding collections of sugar packets, saltine crackers and jams of many flavours. She would like the record to show, incidentally, that she is nothing like as bad a cook as her feckless son persists in portraying her in his books, and I am happy to state here that she is absolutely right.

As for the others who passed through my early life and into the pages of this book, it is difficult to say too much without compromising their anonymity.

Doug Willoughby had what might be called a lively four years at college – it was an age of excess; I'll say no more – but afterwards settled down. He now lives quietly and respectably in a small Midwestern city, where he is a good and loving father and husband, a helpful neighbour and supremely nice human being. It has been many years since he has blown anything up.

Stephen Katz left high school and dived head first into a world of drugs and alcohol. He spent a year or two at the University of Iowa, then returned to Des Moines, where he lived near the Timber Tap, a bar on Forest Avenue which had the distinction of opening for business at 6 a.m. every day. Katz was often to be seen at that hour entering in carpet slippers and a robe for his morning 'eye-opener'. For twenty-five years or so, he took into his body pretty much whatever consciousness-altering replenishments were on offer. For a time he was one of only two opium addicts in Iowa (the other was his supplier) and famous among his friends for a remarkable ability to crash cars spectacularly and step from the wreckage grinning and unscathed. After taking a leading role in a travel adventure story called *A Walk in the Woods* (which he describes as 'mostly fiction'), he became a respectful and generally obedient member of Alcoholics Anonymous, landed a job in a printing plant, and found a saintly life partner named Mary. At the time of writing, he had just passed his third-year anniversary of complete sobriety – a proud achievement.

Jed Mattes, my gay friend, moved with his family to Dubuque soon after he treated me to the strippers' tent at the State Fair, and I lost touch with him altogether. Some twenty years later when I was looking for a literary agent, I asked a publishing friend in New York for a recommendation. He mentioned a bright young man who had just quit the ICM literary agency to set up on his own. 'His name's Jed Mattes,' he told me. 'You know, I think he might be from your hometown.'

So Jed became my agent and close renewed friend for the next decade and a half. In 2003, after a long battle with cancer, he died. I miss him a great deal. Jed Mattes is, incidentally, his real

303

name – the only one of my contemporaries, I believe, to whom I have not given a pseudonym.

Buddy Doberman vanished without trace halfway through college. He went to California in pursuit of a girl and was never seen again. Likewise of unknown fate were the Kowalski brothers, Lanny and Lumpy. Arthur Bergen became an enormously rich lawyer in Washington, DC. The Butter clan went away one springtime and never returned. Milton Milton went into the military, became something fairly senior, and died in a helicopter crash during the preparations for the first Gulf War.

Thanks to what I do, I sometimes renew contact with people unexpectedly. A woman came up to me after a reading in Denver once and introduced herself as the former Mary O'Leary. She had on big glasses that she kept round her neck on a chain and seemed jolly and happy and quite startlingly meaty. On the other hand, a person I had thought of as timid and mousy came up to me at another reading and looked like a movie star. I think life is rather splendid like that.

The Thunderbolt Kid grew up and moved on. Until quite recently he still occasionally vaporized people, usually just after they had walked through a held door without saying thank you, but eventually he stopped eliminating people when he realized that he couldn't tell which of them buy books.

The Sacred Jersey of Zap, moth-eaten and full of holes, was thrown out in about 1978 by his parents during a tragically misguided housecleaning exercise, along with his baseball cards, comic books, *Boys' Life* magazines, Zorro whip and sword, Sky King neckerchief and neckerchief ring, Davy Crockett coonskin cap, Roy Rogers decorative cowboy vest and bejewelled boots with jingly tin spurs, official Boy Scout Vitt-L-Kit, Sky King Fan Club card and other related credentials, Batman flashlight with signalling attachment, electric football game, Johnny Unitas-approved helmet, Hardy Boys books and peerless set of movie posters, many in mint condition.

That's the way of the world, of course. Possessions get discarded. Life moves on. But I often think what a shame it is that we didn't keep the things that made us different and special and attractive in the Fifties. Imagine those palatial downtown movie theatres with their vast screens and Egyptian decor, but thrillingly enlivened with Dolby sound and slick computer graphics. Now that *would* be magic. Imagine having all of public life – offices, stores, restaurants, entertainments – conveniently clustered in the heart of the city and experiencing fresh air and daylight each time you moved from one to another. Imagine having a cafeteria with atomic toilets, a celebrated tearoom that gave away gifts to young customers, a clothing store with a grand staircase and a mezzanine, a Kiddie Corral where you could read comics to your heart's content. Imagine having a city full of things that no other city had.

What a wonderful world that would be. What a wonderful world it was. We won't see its like again, I'm afraid.

BIBLIOGRAPHY

The following are books mentioned or alluded to in the text:

Castleman, Harry, and Walter J. Podrazik, *Watching TV: Six Decades of American Television*. Syracuse, New York: Syracuse University Press, 2003.

DeGroot, Gerard J., *The Bomb: A Life*. Cambridge, Massachusetts: Harvard University Press, 2005.

Denton, Sally, and Roger Morris, *The Money and the Power: The Making of Las Vegas and Its Hold on America, 1947–2000*. London: Pimlico, 2002.

Diggins, John Patrick, *The Proud Decades: America in War and Peace, 1941–1960*. New York: W. W. Norton, 1988.

Goodchild, Peter, *Edward Teller: The Real Dr Strangelove*. London: Weidenfeld and Nicolson, 2004.

Halberstam, David, *The Fifties*. New York: Fawcett Columbine, 1993.

Heimann, Jim (ed.), *The Golden Age of Advertising – the 50s*. Cologne: Taschen, 2002.

Henriksen, Margot A., *Dr Strangelove's America: Society and Culture in the Atomic Age*. Berkeley: University of California Press, 1997.

Kismaric, Carole, and Marvin Heiferman, *Growing Up with Dick and Jane: Learning and Living the American Dream*. San Francisco: Lookout/HarperCollins, 1996.

Lewis, Peter, *The Fifties*. London: Heinemann, 1978.

Light, Michael, *100 Suns: 1945–1962*. London: Jonathan Cape, 2003.

Lingeman, Richard R., *Don't You Know There's a War On?: The American Home Front 1941–1945*. New York: G. P. Putnam's Sons, 1970.

McCurdy, Howard E., *Space and the American Imagination*. Washington: Smithsonian Institution Press, 1997.

Mills, George, *Looking in Windows: Surprising Stories of Old Des Moines*. Ames, Iowa: Iowa State University Press, 1991.

Oakley, J. Ronald, *God's Country: America in the Fifties*. New York: Dembner Books, 1986.

O'Reilly, Kenneth, *Hoover and the Un-Americans*. Philadelphia: Temple University Press, 1983.

Patterson, James T., *Grand Expectations: The United States, 1945–1974*. New York: Oxford University Press, 1996.

Savage, Jr., William W., *Comic Books and America, 1945–1954*. Norman: University of Oklahoma Press, 1990.

ILLUSTRATIONS

Endpapers: An average American family and all the food they consumed in 1951. Hagley Museum and Library, Wilmington, Delaware

The Bryson family photos on pp. iii, viii, x, 32, 98, 296 and 310 are from the author's own collection.

p. 2: Locust Street, Des Moines, 16 February 1953. *Dope Inferno* is showing at the cinema. State Historical Society of Iowa

p. 54: The Paramount movie palace, Des Moines, 1950s. *The Florodora Girl* is showing with Al Morey and Marion Davies. State Historical Society of Iowa

p. 76: Advertisement for Camel cigarettes, with a medical endorsement. Courtesy the Advertising Archives, London

p. 120: 'I dreamed I went to the office in my Maidenform bra'. Courtesy the Advertising Archives, London

p. 136: Naval observers watching a nuclear blast in the Pacific in the 1950s. © CORBIS

p. 154: Schoolchildren practising duck and cover drill in case of nuclear attack, February 1951. © Bettmann/CORBIS

p. 174: Mary McGuire, homecoming queen, in the Drake University Year Book of 1938. Special Collection at Cowles Library, Drake University, Des Moines

p. 214: Chesley Bonestell's vision of Manhattan under nuclear attack. *Collier's*, 5 August 1950. Courtesy Bonestell Space Art

p. 234: Spectators at the Iowa State Fair cake display, Des Moines, 1955. John Dominis/Timepix

p. 266: Charles van Doren on *Twenty-One*, the TV quiz show, 11 March 1957. It was later discovered that the show had been rigged. © Bettmann/CORBIS

SPOKEN SOUL

SPOKEN SOUL

The Story of Black English

John Russell Rickford
and
Russell John Rickford

Foreword by Geneva Smitherman

John Wiley & Sons, Inc.

New York • Chichester • Weinheim • Brisbane • Singapore • Toronto

This publication is designed to provide accurate and authoritative information in
regard to the subject matter covered. It is sold with the understanding that the
publisher is not engaged in rendering professional services. If professional advice
or other expert assistance is required, the services of a competent professional
person should be sought.

ISBN 0-471-32356-X (cloth)

Printed in the United States of America

From Russell John:

For the Almighty, for whom our souls are a witness.

For my godfather Uncle Teddy, the swashbuckler who taught me to take life in my teeth and leap.

For my father, the pacifist who showed me how to skip a rock, build a kite, and be a do-right man.

From John Russell:

For Angela, my beloved, and for our children, Shiyama, Russell, Anakela, and Luke, the pride and joy of our lives.

For my fallen/risen siblings: Peter Howell, Edward Noel, Patricia Stella, and all my kinfolk, here and there. May the circle be unbroken.

For soul speakers everywhere. May their language be better understood and appreciated, and may their enormous potential in school and life be more richly realized.

Contents

Part Five
The Double Self

Foreword

It's been a long time coming, as the old song goes, but the change done come. Back when I was working with the parents and legal team in *King* v. *Ann Arbor* (the "Black English" federal court case, 1977–79), public confusion and misunderstanding about Black English came as a shock to many linguists and scholars. Then shock waves again, almost two decades later, when the Ebonics controversy erupted among the mistletoe and Kinara of the 1996 Christmas-Kwanzaa season. The scholarly community has written volumes of commendable work on Spoken Soul (not by that name, of course), dating back at least to 1884, when Harrison published "Negro English" in the academic journal *Anglia*. However, with one or two exceptions over the past three decades, scholarly research on this language spoken by millions of African Americans has not been written up for the public at large. *Spoken Soul* steps to the challenge. The book breaks it down and makes it plain. At long last, the academic world of morphemes and phonemes reaches beyond ivied walls, connecting town and gown.

The Rickfords—in this case not husband and wife, but father and son—take their title from the name that writer Claude Brown gave to our language back in the 1960s. They present myths and realities about Spoken Soul, and in the process do much soul-speaking themselves, covering topics from the language of great comedians and actors to that of "preachers and pray-ers." In writing that is rich and powerful—and funky and bold when it bees necessary—they dissect black writing and black speech, the grammar and history of Spoken Soul, the Ebonics controversy and media coverage of it.

The story of Spoken Soul is not an easy one to tell because it is not *just* about language. To tell the story right, you have to talk about the culture and lived experience of African Americans. You have to talk about a language inextricable from the complex social structure and political history of people of African descent in these United

States. To get it right, you have to do what the Rickfords have done: you have to represent. Otherwise, there is no way to understand the linguistic double consciousness of black Life, as revealed here in the 1997 Howard University graduation scene with renowned broadcast news pioneer Sista Carole Simpson as commencement speaker, a push-pull scenario reenacted countless times in different versions in African America, and about which the Rickfords write with insight and eloquence in chapter 5, "Singers, Toasters, and Rappers." Their message to us—in a book that is truly da bomb—is that we must "claim both Spoken Soul and Standard English as our own, empowering our youth to appreciate and articulate each in their respective forums," for only then "will we have mastered the art of merging our double selves into a better and truer self."

John Russell and Russell John were both at the Million Man March. And now they have come together to speak the truth to the people about what it means to talk black in America. An African American father and son writing together as a team—now that in itself is a moment of history to be cherished. One a journalist, the other a linguist; one in the academy, the other in public media. *Spoken Soul* is testimony to the power of this combination of *kin*dred spirits.

> —Geneva Smitherman, Ph.D.
> University Distinguished Professor
> Michigan State University
> Author, *Black Talk: Words and Phrases from the
> Hood to the Amen Corner, Talkin and Testifyin:
> The Language of Black America,* and *Talkin That
> Talk: Language, Culture and Education in African
> America*
> October 1999

Acknowledgments

Thanks to the Stanford Humanities Center, where the proposal and much of John's writing for this book were completed, and to the Department of Linguistics and the Program in African and Afro-American Studies at Stanford, which were both supportive throughout. Gina Wein, Trudy Vizmanos, Diann McCants, and Linda Watson were especially helpful. Thanks are due, too, to former Stanford Deans of Humanities Ewart Thomas and John Shoven. Funding from the Martin Luther King Jr. Centennial Fellowship is gratefully acknowledged.

Stanford students Admas Kanyagia, Naomi Levin, Emma Petty, Sarah Roberts, Mary Rose, and Andrew Wong were first-rate research assistants, as were Joy Hsu and Damian Schnyder. Arnold Rampersad, Houston Baker, and Meta Duwa Jones provided helpful feedback with the "Writers" chapter, as did Tom Wasow with the "System" chapter. Lisa Green was generous with her native-speaker intuitions; her theoretically sophisticated work on the structure of Black English is most perceptive, and we look forward to her books. Elaine Ray and Linda Cicero of the Stanford News Service were both encouraging and helpful, and students in John's classes at Stanford, particularly African American Vernacular English, were invaluable in clarifying many points and forcing him to clarify others.

John's study and understanding of Black English have been facilitated by many current and former Stanford students, including Arnetha Ball, Renee Blake, Catherine Chappel, Keith Denning, Dawn Hannah, Raina Jackson, Andrea Kortenhoven, Nomi Martin, Bonnie McElhinny, John McWhorter, and Jacquelyn Rahman. He has also learned from his former research associates and coauthors, Faye McNair-Knox, Christine Theberge-Rafal, and Angela Rickford. His mentors, J. Herman Blake and William Labov, taught him a good deal, respectively, about black life and language. Other scholars and colleagues, many of them cited in the endnotes, also contributed to this learning. But his most significant instructors were the vernacular speakers throughout African America and the Caribbean—particularly in East Palo Alto, Philadelphia, New York City, the South Carolina Sea Islands, Barbados, Guyana, and Jamaica—who gave him the privilege of hearing, observing, analyzing, and appreciating the language.

John wishes, finally, to thank his son Russell for the many pleasures and insights that collaborating on this book involved, and especially for teaching him, by precept and example, how to write for the people. No project has ever been more rewarding.

Many thanks to the brothers of Alpha Phi Alpha Fraternity, Inc., Beta Chapter, Howard University, who guided Russell across the hinterlands of underground hip-hop culture, and who had faith that Spoken Soul was no jive, and to the editors and reporters of the *Philadelphia Inquirer,* whose support and curiosity about this book helped shape its content and style. Thanks also to Venus, who loves books.

Thanks from both of us to Noah Lukeman of Lukeman Literary Management, who first proposed this project and waited patiently for us to sign on, and to Carole Hall, our editor at John Wiley & Sons, without whose faith and convictions this book would not have seen the light of day, and without whose editorial experience and good sense it would not have been the same. Copyeditor Anna Jardine did a fantastic job. We also thank Benjamin Hamilton, associate managing editor, for seeing this book through the production process so efficiently and promptly. For their assistance in procuring photos for this volume, we thank Yaeko Ozaki of the Stanford News Service, and Mary Yearwood and Jim Huffman of the Schomburg Center for Research in Black Culture, New York Public Library. Special thanks are due to the generous cooperation of celebrated photographer Jill Krementz, whose famous photos of distinguished African American writers grace our pages. And for anyone whose contributions we have forgotten to mention, our apologies.

Thanks to Dr. G. (Geneva Smitherman) for righteously encouraging us and for writing the foreword to this book, and to all our colleagues, family members, and friends whose interest in and contributions to this book helped make it what it is. We particularly wish to recognize Angela Rickford, spouse and momma, whose counsel we drew on repeatedly.

Finally, our faith in God sustained us throughout and helped us over many of the bumps along the way.

Part One

Introduction

Part One

Introduction

1

What's Going On?

For what shall it profit a man, if he shall gain the whole world and lose his own soul?

—Mark 8:36

SOUL [*sōl*] *1. The animating and vital principle in humans . . . 5. The central or integral part; the vital core . . . 9. A sense of ethnic pride among Black people and especially African Americans, expressed in areas such as language, social customs, religion and music.*

—*The American Heritage Dictionary of the English Language* (4th edition, 2000)

"Spoken Soul" was the name that Claude Brown, author of *Manchild in the Promised Land,* coined for black talk. In a 1968 interview he waxed eloquent in its praise, declaring that the informal speech or vernacular of many African Americans "possesses a pronounced lyrical quality which is frequently incompatible to any music other than that ceaselessly and relentlessly driving rhythm that flows from poignantly spent lives." A decade later, James Baldwin, legendary author of *The Fire Next Time,* described black English as "this passion, this skill . . . this incredible music."

Now, at the beginning of the twenty-first century, the Spoken Soul these writers exalted is battered by controversy, its very existence called into question. Though belittled and denied, however, it lives on authentically. In homes, schools, and churches, on streets, stages, and the airwaves, you can hear soul spoken every day. Most African Americans—including millions who, like Brown and Baldwin, are fluent speakers of Standard English—still invoke Spoken Soul as we have for hundreds of years, to laugh or cry, to preach and praise, to shuck and jive, to sing, to rap, to shout, to style, to express our individual personas and our ethnic identities ("'spress yo'self!" as James Brown put it), to confide in and commiserate with friends, to chastise, to cuss, to act, to act the fool, to get by and get over, to pass secrets, to make jokes, to mock and mimic, to tell stories, to reflect and philosophize, to create authentic characters and voices in novels, poems, and plays, to survive in the streets, to relax at home and recreate in playgrounds, to render our deepest emotions and embody our vital core.

The fact is that most African Americans *do* talk differently from whites and Americans of other ethnic groups, or at least most of us can when we want to. And the fact is that most Americans, black and white, know this to be true.

In this book, we will explore the vibrancy and vitality of Spoken Soul as an expressive instrument in American literature, religion, entertainment, and everyday life. We will detail the features and history of Spoken Soul. We will then return to the Ebonics firestorm that flared up at century's end, considering its spark (the Oakland, California, School District's resolutions and their educational significance), its fuel (media coverage), and its embers (Ebonics "humor"). In the final chapter we will reflect on the vernacular's role in American life and society, and seek the truth about the dizzying love-hate relationship with black talk that is as old and new as the nation itself. Who needs this information and insight? We all do, because Spoken Soul is an inescapable vessel of American history, literature, society, and popular culture. Regardless of its status, we need to come to terms with this beloved and beleaguered language.

In coming to terms with Spoken Soul, what it is and why it matters, the first thing to know is how high it ranks in the esteem of its maestros. Echoing the sentiments of Claude Brown and James Baldwin, Nobel Prize–winning author Toni Morrison insisted in 1981 that the distinctive ingredient of her fiction was

> the language, only the language. . . . It is the thing that black people love so much—the saying of words, holding them on the tongue, experimenting with them, playing with them. It's a love, a passion. Its function is like a preacher's: to make you stand up out of your seat, make

you lose yourself and hear yourself. The worst of all possible things that could happen would be to lose that language. There are certain things I cannot say without recourse to my language. It's terrible to think that a child with five different present tenses comes to school to be faced with books that are less than his own language. And then to be told things about his language, which is him, that are sometimes permanently damaging. He may never know the etymology of Africanisms in his language, not even know that "hip" is a real word or that "the dozens" meant something. This is a really cruel fallout of racism. I know the standard English. I want to use it to help restore the other language, the lingua franca.

June Jordan, celebrated essayist and poet, in 1985 identified "three qualities of Black English—the presence of life, voice and clarity—that testify to a distinctive Black value system." Jordan, then a professor at Stony Brook College, chided her students for their uneasiness about the colloquial language in Alice Walker's novel *The Color Purple*, and went on to teach them about the art of the vernacular.

The second thing to bear in mind is that between the 1960s and 1990s, a dramatic shift occurred. By the end of the 1990s, we could find scarcely a spokesman or spokeswoman for the race who had anything flattering to say about Spoken Soul. In response to the Oakland school board's December 18, 1996, resolution to recognize "Ebonics" as the primary language of African American students in that California district, poet Maya Angelou told the *Wichita Eagle* that she was "incensed" and found the idea "very threatening." NAACP president Kweisi Mfume denounced the measure as "a cruel joke," and although he later adopted a friendlier stance, the Reverend Jesse Jackson on national television initially called it "an unacceptable surrender, borderlining on disgrace." Jackson found himself curiously aligned with Ward Connerly, the black University of California regent whose ultimately successful efforts to end affirmative action on University of California campuses and in the state as a whole Jackson had vigorously opposed. Connerly called the Oakland proposal "tragic," and went on to argue, "These are not kids who came from Africa last year. . . . These are kids that have had every opportunity to acclimate themselves to American society, and they have gotten themselves into this trap of speaking this language—this slang, really, that people can't understand. Now we're going to legitimize it."

Other African Americans from different ends of the ideological spectrum fell into step. Black conservative academic and author Shelby Steele characterized the Oakland proposal as just another "gimmick" to enhance black self-esteem, while black liberal academic and author Henry Louis Gates Jr., chairman of Afro-American Studies at Harvard, dismissed it as "obviously stupid and ridiculous." Former Black Panther Eldridge Cleaver agreed, as did entertainer Bill Cosby.

The virtual consensus blurred political lines among white pundits as well. Conservative talk-show host Rush Limbaugh assailed the Ebonics resolution, while leading Republican William Bennett, former U.S. secretary of education, described it as "multiculturalism gone haywire." Leading liberal Mario Cuomo, former governor of New York, called it a "bad mistake," and Secretary of Education Richard Riley, a member of President Clinton's Democratic cabinet, declared that Ebonics programs would not be eligible for federal bilingual education dollars, maintaining that "elevating black English to the status of a language is not the way to raise standards of achievement in our schools and for our students." At the state level, anti-Ebonics legislation was introduced both by Republicans, such as Representative Mark Ogles of Florida, and by Democrats, such as Georgia state senator Ralph Abernathy III.

Millions of other people across the United States and around the world rushed in to express their vociferous condemnation of Ebonics and the proposal to take it into account in schools. ("Ebonics" in fact quickly became a stand-in for the language variety and for Oakland's proposal, so the recurrent question "What do you think about Ebonics?" elicited reactions to both topics.) Animated conversations sprang up in homes and workplaces and at holiday gatherings, as well as on television and radio programs, in letters to the editor, and on electronic bulletin boards that were deluged after the Oakland decision. According to *Newsweek*, "An America Online poll about Ebonics drew more responses than the one asking people whether O. J. Simpson was guilty."

The vast majority of those America Online responses were not just negative. They were caustic. Ebonics was vilified as "disgusting black street slang," "incorrect and substandard," "nothing more than ignorance," "lazy English," "bastardized English," "the language of illiteracy," and "this utmost ridiculous made-up language." And Oakland's resolution, almost always misunderstood as a proposal to teach Ebonics instead of as a plan to use Ebonics as a springboard to Standard English, elicited superlatives of disdain, disbelief, and derision:

"Idiocy of the highest form." (December 21, 1996)

"Man, 'ubonics will take me far back to de jungo!" (December 21, 1996)

"I think it be da dumbest thing I'd eber heard be." (December 23, 1996)

These comments, dripping with scorn, are far removed from the tributes that Brown, Baldwin, Morrison, and Jordan had paid to the African American vernacular in earlier decades. Why the about-face? What had happened to transform Spoken Soul from an object of praise to an object of ridicule?

For one thing, the focus was different. The Ebonics controversy of the 1990s was about the use of the vernacular in school, while the earlier commentaries were more about the expressiveness of the vernacular itself in literature and informal settings.

Moreover, the general misconception that the Oakland school board intended to teach and accept Ebonics rather than English in the classroom—perhaps assisted by the resolution's vague wording and the media's voracious coverage—made matters worse. Most of the fuming and fulminating about Ebonics stemmed from the mistaken belief that it was to replace Standard English as a medium of instruction and a target for success.

This misunderstanding was not new, nor was it unique to the United States. The 1979 ruling by Michigan Supreme Court justice Charles Joiner that the negative attitudes of Ann Arbor teachers toward the home language of their black students represented a barrier to the students' academic success was similarly misinterpreted as a plan "to teach ghetto children in 'black English'" (in the words of columnist Carl Rowan). And from the 1950s on, proposals by Caribbean linguists to take students' Creole English into account to improve the teaching of Standard English (in Jamaica, Trinidad, and Guyana) have been similarly misinterpreted and condemned as attempts to "settle" for Creole instead of English.

But the backlash against Ebonics in the 1990s was certainly fueled by new elements, and by considerations unique to the contemporary United States. There is more concern today about what we have in common as Americans, including English. Some who thrashed Ebonics in Internet forums voiced this concern:

> There seems to be a movement with the cultural diversity, bilingualism, and quota-oriented affirmative action campaigns to balkanize the country and build walls between people and dissolve the concept of being an American. This Ebonics . . . will . . . keep a segment of the black community in ghetto mode. (December 20, 1996)

As in this case, critiques of Ebonics were often couched in larger objections to bilingual education, affirmative action, and any measure that seemed to offer special "advantages" to ethnic minorities and women—despite the centuries of disadvantage these groups have endured. A month before Oakland passed its Ebonics resolution, Californians endorsed Proposition 209, outlawing affirmative action in education and employment, and in June 1998, they approved Proposition 227, prohibiting most forms of bilingual education. Many states passed English-only legislation in the 1980s and 1990s, and lawmakers continue to lobby for similar legislation at the federal level.

The 1990s also saw internal divisions within the African American population—by socioeconomic class, generation, and gender—grow more pronounced than they had been in the 1960s. This accounts for some of the stinging criticism of Ebonics that originated "within the race." While the 1960s featured "*The* March on Washington," a united protest by African Americans and others against racial and economic inequality, blacks in the 1990s participated in separate "Million Man" and "Million Woman" marches, and competing "Million Youth" marches. While the proportion of African Americans earning more than $100,000 (in 1989 dollars) tripled between 1969 and 1989 (from 0.3 percent to about 1 percent of all African American households), the proportion earning below $15,000 remained the same (about 43 percent of all African American households), and the mean income actually dropped in the interim (from $9,300 to $8,520). When we consider that Ebonics pronunciation and grammar are used most frequently by poor and working-class African Americans, and that it was primarily the comments of middle- and upper-middle class African Americans heard over the airwaves and read on the Internet in 1996 and 1997, their disdain is not surprising.

What's more, the distance between the younger hip-hop generation and older African American generations—marked by the politics of dress, music, and slang—has in various ways also grown more stark in the 1990s. Some middle-aged and elderly black folk have increasingly come to view baggy-jeans-and-boot-wearing, freestylin' youth as hoodlums who are squandering the gains of the civil rights movement. Not entirely coincidentally, most of the publicly aired comments on Ebonics came from black baby boomers (now in their forties and fifties) or older African Americans. When discussing the slang of hip-hop youth—which they (mis)identified with Ebonics—they often bristled with indignation. So did others, of other races, who vented their prejudices quite openly.

While today's debate is charged with new elements, the question of the role of the vernacular in African American life and literature has been a source of debate among African Americans for more than a century. When Paul Laurence Dunbar was establishing his reputation as a dialect poet in the late 1800s, James Weldon Johnson, who wrote the lyrics to "Lift Every Voice and Sing" (long hailed as "The Negro National Anthem"), chose to render the seven African American sermons of *God's Trombones* in standard English because he felt that the dialect of "old-time" preachers might pigeonhole the book. During the Harlem Renaissance of the 1920s, a similar debate raged among the black intelligentsia, with Langston Hughes endorsing and exemplifying the use of vernacular, and Alain Locke and others suggesting that African Americans ought to put the quaintness of the idiom behind them and offer the world a more "refined" view of their culture. These enduring attitudes reflect the attraction-repulsion dynamic, the oscillation between black and white (or mainstream) poles that W. E. B. Du Bois defined a century ago as "double-consciousness."

This century marks a watershed for the vernacular. One purpose of this book is to help rescue Spoken Soul from the negativity and ignorance in which it became mired during the Ebonics debate, and to correct the many misconceptions people have about black talk. Another is to offer a fresh way to think and talk about Spoken Soul that does justice to its persistence and potency.

Like virtually everyone else, we acknowledge that African Americans must master Standard English, corporate English, mainstream English, the language of wider communication, or whatever you want to call the variety of English needed for school, formal occasions, and success in the business world. But we also believe that Ebonics, African American Vernacular English, Black English, Spoken Soul, or whatever you want to call the informal variety spoken by many black people, plays an essential, valuable role in our lives and in the life of the larger society to which we all belong.

The reasons for the persistence and vitality of Spoken Soul are manifold: it marks black identity; it is the symbol of a culture and a life-style that have had and continue to have a profound impact on American popular life; it retains the associations of warmth and closeness for the many blacks who first learn it from their mothers and fathers and other family members; it expresses camaraderie and solidarity among friends; it establishes rapport among blacks; and it serves as a creative and expressive instrument in the present and as a vibrant link with this nation's past.

If we lost all of that in the heady pursuit of Standard English and the world of opportunities it offers, we would indeed have lost our soul. We are not convinced that African Americans want to abandon "down-home" speech in order to become one-dimensional speakers. Nor—to judge from the ubiquity of the distinctive linguistic style of African American music, literature, and popular culture—do whites and other people in this country and around the world want to see it abandoned either, quiet as that viewpoint is kept. Certainly it is not necessary to abandon Spoken Soul to master Standard English, any more than it is necessary to abandon English to learn French, or to deprecate jazz to appreciate classical music.

Moreover, suggesting, as some do, that we abandon Spoken Soul and cleave only to Standard English is like proposing that we play only the white keys of a piano. The fact is that for many of our most beautiful melodies, we need both the white keys and the black, in the same way that, in the Chinese dualistic philosophy, the *yin* is as essential to the whole as the *yang*. Bear in mind that language is an inescapable element in almost everyone's daily life, and an integral element of human identity. If for that and no other reason, we would all do well to heed the still-evolving truth of the black language experience. That truth promises to help us confront one of the most critical questions of our day: Can one succeed in the wider world of economic and social power without surrendering one's distinctive identity? We hope to transform the conventional wisdom.

Part Two

"This Passion, This Skill,
This Incredible Music"

2

Writers

Perhaps the proper measure of a writer's talent is skill in rendering everyday speech . . . as well as the ability to tap, to exploit, the beauty, poetry and wisdom it contains. "If you say what's on your mind in the language that comes to you from your parents and your street and your friends, you'll probably say something beautiful."

—Paule Marshall (1983)

Whereas black writers most certainly revise texts in the Western tradition, they often seek to do so "authentically," with a black difference, a compelling sense of difference based on the black vernacular.

—Henry Louis Gates Jr. (1988)

Denying or denouncing Spoken Soul requires either missing or forgetting the cadences and capabilities of the vernacular in everyday speech, and the way its "beauty, poetry and wisdom" have been tapped by black and white authors for more than two hundred years.

The earliest representations of black speech in American literature appear in the works of white writers, beginning with eighteenth-century travel books and colonial plays and novels. John Leacock's play *The Fall of British Tyranny; or, American Liberty Triumphant* was published in 1776, the year the Revolutionary War began. In the following excerpt, Cudjo, who has escaped from American slavery, is being interviewed by the Kidnapper on a ship as he and other escapees seek to enlist in the British navy.

KIDNAPPER: Very well, did you all run away from your masters?

CUDJO: Eas, massa Lord, eb'ry one, me too.

KIDNAPPER:	That's clever; they have no right to make you slaves. I wish all the Negroes would do the same, I'll make 'em free—what part did you come from?
CUDJO:	Disse brack man, disse one, disse one, disse one, disse one, come from Hamton, disse one, disse one, disse one, come from Nawfok, me come from Nawfok too.
KIDNAPPER:	Very well, what was your master's name?
CUDJO:	Me massa name Cunney Tomsee.

Derived from the West African name for a male born on Monday, "Cudjo" was a common christening for black men during the colonial period. But Cudjo's language includes several features that are either rare or nonexistent in the speech of African Americans today, such as the use of the verb *come* for past tense (instead of *came*), and the appearance of *me* as subject and possessive pronouns (instead of *I* and *my*, respectively). These patterns are more frequently found in Caribbean Creole English today.

From the 1700s to the present, a legion of white writers put African American vernacular of one variety or another in the mouths of their black characters. Included are some of the most prominent names in American literature: Edgar Allan Poe ("The Gold Bug," 1843), Herman Melville (Fleece's speech in *Moby-Dick*, 1851), Harriet Beecher Stowe (*Uncle Tom's Cabin*, 1851–1852), Joel Chandler Harris (*Uncle Remus*, 1880), Thomas Nelson Page (*In Ole Virginia*, 1887), Mark Twain (Jim's Missouri black dialect in *Huckleberry Finn*, 1885), Thomas Dixon (*The Clansman*, 1905), Margaret Mitchell (*Gone With the Wind*, 1936), and William Faulkner (*Go Down, Moses*, 1942). Some of these renditions (such as Faulkner's) have been praised for their authenticity and imaginativeness. Others (such as Page's) have been severely criticized—and continue to be criticized today—for their stereotypical representations of African Americans. We will return to the work of Harris and Page later in this chapter, because reaction to them helps explain some of the hypersensitivity to black dialect that has shaped literature and criticism in the last hundred years. But our focus will be on the use of Spoken Soul by black writers, who have deployed the idiom for a broader spectrum of purposes and in a wider array of genres (including poetry, the highest mode of self-expression).

As we consider black writers, we might begin with the question: What makes a book black? Not just black enough for a slot on the bookstore's "African American Interest" shelf, but so organically black that it bears witness to a staggering sum of experiences. How does the black author articulate his or her empathy toward these experiences? How does he or she express the marriage of suffering and celebration that binds one African American to the next? What narrative style speaks from the collective soul, amplifying the race's unique pulses and leaving its men and women wondering why they haven't heard their own splendor until just then?

In our attempt to come up with a response, we would do well to borrow Stephen Henderson's notes. Speaking of black poetry, but in terms that could apply to all black literature, Henderson, the late Howard University theorist and a leading spokesman for the Black Arts movement of the 1960s and 1970s, observed: "Whenever Black poetry is most distinctly and effectively Black, it derives its form from two basic sources: Black speech and Black music." In reference to black speech, he went on to say:

> Poets use Black speech forms consciously because they know that Black people—the mass of us—do not talk like white people. They know that despite the lies and distortions of the minstrels . . . there is a complex and rich and powerful and subtle linguistic heritage whose resources have scarcely been touched that they draw upon. . . . For there is this tradition of beautiful talk with us—this tradition of saying things beautifully even if they are ugly things. We say them in a way which takes language down to the deepest common level of our experience while hinting still at things to come. White people and many academicians call this usage slang and dialect; Black people call it Soul Talk.

Charles W. Chesnutt and Alice Walker could have hung with Henderson. Those two, along with a host of black poets, fiction writers, and playwrights spanning more than a century and a half, put this "rich and powerful and subtle linguistic heritage" in the mouths of their characters, and sometimes in their narrative text, sculpting a voice that was—in linguistic and often emotional terms—distinctively black. Of course, on the question of where and how the vernacular should appear, the top thinkers in the nation's black academy rarely harmonized, clashing anew in nearly every decade. And every writer who used the vernacular also used Standard or mainstream English. Nevertheless, almost all leading black writers have exploited or embraced the vernacular at one time or another.

The soul is their witness. Characters with names like Tea Cake, Shine, Simple, and Bigger were soul-generated in the vernacular tradition. Not unlike many real-life dialect speakers, they tended to hail from the working class and to be less "colleged" than the gentry with whom they sometimes shared plot and page. They were heroes and antiheroes, noble or wretched types who, depending on which critics you cared to listen to, shuffled or strode and backpedaled or advanced on race matters. And they turned up at every terminal in the convoy of black American literature. But why have black writers used the dialect when doing so sometimes means catching hell from critics?

For many, it has been to try to express every timbre of emotion while following the true-to-life script of the black playground and pulpit, talking with this evocative tongue, this language that traces a labyrinth of emotions. Through the years, the caravan of black storytellers who spun yarns with the vernacular did so because they acknowledged, publicly or privately, that "homely" speech patterns carried currency in their own community, as in American fiction and popular culture. As we shall see, their use of this currency was motivated by the overlapping considerations of audience, authenticity, and attitude.

Audience

For black writers looking to zero in on their community, Spoken Soul offered a conceptual code that many whites simply could not penetrate. Falling back on an old African American survival strategy, such writers packaged their work in distinctly Afro styles, establishing the principal group they wished to engage—to "conversate" with. Now black writers have mortgages, and certainly want their work to be bought and read by as broad an audience as possible. As we know, the most widely read artists of any ilk use culturally specific material to illustrate universal truths. But the most masterly African American writers of the dialect tradition kept soul people foremost in their minds and slipped them exclusive messages in their works.

Sterling A. Brown (1901–1989) was among them. A pioneering folk poet who produced verse, criticism, and anthologies, primarily in the 1930s and 1940s, Brown homed in on his audience by borrowing the characteristics of the blues. Often he would repeat the initial line of the stanza—a definitive blues feature. But Brown also adopted blues themes, giving hard life a cathartic treatment through the celebration of the melancholy. His pieces crackled with the condition of long labor, the surety of low luck, the promise of death, and the burden of racism as told by iron-forged men. His use of dialect in *Southern Road* (1932) drew praise from James Weldon Johnson, who was generally critical of dialect literature. As the editors of *The Norton Anthology of African American Literature* have noted, *Southern Road* forced Johnson "to reevaluate the place of 'the common, racy, living speech of the Negro' in literature—so much so that he finally found more to praise in Brown's dialect pieces than in the more traditional poems in the same volume." In this verse from the title piece of that collection, a chain-gang prisoner emits a "hunh" with every swing of his hammer:

> . . . White man tells me—hunh—
> Damn yo' soul;
> White man tells me—hunh—
> Damn yo' soul;
> Got no need, bebby,
> To be tole. . . .

Audiences of the time—African Americans in particular—would have been familiar with the Jim Crow policy of condemning black men to a life of servitude in chain gangs on trivial or trumped-up charges, and would have understood the prisoner's bitterness. When you already know damn well that your family's poor, splintered, and black, that the chain gang will "nevah—hunh— / Let me go," and that you're a "Po' los' boy" (revelations from the poem's other verses), your condemnation need not be verbally confirmed. The poem's gritty qualities are derived in part from the fact that, with the exception of *bebby* ("baby"), the speaker's words are all short, forceful, and monosyllabic, befitting a man engaged in hard labor. And the use of dialect helps the poem in more ways than one; the absence of the final *d* in *tole*, for example, facilitates its rhyme with the preceding *soul*.

On the outside, the poem seems a bitter acceptance of white contempt. But inwardly, it amounts to an act of rebellion, a curse of white convention. Bluesmen would not be bluesmen if they did not slyly emancipate the African American spirit with their seemingly straightforward lyrics of heartbreak, backbreak, liquor, infidelity, crime, and death. And Brown would not have been a blues poet if he had shunned the raw language of the blues, with its praise and damnation for life all wrapped up in a bent note. The "hunh" that punctuates the poem is more than an involuntary accompaniment to the prisoner's physical exertion. It's a scoff, a jeer, a private word passed between

Brown and his black reader, a remark that recalls the energetic "hunh" of black preachers at the height of their sermons and simultaneously takes a jab at the presumptions of white folks. This duality of outer and inner meaning is intrinsic to the blues and to African American speech, especially in the sayings of the elders, who have always fought covert battles from society's basement. It is "a *way* of saying" familiar to the dispossessed. Indeed, familiar to those masses magnified by Langston Hughes.

In his verses, Hughes (1902–1967) cast not the blue-veined but the grubby-palmed, not the Negro socialite but the porter or the shoeshine. Everyday people suited him fine. In turn, the masses worshipped the jazz poet (who scraped shoulders with them as a young sailor and a busboy as easily as he did as a scribe) and ultimately granted his lyrics staying power. Even today, of all the names from the Harlem Renaissance of the 1920s, his is the most familiar to the pedestrian on Martin Luther King Jr. Avenue, U.S.A.

A dashing charmer and a prodigious talent, Hughes could talk that talk. For black people his volumes still run it all down, from the deferred dreams to the jubilees. Of course, many of his most recited pieces, such as "The Negro Speaks of Rivers," were fashioned in Standard English. But he often used the vernacular to bear witness that life for the black masses "ain't been no crystal stair." In 1920 he wrote "Mother to Son," one of his most beloved poems, and one that, as an African American journalist recently put it, would not feel the same in Standard English:

> Well, son, I'll tell you:
> Life for me ain't been no crystal stair.
> It's had tacks in it,
> And splinters,
> And boards torn up,
> And places with no carpet on the floor—
> Bare.
> But all the time
> I'se been a-climbin' on,
> And reachin' landin's,
> And turnin' corners,
> And sometimes going in the dark
> Where there ain't been no light. . . .

As his biographer Arnold Rampersad has noted, Hughes's dialect in this poem "allows a humble black woman—and through her all black women—to speak nobly." The overall effect stems from the sustained metaphor of the woman's upward movement on the staircase, despite its tacks and splinters, from the warm conversational tone ("Well, son, I'll tell you") with which she conveys her combination of admonition and encouragement, and from the simple words and phrases (often beginning with "and") that frame her message. Although the immediate audience of the poem is the woman's son, Hughes is speaking for all oppressed people who have overcome daunting circumstances, and to their progeny, male and female, who similarly must learn to persevere and triumph.

Unlike many dialect writers of the nineteenth century, Hughes is sparing in his representation of black pronunciation ("climbing," "reaching," and "turning" are represented as *climbin'*, *reachin'*, and *turnin'*; but "and" is not *an'*, "with" is not *wid*, and "boards" is not *boa'ds*). Thus the poem is easier for readers to follow. The powerful black vernacular effect comes almost entirely from grammatical features, sparingly and skillfully deployed: *ain't* for "hasn't," the double negative (*ain't been no light*), and a few cases of nonstandard verb agreement—*you finds* instead of "you find" (in a line not quoted here) and *I'se* instead of "I'm." Unless it represents contemporary usage that has since vanished, however, the use of *I'se* for "I've" may have been a convention of dialect writing rather than an accurate depiction. We find similar examples in the work of some nineteenth- and early-twentieth-century writers, but *I'se* is not heard today. Even the most pronounced soul speakers regularly use the contracted "I've."

In black speech, cadence is as crucial to meaning as the words themselves. The rhythm, inflection, and rhetorical style are organic to the message, the clues that the speaker provides as to his or her mood and the nature of his or her relationship with the audience. Such is the case with "Queens of the Universe" (1971), an anthem by poet-activist Sonia Sanchez (b. 1934), part of which is reprinted here:

Sisters.
    i saw it to
         day. with
My own eyes.
       i mean like i
got on this bus
      this cracker wuz
driving saw him look/
        sniff a certain
smell and
    turn his head in disgust.

```
sisters.
        that queen of sheba
                perfume wuz
doooooooing it.
                strong/
                    blk/
                        smell that it
    be. i mean
            it ain't delicate/stuff
    sisters.
            when u put it on
                u be knowing it on. . . .
```

For a poem that likens black womanhood to an overwhelming essence, that declares it hip to shun white sensibilities and aesthetics, the swaying tempo fits. One can almost envision the speaker strutting through the bus. There is no question of the intended audience here, and not just because Sanchez comes right out and addresses the sisters. It is the peculiar arrangement of the phrases that gives the verse hips. But it is the extension of the vowel in "doooooooing it" that calls to mind the singsong intonation of a black woman in diva mode. (Recall Don Lee's use of "wooooooooooowe" in "Move Un-Noticed to Be Noticed: A Nationhood Poem.") It is the use of the habitual *be* in "strong/ / blk/ / smell that it / be" that punctuates that strong black smell, adding a consonant stress exuding more attitude than the phrase's mainstream version, "strong black smell that it regularly is." With the line "u be knowing it on," Sanchez makes political use of that *be* once again, signaling pride in the tense-aspect marker *be* and in her people. The versatile word is used here as an appendage, almost like an Afro. But in a deeper sense, it is an affirmation of truths familiar only to those within the double circles of womanhood and blackness. It is an acknowledgment of the shared condition of race (as in, "It *bees* that way sometimes"), and a deliberate signpost of blackness (as in, "How you *be*, sis?").

Sanchez wrote many poems in the vernacular. But when it came to black prose writers, the vernacular was restricted largely to dialogue. This was true of William Wells Brown, who is credited with the first African American novel (*Clotel; or, The President's Daughter,* 1853), and it has been true of virtually all biographers and fiction writers since, including Claude Brown (b. 1937), Mr. "Spoken Soul" himself. In this excerpt from his autobiographical *Manchild in the Promised*

Land (1965), the author/protagonist's parents delete *is* (*he gittin'*), use the double negative, and begin emphatic statements with an inverted *can't*—demonstrating that contrary to the media's misconceptions during the Ebonics controversy, black vernacular usage has never been limited to teenagers or "gangbangers":

> Mama started crying more and saying, "He'll be eleven years old soon, and he gittin' into that shit already."
> Dad said, "Can't nothin' real bad happen before he gits thirteen or fourteen."

The tradition of reserving English for narration and Spoken Soul for dialogue extends even to novels of the 1990s, including the crime fiction of Walter Mosley (b. 1952). In this excerpt from *Devil in a Blue Dress* (1990), the narrator/protagonist comments overtly on the expressiveness of his own dialect, but it is a variety marked primarily by a few pronunciation features (*smilin'*, *front'a*) and vernacular words (*got* for "has," for instance):

> Joppy turned his jagged lips into a frown. "Naw, he must'a come after my time."
> "Yeah, well, Mouse is a lot like Mr. Albright. He's smooth and a natty dresser and he's smilin' all the time. But he always got his business in the front'a his mind, and if you get in the way you might come to no good." I always tried to speak proper English in my life, the kind of English they taught in school, but I found over the years that I could only truly express myself in the natural, "uneducated" dialect of my upbringing.

In a few striking cases, however, black fiction writers have extended the vernacular to narrative text. One of the earliest examples is "Tell Martha Not to Moan," a short story written in 1967 by Sherley Anne Williams (b. 1944), which begins:

> My mamma is a big woman, tall and stout, and men like her cause she soft and fluffy-looking. When she round them it all smiles and dimples and her mouth be looking like it couldn't never be fixed to say nothing but darling and honey.

Close on Williams's heels, June Jordan, whose essays have recorded her high regard for Black English, wrote the first novel entirely in the black vernacular (*His Own Where,* 1971). As in most twentieth-century writing, the effect is carried by the grammar, including unmarked present- and past-tense verbs, and invariant *be* (see chapters 6 and 7 for discussion of linguistic terms that appear in this chapter):

> First time they come, he simply say, "Come on." He tell her they are going not too far away. She go along not worrying about the heelstrap pinching at her skin, but worrying about the conversation. Long walks take some talking. Otherwise it be embarrassing just side by side embarrassing.

Jordan was criticized by some for her extensive use of the vernacular in this novel, especially since it was intended for young readers. But *His Own Where* won her a National Book Award nomination. As Paul Stoller noted, "Jordan shows us that stigmatized varieties of Black English can be poetic, artistic, and moving in a work of fiction."

The autobiographical *Brothers and Keepers* (1984), by John Edgar Wideman (b. 1941), also employs African American English in the narrative text. But the best-known black novel written entirely in the vernacular is *The Color Purple* (1982), which earned its author, Alice Walker (b. 1944), a Pulitzer Prize. As in the works by Williams, Jordan, and Wideman, the vernacular effect is carried by the grammar, including omitted *is (My mama dead)*, unmarked past tense (*die, scream*), double negatives (*don't say nothing*) and invariant *be:*

> My mama dead. She die screaming and cussing. She scream at me. She cuss at me. I'm big. I can't move fast enough. By time I git back from the well, the water be warm. By time I git the tray ready the food be cold. By time I git all the children ready for school it be dinner time. He don't say nothing. He set there by the bed holding her hand an cryin, talking bout don't leave me, don't go. She ast me bout the first one. Whose it is? I say God's. I don't know no other man or what else to say.

The virtually uninterrupted vernacular flow in this novel (found in letters the protagonist, Celie, writes to God and a sister) is particularly effective. By letting Celie recount her experiences in what Stephen Henderson called the "language of feeling," Walker allows her black readers in particular to develop an emotional kinship with the testimony. Walker might have reasoned correctly that they who speak dialect think and dream dialect, too. This rule holds firm in Ntozake Shange's (b. 1948) *for colored girls who have considered suicide / when the rainbow is enuf* (1975), a "choreopoem" in which the artist's stream-of-consciousness technique gets a boost from the lexicon, the unique words, of African American English:

i got drunk & cdnt figure out
whose hand waz on my thigh / but it didn't matter
cuz these cousins martin eddie sammy jerome & bobby
waz my sweethearts alternately since the seventh grade
& everybody knew i always started cryin if somebody actually
tried to take advantage of me
    at jacqui's
ulinda mason was stickin her mouth all out
while we tumbled out the buick
eddie jones waz her lickin stick
but i knew how to dance
    it got soo hot
vincent ramos puked all in the punch
& harly jumped all in tico's face
cuz he was leavin for the navy in the mornin
hadda kick ass so we'd all remember how bad he waz
seems like sheila and marguerite waz fraid
to get their hair turnin back
so they laid up against the wall
lookin almost sexy
didn't wanna sweat
but me & my fellas
      we waz dancin . . .

In this excerpt from Shange's prose poem turned play, the most obvious evidence of audience is vocabulary. References to a *lickin stick* (a dance partner), *jumped all in tico's face* (confronted him), *their hair turnin back* (the wilting and frizzing of black women's straightened hair as their flattened natural coil reacts to the shock of dampness), all expose Shange's desire to engage a specific in-group. There is also some "eye dialect"—spellings such as *cdn't* and *waz*, which don't convey pronunciations different from "couldn't" and "was," but contribute to the impression of vernacular usage. The parlance of black teenagers relays the narrator's experiences effectively. But we must not overlook the *connotation* of the language; the expressed slickness of the joint and the youth trying to be "down" with the scene and the sexual tension and the violent possibility. These ideas don't always translate directly into the language of the white prom going on across town.

Authenticity

Authenticity in African American art and life is paramount. Within hip-hop circles, the mantra is "keep it real," but the same notion exists wherever black people meet. For a people who have been imitated and crossed over and sold out so relentlessly, authenticity is the highly valued sense of what is genuine. It is a question of privilege and access, the password uttered at the door to all that is soulful. And it poses an especially daunting challenge for the black writer. If members of the African American community are to consider a narrative legitimately homespun, they must recognize its origins. Here again, the vernacular can be an invaluable commodity.

It has been observed that the artist creates most poignantly when tapping the wellspring of his or her most intimate memories. Relics from the "oral world" of the African or African American child—phrases, axioms, toasts, boasts, tall tales, prayers—become ore in the imagination of the grown-up author. When the author bores into this source, what often issues forth is the most organic language, the language the author's mother used when scolding or cooing. So Zora Neale Hurston (1891–1960), born in the black township of Eatonville, Florida, must have enjoyed a knowing chuckle when she typed expressions such as these into the pages of her novel *Their Eyes Were Watching God* (1937):

> Ah yeah, she's too smart tuh stay round heah. She figgers we'se jus' uh bunch uh dumb niggers so she think she'll grow horns. But dat's uh lie. She'll die butt-headed.

Such colloquialisms might have swirled about Hurston in the household of her girlhood. Once grown, the accomplished folklorist and anthropologist draped her dialogue with the peculiarities and syntax of black small-town southern living. As Henry Louis Gates Jr. has noted about Hurston and Sterling Brown, "two of the truly great minds of 'the race,'" their

> reverence for the black vernacular and their use of it as the touchstone for rhetorical excellence provide critical models that I have tried to imitate, even if the critical language that I employ might seem to be a different language.

Elsewhere in *Their Eyes*, Hurston's sprite heroine, Janie—ever refusing to live under the heels of men—returns with a wicked tongue an insult her partner, Joe Starks, has hurled at her:

> Naw, Ah ain't no young gal no mo' but den Ah ain't no old woman neither. Ah reckon Ah looks mah age too. But Ah'm uh woman every inch of me, and Ah know it. Dat's a whole lot more'n *you* kin say. You big-bellies round here and put out a lot of brag, but 'tain't nothin' to

it but yo' big voice. Humph! Talkin' 'bout *me* lookin' old! When you pull down yo' britches, you look lak de change uh life.

Besides its deftly timed delivery of Spoken Soul—conveyed primarily through pronunciation spellings (*mo* for "more" and *Ah* for "I") and eye dialect (*uh* for "a")—what makes this passage so convincing is its nod to that ancient African American ritual of putdown swapping known variously as sounding, signifying, capping, snapping, or "playing the dozens." To play, opponents try to outdo each other in a lavishly styled, highly social, lightning-quick display of verbal prowess and improvisation. Hurston's characters observe such rituals again and again as they travel from page to page, lending an authoritative voice to the plot and revealing the author's familiarity with black rhetorical and speech-event traditions.

Hurston's love affair with black speech extended to a passion for black folktales. In many respects the precursors to African American literature, black folktales have always achieved their most memorable recital (and conveyed their most profound message) when delivered with the dramatic inflections of dialect. Daryl Cumber Dance, a leading authority on black folklore, observed as much in the introduction to her anthology of black folklore:

> It is important to note that practically all the jokes included here were delivered in dialect. Even the most sophisticated joke tellers usually revert to dialect in close company. Indeed the tales lose much of their flavor in standard English. As Chapman J. Milling aptly averred, "a Negro story not told in Negro dialect is about as successful as a honeymoon shared by the mother-in-law."

Passed on through generations from elders—descendants of African griots who held the wisdom of nations on their tongues—to youngsters, the various genres of African American folklore serve both to entertain and educate. Decidedly in the entertainment category is this "lie," or tall tale, narrated in 1970 by Walter Simmons, a Baptist deacon from Daufuskie Island, South Carolina, whose powerful prayer is featured in chapter 3. The Gullah roots of the tale are evident in his Creole pronunciations, and in many grammatical features, including the use of *dem* for "those" ("*dem* road," "*dem* wedge"), the occasional use of *um* for "it" ("keep *um* from rollin down"), the use of unstressed *been* for "was" or "were" ("dey *been* bout five thousan people *been* dere"), and the fact that virtually every past-tense verb apart from *was* and *had* is unmarked (*see, grow, roll*):

I see a man raise a watermelon once. Dis watermelon was on a hill, was on de side of a hill, you know, an dey had—just like you gone up on de mountain an had dem road, road on de side of de mountain—it was on de hill, like dat. An dat watermelon grow so large until dey—he roll it up on de side dere in a low place, an been usin it fuh a BRIDGE! People useta come by from everywhere to look at dat watermelon. It was growin so large, until it grow so high until cars couldn't even much go OVUH de bridge! An dey had to—every two or three days dey had to put another wedge on de side of um to keep um from rollin down, you know. An dey been bout five thousan people been dere been lookin at dat melon dat Friday aftanoon. An one of dem wedge slip out, an dat melon start down de hill. An when it strike itself in front of dem rock, it break in half, an de water come out of um drowned over five hundred head o' people.

Walter Simmons is obviously taken with his story, displaying an acute enjoyment in the telling, in the setting up of the drama, and in the satisfying culmination. Note that although this "lie" deals with a watermelon, it has nothing to do with watermelon eating, the ubiquitous black stereotype. The watermelon is, in fact, merely a stage prop for the storyteller's clever exaggerations, piled one on top of another in his deadpan vernacular as his audience expresses mock amazement and rolls with laughter.

Intrinsic to the authenticity of many folk-tale genres is the dialogue between two or more characters, usually rendered in the vernacular. A compelling example of this is children's jump-rope rhymes, which often have the call-and-response structure prevalent in the African American church, in African American music, and in many other aspects of African American performance. The following passage from a jump-rope rhyme, "Aunt Dinah Died," was recorded in Alcoa, Tennessee. Note the use of unmarked *die* for "died," *wear* for "wears," and the omission of *is* in *where she living* and elsewhere:

CALL:	Aunt Dinah died.
RESPONSE:	How she die?
CALL:	Oh, she die like this. (*Does expression and gesture.*)
RESPONSE:	Oh, she die like this!
CALL:	(*excited*) Aunt Dinah's living!
RESPONSE:	Where she living?
ALL:	(*fast*) Oh, she living in a place called Tennessee. She wear short, short dresses up above her knees. She gon' shake that shimmy wherever she go.

Of course, drama is the genre in which dialogue reigns, and plays involving African American characters seem almost to demand authenticity in the form of black vernacular conversation. James Baldwin (1924–1987), one of the most clairvoyant American writers of the twentieth century, penned the essays in *The Fire Next Time* (1963) in artful, incisive Standard English. But to render the dialogue of African Americans in his novels, short stories, and plays, he often chose artful, incisive Black English. This is from his 1964 play *Blues for Mister Charlie:*

PETE: Old Papa D. got something on everybody, don't he?

JUANITA: You better believe it.

RICHARD: He's kind of a Tom, ain't he?

PETE: Yeah. He *talks* about Mister Charlie and he *says* he's with us—us kids—but he ain't going to do nothing to offend him. You know, he's still trading with Lyle Britten?

RICHARD: Who's Lyle Britten?

PETE: Peckerwood, owns a store nearby. And, man, you ain't *seen* a peckerwood until you've seen Lyle Britten. Niggers been trading in his store for years, man, I wouldn't be surprised but if the cat was rich—but that man still expects you to step off the sidewalk when he comes along. So we been getting people to stop buying there.

JUANITA: He shot a colored man a few years back, shot him dead, and wasn't nothing never said, much less done, about it.

In a 1997 article about the Ebonics controversy, Christopher Hitchens, recalling an essay Baldwin wrote in praise of Black English, contended that the writer had defended a "language he didn't speak," as "a duty paid to history." But the Standard English that Baldwin commanded in speech and in prose may well have deceived Hitchens. After all, what's to say Baldwin didn't demonstrate an equally impressive command of the vernacular when he was hanging with his peers? Indeed, given the fact that Baldwin grew up a poor, black Harlemite, it's a safe bet that he could probably deploy some pretty bad jive. Not even nine years in France (1948–1957) could have eroded that competence, which is evident in the vocabulary of the passage (*got* for "has"; *Tom* for "black sellout"; *Mister Charlie* and *peckerwood* for "white man") as well as its grammar. Notice, in addition to linguistic features such as *ain't* and *been* (used here as an equivalent to "have been") and the double negative ("he *ain't* going to do *nothing*"), Baldwin's use of the inverted double negative in "*wasn't nothing* never said" (versus "nothing wasn't never said").

The vernacular also runs throughout the play *A Raisin in the Sun,* by Lorraine Hansberry (1930–1965). This masterpiece, awarded the New York Drama Critics Circle Award for Best Play of 1959, ran for 538 performances on Broadway, and was the longest-running Broadway production by an African American in its time. The opening sentence of the following passage rings as true to the voice of the vernacular today as it did forty years ago, and the grammatical features after it (including *ain't,* and the absence of *are* in *We just plain working folks*) further reinforce this timbre:

MAMA: Now don't you start, child. It's too early in the morning to be talking about money. It ain't Christian.

RUTH: It's just that he got his heart set on that store—

MAMA: You mean that liquor store that Willie Harris want him to invest in?

RUTH: Yes—

MAMA: We ain't no business people, Ruth. We just plain working folks.

RUTH: Ain't nobody business people till they go into business. . . .

August Wilson (b. 1945), whose 1986 play *Fences* won four Tony Awards and a Pulitzer Prize, has provided some of the most credible depictions of black characters in American drama. Wilson deploys a battery of grammatical vernacular features, including completive *done* ("they *done* trumped") and habitual *be* ("he *be* making out"):

BONO: I told Brownie if the man come and ask him any questions . . . just tell the truth! It ain't nothing but something they done trumped up on you 'cause you filed a complaint on them.

TROY: Brownie don't understand nothing. All I want them to do is change the job description. Give everybody a chance to drive the truck. Brownie can't see that. He ain't got that much sense.

BONO: How you figure he be making out with that gal be up at Taylor's all the time . . . that Alberta gal?

In an interview with John Rickford, Wilson explained that while he "values and respects the way that black people talk," when he first tried to write plays, in the early 1980s, he thought that "in order to create art out of it you have to change it." So he would put high-flown language in the mouths of his characters: "Terror hangs over the night like a hawk." In a 1996 article in *People,* he was quoted as saying, "Back then I didn't value and respect the way blacks talked—the everyday poetry of the people I'd grown up with." But then, as he testified in 1999, his feelings changed:

> I was reading a pamphlet by Sekou Touré called "The Artisans and Not the Political Leaders are Representative of the Culture." In that pamphlet he says, "Language describes the ideas of the one who speaks it." It's a very simple and profound statement. Stayed with me, and I began to think about it and analyze it: "Language describes the ideas of the one who speaks it." So there's really nothing wrong with the way that people talk. That is their language and it's describing their ideas. Language describing the ideas is a thought process also; you talk how you think. Once I put those two things together, I said, "Oh, I see, art is within the language of the people. You don't have to change it." . . . Before, [when] I'd try to write, the characters wouldn't sound right. It was stilted, it was stiff, it didn't work. 'Cause I was trying to change it instead of letting it be its own thing. Once I decided to just let it be its own thing, then the characters started talking, and I was writing it down, couldn't shut 'em up. Whereas before, I had trouble writing a dialogue, now it was easy, it flowed because I accepted it.

When asked whether the soulful speech patterns in his plays were relics from his childhood in Pittsburgh, or gems picked up later from observation and listening, Wilson went on to say that the language

> was just in the air. All the people in the neighborhood where I grew up, that's the way they talked. [In Pittsburgh] I spent a large amount of time in a cigar store where the elderly men from the neighborhood would congregate. And they'd sit around there and they'd talk all kinds of stuff and I'd stand there and listen to 'em. There's a lot of this, that's the way they talk: "Yes, I come up, yeah, I come ta Pittsburgh in 'forty-two. Come on da B&O Railroad." "No you ain't!" "You gon tell me . . . ?" "Yeah, hell, yeah, I'm gon tell you, too, 'cause B&O railroad didn' stop in Pittsburgh! B&O Railroad had four stops an' it ain't through heah!" So everybody that came in: "Ey, ey, ey ey, Joe, ey, Fillmore, come on, man. Man talkin', talkin' 'bout how he come up on the B&O Railroad in 'forty-two. Stopped at so-an'-so an' so-an'-so an' so-an'-so." This stuff could go on for two weeks. I found it fascinating.

Wilson's remarks reveal not only that he has a keen ear, but also that he enjoys the vibrant give-and-take of colloquial conversation. His ability to re-create and evoke the beauty, poetry, and wisdom of everyday black speech is a key element in his plays' authenticity and power.

Attitude

Wilson's deployment of Spoken Soul reveals his love for it, and his respect for its speakers. But not every work that employs the vernacular conveys equally positive attitudes, In fact, to trace the origins of some of the widespread condemnation Ebonics received during the 1990s, particularly among African Americans, we must go back more than a century, to the minstrel tradition that was popular in the United States between about 1840 and 1900. As Sylvia Wallace Holton, a professor of English, has noted:

> The minstrel show may have originated on the plantation, first as a means of entertainment by the slaves for themselves and later as a more stylized performance for their masters and their guests. . . . Whatever its origin, it developed rapidly into a ritualized three-part form performed by white men in black face [using grease or burnt cork] to burlesque the black. The image of the black man that grew out of the minstrel show, which became confused with reality in the minds of many Americans, was of a carefree entertainer who could sing about jumping Jim Crow. . . .

The minstrel tradition was infamous for reinforcing demeaning stereotypes of African Americans—as comical, childlike, gullible, lazy, and in the words of Nathan Huggins, "unrestrained in enthusiasm for music—for athletic and rhythmical dance" and "insatiable in . . . bodily appetite." These stereotypes were conveyed in part by a highly conventionalized "Negro dialect" used by the minstrel performers, as in this example in which *am* is used instead of "is"—a peculiarity one didn't hear in black speech of the time, and doesn't hear today:

END: Mr. Cleveland, a fellow was trying to stuff me dat when it am day here it am night in China.

MID: Well, James, that is true.

END: What makes it true?

MID: It is caused by the earth rotating on its axis, but—

END: What am an axis?

Zora Neale Hurston complained in 1934 about the inaccuracy of the dialect in minstrel shows and dialect literature ("If we are to believe the majority of writers of Negro dialect and the burnt-cork artists, Negro speech is a weird thing, full of 'ams' and 'Ises.' . . . Nowhere can be found the Negro who asks 'am it?' nor yet his brother who announces 'Ise uh gwinter' "). Black lawyer, poet, and novelist James Weldon Johnson (1871–1938) voiced in 1933 a more fundamental objection to it, as an instrument so fused to stereotype that it had become a limiting, insurmountable mold:

> I got a sudden realization of the artificiality of conventionalized Negro dialect poetry; of its exaggerated geniality, childish optimism, forced comicality, and mawkish sentiment; of its limitation as an instrument of expression to but two emotions, pathos and humor, thereby making every poem either only sad or funny. I saw that not even Dunbar had been able to break the mold in which dialect poetry had, long before him, been set by representations made of the Negro on the minstrel stage. I saw that he had cut away much of what was coarse and "niggerish," and added a deeper tenderness, a higher polish, a more delicate finish; but also I saw that, nevertheless, practically all of his work in dialect fitted into the traditional mold.

African Americans who resented the prominence bestowed on Ebonics by the 1996 Oakland resolution may have feared a resurrection of some of the vile stereotypes of the minstrel show and the "Negro dialect" tradition of a century before. Ebonics humor (see chapter 11) showed us that such fears were not entirely unfounded.

A century ago, James Weldon Johnson noted perceptibly that the writer working in the dialect conventions of the time was dominated by his white audience, and that "when he wrote he was expressing what often bore little relation at all, to actual Negro life; that he was really expressing only certain conceptions about Negro life that his audience was willing to accept and ready to enjoy." He contrasted this "outside group" orientation with the inward orientations of folk artists: "The latter, although working in the dialect, sought only to express themselves for themselves, and to their *own group*" (emphasis in original).

Not only were nineteenth-century minstrel shows and books containing black dialect intended mainly for white audiences, they also were dominated by white performers and writers. Indeed, the granddaddies of vernacular literature—Joel Chandler Harris and Thomas Nelson Page—were white. Harris, who "played minstrelsy" in his youth, concocted the popular Uncle Remus (*Uncle Remus: His Songs and His Sayings*, 1880), a character who held up all the old stereotypes and who was enormously popular with whites, including President Theodore Roosevelt. Uncle Remus became the star of Walt Disney's Oscar-winning 1946 movie *Song of the South,* a box-office hit until it was withdrawn in the 1960s amid criticism that it perpetuated black stereotypes. Remus, a benign plantation figure, recited tales from the African American tradition for the amusement of a seven-year-old white boy. The first tale in the book, "Uncle Remus Initiates the Little Boy," opens as follows:

> One evening recently, the lady whom Uncle Remus calls "Miss Sally" missed her seven-year-old. Making search for him through the house and through the yard, she heard the sound of voices in the old man's cabin, and looking through the window, saw the child sitting by Uncle Remus. His head rested against the old man's arm, and he was gazing with an expression of the most intense interest into the rough, weather-beaten face, that beamed so kindly upon him. This is what "Miss Sally" heard:
>
> "Bimeby, one day, arter Brer Fox bin doin' all dat he could fer ter ketch Brer Rabbit, en Brer Rabbit bin doin' all he could fer ter keep 'im fum it, Brer Fox say to hisse'f dat he'd put up a game on Brer Rabbit, en he ain't mo'n got de wuds out'n his mouf twel Brer Rabbit come a lopin' up de big road, lookin' des ez plump, en ez fat, en ez sassy ez a Moggin hoss in a barley-patch.
>
> "'Hol' on dar, Brer Rabbit,' sez Brer Fox, sezee. . . ."

Harris has been praised by several generations of scholars for the accuracy of the copiously represented middle Georgia dialect spoken by Uncle Remus. The author has also been credited for his folkloric recording of the Brer Rabbit genre of African American folklore, with its roots in the African trickster tradition, and its invaluable survival lessons for slaves and ex-slaves. But he has also been criticized for his portrayal of Uncle Remus as a doddling, genial throwback to a romanticized period in which whites owned slaves and plantations prospered. As critic Robert Hemenway has noted, linking the Remus stereotype and his language:

> Uncle Remus, an "old time Negro," reminds Southerners of what was "good" about slavery, becoming a wish-fulfillment fantasy for a populace forced to deal each day with black people considerably less docile than the plantation darky. Remus's dialect especially supports this fantasy. The Standard English used by the author to frame the tales contrasts with the vivid dialect in the stories themselves, suggesting that black language is colorful but ignorant, that black people are picturesque but intellectually limited.

Thomas Nelson Page published his collection of dialect stories *In Ole Virginia* in 1887, seven years after Uncle Remus first appeared.

Page is usually hailed as an able chronicler of contemporary eastern Virginia black dialect. But as Sylvia Wallace Horton has noted, Page's representation "is similar to much nineteenth-century dialect writing in that it seems to be bent on representing black speech as 'special' and on suggesting the 'illiteracy' of the black speaker—on eliciting from the reader a patronizing attitude rather than one of empathy." Page's stories generally depicted slaves who were content with their lot and happy to serve their white masters. In this passage from "Marse Chan," Sam, an old black man, bemoans the good old plantation days:

> "Well, when Marse Chan wuz born, dey wuz de grettes' doin's at home you ever did see. De folks all hed holiday, jes' like in de Chris'mas. Ole marster . . . his face fyar shine wid pleasure, and all de folks wuz mighty glad, too, 'cause dey loved ole marster. . . ."

The Clansman (1905), by white novelist Thomas Dixon Jr. (1864–1946), shored up the stereotype Page and other dialect writers had constructed. In one scene of the book, which was billed as an "historical romance of the Ku Klux Klan," a former slave reacts violently to a white northerner's suggestion that he turn on his "ole marster," exclaiming: "Den take dat f'um yo' equal, d—m you! . . . I'll show you how to treat my ole marster, you low-down slue-footed devil!"

As the early decades of the twentieth century clanged to life, black intellectuals increasingly expressed intolerance for such portrayals, and began to prod their own writers to combat old-school images with a new breed of unapologetic, nationalist rhetoric (laid down in Standard English). Black philosopher and critic Alain Locke (1886–1954), a helmsman of the movement, called in the 1920s for African Americans to shed the worn, sentimental skin they had been assigned in the South and subscribe to the boldly independent and refined black spirit then developing in northern cities. He christened the creature produced by this metamorphosis the New Negro. For Locke, whose influence among black intellectuals cannot be overstated, the peddling of dialect by black authors signaled a backslide to the thinking of yesteryear: a return, essentially, to the sensibilities of the Old Negro beloved by Harris, Page, and Dixon. Locke once observed that "the soul of the Negro will be discovered in a characteristic way of thinking and in a homely philosophy rather than in a jingling and juggling of broken English," using words clearly reminiscent of Dunbar's famous lament about dialect poetry, "The Poet."

But other black writers refused to shun the speech of the black masses just because outsiders had misrepresented it. Ever vivacious and perhaps even scandalously outspoken for a woman of her time, Zora Neale Hurston was disgusted by the mere idea, which she said had sprung from the snobbish Negroes she tauntingly dubbed the "Niggerati." She and Langston Hughes, a contemporary and onetime friend, believed that the dialect best signified the black proletariat, the common folk whose stories they endeavored to tell truthfully. In his 1940 autobiography, *The Big Sea*, Hughes squared off with renowned black critics such as Benjamin Brawley and prominent newspaper reviewers who had skewered his second collection of poetry, *Fine Clothes to the Jew*, as "a disgrace to the race, a return to the dialect tradition, and a parading of all our racial defects before the public." Hughes seemed surprised and hurt by the whipping the publication received at the hands of black scholars. After all, weren't the verses true to the roustabouts and the down-and-out blacks who thronged New York City's Lenox Avenue? To those who would have had him stick to upscale Standard English, which he labeled an "un-Negro tongue," Hughes offered this defense:

> Anyway, I didn't know the upper class Negroes well enough to write much about them. I knew only the people I had grown up with, and they weren't people whose shoes were always shined, who had been to Harvard, or who had heard of Bach. But they seemed to me good people, too.

Nevertheless, Hughes acknowledged the minstrel legacy. He understood why black intellectuals, as he put it, wanted to extend to society the race's "politely polished and cultural foot" and parade "not-funny Negroes" before white spectators. But it was a compromise he would not make. Hughes believed that if the Harlem Renaissance was to be a true incubator for self-examination, for rooting out that which was organically African American, for establishing an aesthetic apart from the whims and history of Europeans, then language—the ultimate conduit of culture—had to be given its due.

He had allies. In 1928, the Jamaican-born poet and novelist Claude McKay (1889–1948) published *Home to Harlem*, the first best-selling book by an African American. McKay is often remembered for his sonnets, such as the militant "If We Must Die" (1919), which Winston Churchill later used to rouse England's wartime patriotism. That often quoted poem was delivered in Standard English. But *Home to Harlem*—whose title suggests a return to familial and domestic conventions—was loaded with vernacular dialogue. This was true as well of *The Walls of Jericho,* published also in 1928, by the black physician, fiction writer, and musical arranger Rudolph Fisher (1897–1934). Fisher's book included a ten-page glossary of "Contemporary Harlemese," with terms such as *Boogy* ("Negro. A contraction of Booker T., used only of and by members of the race") and *Mr. Charlie* ("Nonspecific designation of 'swell' whites").

Even before Hughes and Hurston, McKay and Fisher, however, Paul Laurence Dunbar (1872–1906), the first African American poet of national prominence and the dean of the early black-dialect writers, had been taking on genuine African American themes in this medium. In "When Malindy Sings" (1895), for instance, the poet chides his master's "missus," whose croak cannot match his mother's croon:

> G'way an' quit dat noise, Miss Lucy—
> > Put dat music book away;
> What's de use to keep on tryin'?
> Ef you practise twell you're gray,
> You cain't sta't no notes a-flyin'
> > Lak de ones dat rants and rings
> > F'om de kitchen to de big woods
> > When Malindy sings.

Dunbar received stinging criticism in his time for calling up nostalgic images of slavery in some of his poems (such as "The Deserted Plantation," in which a former slave laments the ruin of a glorious plantation). But "When Malindy Sings" does have undercurrents of political awareness. Though its mood is light, its motive is the poet's admiration for the charms of his mother over those of his missus. In praising his mother, he testifies not only to her superior singing voice, but also to her superior graces. The black woman, regarded by whites during slavery as an animal for breeding and portrayed as indelicate and unattractive long after emancipation, is thus elevated over a white woman, the mythical creature blacks had been programmed to worship as the archetype of femininity and beauty.

Dunbar's relationship with dialect was a complex affair, though. He was the master of the dialect genre, and stretched to his colossal stature on the shoulders of the idiom. As he told his contemporary and disciple James Weldon Johnson, he wrote black dialect "as well [as], if not better than, anybody else." Johnson agreed, noting that Dunbar "had carried dialect poetry as far as and as high as it could go," and "had brought it to the fullest measure of charm, tenderness, and beauty it could hold." At the same time, Dunbar was frustrated that while the dialect poetry gained him a hearing, "now they don't want me to write anything but dialect." He was especially frustrated that the many fine poems he wrote in Standard English (among them "Sympathy" and "We Wear the Mask") were not accorded the same recognition by white audiences and the literary world as his dialect pieces. In "The Poet," he expressed this frustration, deploying the word ("jingle") that would be used by other black writers (Locke and Johnson, for instance) to disparage dialect poetry.

> He sang of life, serenely sweet,
> With, now and then, a deeper note.
> From some high peak, nigh yet remote,
> He voiced the world's absorbing heat.
>
> He sang of love when earth was young,
> And Love, itself, was in his lays.
> But ah, the world, it turned to praise
> A jingle in a broken tongue.

Dunbar was only one of many black writers and laymen to display an attraction-repulsion relationship with the black vernacular. James Weldon Johnson, whose works include the black national anthem "Lift Every Voice and Sing" (1900) and *The Autobiography of an Ex-Coloured Man* (1912), began by writing dialect poems "after the style of Dunbar," such as the mournful "Sence You Went Away" (1900), with which he opened a section entitled "Jingles and Croons":

> Seems lak to me de stars don't shine so bright,
> Seems lak to me de sun done loss his light,
> Seems lak to me der's nothin' goin' right,
> Sence you went away.

In his preface to the first edition of *The Book of American Negro Poetry* (1922), Johnson not only praised Dunbar's dialect poetry, but said more generally:

> It would be a distinct loss if the American Negro poets threw away this quaint and musical folk speech as a medium of expression. . . . They are trying to break away from, not Negro dialect itself, but the limitations on Negro dialect imposed by the fixing effects of long convention.

Here he struck a hopeful note for the future of dialect poetry, drawing a conscious distinction between the merits of the vernacular and the curse placed on it by the nineteenth-century minstrel and literary tradition. But in the anthology's revised 1931 edition, Johnson not only nixed a dialect section entitled "Jingles and Croons" (according to Sterling Brown), but was extremely pessimistic about the potential of dialect poetry, observing that "it is now realized both by the poets and by their public that as an instrument for poetry the dialect has only two main stops, humor and pathos." In the preface to *God's Trombones* (1927), a collection of "Negro folk sermons in verse," Johnson explained why he had once again favored Standard English over the vernacular:

> At first thought, Negro dialect would appear to be the precise medium for these old-time sermons: however, as the reader will see, the poems are not written in dialect. . . . although the dialect is the exact instrument for voicing certain traditional phases of Negro life, it is, and perhaps by that very exactness, a quite limited instrument.

Dialect, it seems, was a creature with which Johnson grappled or danced. One moment he would embrace it, unleashing its talents, allowing its cadence to guide his hand. The next moment he would try to hold it at bay, albeit grudgingly, conceding pats of admiration all the while. An ambivalent love affair, to be sure.

But if Johnson was locked in a push-pull relationship with the dialect, he was not alone. Seventy years later, Maya Angelou betrayed the same ambivalence. The renowned African American poet-novelist came across as a vehement foe of vernacular use after the Ebonics controversy erupted in December 1996, saying that she was "incensed" by the Oakland decision. (In fairness to her, she appeared to think, like most people, that Oakland was preparing to teach Ebonics and do away with Standard English instruction). But in applying the art of the vernacular, she had proven herself just as guilty (or as deft) as Dunbar. As many of today's most visible black writers have done, Angelou has distinguished herself in both Standard and vernacular African American English. Her poem "The Pusher" begins:

> He bad
> O he bad
> He make a honky
> poot. . . .

While "The Thirteens (Black)" ends:

> . . . Your cousin's taking smack,
> Your Uncle's in the joint,
> Your buddy's in the gutter,
> Shooting for his point,
> The thirteens. Right On.
>
> And you, you make me sorry,
> You out here by yourself,
> I'd call you something dirty,
> But there just ain't nothing left,
> cept
> The thirteens. Right On.

In both cases, Angelou effectively uses both vernacular vocabulary (*bad, honky, poot, smack*) and grammar (*He bad, there just ain't nothing left*) to convey some of the hard realities of urban life.

Does dialect literature limit or liberate? The question has framed a central conflict among black literati for decades. It is an issue that lives today, still poking a tender spot in the African American psyche. Although many writers seemed unable to hide the profound self-consciousness they felt with respect to Spoken Soul, those sampled above called on it not merely to serve as a curious adornment but also to capture essential elements of the African American experience, an experience that from day to day involves far more than merely pathos or humor. As we have observed, there was (and is) an array of practical and artistic motives behind the use of the idiom. But the most accomplished writers in the vernacular have understood two rudimentary principles: That message cannot be separated from language, and that Spoken Soul often thrives when and where Standard English is left mute. Those who were tormented by that reality swore up and down that they were limited and offended by the vernacular, but they couldn't fully divorce themselves from it either, making spirited use of it in their social interactions as well as in the literature they bequeathed to posterity.

3

Preachers and Pray-ers

But when God speaks, who can but prophesy? (Amen.) *The word of God is
upon me like fire shut up in my bones* (Yes. That's right.), *and when God's
word gets upon me, I've got to tell it all over everywhere. [Shouting.]* (Yes.)
—The Reverend Martin Luther King Jr. (1966)

*I can kick up a little bit of dust sometimes if I got somebody to start de fire
for me, an' kind of warm me up, ya' know what I mean? It'll make yuh rub
yuh eye, anyhow.*
—Deacon Walter Simmons (1972)

With their repertoire of styles and their passion for pageantry and
dramatics, black preachers in the traditional black church don't
merely deliver sermons. They hold court. When they testify for "King
Jesus" in the tradition of the ancestors, the approach is eloquent,
compelling, and certain to kick up dust. For the black church, which
must reward the suffering of the stepped-upon and ward off despair
in hard times, necessitates men and women who are on fire with the
Lord, and who ain't too proud to perspire when delivering the Word.
Ministers who can "take a text" from the Bible and "break it down" to
the level of everyday people are adored. Intensity and fervor are almost always desired; "dead bones" preachers need not apply. In the
many incarnations of the black church, the Living Word tends to be
sung, shouted, clapped, hummed, stomped, and testified to in a ma-
jestic way that moves and moves and moves.

But black preaching is not just a romp. Many young African American ministers strain to perfect that lavish delivery, to tap an old-school

tradition of oral performance that will help them upright toppled souls and earn the respect of the most demanding congregations. But first they must learn to conduct the elaborate exchanges between pulpit and pews that galvanize the black church. To keep members of the flock pressing toward that "mansion in the sky," even to hold their attention fully on a Sunday morning, the black preacher must become a maestro of style, appealing not only to the people's circumstances but to their sense of timing, elegance, tragedy, and humor as well.

So the way in which a sermon is presented becomes almost as crucial as its content. Worshippers must be cued to stand or clap or sway or say "Amen" or wave their palms in testimony through a variety of rhetorical strategies that work them up and draw them in, including innovative metaphors and similes; apt narratives and quotations; appropriate variation in voice quality, gesture, pace, pitch, and volume; and skillful deployment of alliteration, improvisation, humor, repetition, and rhyme. With this mélange, souls on both sides of the altar can be satisfied. As the Bible is "made plain" and the faithful are swept up in the grandeur of the worship experience, the preacher displays an intimate relationship with Christ and struts his or her own verbal panache.

With so many dishes to keep spinning, black preachers cannot forsake Spoken Soul. And many do use the vernacular purposely, effectively, and frequently. In fact, some preach almost entirely in dialect (whether or not they would acknowledge as much if challenged on the matter). Around 1950, a man of the cloth in Macon County, Georgia, described a biblical tragedy as follows:

> Ah, the world swolled up 'gainst man; the seven seas swolled up 'gainst man. Lawd! Telephone wire done come off the post—torn down. Lawd! Gonna make one day—it—Last mountain, Mount Calvery. Man had no salvation. I kin see 'im goin', "I must go to Calvery." Ah, Lord! "Captain's been waiting for me; Captain been looking for me; Captain have been waiting for me—four thousand years ago." Ohhhhhhh, Glory!

Most African American preachers, however, use primarily Standard English in their sermons, making deliberate or not so deliberate excursions into the black vernacular from time to time. So when we talk about Spoken Soul in preaching, we're talking less about a vernacular spree and more about a rhetorical style, an aggregation of vocal and body techniques that overlaps class, geographical region, and denomination.

Blindfold anyone who has ever heard the Reverend Jesse Jackson or Minister Louis Farrakhan preach, march that person into virtually any African American church from New York to Los Angeles, and without hearing a single "ain't" or "sho' nuff," the person will probably be able to identify the minister's race immediately. The Reverend Jackson is Baptist, Minister Farrakhan is Muslim, and both overwhelmingly choose Standard English in their sermons and speeches. But they share an unmistakable and undeniably soulful approach to "running down" the gospel that is reminiscent of the Reverend Martin Luther King Jr. and countless other black ministers and deacons.

Of course, there are many varieties of black churches, and many styles within the black preaching rubric. You may come across a Pentecostal or Holiness minister in Chicago who sings or screams his sermons, and witness a very different tradition in Catholic churches in Philadelphia or New Orleans. Yet it is remarkable that a visit to almost *any* African American church—particularly those in the Baptist and Pentecostal traditions—will yield at least some elements of the soulful preaching tradition, regardless of the educational background of the preacher and the extent to which he or she uses the vernacular itself.

With its quavering falsettos and sonorous baritones, purposeful stuttering, fetching snarls and whispers, singsong melody, rhymes and half-rhymes, interjected exclamations of "hunh," and other trademarks, black preaching is hard to miss and impossible to dismiss. When we examine its themes, functions, and form, we gain precious insight into the souls of black folk, and draw closer to understanding why many of their churches rock like Jericho.

Kickin' Up Dust: Themes and Virtuosity of Black Worship

One Sunday evening in 1970, on a tiny Sea Island off the coast of South Carolina and Georgia, a small group of black Baptists gathered in their praise-house. The Gullah people of Daufuskie Island (which had an almost all-black population of about 110 and—then as now—could be reached solely by boat) were so isolated that only rarely did an ordained preacher from the mainland come to call. Instead of formal church services, the islanders held weekly prayer meetings led by a handful of elders or deacons. That particular morning, Brother Walter "Plummy" Simmons, a subsistence farmer in his sixties, ran the ceremony with the soulful support of his wife, Sister Agnes. After offering the disclaimer "I ain't no preacher—I can't preach," he launched into the prayer that appears below in abridged form. (With the exception of the loss of the final *r*, we have tried to represent faithfully the pronunciation of the original, as well as its grammar.)

Walter Simmons	*Agnes Simmons*
Let us praise God.	*Mmm-hmm*
De day is past an gone.	*Lord, have mercy*
An de evenin shall appear.	*Mmm-hmm*
Oh, may we all remember well	
When de night of death draw nigh.	
We-we'll lay our garment by	
And upon our bed to res.	
An soon, death will corrode us all,	*Lord, have mercy*
An what we have possessed.	
Dis day, dis day, our Father,	*Lord Jesus*
Here is a few, of your own han made.	
We 'semble ourselves together, our Father,	
Not because we could 'semble here,	
Neither to be seen by man.	*Mmm-hmmm*
But, our Father, I ask you please,	
Oh please, our Father, while you ridin,	*Oh, please*
On de route one ridin on to Jericho,	*Have mercy*
Please, stop by dis house dis day, our Father,	
'Cause I want to give you thanks, our Father,	
For how las night's sleep has not found me dead.	
Here our early rise dis mornin	
Hasn' found us to dead man's bed.	*Oooh, yes*
Den, den, den, our Father,	
You lay me down las night,	
An you sen your angel	
An you guard me allll night long.	*Lord, have mercy*
An sooon dis mornin, our Father,	
You wake us up. Our Father,	
We are clothed, in our right mind.	*Lord, have mercy*
An our Father, we want to	
Give you another thanks,	
Our Father, dat when you	
Wake us up dis mornin,	
We found here a coool worl,	*Mmm-hmm*
Where yo prayers can be ascendin	

An your sins can be forgiven.
An den, den, den, our Father,
We—we got some boys,
An we got some girls,
Walkin up an down wid a
Stiff neck an a rebellious heart.
Pleeaase, oh pleeaaase, my Father,   *Oh, please God*
Call dem, my Father, an tell em
Dat de wages of sin is Death,
An de gift of God is Eternal Life.   *Mmm-hmm*
Tell dem, our Father, dat
De train dey ridin on
Is full of dead man's bones.
Make dem know, our Father,
Dat de house is on fire,
An de roof is what burnin down.   *Lord, have mercy*
Make dem know, our Father,
Dat you is de God,
An beside you is no other.
Make dem know, our Father,
Dat you can defen,
An you will destroy.
An our Father,
Make dem know, our Father,   *Mmmmmmmmm*
Dat when you thunder in de eas,   *Mmmmmmmmm*
No man can thunder in the west   *Mmmmmmmmm*
After you.   *Mmmmmmmmm*

Brother Simmons's prayer was not so much spoken as chanted and performed, and there is no way to represent its resplendent quality fully on paper. The chanting of the phrases, the rich modulation of the voice, the variations in volume and tempo, the metrical beat, and the stress patterns and intonations must be heard to be appreciated. While his pronunciation reflects the Gullah background of most (especially older) African Americans on the islands, his grammar, with the exception of a few zero copulas ("you ridin"; see the explanation of zero copulas in chapter 7) and unmarked pasts (*lay, sen, guard, wake;* "You wake us up"), is relatively standard. His word choice is rather ornate and his sentence structure rhetorically balanced: note the parallelism in such phrases as "You can defen' / An you will destroy," and "when you thunder in the eas / no man can thunder in the west." In these respects, Brother Simmons's prayer is similar to those in the devotional phase of Afro-Baptist churches elsewhere in the United States, as was observed in Walter Pitts's 1993 study of a Texas church.

The vocalizations and phrases Sister Simmons uttered and intoned in the background were organic to the prayer, accenting the deacon's especially plaintive or prophetic remarks—and letting him know when he was really cookin'. Toward the end of the prayer, her accompaniment was marked by a soft, continuous humming that gradually swelled into song ("Mmm . . . Oh, sinner, what you doin' 'bout the Lord? Sinner, what you doin' down there? . . ."). Worship among black folk is often characterized by expressiveness rather than solemnity (though not necessarily *unrestrained* expressiveness). Thus Sister Simmons's song both articulated and released the spirit that had been building inside her during her husband's recitation. Yet only the most evocative of words and phrases stir such spirits. Only images and metaphors consistent with the ideologies and experiences of the culture they serve are intimate enough to conjure the Holy Ghost.

Brother Simmons knew this. Without the benefit of divinity studies or a theology degree, he had an impressive awareness of black Baptist themes and how they might be used to dazzle his peers and hitch them emotionally to the prayer. He appealed, for instance, to "our Father, while you ridin'," summoning the image of a supreme warrior who journeys in his fiery chariot as if "on to Jericho," the biblical city of sin whose walls tumbled at the sound of the horns of the righteous (Joshua 2 and 6). A hymn heard in black churches similarly entreats, "O my Good Lord, show me the way—enter the chariot, travel along." And one of the most recognized spirituals calls for deliverance from the miseries of slavery with the refrain "Swing low, sweet chariot, coming for to carry me home."

Two classic African American prayer motifs are combined in Brother Simmons's allusion to a train brimming with "dead man's bones." One is the train, which appears within both sacred and secular categories of African American life. Think of the notion of the "freedom train," whether manifested by the underground railroad that escaped slaves "rode" to liberation, or by the railcars that during the early twentieth century hauled legions of southern blacks toward the promise of greater tolerance and opportunity "up North." Then there is the religious idea of the train, mentioned in the introduction to James Weldon Johnson's book of "old-time Negro sermons," *God's Trombones:* "Both God and the devil were pictured as running trains, one loaded with saints, that pulled up in heaven, and the other with sinners, that dumped its load in hell."

Brother Simmons opened his prayer (in the grand tradition of black preachers) by praising God for another morning that had found the dearly assembled not stretched upon "dead man's bed," but "clothed in our right mind." Extravagant thanksgiving in the black church is often in order if, during the previous night, "our sleeping couch was not our cooling board" and "our cover was not our winding sheet." One of the prayers that the late linguist Walter Pitts recorded at St. John Progressive Church in Austin, Texas, in the 1980s, included virtually the same phrasing as Brother Simmons's: "We thank Thee, our Heavenly Father, early this morning. / For waking up us, Oh Heavenly Father, clothed in our right mind." As Pitts notes, prayers recorded in Tennessee during the 1920s and in Texas during the 1930s employed very similar language. Brother Simmons's prayer, like others, followed the topical structure that anthropologist Patricia Jones-Jackson found on the South Carolina Sea Islands: formal opening, proem (expression of humility), thanksgiving, appeals, and peroration (including references to the end of life).

Like the most enduring folktales, the themes of Brother Simmons's prayer conformed to a cultural tradition. The deacon, a subsistence farmer, was able to lace together metaphors and biblical themes (for instance, the train brimming with "dead man's bones") that his fellow worshippers could easily internalize. And though his prayer borrowed its framework and some of its phrases from the black Baptist tradition, his genius for metaphor, delivery, and improvisation clearly helped elicit his wife's "Lord have mercy's" and nudge his listeners toward spiritual rhapsody. Brother Simmons was not a preacher. Still, he exhibited all the poetry, majesty, and virtuosity of black preaching and praying. That's how deeply and universally this tradition of ornately rendering words is entrenched in black culture.

In terms of education and fame, Dr. Martin Luther King Jr.—a reverend, a scholar, and a prodigy of Southern Baptist preaching—existed in a stratosphere well above Brother Simmons. But he was similar insofar as he "delighted in euphony, the sweet sound of words and rhythms." The public today tends to think of Dr. King as a dreamer, and to remember him primarily in terms of the constantly recycled conclusion of his "I Have a Dream" speech. Few recall the philosopher, the social engineer, and the Christian warrior who was King. Even fewer still acknowledge the preaching phenomenon who was reared in the black church and who relied on, even perfected, the rhetorical strategies of the black preaching tradition.

One such strategy is repetition, evident in this passage from one of Dr. King's sermons:

> Sir, we would see Jesus, the light of the world.
> We know about Plato, but we want to see Jesus.
> We know about Aristotle, but we want to see Jesus.
> We know about Homer, but we want to see Jesus.

As his biographer Richard Lischer has pointed out, Dr. King's "voice stabs at the first syllable of Pla-to and Ho-mer and drops at the end of each sentence to a gravelly and intimate Jee-sus." As this book was being written (and surely long after its publication), the same pronunciation of "Jesus" was and will be heard in black churches across the country. And yet people don't recognize the jewels of Spoken Soul that fell from Dr. King's lips. Many might indeed consider it blasphemy to suggest that the martyr even dabbled in down-home talk. But Dr. King probably could not have become such a trusted national spokesman for the black masses, and might not have been able to lead garbagemen and porters and church mothers as effectively as he did, if he had not had control over not only Standard English, but also the pauses, inflections, cadences, and other devices of the black rhetorical and preaching tradition—the same devices that put the swing in Brother Simmons's prayer.

Alliteration is another "sweet sound" rolling down from the black pulpit. Addressing visitors to a Baptist church in Palo Alto, California, in 1992, the Reverend Emil Thomas said:

> We want you to know that you are *w*elcome and you are *w*anted at Jerusalem Baptist Church. If you're looking for a church home, you might find some churches that are *b*igger, but you won't find any that is *b*etter. And you can make it straight to heaven from Jerusalem, if you *b*een *b*orn again! (All right! Amen!) So, as you worship with us today, we hope that you will *p*rayerfully *p*onder the *p*ossibility of joining with us on this *p*ilgrimage from time to eternity.

Alliteration is not an isolated trick. The genius of black preachers lies in their ability to use many tools of language simultaneously. Linguist Geneva Smitherman praised such displays of dexterity, calling them a function of "tonal semantics":

> Tonal semantics . . . refers to the use of voice rhythm and vocal inflection to convey meaning in black communication. In using the semantics of tone, the voice is employed like a musical instrument with improvisation, riffs, and . . . playing between the notes. This rhythmic pattern becomes a kind of acoustical phonetic alphabet and gives black speech its songified or musical quality.

Contributing to the songlike lilt of the black sermon is the "hunh" many preachers use at the end of chanted breath groups as an energizing punctuation, as in this extract:

> You got to persevere . . . hunh?
> You got to give yo' all . . . hunh?
> You got to be long-suffering . . . hunh?
> You got to *do* right!

As she circled the pulpit with microphone in hand, speaking first to the choir, then to the Amen corner, a pastor at a Pentecostal church in Berkeley, California, used a variation on this "hunh" to cap her most ecstatic phrases. Every pause she took was occupied by the peals of an organ, and the result was a delightful conversation between human voice and musical instrument:

> You wouldn't be here today, hunh-hunh-hunh,
> Hadn't God comforted you, hunh-hunh-hunh,
> Hadn't God had understanding for you, hunh-hunh-hunh,
> Hadn't God had love for you.
> Whoooooa, Lawd! Thankya, Jesus!
> When He receeeived you, hunh-hunh-hunh,
> Some o' you were prostitutes, hunh-hunh-hunh,
> Some o' you were dope addicts, hunh-hunh-hunh.
> When He receeeived ya, hunh-hunh-hunh,
> Some o' you were layin' with men, hunh-hunh-hunh.
> When He receeeived ya, hunh-hunh-hunh,
> Some o' you were bar-hoppers, hunh-hunh-hunh.
> When He receeeeived ya, hunh-hunh-hunh,
> Some o' you were backsliders. Ooohhhh, Lawd!

Other calling cards of the traditional black preaching style include deliberate stuttering or the manipulation of voice texture and inflection to produce a grating, gravelly, or mellifluous tone. There are often abrupt starts and stops, bursts of acceleration that disrupt an otherwise plodding pace, and wild fluctuations in volume that come without warning. There is the exploitation of rhyme ("God don't bless mess") and the elongation of syllables, as in Dr. King's last great speech, in which, his pitch soaring as if to reach the providential summit he was envisioning, chanted, "I've *been* to the moun-tain-top."

Grace Sims Holt dedicated an essay to the black preacher's gift for "stylin' outta the pulpit." By "stylin'" she meant the process of strutting back and forth behind the pulpit with hand on hip or on the small of the back, or firing up a congregation by "stomping out the devil" with a polished wingtip heel, or "tearing down the gates of hell" with a violent kick. Even when a sermon is presented largely or entirely in Standard English, the signature of black preaching remains, as in James Weldon Johnson's poem "The Creation," based on the sermon of an old-time black preacher who originally spoke in dialect. The rich metaphors linked to the local environment ("Blacker than a hundred midnights / Down in a cypress swamp"), the direct speech quotations, the repetitions within a simple sentence structure ("And the light broke, / And the darkness rolled up") conjure the sense of being in the presence of the traditional black preacher, and one hears the words with the stretched-out vowels the preacher would give them ("And faaaaaar as the eye of God could see . . . "):

And God stepped out on space,
And he looked around and said:
I'm lonely—
I'll make me a world.
And far as the eye of God could see
Darkness covered everything,
Blacker than a hundred midnights
Down in a cypress swamp.

Then God smiled,
And the light broke,
And the darkness rolled up on one side,
And the light stood shining on the other,
And God said: That's good!

Then God reached out and took the light in his hands,
And God rolled the light around in his hands
Until he made the sun;
And he set that sun a-blazing in the heavens.

And the light that was left from making the sun
God gathered it up in a shining ball
And flung it against the darkness,
Spangling the night with the moon and stars.
Then down between
The darkness and the light
He hurled the world;
And God said: That's good!

The Worship Spiral

Few rituals in the black church are sedentary. Instead, they whirl and
surge and ebb as if choreographed at sea. The service may begin
slowly and sedately, with a deacon droning on about the upcoming
Bible training classes or church picnic, with prayers and devotions being offered by the deacons and other church members, with the pastor scolding worshippers for falling short of their tithing and offer-
tory duties, and dispensing with routine duties such as baptism. But as
the morning wears on, often even before the sermon has begun, fans
flutter, bodies sway, tambourines shiver, hands clap in response to
"Onward, Christian Soldiers," "I Love the Lord," or another hymn,
and a symphony of movement sets the rafters jumping.

Women generally initiate the hand-clapping that accompanies a
hymn, and are usually the first to exhibit that they have caught the
spirit—dancing, swooning, or (in Pentecostal churches) talking in
tongues as ushers encircle them for their own safety and the protection of others. Later in the service, members of the congregation—
again, women in particular—may stand and offer personal testimonies.
Testifying is an impromptu act sometimes solicited by elders or deacons who set aside a section of the service for "moments of medita-
tion and praise" and "ministry in music." But testifying can be just as
lavish and stylized as any prepared portion of the service. The ritual
consists of congregants' making short statements about how Jesus
saved their soul from a life of gangs, drugs, alcohol, gambling, infidelity, or any of the devil's other works, or about how Jesus' hand
guided them when they were laid off from work and their daughter
was sick, or how He turned their face toward the rays of Everlasting
Life when they didn't deserve salvation in the first place.

As the service intensifies, men, too, may shed whatever macho in-
hibitions they may have walked in with, stand up stiffly, stomp and
shout, or wave at the preacher in an encouraging gesture that may

seem dismissive to an outsider. There is at least a twofold explanation for such displays. First, in the tradition of the ring shout, each member of the black church is expected to fuel the worship experience through emotional investment and participation in the call-and-response ritual; second, the Holy Ghost is believed to inhabit the body at the height of spiritual ecstasy.

On a Sunday morning at Mount Calvary Baptist Church in Washington, D.C., a choirboy overcome by the crescendo of a rousing service leaped from his seat behind the minister, made his way to the front pews, and proceeded with a quick jog around them. Black denominations shaped by such a tendency to submit to the physically possessing properties of the Holy Spirit include the African Methodist Episcopal, African Methodist Episcopal Zion, Christian Methodist Episcopal, the various Baptist affiliations, the Church of God in Christ, and other Pentecostal, Holiness, and Sanctified churches.

Even in the many black churches where no shouting or speaking in tongues is heard, and no one is seen convulsing or weeping after receiving the Holy Spirit, congregations and preachers alike are governed by a spiral of conventionalized social cues—both spoken and acted out—within the worship service. The minister sets this spiral in motion by using one or more of the evocative rhetorical tools available, or by overtly seeking feedback from the congregation ("Can I get a witness?"). Worshippers receive the message and respond (by standing, clapping, testifying, waving, stomping, nodding their heads, clucking their tongues, or letting loose a "Hallelujah!").

The original message is thus amplified, and the minister is encouraged to continue while the spirit escalates, passed around the sanctuary by the choir, the congregation, the deacons, and others in the church. If the spiral peaks during the sermon and is sustained through the benediction, the pastor may remark that the spirit of the Lord "has taken hold" of the church. But do not be misled. No gesture from pews or pulpit is ever superfluous, or made for sport. A subtle order exists, even amid the apparent frenzy. It is always understood, for example, that the preacher's fundamental role is to explicate the Bible, while the congregation's fundamental role is to back up and build up the preacher. Such unwritten rules of behavior are learned over time as children are raised in the church, watching their mothers testify and their fathers say "Amen."

Anyone who has worshipped in an African American church knows that the most exhilarating exchanges evolve unrehearsed as the morning proceeds, and that some of the most prodigious preaching comes after the minister has folded up notes. Improvisation, a cornerstone of black preaching, was critical to the Daufuskie faithful, as chapelgoers could stand up at virtually any time in the fellowship—if the spirit so moved them—to offer testimony or song. Indeed, if the vibrations of worship are to reach a divine pitch (and this tends to hold true in large urban African American churches as well), some improvisation must occur.

Consider the sermon "When You Fail in Your Trying," delivered in 1998 at Chicago's Trinity United Church of Christ. The pastor, the Reverend Dr. Jeremiah Wright, amped up the congregation that morning with a footloose style steeped in spontaneity and informality. Drawing from Genesis 29, the Reverend Wright preached about the shortcomings of Leah, the misguided figure who slept with Jacob and bore him sons in a vain attempt to wrest his affections from her beautiful sister Rachel. The Reverend Wright used a conversational tone (and, as the sermon went on, more and more vernacular) to depict the Old Testament characters as everyday folk one might imagine hanging in one's own 'hood.

At one point, the reverend asked his congregation a question:

> Do you all know any Jacobs? Sleeping with a woman that he does not love. Having sex with a woman that he does not love. And Dr. Weems reminded us on Monday night one ain't got nothing to do with the other. You missed that: Having sex with a woman ain't got nothing to do with loving a woman!

Black preachers are famous for demanding answers to rhetorical questions. When the Reverend Wright asked, "Do you all know any Jacobs?" he paused to allow the congregation to chorus, "Yessir." Church folk will supply speedy responses to such inquiries; they are obliged to do so for reciprocity's sake (hence the worship spiral). Proper etiquette dictates that when the "Rev" calls for support one must "get his back" and demonstrate that one is following along with the lesson. Black preachers demand participation from their congregations. If they so much as sense a lull, they will not hesitate to ask, "I'm not boring y'all, am I?" or "How much time I got left?" To which the only proper response, of course, is a hearty "No sir!" or "Take your time, Preach!" If an even more enthusiastic response is desired, or if the preacher arrives at a particularly transcendental point in the sermon, he or she will drop a hint: "Somebody ought to say 'Amen,'" or "Let the church say 'Amen.'" Using a similar strategy, the Reverend Wright, when preparing to broach a delicate topic, instructed his congregants to "turn to your neighbor and tell them, 'He's going there.'" Then he directed them to "turn to the other side and say, 'I wish he wouldn't.'"

Strategies for encouraging participation are common, for in the black church, sluggishness is tantamount to spiritual hibernation. As Grace Sims Holt observed:

> The preacher's beginning is slow-moving (funky) to get the audience physically involved. The preacher walks, body swaying from side to side, slightly bent, from one side of the pulpit to the other, or from one end of the platform to the other. He waits until he gets to one side, stands up straight, and makes a statement about sin. If a husband "ain't acting right," if he's running around with another woman, or gambling, and not bringing his money home to his wife and children, the preacher must "get on his case" with a strong use of melody and rhythm.

When they are about to introduce a crucial point, many black preachers alert their congregations. "Watch this," they'll say, or "Follow me close, now." Notice how the Reverend Wright warned the Trinity members, "You missed that," before echoing the sentiment that sex "ain't got nothing to do with loving."

Beyond embellishing the sermon and delivering the gospel, a black preacher is expected to display a keen cultural understanding of the congregants. The preacher must be intimately familiar with their ways and weaknesses in order to be taken seriously when coaxing them down a righteous path. A preacher must be able to relate, and at the very least must have the capacity to talk congregants' plain talk. When he began to dig into the meat of his sermon, the Reverend Wright changed Leah's speech from the biblical to the colloquial:

> And on the third baby, she said, "This time I got him. He can't go nowhere. Now he is joined to me. He's mine." Y'all know Leah, don't you? [Congregation: "Yes!"]

At that moment Leah stood transformed. Suddenly she was a sister who talked as many of the congregants did in their most informal moments. Suddenly it was much easier for them to relate to her circumstances. "I think somebody here knows what street Leah lives on," the

Reverend Wright said. "I think somebody here still living on that street." To this, a man in the pews cried out "Preach-uh!" The Reverend Wright continued:

> Leah conceived again and bore a son and said, "*This* time—I made a mistake once. I was too blind to see the second time. And I was a fool for you, baby, on the third time. But *this* time, I finally woke up. *This* time, I see my mistake. *This* time, I ain't falling for it, babycakes. *This* time, me and the Lord got this thing going on."

By now, secular references had crept into the sacred context. One might in fact expect to find such phrases as "I was a fool for you, baby," and "got this thing going on" on the pop charts. The informal flavor had at least two obvious benefits: it perked up the congregation, and it prompted laughter. Austere members of the church might have turned to one another and remarked that the Reverend Wright "sure is cuttin' up," but they were paying attention to the lesson, despite themselves.

The most accomplished black preachers—like the best black comedians—use levity to wade into sensitive discussions. In his sermon, the Reverend Wright used two very informal expressions for sex: "C'mon baby, we gon tear the roof off the sucka tonight," and "You got to give it up, tonight" (to which members of the church responded with hoots, laughter, and exclamations of "Wellll!"). Blurring the line between the sacred and the secular is permissible, as long as the preacher stays within the guidelines of the Bible, as long as the goal is to increase participation in the service and understanding of the Scriptures, and as long as the congregation is convinced that the preacher knows the deal.

In his book *Black Preaching*, Henry Mitchell observed that "black preaching requires the use of black language." Certainly the idea of a sentence like "We gon tear the roof off the sucka tonight" echoing in the house of the Lord may shock some critics. But in many black churches, as the emotions of congregants are stirred and the accoutrements of the starched work week are shed, use of the black vernacular peaks. Richard L. Wright demonstrated this in a 1976 study of five Afro-Baptist preachers. He showed that deletion of *is* and *are*, double negatives, and other markers of Spoken Soul in the speech of preachers occurred four times more frequently during the sermonic climax than during earlier portions of the service, such as the devotional.

Walter Pitts, replicating this analysis in 1993, found that preachers' use of black vernacular features during the sermonic climax was twice as high as in their conversational speech earlier in the service. P. K. McCrary was perhaps conscious of this when she introduced her "black Bible series," which translated the Scriptures into Spoken Soul. Intended for young people who have trouble relating to or decoding the King James Version, the series featured distinctive black vocabulary and grammar, as in this extract from the Gospel of Matthew:

> And when these things go down like Daniel of a long time ago talked about, ya'll better run to them hills. Those on top of the house should stay put and those who are out in the field, don't worry 'bout packing a suitcase. . . . Folks will be stabbing you in the back and calling you names. Worse, they'll want to waste you for what you believe.

The Rev. Ervin Green, pastor of Brick Baptist Church on St. Helena Island, South Carolina, and a collaborator on the Gullah version of the Gospel According to Luke (*De Good Nyews Bout Jedus Christ wa Luke Write*), reports that a parishioner who'd read it told him excitedly, "Rev, dis de firs' time God talk to me de way I talk!"

Few of black America's most sought-after preachers and pray-ers have abandoned black preaching traditions, even if they speak (inside and outside the church) with the gloss of Standard English. Nation of Islam helmsman Minister Louis Farrakhan, speaking on the unwieldy subject of a "black agenda" in 1988, offered a good example of this double-consciousness:

> I saw in the newspaper this morning . . . they said we have got to find a way to accommodate Reverend Jackson and pacify his constituency. There it is! There it is! Do we need accommodation? [Audience: "No!"] And moral pacification? [Audience: "No!"] Tell me how accommodation feeds the hungry? And gives jobs to those who have no employment? And gives housing to those who are homeless? Tell me how does accommodation and pacification give justice to those who cry out for justice? [Audience: "Go 'head, brother, go 'head! Yessuh! Talk to the people, Brother Minister!"]

When Minister Farrakhan exclaimed, "There it is! There it is!" it was for the same reasons that the Reverend Wright proclaimed, "You missed that"—as a signal that a significant statement had just been made or was about to follow. A beguiling rhetorician, Minister Farrakhan knows that not even he can secure the optimal feedback from a black audience unless he is perceived, fundamentally, as a people's preacher. So the Muslim leader kept the rhythms of a black church's Amen corner in mind. Once again, the widest range of expression is the highest goal. Speaking before a younger audience of New York college students, Minister Farrakhan selected an even more overt vernacular style:

> When I was comin' up as a youngsta I used to smoke reefer. What? Well, wait a minute . . . I don't want you to think I came down from heaven. I-I-I-I came up from hell jus' like everybody else. But I knew where the reefers were. Anytime I wanted some I knew where to go. Don't you know where to go? You know where the coke is. You know where the man is that got the good stuff. You know where the man is that waters it down.

When Minister Farrakhan was fishing for feedback, he asked, "Are y'all all right?" or "Do I have a few more minutes?" just as the Reverend Wright did when he felt Trinity's members growing restless. Minister Farrakhan was able to swivel between the street and the standard in order to narrow the gap between himself and his audience, using commonalities of the culture.

Black preaching's rhetorical style—including its tendency toward repetition—also bled through the Reverend Jesse Jackson's speech before a mainstream audience during the 1988 Democratic National Convention:

> They work hard every day. I know. I live amongst them. I'm one of them. I know they work! I'm a witness; they catch the early bus. They work every day! They raise other people's children. They work every day. They clean the streets. They work every day. They drive dangerous cabs, they work every day. They changed the beds you slept in in these hotels last night, and can't get a union contract. They work every day!

Jackson tends to avoid heavy black vernacular grammar and syntax, particularly when speaking before mixed or predominantly white audiences. Yet he evidently "sermonizes" his speeches, drawing on the inflection, cadence, and rhyme of the same preaching tradition that produced his colleague the Reverend Martin Luther King Jr.

Because black preachers tend to seek as broad a verbal and stylistic range as possible, the vernacular is an empowering element of their craft. As we have seen, it isn't the only element. In the end, black preachers are expected to be graceful and versatile wordsmiths capable of wielding the language of prestige—Standard English. However, one rule is true of almost all black churches, working-class or middle-class, rural or urban: The preacher who uses Standard English exclusively, without any of the motifs, rhythms, and gestures of the soulful preaching style (as rare as he or she would be to come across) is in serious risk of appearing detached or "uppity," and thereby of losing the interest of a good portion of the congregation. When the Reverend Jeremiah A. Wright Jr. went on his dialect jaunts, he was not out to sound ignorant. And he didn't: He was strutting. It was a testament to his preaching virtuosity that he could switch so effortlessly between the diction of the evening news and the lingo of Chicago's South Side.

4

Comedians and Actors

The black comedian of today uses the language of the streets, and in doing his characterizations, he speaks the same way.

—Redd Foxx (1979)

Even the most sophisticated joke tellers usually revert to dialect in closed company. Indeed the tales lose much of their flavor in standard English.

—Daryl Cumber Dance (1978)

One of the surest indications that Spoken Soul is alive and deeply cherished, despite assertions to the contrary, is its pervasive and vibrant use among black comedians. To these performers, and their appreciative audiences, Spoken Soul is a mechanism for slipping the fetters of polite convention, and a source of intense pleasure.

Ground-breaking humorists such as Bert Williams, Sammy Davis Jr., Dewey "Pigmeat" Markham, Dick Gregory, Redd Foxx, Jackie "Moms" Mabley, and Richard Pryor should all be regarded as connoisseurs of the tongue, and contemporaries such as Adele Givens, Whoopi Goldberg, Steve Harvey, Eddie Murphy, and Chris Rock have proven themselves equally comfortable in mainstream English and black talk. These and other black comedians have mined Spoken Soul to enrich their comic routines, and sometimes have talked frankly about the critical role the vernacular has played in their comedy, especially through its dramatic contrast with mainstream English.

Bert Williams, one of the earliest black comedians to make a name for himself, did so as part of a comedy team with George Walker (the Two Real Coons) that began playing in San Francisco in 1893 and moved to New York in 1896. The duo had a string of successes there in the early 1900s, including the 1906 hit *Abyssinia*, in which Williams sang the amusing but poignant song "Nobody," built around a series of multiple negatives:

> I ain't never done nothin' to nobody,
> And I ain't never got nothin' from nobody,
> And until I get somethin' from somebody,
> Sometime . . .
> I ain't never gonna do nothin' for nobody,
> No time.

In the 1920s, with segregation still firmly entrenched, a series of black comedians performed in black theaters throughout the Midwest and the South under the auspices of the Theatre Owners' Booking Association, or TOBA; their tours were known as the Toby circuit. Pigmeat Markham, Ethel Walters ("Sweet Mama Stringbean"), Bill Robinson, and a number of other black performers became famous on the circuit. Especially relevant to our topic is Sammy Davis Jr., who started out on the circuit in blackface at the age of four as part of his uncle's act, passed off (to circumvent child labor laws) as a forty-four-year-old midget. In an interview with Redd Foxx, Davis was explicit about the role of dialect in the humor of the day:

> Comedy at that time was done by the great dialecticians of that era. The black style of comedy was the same for the black man as for the white man. You had the Jewish comics who wore baggy pants, the Dutch comedians who had accents that were so strong you could cut them with a knife, and then there was the Irish comic. All of the comedy in those days was ethnic. . . .
> My concept of black humor is very nonracial in a way, until it reaches the punch line. At that time I color it with typical black sounds. For instance, I pretend that I'm walking up to a desk clerk and, in a very white-style voice, I'll say, "Good evening, my good man. My name is Sammy Davis, Jr. Do you have my reservation?" The desk clerk would answer, "I don't have your reservation and I don't know you." My answer, which would be the punch line, would be a switch to a typical black voice, "Whatcha mean ya don't know me!" It's not the words that are funny, it's when I switch voices and become colored that is funny.

In 1975, decades after the TOBA circuit, Richard Pryor embodied this same principle—that humor lay in the swapping of voices—in his routine of a black minister delivering a eulogy. Note the omission of the plural *s* ending ("In other word") and the *is* copula ("the nigger

dead"; see chapter 7 for a discussion of copula), and the introduction
of *been* and *ain't* as the minister switches registers:

> We are gathered here today, on dis so[rrow]fu[l] occasion, to say
> goodbye to the dearly departed. He was dearly, and he has departed.
> Thus, tha's why we call him the dearly departed. In other word, the
> nigger dead! [Laughter.] As you can see him laying here—I been here
> three days, the boy ain't move a muscle. So I know the nigger dead!

Leap forward to the 1990s—when black comedians' live performances before largely black audiences reached vast interracial and international populations through BET's *Comic View* and other television broadcasts—and you can still see the principle in effect. In her
irreverent "Fake Bitch" bit, Adele Givens recalls how her mother used
to switch from vernacular to straight English, depending upon who
was on the telephone:

> Because everybody here, when you were little, you could tell who yo'
> mama—who she was talking to on the phone. . . . You just heard the
> "fake bitch" when she took over, didn't you?
>   'Cause when her friends call it's like, "Hello . . . ? Oh, hey, how
> you doin', girl? I ain't doin' nothin'. . . . Cookin' these beans! Yeah,
> I know we had them yesterday, but beans taste better the second day,
> ya know? Girl, I can't hardly hear nothin' you sayin', these kids with all
> that damn noise. Yah, yah. Hold on. Let me— Y'all kids stop all that
> damn noise! People think I ain't taught you nothing."
>   That's how she talk to her friends. But you let the principal . . . or
> the insurance man . . . or somebody white calling: "Hello. Oh, hi, Mr.
> Kennedy, how are you? Gee, you haven't received it yet? I mailed it out
> on Tuesday. Well, don't you worry. I've got the account number. I'm
> gonna track it down. Can you hold on for just a second, Mr. Kennedy?
> I can barely hear you. Children, Mommy's on the phone now!"
>   Get to know me, white people, so I can relax and just talk to you
> like I talk to everybody else. . . .

The last sentence explicitly associates the vernacular with speaking in a relaxed and natural mode, a mode Givens obviously values.
But note, too, apropos of the theme of cultural duality in this book,
that after this passage she adds the disclaimer that she doesn't "bash"
the "fake bitch" and her change to Standard English, because "she
the one got your ass where you at today!" After this, she tilts back toward the genuine and the vernacular, exemplifying Du Bois's push-
pull dialectic: "But sometimes you got to reel her in. 'Cause sometimes she come out when it's unnecessary!"

A more extended example of how the contrast between black and white styles of speech are exploited for humorous effect comes from a live 1997 performance by Steve Harvey, broadcast on national television. Harvey, wisecracking emcee for years on the program *It's Showtime at the Apollo,* had his own weekly sitcom, but he displayed his linguistic and comic versatility fully in solo performances. The routine we'll examine involves two ill-fated workers, one white, one black, who are about to be fired by their white boss, Tom.

Harvey gets into the character of Tom, clenching his rear end and striding stiff-backed across the stage as if making his way out of a private office and into the cubicle of a low-level white drone, Bob, who is asked to enter the boss's office. Harvey also impersonates the doomed employee, who trots after his supervisor.

TOM: Ya know, Bob, at the end of the board meeting this past week, and after going over the board, we were kinda looking at your evaluation. And well, to tell you the truth, you're just not cutting it.

BOB: Tom, what're you saying? [Harvey slips out of character and speaks to the mostly black audience: "You know good and hell well what he sayin'. Yo ass is almos' outta here. You see what da hell's goin' on. But *denial.*"]

TOM: Listen to me. You're making this so difficult. I know you're going to have a tough time explaining this to Becky, but we're going to have to let you go.

BOB: Oh! Oh, Jesus! Oh Tom, what am I going to do? What about the mortgage? What about the children's college fund? Oh, Father God!

To mimic, or "mark" (see below), the white characters Tom and Bob, Harvey puts on an outlandish nasal voice and keeps their speech close to Standard English (vernacular features such as zero copula, *r* deletion, and *s* deletion are absent from their speech, but resurface in his aside to the black audience: "what he sayin' "; *Yo; almos'*). The white characters' speech comes across as stilted and, in Bob's case, corny ("Oh, Father God!"), accommodating, and hopelessly submissive.

When Tom tries to fire the black employee—brotha Willie—in the same manner, the employee's attitude and language change dramatically. Willie lets off sparks of defiance from the jump ("What da hell" replaces "Oh Father God"), and the pronunciation (*fo'; goin'; da; sompn*) and grammar ("we goin'"; *ain't*) of Spoken Soul emerge. Harvey's commentary to the audience—who absolutely delight in it—is also rife with vernacular features, including zero third-singular-present *-s* ("He know"), immediate future tense *fitna* ("Sompn *fitna* go down!"), and a series of black colloquialisms (*show his whole ass; act a damn fool*):

TOM: Willie, can I see you in my office for a moment, please?

WILLIE: What fo'? What da hell we goin' in da office fo', Tom? You got sompn to tell me, you tell me right here. I got a desk right here. I ain't goin' in da office. You got sompn to tell Willie, you tell Willie right here! [To audience: "Now . . . Tom know he got a problem. He know he got to get this altercation behind closed doors right now. 'Cause he know Willie fitna show his whole ass! Awww—Willie fitna act a damn fool out here! Willie fitna tear up all these cubicles in this office. Sompn fitna go down!"]

Even after Tom coaxes the black employee into his office, things don't go much smoother:

TOM: Ya know, Willie, we were at the board meeting the other week. We were going over your evaluation. . . .

WILLIE: What 'valuation? I ain't see no goddamn 'valuation! When did you have the 'valuation? I didn't—I wadn't dere fo' it. Did ya pos' it on da board in da cafeteria las' week? I ain't seen nothin'. I ain't signin' shit!

The audience roars at that one. But what is it that makes the routine so funny? The crowd of course recognizes the cultural contrast between Bob and Willie. One can easily differentiate between the rhetorical styles and dispositions of the two characters. Willie has much more bass to his voice, and his street demeanor and suspicious attitude run contrary to Bob's sprightly naiveté and accommodation. Willie is boorish, but he's also savvier than Bob, and more confrontational in his defense. The portrayal of blacks as more astute than whites and more capable of vigorous self-defensive or self-assertive talk is recurrent in black folk humor, and provides psychic rebuttal to the dominant society's stereotype that blacks are less sharp or less articulate. Two genres in which this is well represented are jokes about outsmarting the master, or "puttin' on ole massa," in the days of slavery and stories about blacks "shuckin'" and "jivin'" their way out of confrontations with police in modern times.

In Harvey's skit, the audience associates Willie's speech with expressiveness and spunk, and Bob's with detachment and restraint. Communications consultant Thomas Kochman has suggested that this may be true more generally:

> The modes of behavior that blacks and whites consider appropriate for engaging in public debate on an issue differ in their stance and level of spiritual intensity. The black mode—that of black community people— is high-keyed: animated, interpersonal, and confrontational. The white mode—that of the middle class—is relatively low-keyed: dispassionate, impersonal, and non-challenging. The first is characteristic of involvement; it is heated, loud, and generates affect. The second is characteristic of detachment and is cool, quiet, and without affect.

Whether this characterization is valid in all real-life cases is open to debate, but it does hold true in the Harvey piece. The cultural difference is familiar, and that hint of familiarity is entertainment enough for the ladies and gentlemen of the audience, who have paid to laugh not at a comedian but at themselves. Laughter, we must remember, is often nothing more than that fleeting and reflective moment when one lays aside pretension and peers into the shadowy corners of one's own self-image.

Even as Harvey mocks white speech and white mannerisms (with Bob's stilted walk), he pokes fun at his own folk (with Willie's emotional eruptions). There's no question that this self-chiding instinct is a cornerstone of black humor, a long-standing strategy for taking the edge off slanderous caricatures of the race established by outsiders. But the most compelling aspect of Harvey's skit is the clash of black and white styles themselves. And the most fundamental conveyor of those styles is the manner in which the characters talk, a fact the audience acknowledges and delights in.

To set up the contrast that really lends the scene humor, Harvey must master the linguistic extremes of both cultures. From his verbal repertoire, he must be able to produce the diction and delivery of not just a Bob but a Willie, too. He must capture the absurdity of Bob's feeble reaction to the news that his "ass is almos' outta here," as well as the novelty of Willie's theatrics in the middle of the office. And he must do so mainly with language. The routine demonstrates that Harvey, like many other black people in this country who deal with whites on a daily basis, is able to switch effortlessly between the most proper "whitese" and the most exaggerated "soulspeak." This talent for playing dialect hopscotch, at least to the degree we see here, is not as exercised in mainstream culture. Few white comedians, for example, can parrot the black vernacular as convincingly as Givens or Harvey. Of course, one source of increasing concern today is that many black youngsters seem unable or unwilling to shift into Standard English when the social or educational environment seems to require it. But it remains true that many blacks—ordinary people as well as celebrated comedians like Harvey—control a broad range of linguistic registers, and flex them in everyday life and in their narratives and jokes about everyday life.

In the routine, Harvey is "marking" his characters, using a narrative technique that anthropologist Claudia Mitchell-Kernan has described as follows:

> A common black narrative tactic in the folk tale genre and in accounts of actual events is the individuation of characters through the use of direct quotation. When in addition, in reproducing the words of individual actors, a narrator affects the voice and mannerisms of the speakers, he is using the style referred to as marking (clearly related to standard English "mocking"). Marking is essentially a mode of characterization. The marker attempts to report not only what was said but the way it was said, in order to offer explicit comment on the speaker's background, personality, or intent.

Mitchell-Kernan offers an instructive example in which the "marker" (S2 in the dialogue below) conveys the Uncle Tom character of a black company man by transforming his words at a corporation meeting (reported by S4) into the drawling speech of a "handkerchief head":

S1: What did he say?

S2: [Drawling] He said, "Ah'm so-o-o happy to be here today. First of all, ah want to thank all you good white folks for creatin so many opportunities for us niggers and ya'll can be sho that as soon as we can git ourselves qualified we gon be filin our applications. . . ."

S1: Did he really say that?

S3: Um hm, yes he said it. Girl, where have you been? [Putdown by intimating S1 was being literal.]

S1: Yeah, I understand, but what did he really say?

S4: He said, "This is a moment of great personal pride for me. My very presence here is a tribute to the civil rights movement. We now

> have ample evidence of the good faith of the company and we
> must now begin to prepare ourselves to handle more responsible
> positions. . . ."

In a sense, all comedians and dramatists—and where the use of
Spoken Soul is concerned, black comedians especially—are markers.
Chris Rock, who is relatively standard in many of his routines, deploys
the vernacular for an affectionate marking of his father in this bit:

> I [was] supposed to go on tour with Run DMC? Tol' my father, say,
> "Dad, I'm goin' on tour with Run DMC—they gon let me open up for
> dem, make a lot o' money!"
> "Dem boys ign'ant [ignorant]! Dem boys are ign'ant! Why dey got
> dem hats on dey head? Dey ain't Jewish! An' what's that thing around
> dey neck?"
> "A rope chain, dad."
> "I tol' you dem boys ign'ant! What nigger in his right mind wants
> a rope aroun' his neck?!"
> . . . Father was nuts, man.

Ironically, or perhaps predictably, Bill Cosby, caustic critic of Black
English in the seventies (see below) and Ebonics in the nineties (see
chapter 1), unspooled the vernacular (italicized segments below) to
represent himself and his mother in his 1972 routine "The Lower
Tract":

> My wife is from the South. Now, I'm from Pennsylvania. I *don' eat
> no—no* chitlins. My mother loves chitlins. . . . You say, "Somebody is
> *cookin'* chitlins!" she'll get in the car *an'* drive, man! She noses in:
> "Hi, *you havin' chitlins?* I'll be right in." *An' jus'* sit down, and eat *'em.*
> I can't eat *'em,* man. *Firs'* time she ever brought *'em* to me, I looked
> at *'em,* I *say,* "What is this?" They *was* all in the plate, like that.
> [Laughter.]
> She said, "Chitlins."
> I *say,* "What?"
> She *say,* "Chitlins."
> I *say,* "I *don' want none.* What is chitlin?"
> She *say,* "Well, it's the intestines of the pig."
> I *say,* "Noooo, I *don' want none* o' that! [Laughter.] Nooo, *'cause* if
> I know anything about anatomy, you know, you got the lower tract in
> there, *ain't* you? [Loud laughter.] *An' ain't no* food down in that area!
> Matter of fact, I think you better check it out—somebody misspelled a
> word! [Laughter and applause.]

This seems a far cry from the comedian whose position on Black English in the 1970s was represented by author Ronald Smith as follows:

> [Cosby's] conservative viewpoints seemed out of touch with the times. Guys like [Richard] Pryor were putting on the toughest of street-jive dialects, while Cosby took a dim view of black English: "We're lighting a fire that has no use, a fire that doesn't warm anybody, where you're going to make up your own language, your own mathematics and sciences. That's just an easy way out. We need black people in space and science programs and in many other areas. While these hoodlum packs are out roaming the streets and saying 'what it is, what it is' and 'right on' and giving handshakes and challenging each other over a piece of cement that the city owns, there are some very bright ones . . . who could contribute something to society."

As "The Lower Tract" and other Cosby skits showed, the funnyman did have a use for the black vernacular, drawing on it to re-create warmly the natural conversation among black friends and family. While the contrast between his statements about black talk and his use of Black English might be rationalized on a number of grounds (the derogatory statements quoted by Smith occur in an educational "future of the race" context, for instance, and they seem to focus on contemporary slang rather than grammar), it is ultimately a reflection of the larger love-hate relationship with Spoken Soul that has provided this book with both its subtitle and subtext.

Lest we leave the impression that black comedians use Spoken Soul only for routines about home and family, and reserve Standard English for more "lofty" themes such as civil rights and politics, we should remember that icons including Moms Mabley and Redd Foxx all possessed an unrestrained mystique, a self-issued license to say just about whatever they pleased, however they wished to say it. Because they were so wickedly funny, they got away with confronting even the most politically hot-wired or taboo topics head-on—poverty, crime, sex, homosexuality, drugs, and race, race, race. Vernacular simply re-inforced their footloose styles, adding, for instance, to the wry flavor of Gregory's political remarks:

> I spent six months, once, sitting at an Alabama lunch counter. And when they finally served me, they didn't have what I wanted! . . .
> My brother is so sure he isn't going to get waited on, he don't even take no money with him. . . . Wouldn't it be funny if they finally decided to serve him? If they was ready, and he wasn't?

Mabley was equally incalculable. The "chitlin circuit" darling addressed topics such as the fall of President Nixon with homespun wisdom and a demeanor as deceivingly innocuous as the housecoat she always wore:

> Even old Moms couldn't do nothin' for that man 'cept give him a few licks upside the head . . . he was just too far gone. Only thing I got to say about him is, your sins will find you out. Like old Joe Louis says, you can run, but you can't hide.

Redd Foxx, popular for his stand-up comedy performances and recordings long before his starring role in the 1970s TV series *Sanford and Son,* reflected on the civil rights movement with similar downhome pragmatism:

> And when the civil rights marchers was parading through Selma and getting it from the white-sheet wearers, I used to say, "I ain't gonna do no marching nonviolently. Ain't no way I'm gonna let a cracker go upside my head with a stick and I do nothing but hum 'We Shall Overcome.' I'm going to cut him. I'm from St. Louis, and we wake up bucknaked with our knife on."

Redd Foxx not only exploited the language of the black community in his routines, but talked explicitly about doing so:

> The black comedian of today uses the language of the streets, and in doing his characterizations, he speaks the same way. . . . There is no doubt that black street language has spilled over to every walk of life in our society today, thus making the American English language that much more (if you'll pardon the expression) colorful.

This comment in fact closes a seven-page exposition, "Black Language," that concludes *The Redd Foxx Encyclopedia of Black Humor.* It includes a discussion of the history of black language, explanations of various slang terms, and recollections of how the vernacular was used by various entertainers. Foxx's delight in the vernacular is obvious. But in the immediately preceding chapter, it was the same man who wrote:

> When I first started out in the business, the blackface comedian was something I resented strongly. I used to see this in St. Louis and Chicago where I grew up and couldn't figure out why a man being black had to black up his face. I just couldn't see no reason for it.
>
> Even the dialect I resented. When Slappy White and I first began to work together back in 1948, the first thing I did was to take the de's and dem's and doe's out of his mouth. We were not going to talk like that. I knew I didn't need no dialect to be funny, so I never used it.

To understand the conflict between Foxx's expressed resentment for "the dialect" and his demonstrated affinity for "black street language," we need to remember that the dialect to which he objected was that stereotyped and tired characterization of late-nineteenth- and early-twentieth-century minstrelsy and the blackface performances that succeeded it. In this respect Foxx echoed James Weldon Johnson, who in 1933 took exception to the use of "conventionalized dialect" in poetry, rooted as it was in a despised minstrel tradition. In fact, the language in which Foxx reveled during his stand-up routines also included *des*, *dems*, and *doses*, and some of the vernacular features found in the blackface comic tradition, though not the shuffling, self-demeaning characterizations most endemic to that tradition. So Foxx, like Cosby and Givens, exemplified the same oscillating relationship with black language that such writers as Johnson and Dunbar and Angelou did, and that still has Americans of all stripes eating their words, as it were.

As we have emphasized throughout this book so far, the variously named vernacular of African Americans does have a remarkable capacity to elicit denial and shame from blacks (not to mention others). But if comedy is what happens when folks relax, "get down," and "let it all hang out," then one would expect to find vernacular—the variety of informality—where there is laughter. Indeed, the "dialect" of black jokesters—professionals or the sidewalk variety—is more than a prop for the burlesque (it remains vastly more essential than, say, Richard Pryor's casually dangled cigarette). It is organic to the culture of the man and woman of words, organic to the signifying tradition, and organic even to the types of scenarios African Americans consider funny.

In the 1990 movie *House Party,* which became something of a cult hit among black youth of the time, Robin Harris's character Pop comes off as comical and irreverent because he uses the vernacular, but also because he uses the "trash-talking," insult-trading style that is a mainstay of everyday humor within the black community. In one scene, the stern working-class father confronts two teenagers after showing up at a house party in search of his wayward son, who is supposed to be home as punishment:

POP: Bilaal, whateva yo name is. Sounds like something you catch
          under yo feet. You see my boy?

BILAAL: Nah, I haven't seen him, sir.

POP: You sure?

BOY: Yo, why don't you go home and watch the late show, Pops?

POP: Why don't you jus' go home? Test-tube baby. Wha's yo name?

BOY: Clinton.

POP: Clinton what?

BOY: Clinton, ahm, X.

POP: Clinton X, huh?

BOY: Yeah, Clinton X. Ahm a Muslim.

POP: Well, go home and bring me back two bean pies and a poke chop sandwich, li'l trout-mouf heathen. (*Turns to face another partygoer.*) Ohh, how you doin'? I shoulda known you was in here. I saw the drip in front of da driveway. You know som'n, wit dat Jheri Curl you got on yo head you betta not eva do a crime. Ain't no problem findin you—follow da drip, follow da drip.

The scene is not just cinema. Almost every African American has a father or an uncle or a grandmother or a cousin or a friend who "talks trash" relentlessly. In fact, the art of "clowning," "dissing," "busting caps" (or "snaps"), or "playin the dozens" by ritually insulting an individual and his kin (especially his or her mother, although some people draw the line there) is traditional and widespread in Soulsville. The following snaps were recorded among sixth-graders on a basketball court in East Palo Alto, California:

Went to yo house, I ask where the bathroom was, she said two bushes to the left.

I can tell by that neck, you bin in a helluva wreck.

Bobby, yo nose so big, you can go skiin' in it.

Yo granny got three teeth—one in her mouth, two in her back pocket.

Yo motha got a wooden eye, every time she blink she get a splinter.

Yo mama so fat, instead of usin a beeper, she use a VCR.

As James Percelay, Monteria Ivey, and Stephan Dweck observe in their book *Snaps:*

The dozens is the blues of comedy. It is a ritual that crosses generational, regional and class boundaries. The dozens illustrates the force of the spoken word, and is the ultimate expression of fighting with your wits, not your fists. This oral tradition is another example of the originality and verbal innovation that distinguish . . . African American culture.

Their compilation includes more than four hundred fifty snaps, of which the following represent only a small sample (we have skipped the popular but "dirty" snaps):

> Your mother is so fat, she broke her arm and gravy poured out. (From the movie *White Men Can't Jump*)
>
> Your mother is so fat, she puts on high-heel shoes in the morning, and by the end of the day, they're flats.
>
> Your sister is so fat, they had to baptize her at Sea World. (From the TV show *In Living Color*)
>
> If ugliness was a crime, you'd get the electric chair.
>
> Your brother is so ugly, when he sits in the sand the cat tries to bury him.
>
> Your family is so poor, the last time you had a hot meal was when your house was on fire.

Potent vernacular use on the schoolyard and stage notwithstanding, Black English in comedy has often been linked with some of the most crippling and one-dimensional portrayals of African Americans. In the 1950s, the television show *Amos 'n' Andy* raised the ire of the NAACP and other groups who contended that its slapstick humor and its characters' antics depicted blacks as inept and foolish. Two decades later, the myth that black life is rife with capers and jovial misadventure was still being pandered to on the tube (though to a lesser degree). *Good Times* (1974–1979) chronicled happenings in the life of a black working-class family living in a public housing development. The sitcom's premise was that despite insecure employment, paltry wages, pitiful health care, the specter of crime, a corrupt police force, and other circumstances of poverty, black people still manage to smile, hum, and exclaim in Pollyanna fashion, "Ain't we glad we got 'em . . . good times!" Although it represented one of television's first authentic portrayals of Spoken Soul, the program's content soon disappointed some blacks. In one typical family crisis, J.J. (the show's most memorable character) was jailed on bogus robbery charges. Unable to come up with the $500 he needed to make bail, his parents, Florida and James, spent the night at the police station. Friend Willona and brother Michael showed up the following morning:

FLORIDA: James? James!

WOMAN: You betta answer, cuz I ain't no James!

JAMES: I'm sorry, baby, I—I musta been dreamin'.

FLORIDA: Yeah, yo' dream musta been in a dance hall, cuz you changed partners.

WOMAN: People ain't safe no place. You even get molested in a po-lice station.

JAMES: I'm sorry, baby.

FLORIDA: Ah, that's awright, honey, I was dreamin' too. . . . I dream we was home and everything was awright. . . . You know, James, I was thinkin' dis experience might teach J.J. not to make a joke outta findin' things.

WILLONA: Good morning, y'all.

MICHAEL: Hi Ma, hi Dad.

JAMES: Hey, Michael. What choo got dere?

MICHAEL: I made a picket sign: "The fuzz unfair to brothers especially mine."

WILLONA: You think that one's bad, you shoulda seen the one he was gonna bring.

FLORIDA: What we gonna do with this boy?

JAMES: I don't know what choo gonna do, babe, but I'm 'onna get him some more cardboard so he can keep on makin' these signs.

MICHAEL: Right on, Dad.

Two years before *Good Times* premiered, *Superfly,* one of the most successful blaxploitation movies (with a reported gross of $6.4 million), arrived in theaters. The film, which glares like a Polaroid flash from a time when black men were painted as rifle-toting pimps and pushers who lorded it over urban streets, featured Ron O'Neal as the shadowy cocaine peddler named Priest. In an opening sequence, two huddled junkies prepare to rob Priest for his dope loot:

JUNKIE NO. 1: Did you get the money?

JUNKIE NO. 2: I ain't got nothin'. She wouldn't give it to me.

JUNKIE NO. 1: Wastin' all this goddamned time. We do it my way.

Fed up with such narrow big-screen roles, comic Robert Townsend lampooned the film industry's portrayals of blacks in his 1987 movie *Hollywood Shuffle.* The opening scene finds Townsend, who plays an aspiring actor looking for his first gig, rehearsing the part of a gangster in the bathroom mirror as his amused little brother looks on:

TOWNSEND: Tommy. Tommy. You kill-ded mah bro-tha. He was mah only bro-tha. I love-ded dis dude, babee. An you gonna pay, jive sucka. You done messed wit da wrong dude, babee. Ahm gon be on yo' ass like a pair of Fruit-of-the-Looms. Ahm gon' bounce you harder than a canceled check. As soon as you get yo' foot off ma face, I'm gon hurt ya, man. I'm gon hurt chyoo. Dis be ma turf, babee. Ah owns da East Side. Listen . . . listen . . . Oh! You tough now! Oh, you tough now! Becuzin' you be got yo' gang. You be got yo' gang. But when ma gang finds out . . . Oh. Oh! Why you gotta pull a knife, man? Why you gotta pull a knife? (*Slips out of character and addresses younger brother:*) What's the line?

BROTHER: I ain't be got no weapon.

The spoof is hilarious, of course, because of Townsend's outrageous, whiny inflection, and because some of the dialogue ("kill-ded," "love-ded"; "Becuzin' you be got yo' gang"; "I ain't be got no weapon") is contrived gibberish, involving a fracturing of some of Spoken Soul's genuine rules. In fact, this is how African American Vernacular English might sound if, as countless black and white columnists, policy makers, and pundits have maintained, it followed no hard-and-fast rules. Townsend uses the absurd script to illustrate Hollywood's apparent ignorance about black life and its penchant for churning out the most stereotypical of images. But he also pokes fun at a more widespread lack of awareness on the part of the larger culture about the nuances of black speech itself.

With the black vernacular so misunderstood, and so often placed in the mouths of jesters such as *Good Times*'s J.J. and criminals such as *Superfly*'s Priest, it's not surprising that many blacks let out a collective sigh when *The Cosby Show* came on the air in the 1980s. Clifford and Clair Huxtable, well-to-do professionals who spoke proper English and meted out textbook-perfect guidance and affection to their children, were redemptive in many ways. Once a week, like clockwork, black American families were ushered into that idyllic brownstone where Standard English and hundred-dollar sweaters—rather than jive and food stamps—were the norm. Now there are many such real-life households in black America. But there are many more black households in which neither parent holds an advanced degree—or any degree, for that matter. And in many of these homes, Black English is the lingua franca.

   As Givens's and Harvey's routines imply, though, the black community's linguistic chameleons—and a chameleonlike existence remains an imperative of black life—probably have as much Bill Cosby coursing through their veins as they do Redd Foxx. In a very real sense, both are the result of cultural confluence. And black folk are better off for having them both around. For together they speak to both halves of the soul, allowing us to play doctor on the job and the dozens after quitting time.

5

Singers, Toasters, and Rappers

If the music of the Negro in America, in all its permutations, is subjected to a socio-anthropological as well as musical scrutiny, something about the essential nature of the Negro's existence in this country ought to be revealed, as well as something about the essential nature of this country, i.e., society as a whole.

——Leroi Jones (now Amiri Baraka; 1963)

In this present day, someone in Cairo is feelin' *Tupac's philosophy and graffing it on an ancient wall. They're doing the same in Tokyo. . . . In the last decade,* Black Street Speech *has become a planetary phenomenon, with global hip hop heads spittin' phrases like* da bomb! *and* you know what I'm saying?

——James Spady and H. Samy Alim (1999)

Some Americans embrace Spoken Soul (albeit subconsciously) only when it's delivered over the FM dial, crooned in a ballad, or draped atop the *thud-thud* of a funky baseline. Not that vernacular pronunciation and syntax are obscured when set to music, for they often take on an even grander flavor—becoming even more evocative and "in your face"—when jazzed up for twelve bars or worked over a catchy hook. It is then that Spoken Soul's aptness for expressing the exotic in the plainest of terms, for expressing the unremarkable with the greatest flamboyance, and occasionally, for expressing concepts that Standard English simply cannot becomes most obvious. Duke Ellington might have meant this, in part, when he observed in 1932 that "it don't mean a thing if it ain't got that swing." With that pronouncement, Ellington lent the era its jingle and proclaimed mainstream

America square. And she *was* square when compared with the dancing, jazzing culture then emerging from New York and other cities, a culture in which black vernacular was the parlance of the hip.

Americans of all types tend to bad-talk soul talk, even though it is the guts of the black music they so relish, and even though this would be a much duller country without it. It is an absurd contradiction, and as we observed on a drizzling May morning in 1997, one that often goes unnoticed.

It was commencement time at Howard University, the Washington, D.C., campus said to have placed the capstone on black education. African America appeared to have sent delegates from every city block, cul-de-sac, and country lane, and black vernacular could be heard everywhere among the crush of bodies. After the faculty procession, African American broadcast-news pioneer Carole Simpson began her keynote speech, enunciating with broadcast-news diction. She blurred through a medley of race matters, praising affirmative action and snubbing biracial blacks who had petitioned the federal government for a census classification other than "African American." They threatened to undercut black political clout by denying a part of their heritage that society would ascribe to them entirely anyway, she suggested. The audience offered scattered Amens.

Then she turned to the matter of racism in America, some of which, she said, was "the fault of white people, [but] not all. Some of the negativism we bring on ourselves." Simpson offered two examples. The first was rap music, which, she maintained, cast black men as "criminals, gun-toting gangsters, malt liquor–swilling, drug-taking women-haters." She went on:

> You'll tell me it's about keeping it real—the beat, the rhyme, the message . . . *Please!* Most African Americans are like you—hardworking, law-abiding, family-loving, goal-oriented, patriotic people. You suffer— we *all* suffer—because white Americans think we are all the blacks portrayed in popular culture, which is produced by white people.

The second example, significantly enough, was the Oakland Ebonics controversy, which had erupted six months earlier and was finally fading from the headlines:

> I was in Oakland, California, last week, the birthplace of Ebonics. [Scattered laughter from crowd.] I came in contact with many black people, and black children. I did not hear *one* person talking in Ebonics or Black English, or what when I was growing up we used

to simply call "street slang." What was Ebonics all about? . . . The story
was distorted when it first came out, but to suggest that black children
cannot speak good English makes me crazy. . . . Nobody is happier than
I am that Ebonics has been stopped dead in its tracks!

After Simpson had finished, members of the Howard University
Choir and Orchestra rose and offered their rendition of a spiritual.
Their voices were buoyant, and Simpson and the crowd nodded and
swayed approvingly:

> Lord, I done done,
> Lord, I done done,
> Lord, I done done,
> I done done whatcha tole me ta do.

It wasn't long before the final remarks were made, the last strains
of "Pomp and Circumstance" subsided, and the graduates dashed
down the hill with their extended families in tow. No one, evidently,
had caught the contradiction. No one appeared to realize how odd
the disdain for Ebonics (expressed by the keynote speaker and
some—though not all—members of the crowd) seemed when paired
with the obvious delight in such utterly idiomatic lyrics. This spiritual
draws much of its poignancy and soul from the vernacular itself—
note the completive *done* in "I *done* done," the dropping of the final
consonant sound in *tole,* and other features—and from the image it
conveys of an erstwhile slave or modern-day long-sufferer who has remained spiritually faithful despite the "trials of this world." But getting folks *consciously* to celebrate their ancestors' innovations on English—the living evidence of an African encounter with a socially and
linguistically hostile New World—can be as exacerbating as getting
them to confront the legacy of slavery itself. There will probably always be an astonishingly large number of blacks in this country who
applaud the black vernacular only when they don't realize it is the
black vernacular they're applauding.

Contemplate that audience's appreciation for the ebony phonics
of the spiritual and the simultaneous distaste for "Ebonics" (again,
this was taken to mean both the variety of speech and Oakland's public relations nightmare), and you may come to the following conclusion: Appreciating sung soul is one thing, but appreciating soul as
it is spoken is something else entirely. It might well be said that music
that draws heavily on non-Standard English (and by this we mean almost all popular music, including jazz, blues, rock and roll, soul, and

rhythm and blues) has generally been embraced by the mainstream. Though its lexicon and sensibilities have seeped into mainstream talk for centuries, however, nonstandard English itself has generally been scorned or ridiculed by the dominant culture. In fact, middle America has quite often jeered those who speak "jive" in the same breath and with the same enthusiasm that it has grooved to black sounds à la Bessie Smith and Mahalia Jackson and Ray Charles and Lauryn Hill (all of whom were and are far less concerned with speaking "proper English" than with singing soulfully and unabashedly).

African Americans themselves pay tribute to those and other dialect-slingers precisely because of the abundance of their soul—that gift for articulating the most intimate spiritual and aesthetic selves of African America, with all its drama, irony, and poignancy. In fact, most blacks will acknowledge their own conventionally soulful characteristics (such as a fondness for certain foods, and distinction in a variety of musical genres including spirituals, jazz, the blues, and hip-hop), even if they denounce the soulful shadows of their most private speech. Many soul people feel at ease rooting for outsiders who ridicule or condemn Black English, but most would bristle if anyone dared to dismiss as primitive the notional attribute of soul itself, or suggest that it didn't even actually exist.

The idea of "soul" reached new heights in the 1960s (when blacks became "soul brothas and sistahs"), and found a champion in James Brown. Wrapped in bodysuits and capes, Brown would tattoo the stage with magical feet, slinging sweat and exchanging indecipherable calls and responses with his band. That sapsucker had him some soul—a fact that he articulated succinctly in his 1971 hit "Soul Power":

> I got something that makes me wanna shout,
> I got something that tell me what it's all about,
> I got *soul*, and I'm supa-bad.

When Brown did his "thang," he impressed even himself, and would exclaim, "Good God! I gotta jump back and kiss myself!" Such is the exuberance of soul power. And it sells, too: Brown had fifty-six R&B top-ten hits, eighteen number-ones and more than forty million-plus sellers. Americans of all colors went wild for the audacious, outrageous performer who dripped attitude and unleashed dialect. Now, imagine what those fans might have thought had they hustled to the music store for the latest James Brown album, and dashed home only to hear an announcer's broadcast-news diction pouring from their record players: "I have something that makes me want to shout, /

I have something that informs me what is happening, / I have soul, and I am super-good." Sure, that sort of syntax suits the evening news. Crisp broadcast talk has its place. But such language would not have gone over well with Brown's audiences. Feeling *hip, outta sight, cool, funky, bad,* or *fly* themselves, they prefer Spoken Soul, which, by virtue of the experience that produced it, conveys the intoxicating feel of *cool.*

The point was not lost on the Rolling Stones. Like other bands that emerged while rock and roll was young, they became famous by borrowing black styles and black talk, and often without attribution. Several of their hits can be loosely traced to black standards of the South; a few are plain knock-offs. When recording "You Gotta Move" in 1971, for instance, the band did nothing more than lay a grinding electric guitar behind old, old African American lyrics:

> You gotta move, you gotta move, child,
> Oh, when the Lord gets ready,
> You gotta move.

The original "I Gotta Move" was sung in black churches for years, particularly on the Carolina and Georgia Sea Islands and elsewhere in the South, and is likely still being sung there. It contains many of the classic characteristics of ring shouts, the praise sessions of slaves who rekindled faith and resisted misery by drawing themselves into animated worship circles. Ring shouts tended to carry simple messages through simple lyrics. It was their rendering that was adorned. The following version of "I Gotta Move," recorded in the 1960s during a live a cappella performance by a group of Georgia Sea Island women, began almost liltingly, with booming voices, syncopated claps, and stomps on a naked floor creating an orchestra without instruments. One woman alone introduced each line, but she was soon accompanied by the harmonizing wails of the others. A few bars into the plaintive melody, the footfalls sped up and the clapping went double-time. The resulting sound was layered and throbbing and sepulchral, as if it had wafted up from a sad netherworld:

> I got to move, we got to move,
> We got to move, we got to move,
> Oh, when the Lord, Lord get ready,
> You got to move. Oh,
>
> You may be rich, you may be poor,
> You may be high, you may be low,

But when the Lord get ready,
You got to move. Oh,

My brother move, my brother move,
My brother move, my brother move.
Oh, when the Lord get ready,
You got to move.

Sometime I'm up, sometime I'm down,
Sometime I'm almost to da groun'.
Oh, when the Lord get ready,
You got to move. . . .

There are layers of meaning here as well as of sound. You got to move when the spirit says move, the song suggests, as when the Holy Spirit winds you up on Sunday morning. But you've also got to move on home to Jesus when He says it's time to rest. And this is the great equalizer, for as is observed, the rich and high-ups must go before Him when He is ready, just as the poor and low-downs. Such a profound faith in the equal opportunity of mortality might have scraped a slaver's spine like an icy finger. Lord knows all men were created equal, the lyrics imply. And in the afterlife, you will be equal too.

But to understand fully the original song's character and intent, we must also scrutinize its language, which plainly shows its folk roots: *got to,* not "have to," *Sometime,* not "Sometimes," *groun'* not "ground," *the Lord get ready,* not "gets ready." Tense in particular must be considered at some length, because it forces us to wrestle with this question: When those Sea Island women sang, "My brother move," were they omitting the present-tense suffix ("My brother move*s*") or the past ("my brother move*d*")? In African American English, "he move" can denote either. Yet the significance of the song hinges in part on which of the verb's two forms was originally intended. Did the first soul to wail these lyrics mean to convey that his or her brother was moving at that moment—which would suggest that the sibling in question was still present—or that his or her brother had already "moved," and was, as the old folks say, "resting in the bosom of Jesus"?

Maybe both. Human capitulation to the will of the Lord is the song's main concern. But "I Got to Move" might also be viewed as a carry-over from the African faith system that tells us that departed kinfolk inhabit a dynamic spirit world, a realm from which they can participate in and guide the affairs of the living. If your brother had passed on, or even if he had escaped or been purchased by a plantation owner far away, you and he would still have been wrapped in a quilt of co-dependency—a notion perhaps articulated by the haunting phrase "We got to move."

So the vernacular is a survival tool, encoding the culture's semantic dualism and expressing the "double consciousness" necessary to negotiate the world as it is and envision it as it could be. Spoken Soul can camouflage or elucidate. Its sleight of tongue can hide a message from members of the larger culture, or feed it to them on the sly. It is, necessarily, the language of double entendre:

> Steal away, steal away, steal away to Jesus,
> Steal away, steal away home,
> I ain't got long to stay here.

> My Lord, He calls me,
> He calls me by the thunder,
> The trumpet sounds within-a my soul,
> I ain't got long to stay here.

> Steal away, steal away, steal away to Jesus,
> Steal away, steal away home,
> I ain't got long to stay here.

> Green trees a-bending,
> Po' sinner stands a-trembling,
> The trumpet sounds within-a my soul,
> I ain't got long to stay here.

> Steal away, steal away, steal away to Jesus,
> Steal away, steal away home,
> I ain't got long to stay here.

The slaves who uttered those words were not just gazing longingly into the firmament, but picturing a homecoming they intended to experience *during their lifetime.* The scene of redemption could have been a free state in the northern United States, or it could have been Canada or the continent of Africa. No matter where the jumping-off point, the belief that the sons and daughters of Africa could "fly" out of bondage manifested itself both in everyday oral abstractions and in real designs to flee the plantation. Though many went barefoot in North America, the old Negro wisdom reassured that "all God's children got traveling shoes." The implication perhaps being that some fortunate Negroes were even going to get their running shoes here on earth.

Many a slave master must have dismissed the ditties and dirges of his bondmen and bondwomen as wishful thinking, as cryptic pleas for the deliverance of death, or as quaint noise-making, never suspecting that his singing slaves were tacitly resisting psychological bondage, concealing subversive messages, possibly plotting uprisings or escape. Nevertheless, most spirituals can be linked to philosophies of liberation, and their genealogy traced to the first moment a kidnapped African paused from the labor imposed by the white man to observe the ancient custom of chanting one's discontent.

Makers of black music have always defined themselves, with the gloss of Spoken Soul, in terms of who they were to become once they had reached the Other Side. Whether the Other Side was seen as a trouble-free afterlife or an earthly life of liberation, a wistful paradise or a destination well worth holding on for (or throwing down for) in this world, black folk have always used their music to project themselves into a place where they are in control, where they do not have their humanity gouged out for their having been born black, where they overcome, or get even:

> Monday morning, gonna lay down my cross, get me a crown
> Late in the evenin'. Oh, I'm goin' home, live on high
> Soon as ma feet strike Zion, gonna lay down ma heavy burden
> I'm gonna put on ma robe in glory
> I'm goin' home one day an' tell ma story
> I've been comin' up hill and mountain
> Gon' drink from the Christian fountain.

Mahalia Jackson, often hailed as the world's greatest gospel singer, recorded "I Will Move On Up a Little Higher" in 1947. The song explores the exhilarating conviction that black folk will shed earthly constraints and be richly rewarded on that "great gittin'-up morning" when they see Christ and are reunited with long-gone kinfolk. An end to the toil of slavery and poverty is envisioned, and the spiritual metaphors of "goin' home," walking without weariness, and drinking from the fountain become sweet music for the thirsty, the dispossessed, the displaced and overworked. These are powerful Christian ideas, and Jackson expresses them with every ounce of her sanctified self. The phrase "get me a crown," for instance, conveys a sense of entitlement and self-righteousness that the Standard English translation ("I'm going to get a crown for myself") cannot.

But not all representations of the Other Side have been as pious. When blacks set out to articulate heartache and a vision for deliverance in secular terms, what came up was foot-thumpin', name-takin', raunchy, bad, and blissful. It was the blues:

Now when I was a young boy, at the age of five,
Ma mutha said I was gon be the greatest man alive.
But now I'm a mahn, way past twenty-one,
I wan choo ta believe me baby, I have lots of fun.
I'm a mah-yun!
I spell M, A child, N
That represent man! (Yeah)
No B (Whooo), O child, Y (Yeah)
That mean mannish boy!
I'm a mah-yun! (Yeah)
I'm a natural-born lover's man!
I'm a mah-yun!
I'm a rollin' stone!
I'm a mah-yun!
I'm a hoochie-coochie man.

When a black youngster is giving too much lip, showing out, acting up, or generally behaving "too grown" for his own good, his
grandmother is likely to snap, "Quit actin' so mannish, boy!" So with
this song's title, "Mannish Boy," Muddy Waters was playing on an expression organic to African American childhood. It's easy to hear this
blues classic and attribute it just to braggadocio. But between the
ecstatic cries from the audience heard on the original recording,
beneath the gusto of the legendary voice and the virility with which
Waters growls "I'm a mah-yun," a deeper message percolates. We must
not forget that at the time of this recording (1955), black men were
still being called "boy" well into their advanced years, an indignity
that Waters—born the son of a Mississippi sharecropper in 1915—
was no doubt all too familiar with. Stripped to its core, then, "Mannish Boy" is a rousing affirmation of black manhood, the unequivocal
resolution to the slave plea: "Am I not a man and a brother?"

Of course, with boasts such as "The line I shoots, it will never
miss— / when I make love to a woman, she cain't resis'," Waters also
exemplifies the swagger typical of the "signifying" tradition. This ritu-
alized wordplay, a highly stylized lying, joking, and carrying on with
such virtuosity as to inject one's message with metaphor and eloquence while elevating one's social status and parodying one's inter-
locutors or their attitudes and behaviors, goes on every day in the
backyards, poolrooms, and front porches of Soulsville. It's hard to attach a textbook definition to such an inclusive speech event, but anthropologist Claudia Mitchell-Kernan has suggested that it is "a way of

encoding messages or meanings in natural conversations which involves, in most cases, an element of indirection."

> The black concept of *signifying* incorporates essentially a folk notion
> that dictionary entries for words are not always sufficient for interpret-
> ing meanings or messages, or that meaning goes beyond such inter-
> pretations. Complimentary remarks may be delivered in a left-handed
> fashion. A particular utterance may be an insult in one context and not
> in another. What pretends to be informative may intend to be persua-
> sive. Superficially, self-abasing remarks are frequently self-praise. The
> hearer is thus constrained to attend to all potential meaning carrying
> symbolic systems in speech events—the total universe of discourse.

Signifying, then, is the verbal artistry you're likely to overhear
whenever black folk get together in an informal forum, whether that
is a fish fry or a barbershop. It's part of an appreciation for "rapping,"
for fluid speech that brings the speaker and the listener immeasurable pleasure. One of the signifying tradition's most outlandish
genres—generally the province of adult (especially older) males—
are "toasts," including "The Signifying Monkey," "Stagolee," and
"Shine and the *Titanic*." Linguist William Labov and his colleagues
define toasts as "long oral epic poems." Folklorist Roger Abrahams,
the first scholar to reprint and discuss toasts at length, offers this
characterization:

> The toast is a narrative poem that is recited, often in a theatrical
> manner, and represents the greatest flowering of Negro verbal talent.
> Toasts are often long, lasting anywhere from two to ten minutes. They
> conform to a general but by no means binding framing pattern. This
> consists of some sort of picturesque or exciting introduction, action
> alternating with dialogue (because the action is some kind of struggle
> between two people or animals), and a twist ending of some sort,
> either a quip, an ironic comment, or a brag.

Toasts (which may be compared to the less-than-genteel "'Twas
the Night Before Christmas" poem in chapter 11) often contain pro-
fanity, lawless capers, improbable sex romps, and exploits of heroes
who, as Abrahams notes, fall into two main categories: tricksters and
badmen. Into the trickster-hero category falls "The Signifying Monkey," perhaps the best-known toast, and one that forms the center-
piece for a theory of black literary criticism developed by Harvard
Afro-American studies professor Henry Louis Gates Jr. One version of
this toast begins:

Down in the jungle near a dried-up creek,
The signifying monkey hadn't slept for a week.
Remembering the ass-kicking he had got in the past
He had to find somebody to kick the lion's ass.
Said the signifying monkey to the lion that very same day,
"There's a bad motherfucker heading your way.
The way he talks about you, it can't be right,
And I know when you two meet there going to be a fight."

In the badman tradition is "The Great MacDaddy," whose hero defies the judge he faces two hours after he's picked up "on a lame rap." As in many toasts, characters speak in the vernacular:

Later on, 'bout ten past ten,
I was facing the judge and twelve other men.
He looked down on me, he said,
"You're the last of the bad.
Now Dillinger, Slick Willie Sutton, all them fellows is gone,
Left you, the Great MacDaddy, to carry on."
He said, "Now, we gonna send you up the way. Gonna send you up
  the river.
Fifteen to thirty, that's your retire."
I said, "Fifteen to thirty, that ain't no time.
I got a brother in Sing Sing doing ninety-nine."

Somewhat intermediate between the trickster and the badman traditions, as Abrahams pointed out, is Shine, a powerful, quick-witted, metaphorical black man who stoked the coals in the belly of that ill-fated cruise ship, the *Titanic,* and whose exploits are celebrated in a series of toasts of the same name. Shine is the first to notice the water coming in after the boat runs up against an iceberg, but his initial attempts to address the situation are all rebuffed by the captain, overconfident about his vessel and disdainful of this black boiler-room boat-hand. Eventually, Shine leaps overboard and begins to swim:

Shine took off his shirt, took a dive. He took one stroke
And the water pushed him like it pushed a motorboat.
The captain said, "Shine, Shine, save poor me,
I'll give you more money than any black man see."
Shine said, "Money is good on land or sea.
Take off your shirt and swim like me."

In almost every version of this toast, Shine also turns down the entreaties of both the captain's wife and his daughter, who, from the deck of the doomed ship, offer him their affections in return for salvation. Shine swims on, besting a shark in the open sea and making it to shore, where, it is said, he gets himself good and soused by the time the *Titanic* goes under.

Shine possesses the superhuman abilities typical of many toast protagonists. Similarly incredible traits are exhibited by Dolomite, a notorious character (often portrayed by entertainer Rudy Ray Moore) who was so bad that he kicked African lions "to stay in shape" and who conquered scores of women (almost always presented as loose and scurrilous). It was said of Dolomite:

> At the age of one he was drinkin' whiskey and gin,
> at the age of two he was eatin' the bottles it came in.
> Now Dolomite had an uncle called Sudden Death,
> killed a dozen bad men from the smell of his breath.
> When his uncle heard how Dolomite was treatin' his ma and his pa,
> he said, "Let me go and check on this bad rascal before he go too far."
> Now one cold, dark December night,
> his uncle broke in on Dolomite.
> Now Dolomite wasn't no more'n three or four,
> when his uncle come breakin' through the door.
> His uncle said, "Dolomite,
> I want you to straighten up and treat your brother right,
> 'cause if you keep on with your dirty mistreatin',
> I'm gonna whup your ass till your heart stop beatin'." . . .
> He led off with a right that made lightnin' flash,
> but Dolomite tore his leg off, he was that damned fast.

For black men, who have been physically and psychologically castrated during their North American internment, assertions of manhood—of strength, potency, and bravado—must be larger than life. The badmen of toasts thus represent irreverent heroes of redemptive proportions. They're immortal, and they're worth mentioning in a chapter on singers because they help us understand first, the continuum of oral dexterity that blurs the distinction between black speech and song, and second, the wicked self-aggrandizement found in the newest chapter in the African American book of folklore, hip-hop:

> When rap begin then I gotta join in and
> Before my rhyme is over, you know I'ma win
> Cool J has arrived so you better make way
> Ask anybody in the crowd they say the kid don't play

Sparring competition that's my hobby and job
I don't wear a disguise because I don't own the mob
Got a pinpoint rap that makes you feel trapped so many girls on my jock
I think my phone here is tapped

I'm bad
(Cool J)
(Cool J)
(Cool J)
(C-C-C-C-Cool J)
(C-C-C-C-C-C-C-Cool J J J J J)

I'm like Tyson icin', I'm a soldier at war
I'm makin' sure you don't try to battle me no more
Got concrete rhymes, been rappin' for ten years and
Even when I'm braggin' I'm bein' sincere

The precise origin of hip-hop is a matter of dispute, but the originators appear to have been New York City youths who, in the middle and late 1970s, with nothing more than turntables and their imagination, began mixing old-school jams by funk prophets such as James Brown and George Clinton. The parents of the hip-hoppers (who were themselves of the Dolomite generation) must have groused when their Ohio Players, Isley Brothers, O'Jays, and Sly and the Family Stone records were returned scratched. But by the time the Sugarhill Gang dropped "Rapper's Delight" ("I don't mean to brag, I don't mean to boast, / but we like hot butta on our breakfast toast") in 1979, and Grandmaster Flash and the Furious Five released "The Message" ("It's like a jungle sometimes, / it makes me wonder how I keep from going under") in 1982, rap culture was oozing from the streets of urban America.

Remember, no creation in the Spoken Soul universe emerges from a vacuum. LL Cool J, the MC responsible for the immodest lyrics above, is as much a son of Rudy Ray Moore as he is of Muddy Waters. The braggadocio of his 1987 ballad "I'm Bad" (in which the musical theme from the blaxploitation movie *Shaft* was sampled) in a sense represents the incarnation of a Dolomite chant, or the ranting of a "Mannish Boy" in the 1980s. And boasts delivered Gatling-gun style remain the bread and "butta" of rap. In much the same way that Muddy Waters had enumerated his hustling credentials ("I'm a rollin' stone! . . . I'm a natural-born lover's man . . . I'm a hoochie-coochie man") four decades earlier, Smooth Da Hustler testified to his badness in a 1997 joint that earned him some underground acclaim:

> The money stasher, gun-blastin' razor slasher
> The human asthma breath-taker
> Body dump waster
> The Glock cocker, block locker, the rock chopper
> The shot popper, the jock cock Glocker
> The face splitter, human-disgrace getter

But the rap game wasn't all about getting "big ups" or "mad props" (respect and acclaim). Hip-hop artists also inherited the struggle to "get ovah" to the Other Side. Some, such as bawdy material girl Lil' Kim, envision "Money, Power, Respect" as the keys to transcendence. Others offer a more complex scenario. Nas's single "If I Ruled the World" (1996) imagines the ghetto turned B-boy utopia, and blends an appetite for luxury cars with a longing for liberated black minds:

> Brand-new whips to crash then we laugh in the iller path
> The Villa house is for the crew, how we do
> Trees for breakfast, dime sexes and Benz stretches
> So many years of depression make me envision
> The better livin', the type of place to raise kids in
> Open they eyes to the lies history's tole foul

Nas pictures *whips* (cars) and *dimes* (fine women) as playthings for his *crew* (posse) on a track teeming with insider lingo. Slick lexicon is hip-hop's Magna Carta, establishing the rights of its disciples to speak loudly but privately, to tell America about herself in a language that leaves her puzzled. This glossary is forever morphing, constantly reinventing itself, bumping off words that were considered tony just the other day (but that have now been mainstreamed and co-opted by Madison Avenue to hawk everything from cereal to soda pop). Many of the more or less new hip-hop terms for, say, cash—including *bank, bank roll, benjamins, cheddar, cheese, cream, dead presidents, dividends, ends, g's, loot, mail, papers, papes,* and *scrilla*—are guaranteed to go stale soon, maybe inside a few years.

Any MC who wishes to maintain street validity had better be able to wield the most contemporary slang. For this, along with a raw, unslurred delivery, is what determines much of prowess when it comes to freestyling, a ritual in which "hip-hop heads" form a circle and "bust" improvised rhymes "off the top of the dome." Holding only a slightly lower profile than slang in the rap game, of course, is bona fide Black English, which encompasses vocabulary—and thus slang—

but is also composed of distinct grammatical and phonological elements. There is no question that black talk provides hip-hop's linguistic underpinnings, but manifested strikingly in "The Day After" (1995) by the ultraconscious Atlanta-based group Goodie Mob:

> I been this way since birth
> Heaven above sent a newborn to tell it like he see it
> No lies through the eyes of an angel suggest you don't table
> Every angle be obtuse, ain't no truce, it's war
> It won't stop, to compromise wouldn't stop the bloodsheddin'
> It's Armageddon in the streets of each inner city
> Ain't takin' no pity on the unjust callin' it trust
> I'm on the bus starin' out of a window
> Thankin' 'bout them happy days I had

Rap aficionados gush about this group's talent for flowing in the "cipher," the supercharged circuit of rap knowledge and creativity (something not dissimilar—in the vein of highly communal, responsive rituals—to the ring shout). What many hip-hop heads probably don't realize is that Goodie Mob owes plenty to Spoken Soul. Not just for sledgehammer lyrics and the style in which they're delivered, but for its coveted, noncommercial status within the industry. After all, the Mob is regarded as "real" and truthful because of its image of fierce nonconformity, and nothing thumbs its nose at conformity like the unrestrained African American vernacular. Although white suburban youngsters eat up hip-hop's edgy tales of money, sexual adventure, ghetto life, and racial injustice (and keep ghetto rhymes atop the pop charts), black urban youngsters are the genre's target audience. And black urban youngsters follow artists who roam the world implied by the neighborhood language of black urban youngsters. "Peep" (look at) rapper DMX's "How's It Going Down":

> What type of games is bein' played, how's it goin' down
> If it's on til it's gone, then I gots to know now
> Is you wit me or what, they gon try to give me a nut
> Just honeys wanna give me the butt, what

These lyrics reverberated from car speakers throughout 1998. It is a good example of hip-hop's allegiance to both slang and the grammar of Black English. But it's safe to say that of those who turned up their radios when "the jam bumped," few if any were contemplating hip-hop's ties to the blues, old-school toasts, or jazz, or even considering its developing role as the new conventional wisdom of pop culture, or as folklore transformed. Few hip-hop heads are inclined to trace their music culture to the fast-talking of Fats Waller and Cab Calloway, or even to the scatting of Louis Armstrong. But jazz is in the energetic nonsense words that kick off "Rapper's Delight":

> I said a hip hop the hippie the hippie to the hip hip hop
> a you don't stop a rockin' to the bang bang boogie
> said up jump the boogie to the rhythm of the boogie da beat.

It is a tribute to the resilience of a people who resisted annihilation for centuries, then came out swinging, bebopping, and now hip-hopping, that they are able, with each new generation, to reinvent themselves artfully using the same essential mortar.

The Howard University crowd that found itself swept away by a spiritual's sentiment unwittingly paid homage to the language of "soul power." Members of that audience who experienced a flash of recognition, a starburst of emotion from their communal experience, should acknowledge that the disposition, the very organization of the phrase "I done done" helped trigger those feelings. And if the students in that audience had listened, really listened, to their *own* music, perhaps they would have discovered not only the lingering growl of Muddy Waters and wail of Mahalia Jackson, but the talk of the spirituals as well. Consider 1999 Grammy Award winner Lauryn Hill's "Lost Ones," a hybrid hip-hop-and-reggae tune that did some serious radio rotation in 1998:

> You might win some but you really lost one
> You just lost one, it so silly how come
> When it's all done did you really gain from
> What you *done done,* it so silly how come [Emphasis added.]

As Hill herself submits, there is "not a game new under the sun." Her use of Spoken Soul features such as the completive ("done done") and the deletion of the contracted *s* ("*it so* silly") are natural, accepted, even appreciated elements of a linguistic convention that has sustained the soul. There are many black singers, including Nat King Cole and Sam Cooke, who produced exhilarating, beloved music in "mainstream" English. But if the Rolling Stones flattered the language of our black ancestors with constant imitation, why must the direct heirs to that language disparage it on the street? Why indeed, when the next hip-hop generation busies itself sampling and resampling James Brown, and the parlance of soul still crowns the pop charts?

Part Three

The Living Language

6

Vocabulary and Pronunciation

*Ebonics has no dictionary, no text books, no grammar, no rules. It is
rebellious and outside rule-based language.*
—America Online contributor (December 23, 1996)

*You are 100% incorrect that "Ebonics" has no rules, structure, or
dictionary. Africanized English has a consistent structure and rules. . . .
Please do not confuse street slang with Africanized English.*
—America Online contributor (December 23, 1996)

For most people, languages and dialects are distinguished primarily
by their words and expressions. French speakers say *"Bonjour,"* English
speakers "Hello." The British say "lorry" where Americans say "truck."
Bostonians use "tonic" for what other northeasterners refer to as
"soda" and midwesterners call "pop." And so on. Similarly, for most
casual commentators, what sets black talk apart is its distinctive word
usage, particularly the informal and usually short-lived "slang" expressions known primarily to adolescents and young adults. The only
examples of Black English in James Baldwin's 1979 tribute to the vernacular ("If Black English Isn't a Language, Then Tell Me, What Is?")
are expressions, especially slang, that have crossed over into general
American use, such as *jazz, sock it to me, let it all hang out, right on, uptight,* and *get down.* And for nine out of ten people who contributed to
the America Online discussion of Ebonics in December 1996, Ebonics
was "just a bunch of slang."

But Spoken Soul, like any other language variety, is much more
than slang, and much more than the sum of its words. For linguists,

the scientists who study human language, two other aspects of any language variety are as important as vocabulary, if not more so: its rules for pronouncing words, or pronunciation patterns, and its grammar—including its rules for modifying or combining words to express different meanings and to form larger phrases or sentences. African American vernacular has, for instance, a rule of grammar that allows speakers to move negative helping verbs such as *ain't* and *can't* to the front of a sentence to make the sentence more emphatic, so that "Nobody ain't going" can become "Ain't nobody going!" (This is an emphatic utterance, not a question, and usually such a phrase has the falling intonation of a statement or exclamation.) The verb can be moved to the front only if the subject of the sentence is a negative quantifier such as *nobody* or *nothing*. If the subject is not a negative quantifier—say, *John* or *the boy*—the rule does not apply. You can't convert "John ain't going" into "Ain't John going," at least not as an emphatic statement. (With rising intonation, of course, "Ain't John going?" would be an acceptable question.)

From this example, it should be clear that by "rules" we don't mean regulations that are prescribed in grammar books or consciously memorized. Nobody sits a kid down at the age of six and says, "Okay, time to learn the negative fronting, or inversion, rule." But through exposure and experimentation, children in every speech community around the world learn the conventional and systematic ways of pronouncing, modifying, and combining words that are characteristic of their community's language variety (or varieties). It is these conventional and systematic ways of using language that we refer to as rules.

Every human language and dialect studied to date—whether loved or hated, prestigious or not—has regularities or rules of this type. A moment's reflection would show why this is so. Without regularities, a language variety could not be successfully acquired or used in everyday life, and this applies to Spoken Soul, or Ebonics, as much as to the "Received Pronunciation," or "BBC English," of the British upper crust. Characterizations of the former as careless or lazy, and of the latter as careful or refined, are subjective social and political evaluations that reflect prejudices and preconceptions about the people who usually speak each variety. In contrast, linguists try, as objectively as possible, to understand and reveal the systematic regularities that every language inevitably possesses. That is our goal in this chapter and the next, beginning with the vocabulary and pronunciation of Spoken Soul, and then considering its grammar. Whereas pronunciation and grammar vary less than vocabulary from one region to another, they tend to vary more by social class. And because of their impact on verbal expression and literacy, they loom large when we consider the education of African American children.

Vocabulary

The claim that Ebonics has no dictionary (see the first comment at the beginning of this chapter) is incorrect. Since 1994 there have been two authoritative guides: Clarence Major's 548-page *Juba to Jive: A Dictionary of African American Slang* (a revised, expanded version of his 1970 *Dictionary of Afro-American Slang*), and Geneva Smitherman's 243-page *Black Talk: Words and Phrases from the Hood to the Amen Corner* (a revised and expanded edition of which will appear in 2000). There has also been no dearth of shorter, more informal glossaries, from "Introduction to Contemporary Harlemese" in Rudolph Fisher's 1928 novel *The Walls of Jericho,* through *The New Cab Calloway's Hep-ster's Dictionary* (1944), to more recent word and phrase books such as *A 2 Z: The Book of Rap and Hip-Hop Slang* (1995). Add to this dozens of scholarly articles and a number of book-length studies, including J. L. Dillard's *Lexicon of Black English* (1970) and Edith Folb's *runnin' down some lines* (1980), and it's clear that there is substantial information on the vocabulary of Spoken Soul, past and present.

Since vocabulary, especially slang, is always changing, new studies will always be needed. And a full-fledged Ebonics dictionary with pronunciation, etymologies, and historical attestations, to parallel the *Oxford English Dictionary* or *Webster's Third,* remains to be written. But we know enough from existing studies to make a number of generalizations.

One of the many fascinating features of black vocabulary is how sharply it can divide blacks and whites, and how solidly it can connect blacks from different social classes. In 1992, sociologist Teresa Labov published a study that examined the extent to which adolescents used and understood eighty-nine slang terms. Of all the social variables she considered, race turned out to be the most significant factor, with blacks much more familiar with terms like *bougie* ("an uppity-acting African American"), *busting out* ("looking good"), and *fresh* (for "cool"), and whites much more familiar with terms like *schlep* (for "to drag along") and *bombed* or *smashed* (as a synonym for "drunk"). That the black respondents knew the black terms is significant: they were college students at predominantly white institutions. Although "bloods from the 'hood" and those from the hills certainly differ in the range and kinds of black slang they use (see the comments quoted by Edith Folb later in this section), familiarity with distinctive black vocabulary is one of the ways in which virtually every African American can be said to speak some form of Ebonics, or Spoken Soul.

In 1972, Robert L. Williams, the psychologist who coined the term "Ebonics," created the so-called BITCH test, which, like Teresa Labov's study, highlighted differences in black and white vocabulary and experience. Williams's aggressive acronym stood for "Black Intelligence Test of Cultural Homogeneity," which was designed to give blacks an advantage, unlike the usual intelligence tests that privileged the experience of whites. The test included one hundred multiple-choice questions, most of them requiring the test-taker to select the right gloss for words and expressions "from the black experience." Test items (with Williams's glosses) included: *blood,* "a brother of color"; *to hot-comb,* "to press [one's hair]"; *HNIC,* "head nigger in charge"; and *playing the dozens,* "insulting a person's parents."

What is revealing about Williams's test is that many of the terms are not slang—relatively new and informal usages that are most common among teenagers, and likely not to last long—but words familiar across all age groups in the African American community, and words that have been around for a long time. As the preceding examples show, many of these historically "black" words refer to unique aspects of the black experience, including the physical attributes, social distinctions, and cultural practices and traditions of African Americans. Other examples in this category include the following (definitions are from Smitherman's *Black Talk*):

> **Ashy:** The whitish or grayish appearance of skin due to exposure to wind and cold; shows up more on African Americans due to Black people's darker skin pigmentation.
>
> **Bad:** Good, excellent, great, fine. [In] the Mandingo language in West Africa, *a ka nyi ko-jugu* [is] literally "It is good badly," meaning "It is very good."
>
> **Juneteenth:** The day, usually in mid to late June, when African Americans celebrate emancipation from enslavement; originally June 19, 1865, the date enslaved Africans in Texas learned they had been freed.
>
> **Kitchen:** Hair at the nape of the neck, inclined to be the most curly (*kinky*) and thus the hardest part of *straightened* hair to keep from *going back.*

Tom, Uncle Tom: A negative reference to a Black person, suggesting that he/she is a sell-out, not down with the black cause. Tom comes from the character Uncle Tom in Harriet Beecher Stowe's *Uncle Tom's Cabin,* who put his master's wishes and life before his own. . . . For women, *Aunt Thomasina, Aunt Jane.*

Yelluh, high yelluh: A very light-complexioned African American.

Many [illegible] words
differs fr[illegible] *yelluh,*
which hav[illegible]rd from
other wor[illegible] college
students v[illegible] was not
standard [illegible]ning in
standard [illegible]ey were
bowled ov[illegible]ducted
that the i[illegible]976, for
example, [illegible]evealed
that black[illegible]ords for
visual and [illegible]r anger
at the per[illegible] blacks
(94 perce[illegible]familiar
with *cut-ey*[illegible]iar with
suck-teeth, [illegible]

When [illegible] *English* (DARE) was being prepared in the 1970s, an even larger survey was conducted in which 2,777 American informants—representing various races, age groups, and education levels—participated. One result was a comprehensive picture of which terms were used "among Black speakers" (e.g., *ace-boon-coon,* "a very close friend") or "chiefly among Blacks" (e.g., *bid whist,* "a variation of the card game whist in which players bid to name trump"), and which were "especially common among Blacks" (e.g., *bubba,* "term of address for a brother"). Some of the terms DARE identified as black were compounds involving body parts, such as *bad-eye* ("the evil eye: a curse or threatening glance"), *bad-mouth* ("to speak ill of someone"), and *big-eye* ("greedy, covetous"). Like *suck-teeth,* these are translations into English of literal and metaphorical expressions in West African languages (e.g., Mandingo *da-jugu* and Hausa *mugum-baki* for *bad-mouth,* and Igbo *íma osò,* Yoruba *kp̀ošé,* Hausa *tsaki,* Efik *asiama,* Kikongo *tsiona,* and Wolof *cipu* for *suck-teeth* sound).

The mention of African languages raises a larger question about the major sources and domains of black vocabulary. Besides African languages, these include music, especially the blues (*jazz, gig, funky, hep, boogie*); religion and the church (*shout, Amen corner*); sex and love-making (*grind, johnson, mack*); superstition and conjure (*obeah, voodoo, mojo*); street life, including prostitution, drugs, gangs, fights, and cars (*trick, pimp walk, numbers, cracked out, bus a cap, hog*); people (*cuz, posse, saddity/seddity, the Man*); abbreviations (*CP time, HNIC, on the DL*); and slang or youth culture (*fresh, phat, bustin out*).

When it comes to slang, which overlaps to some extent with the other categories (e.g., sex and lovemaking), variation by region and social class is widespread, as is rapid change over time. Edith Folb's two-decade-old study of the language of black teenagers in Los Angeles documents how slang use there varied according to age, gender, region, social class, and life-style. Her comments on class differences are worth quoting, if only to counteract the impression one might otherwise get that all blacks are hip to exactly the same range of black slang (if the slang sounds dated, it's because Folb's fieldwork was conducted in the late sixties and early seventies):

> There are ghetto realities that most middle-class teenagers simply have no contact with. As one politically active middle-class youth put it, "Sure, I know a lot of the words [in the lexicon], but I'm not livin' down there. It's different. Can't pretend it isn't. Some of those terms just not part of my life." His ghetto peer agrees: "Dig. The brothers up dere in dem Hollywood Hills, out dere at UCLA and all dem li'l ol' colleges, they okay—hear what I'm sayin'? They hip to some o' d' happ'nin's, they blood. But when dude come down here, better take it slow, 'cause gon' be lot shit he ain' got together. Some blood blow his mind, send 'im on a hombog. Run down some lines he done never heard!"

Although some slang words do hang around for a long time (*pad*, for instance, has been used for "apartment" or "home" since the 1800s), slang is *the* most rebellious and dynamic aspect of any language. As noted by Clarence Major:

> Black slang is a living, breathing form of expression that changes so quickly no researcher can keep up with it. A word or phrase can come into existence to mean one thing among a limited number of speakers in a particular neighborhood and a block away it might mean something else or be unknown entirely—at least for a while.

The regional and rapidly changing aspects of slang account for the variations in vocabulary that people notice between East Coast and West Coast (not to mention southern and midwestern) rap. In Philadelphia, "That's whassup" affirms a statement. In Washington, D.C., it's "I'm with it," and in New Orleans it's "I'm 'bout it." To learn the state of affairs, ask a New Yorker, "Yo, what the deal?" and a Chicago native, "What the demo?" Because the life span of slang verbiage is so short, many of the most contemporary terms cannot be found in the 1994 dictionaries of Major and Smitherman. Both dictionaries, for instance, include *player*. In Major, one of the definitions is "a lady's man; a sexually active male; male with more than one woman"; Smitherman has a similar gloss, but adds: "a flamboyant, flashy, popular man or woman, who may or may not have many women or men." But neither includes the more recently coined *player-hate* (pronounced *playa-hate*), "to be jealous of or to impede the success of a player or anyone who is doing well." Similarly, while they both include *short,* slang for "car" that goes back to the 1930s, neither has *shorty* (pronounced *shawty*), a newer term for "girlfriend" or "female" (as in "Shorty, what your name is?") popular on the East Coast and in the South. (However, both terms appear in the 2000 edition of *Black Talk*.)

Claude Brown confronted the changing nature of slang back in 1968:

> The expression "up-tight," which meant being in financial straits, appeared on the soul scene in the general vicinity of 1953. Junkies were very fond of the word and used it literally to describe what was a perpetual condition with them. The word was pictorial and pointed; therefore it caught on quickly in Soulsville across the country. In the early Sixties when "uptight" was on the move, a younger generation of people along the Eastern Seaboard regenerated it with a new meaning: "everything is cool, under control, going my way."

Clarence Major comments on the subsequent evolution of *uptight:* "Later, in the late sixties, early seventies, it was adapted by white teenagers to mean mental or emotional disorder."

Which brings us to another point. Quite apart from words such as *bubba, big daddy, grits,* and *chitlins/chitterlings*—which long ago diffused among southerners as a group (from black to white in the case of *bubba* and *big daddy,* from white to black in the case of *grits* and *chitlins*)— black slang has been spreading to teenagers of other ethnic groups more generally (primarily through music), and thence to mainstream

America, for quite some time. James Baldwin remarked on this in 1979:

> Now, I do not know what white Americans would sound like if there had never been any black people in the United States, but they would not sound the way they sound. *Jazz*, for example, is a very specific sexual term, as in *jazz me, baby*, but white people purified it into the Jazz Age. *Sock it to me*, which means roughly the same thing, has been adopted by Nathaniel Hawthorne's descendants with no qualms or hesitations at all, along with *let it all hang out* and *right on!*

And in 1998, Hampton University professor Margaret Lee listed more than sixty black expressions that had crossed over into mainstream newspaper use, including *chill out; threads; all that; boom-shaka-laka; main squeeze; you go, girl; high-five; homeboy; soulmate;* and *got game.*

Although many blacks complain about white and mainstream adoption of black slang, new slang terms that provide secrecy and reflect rebelliousness are constantly being created within the black community. Furthermore, as Clarence Major reminds us, the process of diffusion is not just normal, but unavoidable:

> This evolution from private to public is not only essential to the vitality at the crux of slang, but inevitable. By this I mean, African-American slang is not only a living language for black speakers but for the whole country, as evidenced by its popularity decade after decade since the beginning of American history. The most recent example of this popularity is rap and hip-hop during the 1980s and 1990s.

Pronunciation

Claude Brown, who paid homage to the "communicative and meaningful" sounds of Spoken Soul, insisted that it was such sounds ("soul vocalization"), rather than slang, that represented the distinctive identity of the black vernacular. As he noted:

> Spoken soul is distinguished from slang primarily by the fact that the former lends itself easily to conventional English, and the latter is diametrically opposed to adaptations within the realm of conventional English. Police (pronounced pō′ lice) is a soul term, whereas "The Man" is merely slang for the same thing.

Brown was not a linguist, and most of the 1968 article in which he wrote this was about slang. But he did realize that the system represented by black pronunciation was a more fundamental part of

Spoken Soul. As he observed, this system allowed virtually any word in "conventional English" to be converted to the sounds of a black vernacular:

> There are specific phonetic traits. To the soulless ear, the vast majority of these sounds are dismissed as incorrect usage of the English language . . . To those so blessed as to have had bestowed upon them at birth the lifetime gift of soul, these are the most communicative and meaningful sounds ever to fall upon human ears: the familiar "mah" instead of "my," "gonna" for "going to," "yo" for "your."

The first example he offered was the pronunciation of "my" as *mah*—to which one could add other examples: "I" as *Ah*, "side" as *sahd*, and so on. In these cases, what linguists call a diphthong (a two-vowel sequence) involving a glide from an *ah*-like vowel to an *ee*-like vowel, is produced as a long monophthong (a single vowel) without the glide to *ee*. Like many other pronunciation features of Spoken Soul, this monophthongal pronunciation is characteristic of southern white speech, as shown by the first entry in a popular little glossary entitled *How to Speak Southern:*

> **Ah:** The things you see with, and the personal pronoun denoting individuality. "*Ah* think *Ah*'ve got somethin' in mah *ah*." ["I think I've got something in my eye."]

Another instance in which Spoken Soul resembles southern white speech is in the similar pronunciation of *e* and *i* before nasals (sounds like *m*, *n*, and *ng*, which require air from the lungs to flow through the nose as well as the mouth), so that *pin* and *pen* sound like *pin*, and one might have to ask, "Do you mean a sticking *pin*, or a writing *pen?*"

That white southerners also say *mah* and *Ah* and merge *pin* and *pen* does not detract from the significance of these features as markers of Spoken Soul. For one thing, in the vast areas of the North, East, Midwest, and West where African Americans now live, *mah, Ah,* and the *pin/pen* merger are regularly used and interpreted as distinctive elements of "sounding black." In a recent study in Detroit, for instance, linguist Walter Edwards found that working-class blacks used monophthongal pronunciations like *mah* and *Ah* 60 percent of the time, while working-class whites used them only 12 percent of the time. It is possible that in these as in other cases (e.g., *r*-lessness, as in *yo* for "your"—an example that Brown also cites), white southerners adopted the feature from blacks rather than vice versa.

Recall that until the northern and western migrations of the early twentieth century, 90 percent of the country's black population was concentrated in the South. The fact that it is southern white speech that most resembles black speech is probably not an accident, and some observers have explicitly attributed the features of southern white speech to black influence, most recently linguists Erik R. Thomas and Guy Bailey:

> Campbell (1746), Barker (1855), Jackson and Davis (1908), and Cash (1941) all report that White children on plantations often adopted features from the slave children who were their playmates. Feagin (1990) uses such historical evidence as a basis for postulating that African American influence promulgated r-lessness among whites in the South. It is important to remember that on smaller plantations and farms (where the vast majority of slaveholders lived), the owner and his family often worked alongside slaves in the fields. Moreover, after the Civil War, Whites often fell victim to the system of tenancy so that in many cases Blacks and Whites worked alongside each other as tenant farmers.

In at least some cases, blacks who influenced southern white speech in the nineteenth and twentieth centuries might have been transmitting features their ancestors in turn had acquired from English, Irish, and Scots-Irish indentured servants and peasant settlers in the seventeenth and eighteenth centuries, better preserved by them for a variety of historical reasons. (Compare East Indians in Guyana, who acquired deep Guyanese Creole from the newly emancipated Africans when the former group first came to what was then British Guiana as indentured servants in the 1830s. Today, because East Indians are more heavily represented in the peasant farming areas where deep Creole speech thrives, they are statistically more likely to exemplify it than are the more urban descendants of the Africans.)

But despite mutual influence between blacks and whites, it would be a mistake to assume that black and white pronunciations are identical, even in the South. Thomas and Bailey in fact point to two other features of vowel pronunciation distinguishing blacks and whites, even those from the same area. One is the pronunciation of the *a* (phonetically [e] in *name, state, pay, say, baby, slaves,* and similar words) and the *o* (phonetically [o] in *go, so, no, home,* and similar words), as pure monophthongs, or words with little variation or change in sound from beginning to end. Ex-slaves born in the 1840s and 1850s had this feature, in common with older African Americans born before World War I and Caribbean English Creole speakers. White Americans born in the 1840s and 1850s did not have this feature, displaying a more diphthongal pronunciation, in which the tongue rises at the end. Younger African Americans follow their white counterparts in this respect, but in their pronunciation of the second feature, the [ɑ] onset of the [ɑʊ] diphthong in words like *down* and *house,* they differ from whites of all ages, and follow older African Americans and their Caribbean English Creole brethren in using nonfront pronunciations, more like the vowel of *father* than like the vowel of *cat.* In a recent study, nearly 70 percent of black Texans began the diphthong of *thousand* with a nonfront pronunciation, while less than 20 percent of white Texans did.

The issue of whether blacks can be distinguished from whites by the sound of their voices alone came to national attention during the O. J. Simpson murder trial in Los Angeles. On July 12, 1995, prosecutor Christopher Darden tried to have witness Robert Heidstra validate an earlier statement he had allegedly made that one of the two voices he heard near Nicole Brown Simpson's house on the night of her murder sounded like that of a black man. Defense attorney Johnnie Cochran objected immediately, and Judge Lance Ito sustained his objection. In a dramatic moment, the jury and the witness were asked to leave the courtroom, and Mr. Cochran angrily explained the basis of his objection:

> You can't tell by somebody's voice whether they sounded black. . . . I resent that [as] a racist statement. . . . This statement about whether he sounds black or white is racist and I resent it and that is why I stood and objected. And I think it is totally improper in America [that] at this time . . . we have to hear and endure this.

However, as linguist John McWhorter has noted in a recent book:

> In fact . . . Cochran got away with murder on that one. . . . Most Americans, and especially black ones, can almost always tell that a person is black even on the phone, and even when the speaker is using standard English sentences.

The evidence lies in more than a dozen studies that have been conducted over the past three decades showing that listeners are able to identify accurately the ethnicity of black and white speakers on the basis of tape-recorded samples of their speech, some less than 2.5 seconds long. The overall accuracy of identification is typically between 80 and 90 percent in these studies, and the pronunciation cues (in many cases the speakers are using identical Standard English grammar) include differences in vowel quality of the type described above, and other features. In a 1972 study by John Rickford, speakers uttering "Hey, what's happening" and other phrases were accurately identified as black or white 86 percent of the time, apparently on the basis of what listeners described as their "inflection," "variation in pitch and rhythm," "intonation," and "tone." Acoustic phonetic analysis revealed that the two black speakers did indeed show wider variation in pitch and intonation (with their voices rising higher and falling lower) than the whites, even when their pronunciation of individual consonants and vowels was more similar.

The speech of highly educated black speakers was identified much less accurately in early studies by researchers Richard Tucker and Wallace Lambert (around 50 percent), and Roger Shuy (8 to 18 percent). These results, along with a subsequent study by William Labov and his colleagues in which listeners were only moderately successful (30 to 66 percent correct) in identifying the ethnicity of "difficult cases"—whites who had been raised in the South or who otherwise showed strong black influence, and blacks who had been raised entirely in white communities—firmly established that "sounding black" (or "white") is not rooted in genetics or physiology, but influenced by society and culture. Cochran was right to resist the "racist" insinuation that *any* black person, regardless of education, cultural upbringing, and association, could be infallibly identified as black by the sound of his or her voice alone. Yet it was not "totally improper" for Darden and the prosecution to allege otherwise, for in the vast majority of cases, cultural and sociological factors have conspired to make blacks and whites sound different, and they do.

So far we have been talking about "soul vocalization" almost entirely in terms of vowels and intonation. But sometimes what's distinctive happens with syllables. Take, for instance, the fact that blacks place the stress on the first rather than the second syllable, as in *PO-lice* and *HO-tel,* or the fact that blacks (especially older ones) delete the unstressed initial and medial syllables in words like *(a)bout, (be)cause, (a)fraid,* and *sec(re)t(a)ry* more often than whites do.

Moreover, it is often the pronunciation of *consonants* that distinguishes the speech of blacks from the speech of other ethnic groups in the United States, quantitatively as well as qualitatively. Some black consonant pronunciations—such as *aks* (or *axe*) for "ask"—are shibboleths of vernacular black speech. In a March 1995 segment of *60*

Minutes, television news reporter Morley Safer asked Arch Whitehead, a well-suited African American who recruits corporate executives, what would happen if a black man applying for a Wall Street job were to say, "May I *aks* you a question?" versus "May I *ask* you a question?" Whitehead laughed and said, "He won't get to *aks* that very often, I'll tell ya," and the two men agreed that he wouldn't even "get a foot in the door."

But two things should be noted about this widely stereotyped and stigmatized pronunciation, which is often a focus of "speech improvement" classes taken by black students. The first is that it was widespread in British English in earlier times. In Old English for example, as the *Oxford English Dictionary* or *Webster's Third New International Dictionary* will tell you, *a-csian* alternated with *a-scian* as the word meaning "to ask." Even in Middle English, the spelling alternated between *axen* and *asken,* although the latter won out to become the Standard English pronunciation of modern times. Second, *aks* for "ask" is an example of metathesis—switching two consonants in a word, often to achieve an easier articulation. (An example from Standard English is "comfortable," where the *t* is sometimes pronounced before the *r,* even though it's spelled with *r* before *t.*) Another example in Spoken Soul is the pronunciation of "wasp" as *waps,* but that is much less common than *aks* for "ask."

Much more widespread in their effects are rules deleting *l* and *r* after vowels, as in *he'p* for "help," *afta* for "after," and *yo* for "your" (one of Claude Brown's examples of soul vocalization). These processes are found also in the speech of whites and other ethnic groups, but they tend to occur more often in black vernacular speech, and they sometimes affect *r* between vowels (as in *Ca[r]ol*), unlike other dialects. Note that the deletion of contracted *'ll* from *will* allows invariant *be* to function sometimes as a future marker, as in "He('ll) *be* here in a few minutes"—a point we'll return to in chapter 7.

Another pronunciation that is often described as deleting a consonant—the practice of dropping the final *g* in words like *walkin'* and *singin'*—does not actually involve deletion, but the replacement of one type of nasal (the *eng*-like velar nasal, as at the end of *thing,* formed with the back of the tongue raised toward the back of the mouth) with another (the *en*-like alveolar nasal, as at the end of *thin,* formed with the front of the tongue raised behind the upper teeth). Other examples of consonant replacement rather than deletion are the pronunciation of "street" as *skreet* and "stretch" as *skretch* (with *k* replacing *t* in *str* sequences, especially in the South), and the use of *b* for *v* (as in *hebben* for "heaven" and *nebba* for "never").

What all this talk about consonant deletions and replacements tends to miss is the fact that these processes are highly systematic, and not the careless or haphazard pronunciations that observers often mistake them for. (Recall the America Online contributor quoted at the beginning of this chapter who said that Ebonics has no rules, and the William Raspberry column, quoted in chapter 11, in which Ebonics is said to have "no consistent spellings or pronunciations and no discernible rules.") To appreciate this, let us consider two well-known features of Spoken Soul—the simplification of consonant clusters (by deletion of the final consonant) at the end of words, as in *tes'* for "test," *des'* for "desk," and *han'* for "hand," and the replacement of *th* by *t, f, d,* or *v,* as in *tin* for "thin," *Rufe* for "Ruth," *dem* for "them," and *bave* for "bathe." Not just any consonant cluster at the end of a word can be simplified; you can't simplify "jump" to *jum'* or "pant" to *pan'*, and the *th* in "Ruth" can't be replaced by *v* instead of *f,* nor can the *th* in "them" be replaced by *t* instead of *d.* In order to produce the correct vernacular pronunciations in each case, speakers of Spoken Soul have to attend to whether the corresponding Standard English pronunciations are voiced or voiceless.

Voiced or voiceless, you say? What you talkin' 'bout? We're referring to whether your vocal cords are held closely together, vibrating noisily (voiced), or whether they are spread apart and not vibrating (voiceless). The consonants *s* and *z* are identical sounds, except that *s* is voiceless and *z* is voiced. If you put your fingers in your ears and say a prolonged *s* followed by a prolonged *z*—*sssszzzz*—you'll hear the difference quite dramatically as voicing begins for *z* and the vibrations resonate from your throat through your entire head. The consonants *s, f, p, t,* and *k* (among others) are voiceless, and *z, v, b, d,* and *g* (among others) are voiced. Now, we'll bet your parents or teachers never taught you about voicing. But if you're a native speaker of English, it's something you've been attending to every day of your life, at least from the time you learned to form plurals. Although grammar books tell you that you simply add *s* or *es* to the end of a word to form a regular English plural, the rule holds true only for writing. In speech, it's slightly more complicated. If the word ends in a sibilant (a hissing sound like *ch* or *s*), the pronunciation becomes *uhz* or *ihz,* as in *rozuhz,* "roses," or *churchihz,* "churches." If the word ends in a vowel (all English vowels are voiced) or a voiced nonsibilant consonant, like *b* or *g*, you add a voiced *z*, as in *teaz*, "teas"; *cabz*, "cabs"; or *bidz*, "bids"; if the word ends in a voiceless nonsibilant sound like *p* or *t*, you add a voiceless *s*, as in *caps* or *bits*.

Let's return to Spoken Soul. The unconscious but very regular rule for simplifying consonant clusters by deleting the final consonant at the end of a word applies only if both (or all three) consonants are voiceless (as in *test*) or voiced (as in *hand*). If one of the consonants is voiced and the other is voiceless, as in *jump* and *pant*, you can't simplify them. Of course, all good rules have exceptions (compare *oxen* and *sheep* as English plurals). Spoken Soul is no exception, but even the exceptions are regular. Negatives like *can't*, *won't*, and *shouldn't* regularly lose their final voiceless *t* (as in *can'*, *won'*, *shouldn'*) even though it's preceded by a voiced *n*. Many colloquial dialects of English have similar rules for consonant cluster simplification, but Spoken Soul applies it more often than most. And for speakers who regularly simplify the final cluster in "test" to *tes'*, the latter becomes the base form in their mental dictionary, and its plural becomes *tesses* (*tessuhz*) instead of "tests" (which ends in a triple consonant cluster) because of the rules for plural formation outlined in the preceding paragraph. (Compare also *desses* instead of "desks.")

In the case of *th*, voicing is relevant because English *th* comes in both a voiceless variety, as in "think," and a voiced variety, as in "them." English spelling masks the difference, but you can hear it by taking the initial voiced sound in "them" (more like a *dh* than a *th*) and substituting it for the initial sound of "think" (yielding something like *DHink*, which sounds funny), or taking the initial voiceless sound of "think" and substituting it for the initial sound of "them" (*THem*, which also sounds funny). The rules for replacing "th" in Spoken Soul depend crucially on voicing. Voiceless *th* can be replaced by voiceless *t* or *f* (the latter primarily at the end of words, as in *toof*, "tooth"; the former almost anywhere: *tink*, "think"; *nutten*, "nothing"; *toot*, "tooth"); voiced *th* can be replaced by voiced *d* or *v* (the latter in the middle or at the ends of words, as in *muvva*, "mother," and *bave*, "bathe"; the former anywhere: *dem*, "them"; *mudda*, "mother"; *bade*, "bathe"). The ways in which English *th* is pronounced in black vernacular therefore reveal in a very systematic way whether it is voiced or voiceless, even more so than English spelling does.

Finally, voicing is relevant to another pronunciation feature of Spoken Soul, which shares with many English-based creoles a rule deleting *b*, *d*, or *g* (all voiced "stops" when any one of them is the first consonant in tense-aspect markers or auxiliary verbs). Examples include the *d* of *don't* (*Ah 'on' know* = "I don't know") and *didn't* (*He ain't do it* = "He didn't do it") and the *g* of *gonna* (*ah ma do it* = "I'm gonna do it," with the *g* and most of *gonna* deleted). Among U.S. dialects, this rule is apparently unique to the black vernacular or very nearly so, and it provides one indication among others that Spoken Soul may have had Creole English ancestry or been influenced in its history by Creole speech. (See chapter 8.)

Variation in Pronunciation

As we have indicated, despite a certain cohesiveness of vocabulary use among blacks as opposed to whites, social class and other factors differentiate vocabulary even among blacks. This is more true of pronunciation. One of the most careful studies of social-class differences in black pronunciation, conducted in Detroit by linguist Walt Wolfram more than thirty years ago, showed that while upper-middle-class (professional) blacks simplified their consonant clusters quite often— an average of 51 percent of the time in their recorded speech—lower-working-class blacks (unskilled workers) did so even more frequently— an average of 84 percent of the time. Catherine Chappell's 1999 replication study in Oakland also showed lower-working-class blacks there simplifying their final consonant clusters 84 percent of the time. She had no upper-middle-class blacks in her study, but her lower-middle-class blacks simplified their clusters 72 percent of the time, similar to the 66 percent simplification figure for the lower-middle-class blacks in Detroit whom Wolfram wrote about in 1969. When it came to pronouncing the voiceless *th* of *tooth* as *t*, the class differences in Wolfram's study were even more dramatic, with working-class blacks using the *t* pronunciation 70 to 73 percent of the time, while the middle-class blacks did so only 23 to 25 percent of the time. The pronunciation features we've associated with Spoken Soul in this chapter are most characteristic of the working classes. This is why the middle-class blacks who serve as media spokespersons on Ebonics and other language-related matters are so sensitive about—even hostile toward—the suggestion that black people as a group speak "Black English" or have a distinctive vernacular.

But virtually all African Americans use some of the pronunciation features identified in this chapter at least some of the time, especially in their most informal moments. A recent study showed, for instance, that Oprah Winfrey, perhaps the country's most popular talk-show host, pronounced her *ay* diphthongs like monophthongs (*ah* for "I," *mah* for "my") significantly more often (38 percent of the time) when introducing or discussing someone black than when referring to someone who was not black (10 percent of the time). Arch Whitehead, the executive recruiter who on *60 Minutes* laughingly dismissed the prospect of blacks' getting or keeping executive jobs if they said *aks* instead of *ask*, went on to make these remarks:

> When I get home, I don't want to think about all that nice English. I wanna go back to my golden years, when I could say *dis* and *dat*, when I could say "How ya doin?" instead of "Hi, guys!" When I didn't have to belong and fit.

The significance of style in black pronunciation was illustrated in Walt Wolfram's 1969 Detroit study; black speakers of *every* class used the vernacular variants (e.g., *t* or *f* for voiceless *th*) less often when reading a text than when talking with the interviewer.

Other factors that were correlated with the extent to which speakers used black pronunciation in Wolfram's study included age (preadolescents and teenagers generally using the black vernacular variants more often than adults), gender (males using the vernacular variants more often than females), and racial isolation (blacks with predominantly black social contacts using the vernacular variants more often than blacks with predominantly white social contacts).

Interestingly, a replication study in Detroit by linguist Walter Edwards, published in 1992, showed similar correlations, but not always in the same way. Although age was a significant factor in the extent to which blacks used *ah* instead of [ay] in words like *find*, it was the oldest rather than the youngest age-groups who did this most often, and this was true also of *r* deletion after a vowel, as in *store*. However, Edwards's study did not include any teenagers below the age of eighteen, as Wolfram's study did, and, on the other side of the coin, Wolfram's study did not distinguish the four "adult" age groups that Edwards's did. Furthermore, in Edwards's study, gender was not significant overall, although females tended to use more of the vernacular variant than did males; the one exception was in the oldest (sixty-plus) age group, where men deleted *r* after a vowel more often (59 percent of the time) than the women did (46 percent of the time).

Edwards's 1992 study showed that individuals in Detroit who were relatively restricted to their inner-city neighborhoods and/or more positively oriented toward it used black vernacular pronunciations more often than individuals who had more interactions with people outside the neighborhood and/or more negative attitudes toward it. (More succinctly: If you stay in the 'hood and you're cozy there, you'll likely speak more soul than a neighbor who often roams beyond and/or tends to dis it.) In this respect, Edwards's study agreed more substantially with Wolfram's. Both concur with our own informal experiences and observations in reminding us that language use in the African American speech community, as in every other, is variable, influenced by such factors as social class, gender, social network, and style.

One factor in phonological variation that people who aren't linguists are less aware of is variation according to linguistic "environment"—where in a word a particular sound occurs, for instance, or what kind of word it is, and whether the following word begins with a consonant or vowel. We've referred to these sorts of factors throughout this chapter, when we talked about rules "deleting *l* and *r after vowels.*" The italicized qualification is necessary to rule out the deletion of *l* and *r* before vowels, as in **ed* for "red" or **ast* for "last"— something that doesn't happen in Spoken Soul or other varieties of English (hence the asterisks, indicating nonoccurring forms). The exception is a pronunciation like *tho* for "throw," where *r* follows *th* and precedes *o*. (Note that even for such exceptions, we have to specify the linguistic environment; in Spoken Soul, as in all other language varieties, language is not random but systematic.)

The effect of linguistic environment we want to close with here is not qualitative, as in these cases, but quantitative. Several studies have shown that consonant cluster simplification, as in *jus'* for "just," is more common before a word beginning with a consonant (as in "just *g*lad") than before a word beginning with a vowel (as in "just *e*nough"), and least common when the deleted consonant represents the past tense (as in "miss*ed*"—spelled *ed* but pronounced *t*). In their most informal group interactions, the New York City adults recorded by Labov and his colleagues deleted the final *t* in words like "just" 79 percent of the time before a consonant, and only 32 percent of the time before a vowel; in words like "missed," where the final *t* sound represents the past tense, they deleted it 30 percent of the time before a consonant, but never before a vowel. Wild, huh? This regular symphonic variation, it should be remembered, occurs far below the level of consciousness.

7

Grammar

*In sentences like "An' so I comin' down an' she out there blabbin' her
mouth told my sister I was playin hookey from school" there are no words
which are not in Standard English, and no word forms which white dialects
do not have. . . . A syntactic analysis, however, reveals a greatly different
system. Syntax, the focus of more modern linguistics, is the area in which
the analysis of Black English is most revealing.*

—J. L. Dillard (1972)

*Linguistically speaking, the greatest differences between contemporary Black
and White English are on the level of grammatical structure.*

—Geneva Smitherman (1986)

The claim that Ebonics, or Spoken Soul, has no grammar is as bogus
as the claim that it has no dictionary. If this is taken to mean, as it often is, that African American vernacular is unsystematic, without rules
or regularities, then it is blatantly false, as we will show several times
over in this chapter. If it is taken to mean that no one has studied or
written about the rules and regularities of African American Vernacular English (AAVE)—the most popular name for Spoken Soul among
linguists—then it's equally absurd. Since the 1960s, at least (there
were occasional studies even earlier), scholars have produced detailed accounts of AAVE pronunciation and grammar. Two of the
best-known, dealing with black speech in New York City and Detroit,
were conducted in 1968 and 1969, respectively. Now, as is true of most
languages and dialects, much remains to be discovered and published
about the linguistic features or attributes of black vernacular. But linguists (who study the sounds, words, and grammar of languages and

dialects) already know enough to present an informed picture of the system—the "systematicity," if you will—of the tongue.

When discussing grammar we'll use mostly snatches of actual conversations among blacks recorded by us and others in East Palo Alto, California; Philadelphia; the South Carolina Sea Islands; and elsewhere. These might be thought of as instances of Spoken Soul in spirited use by ordinary, everyday people—the folk who in some neighborhoods are said to "talk regular." Their usage extends the discussion of the spirited and pleasurable use that black writers, preachers, entertainers, and other men and women of words make of the vernacular that we explored in chapters 2 through 5.

Let's begin with a quotation from East Palo Alto's Foxy Boston, whom we have recorded periodically since 1968, when she was a teenager. (Here, as elsewhere, we'll use the symbol for zero, Ø, to show where the copula—usually *is* or *are*—is absent.)

> But *i's*—*i's* a lot of girls . . . it *seem* like, when I *be* driving, it *seem* like every corner I drive around, there *go* somebody you know pushing a baby. . . . Me and Teresa *and them be* like, "Tha's a shame, huh?" . . . I *be* like, "Dang, Teresa, she Ø in the same grade with me and she *have* three kids!"

Plural *s* and *dem*.   We must acknowledge from the start that AAVE shares an array of grammatical features with mainstream English and other dialects. In fact, as linguists Stefan Martin and Walt Wolfram point out in a recent article:

> The distinctiveness of AAVE does not particularly reside in the structure of its sentences. Basic utterance types—e.g. declarative, interrogative, and imperative sentences—are all formed in essentially the same way as they are in other dialects.

Plural formation is really an aspect of inflectional morphology—the different forms words take to show grammatical relationships—rather than of sentence structure, but it illustrates the same point. Take, for instance, the elementary rule that says you add *s* to most nouns to form the plural—that is, to refer to more than one person, place, or thing. AAVE speakers sometimes ditch the plural *s*, but not often (1 to 10 percent of the time, in studies to date). In the passage above, *girls* and *kids* hold fast to the final *s*.

AAVE has other ways of marking plurality, as with *dem*. One way is to use *an dem* after the name of a person, to refer to others associated with that person, as in *John an dem,* for "John and his friends." This associative plural, as some linguists call it, can be used also with definite nouns (i.e., preceded by "the") that refer to people, as in *the judge an dem,* for "the judge and people like him." In the Gullah of coastal South Carolina and Georgia, as in many Caribbean Creoles, the *an* may be left out, but this is less common in urban Spoken Soul. Another way of using *dem* to mark plurality is by putting this form before the noun, as in *dem books,* "those books." In this construction, the *dem* does not simply indicate that more than one book is being referred to; it also indicates that it is "those" and not "these" books, and the plural is simultaneously or redundantly marked by the *s* ending on *books.* In Gullah, as in the Caribbean Creoles, the plural marking function is clearer, because the construction can be used without plural *s,* as in *dem book,* meaning "those books."

Existential *it is.*   The italicized portions of Foxy Boston's speech indicate points at which AAVE diverges from the English of the nightly news. Instead of "there is" or "there are," she uses the characteristic AAVE alternative, *it's* or *i's* (reduced forms of *it is*), which may be used with singular or plural nouns, as in:

> *i's* a lot of girls (= there are a lot of girls)

Absence of third-person singular present-tense *s.*   *Seem,* the next italicized word in Foxy's quotation, exemplifies another typical AAVE feature: "it *seem* like, when I be driving, it *seem* like every corner I drive around." Like *go* in the subsequent line, *seem* snubs the *s* that mainstream English requires, in "it seem," or "the man seems," or as a high school English teacher might put it, when you have a present-tense verb with a third-person-singular subject. To make it clearer, "third-person-singular subject" means that the subject refers to a single person, place, or thing, neither the speaker in a conversation (*I,* the first person), nor a person being addressed (*you,* the second person).

Standard English is somewhat fickle because it requires adding an *s* (or *es*) to verbs with third-person-singular subjects ("he go*es*") but requires the bare verb (the form with *to,* as in "to go") for all other subjects ("I go," "you go," "we go," "they go"). In getting rid of third-person *s,* you might think of AAVE as making the rules of English more regular, or as an advocate for equal opportunity: the verb doesn't have special endings with other subjects, so it shouldn't with third-person-singular subjects.

Since it lacks the Standard English *s* ending, *it seem* is a clear case of the AAVE rule, "Thou shalt not treat present-tense verbs with third-person-singular subjects any differently from verbs with other subjects." Somewhat less obviously, *she have* (instead of "she has") in the last line of Foxy's quote ("Dang, Teresa, she in the same grade with me and she *have* three kids!") also exemplifies this rule. In Standard English, *has* is the third-person-singular form of *have* in the present tense, as one can see by contrasting "he has" with "I have," "you have," "we have," and "they have." The use of *he do* and *he don't* instead of "he *does*" and "he *doesn't*" are yet other examples of the rules, beautifully illustrated (along with the absence of third person *-s* in Oprah's vernacular) in this *People* magazine account of an encounter between Oprah Winfrey and a man looking for her house: "He said, 'Hey, I was going down the road to see Oprah Winfrey's house. *Don't* she have a house down there?'" she recalls. The multimillionaire television star looked the stranded traveler deep in the eyes and said in her best down-home accent: "I believe she *do.*"

This tendency of soul speakers to drop the third-person-singular *s* was evident in earlier studies of working-class folk in New York and Detroit, where *s* was absent from 56 to 76 percent of the time. For Foxy Boston and Tinky Gates, another East Palo Alto teenager we have recorded in multiple interviews, the rate was even higher—97 and 96 percent, respectively. In other words, in virtually every case, the girls used forms like "John *go*" instead of "John *goes*" and "John *have* a car" instead of "John *has* a car."

Absence of possessive *'s*. Although this particular feature doesn't show up in Foxy's quotation, it's worth mentioning while we're on the subject of Standard English *s* forms that get zapped in AAVE. For an example of a noun without the *'s* ending that Standard English relies on to indicate possession (as in "girl*'s* house"), we'll turn to Tinky:

This one day, Nito came over to that *girl* house.

In this case, AAVE indicates possession through the juxtaposition of the two nouns (*girl house*) rather than with an *'s* ending. As in many pidgin and creole languages—produced by fusing and simplifying two or more languages when their speakers come in contact (see chapter 8)—the possessor comes immediately before the thing possessed. We pointed out earlier that AAVE speakers rarely toss out the plural *s*. But it's quite common for them to chuck the *possessive 's*. A group of working-class teenagers in New York, for example, did so between 57 and 72 percent of the time. For Tinky and Foxy, the rate was 53 and 86 percent, respectively.

Invariant *be*. The verb *be* is one of the most celebrated features of Spoken Soul. Over the past thirty-five years, linguists have studied it to death—or nearly so, since it's still kicking, and every few years we discover something new about it. *Be* comes in two basic flavors: (1) conjugated, or inflected, which *varies* in form (*am, is, are, was, were,* and so on), depending on the subject (*I, you, he/she/it, we, they*) and whether it refers to present or past; and (2) invariant, which, as its name suggests, doesn't vary (although it occurs occasionally as *be's* or *bees*). One of the interesting things about the first *be* is that some of its forms (*is* and *are*) can disappear, yielding zero copula, about which we'll say more below. For now we want to focus on the second, invariant *be*.

There are a few different kinds of invariant *be* in AAVE. One—the kind that comes in imperatives ("*Be* good!"), in infinitives with *to* ("He tried to *be* good"), and after helping verbs like *can* and *must* ("He must *be* good")—is used much the same as in mainstream or Standard English. A second kind results from leaving out *will* or *would* (more accurately, their contracted forms *'ll* and *'d*) and produces sentences with future or hypothetical reference:

> Wait awhile. She *be* [= *'ll* be] right around. (Johnny Guitar, forty-four, Philadelphia)
>
> Well, if I be the winner, I *be* [= *'ll* be or *'d* be] glad. (thirteen-year-old, New York City)

The third and most distinctive kind (distinctive because it occurs rarely or not at all in white vernaculars) is the invariant habitual *be* that occurs twice in Foxy's passage: "when I *be* driving . . . Teresa and them *be* like . . ."

This invariant habitual *be* is probably the best-known but least understood of AAVE's grammatical signposts. Many outsiders to Spoken Soul believe that black folk replace Standard English *is* and *are* with invariant *be* all the time, as in, "He *be* talkin' to her right now." But AAVE is actually more discriminating. For one thing, invariant habitual *be* describes only an event that is performed regularly or habitually, as in "He *be* talkin' with his lady every day." Contrast this habitual sense with "He Ø talkin' to her right now"—which is what a speaker of Spoken Soul might say when describing an event taking place at the moment of speech, without any implication that it happens regularly.

Furthermore, unlike *ashy*, invariant habitual *be* is more than an isolated AAVE word; it is part of the grammatical system, an integral tile in the mosaic of the dialect. Each piece has its place and its purpose, and reacts predictably with other pieces to create the collage we call conversation. Indeed, we can prove that invariant *be* is not random, because it minds its grammatical manners. To form the negative version of a sentence in AAVE, you usually use *ain't* ("John isn't walking" becomes "John *ain't* walkin'"). But to form the negative with habitual *be*, you have to use *don't*: "John *don't be* walkin'." If you said, *"John ain't be walkin'"* (as before, the linguistic convention is to put an asterisk before a sentence or form to show that it is a nonoccurring form or ungrammatical), not only would you be speaking improper Ebonics, you'd probably get some funny looks. Here is a grammatical example with *don't*, courtesy of Foxy:

> An she *don't be* listenin'. So I be like, "Hey, I tried to tell you . . ."

Ebonics speakers also use *do* and *don't* to phrase questions with invariant *be*, as in *"Do* John be listenin'?" This is true also of so-called tag questions, in which the speaker assumes a positive response, as in "John *be* listenin', *don't* he?" or a negative response, as in "John *don't be* listenin', *do* he?"

When an AAVE speaker wants to intensify, or stress, the continuous, persistent nature of an action, he or she will sometimes hitch on a *steady*, as in this sentence made famous by John Baugh, the linguist who introduced us to *steady:* "Ricky Bell *be steady* steppin in dem number nines."

Zero copula (absence of *is* or *are*).   The last noteworthy AAVE feature in Foxy's quotation is known among linguists as zero copula—that is, the absence of *is* in "she Ø in the same grade." *Is* and *are* are called copulas because they couple, or join, a subject (in this case, "she") and a predicate (what's said *about* the subject—in this case, that she's in the same grade). Here's an example from a twenty-six-year-old Philadelphia woman who doesn't use the copula *are* in her first sentence but includes it when she repeats the sentence, with emphasis:

> People Ø crazy! People *are* stone crazy!

Zero copula provides a clear demonstration that the grammar of Spoken Soul is systematic and rule-governed. To begin with, there are some copula forms that cannot be left out. You can't delete the past-tense copulas *was* and *were*, both of which are left intact in the following sentences from forty-four-year-old Johnny Guitar of Philadelphia, as they are in the speech of virtually all speakers of black vernacular:

> You *were* a thousand miles away.
> He been doin it since we *was* teenagers, and he Ø still doin it.

Even in the present tense, you can't delete *am*. "I am" is often contracted to *I'm* in AAVE, but the *'m* is not deleted. In Caribbean Creole English, you can delete *am* or *'m* ("I Ø cuttin off de heads," a young Barbadian fisherman explains, as he deftly slices up fish on a tray). But you can't do this in African American Vernacular English.

You can't delete infinitive *be* in AAVE, either (for instance, after *to, can, may, must, shall, should, would, will*), as this forty-six-year-old in East Palo Alto shows by retaining *be* in the first half of this sentence while deleting *are* in the second half: "You can *be* sitting up in class, an nex' thing you know, you Ø out of it."

The only copula forms you *can* leave out in Spoken Soul are *is* and *are*, but even so, there are restrictions. If *is* or *are* comes at the end of a sentence, or is stressed, it can't be deleted ("That's what he *is!*" but not *"That's what he Ø!"). When negative *is* or *are* becomes *ain't*, the *ain't* cannot be erased, either. The forms *what's, it's,* and *that's*—which contain contracted *is* and often lose their final *t* as well (*wha's, i's,* and *tha's*)—behave somewhat like *am*. That is, you can't delete the contracted form of the copula (in this case *'s*), except in some greetings, for instance, *Wa'apnin* as a variant of "What's happenin . . . ?" and *What up?* as a variant of "What's up?"

That's a pretty complex set of rules and restrictions. As with most rules of spoken language, no AAVE speaker has ever been taught these things formally, and few speakers could spell them out for you (unless, perhaps, they had learned them in a linguistics course). But AAVE speakers follow them, almost religiously, in their daily speech. In these animated words from fifteen-year-old Tinky Gates, the copulas that cannot be omitted are intact (and are shown in boldface), and the copulas that can be omitted have indeed been zapped (*are* and *is,* with Ø showing where they might have occurred):

> I'm gone! Maria **was** gone! She **was** up under a tree. She say, "Cops! Oh gosh, wha's gon happen? How Ø we gon get home?"
> "Uh, uh," I said. "Oh gosh," I said. "My mama think we Ø at this shirt party havin a goo' time," and I said, "I **ain'** tellin her this, 'cause she **ain'** gon never let me go back!"

In allowing the deletion of present-tense *is* and *are* but not past-tense *was* and *were*, Spoken Soul differs from mainstream English but is similar to many other languages, including Arabic, Hungarian, Russian, and Swahili.

So far we've told you which copula forms speakers of Spoken Soul can and cannot delete. But there's more. Soul speakers from New York to Detroit to Atlanta to Los Angeles are remarkably similar in terms of *how often* they delete the forms of the copula that can be deleted (basically, unstressed *is* and *are*). For instance, AAVE speakers delete *are* ("They Ø happy") more often than *is* ("He Ø happy"). They delete both *is* and *are* more often when these copulas come after a pronoun ("They Ø happy") than when they come after a noun ("The boys Ø happy"). And they delete *is* and *are* least often before a noun ("He Ø a man"), more often before an adjective ("He Ø happy") and most often before *going to* or its reduced forms, *gonna* and *gon* ("He Ø gon tell Mama").

Want proof? See the chart below, which showed how often zero copula was observed in recordings with different groups of AAVE speakers across the country. For each group, copula deletion was least frequent before a noun, more frequent with a following adjective, and most frequent with a following *gon(na)*. In this respect, AAVE is similar to pidgin and Creole English elsewhere in the world—in Barbados, Jamaica, Guyana, Hawaii, and Liberia. That's a crucial commonality, and as we argue in chapter 8, it's strong evidence that AAVE may have had Creole roots and influences itself.

Copula form and AAVE group studied	Copula deletion before noun ("He Ø a man")	Copula deletion before adjective ("He Ø happy")	Copula deletion before *gon(na)* ("He Ø gon go")
is, New York City Thunderbirds (teenage gang)	23%	48%	88%
is + are, Detroit working class (all ages)	37%	47%	79%
are, Los Angeles (all ages)	.25	.35	.64
is + are, Texas youngsters	.12	.25	.89
is + are, East Palo Alto, California (all ages)	.27	.45	.83
is + are, ex-slaves (mainly from South, recorded 1930s)	12%	29%	100%

Been, BEEN, and Toni Morrison's "five present tenses." Now that we've gone through zero copula, *be*, and *steady*, we're almost ready to exemplify the "five present tenses" that Toni Morrison was probably referring to in the passage cited in chapter 1: "It's terrible to think that a child with five different present tenses comes to school to be faced with books that are less than his own language." We have to say "probably" because the good sistah didn't give us any examples of the different present tenses she was referring to when she praised Spoken Soul, and because "five" might have simply been meant to indicate more present tenses than in Standard English, rather than a precise number. And we have to say "almost ready," because we first have to introduce *been* and *BEEN* (sometimes spelled *bin* and *BIN*, to indicate their pronunciation better).

Been is an unstressed form, lacking in the stress that speakers put into *BEEN*. It's pretty much (but not completely) equivalent to "has been" or "have been" in mainstream English, as shown by these sentences from thirty-nine-year-old "Bomb" Jones of Philadelphia and her husband, Johnny Guitar.

I *been* playing cards since I was four. (Bomb)
He *been* doin it since we was teenagers, and he still doin it. (Johnny)

Sometimes *been* occurs with *has* or *have,* or their contracted forms *'s* and *'ve:*

'Cause I*'ve been* through it. I*'ve been* through them changes. (Johnny)
Here's a guy, live next door to him. He*'s been* a gangsta all his life. (Johnny)

The differences between *been* in Black English and *has been* or *have been* in Standard English are sometimes discernible in the kinds of verbs and adverbs with which they can be linked. Johnny uses *been* with *knowing* in the following sentence, where a speaker of Standard English would use *have known:* "I *been* knowing her for a long time. I *been* knowing her for twenty years." And in the following sentence, Joe, a twenty-nine-year-old man who regularly hung out with Johnny and Bomb, uses *been* to refer to a specific time where a mainstream English speaker would use *was:* "About eleven or twelve o'clock he *been* eating everything."

This phrasing resembles that of the Gullah, or "Geechee," variety of black vernacular spoken on the Sea Islands off the South Carolina and Georgia coasts (the setting for Julie Dash's movie *Daughters of the Dust*). In the following Gullah example, a fifty-nine-year-old black man from Daufuskie Island, South Carolina, alternates between *was* and *been*: "I don't know if dat snake *was* coil, or either *been* stretch out or what." Gullah, like Jamaican patois—its Creole English counterpart in the Caribbean—uses *been* before a verb stem (*thief* in the example below) to mark an action in the past:

> We *been see* [Gullah = saw] that man thief that man car. (Cited in Cunningham)
> Me *been know* [Jamaican Creole = knew] say him wouldn come. (Cited in Bailey)

You wouldn't hear this *been* much in mainland (especially northern) varieties of AAVE these days, although it may have been more frequent in earlier centuries. An example occurs in A. B. Lindsey's 1807 play *Love and Friendship:* "I tink dey *been like* [= liked] sich a man de bess."

What you're much more apt to come across, both on the Sea Islands and in Detroit, Philadelphia, New York, or Los Angeles, is stressed BEEN (with increased emphasis on the word). This exaggerated BEEN describes an action that took place or a state that came into being a long time ago, which is why stressed BEEN is often called a "remote time" marker:

> She ain't tell me that today, you know. She BEEN tell me that. (thirty-one-year-old woman, Sea Islands)
> He [the dentist] finish so quick. I ask him was he finished, and he say, "I BEEN finished!" (seventy-two-year-old black woman, Philadelphia)

One crucial point about BEEN: Unlike its milder twin, *been,* it can't be used with adverbial phrases that mark the passage of time. The contrast is clear in this sentence, in which Philadelphian Johnny Guitar alternates between the two forms:

> INTERVIEWER: I see your friend's doing good business.
>
> JOHNNY: Oh yeah—you mean the fruit seller? I BEEN know that guy. He's a numbers runner—*been* doing that *for years.*

Note, too, that when BEEN brings a state into being, that state remains in effect up to the moment of speech. When Johnny says he "BEEN know that guy," he means that he not only has known him for a long time, but still knows him. These nuances can be confusing to those who don't speak the vernacular. Some years ago, twenty-five whites and twenty-five blacks were asked whether "She BIN married" meant that the woman was still married or not. Twenty-three of the blacks said yes (the correct answer for AAVE), as compared with only eight of the whites. The vast majority of the whites thought that the person was not married—a misunderstanding that could lead to embarrassment, or worse.

Two final notes about BEEN. First, the "remoteness" of the time involved is a subjective matter. In many cases, people front, or pretend, that they've had a particular possession for quite a while, when in fact they just acquired it. You may have complimented someone on an outfit only to hear the person say dismissively, "Aw, man, I BEEN had this!" Second, stressed BEEN can be combined with *had, coulda, shoulda,* and other forms to create complex constructions in which the period designated by BEEN remains in effect until a time earlier than the moment of speech:

> We had BEEN married when this lil' one came along. (seventy-one-year-old Philadelphian; cited in Dayton)
>
> They coulda BEEN ended that war. (twenty-nine-year-old Philadelphian)

Now that we've seen the workings of *been* and *BEEN*, let's return to Toni Morrison's "five present tenses" of AAVE, which might look like this (the Standard English equivalent is given in parentheses):

1. He Ø runnin. (He is running.)
2. He *be* runnin. (He is usually running, or He will/would be running.)
3. He *be steady* runnin. (He is usually running in an intensive, sustained manner, or He will/would be running in an intensive, sustained manner.)
4. He *been* runnin. (He has been running—at some earlier point, but probably not now.)
5. He *BEEN* runnin. (He has been running for a long time, and still is.)

Pretty impressive, isn't it? As you can see from the glosses, you can't convey quite the same idea in Standard English without adding adverbs and lengthy explanations.

Done, be done, finna, had, **and other tense-aspect markers.** By now you may have realized that the grammar of Spoken Soul is quite distinctive in its tense-aspect markers—forms such as *be, steady,* and *BEEN* that come just before or after the verb and tell when (tense) or how (aspect) something happened. The vernacular has other forms like these, which we'll go through quickly in this section.

Done, which emphasizes the completed nature of an action, and/ or its relevance to the present, is one of the best-known vernacular forms. As these examples show, it's often more or less equivalent to Standard English forms with *has* or *have* and *already:*

> I *done* had [= have had] enough. (Renee Blake, New Yorker in her thirties)

> They *done* tore [= have already torn] the school up. (Sue, sixteen, Philadelphian)

> Even though he *done* took [= has already taken] all the bullets out . . . he still may shoot me because I got a gun. (Calvin, forty-four, Alabama resident)

Done is not identical, however, to *has/have.* For one thing, soul speakers report that *done* feels and sounds more intense, more forceful. And there are subtle linguistic differences between the forms, including the fact that *has/have* can be used with negatives (e.g., "He *hasn't* gone"), while *done* cannot: *"He ain't done gone" is ungrammatical, and *"He donen't gone" is even worse.

Done can be hitched up with *be* to make matters more interesting. Since *be,* as noted above, can have future, conditional, or habitual meaning, *be done* sentences combine each of these meanings with the completive sense of *done,* as in:

> Another few weeks, the Puerto Ricans *be done* took [= will have taken] over. (Future completive; Joe G., thirty, Philadelphia)

> If she [= dog] wasn't spayed, she*'d be done* [= would have] got pregnant cause she gets out. (Conditional completive; Philadelphia speaker; cited in Dayton, p. 655)

> The children *be done* ate [= have usually eaten] by the time I get there. (Habitual completive; cited in Green, p. 43)

Be done is most common with the future completive or future perfect, and sometimes occurs with the future marker *will* or *'ll* before it, as in:

> I*'ll be done* bought my own CB waitin on him to buy me one. (Los Angeles speaker; cited in Baugh, p. 78)

This is a complex construction—the future perfect equivalent in mainstream English ("John will already have left by the time Mary arrives") is fairly rare—and it has developed a number of additional subtleties in Spoken Soul. See the notes for further reading on this.

Another striking tense/time marker in Spoken Soul is *finna,* which is used for immediate futures (events just about to happen), as in these sentences from Tinky Gates, the East Palo Alto, California, teenager. She is talking about the moment when she and her friend Ruth decide to leave a party because a fight has broken out and things are on the verge of "getting turned out"—becoming even more rowdy:

> I'm serious! I foun' Ruth an' I said, "Word." I said, "This thang *finna* get turned out, so y'all better get in yo' lil car an' . . . go home." Ruth said, "I'm *finna* get up out of here, 'cause i's gettin' rowdy." So I found her an' we left.

Finna is derived from *fixing to,* which both blacks and whites use for the immediate future throughout the South, as in "He is *fixin' to* go." But in vernacular black speech all over the United States, especially among teenagers, *is* or *are* is almost always dropped (but not *am, 'm, was,* or *were;* recall the rules for copula deletion outlined earlier), and *fixing to* is reduced to *finna, fidna* or *fitna.* Again, you can't use it for things in the distant future (e.g., you can't say, *"I'm finna get married five years from now"), but only for things that are just about to happen.

Somewhat different from *finna* is the use of stressed BE for states that exist now and are likely to continue for a long time in the future. Johnny Guitar's response in this sequence was recorded in Philadelphia some years ago:

> J: How long is your brother gonna be here?
>
> JOHNNY GUITAR: Oh, he gon BE here. I ain't seen him for a long time, so he's gon' BE here.

Although this use of stressed BE is rare—this is the only example we have in our files—it is a logical extension of stressed BIN, and was immediately understandable when it was used. That is, stressed BEEN can refer to a situation that exists now and began long ago in the past (*He BIN here* = "He is here now and has been for a long time"). Stressed BE, by analogy, refers to a situation that exists now and will continue long into the future. We aren't crystal-ball gazers, but we won't be surprised to record other examples, and to see stressed BE become even more common in the future.

One tense-aspect marker that does appear to have become more common over the past two decades is the use of *had* plus a past-tense verb to refer to narrative events that would usually be referred to just with a past-tense verb, as in this example:

> This is a story that happened to me Monday, not too long ago. I was on my way to school, and I *had* slipped and fell [compare "I slipped and fell"], and I ran back in the house to change my clothes.

The speaker here is Dafina, a twelve-year-old girl from East Palo Alto who, like other preadolescents from this area, uses *had* to refer to the high point of a story. In East Palo Alto, speakers seem to abandon this use of *had* over time; older teenagers including Foxy and Tinky showed no use of it (they use *had* in the pluperfect, as in Standard English "By the time I got there, he *had* already left"). In Texas and other parts of the country, however, examples of Dafina's *had* have been recorded among older teenagers and even among people in their twenties, so it might not be as age-restricted as we first thought.

One other thing we've said little about is the use of *come*, usually before a verb ending in *ing*, to express the speaker's indignation or anger about an event, as in this sentence:

> He *come* walkin in here like he owned the damn place!

This isn't a tense-aspect marker—it tells us not when the event occurred, or how it occurred, but how the speaker *felt* about the event that occurred (i.e., he didn't like it—was mad, angry, or resentful). In that sense, it's really more of a modal marker—representing the speaker's mood or feeling about an event. But we include it with forms like *finna* and *had* and BEEN because it's one of the rich set of "helping" verbs (or auxiliaries) that soul speakers use before other verbs to encode fine nuances of meaning about situations and events around them. Far from being deficient, Spoken Soul is very impressive in this regard.

Negative forms and constructions.   The most common negative form in Spoken Soul—and the main feature some writers use to represent the vernacular—is *ain't*. As in other vernacular varieties in the United States, *ain't* can be used as the equivalent of Standard English *am not, isn't, aren't, don't, hasn't,* and *haven't*:

> I *ain't* [= am not] lyin'. (Bomb Jones, Philadelphia)
>
> He *ain't* [= is not] comin' in now. (John, Trenton, New Jersey)
>
> No you *ain't* [= are not]. (Bomb Jones)
>
> He thinks I *ain't* [= don't] got no more aces. (Bomb Jones)

He *ain't* never [= hasn't ever] had a job in his life. (Johnny Guitar, Philadelphia)

Contrary to most white vernaculars, however, *ain't* can be used as the equivalent of "didn't" in the African American vernacular, as in:

He *ain't* go no [= didn't go any] further than third or fourth grade. (Johnny Guitar)

This unique usage has historical implications for the origins of AAVE, as we explained in the pronunciation section of chapter 6.

One of the most commonly discussed features of the black vernacular—and other English vernaculars—is the double negative, in which a negative verb such as *ain't* or *don't* or *wasn't* is used with a negative noun or pronoun such as *no . . . lady, neither,* or *nothing* instead of Standard English equivalents "any . . . lady," "either," or "anything":

She *wadn't no* young lady, *neither.* (She wasn't any young lady, either— Larry, late sixties, outside Philadelphia)

I *don't* want *nothing nobody can't* enjoy. (I don't want anything nobody can enjoy—Dorothy, thirty-five, Philadelphia)

Contrary to what purists often allege, double negatives are virtually never interpreted as positives (as the logical "two negatives make a positive" rule would predict), even by Standard English speakers. That is, no one thinks that "She wasn't no young lady" means "She was a young lady"—any more than they thought this in Chaucer's or Shakespeare's time, when double negatives were used even in literary British English, as in:

Ther *nas no man nowher* so vertuous. (Chaucer, referring to the Friar)

I *cannot* go *no* further. (Shakespeare, *As You Like It,* act 2, scene 4)

Even in the second Spoken Soul sentence above, which is more complex because it joins two double negative sentences (*I don't want nothing* = "I don't want anything"; and *Nobody can't enjoy* = "Nobody can enjoy"), the meaning is crystal clear in context.

Less often discussed but more unusual among English dialects are Spoken Soul sentences like these that begin with a negative verb such as *ain't* or *can't,* followed by a negative noun or pronoun such as *nobody* or *nothing:*

Can't nobody beat 'em. (Cited in Labov et al., ex. 367)

Ain't nothin' went down. (Cited in Labov et al., ex. 359)

In these examples, the negative verb appears to have changed positions with the subject (i.e., *"Nobody can't* beat 'em → *Can't nobody* beat 'em"), and so linguists frequently describe this as negative inversion. But bear in mind that these are statements—often emphatic statements—not to be confused with Standard English questions, which also involve inversion ("Isn't John going?" from "John isn't going"). Bear in mind too that the uninverted order is sometimes impossible (e.g., "Ain't nothing I needed" comes not from *"Nothing ain't I needed" but from "There ain't nothing I needed" or "It ain't nothing I needed").

Questions, direct and indirect. Inversion is curious in AAVE, because when it comes to questions, AAVE speakers appear to be doing exactly the opposite of what Standard English requires. In simple direct questions, AAVE speakers often do not invert the subject and the verb, as formal Standard English requires, but use rising intonation to signal that they are asking a question instead of making a statement (as, of course, do many Standard English speakers in their colloquial speech):

> This is a microphone, too? (Is this a microphone, too?—Arnold, ten, East Palo Alto, California)

Contrarily, where Standard English uses the noninverted word order with *if* or *whether* in embedded or indirect questions ("I asked him *if he could* come with me"), AAVE speakers typically use inverted word order without *if* or *whether* in such questions:

> I asked him *could he come* [if he could come] with me.
>
> Could you ask her *is she* [whether she is] Miss or Ms? (Dawn, sixties, Philadelphia)

In the 1960s, an experiment was done in which African American adolescent males in Harlem were asked to repeat sentences like "I asked Alvin *if he could* go." About half of the respondents would repeat the sentences as "I asked Alvin *could he* go," showing that while they understood the Standard English formulation with *if,* they preferred—in fact were almost wedded to—the inverted vernacular formulation without *if.* Similar results were obtained in experiments done in Baltimore and Washington, D.C.

We can't do justice to all the features of the African American vernacular in a chapter of this length. But to help you understand them if you're a speaker of Spoken Soul, and to help you recognize them in speech or writing if you're not, we'll briefly discuss some other features of Spoken Soul under two headings: "Pronouns" and "Verbs Once More."

Pronouns.   In this category is the feature double subject, sometimes referred to more technically as pleonastic or appositive pronoun.

> *My mother, she* told me, "There's a song I want you to learn."
> (vs. "My mother told me"—Helen B., black gospel singer on radio, San Jose, California, 1999)
> *That man, he* walks to the store. (vs. "That man walks to the store.")

Here a pronoun corresponding to the subject noun is inserted after it, creating a second, or double, subject. Standard English sometimes does this for emphasis, or with very long noun phrases in which the subject is in danger of getting lost (as in "The little old man who lives down the street and who I was telling you about earlier, *he* walks to the store"), but in the African American vernacular it seems to occur more frequently, and even when the subject noun phrase consists of only one or two words, as in the examples above.

Another instance in which AAVE inserts a pronoun where Standard English does not or need not is in dative pronoun, or benefactive pronoun, constructions like this: "Ahma git *me* a gig" (I'm going to get [myself] a job). This usage is shared with white vernaculars. At the other extreme are cases in which AAVE deletes a relative pronoun (*that, who, whom, which*), as in:

> Alan saw the car [that] Charlie sold. (Martin and Wolfram)

Sentences like this, in which the deleted *that* refers to an object noun (*the car* is the object of the verb *sold*), are not uncommon in Standard English. Somewhat more distinctive is the fact that Spoken Soul allows you to delete relative pronouns that are the *subjects* of verbs, as in these sentences from recent work by linguists Stefan Martin and Walt Wolfram:

> He the man [that] got all the old records.
> Wally the teacher [who] wanna retire next year.

Verbs once more.   By now it should be clear that verbs (zero copula as well as tense-aspect markers) are where a lot of the action is in Spoken Soul, where much of what is distinctive and identity-affirming about the vernacular is marked out. One special construction that we haven't talked about is the use of double and sometimes triple modals (verbs such as *can, could, might,* and *should* that indicate ability, possibility, or obligation), as in these examples; this usage is found also in some white vernacular dialects, especially in the South:

> He *might could* do the work.
> She *may can* do the work.
> They *should oughta* go.
> They *might should oughta* do it.

AAVE speakers also sometimes use a singular verb with a plural or second-person-singular subject, as in *they is* instead of "they are" or *you was* instead of "you were." This is sometimes referred to as verb generalization or verb nonagreement. The former term (referring to the generalization of the singular form to the plural) is probably better, since the latter term suggests that AAVE speakers would just as readily use a singular verb form with a plural subject as they would a plural verb form with a singular subject. In fact, sentences like "I *were* happy" (instead of "was") are very rare; much more common is the generalization of the singular verb form to the plural (*we was, they is*).

Variation in Grammar

The kind of variation by *social class* that occurs with Spoken Soul pronunciation patterns is even more dramatic with its grammar. In Walt Wolfram's 1969 Detroit study cited in the last chapter, blacks from the lower working class (unskilled workers) and upper working class (skilled workers) used multiple negation, as in "He can't see nobody" on average 78 and 55 percent of the time, respectively. But blacks from the lower middle class (white-collar workers) used multiple negation only 12 percent of the time, and blacks from the upper middle class used it only 8 percent of the time. In short, this feature provided an example of what Wolfram called "sharp stratification," with a much clearer line between the middle and the working classes than seen in the case of consonant cluster simplification in the preceding chapter, which showed a more "gradient" stratification between the social classes. Other grammatical features of Spoken Soul showed even sharper stratification by social class. The deletion of the *s* suffix on third-person present-tense verbs, as in "He walk," occurred 71 percent of the time in the recorded speech of lower-working-class black speakers in Detroit, and 57 percent of the time among upper-working-class black speakers. But among lower-middle-class blacks, the feature fell to 10 percent, and among upper-middle-class blacks to only 1 percent.

Grammatical variation is influenced by *gender* as well. In Wolfram's Detroit study, lower-working-class black men deleted copulas (e.g., "He Ø walkin" and "She Ø nice") 66 percent of the time, while lower-working-class females did so less often, 48 percent of the time. This association of black vernacular speech with maleness and toughness was common in early studies, and it may still be true today. But many of the early studies were conducted by men, who did not get down with the sistahs as effectively as they did with the brothas. In more recent studies in the black community of East Palo Alto, California, a black woman, Faye McNair-Knox, who grew up in the same community, established a close rapport with her female interviewees; the teenage girls she recorded deleted their copulas a striking 81 to 90 percent of the time.

Of course, variation by *age* is also relevant. In virtually every study, younger people use vernacular grammar more often than older speakers do. In Wolfram's Detroit study, lower-working-class black teenagers (fourteen to seventeen years old) deleted their copulas (e.g., "He Ø happy") 68 percent of the time, almost twice as often as their lower-working-class adult counterparts (38 percent of the time), although the difference in copula deletion rates between teenagers and adults for the other social classes were much less significant (e.g., 30 and 27 percent for upper-working-class teenagers and adults, respectively). Among the East Palo Alto speakers recorded by McNair-Knox, fifteen-year-old Tinky Gates deleted her copulas 81 percent of the time, but her mother, Paula Gates, deleted her copulas only 35 percent of the time, and a seventy-six-year-old woman in the community, Penelope Johnson, deleted her copulas even less often—15 percent of the time. It isn't always true that younger people use the grammatical variants of Spoken Soul more often than their elders. For instance, Tinky Gates used unmarked past tenses (e.g., *he say* for "he said") 11 percent of the time, while senior citizen Penelope Johnson did so 14 percent of the time, and eighty-eight-year-old John Carbon did so even more often—20 percent of the time. But cases like these are more the exception than the rule.

In discussing copula deletion, we've already shown variation by linguistic environment (recall the table showing that zero copula was least common before a noun, as in "John Ø a man," and most common before *gon(na)*, as in "He Ø gon do it"). It remains only to show how grammatical variation in Spoken Soul varies with speakers' styles. This was demonstrated quite dramatically in a recent detailed study of how often East Palo Alto teenager Foxy Boston deleted her copula in different contexts. In one interview conducted by a black person with whom she was familiar, Foxy was very comfortable, and used Spoken Soul more extensively, deleting her third-person-singular present-tense *s* inflections ("He walk") 73 percent of the time, and deleting her *is* and *are* copulas 70 percent of the time. But subsequently, with a white interviewer whom she didn't know, Foxy used the black vernacular less often, deleting the *s* inflections only 36 percent of the time and copulas only 40 percent of the time. Within each of the interviews, however, her use of these and other vernacular features varied by topic. When talking with the black interviewer about graduation and plans for college and career, Foxy's copula deletion rate fell to 43 percent, but when talking more animatedly about boy-girl relations, it rose to 86 percent.

Our overall point is that although it is common to think of Spoken Soul as a fixed entity, in everyday use it is dynamic and variable. Like dress and other kinds of social capital, speakers deploy it to greater or lesser extents to delineate identity, to mark differences of social class, gender, and age, and to express how comfortable they are with their audiences and topics. In short, it is a resource or commodity that speakers exploit or avoid, depending on their social backgrounds, relations, and attitudes, on what they want to achieve, and on how they want to come across in each interaction.

8

History

*Pupils were made to scoff at the Negro dialect as some peculiar possession
of the Negro which they should despise, rather than directed to study the
background of this language as a broken down African tongue.*

—Carter G. Woodson (1933)

*There is not a single sentence structure in Black English that is traceable
to West African languages. . . . We would die trying to find any African
language that worked anything like Black English. On the other hand,
if we went to England and took a train into the countryside, we would
find much of what we were looking for.*

—John McWhorter (1998)

While the issue of whether Spoken Soul is a dialect of English or a
separate language fascinates the public, other questions have kept
scholars arguing for the past thirty years: How did Spoken Soul come
to be the way it is, and where is it headed now?

Some scholars contend that the African American vernacular
bears the vivid imprint of the African languages spoken by slaves who
came to this country in waves from the seventeenth to the nineteenth
centuries. Others maintain that the devastating experience of slavery
wiped out most if not all African linguistic and cultural traditions, and
that the apparently distinctive features of Spoken Soul come from
English dialects spoken by white (British) peasants and indentured
servants whom Africans encountered in America. For many scholars,
the central question is not the "Africanness" of the black vernacular,
but its "creoleness"—whether it was ever as different from Standard

English as the "creole" varieties spoken today in such places as Jamaica, Trinidad, Guyana, and Barbados, or whether it was ever influenced by them.

The newest question, posed only over the past fifteen years, concerns whether African American English is currently diverging or veering farther from white vernacular and Standard English.

According to one hypothesis, some of the central linguistic features of Spoken Soul developed only in the twentieth century, as blacks migrated north and west to segregated inner cities and their English became less and less like that of whites. If so, the future portends an even greater rift between these varieties unless the separate continents of white and black America reverse their drift.

If we had a time machine equipped with tape recorders and videocameras, we could answer these questions about the development of Spoken Soul. Instead, we must seek the truth by considering evidence of various kinds:

- Sociohistorical information about how many blacks were in contact with how many whites, when, were, and how—which allows us to gauge whether conditions in the United States were similar to those in Caribbean countries where more African features were retained

- Samples of black speech from earlier times, which are unfortunately not as numerous or as old or as reliable as we would wish

- Comparisons of current Black English with West African languages

- Comparisons with Caribbean English

- Comparisons with white nonstandard dialects of English, especially in Britain, but also in the United States

- Evidence from the African American diaspora—e.g. Liberia, Samaná (in the Dominican Republic), and Nova Scotia, where African Americans emigrated in the eighteenth and nineteenth centuries and where their descendants remain in linguistic and cultural enclaves

- Comparisons of the speech of older, middle-aged, and younger African Americans—which give us some idea of how Spoken Soul is evolving today

A Thumbnail, Century-by-Century History of African Americans

Let's begin our search by taking a walk through the history of African Americans, concentrating on sociohistorical events potentially relevant to the development of Spoken Soul.

The seventeenth century. The earliest Africans brought to what is now the United States are believed to have been one hundred slaves who formed part of a Spanish colonizing expedition of six hundred that attempted to settle in Virginia in 1526. But as far as the development of African American English is concerned, the colonization of the American mainland by English settlers is more important. That did not begin until the seventeenth century, with the successful English settlement at Jamestown, Virginia, in 1607. A dozen years later, the Jamestown settlers acquired twenty Africans as indentured servants. Indenture, the arrangement under which most white servants and laborers came to America, involved contracted work for a period (often five to ten years), after which the laborer might receive land and would be free to work for himself or herself. As historians John Hope Franklin and Alfred A. Moss Jr. have noted:

> As late as 1651 some Negroes whose period of service had expired were being assigned land in much the same way that it was being assigned to whites who had completed their indenture.

By the end of the seventeenth century, twelve British colonies had been established on the North American mainland: the New England colonies of New Hampshire, Massachusetts, Rhode Island, and Connecticut; the Middle colonies of New Jersey, New York (acquired from the Dutch in 1664), Pennsylvania, and Delaware; and the Southern colonies of Virginia, Maryland, North Carolina, and South Carolina. Neighboring Georgia, the last of the original "thirteen colonies," was not settled until 1732.

Although Africans were present in each of these colonies in the seventeenth century, they generally did not constitute a large segment of the population. English, Irish, and other indentured servants were the main workers, and labor-intensive crops such as tobacco, rice, and cotton had not yet become the norm. (Virginia began tobacco cultivation in the 1620s, and until about 1680 most of its workers were white indentured servants.) In 1671 there were only some two thousand blacks in Virginia, 5 percent of a total population of forty thousand.

In most of the New England and Middle colonies blacks were even sparser. These low proportions have led observers to suggest that the newly arrived Africans might have acquired relatively quickly and successfully, although of course not instantly, the English of the indentured servants and other colonials they met in America. As in naturalistic, unschooled second-language learning everywhere, Africans arriving in America in the seventeenth century might have transferred words and other features from their native languages, and simplified or generalized features of the target language. But they were perhaps less likely than their Caribbean counterparts to have drastically restructured it.

By 1690, Africans in Jamaica constituted 75 percent of the population. By 1746, that percentage had climbed to 92 percent. In Suriname (Dutch Guiana), Africans represented 93 percent of the population in 1700. And in both places, new creole languages based on English had begun to emerge—Jamaican Creole in Jamaica and Sranan in Suriname. Linguist Derek Bickerton has suggested that creoles develop only when the language learners constitute at least 80 percent of the population in a contact situation. Creoles have arisen in Martinique and Haiti, where the language learners (in these cases Africans) were only 35 or 50 percent of the population in the first twenty-five years. But Bickerton's figure captures the reality that creoles emerge when language learners have limited opportunities for contact with target-language speakers, and essentially work out their own norms based on their native languages and universal principles of language.

What's a creole, you might ask. To understand that, you have to know what a pidgin is. When speakers of different languages come into contact with one another (e.g., slaves speaking Yoruba, Twi, Igbo, and Mende on a Jamaican plantation), they may develop a simplified variety of the socially dominant language (in this case English) to communicate with one another. Such a variety is called a *pidgin* language. In addition to being simpler than any of the contact languages, the pidgin is usually mixed, in the sense that it shows strong grammatical influences from the languages of the socially subordinate speakers who bear the primary burden of linguistic accommodation and play the central role in creating it. If that pidgin is acquired and used as a native language (for example by slave children born on the plantation), it is called a *creole*. Because they are used as native languages—to talk about everything—creoles usually develop more words and more complex grammars than pidgins, but they often remain simpler than their input languages in several respects.

The following Sranan version of the sentence "Dogs are walking under the house" reveals how radically English can be transformed by pidginization and creolization, and how much it can show grammatical influence from socially subordinate languages (in this case Ewe and the Niger-Congo family of languages from which it derives, especially the Kwa subgroup):

Sranan:	Dagu	e	waka	go na	oso	ondro
Ewe:	Avu	le	tsa	yi	xo	te
English:	Dog	are	walk	go at	house	under

Even if we accept that seventeenth-century Africans in America might not have arrived in sufficient numbers and with sufficient distance from English norms to create pidgin and creole varieties, such varieties might have found their way into America via slaves imported from the Caribbean, or from those who arrived already speaking Guinea Coast Creole English that they had acquired in holding forts on the West African coast. In the seventeenth and early eighteenth centuries, many slaves came to what is now the United States not directly from Africa, but after having lived and worked in Jamaica, Barbados, and other colonies, where pidgin and creole-like speech had already begun to form. After South Carolina was founded in 1670, the first blacks it imported came from the Caribbean. In New York, between 1701 and 1726, twice as many slaves were brought from the Caribbean as from Africa.

We have virtually no samples of slave speech from the seventeenth century. One exception is the 1692 testimony of Tituba at the Salem witch trials, recorded by Magistrate John Hathorne and published 174 years later by Samuel Drake. Tituba was actually an Amerindian slave, reared by an African family in Barbados before being transported to Massachusetts in 1680 as a teenager. Her testimony included the sentence:

He tell me he Ø God. (He told me he is / was God.)

Two features common to creoles are found here—absence of the copula, which can be deleted in Caribbean Creole English whether it is present (*is*) or past (*was*), and use of an unmarked "action" verb (*tell*) for past tense, without an *ed* suffix or other verb change (as in *told*).

The eighteenth century. Throughout the eighteenth century, the proportions of blacks in the American colonies increased steadily, as did the numbers who were brought directly from Africa. Disparities between the three colonial regions became even more marked. By 1750, blacks represented only 3 percent of the population in New England, 7 percent of the population in the Middle colonies, but nearly 40 percent of the population in the plantation-rich South. Since 87 percent of all blacks in the American colonies at the time were in the South, it is this region that we must concentrate on when we consider the development of the African American vernacular.

By 1708, blacks outnumbered whites in South Carolina, representing 65 percent of the colony's population in 1720, and 69 percent in 1730. In 1776, on the eve of the War of Independence, there were more than twice as many blacks—the main labor force in the cultivation of rice and indigo—as whites in this colony: ninety thousand blacks to forty thousand whites. In neighboring Georgia, which was founded as a colony only in 1735, and which began importing slaves only in 1750, the black proportion was not as large, but it grew rapidly. Between 1760 and 1773 the black population almost doubled, increasing to fifteen thousand, as against eighteen thousand whites. In the swampy rice-cultivating coastal and Sea Island areas of South Carolina and Georgia, blacks represented even higher proportions— 70 percent and more in some parishes, 90 percent and more on some islands and plantations. The clearest example of Creole English in America—Gullah, or Sea Island Creole—developed in these regions and is still found there.

In eighteenth-century Virginia, Maryland, and North Carolina, the overall proportions of blacks were not as high as in South Carolina and Georgia, but they were still substantial, and black slaves significantly outnumbered white servants. By 1750, for instance, blacks constituted 27 percent of the population in North Carolina, 31 percent in Maryland, and 44 percent in Virginia. But as historian Philip S. Foner has noted, blacks outnumbered whites in three southern counties of Maryland as early as 1712, and "by the mid–eighteenth century, the Negro population had outstripped many times the white laboring class—46,356 Negroes to 6,781 white servants."

Two side effects of the black population explosion of the eighteenth century may themselves have had significant linguistic consequences. The first is that blacks increasingly learned their English not from whites, but from other blacks, who may have been speaking highly vernacular dialects themselves; this reflects the process of language acquisition and the influence of African languages. Historian Peter Wood made this observation in 1974, referring to South Carolina:

> After the first generation, contrary to accepted dogma, most new Negroes learned the local language not from Englishmen but from other slaves, a fact which reinforced the distinctiveness of the dialect.

The second is that whites, feeling threatened and wanting to ensure their economic and social dominance, passed increasingly harsh laws restricting the rights of blacks, stipulating their status as property for life, and prescribing draconian punishments for them. This process had begun since the middle seventeenth century in Maryland and Virginia, but the legislation spread to all the colonies and became harsher in the early eighteenth century. In Virginia, blacks were distinguished from whites as early as 1639 by an act allowing the latter but not the former to receive arms and ammunition. The following year, lifetime service was instituted for blacks but not whites. A series of laws throughout the seventeenth century chipped away at other rights of slaves, such as the right to assemble. But the slave code of 1705 consolidated all the former laws and, in the words of Philip Foner, "fastened the chains of bondage on Negroes more tightly." As he notes, the measure

> increased punishments for slaves by providing that for petty offenses, slaves were to be whipped, maimed or branded; for robbing a house or a store a slave was to be given sixty lashes by the sheriff, placed in the pillory with his ears nailed to the posts for a half-hour, his ears then to be severed from his head. . . . For the first time too, the law prescribed the castration of recaptured fugitive slaves.

Laws like these might have erected or reinforced sociopsychological barriers between blacks and whites, fomenting black resentment and leading to the crystallization of a black identity expressed, in part, through a distinctive vernacular. No slave who had had his ears nailed to a post and severed from his head would have wanted to speak exactly like his persecutors, no matter how many hours he had worked alongside them in the fields.

We begin to find in the eighteenth century not only several literary attestations of slave speech, but also explicit comments about the language of the Africans and about the ways in which black language and culture differed from white. Historians Marvin Kay and Lorin Cary cite the following from contemporary observers:

> Philip Reading, Anglican minister in Delaware, wrote in 1748 that slaves there "have a language peculiar to themselves, a wild confused medley of Negro and corrupt English . . ."

> J. F. D. Smyth, "an English visitor to the colonies at the beginning of the American revolution," described the language used by the Virginia and North Carolina slaves in the 1770s as "a mixed dialect between the Guinea and the English."

> The Reverend James Marye Jr. wrote from Orange County, Virginia, in 1754 that "there are great Quantities of those Negroes imported here yearly from Africa, who have languages peculiar to themselves, who are here many years before they understand English; and great Numbers there are that never do understand it."

Historian Allan Kulikoff explicitly suggests that

> a new creole language may have emerged in the Chesapeake [Virginia and Maryland] region combining the vocabulary of several African languages common among the immigrants, African linguistic structures, and the few English words needed for communication with the master.

And the language that Daniel Defoe put in the mouth of a Virginia slave in his novel *Colonel Jacque* seems to prove Kulikoff right, for it includes such creole features as *me* as subject pronoun (instead of "I" or "Ah") and *no* as negator:

> "Yes, yes . . . me know, but me want speak, me tell something. O! me no let him make de great master angry."

Moreover, as linguist J. L. Dillard has noted in relation to these very sentences:

> The Virginia and Maryland Negroes in *The Life of Colonel Jacque* speak the same Pidgin English which Defoe attributes to his other Africans. The white indentured servants who work beside them speak an entirely different variety of English.

Allan Kulikoff, considering the testimony of late-eighteenth-century observers, noted that black/white differences at the time extended to other aspects of culture besides language:

> White observers agreed that the music, dance, and religiosity of black slaves [in Virginia and Maryland] differed remarkably from those of

whites. . . . The practice of a distinctive culture within their own quarters gave them some small power over their own lives and destinies.

This notion is reinforced by the eighteenth-century observation of the Reverend Alexander Garden that blacks in South Carolina were "a Nation within a Nation. . . . They labour together and converse almost wholly among themselves."

During the War for Independence, fought between 1776 and 1783, thousands of slaves, attracted by promises of freedom, fled to (and sometimes fought for) the British side. John Leacock depicted one of them, Cudjo, in his 1776 play, *The Fall of British Tyranny*. In the passage quoted in chapter 2, Cudjo's speech shows possible influences from creole and/or West African languages, such as copula absence and the use of *me* as both subject and possessive ("*me* come from Nawfok," "*Me* massa Ø name Cunney Tomsee"), and the addition of an extra vowel (a process called epenthesis by linguists) in *disse* (this), and other words to make them conform to the common West African consonant-vowel syllable pattern. Many slaves and ex-slaves like Cudjo settled in Nova Scotia after the war, some eleven hundred of them moving on from there to Sierra Leone, where they founded Freetown in 1792. The descendants of these diasporic African Americans in Nova Scotia and Sierra Leone and Liberia would be recorded by linguists in the latter half of the twentieth century, and their speech used to reconstruct the nature of the African American vernacular of the late eighteenth century.

Evidence on slave speech in the eighteenth century can also be gleaned from newspaper ads about runaway slaves. Assessments of the English of slaves in these ranged from very low ("can't speak English"; "speaks broken English"; "speaks fast and bad English") to very high ("speaks very good English"; "speaks exceedingly good English"; "speaks very proper"), depending on how long the slaves had been in America and other factors. These assessments confirm what might be suspected anyway—that there was variation in slave speech resulting from the varying social circumstances and history of individuals and subgroups. Even J. L. Dillard, a linguist who firmly believes that both West African English and Plantation Creole were in use in eighteenth-century America, also insists that some blacks at the time spoke Standard English, and perhaps other varieties. Insofar as wide linguistic variations existed, eighteenth-century African America was much like the African America of today, although the sociohistorical circumstances shaping the variations were quite different.

The nineteenth century. The 1793 invention of the cotton gin—a machine that facilitated the separation of the cotton fiber from the seed—significantly expanded the production of cotton. Cotton replaced tobacco and other staples as the plantation crop in most parts of the Old South, and fueled the development of new states in the Midwest and Southwest, including Alabama, Arkansas, Louisiana, Mississippi, Missouri, Ohio, and Texas. Not surprisingly, U.S. slave populations underwent massive increases as a result—from seven hundred thousand in 1790 to nearly four million in 1860.

Some of this increase stemmed from the legal importation of slaves from Africa and (to a much lesser extent in this period) the Caribbean, which continued until January 1808, when the importation of slaves was outlawed. But there was also a thriving market in the illegal importation of African slaves that continued well into the nineteenth century, particularly in coastal regions of the South where ships could slip in and unload their cargo quickly and easily. (In 1858—fifty years after the slave trade had been outlawed—more than four hundred African slaves were brought to Jekyll Island, Georgia, on the slave ship *Wanderer.*) A third factor behind the black population spike was "natural" increase, spurred on by prolific slave breeding and the incentives that encouraged it: among them, reduced workloads, gifts of food and livestock to mothers of newborn children, and promises of freedom to women who bore ten or fifteen children.

The main source of new slaves in the newly settled states, however, and in parts of the Deep South where cotton became king, was the domestic or internal slave trade. Under this trade, slaves were moved en masse, by boat or train or, most often, on foot (via forced marches in slave coffles), from Virginia, Maryland, Kentucky, Tennessee, and other states to key cotton-producing states in the lower South—Arkansas, Louisiana, and Texas. Historians Daniel Johnson and Rex Campbell estimate that

> three quarters of a million slaves were removed from the old slave
> states of Delaware, Maryland, Virginia, [and] North Carolina and
> the District of Columbia to states in the Deep South and Southwest.
> . . . In the last decade for domestic slave trading, 1850–1860, migra-
> tion accelerated, with 193,000 slaves transported over state lines.

One effect of this domestic slave trade was the spread of the black vernacular westward, in a pattern that would be repeated and accelerated in black migrations from the South in the twentieth century.

Much of the apparent uniformity of Spoken Soul may be due to this population diffusion from the South. Another effect was to break up the black family, as mothers, fathers, and children were often separated from each other in the profit-making fervor that drove the nineteenth-century domestic slave trade. Josiah Henson's remembrances of his own forceful separation from his mother at an auction block in Maryland in the early nineteenth century, when he was five or six, make painful reading:

> I seem to see and hear my poor weeping mother now. This was one of my earliest observations of [white] men; an experience which I only shared with thousands of my race, the bitterness of which to any individual who suffers it cannot be diminished by the frequency of its occurrence, while it is dark enough to overshadow the whole after-life with something blacker than a funeral pall.

Such traumatic separations were probably similar to the ear-nailings of the eighteenth century that we cited earlier, in the sense that they would have created or increased the psychic distance between blacks and whites. Blacks experiencing, witnessing, or even hearing about such cruelty would probably not have wanted to talk like their oppressors, and they would probably have become more determined to develop or maintain their own communicative and expressive styles. The fact that Spoken Soul often marks the oppositional identity of blacks vis-à-vis whites and "mainstream culture" is undoubtedly part of the reason for its vibrant existence to this day.

Another key historical development of the nineteenth century was the War of 1812 with Britain, which led to further emigration of blacks to Canada and to a lesser extent the West Indies. In the 1820s and 1830s, colonization movements resulted in the emigration of thousands of blacks to Samaná and other parts of the Dominican Republic and, in even greater numbers, to Liberia. Analyses of modern-day Samaná English and Liberian English have become, in the last decade and a half, important indicators of what the black vernacular may have been like in earlier times.

Of course, the major historical events of the nineteenth century for African Americans were the Civil War between the North and the South, which began in 1861, and their achievement of freedom in the ensuing years. Abraham Lincoln's Emancipation Proclamation of September 1862 offered freedom to all slaves in rebellious Confederate states in January 1863, and the Thirteenth Amendment of 1865 constitutionally abolished slavery everywhere in the United States.

In many parts of the South, slaves achieved their "day of jubilee" even earlier, once Union forces defeated the Confederate forces. Wallace Quarterman, born a slave in Georgia in 1844, gave Zora Neale Hurston and others in 1935 this gripping first-person account of how freedom came to his plantation after the "big gun shot." The event probably took place at or close to the time that fifty Union vessels steamed into Port Royal and the surrounding South Carolina Sea Islands in 1861, and defeated the weak Confederate forces there:

> The overseer ask me what is that, if that is thunder? I tell um I don't know. I know was the Yankee come. . . . An' he call me an' tol' me to run down in the fiel', and tell Peter to turn the people loose, that the Yankee come. An' so I run down in the fiel', an', an' whoop and holler. . . . An that, the people them throw 'way they hoe them. They throw away they hoe, an' then they call we all up, you know, an', an' give we all freedom 'cause we are jus' as much as free as them.

Despite the achievement of legal freedom, the post–Civil War period was one of severe economic hardship for most blacks in the South, ravaged as the region had been by the war and the breakup of the plantation economy. One response was black migration within and out of the region—to bigger cities within the South, to south-western frontiers such as Kansas and Oklahoma, and to the industrial states of the North. Between 1860 and 1880, the black population in Kansas increased from 627 to 43,100. During the 1880s more than 30,000 Southern blacks migrated to Pennsylvania, New York, and New Jersey. And between 1890 and 1900 more than 105,000 southern blacks migrated to the North. Linguist Don Winford has suggested that "the concentration and intense contact of African Americans of various regional backgrounds in northern and southern cities set the stage for further leveling or convergence among AAVE [African American Vernacular English] varieties, and the emergence of the relatively focussed and uniform urban vernacular."

While the attainment of freedom was replete with hardships, it did allow many blacks to earn a living, especially in the industrial North, and it resulted in increased opportunities for education, in both the North and the South, for election to public office, and for involvement in leadership positions in the church. Those who were fortunate enough to move up economically, educationally, and otherwise would undoubtedly have had more access to standard or mainstream speech.

Although its accuracy is sometimes open to question, the contemporary evidence on black speech in the nineteenth century is voluminous. One finds it in novels, short stories, travelers' accounts, descriptions of minstrel shows, slave and ex-slave narratives, semitechnical studies, dialect sermons, music, and poetry. For a discussion of some of this literary material, see chapter 2.

The twentieth century. Despite the migratory movements blacks had participated in throughout the nineteenth century, nothing matched in scale and significance the "Great Migration" to the North and West (and specifically to urban centers there) that began around 1916. The initial pull factor was World War I, which increased the need for labor in northern industries at the same time that it caused a precipitous drop in European immigration—from one million in 1914 to a fourth of that in 1916 and a tenth in 1918. Recruiters from the North went south and found many willing migrators among blacks, who were attracted by the promising economic prospects of the North and repelled by the economic stagnation, overt discrimination, inferior education, exclusion from the electoral process, and racial violence (including lynching) that they experienced in the South.

According to one estimate, some 1.8 million black southerners migrated to states in the North or West between 1914 and 1930, about *four* times as many as had done so in the preceding forty years. This process continued in later decades, so that whereas 90 percent of the black population lived in the South in 1900, only 68 percent of the black population lived there in 1950; 15 percent were in north or central states, 13 percent in the Northeast, and 4 percent in the West. By the time of the 1960 census, 1.5 million, or 47 percent, of blacks living in the north central region had been born elsewhere, but only 1.4 percent of the South's black populations had. Illinois showed a net increase of 189,000 black immigrants between 1950 and 1960, and California an increase of 176,000 over the same period. By contrast, Mississippi showed a net decrease of 323,000 blacks from 1950 to 1960, and South Carolina and Georgia a net decrease of more than 200,000 blacks each during this period. It was not until the 1970s that the South, newly industrialized and with good housing and job opportunities, began to show increases in net in-migration, mainly people who had lived or grown up in the South before moving to the North or West, and who were returning rather disillusioned.

Black migration in the twentieth century was not only from South to North and West, but also from rural to urban areas. This was true even for blacks who remained in the South, driven from farms to cities by the collapse of the tenant farming system, by mechanization, and by crop disease. In 1920, 25 percent of southern blacks were urban, but by 1940, that figure had increased to 36 percent, and by 1950 to 48 percent. Urban living was even more characteristic of the North and West. In 1920, 87 percent of north/central blacks were urban, and by 1940, 89 percent were, versus 57 percent of whites. By 1950, fully 94 percent of blacks in the north/central area were urban. By 1970, 74 percent of blacks in the United States as a whole lived in metropolitan areas, and the proportions increased as white flight to the suburbs continued.

Throughout the twentieth century, and especially before the civil rights struggles and legislation of the 1960s, what blacks encountered both in the South and in the "promised land"—the North and the West—was discrimination in jobs and unions, segregation in housing, and distinct inequalities in education. In the 1920s, most blacks in the urban north were working-class, mostly in unskilled occupations (porters, elevator operators, janitors, domestics, and so on). Access to most higher-paying, skilled jobs and their labor unions was blocked by a process of "affirmative action" for whites and "rejective action" for blacks; of the ten thousand apprenticeships in skilled trade unions in New York City in 1920, only fifty-six were held by blacks. In the 1940s, blacks were excluded from most defense industry jobs until the Committee on Fair Employment Practices was established in 1941; between 1942 and 1944, the percentage of blacks in shipbuilding and other war industries increased from 3 to 8 percent, and cities with such industries experienced huge gains in black immigration as a result. Between 1940 and 1944, for instance, the number of blacks in Portland, Oregon, swelled from 2,000 to 15,000, and in the San Francisco Bay Area from 20,000 to 65,000.

Segregation in housing—usually in the form of restriction to overcrowded inner-city ghettoes—was high. In Baltimore in 1941, to name one city, approximately ninety thousand black residents were crammed into an area of one square mile. And in at least 109 cities in the North, South, and West, segregation actually increased between 1940 and 1950. The average index of black segregation for 207 cities surveyed in 1960 (defined by Daniel Johnson and Rex Campbell as "the percentage of blacks [who] would have to move from one block to another to effect an even, unsegregated residential distribution") was 86.2 percent. As upper- and middle-income whites moved to the suburbs, and jobs and industries followed them, the tax base for many cities dropped sharply, and the amount of spending for inner-city schools and other facilities for blacks also plummeted. Linguists William Labov and Wendell Harris, among others, have argued that this intense mid-century segregation in housing and schools led to changes in the grammar of Spoken Soul and increased divergence between black and white vernaculars—an idea we'll take up later.

The civil rights struggles of the 1950s and 1960s—culminating in the 1963 March on Washington, led by the Reverend Martin Luther King Jr.—represented a major attempt to overcome these disparities. The Civil Rights Act of 1964, which legislated an end to segregation in public accommodations and forbade discrimination in hotels and restaurants and in federal spending, was its most spectacular achievement. Voting rights for blacks increased, as did opportunities for education, employment, and access to social services. Affirmative action, providing for preferences in employment for minorities (and women) who had been the earlier victims of discrimination and what we regard as "repressive action," also began in the 1960s. As historian Kennell Jackson has noted: "After the Watts riots in 1965, [President] Johnson signed Executive Order 11246, which required employers using federal funds to set goals for hiring minorities."

Economist Martin Carnoy has argued that such federal interventions as New Deal legislation, the Civil Rights Act, and affirmative action helped produce real gains in black employment and income:

> Between 1939 and the early 1970s, a black male worker pushed his average earnings from 42 to 67 percent of a white male worker's earnings. . . . Black women did even better, almost reaching parity with white women by the end of the 1970s. . . . Black men moved from agricultural to higher-paying, higher-skilled factory jobs, and eventually, office jobs. Black women shifted from domestic service and low-paying factory jobs into retail sales and office work. The fact that black men *and* women were getting more pay helped change the position of the black family. Two-parent black families earned 60 percent of what white, two-parent families were making in 1960, a figure that leaped to 80 percent by 1979—a period of only two decades.

Between the 1970s and the 1990s, however, a series of Supreme Court decisions effectively restricted and outlawed federal affirmative action based on race and gender, and black gains in employment, income, and access to higher education are being eroded. While some blacks have been upwardly mobile (those earning $100,000 or more represented 0.3 percent of all blacks from the 1960s to 1984, but increased to 1 percent in 1987–1989), black-white disparities in employment and income remain very sharp, particularly at the lower levels. In the United States, more than twice as many blacks as whites were unemployed in 1993, and among blacks aged sixteen to twenty-four, nearly 32 percent were unemployed, nearly *three* times as many as whites aged sixteen to twenty-four. Economist Martin Carnoy has argued persuasively that economic and social progress made by blacks between 1940 and the mid-1970s stopped and in some respects reversed since then, and he blames this squarely on reduced government activity and involvement in minority matters. In 1994 he noted some of the grim effects:

> One of two black children now grows up in poverty, a much higher fraction than twenty years ago. One of two young black males has a criminal record, and half of the total prison population is black. One of two black children is born out of wedlock. Again, that number is up over the past two decades. . . . As blacks have moved out of cities into the suburbs, segregated housing has moved with them. Almost all black children grow up in such informally segregated neighborhoods, North and South, most with low-quality services and low-quality schools.

Furthermore, although blacks now occupy some of the highest positions in the land, as congressional representatives, mayors, and police chiefs, among others, they are still disproportionately the victims of criminal injustice and police violence. The 1992 not-guilty decision of an all-white jury for the four Los Angeles police officers who were recorded on videotape savagely beating Rodney King touched off the "largest peacetime civil disturbance of this century," in which fifty-two people died. Even as we write, investigations are proceeding into various incidents of premature and excessive police violence against blacks in New York, New Jersey, and other states across the country.

Some may argue that in summarizing the history of African Americans in the twentieth century we have highlighted the negatives rather than the positives. That may well be so. But the negatives are real, and they explain the existence of the seething "oppositional identity" that anthropologist John Ogbu finds alive and well in the

African American community. That attitude in turn fuels the continued existence and development of the African American vernacular—Spoken Soul.

Sources for studying the nature and development of Spoken Soul in the twentieth century are superabundant, but they have only recently begun to be tapped. In addition to literary sources even richer than those of the nineteenth century (including the works of black writers from the 1920s Harlem Renaissance and their successors), we have the ex-slave narratives and recordings of the 1930s; hoodoo (voodoo) material recorded between 1935 and 1961; recordings made between the 1970s and 1990s of the descendants of African Americans who emigrated to Liberia, the Dominican Republic, and Nova Scotia in earlier centuries; and a wide range of systematic linguistic studies of black speech made in selected cities across the nation from the 1960s to the present. Spoken Soul has come into media prominence during the same period, and the evidence of that coverage is discussed in chapter 10.

Having laid the historical groundwork, we now return to the major linguistic questions about the development of Spoken Soul—the extent of African, English (especially British), and Creole influences on Spoken Soul, and the question of whether it is currently diverging from white vernacular.

African, English, and Creole Influences on the Vocabulary of Spoken Soul

The vocabulary of Spoken Soul is overwhelmingly English in origin, and about that there has never been any dispute. Even the most ardent Africanists and Afrocentrists concede this, contending that African influence is strong in grammar, not vocabulary. Molefi Asante, the leading Afrocentrist scholar in America, notes that "although African lexical items may be found in limited supply among African Americans, they do not make the argument for a more general retention of African linguistic behavior applicable to most black Americans."

At the same time, research over the past half-century has helped dispel the contentions of earlier scholars that "the African brought over or retained only a few words of his jungle-tongue." That indelicately phrased assessment was made in 1922, by Ambrose Gonzales, the same "scholar" who displayed his racism and his ignorance of the fact that physiological factors have little or nothing to do with lan-

guage features, by hypothesizing that South Carolina and Georgia
Gullah originated as follows:

> Slovenly and careless of speech, these Gullahs seized upon the peasant
> English used by some of the early settlers and by the white servants of
> the wealthier colonists, wrapped their clumsy tongues about it as well
> as they could, and, enriched with certain expressive African words, it
> issued through their flat noses and thick lips as so workable a form of
> speech that it was gradually adopted by the other slaves and became in
> time the accepted Negro speech of the lower districts of South Carolina
> and Georgia.

Gonzales's successors avoided putting their feet in their mouths
quite so firmly, but even in relation to Gullah—widely regarded as the
most African and creole-like variety of Spoken Soul—Samuel Stoney
and Gertrude Shelby in 1930 estimated that it had only about twenty
African words, "of which six or seven are in common use." And Mason Crum, writing in 1940, essentially agreed: "perhaps a score of
African words remaining." By contrast, Lorenzo Dow Turner, after
nearly two decades of research, revealed in 1949 that Gullah had approximately four thousand words with plausible African sources. Most
of them were personal names (e.g., *Shiyama,* from a Kongo word
meaning "strength," "security"), but more than two hundred fifty were
words used in conversation (e.g., *goober,* or *guba,* from *ngguba,* a Kim-
bundu word meaning "peanut").

Scholars David Dalby, Joseph Holloway, and Winifred Vass, among
others, have extended Turner's work in regard to African American
English and American English more generally, arguing that even
common expressions such as *jazz, tote* (carry), *okay,* and *do one's thing*
have plausible African sources. Africanisms in vocabulary include not
only direct retentions or borrowings from African languages (*goober/
guba*), but also loan translations into English of African compounds
or concepts (*cut-eye, bad-mouth*). Because loan translations "pass" as
English words, they tend to survive longer than direct loans.

Arguments that African American English shows creole influences
are, like arguments that it shows African influences, made almost entirely in relation to its pronunciation and grammar rather than its
vocabulary. There are some striking vocabulary parallels between
Caribbean Creole English and African American English, but these
generally involve shared Africanisms such as *tote* and *cut-eye.* Shared
grammatical markers such as *steady* and *come* that do not appear to be
Africanisms are also noteworthy, however.

It should be noted that in addition to the vocabulary obtained from African, English, and Creole sources, Spoken Soul created and innovated many words on its own, as shown by the extensive slang and other expressions that can be found in the dictionaries *Juba to Jive* and *Black Talk*, cited in the notes. Chapter 6 offers several examples.

African, English, and Creole Influences on the Pronunciation of Spoken Soul

Africanists, those who argue for extensive African influences, and Anglicists, those who argue for extensive English—especially British nonstandard—influences, both yield little or no quarter when it comes to the pronunciation of Spoken Soul. For the Africanists, the reason many African Americans pronounce English *th* as *t, f, d,* or *v* (as in *tin* for "thin," *Rufe* for "Ruth," *dem* for "them," and *bave* for "bathe") is simple: The West African languages spoken by the ancestors of today's African Americans did not include the *th* sound, and when acquiring English in the seventeenth through the nineteenth centuries, Africans substituted the consonants most similar to *th* in their own language. Linguist Geneva Smitherman puts it quite plainly. In a column headed "Sound Rule in West African Languages" she gives the feature "no /th/ sound," and in the corresponding column headed "Black English," she gives the result: "Black English speaker substitutes /d/ or /f/ for /th/: thus *souf* (for 'south') and *dis* (for 'this')."

Anglicists are just as adamant that this and other pronunciation features of Spoken Soul are carry-overs from the nonstandard language spoken by settlers from Britain. Most of these settlers, they remind us, were peasant and low-class social types (indentured servants) who were likely to have been speaking vernacular rather than Standard English. As linguist John McWhorter has observed:

> Rural nonstandard dialects in Great Britain are chock full of the very structures that define Black English. In fact if Black English were spoken there, the African Language System notion wouldn't have even made it out of the starting gate because the actual models for most of its constructions would have been closer to hand.
>
> The substitution of *f* for final *th* (*mouf*), the substitution of *d* for *th* at the beginnings of words (*dem, dese* and *dose*), and the simplification of consonant clusters at the end of words are all common in nonstandard British dialects.

Cleanth Brooks, well-known author and literary critic, and a self-styled "amateur" in linguistic matters, is equally obdurate in his claim that such pronunciations as *de, dis,* and *dat* in southern Black English came from southern British dialects, such as that of Sussex, rather than from African languages. He cites evidence from an 1860 pamphlet that such pronunciations were being used in Sussex in the mid-nineteenth century and that they were in use there even earlier, since the sixteenth century. The rural folk in Sussex, he argues, could not have gotten their *des, disses,* and *dats* from blacks, because they had never encountered any, but the black folk in America could and did learn their English from white folk like those who came from Sussex. The blacks kept these and other pronunciations longer and used them more frequently than whites, he claims, because

> the blacks, who were denied education and later on only got a rather poor and limited "book learning," held on to what their ancestors had learned by ear and [what] had been passed on to them through oral tradition. In short, they rather faithfully preserved what they had heard, were little influenced by spelling, and in general actually served as a conservative force.

Is it possible that some of the British settlers might have come to America using the *th* pronunciations? Not really, Brooks avers, for "at this time the standard language had hardly settled down to a generally acknowledged form," and upper-crust Britishers "were few enough in the new American colonies." And is it possible that Africans modified English *th* pronunciations for the same reasons the French do (*zee boy* for "the boy") because this consonant sound is "completely unfamiliar" in their language? Brooks says maybe so for Gullah on the South Carolina and Georgia Sea Islands, where the speakers were "relatively isolated and had little contact with the whites," but outside of this area, no.

We cite Brooks at some length to indicate the uncompromising character of debate on the "origins" issue—concessions are rarely granted to the other side(s)—and to show that arguments are rarely as watertight as they are made to appear. For one thing, while it is certainly possible that Africans learned from whites to pronounce *th* as *d, t,* and so on, it is not necessary to assume this, for influence or "interference" from West African languages, which generally lack *th*, would almost certainly have produced the same result, as Smitherman and others have suggested. This much is clear from the English spoken by

Nigerians, Jamaicans, Gullahs (the one concession Brooks makes), and others in areas where contact between African languages and English took place without the presence of large numbers of British indentured servants and dialect speakers. Moreover, the claim that virtually every British immigrant to America was using nonstandard dialect pronunciations of *th* throughout the more than two hundred years that Africans were being brought to America can hardly be valid, especially since *th* pronunciations are more common among their white descendants today, even those with limited book learning. One problem with the argument of some Anglicists, in fact, is their failure to tell us anything about the frequency with which putative nonstandard features of British dialects occurred in America in the past and occur in Britain today; it is almost as if the attestation of a feature from one British speaker, once, could be the source of the high-frequency use of a similar feature among many if not most African Americans. Since Spoken Soul is often distinguished from surrounding white dialects today by how often particular pronunciations or structures are used, frequency considerations are important in reconstructing its history.

In any case, it is very likely that some Africans coming to America encountered *th* pronunciations among the English speakers they encountered, and produced pronunciations with *t, d, f,* and *v* instead because of the influence of their African languages. It is even more likely that this is one of several features that show mutual or convergent influence from British dialects *and* African languages. Linguist Norma Niles, one of the first to argue British dialect origin for Barbadian Creole English, made precisely this point twenty years ago:

> There may be a significant number of features, grammatical and lexical, with dual African and dialect origins. More significant though is that the similarity of features of the contact languages strengthens the chance of retention and persistence of these features in the developing languages.

In this regard she concedes strikingly more than those who argue for Anglicist origins of Spoken Soul.

Before leaving the subject of *th* pronunciations, we should mention that pronunciations like *t* and *d* could be attributed also to "simplification" from pidgin/creole influence, since *th* consonants are rare, or "marked," among the world's languages, and they are almost universally converted to non-*th* pronunciations in pidgin and Creole

English worldwide, even in the Pacific (Solomon Islands and China Coast Pidgin English, Australian Creole), where African influence is unlikely. This is a feature that could have come from African, English, or creole sources, either individually or jointly.

Another black pronunciation that is claimed by both Anglicists and Africanists is the simplification of consonant clusters by deletion of the final consonant, as in *tes'* for "test" and *han'* for "hand." McWhorter's comment quoted above includes the claim that this, too, is "common in non-standard British dialects," while Smitherman attributes it equally to a sound rule in West African languages disallowing consonant clusters. Ernie Smith elaborates on the Africanist position:

> In the deep phonology of African American speech there is a distinctively West and Niger-Congo African CV (consonant vowel) vocalic pattern that has been retained. As a result of having retained this CV rule, in the deep phonology of African American speech, in consonance with the rules of the West and Niger-Congo African languages, certain consonant clusters or consonant blends do not occur.

Smith's claim receives support from the observation by William Welmers, a leading expert on African languages, that "in Nilo-Saharan as well as in Niger-Congo, consonant clusters are generally rare." And given the evidence of Gullah, Nigerian English, and Caribbean Creoles that Africans with only minimal contact with English speakers simplified their consonant clusters, it is again clear that it is not necessary to appeal to English dialects to explain the presence of this feature in African American speech. Niger-Congo speakers learning English three hundred years ago would have been likely to simplify English consonant clusters because of their African language patterns, just as Africans learning English today do.

Smith makes a further claim that the restriction of consonant cluster simplification in African American speech to homogeneous, or "same voice," clusters (e.g., *nd* in *hand* but not *nt* in *pant*) is also "in consonance with the phonological rules of Niger-Congo African grammars." But no specific Niger-Congo languages are cited in support of this claim, and we could find no evidence in Welmers and other sources for it. On the contrary, the existence of heterogeneous, or "mixed voice," sequences in KiKongo (e.g., *nti,* meaning "tree") weakens the validity of the claim. Although these sequences are not quite the same as the simplified clusters of Spoken Soul (they occur at the beginning or in the middle of words rather than at the end),

Welmers argues for treating them as clusters, and they do involve mixed voicing (*n* is voiced, *t* voiceless).

What of *r* deletion after vowels, for example *afta* for "after," and *yo* for "your"? As in the case of the other Spoken Soul pronunciations discussed in this section, Geneva Smitherman attributes this to a West African language sound rule. Don Winford, while attributing *dem, ting,* and *tes'* pronunciations primarily to West African or creole influence, feels that *r* deletion after vowels, like the use of final *in* for *ing,* comes primarily from British English dialects spoken by indentured servants and other British settlers. However, the normally Anglicist John McWhorter concedes the possibility of West African influence here:

> It is reasonable to trace the absence of *l* and *r* after vowels (*stow* for 'store,' *co'* for 'cold') to West African languages. British dialects did not start dropping *r* in this position until the mid-1700s, after the basics of slave speech here were almost certainly long established, and only a few British dialects are known for dropping *l* after vowels at all.

Although pidgin and/or creole influence is a possibility in the preceding cases, one black pronunciation that seems to make the case for creole influence more strongly than for anything else is the rule deleting *b, d,* or *g* in the preverbal tense-aspect markers, as in "He ain't do it" (He didn't do it) and "Ahma do it" (I'm gonna do it). Parallels to this in Caribbean and other pidgin/creole languages are common (*'on* for *gon, 'a* for *da, 'en* for *ben*) and the feature is unknown in British English dialects. Whether African sources lie behind these creole similarities is not yet clear.

Another feature with strong creole rather than British dialect parallels and possible West African sources is the monophthongal pronunciation of vowels, as in *pay* and *go,* discussed in chapter 6. As linguists Erik Thomas and Guy Bailey recently observed:

> Older AAVE [African American Vernacular English] shows a much higher incidence of monophthongal /e/ and /o/ and of non-front /au/ than Southern White English, and it shares these features with Caribbean creoles. These features may ultimately be derived from African languages.

The authors note that the West African languages seem to favor monophthongal pronunciations, too: "none of the West African systems that have been described by linguists seem to have upgliding diphthongs for /e/ and /o/."

African, English, and Creole Influences
on the Grammar of Spoken Soul

Arguments about the sources of the grammar of Spoken Soul are sometimes as trenchant and diametrically opposed as those about its grammar, sometimes even more so. John McWhorter has claimed that "there is not a single sentence structure in Black English that is traceable to West African languages" (see the opening of this chapter) and that virtually all its nonstandard grammatical features come from British dialects of English. At the other extreme, Ernie Smith contends that "Black English" is itself an oxymoron, since "African American speech does not in any way follow the grammar rules of English" but is "the linguistic continuation of Africa in Black America."

The claim that African American speech does not in any way follow the grammar of English is easily refuted. As several linguists have noted (recall the quotation from Stefan Martin and Walt Wolfram cited in chapter 7), Spoken Soul is essentially if not overwhelmingly English in its word order and sentence structure. Moreover, some of the vernacular grammatical features that make it seem distinctive today do indeed have striking parallels if not sources in British dialects. The list includes existential *it* instead of "there" ("*it*'s a lot of girls") and inverted word-order in indirect questions ("I asked him *could he come* with me"). As far as we know, neither of these has parallels in West African or creole languages. Some features of Spoken Soul do have counterparts in Caribbean Creoles, but they may derive from British dialects, in form if not in precise meaning and use. This category includes double negatives ("I *don't* want *nothing*"), double modals ("He *might could* do it"), the use of *ain't* as an all-purpose negator ("I *ain't* lyin"; "He *ain't* gone"), and the use of *done* as a completive ("I *done* had enough"). As Don Winford has recently suggested, however, the meaning of *done* in Spoken Soul and southern white English vernacular, "particularly the sense of 'already,'" differs from that of the British *have / be done [verb](ed)* (e.g., "He *has done* petuously *devour* the noble Chaucer" from Scottish poet William Dunbar, 1460–1513) construction that was its "putative source" and "suggests some degree of creole semantic transfer."

The case can be made for African influence in several aspects of grammar of Spoken Soul, however. For instance, the use of *say* to introduce a subordinate clause, as in this sentence from a Philadelphia man, "They told me *say* they couldn't get it in time," might at first appear to involve nothing more than a nonstandard form (*say* instead of "said"). However, the similar use of *say* with verbs like *think, know,* and *believe* in Gullah and Jamaican Creole—where no "saying" is involved—suggests that more is going on:

> You wouldn't *believe say* i's a colored woman own dat house.
> (Gullah woman)
>
> Me been *know say* him wouldn come. (Jamaican Creole)

Here *say* is functioning much more like English *that,* serving to introduce the complement of a verb. And Lorenzo Dow Turner, who commented on the use of *say* after verbs of saying, thinking, and wishing in Gullah, pointed out that a parallel "use of *sɛ* or a synonym of it [Ewe *be₃*, where the ₃ marks a high tone; Mende *yɛ*] is common in many West African languages." He gives an example from Twi: *ɛnna o susuwi sɛ ɛyɛ ɔkramaŋ foforo bi,* meaning "Then he thought *that* it was some other dog." It is conceivable that in "They told me *say*" we have a West African structure masquerading in English guise, or at least a convergence between West African and English forms.

Molefi Asante has argued that there are some African American parallels to the common West African phenomenon of "serial verbs," in which two or more verbs occur next to or close to one another in a sentence with only one surface subject and special semantic meanings, as in the Vagala sentence that translates literally as "He took knife cut meat," meaning "He cut the meat with a knife." Spoken Soul does not appear to have the wide range of serial verb constructions (inceptive, instrumental, benefactive) one finds in the Caribbean Creoles, but there are suggestive parallels in such structures as "I hear tell you went home," "Go home go see about those children," "He picked up and went to town," and "I'll take a switch and beat you good." This last sentence is instrumental, reminiscent of the Vagala example above ("He took knife cut meat").

Another feature of Spoken Soul that Asante and others attribute to African influence is the primacy of aspect (the manner in which an event occurs) over tense (when it occurs). There is no evidence that tense is unimportant in Spoken Soul, as it is in some West African languages. On the contrary, past-tense marking is very common in black American speech, especially with strong verbs such as *went* and *came,* where there is no possibility for consonant cluster simplification or other pronunciation rules to eat away a final *ed* (as may happen with, for example, *walked*). And Spoken Soul makes distinctions among degrees of future and past (*fitna* is immediate future; BEEN is remote past), which certainly involve tense, the marking of event time.

But the very presence of certain aspect categories in Spoken Soul—particularly the completive (marked by *done*) and the present durative, or habitual (marked by *be*)—may be attributed to their prevalence in West African languages, which is well documented in work by William Welmers and others. Even the existence of a category of remote past (marked by BEEN) may go back to distinctions in languages like LuGanda and KiKongo. Moreover, the tendency of Spoken Soul to encode its most important tense-aspect distinctions through a series of preverbal markers (*be, bin, done*, BIN, *fitna, had*, and so on) rather than through verbal affixes strikingly parallels the pattern in Caribbean Creoles.

In recent years, arguments about African, creole, or British/English sources for Black English features have become more complex, involving frequency considerations, evidence from the African American diaspora, and subtle questions about linguistic constraints. To give an idea of items often discussed and debated, we close this section with two features: copula absence and negation.

Copula absence (as in "He Ø happy" for "He is happy") provides one of the strongest arguments for possible creole and African influences on the grammar of Spoken Soul. In the first place, British dialects of English do not appear to delete their copulas now, nor do they appear to have done so in the past, so the predecessors of today's African Americans cannot be said to have picked up this feature from indentured servants and other English-speaking settlers. Most American white vernacular doesn't delete copulas, either, except for varieties in the South, which, arguably, "learned" to do so from black vernacular. In fact, recent studies of coastal North Carolina communities in which blacks and whites have resided for decades show that the two groups are similar in a number of distinctive pronunciation patterns but differ sharply on some key grammatical features, including copula absence: the blacks deleted *is* 15 to 20 percent of the time, the whites only 1 percent of the time; the blacks deleted *are* 30 to 58 percent of the time, the whites only 4 percent of the time. A study of an old white man and an old black woman who had spent all or most of their eighty-plus years on a South Carolina Sea Island showed similarly dramatic differences with respect to plural marking and other grammatical features, and it was suggested that these linguistic differences reflect differences in both informal socialization networks and expected community norms. Copula absence is one of a number of grammatical variables distinguishing blacks from whites in the present and in the past. While some features of British dialects were adopted, others were not, and differences were either maintained or intensified as part of the social construction of how blacks should talk and how whites should talk. That is something even the most ardent Anglicist has to recognize and explain.

Second, many West African languages and the deep, or basilectal, varieties of Creole English in the Caribbean regularly have no copula before adjectives (Ewe: $a_1 ti_3 \ la_3 \ k\jmath_3$ = Tree the tall, "The tree Ø tall"; Guyanese Creole: *De tree Ø tall*), so this could be one model for copula absence in Spoken Soul. Beyond adjectives, both the Caribbean and creole varieties do have copulas, but these differ in form depending on the following grammatical environment. Before nouns, many Caribbean Creoles have *da* or *a* (*He a de teacha*), and Gullah has *duh;* and before locatives, which tell where a person or thing is, many of them use *deh* (*He deh home*). This use of different copulas before different kinds of predicates cannot have come from English, for English uses the same copula form regardless of whether it precedes a noun ("He *is* the teacher"), an adjective ("He *is* sick") or a locative ("He *is* at home"). A much more reasonable source is African languages, which regularly use different copulas according to the following grammatical environment. Yoruba, for instance, uses *ṣe* and *jẹ́* for following nouns, *wà* and *sI* for following locatives, Ø and *ri* for following adjectives, and *ń* for following verbs. The West African system is not perfectly preserved in the basilectal creole equivalents, for different kinds of nouns, locatives, and adjectives are not distinguished by different copula forms. But an African-like distinction among nouns, locatives, adjectives, and verbs is maintained by the different copulas used in the creoles.

When we consider variation in these creoles, especially in mesolectal, or intermediate, varieties somewhat closer to Spoken Soul, things are even more interesting. For the various creole copulas are sometimes deleted and sometimes replaced by English copula forms (*is, are*), and the relative frequency with which you get zero in the different grammatical environments mirrors the relative frequency with which you get zero in Spoken Soul. This is true also for the African American diaspora varieties spoken by the descendants of eighteenth-

and nineteenth-century African Americans who emigrated to Samaná, Liberia, and Nova Scotia, as shown in the table below, which should be compared with its equivalent in chapter 7. It could be argued that the percentages of copula absence that regularly differentiate these following grammatical environments in Spoken Soul and its diasporic and creole cousins essentially maintain the deep creole and African differences among following nouns, adjectives, and verbs that were originally marked with different copulas.

Creole variety or African American diaspora group studied	Copula deletion before noun ("He Ø a man")	Copula deletion before adjective ("He Ø happy")	Copula deletion before gon(na) ("He Ø gon go")
Jamaican Creole	4%	59%	93%
Trinidadian Creole	1%	79%	97%
Barbadian Creole	.08	.42	.77
Liberian Settler (Albert)	32%	65%	100%
Samaná, Dominican Republic	.12	.44	.93
African Nova Scotian English	.31	.46	.73

What about negation? For this we will draw primarily on a recent discussion by linguist Darrin Howe. He begins by noting three respects in which the negation system of modern black speech—as exemplified in studies done in Ohio and New York—differs from white vernacular English and seems closer to Caribbean Creole. They are the use of *ain't* for "didn't" (as in "I *ain't* do it"), the use of *ain't* for "don't" (as in "He *ain't* got none"), and the fact that double or multiple negation is obligatory when there's an indefinite in the same clause ("Nobody *don't* know about *no club*"), just as it is in Guyanese Creole.

But a quantitative analysis of negation in three data sets that provide evidence on nineteenth-century and/or early-twentieth-century speech—African Nova Scotia English, Samaná English, and ex-slave recordings—reveals *less* Creole influence rather than *more*. For instance, *ain't* was used for "don't" only eleven times in the ex-slave recordings and Samaná English corpus combined, and never in the African Nova Scotian English sample. Similarly, *ain't* was used for "didn't" only 6 percent of the time in the Samaná English sample, 3 percent in the ex-slave recordings, and 2 percent in the African Nova

Scotian English data, compared with 40 percent of the time in a modern Spoken Soul sample from Columbus, Ohio. Finally, double negation with an indefinite (*anything, nothing*) in the same clause occurred only 66 percent of the time in Samaná English, 80 percent of the time in the ex-slave recordings, and 89 percent in African Nova Scotian English. These rates are closer to the rate of 75 to 81 percent reported for white nonstandard dialects in the North and South of the United States, but lower than the 98 percent reported for modern African American Vernacular English. It is these data, together with other aspects of negation in the three earlier Black English samples that make them appear more similar to white vernacular varieties, that lead Howe to conclude that the negation system of these early varieties "can be said to have derived exactly from English."

Of course one could temper Howe's conclusion by suggesting that his early Black English texts do not go back far enough, and that they may not have been as vernacular and informal, in terms of the circumstances of recording, as more recent data sets. But his conclusions converge with those of others who have explored the sources of negation in African American speech, and they serve to remind us that African, Creole, *and* British English sources must be acknowledged as having contributed to the development of Spoken Soul.

Divergence

Most of our discussion until now has been about historical influences on Spoken Soul between the seventeenth and eighteenth centuries. The divergence hypothesis, however, brings us into the twentieth century, for it suggests that the Great Migration of blacks to inner cities in the North and West in 1915 and after has led to increasing divergence between black and white vernaculars in the twentieth century, particularly since World War I.

This hypothesis was first presented in the mid-1980s by two Philadelphia-based researchers, William Labov and Wendell Harris, who began by noting that the black population in that city had become increasingly segregated between 1850 and 1970. The proportion of blacks in each census tract had, for instance, increased from 11 percent in 1850 to 35 percent in 1930, 56 percent in 1950, and 74 percent in 1970, and the number of census tracts with 75 percent or more blacks was growing in 1980. For those who believed that segregation had been decreasing since the 1960s because civil rights legislation had dismantled the legal barriers to integration, data like these were a shock; but they reflect white flight to the suburbs and the increasing presence within inner cities of blacks and other people of color. Labov and Harris argued that the increasing segregation of blacks and whites was accompanied by increasing divergence of black and white vernaculars, and they produced two kinds of evidence to support it.

The first kind was the development of new pronunciations among whites that were not spreading to blacks. For instance, whites had begun to produce the diphthong in words like *out* and *doubt* with the tongue farther front, beginning with the vowel of *day* rather than *bat*, and ending with the vowel of *ought*. However, blacks had not adopted this change, beginning their *out* diphthongs with the vowel of *father* and ending them with the vowel of *too*, as in most northern dialects. Independently, Guy Bailey and his students have produced similar evidence in Texas. Of seven ongoing sound changes in Texas, blacks and whites use about the same proportions of the innovative pronunciation for three of them, but the whites are clearly in the lead for the remaining four changes. The difference between the two groups of changes, however, is that those in which blacks and whites appear to be equally involved (such as the pronunciation of *Tuesday* as "*toos*-day" rather than "*tyews*-day") are older changes, which began early in the twentieth century. By contrast, the changes in which blacks are less involved (the pronunciation of the vowel in *night* as long [aa] rather than [ai]) are newer changes, which began to spread rapidly only after World War II. This, together with evidence from other grammatical features, suggests that World War II was a watershed for black-white linguistic divergence.

The second kind of evidence that Labov and Harris pointed to was grammatical usage within the black community. Blacks who had the least contact with whites and were most involved with other blacks in the culture and values of the street used third-person singular present-tense *s* ("he *walks*") and possessive *'s* ("*John's* hat") least frequently, less than 25 percent of the time, and sometimes not at all. Blacks who had the most contact with whites (for instance, musicians) and/or were relatively isolated from street culture, had much higher frequencies of these Standard English features, using them between 60 and 100 percent of the time. Moreover, the black inner-city core group seemed to be using verbal *s* not to mark the third-singular present tense, but to mark the narrative past, and they would frequently put an *s* on the end of the first verb joined by *and* but not the second

("This white guy *runs* behind me an' *bend* down"). However, these findings about the use of *s* as a marker of narrative past were not replicated in the Texas studies (and have not been elsewhere as yet). And although the correlations between contact patterns and vernacular usage that Labov and Harris found seem valid enough, it isn't clear that they represent change from any previous situation, as "divergence" would require.

Bailey and his associates have, however, pointed to other changes in grammatical usage within the black community that have been confirmed from other communities and that qualify better as (mid-) twentieth-century developments. One is a sharp increase in the frequency of invariant durative or habitual *be* over the past fifty years, especially in urban areas, and especially before [verb]*ing* (as in "He *be* dancing"), making it almost the exclusive marker of extended duration or habituality in this linguistic environment. (But contrary to a widespread misconception that *be* was invented from scratch by the youngest generation, note that the adults in this study used *be,* too, and almost always with habitual or extended durative meaning. Urban youth eleven to fifteen years old used invariant *be* 135 times, or 10 percent of the time in the present tense, *am, is, are,* and zero representing the other options. For adults twenty-five to forty-five years old and fifty to one hundred years old, the proportional use of invariant *be* was lower—6 and 2 percent, respectively, of all present-tense copula forms—but this still amounted to a sizable number of *be* tokens, 64 and 72 in each case, respectively.) Another feature that shows twentieth-century change is the use of *had [verb]ed* to mark a simple past rather than a pluperfect, or past-before-the-past (*He had walked* for "He walked"). In Texas, this usage appears to have begun with speakers in the twenty-five-year-old group and to have accelerated among teenagers.

Although these features and others—including *fitna* or *finna* increasingly used as an immediate future—show that Spoken Soul is innovating, like all living speech varieties, its changes are not all away from Standard English and white vernaculars. For instance, the frequency with which black speakers delete the initial unstressed syllables of words like "afraid" (*'fraid*) and "electric" (*'lectric*) in Georgetown County, South Carolina, steadily drops by age group—from 85 percent among sixty- to ninety-two-year-olds, to 70 percent among forty- to fifty-nine-year-olds, to 52 percent among eight- to twenty-year-olds. And in East Palo Alto, California, lax pronunciations of the final vowel in *fifty* and the absence of past-tense marking ("He *go* there yesterday") are both less common among younger age groups; this represents convergence with white norms. In short, while the twentieth century has witnessed the divergence of Spoken Soul from white vernaculars and Standard English in some respects, it has witnessed its convergence with these varieties in other respects.

Author Claude Brown, who coined the term "Spoken Soul" for black talk, praised its "pronounced lyrical quality." (*AP/Wide World Photos*)

Writer James Baldwin described Black English as "this passion, this skill, this incredible music" in a 1979 article. (*Photograph © by Jill Krementz. Courtesy of the photographer.*)

Author Toni Morrison: "The worst of all possible things would be to lose that language [Black English]. I know the standard English. I want to use it to help restore the other language, the lingua franca." (*Photograph © by Jill Krementz. Courtesy of the photographer.*)

The Rev. Jesse Jackson at first called the Ebonics resolution "an unacceptable surrender, borderlining on disgrace." A week later he reversed his position, urging Oakland school board officials to revise the resolution because "your message is not getting through." (*Chuck Painter, Stanford News Service*)

Poet Maya Angelou was "incensed" by the Oakland school board's resolution, but has used Black English in her poems—e.g., "The Thirteens (Black)" and "The Pusher." (*Photograph © by Jill Krementz. Courtesy of the photographer.*)

Paul Laurence Dunbar, renowned for his black dialect poetry, was frustrated that his poems in mainstream English were ignored. (*Schomburg Center for Research in Black Culture*)

James Weldon Johnson, who wrote the Black National Anthem, alternately praised and critiqued the use of black dialect in literature. (*Schomburg Center for Research in Black Culture*)

Zora Neale Hurston used Black English copiously in her novels and critiqued its inaccurate representation in minstrel performances. (*Schomburg Center for Research in Black Culture*)

Alice Walker's *The Color Purple* is the best-known black novel written entirely in Black English. (*Photograph © by Jill Krementz. Courtesy of the photographer.*)

Playwright August Wilson's dialog draws extensively on black talk. As he notes, "Art is within the language of the people." (*Linda Cicero, Stanford News Service*)

Comedian Redd Foxx included a chapter on "Black Language" in *The Redd Foxx Encyclopedia of Black Humor.* In his words, "the black comedian of today uses the language of the streets." (*Schomburg Center for Research in Black Culture*)

Like many black preachers, the Rev. Jeremiah A. Wright Jr. incorporates Black English for dramatic effect, especially in the sermonic climax. (*Erv Cupil, Trinity United Church of Christ, Chicago*)

Oakland school board member Toni Cook, at the center of the 1996 Ebonics firestorm, now manages the African American Literacy and Culture Project. (*John R. Rickford*)

Linguist William Labov, who has been studying Black English since the 1960s, testified before the U.S. Senate's Ebonics panel in 1997. (*John R. Rickford*)

Psychologist Gary Simpkins, coauthor of the *Bridge* readers, which produced big reading gains but were withdrawn because they incorporated Black English. (*John R. Rickford*)

Educator Kelli Harris-Wright, whose bidialectal program for nonstandard dialect speakers in Georgia has produced "improved verbal test scores at every school." (*John R. Rickford*)

A teacher and students in the Academic English Mastery Program for Speakers of Nonstandard Language Forms in Los Angeles. The program is directed by Noma LeMoine, author of *English for Your Success: A Handbook of Successful Strategies for Educators.* (*John R. Rickford*)

Chattanooga Times, cartoon by Bill Plante, December 20, 1996.

San Jose Mercury News, cartoon by Scott Willis, December 22, 1996.

A Beavis and Butt-head Ebonics cartoon by Mike Luckovich that appeared in the *Atlanta Constitution* and other papers early in 1997.

Jeff Danziger's Ebonics *Hamlet* cartoon, which appeared in the *Christian Science Monitor* on January 2, 1997.

Part Four

The Ebonics Firestorm

9

Education

*Your message is not getting through. The language and the message must
get synchronized.*

—The Reverend Jesse Jackson (1996)

*Without familiarity with student's traditions, how will teachers see them
clearly? How will they recognize their strengths and envision their potential?*

—Terry Meier (1998)

On December 18, 1996, the Oakland Unified School District approved
its Ebonics resolution and ignited a firestorm. But the measure was
only one response to a series of recommendations that the Task Force
on the Education of African American Students, established earlier
in the year at the request of school board member Toni Cook, had
developed in response to evidence that African American students
were doing poorly in Oakland schools—worse, in fact, than any other
ethnic group. In a school district where more than half the student
body and the board of education was black, the concern was well
warranted.

It is important to remember—since this fact was obscured in subsequent debates about whether Ebonics (Spoken Soul) was a dialect
or a language and whether it was or was not genetically based—that
the concerns that led Oakland to establish a special task force and to
pass its resolution were not linguistic, but educational. African American students, particularly the majority, who come from working-class
and underclass backgrounds, have been failing in schools nationwide.
Or rather, schools nationwide have been failing African American
students.

Despite media suggestions to the contrary, Oakland schools were not alone in this respect. In 1992–1993, for instance, data from fifty large urban school districts across the country indicated that the reading achievement scores of black students were considerably below grade level. Only 31.3 percent of black elementary students scored above the national median, and only 26.6 percent of black high school students did so. (If these students were representative of American children nationwide, then 50 percent of them should have scored above the national median.) By contrast, 60.7 percent of white elementary students scored above the median, and 65.4 percent of white high school students did so. Data from the 1994 National Assessment of Educational Progress show the same depressing trend: on a 500-point scale, African American students at the age of nine are an average of 29 points behind the scores of their white counterparts; by age thirteen, they are 31 points behind; and by age seventeen, they are 37 points behind.

National findings like these are alarming, and Oakland was in no better shape. The district, concentrating on its own maladies, found more than enough to warrant concern and action. While African Americans constituted 53 percent of the nearly fifty-two thousand students in Oakland, they accounted for a disproportionate number of the youngsters who were facing crisis in the district. Fully 80 percent of suspended students and 67 percent of students classified as truant were black. African Americans constituted 71 percent of students enrolled in Special Education, but only 37 percent of those enrolled in Gifted and Talented Education classes. Nearly one-fifth (19 percent) of twelfth-grade African American students failed to graduate, and the mean grade point average of black students (1.80, or C−) was the lowest of all ethnic groups in the district.

The Task Force's initial recommendations.   In 1996, in an effort to remedy these and other problems, the Task Force came up with nine recommendations, including new criteria to identify, assess, and admit youngsters to Special Education and Gifted and Talented Education classes; improved parental and community involvement; increased funding; and stepped-up efforts to hire African American teachers and staff members. The primary recommendation, however, dealt with language:

> African American students shall develop English language proficiency as the foundation for their achievements in all core competency areas.

This alone would not have provoked objection from anybody. In fact, given the fuss people made about the importance of English in the wake of the Oakland resolution, it was clearly a standard upon which the whole country agreed. But the kindling for controversy lay in the preamble to the Task Force's report. In addressing the challenge of helping students make the transition "from their home language, Ebonics, to achieve greater proficiency in standard English," the Board was challenged "to take bold measures" to:

> 1. Recognize African American Language/Ebonics as the primary language of many African American students. Add African American Language/Ebonics to all district documents offering optional placement of students in classes or programs serving limited English proficient students.
> 2. Provide access to all services, current or planned, for limited English proficient students to Limited English African American Language/Ebonics students.

Word of these proposals began to leak to the press nearly three weeks before the school board had approved the resolution. On December 1, 1996, the *Sunday Times* of London ran the following report, hinting, in the editorializing frame within which the information was presented, and in the appended comment by Joan Rattary, at the maelstrom that was to follow:

> Despite the move to return to traditional methods, "progressives" have still not given up the fight. In California last week, the Oakland School Board of Education argued that blacks who speak "black English" should qualify for federal bilingual education funds because they speak an authentic language other than English.
> The African English is known as Ebonics and the speakers say, for example, "I been done walk" instead of "I have walked."
> "I don't call it Ebonics, I call it incorrect English," said Joan Rattary, president of the Institute for Independent Education, a Washington think tank.

Then the December 18 vote was cast. Within days, the resolution had become *the* media story nationally, and while a few people praised the decision, many more were laughing, howling, complaining, and venting about Ebonics. In response to the confusion and criticism greeting the proposal, the school board hired a publicist to serve as go-between with the media, and issued a revised resolution on January 15, 1997. The amended document came on the heels of a series of back-and-forth communications between the Reverend Jesse Jackson, who had become the resolution's most quoted critic, and Oakland administrators, who were determined to set things straight with this powerful potential ally. The culmination of these communications was a couple of tense, closed-door meetings of school board and Task Force members with Jackson, local politicians and educators, and community activists at Oakland School District headquarters on December 30, 1996. While some insiders calmly explained the rationale for the Oakland resolution, one or two participants, stung by Jackson's earlier criticisms, demanded that he issue an apology. But the diplomatic minister deftly sidestepped these demands by listening quietly, talking passionately about the larger problems of education and criminal justice affecting black people, and saying, "Shall we bow our heads in prayer?" Jackson emerged from the huddles with a clearer picture of the Oakland plan, a conviction that the school district had the best interests of black students at heart, and a hope that a national showdown on Ebonics would bring attention to the crisis of black youth. In an auditorium brimming with reporters and cameramen, Jackson reversed his stance on Ebonics publicly, but not before he had delivered an unequivocal message to the Oakland educators: "Your message is not getting through. The language and the message must get synchronized."

In a final effort to clarify its objectives and shake the media loose, the board approved a revised set of Task Force recommendations in May 1997 that made no reference to "Ebonics." But the focus on the "development of a comprehensive English language development program for African American students" remained.

The Oakland school board's resolution.   We provide below the full text of the original resolution, including the January 1997 modifications, and follow this with a discussion of each of its key clauses.

> RESOLUTION (No. 9697-0063) OF THE BOARD OF EDUCATION ADOPTING THE REPORT AND RECOMMENDATIONS OF THE AFRICAN-AMERICAN TASK FORCE; A POLICY STATEMENT, AND DIRECTING THE SUPERINTENDENT OF SCHOOLS TO DEVISE A PROGRAM TO IMPROVE THE ENGLISH LANGUAGE ACQUISITION AND APPLICATION SKILLS OF AFRICAN-AMERICAN STUDENTS
>
> [Clause numbers have been added here; italicized words were present in the original resolution of December 18, 1996, but deleted in the amended

version of January 17, 1997; wording that was added at that time to replace or supplement the original wording appears in bold, in brackets; otherwise, in the words of the secretary of the Board of Education, this "is a full, true and correct copy of a resolution passed at a Regular Meeting of the Board of Education of the Oakland Unified School District held December 18, 1996."]

1. WHEREAS, numerous validated scholarly studies demonstrate that African-American students as a part of their culture and history as African people possess and utilize a language described in various scholarly approaches as "Ebonics" (literally "black sounds") or "Pan-African Communication Behaviors" or "African Language Systems"; and

2. WHEREAS, these studies have also demonstrated that African Language Systems *are genetically based* [**have origins in West and Niger-Congo languages**] and *not a dialect of English* [**are not merely dialects of English**]; and

3. WHEREAS, these studies demonstrate that such West and Niger-Congo African languages have been officially recognized and addressed in the mainstream public educational community as worthy of study, understanding *or* [**and**] application of their principles, laws and structures for the benefit of African-American students both in terms of positive appreciation of the language and these students' acquisition and mastery of English language skills; and

4. WHEREAS, such recognition by scholars has given rise over the past fifteen years to legislation passed by the State of California recognizing the unique language stature of descendants of slaves, with such legislation being prejudicially and unconstitutionally vetoed repeatedly by various California state governors; and

5. WHEREAS, judicial cases in states other than California have recognized the unique language stature of African-American pupils, and such recognition by courts has resulted in court-mandated educational programs which have substantially benefited African-American children in the interest of vindicating their equal protection of the law rights under the Fourteenth Amendment to the United States Constitution; and

6. WHEREAS, the Federal Bilingual Education Act (20 U.S.C. 1402 *et seq.*) mandates that local educational agencies "build their capacities to establish, implement and sustain programs of instruction for children and youth of limited English proficiency"; and

7. WHEREAS, the interests of the Oakland Unified School District in providing equal opportunities for all of its students dictate limited English proficient educational programs recognizing the English language ac-

SPOKEN SOUL

quisition and improvement skills of African-American students are as fundamental as is application of bilingual education **[or second language learner]** principles for others whose primary languages are other than English **[Primary languages are the language patterns children bring to school]**; and

8. WHEREAS, the standardized tests and grade scores of African-American students in reading and language arts skills measuring their application of English skills are substantially below state and national norms and that such deficiencies will be remedied by application of a program featuring African Language Systems principles *in instructing African-American children both in their primary language and in English* **[to move students from the language patterns they bring to school to English proficiency]**; and

9. WHEREAS, standardized tests and grade scores will be remedied by application of a program that teachers and *aides* **[instructional assistants]**, who are certified in the methodology of featuring African Language Systems principles *in instructing African-American children both in their primary language and in English* **[used to transition students from the language patterns they bring to school to English]**. The certified teachers of these students will be provided incentives including, but not limited to salary differentials;

10. NOW, THEREFORE, BE IT RESOLVED that the Board of Education officially recognizes the existence and the cultural and historic bases of West and Niger-Congo African Language Systems, and each language as the predominantly primary language of **[many]** African-American students; and

11. BE IT FURTHER RESOLVED that the Board of Education hereby adopts the report, recommendations and attached Policy Statement of the District's African-American Task Force on language stature of African-American speech; and

12. BE IT FURTHER RESOLVED that the Superintendent in conjunction with her staff shall immediately devise and implement the best possible academic program *for imparting instruction to African-American students in their primary language* for the combined purposes of *maintaining the legitimacy and richness of such language* **[facilitating the acquisition and mastery of English language skills, while respecting and embracing the legitimacy and richness of the language patterns]** whether *it is* **[they are]** known as "Ebonics," "African Language Systems," "Pan African Communication Behaviors" or other description, *and to facilitate their acquisition and mastery of English language skills;* and

13. BE IT FURTHER RESOLVED that the Board of Education hereby commits to earmark District general and special funding as is reasonably neces-

sary and appropriate to enable the Superintendent and her staff to accomplish the foregoing; and

14. BE IT FURTHER RESOLVED that the Superintendent and her staff shall utilize the input of the entire Oakland educational community as well as state and federal scholarly and educational input in devising such a program; and

15. BE IT FURTHER RESOLVED that periodic reports on the progress of the creation and implementation of such an education program shall be made to the Board of Education at least once per month commencing at the Board meeting of December 18, 1996.

The first notable aspect of the resolution is its uppercase title, which, even in the original version, proclaimed as its mission "to improve the English language acquisition and application skills of African-American students." Nowhere does the board state that its wish is to replace English with Ebonics, or to give up on English, as feared by commentators, many of whom apparently did not read the resolution itself. The resolution's wording clearly indicates (as does the primary Task Force recommendation—see page 164) that the board was concerned about enhancing students' English. The dispute lay in *how* this goal was to be achieved, although many people misunderstood that it was the merits of Standard English at issue.

Clause 1 is less noteworthy for what it includes than for what it excludes. The list of alternative terms for the African American vernacular omits "Black English (Vernacular)" and its successor "African American Vernacular English," the labels that have been most common in scholarly studies by linguists over the past quarter-century. "Black English (Vernacular)," and its predecessor, "Negro Non-Standard," were coined by white linguists including J. L. Dillard, Ralph Fasold, William Labov, William Stewart, and Walt Wolfram, who pioneered the serious study of the African American vernacular in the 1960s. ("Black English" and "African American Vernacular English" continue to be used by the vast majority of linguists, white and black, who entered the field between the 1970s and 1990s.) But these terms were considered derogatory and insufficiently suggestive of African origins by Afrocentric scholars such as psychologist Robert L. Williams and social studies professor Robert Twiggs, who created alternatives in the 1970s.

Twiggs came up with "Pan African Language in the Western Hemisphere" in 1973. This never really caught on, yet it resurfaced in the

Oakland resolution as "Pan African Communication Behaviors." Williams and other African American scholars attending a conference on cognitive and language development of the black child in 1973 coined "Ebonics" (from *ebony* and *phonics*—"black sounds") to avoid the "white bias" and inaccuracy they saw in older terms like "nonstandard English" and "broken English," and "to define black language from a black perspective." But the term "Ebonics" never gained much momentum, either. In fact, Oakland's 1996 resolution gave it more recognition and mileage in twenty-four hours than it had enjoyed in the preceding twenty-three years.

Ernie Smith, professor of medicine, ethnology, and gerontology at Charles R. Drew University of Medicine and Science in Los Angeles, was the scholar who most influenced the wording and philosophy of the Oakland resolution. Smith, who was present at the 1973 meeting where *ebony* and *phonics* were fused, had in the intervening years become the staunchest advocate of the idea that Ebonics was a separate, Niger-Congo–based language rather than a dialect of English. Nabeehah Shakir, a key player in the framing of the Oakland resolution, and a supporter of Smith's ideas, distributed at the height of the controversy a copy of Smith's 1995 paper "Bilingualism and the African American Child." In it Smith insists that

> Afro-American and Euro-American speech emanate from a separate linguistic base. . . . African Americans have, in fact, retained a West and Niger-Congo African thought process. It is this thought process that is dominant in the substratum phonology and morphosyntax of African American speech but stigmatized as being Black English. According to the Africanists the native language of African Americans is Ebonics— the linguistic continuation of Africa in black America. . . . The Africanists posit that Ebonics is not genetically related to English. Therefore the term Ebonics is not a mere synonym for the more commonly used Black English. . . . In fact, they argue that the term Black English is an oxymoron.

Not only does this passage explain the exclusion of "Black English" from the resolution's first clause, but it also clarifies the source and meaning of the resolution's second clause. The initial wording of clause 2, however, ran into a buzz saw of criticism from people who thought that genetics in the biological sense, with all its racist historical baggage, was intended. What Smith meant—and this is quite clear from his 1995 article—was that Ebonics was genetically related to West African languages in the sense that linguists use the word to denote descent from a common origin. But the original phrasing that the resolution's framers chose ("are genetically based") was unusual even in linguistics, and was wide open to misinterpretation. Not surprisingly, this clause was one of the first to be deleted from the January 1997 amendment, although the amended version ("have origins in West and Niger-Congo languages and are not merely dialects of English") betrayed the influence of Smith's article even more overtly. For instance, the "West and Niger-Congo" collocation—a unique mixture of geographical ("West") and language classification ("Niger-Congo") labels—occurs in both. As Caribbean linguist and Afrocentrist Hubert Devonish has noted, highlighting the novel nature of the collocation, "We must presume that what is intended by the phrase 'West and Niger-Congo languages' is the Niger-Congo languages of West Africa."

Clauses 3 and 4 refer, in part, to the Standard English Proficiency program for African American Students (SEP), first approved for use in California in 1981. And the "judicial cases" referred to in clause 5 undoubtedly include the 1979 ruling by Justice Charles Joiner that the Ann Arbor, Michigan, school district had failed to take the "Black English" of students at Martin Luther King Jr. Elementary School into account. (See chapter 10.) Neither the SEP program nor the Joiner decision had hinged on the strongly Afrocentric view that Smith and the Oakland resolution writers were promoting, however. In fact, several linguists, black and white, many of whom were either neutral or negative on the African origins issue, had played key roles in developing the SEP program and winning the Ann Arbor case. In both instances, they had argued that African American speech was distinctive and systematic enough to merit special consideration in schools.

Clauses 6 and 7 make the first link between the language of African American children and federal bilingual education and limited-English-proficiency programs, for which African Americans are not normally eligible. But this connection had already been drawn in Smith's 1995 paper, where he argued that African American children should be treated like "Asian American, White, Hispanic American, Native American, Middle Eastern, and East European children whose limited and non-English proficiencies are acknowledged as being a function of interference from their primary languages." There he urged also that the "discriminatory denial of English as a Second Language (ESL) and Bilingual Education programs for African American children" should be brought to an end. Although they insisted that this was never their intent, Oakland School District officials earned plenty of criticism for the apparent attempt to go after bilingual-education dollars for speakers of what most people considered at best a dialect of English. In February 1997, California assemblywoman Diane Martinez successfully introduced Assembly Bill 1206 to block efforts of this kind. California voters rendered the issue moot by approving Proposition 227 in June 1998, outlawing bilingual education for everyone except as a temporary measure when parents individually requested it.

The original versions of clauses 8, 9, and 12 wound up in the eye of the Ebonics storm because in them lay the suggestion that African American children would be instructed not only in English, but also "in their primary language," namely Ebonics. Many observers took this to mean that teachers would now be expected to teach *in* Ebonics, and to teach Ebonics itself, helping students therefore to master "I be goin', you be goin', he/she/it be goin'," and so on. To clarify matters, the school district issued a supplementary statement in December 1996 emphasizing that:

1. The Oakland Unified School District is not replacing the teaching of Standard American English with any other language.
2. The District is not teaching Ebonics.
3. The District emphasizes teaching Standard American English and has set a high standard of excellence for all its students.

In its January 1997 amendment, the school district tried to erase all doubt on this score by excising the phrases about instruction in the primary language and stressing movement or transition from Ebonics to English proficiency. While we do not believe that the school district intended to teach its students Ebonics, or teach them *in* Ebonics, it should be noted that in helping students switch from the language of Jump Street to the language of Wall Street, teachers must be familiar with the former in order to help children compare and contrast it with the latter—a point we elaborate in the final section of this chapter. In this sense, students would indeed be taught *about* their primary language. But that is a far cry from being taught the vernacular itself. Since many of the students who would benefit from the compare-and-contrast method, known as contrastive analysis, are already fluent vernacular speakers, tutoring them on Ebonics would be like giving a veteran angler a lesson on baiting hooks.

The minor amendment that clause 10 underwent is noteworthy. The word "many" was inserted before "African American students" to counter the insinuation of the original wording that all black students speak Ebonics or African Language Systems as their mother tongue.

Two more comments might be made about the resolution before we briefly consider the May 1997 recommendations. The first is that in the midst of the linguistic and political discussions sparked about whether Ebonics was an English dialect or a separate language, whether it had African roots, whether Oakland was just pursuing bilingual-education funds, and whether it planned to teach in Ebonics, the central educational problems that led to the creation of the Task Force and to the framing of the resolution in the first place (rehashed in clause 8) were lost. And with them was lost a rare opportunity to discuss the devastating malaise of many African American students.

What's more, the resolution's framers did not include or cite any experimental data showing that taking the vernacular into account when teaching Standard English had worked elsewhere. There are several studies from Europe and the United States that support the soundness of Oakland's general approach (we summarize these at the end of this chapter). Failure to cite these experiments—perhaps because the resolution's framers did not know they existed—led California state schools superintendent Delaine Eastin to complain immediately after the resolution was approved that "we are not aware of any research which indicates that this kind of program will help address the language and achievement problems of African American students." Her sentiments were echoed by other educators and policymakers, and potential solutions to the educational predicament faced by African American children everywhere were largely ignored in the media's six-month frenzy.

The Task Force's revised recommendations of May 1997.   The Ebonics furor fizzled, then died, in the spring of 1997, when the school district released to the media the revised recommendations of its Task Force on the Education of African American Students. In her accompanying statement, Superintendent Carolyn Getridge explained that after the media attention elicited by the December 1996 resolution,

> it became increasingly clear that if the nation, and particularly the Oakland community, was to completely understand the driving factors for the resolution and the recommendations, the Task Force needed to pave the way toward a more accurate and meaningful dialogue.

To this end, the Task Force had assembled for four weeks in February and March 1997, intent on revising recommendations and drafting a detailed plan for setting them into action. Getridge herself had then spent a month poring over and modifying the committee's wording before submitting the amended proposal to the school board and putting it in the hands of the press.

In the revised recommendations, the word "Ebonics" had vanished, apparently stripped from the report by Getridge. The omission seemed to surprise Task Force chairman Sylvester Hodges, who told the *Oakland Tribune:* "I felt sure we had that [word there]." But he conceded that "we did not want to focus on the word," which would have likely meant more searing media scrutiny.

Also missing from the seventeen-page recommendation was any suggestion that bilingual education funds be funneled into the district to help African American students improve their English. Instead, the board itself proposed to spend nearly $2 million over the next five years to implement the Task Force's eight main recommendations (which, again, encompassed a broad set of strategies, including reinforcing career training programs for youngsters).

Yet the spirit of the original Ebonics proposal was unbroken. The first recommendation of the finalized report remained the "development of a comprehensive language development program for African American students" with an emphasis on "the need for . . . children to learn Standard English in the schools." The touched-up proposal stressed a "phonics" approach to reading and urged the use of Afrocentric and culturally relevant literature, but it also continued to emphasize respect for home languages, and to suggest that comparisons be made between a student's mother tongue and mainstream English. In fact, the Standard English Proficiency program, previously offered in only a few Oakland schools, was now to be incorporated in all pre-kindergarten to third-grade classrooms where African Americans constituted 53 percent or more of the student body. The SEP strategies were also to be expanded to sixth- through ninth-grade students as the first phase of a broader approach.

After praising these May 1997 recommendations, the media finally left the Oakland School District alone and allowed the African American vernacular to retreat from the spotlight, at least for the time being.

In a subsequent development completely unnoticed by the press, Congress in late 1997 approved a $1 million grant allowing Oakland to continue exploring techniques for tapping the linguistic and cultural resources of black students in order to enhance their school performance. Toni Cook, a former school board member and an administrator centrally involved in the Ebonics controversy, is project manager. Educator Etta Hollins, author and editor of several well-known texts on race, ethnic identity, and culturally responsive teaching, is research director of the cultural component of the research program, based in Oakland. University of Pennsylvania linguist William Labov is the research director of the grant's linguistic component. Labov had testified before U.S. Senate subcommittee hearings on Ebonics chaired by Senator Arlen Specter (Republican, Pennsylvania) in January 1997; Specter's subcommittee (Labor, Health and Human Services, and Education) sponsored the line item in the budget, and Labov worked in Specter's home state. Labov works mostly with children in Philadelphia, but he collaborates with the Oakland School District and with California linguists in analysis of the decoding errors made by black students in reading (e.g., reading *bite* as *bit*), and in development of new texts and exercises to help them improve.

At various times during the Ebonics controversy, a line was drawn by some between linguists in the Afrocentric camp (who attribute Ebonics' origins almost entirely to Africa) and those who were either skeptical or neutral on this matter. This is an intellectual issue on which research and debate should continue, with, one hopes, more substance and less acrimony than we have seen in the past. But the Ebonics controversy confirmed that linguists—whether or not they describe themselves as "Afrocentric"—are generally united in their respect for the legitimacy and complexity of the language spoken by many African American children. This perspective clashed with the more widely held public opinion that Ebonics was simply slang and gutter talk, or the product of laziness and carelessness.

Most linguists supported the educational philosophy behind Oakland and Los Angeles school district attempts to teach children mainstream English by constrasting it with their home language. The roughly six-thousand-member Linguistic Society of America in January 1997 issued an endorsement of Oakland's strategy as "linguistically and pedagogically sound." Other language organizations, among them the American Association for Applied Linguistics and Teachers of English to Speakers of Other Languages, subsequently adopted similar resolutions. And although differences and tensions remained between advocates of Afrocentric and cultural approaches and advocates of English-oriented and linguistic approaches, enough of a consensus was struck on the overarching educational dilemma of teaching

English to black inner-city students that the two intellectual camps could cooperate to seek a cure. And they began to do so—away from the public eye.

The ultimate value of the approach Oakland announced to the world in December 1996 remains to be seen. We are hopeful. Far too many black children in that California school district, and in comparable urban districts nationwide, are not making the grade when it comes to reading, writing, and the language arts—areas that are critical for success in school and the workplace.

Research on taking the vernacular into account in teaching Standard English and reading. As we have seen above, the Oakland school board never intended to replace the teaching of Standard, or mainstream, English with the teaching of Ebonics, or Spoken Soul. But it did intend to take the vernacular into account in helping students achieve mastery of Standard English (reading and writing in this variety in particular). And while the board perhaps erred in not citing studies to support its position, such evidence does exist.

One of the earliest studies was done in the Oakland School District itself, in the early 1970s. The researcher, Ann McCormick Piestrup, studied two hundred Oakland first-graders, most of them black, and the ways in which different styles seemed to correlate with their success in school. Of the several styles she investigated, two were especially significant. Students who were taught with the "Interrupting Approach"—by teachers who constantly interrupted and corrected them when they read or spoke in Spoken Soul—withdrew from participation, became hostile to the classroom enterprise, and posted some of the lowest reading scores. By contrast, students taught with the "Black Artful Approach"—by teachers who used rhythmic play and exposed children to Standard English distinctions, but who did not constantly interrupt or correct their Spoken Soul—participated enthusiastically in the classroom, and recorded higher scores on reading tests. This study confirms what we know from other studies: that negative and uninformed attitudes toward children's vernacular can be counterproductive, and even harm performance.

Programs such as California's Standard English Proficiency (SEP), started in the early 1980s and now in use in more than three hundred schools statewide, attempt to do more than improve teachers' unfavorable attitudes toward Spoken Soul and discourage them from constantly interrupting and correcting dialect speakers. The basic strategy is contrastive analysis, which involves specifically drawing students' attention to differences between their vernacular and the mainstream or standard language, and helping them develop competence in the latter through a variety of drills and other exercises. In a recent book, Henry Parker and Marilyn Crist extol the virtues of contrastive analysis, noting that they have used the approach successfully to teach "corporate language" to vernacular speakers in Tennessee and Chicago at the preschool, elementary, high school, and college levels.

California's SEP program has a fat handbook of several hundred pages designed to help teachers help their students switch between Spoken Soul and Standard English. The Los Angeles and Oakland school districts don't use the handbook directly, but they do follow the principles of contrastive analysis, asking children to switch between "African Language," or "Nonstandard Language," and "Standard English," or "Academic English," in their classroom exercises.

Unfortunately, the SEP's success has never been closely monitored, via control and experimental groups, so we have no hard evidence of its success. We have, however, seen and read about teachers, ostensibly doing SEP, who ask students to "correct" sentences like "Us wented to the store," which are artificially and exaggeratedly nonstandard, including features (*us* as subject; *wented* as verb) that virtually never occur in real speech. The value of such exercises is questionable, although in fairness to the program, the handbook's exercises are much better.

Much better documented is the ten-year-old program in DeKalb County, Georgia, in which fifth- and sixth-grade students in eight schools are taught to switch from "home speech" to "school speech," using contrastive analysis. As newspaper columnist Doug Cummings noted:

> The program has won a "center of excellence" designation from the National Council for Teachers of English. Last year, students who had taken the course had improved verbal test scores at every school.

The program director, Kelli Harris-Wright, has recently presented results showing that between 1994 and 1997, students in the bidialectal contrastive analysis program showed bigger improvements in their reading scores (as measured by the Iowa Test of Basic Skills) than students in the control group, who were taught by conventional methods. In fact, in the 1994–1995 and 1996–1997 school years, students in the control group scored worse at the end of the school year than they had at the beginning (in a pattern sadly reminiscent of many black students' school performance elsewhere), while the scores of students in the experimental contrastive analysis group steadily improved.

More concrete evidence of the success of contrastive analysis with speakers of Ebonics comes from research on writing done by Hanni Taylor in the late 1980s. She reported that a group of inner-city Aurora University students from Chicago who were taught with contrastive analysis techniques showed a 59 percent reduction in the use of Ebonics features in their Standard English writing, while students taught by traditional methods showed an 8.5 percent increase in the use of such features. In short, the goal of developing proficiency in Standard English, an important one for most of the people who criticized Oakland's resolutions, was better achieved by explicitly contrasting it with Ebonics than by ignoring or degrading the latter, as critics seem to favor doing.

Although it is not what Oakland proposed, we should mention that another approach that takes the vernacular into account—teaching students to read first in their native dialect and then switching to the standard language—has some notable successes to its credit. One of the earliest dialect-reader studies was done by Tore Österberg in Sweden in the early 1960s. One group of dialect speakers was first taught to read in the vernacular, and then taught in standard Swedish, while another group was taught entirely in standard Swedish. After thirty-five weeks, the vernacular-to-standard method showed itself superior in both reading speed and comprehension.

A similar study, reported by Tove Bull, was conducted in Norway in 1990. Ten classes of Norwegian first-graders were taught to read and write either in their Norwegian vernaculars and then in standard Norwegian, or entirely in standard Norwegian. Bull's findings were similar to Österberg's: "The vernacular children read significantly faster and better . . . particularly the less bright children."

The most similar experiment in the United States involved the Bridge readers, coauthored by Gary Simpkins, Grace Holt, and Charlesetta Simpkins in 1977. These provided reading materials in black vernacular, a transitional variety, and Standard English. The 417 students across the United States taught with Bridge showed an average reading gain of 6.2 months over four months of instruction, while the 123 taught by regular methods gained only 1.6 months—showing the same below-par "progress" that leads many Spoken Soul and other dialect speakers to fall further and further behind. Despite their dramatic success, the Bridge readers were discontinued because of hostile, uninformed reactions to the recognition of the vernacular in the classroom. William Stewart and Joan Baratz's promising attempts to introduce dialect readers in a school in Washington, D.C., in 1969 were similarly squelched.

John McWhorter, a critic of contrastive analysis, has recently highlighted a number of studies done in the 1970s that suggest that children tested with Standard English materials performed essentially the same as those tested with Black English materials. However, those studies involve one-time tests and do not systematically help children bridge the gap between the vernacular and the standard over a period of time, as the successful experiments by Harris-Wright, Taylor, and Simpkins, Holt, and Simpkins all do. Moreover, while we agree with McWhorter that more positive attitudes toward the vernacular and Afrocentric curricula could help reverse black students' devastating school failure (they should be a feature of *all* programs), we are skeptical about his suggestion that "immersion" in Standard English— by itself—could significantly improve their ability to read and write fluently in this variety. "Immersion" is what black students already receive in the thousands of schools nationwide that teach entirely in Standard English and ignore Spoken Soul. Yet they show steadily declining scores on language arts tests. With only a few exceptions, Standard English is what black students are exposed to in the media. The evidence is that this passive exposure makes very little difference to their productive control of Standard English. Many have difficulty distinguishing their native vernacular (Spoken Soul) from Standard English when attempting to use the latter. We need more explicit measures to help them bridge that gap.

We are aware that the schools in which speakers of Spoken Soul are concentrated often suffer from larger systemic problems—including limited funding, poor facilities, and undertrained teachers—and that these contribute significantly to the devastating failure rates of black children nationwide. In the face of these looming problems, the relevance of Spoken Soul might seem minimal. But success in reading and writing, especially in Standard English, is central to school success, and the evidence is compelling that black students can be led to success by methods that build on their already developed competence in the vernacular. Although contrastive analysis and dialect readers are not the only viable approaches to teaching the standard, these innovative methods do work. School districts like Oakland that experiment with them to reverse the devastating failures of their dialect speakers should not be hamstrung by carping and criticism from the uninformed.

10

The Media

Language prejudice remains a "legitimate" prejudice; that is, one can generally say the most appalling things about people's speech without fear of correction or contradiction. . . . Let a Fuzzy Zoeller deal with Tiger Woods in an overtly racist manner and he must immediately apologize, drop out of a major golf tournament, and lose his Kmart endorsements. This is not the case for anyone reviling African Americans in general for their language.

—Wayne O'Neil (1997)

In trying to understand the reactions to the Oakland resolution, what was not said—the conversations that did not occur, the topics left unexplored, the voices not heard—is as important as what was said.

—Theresa Perry (1998)

The Oakland Ebonics controversy broke a week before Christmas 1996, amid the slow news season journalists generally spend playing solitaire and praying for a bank heist or a collapsed bridge on their beats. So when Ebonics arrived like an exotic holiday traveler, the media went berserk. Radio talk shows chattered, news wires buzzed, television sets hummed, and magazines and newspapers from coast to coast churned out article after article chronicling, analyzing, and in many cases misinterpreting or maligning the Oakland initiative. The morning after the December 18 resolution was adopted, The *San Francisco Chronicle* announced:

> The Oakland school board approved a landmark policy last night that recognizes Ebonics, or Black English, as a primary language of its African American students, making it the first school district in the United States with such a systemwide approach.

Weeks earlier, the UPI news service had reported that Oakland was considering the measure. On December 20, the *New York Times* and the *Washington Post* published their first articles, etching the story into public record. Over the next two weeks, the *Times* ran six more stories on Ebonics, along with a column, an editorial, a few op-ed pieces, and three letters to the editor. Four days after the school board vote, the Reuters wire service had printed more than fourteen hundred words on the topic. If Ebonics was a pop-in guest, it showed no signs of wearing out its welcome.

In fact, by the first week of 1997, Oakland's "landmark policy" had spawned more than twenty-five hundred articles, editorials, columns, and letters in daily U.S. newspapers from Seattle to New Orleans to Boston, to say nothing of the avalanche of coverage on television and in journals, magazines, and newsletters. The fever would run through much of the winter, with Ebonics stories splashed on page one and delivered at the top of the evening news.

The nation had never witnessed such intense and widespread scrutiny of the vernacular. But Black English as a novel (if not white-hot) story was far from new. The media had for years "known the four-one-one" on inner-city dialect—had been aware, that is, that attitudes toward the tongue could be a complicating matter (educationally, socially, and otherwise) for those who relied on it for communication. In 1987, for instance, no less an agenda-setter than Oprah Winfrey hosted a discussion of Standard and Black English on her daytime television show. (Though mostly unfavorable toward the vernacular, the aired comments of Oprah, her guests, and her audience included some strong positives and were more balanced than those prompted by the Ebonics conflagration a decade later.) In 1994, the *New York Times* published a long feature, "Lingering Conflict in the Schools: Black Dialect vs. Standard Speech," which attributed the persistence of Black English to:

> the growing resistance of some black young people to assimilate and their efforts to use language [for] cultural distinction. It also stems from the increasing isolation of black inner-city residents from both whites and middle-class blacks, and . . . from a deep cynicism about the payoffs of conforming.

And the following year, producers of the respected program *60 Minutes* dedicated a segment of one of the television newsmagazine's shows to African American vernacular, with Morley Safer beaming as black adolescents taught him the latest slang and discussed the question of learning Standard English.

Americans who weren't hip to the complexities of Black English, or who had known the variety only as "jive," were probably as intrigued as they were puzzled by these mainstream reports, and by dozens of less notable dispatches on Spoken Soul. But to judge from the many incredulous reactions to the Oakland affair, what some members of the public must have forgotten by 1996 (and others may never even have realized) is that *every decade in the latter half of this century has contained at least one Ebonics flare-up.* One author even theorized that the mass media's relationship with Black English over the past two centuries has followed major twenty-five-to-forty-year cycles and lesser ten-to-twenty-year "intercycles," during which lapses in interest have been broken at fairly regular intervals by periods of intense attention. We won't go back two hundred years, but consider the last thirty:

■ In 1985, University of Pennsylvania linguist William Labov prompted some hand-wringing when he warned that Black English and Standard English were diverging—drifting steadily apart as they evolved.

■ In 1979, ruling on a lawsuit filed on behalf of eleven black children, a federal judge drew the most intense media coverage of Black English up to that point when he ordered the Ann Arbor, Michigan, school district to educate teachers about Black English in order to allay their negative attitudes toward the dialect.

■ In 1977, a trial program involving Bridge readers, a series of short stories written with diminishing doses of dialect and designed to help inner-city children "decode" Standard English more efficiently, vexed community leaders, even as researchers reported striking successes with the readers.

■ In 1969, in Philadelphia, the book *Teaching Black Children to Read* sparked a number of misunderstandings, and much defamation of the dialect.

In each case, educators, researchers, and the public jumped into a dispute prompted by a new suggestion that acknowledging and understanding black vernacular might empower inner-city schools to help children take that first stumble, then stride down the path to boardroom English. And in each case, the dispute sent reporters and critics running for their keyboards.

In the May 5, 1985, *Philadelphia Inquirer Magazine,* Neal Peirce, a founder of the *National Journal,* took on Labov's divergence theory:

> But blacks, Labov says, don't share in the evolving local white dialects. Instead, the black vernacular—black English—lives in its own world. The language gap, he warns, is just another reflection of "increasing residential segregation, fewer jobs, fewer contacts between the races." Many young blacks, he says, begin school without ever having conversed before with a white person.

Peirce acknowledged that Black English was the "legitimate and chosen language form of millions of Americans." But he insisted that poverty (rather than race) was to blame for linguistic isolation:

> No one disagrees that young people deprived of learning standard English face bleak, often jobless futures. If you can't speak the language, it's impossibly hard to get ahead except, perhaps, in underclass peer groups. Yet for all the public schools' failings, they do teach standard English. With television blaring away in people's houses "24-seven," who's to say that black America—and for that matter Hispanic or Asian America—doesn't get plenty of exposure to standard English?

Eight years earlier, the remedial reading strategy of dialect readers (see chapter 9) had been at the crux of contention, with the Bridge readers—believed by some researchers to help students swivel more smoothly between Black English and Standard English—were crushed beneath a riptide of condemnation despite their positive results. The *Philadelphia Daily News* had fueled a similar climate of outrage in 1969, when it learned of an internal memo written by a Philadelphia School District administrator and distributed among district personnel; "Order to OK 'Black English' in Schools Comes under Fire," the paper announced. Actually, the memo had only suggested that staff members glance at *Teaching Black Children to Read,* an edited book of papers by linguists who insisted, among other things, that Black English was systematic and legitimate, and that ignoring it or sneering at it could lead to disaster. But the recommendation was misinterpreted as an edict to allow or teach Black English in the classroom.

Of course, the mother of all Black English controversies before the 1990s was the 1979 Ann Arbor decision, sometimes referred to as the "King case." In July 1977, a lawsuit was filed on behalf of fifteen African American students, all of whom attended Ann Arbor's Martin Luther King Jr. Elementary School, alleging that the school, the district, and the state had "failed to properly educate the children, who were thus in danger of becoming functionally illiterate." Judge Charles W. Joiner narrowed the case to whether the school had taken adequate measures to recognize and overcome the barriers to equal educational opportunity posed by the children's home language, Black English. Two years later, the judge ruled in favor of the students in federal court, stating that "the unconscious but evident attitude of teachers toward the home language causes a psychological barrier to learning by students.

The decision did not set a legal precedent. It did, however, set off sirens. Syndicated black columnist Carl Rowan, writing one day before Judge Joiner's decision was released in July 1979, was among the many who bemoaned the impending "tragedy":

> For a court to say that "black English" is a "foreign tongue" and require schools in Ann Arbor, Mich., or any place else *to teach ghetto children in "black English"* would be a tragedy. For that would consign millions of black children to a *linguistic separation* that would guarantee that they will never "make it" in the larger U.S. society.
>
> What black children need is an end to this malarkey that tells them they can *fail to learn grammar, fail to develop vocabularies, ignore syntax and embrace the mumbo-jumbo of ignorance*—and dismiss it in the name of "black pride." [Emphasis added.]

Of course, no one had proposed teaching children in "black English," or telling them that they could ignore syntax and vocabulary. The anxieties surfaced nevertheless. By contrast, Vernon E. Jordan Jr., then president of the Urban League got the story straight:

> Black English became a barrier to learning not because of the children's use of it, but because teachers automatically assumed its use signified inferior intellectual intelligence, inability to learn or other negative connotations. . . . By focusing on the teachers, the judge made the right decision. Sensitizing teachers to Black English will equip them to communicate better with pupils who use the language in their daily lives. And it should help them to make better assessments of their students' ability to read and speak public English.

But even Jordan went on to stress, lest anyone get ideas, that it would be "a big leap from that to advocate teaching Black English in the schools. That would be a big mistake."

Not surprisingly, the King case would roil Michigan and rattle the presses for some time. Between July 1977 and February 1981, nearly five hundred news stories on the case were published. The prim community of Ann Arbor was not to become ground zero for Ebonics on the scale of Oakland (the city where Black Panther radicalism started, after all), but shock waves from the judgment would indeed be felt throughout the country, with dozens of newspaper commentators piling on to snuff out any sympathy for Black English. With the next big tumult over Ebonics, nearly two decades later, the angry sentiment was an echo through the years.

What made Ebonics such a scintillating story in 1996 and 1997? The same characteristics that made it compelling in the sixties, seventies, and eighties, and that all but guarantee another flare-up in the future: that is, its explicit mingling of questions of race and educational justice, and its implicit blending of questions of class, power, identity, and money. Indeed, language is often bound up with volatile political, social, and cultural issues (witness black opposition to Afrikaans in South Africa and jingoistic reactions to what some consider the encroachment of Spanish on the English domain in the United States). Any newsman or newswoman aware of these issues might have predicted that the discussion would grow noisy. But few journalists could have anticipated the intensity of the eruption on December 19, 1996. And after it finally subsided, fewer still would admit they had helped manufacture it.

Although many journalists were confused about how to handle Ebonics, some were fair and thorough. Some did their best to dissect Ebonics and make the story plain for a largely baffled public, even in the face of growing hysteria. Some struggled to understand the Oakland school board's intent, and to translate the convoluted wording of its manifesto. Others tried to trace Ebonics' history, and to unearth the deeper motivations behind the resolution. A precocious few even used the opportunity to scrutinize urban schools that had been overlooked for years, posing such fundamental questions as: Why are so many inner-city African American children having such a tough time mastering Standard English, and what should be done about it?

Overall, though, the coverage had some serious flaws. When Ebonics first hit the scene, journalists hastily identified the handful of public figures who were creating the loudest hullabaloo. The problem was that many of the follow-up articles to appear on or after December 20 and 21 seemed dedicated more to chronicling the ways in which these mouthpieces were spurning the proposal than to examining the curriculum changes Oakland administrators were considering. As is their wont, the media called upon the same handful of pundits to weigh in again and again; Kweisi Mfume, Maya Angelou, and Jesse Jackson appeared to fume anew in every article, but each had in fact issued only one initial statement, which newspapers, radio, and television kept recycling. The debate raged for weeks before advancing beyond pithy sound bites and rhetoric. The country was well into the mess before linguists—among the most informed commentators—were sought out in force. When reporters finally began to call him, University of Pennsylvania professor and Black English expert William Labov told them that Ebonics had been "too emotional a subject to get accurate reporting up to now."

By allowing the same stable of intellectuals to bash the dialect, while ignoring or failing to seek out those of equal caliber who might have praised it (such as novelist Toni Morrison, poet Ishmael Reed, or playwright August Wilson, who in an interview for this book remarked that "art is within the language of the people"), the media overstated the case and almost created a national consensus of scorn. (Indeed, when Reed wrote an op-ed piece to the *New York Times* decrying America's chorus of contempt for Black English, not only did the newspaper decline to publish it, but he was reportedly urged to rethink his position.) And even after Oakland schools superintendent Carolyn Getridge insisted publicly that the school district wasn't making a lunge for government money, newspapers continued to suggest that the Ebonics affair was merely a ploy for federal bilingual education funds. At the same time, Ebonics itself was portrayed, quite deceptively, as a made-up language, a creature engineered overnight in an Oakland basement.

It was the opinion writing that made some people cringe. Several newspapers (among them the *Atlanta Journal-Constitution*) ran almost seven times as much commentary on Ebonics as straight news. Respected periodicals such as *Vanity Fair, Liberty,* the *New Yorker,* the *New Republic,* and *Newsweek* published one-sided essays on the subject. While there were opportunities for clear-headed, well-researched debate, many columnists, editorial writers, and op-ed contributors instead relied on spurious arguments, distortion, condescension, parody, ridicule, and pseudohistory to malign liberal educators, black children, their parents, their communities, and their talk. The diatribes of many of the more reactionary columnists contained little or no discussion of the poor academic performance that had prompted the resolution. Few of these critics seemed to care, or cared to mention, that the average GPA of African American students in Oakland was 1.8, and that traditional strategies for teaching the language arts were failing miserably in a school district filled with speakers of Spoken Soul. As one African American parent complained, "No one worried about what our kids were being taught until this Ebonics thing."

News

The first Ebonics mistake many journalists made was to suggest that Oakland teachers had discarded Standard English and were preparing to give lessons in and on the vernacular. One of the most visible examples of this was seen on NBC's *Meet the Press,* when host Tim Russert asked Jesse Jackson what he thought of the proposal that "Black English, Ebonics, should be taught as an official language." Jackson responded with his oft-quoted statement that the very suggestion was "an unacceptable surrender borderlining on disgrace." As other mainstream television news programs (among them, *Crossfire* and *Talk Back Live*) and talk shows (*Geraldo*) featured discussions on Ebonics, the false assumption underlying Russert's question—that Oakland intended to teach Ebonics—became epidemic.

The January 17, 1997, taping of *Rolanda,* a daytime talk show hosted by Rolanda Watts, an African American woman, offered an almost comical example of how this runaway misconception clouded the national conversation. A cluster of black teenagers on a New York sidewalk were commissioned by the show's producers to provide samples of Ebonics from their everyday speech. Gesticulating dramatically in oversize jackets, the youngsters ran down a brief glossary of hip-hop lingo: *He flooded* or *He iced down* meant "He's got a lot of nice jewelry on," they explained. *I'ma jump in my whip* meant "I'm going to get in my car." *Homeboy flossin'* meant he was "lookin' good" and enjoying a lavish life-style, but *Homeboy flossin' too much* or *frontin'* meant he was looking for trouble. Rolanda's racially mixed studio audience chuckled at the colloquialisms. But believing that this sort of talk was to be encouraged in Oakland classrooms, despite the protests of scholarly guests, they grew serious, and rallied behind a teenager who declared, "You can't progress in society with slang. Slang is for you to get around the hood and all dat." (Linguist and Black English expert

Geneva Smitherman, who was originally featured as a guest, was so incensed that she withdrew and had the producers edit her segments out.) Similar discussions based on misleading information took place on radio programs, fueled by newspapers such as the *Times-Picayune* of New Orleans, which trumpeted, "Oakland to Teach 'Black' English," and the *Sacramento Bee*, which proclaimed, "Oakland Schools OK Teaching of Black Dialect."

Those last two pronouncements represent among the poorest elements of Ebonics coverage: the headlines. A good example of their consistent ambiguity came in March 1997, when the *Toronto Star* titled a story "Ebonics' Garbled Message." The headline implied not only that Oakland administrators had been vague about their intentions (true enough), but that the dialect they wished to redeem was itself garbled, unintelligible, mere gibberish (totally false). There was no such suggestion, however, in the article itself, which mainly probed the motivations of the resolution's framers and punctured the myth that the "home language" they were referring to was, linguistically, a new kid on the block. "While it's as old as slavery in the South," the article stated, "the new debate is about the legitimacy of ebonics, whether it's in the 'hood or in the classroom."

Sometimes the biases were subtle, almost unavoidable, because they came tangled with the attitudes and prejudices that bind our nation's consciousness. Consider the *New York Times,* which on December 30, 1996, announced: "Voice of Inner City Streets Is Defended and Criticized." Now, some speakers of the vernacular may be accurately associated with "the streets." But the streets are certainly not the vernacular's only, or even primary, domain. Indeed, African American vernacular can be heard in black homes and schoolyards, and even in churches (see chapter 3), across the country. Many middle-class readers of all colors got the impression, though, that the dialect was restricted to the streets, and to the "mean streets" at that. For them, "Ebonics" and "hoodlum" had become a natural equation, a duo nicely wed in the shadows of the imagination.

In the same *Times* article, Black English was described as a collection of "idiosyncratic speech patterns." The phrase sounds innocuous enough, but it helped trivialize the dialect, suggesting a linguistic quirk or an absence of the orderliness that is in fact the hallmark of all language varieties, and adding to the sense of weirdness surrounding the already rather alien term "Ebonics." There was much skepticism as far as the legitimacy of Black English (whether spoken inside or outside the classroom) was concerned, and the media often took great pains to avoid presenting it as a credible or even real way of speaking (which it undeniably is).

One reason the press fussed over Ebonics for so long was the emotional outcry the topic continued to evoke. On December 20, 1996, the *San Francisco Chronicle* published an article in which an African American senior at San Francisco High School dismissed Black English as "slave language." On January 5, 1997, the *San Francisco Examiner* ran a feature in which a Bay Area seventeen-year-old commented on Ebonics: "It's rooted in me. I'm very proud of my culture." Elsewhere and at other times, when asked about Ebonics, Spike Lee blistered, rapper Chuck D scoffed, San Francisco 49ers wide receiver Jerry Rice shook his head, and University of California regent Ward Connerly sputtered that it was "just ass-backwards." And yet most of the residents at an Oakland town hall meeting covered by the *San Jose Mercury News* in January supported Ebonics. Said one resident, "If we be cookin', we be cookin'!" Another felt that it was just common sense that a respect for language was elementary to learning: "I saw my peers frustrated and made to feel inferior by teachers and instructors who did not have a background in Black English."

Two weeks before the forum, a white accountant interviewed in an upscale San Francisco shopping center had spoken out against Black English: "They're encouraging kids to use improper language." In an African American section of the same city, an unemployed black welder had staunchly defended it: "They [the school board] said it's all right to talk the way you talk—that you're not stupid, just different." These perspectives reveal as much about our country as they do about the media's approach to covering Ebonics. Despite the distance between the views of the accountant and those of the welder, Ebonics had, in a superficial sense, bridged America's racial gap. People of all complexions were giggling or fuming. But the debate also unveiled the deep socioeconomic fissures within the African American community. The welder's comments, for instance, remind us that while the black middle class was overwhelmingly denouncing Ebonics, many members of the black working class, whose views rarely found their way over the airwaves or onto newsprint, were championing it, or at least grumbling about its getting slammed. In any case, that the *San Francisco Chronicle* would publish the statements of the white accountant and those of the out-of-work black welder one right after the other smelled funny. The implication seemed to be that you could find scarcely anyone with a job who had anything polite to say about Black English.

Reporters committed their most grievous mistake, though, not by using loaded words or sensationalizing headlines or indulging in bits of editorializing, but by excluding from their articles national evidence showing that black students were lagging perilously behind whites when it came to academic achievement. This disparity, after all, was the number-one motivation behind the Ebonics plan in the first place. In the final days of 1996, just as the Ebonics controversy was peaking, the Education Trust released a report indicating that African American students had begun losing ground in reading and writing after years of gaining academically. Minorities had made moderate or significant academic progress in the 1970s and 1980s. But according to a study conducted by the national research group, blacks in the mid-1990s were backsliding in all disciplines, including reading and writing, when compared to whites.

Yet those numbers seldom appeared in articles about Ebonics. This is not to suggest that the press ignored *all* the statistics; many newspapers recounted the discouraging performance of African American students in Oakland schools, and a few even made the crucial point that the district was looking to its Ebonics policy as just one possible solution. But few publications explored the notion of Black English as a universal classroom hurdle as thoroughly as the *Washington Post*, which on January 6, 1997, held that

> in the nation's urban public schools, the scenario is familiar. The academic record of many poor black students is dismal and getting worse. Frustrated educators search for dramatic new ways to get at one root of the problem: language skills.

The *San Jose Mercury News* was also on target, placing Oakland's "disheartening" academic circumstances in the context of a U.S. Department of Education report that revealed that seventeen-year-old blacks were reading at the level of thirteen-year-old whites, and that SAT verbal scores for blacks were on the average almost 100 points lower than those for whites. Clearly, Oakland had no monopoly on failure. Urban schools across the country were reeling. So why did the media often fail to consider these symptoms in the Ebonics diagnosis? We're not entirely sure. That many journalists refused to believe that language could be a central factor in the poor academic performance of many African American students played a part. And certainly, the reality that the educational system, through traditional but often inept teaching methods, was preparing hundreds of thousands of black children for nothing more than poverty was less sexy a story than the prospect of "I be goin' to da sto" replacing "Reading, writing, and arithmetic" as the classroom mantra. As one Stanford University graduate student observed in the aftermath of the Ebonics inquisition, there is often a good distance between what is worthy and what is deemed newsworthy.

To be fair, however, we should recognize what many journalists came up against while trying to tough their way through the wilds of the Ebonics story. It was undoubtedly a story caught in the crosshairs of race and class, and trapped in an elaborate historical web of slavery, segregation, and economic and educational inequity. Folks, white and black, grew touchy or indignant or just plain silly when asked to talk about Black English. Modern scientists themselves had been seriously researching Ebonics only for a matter of decades, and already it had spurred more than its fair share of scholarly quibbling. Even Oakland administrators were conspicuously tight-lipped at first when it came to discussing how the Ebonics plan might be implemented, and at what cost, and who was to pick up the tab—probably because many of these details had yet to be worked out.

The media's later and longer efforts to rescue Black English and the Oakland policy from the muck of public ignorance were, nonetheless, far more auspicious. Just before the new year, for example, the *Oakland Tribune* was one of the few newspapers in the country to publish the full text of the resolution, giving readers a chance to scrutinize the gnarled wording of the document firsthand, "unfiltered by the news media, school officials or their spin doctors." The same day, the *New York Times* reminded readers that Black and White American Englishes, in their slang at least, were "not so separate," pointing out that *uptight, outta sight, groovin', dissin', wannabe, You go, girl,* and *my man* all originated in the 'hood. And to demonstrate that journalists willing to sleuth out the more enduring questions beneath the debate would continue to find plenty of cultural fodder, the *Washington Post* in early January 1997 stated:

> So crucial is a common language to people's sense of security, experts say, that the smallest difference—whether it's a foreign accent or a nonstandard grammar, as occurs in Ebonics—can quickly bring to the surface deep-seated ethnic fears.

In mid-February, the *San Jose Mercury News,* one of the few newspapers to examine some of the instructional strategies used in Oakland's Standard English Proficiency program, offered readers a sample of contrastive analysis, the controversial but promising core of science at the center of the resolution. This was a crucial piece of reporting, as many newspapers failed to provide even one sample of how Black English was being used to teach the standard. The *Mercury News* wrote:

> Haynes cited as an example a lesson in which students are asked to translate into standard English sentences such as "Michael Jackson be dancing. Michael Jackson be the best dancer I know." Supporters of the SEP program have stressed that teachers never instruct in black English. They do, however, ask students to identify the differences between black English and standard English and have students translate black English phrases into standard English.

When Peter Applebome of the *New York Times* went in search of substance, he was able to capture the desperation, the ideology, and the personalities behind the Oakland plan, and after what must have been hours of research, to pen the best Ebonics article of the bunch. But Ebonics as a national topic was a phenomenon of the winter frost, and Applebome's piece didn't appear until March 1997, well into the thaw. Truth came too late, and too little.

Opinion

As 1996 made way for 1997 and Ebonics mania wore on, everyone seemed to be vying for a piece of Oakland. Pundits of all stripes set out to indict Ebonics, to apologize for Ebonics, to try to fix Ebonics, to look for the spin on Ebonics that would suit their own agenda. In the end, the resolution was used to prop up virtually every political platform imaginable. A socialist newsletter, the *International Workers Bulletin,* for instance, claimed that Ebonics had been conjured up by the American aristocracy in order to divert attention from the injustices of class disparity. Another such organ, *Socialist Action,* defended the Oakland school board against the "racist assault" of fascist politicians. Mouthpieces for the mainstream media dug trenches of their own, seeking to resolve some central questions: What is Ebonics, and where did it come from? Who and what is behind the Ebonics movement? And what should be done about it?

Black conservative Thomas Sowell, for one, took the position that
Black English "is just as white as any other English." In a newspaper
column, Sowell stated that Ebonics apostles were endorsing fairy tales
by suggesting that the continent of Africa had anything to do with the
way black people talk today. Black English, he maintained, represents
nothing more than the last murmurs of an obsolete British dialect
(see chapter 8 for our remarks on this):

> From what African language did "ain't" come? And why were whites
> saying it in England before they ever crossed the Atlantic or ever saw
> anybody of African ancestry?

Black columnist Walter Williams also insisted that "'I be' talk has
no ties to any African heritage." He was among the dozens of critics
who wrote a portion or all of their columns in dialect (or some approximation thereof), presumably to illustrate its backwardness most
colorfully. In Williams's words: "Y'awl might axin me why Ah be writin
dis way." Williams guessed that many of his readers, "intellectual
multiculturists" included, would misinterpret the preceding passage
as Black English. In fact, he maintained, it was an amalgamation of
"regional dialects spoken throughout the south and west of England
during the Seventeenth Century" and transplanted to America in
later years. Poor whites and blacks in the American South had simply
retained such "ill-bred" speech patterns. Williams concluded that
"the language we often hear spoken among blacks has little or nothing to do with Africa. It's as English as you want to get."
    Williams and Sowell hadn't come up with anything new. Again
and again, black intellectuals have tried to drop Black English into
the laps of whites and run. As early as 1971, for example, civil rights
leader Bayard Rustin, then executive director of the A. Philip Randolph Institute, wrote in a column published as a paid advertisement
in the *New York Times:* "'Black English,' after all, has nothing to do
with blackness but derives from the conditions of lower-class life in
the South (poor Southern whites also speak 'black English')." Shunting off the vernacular, ascribing it to an entirely separate neighborhood, seems to be a much easier policy than confronting it head-on.
Some blacks grab whatever convenient scraps of linguistic data they
can, and sketch a genealogical chart for Ebonics that they hope will
exonerate their great-grandfathers. (But we're all implicated, for as
we have shown in chapter 8, the real origins of the dialect are quite
diverse and complex.)

White critics tended to fall in with Williams and Sowell, at least in asserting that Ebonics is not what it pretends. Columnist George Will, on an edition of the television program *This Week with David Brinkley,* declared uninformedly that Ebonics

> is clearly not a language. Is there an Ebonics dictionary? No. Is there a canon of Ebonics literature? No. It's not a language. . . . It contributes to the ghettoization of young African Americans.

Other journalists joined Knight-Ridder national correspondent Rachel Jones, an African American, in recognizing that Black English was a "valid part of our cultural history." But many more joined editorial writer Bill Johnson in assailing it as a "linguistic nightmare that refuses to die a natural death." Other less than flattering descriptions of and appellations for the tongue included "mumbo jumbo," "mutant English," "broken English," "fractured English," "slanguage," and "ghettoese." A *New York Times* op-ed went so far as to condemn the "Ebonic Plague." And even Jones's *Newsweek* piece, which began by complimenting the vernacular, ended up as more of a call for "proper speech" than anything else, with Standard English touted as the panacea for much of what was ailing black folk:

> My skill with standard English propelled me from a life of poverty and dead ends to a future I could have scarcely imagined. It has opened doors for me that might never have budged an inch for a poor black girl . . .

Jones testified that she herself didn't "talk white," just "right." Though she was willing to confer on Black English all the validity of an anthropological relic, she apparently still considered it categorically wrong. Standard English, she seemed to suggest, had cornered the market on clarity, eloquence, and when you got down to it, any sort of inherent value. Whether or not they came right out and said it, this was the fundamental conviction of many of the black journalists who sounded off on Ebonics. Whether liberal or conservative, Black English in their minds represented a dark side, a streak of backwardness that had to be shunned, purged, stripped away, or lopped off like an unsightly carbuncle in order for the race to advance. Researchers could have lectured these intellectuals all day long, arguing that the goal of Oakland's Ebonics policy was actually Standard English and that a youngster who has mastered a home language can be taught to use the same cognitive abilities to master a school language. But as

soon as the word "Ebonics" left their lips, the debate, as far as many
African American pundits were concerned, was over. Something deep
in the psyche of many blacks refused to accept that anything good
could come of this "I be" jive.

A handful of writers, however, considered Black English a commodity. Writing in the *Boston Globe,* Derrick Jackson suggested that
Ebonics was just good marketing:

> Oakland said it wants to recognize Ebonics as a way of helping youths
> bridge the gap to mainstream English. This is a source of outrage?
> White people have no problem bridging the gap to black English
> when they make money off it, like sneaker and insurance companies
> that borrow "You go, girl," like white editors of rap magazines, like
> John Belushi and Dan Aykroyd parading as "Blues Brothers," or like
> white college basketball and football recruiters who talk more jive than
> Cab Calloway to get black men to come to their school to play ball.

Author Ishmael Reed insisted in *Newsday* that the dialect was a
currency no American lacks:

> Like other forms of African-American culture, Ebonics is something
> that whites sleep with at night and don't recognize during the day.
> When they do recognize it they give it a stepfather. Many young whites
> believe that Bill Haley invented rock 'n' roll.

But Reed took exception with the Oakland school board and others
who casually lumped Ebonics together with African languages:

> I have studied Yoruba, which is still spoken and written in Cuba and
> Brazil, and have found only superficial resemblances between it and
> black English. I wonder how many of the op-ed writers who've claimed
> that there are strong connections between "African language systems"
> and black English have actually studied one of these West African
> languages.

What made Reed bristle, this "everybody's an expert" attitude,
also makes linguists crazy. They often complain about the popular
perception that anybody and everybody who *uses* language is qualified
to speak with authority *about* language. To scholars who spend much
of their lives contemplating the nuances of human communication,
that's like saying that anybody with a belly button is qualified to perform brain surgery. But that didn't stop many an individual with
access to a keyboard from pontificating about the source and system
of Black English during the Ebonics controversy.

As to the question of who and what was behind Ebonics, most commentators, again, were less than complimentary. On one edition of *Forum*, a KQED public education radio program, *Oakland Tribune* urban affairs reporter Chauncey Bailey ripped into the Oakland school board and its defenders, calling them all "poverty pimps in Kente cloth." No doubt Oakland educators eventually got used to that kind of talk; again and again they were accused of being radical Afrocentrists, wild-eyed separatists, and racist crackpots. More often than not, though, anti-Ebonics crusaders left the authors of the resolution alone after one or two jabs. Unfortunately, it was the black community at large that sometimes took the roundhouse punch.

This was the case with "Ebonics: Bridge to Illiteracy," a long, searing five-page essay penned by Nicholas Stix and published in a libertarian political magazine. Like many other columnists, Stix believed Ebonics to be a dangerously subversive scheme. And like several other columnists, he wound up revealing some of his own deep-seated stereotypes and animosities while slamming the proposal. Arguing that a federal government with a jones for "counter-institutions" was coaxing Afrocentrists out of the cracks, Stix declared that

> the movement for Ebonics is just one division of the movement for bilingual education in which we see the partnership of the welfare state and racism in making the world safe for illiteracy.

Stix certainly had a right to protest the possibility that national funds would be spent on an Ebonics program he considered backward and sure to fail. But not only is the notion that illiteracy is a necessary consequence of Ebonics ignorant and insulting, it requires us to look at peculiarities of culture as if they were determinants of ability, an exercise that leads irrevocably to racism. And yet this antagonism toward Ebonics, bilingual education, and other perceived tabernacles of "liberalism" was merely symptomatic of the fever for "pure" English and for a homogeneous America that we were suffering from during the time of the Ebonics affair—and that we will likely continue to suffer from well into the twenty-first century. In such a climate of intolerance, it's only natural to blame the victim.

Stix was not alone in crying racism while propping up distinctly racist attitudes. Jack White fell into the same trap when he wrote "Ebonics According to Buckwheat" for *Time* magazine. Common sense dictates that teachers in the inner city recognize that some black youngsters speak differently from how other students do. White was willing to allow that much. And faced with such an alarming rate of high school dropouts, Oakland had to try something new, he conceded. But White sneered at the hypocrisy of the "Afrocentric jargon and education-speak" of the resolution. Yet in trying to satirize the Ebonics policy by resurrecting Hollywood's old racial caricatures, White succeeded in doing little more than just that—resurrecting racial caricatures:

> I put in a call to the Home for Retired Racial Stereotypes in a black section of Hollywood. The Kingfish answered. "Holy mack'rul dere, Andy, somebody wants to talk 'bout dis 'ere Ebonics. Could you or Tonto tell Buckwheat come to da phone? He de resident expert."

Protests to the editor followed, mostly because the article contained some of the same minstrel-style speech ("paragiraffe" for *paragraph*) that blacks had long worked to erase from literature and the American stage (see chapter 2). But many people agreed with the point White was trying to make, that tolerance for Ebonics was a shuck-and-jive that would ultimately only validate stereotypes and send the race backsliding. And it was this same unmitigated intolerance for Ebonics that drove some white writers, perhaps unwittingly, to make the most condescending and paternalistic statements about blacks. In an article entitled "Hooked on Ebonics," for instance, *Vanity Fair* contributor Christopher Hitchens stated:

> There is tragedy and history and emotion involved in the survival of a black speech in America, and giggling at its expense is not good manners. But the worst irony of all would be to congratulate, hypocritically, the "richness" of something that threatens to imprison its speakers . . .

And in the *New Yorker,* an essayist submitted that

> multiculturalism, of the strident sort that the Oakland board has espoused, is no favor to American subcultures. In the short run, it may enliven everyone's appreciation of the variety of American styles, but in the long run it can only turn that variety into mainstream mush.

Both these excerpts reveal a tendency to belittle the dialect, to encapsulate it, to write it off as just one more spirited attempt at multiculturalism, or as nothing more than the gurgling of a "subculture." Once defined as such, some writers must have figured, the thing could be shelved away and perhaps forgotten. But such dismissive attitudes indicate a profound disrespect for the experience of blacks in America. To attribute a system of communication used consistently by millions to a quaint emotion or to liken it to a plaything to be pulled out for cultural show-and-tell is to subscribe to the same one-dimensional matrix that produced the great mascots of white fantasy—Buckwheat included.

Occasionally, though, someone sounded a note of praise for Black English. Several newspapers joined the *San Diego Union-Tribune* in cautioning that "the backlash against Black English overlooks the beauty of the words." In some cases, recognized columnists such as the *Miami Herald*'s Leonard Pitts and the *Washington Post*'s William Raspberry rethought their initially negative positions and adopted more moderate stances on the vernacular. While Pitts swore in December 1996 that he was "insulted" by black "slanguage," by the next month he was ready to acknowledge that Ebonics could be "a bridge to success" and to make a plea for tolerance:

> We come here, we Americans, from a thousand different bypasses, back yards, bayous and boulevards, from outposts of culture and enclaves of speech, any one of which has potential to seem strange and outlandish to the rest of us.

Other writers cautiously sided with some of the Oakland school board's philosophies. There was the *Essence* magazine contributor, for instance, who reasoned that

> it can't help our children to be told at every utterance that their mode of expression—which is intimately linked to their identity—is wrong, wrong, wrong, when others who plagiarize them are getting paid.

And in an unusual move, the *Oakland Tribune* produced an editorial that gave the Oakland school board the benefit of the doubt:

> We hope good news eventually comes out of this controversy, because Oakland school children need and deserve success. If as the district tells us, the Ebonics program is one way we can raise the achievement level of African-American students, we have to say, "Go for it."

Of course, these were the exceptions. Far too many columnists, editorial writers, and op-ed contributors saw the Ebonics story as an opportunity to poke fun at black policy-makers, ridicule an act of black self-determination, and smear the vernacular spoken by the black masses while still enjoying the applause of the black middle class. And all this at a time when minorities, having finally added a dash of color to what for years were milk-white newsrooms, were increasingly taking their editors to task for slanted or stereotypical representations of their communities.

For those who sought balance and reason rather than a blind backing up or vicious hacking up of Black English—one of the most organic and distinctive speech varieties in the United States—these were confusing, even troubling times. Amid the fray, the question of whether Ebonics was a language or a dialect kept recurring. But the real question was: Who would decide? As long as Ebonics could be kept underfoot and condemned publicly as bastardized speech, who cared whether the variety lived or died in the ghetto, or that it was spreading to the tongues of young white suburbanites? The debate seemed at times to hinge less on why black inner-city children were doing so badly on tests of Standard English proficiency than on which critics would triumph in a battle too often waged with deception on behalf of ethnic fear or embarrassment.

And as for what should be done about Ebonics? Most of the media had an easy answer: Spin it to death. In an op-ed that appeared in the *New York Times* in January 1997, Frank Rich wrote:

> There isn't a public personage of stature in the land . . . who doesn't say that the Oakland, Calif., school board was wrong, if not deranged, to portray black English as a "genetically based" and "primary" language . . . and to imply that it was worthy of public funds set aside for bilingual education.

Rubbish. Actually, at least half a dozen people that we know of, including a well-published and widely acclaimed writer, a documentary film director, an education council director who testified at the congressional hearing on Ebonics, and three leading linguists, all sent op-eds to the *Times* defending the vibrancy and legitimacy of Black English, espousing its potential as a bridge to Standard English, or decrying its widespread condemnation. But the *Times* published none of these. The contribution by University of Chicago Linguistics Chair Salikoko Mufwene, solicited by the *Times,* was rejected in favor of one written by a lawyer opposed to Ebonics. While the paper must of course be selective about op-ed submissions, it is striking that it never printed an opinion piece on this issue that was neutral, much less positive, and that it ignored the contributions of experts in the field.

Ebonics coverage, by and large, was yet another case of the mainstream media's not merely establishing the national agenda, but shaping the national consciousness in the style described by linguist and social critic Noam Chomsky in *Manufacturing Consent.*. The beating the vernacular was getting in the press encouraged the bruising it was getting on the street, and created a lasting climate in which the very mention of Ebonics elicited funny looks, giggles, or tirades of intolerance.

On October 9, 1998, the *Times* set off a fresh wave of tremors among linguists and educators by running, free of charge, an arresting quarter-page anti-Ebonics ad. Created by the Ketchum advertising agency (of Pittsburgh) for a group identified as "Atlanta's Black Professionals," the ad had won the prestigious $100,000 Athena award (Award to Honor Excellence in Newspaper Advertising) from the Newspaper Association of America. Depicting a rearview silhouette of the Reverend Martin Luther King Jr. superimposed with "I has a dream" in large, bold letters, the ad included this message:

> Does this bother you? It should. We've spent over 400 years fighting for the right to have a voice. Is this how we'll use it? More importantly, is this how we'll teach our children to use it? If we expect more of them, we must not throw our hands in the air and agree with those who say our children cannot be taught. . . . The fact is, language is power. And we can't take that power away from our children with Ebonics. . . . If you haven't used your voice lately, consider this an invitation. SPEAK OUT AGAINST EBONICS.

Advertising executives at the *Times* ran the ad for free in recognition of the Athena award. But when more than two hundred linguists and educators wrote to the *Times* in protest, urging that it publish the Linguistics Society of America's pro-Ebonics resolution for the sake of balance, the newspaper turned them down, explaining that it had "a policy that mandates against giving away advertising space."

But the "I has a dream" represents just another of the many Ebonics blunders catalogued in this chapter and this book. First, contrary to the widespread misconception that any sentence with "bad" Standard English grammar would be "good" Ebonics (the "anything goes" fallacy), "I has a dream" is *not* acceptable in Ebonics or Spoken Soul. Although speakers of this vernacular commonly use *have* where SE requires *has* (with third-person-singular subjects, as in "He *have* a car"), they never or very rarely use *has* where SE requires *have* (with non-third-person-singular subjects, as in *"I *has* a dream"). In the recorded speech of a sample of forty-four black teenagers in New York City, for instance, *have* for "has" occurred 67 percent of the time, but *has* for "have" (the nonstandard construction maligned in the ad) occurred 0 percent of the time—that is, never.

Second, the ad falsely suggests that those who framed and supported the Ebonics resolutions wanted to teach children Ebonics and deny them access to the English of Martin Luther King Jr. and other leaders. But the intent, as observed in chapter 9, was to use the former to increase proficiency in the latter, and as noted in chapter 3, Dr. King is but one titan in a rhetorical tradition that includes both Standard English *and* Spoken Soul. Finally, although the *Times'* version of the ad appeared to have been sponsored by the National Head Start Association (its name and address were listed at the end of the ad), it was not. Head Start's board had not approved the use of its name and had not taken a position on Ebonics, and after the controversy created by the publication of the ad, Head Start made that known publicly. The *Times,* which normally checks such attributions, did not do so in this case.

In fairness, it was the *Times* that had published James Baldwin's paean to Black English (see chapter 1) three decades earlier, and that provided some of the best reportage on the subject. But in its one-sided selection of opinion pieces on the Ebonics issue, and in its generous publication of the misleading "I Has a Dream" ad, the nation's newspaper of record appeared to be as much under the sway of the dominant ideology on this issue as the rest of the media were.

11

Ebonics "Humor"

It was a funny type of humor, which on its surface appeared to be of the ha-ha! type, but at a deeper level of the more serious uh-hmm type.

—Jerrie C. Scott (1998)

Mock Ebonics on the Internet blurs the distinction between public and private discourse, thereby distancing producers and consumers from responsibility for language that would be highly offensive in other public venues, such as call-in talk shows, neighborhood bars, and letters to the editor.

—Maggie Ronkin and Helen E. Karn (1999)

Long after the media abandoned Ebonics, humorists continued to stoke the coals. In fact, Ebonics seemed to have become a national punch line the very instant the Oakland school board released its resolution. At first, the raillery was part of the media's response, as cartoonists and columnists wove their wit into pages crowded with serious news reports, headlines, letters, and op-ed pieces. But before long, comedians, public speakers, preachers, and people on the street and on the World Wide Web—especially on the Web—jumped in to create and spread new varieties of Ebonics humor.

John Leo suggested in a *U.S. News Online* column that "the nationwide roar of laughter over Ebonics is a very good sign." He took the open laughter as an indication that Americans in the later 1990s had less tolerance for political correctness than they had had before, and that they were more willing to respond to what they considered wrongheadedness with chuckling, satire, and ridicule. While Ebonics humor revealed that political correctness had fallen out of favor, some of it revealed also that crude racial stereotyping and overt expressions of racism were as much in vogue as they ever were. More often than not, the satire proved how little most people understood not only Ebonics itself but also Oakland's proposal to use it to teach Standard English.

Ebonics jokes fall into four main categories: -onics jokes; jokes involving the verb be; translation humor; and racial caricatures. As is evident below, there is a considerable gap between the first and last categories in terms of how closely they relate to Ebonics and how sinister the humor is.

-onics jokes.   The earliest and most innocuous jokes to emerge often poked fun at the term "Ebonics"—which sounded to many like some weird science—and mocked the claim that it referred to a distinctive way of speaking. Fanciful varieties of -onics languages sprang up on the Internet, and circulated on fliers that were nearly indecipherable because they had been photocopied so many times:

> *Languages Being Taught in Oakland, California*
>   Afro-American Speak—Ebonics ("Ebony" + "Phonics")
>   Irish-American Speak—Leprechaunics
>   Native-American Speak—Kimosabics
>   Italo-American Speak—Spumonics (or Rigatonics)
>   Chinese-American Speak—Won-tonics
>   Japanese-American Speak—Mama-san-ics
>   Jewish-American Speak—Zionics
>   Russian-American Speak—Rasputonics
>   Spanish-American Speak—Burritonics
>   Eskimo-American Speak—Harpoonics
>   German-American Speak—Autobahnics (or Teutonics)
>   French-American Speak—Cornichonics (or Escargonics)
>   Oakland-School-Board Speak—Moronics

Here the humor stems from the play on ethnic stereotypes, in some cases more entrenched than in others. The list is perhaps less offensive than it might have been, because the strings of virtually every ethnic group are yanked. Two points are noteworthy: First, the etymology (or origin) of "Ebonics" is given at the outset. Second, the final item names the school board. So whether one thinks it lame or clever, the joke is firmly based in the substance of the Ebonics issue—educational policy and language.

Other -onics gags resembled this list. In the first cartoon following page 160, notice that the linguistic subtypes are not only ethnic but geographic and occupational. The second cartoon, by Scott Willis, even includes a new term, "Waveonics," for the speech of surfers.

These cartoons imply that there are so many different ways of speaking in America that to recognize and cater to them all would be lunacy. The case is made more explicitly in a cartoon by Barbara Brandon that was published in the *Detroit Free Press* on January 12, 1997. It ends with the lines, "What's next? Will we validate poor English spoken by white folks by calling it . . . Ivoronics?" A cartoon by Mike Keefe that appeared in the *San Francisco Examiner* on December 29, 1996, has a teacher introducing to her class "your new Ebonics interpreter . . . and your interpreters for Brooklynese, east Texan, Appalachian, Minnesotan, Down Eastern, Deep Southern, Chicagoan, Valley Speak, Surfer, Cajun, Clevelandic . . ." The point that's lost, however, is that Ebonics is more than the narrow, specialized, and often ephemeral words that characterize such dialects or styles. In fact, Ebonics is a full-fledged language variety with distinctive features of pronunciation, grammar, and vocabulary. And its deep-rooted and widespread use among African Americans affects the teaching of reading and the language arts in ways that most other American dialects do not.

The suggestion in the next cartoon that even the inane "huh-huhs" of MTV characters Beavis and Butt-head would qualify as a "distinct language" in Oakland illustrates how nonchalantly many critics dismissed Ebonics as gobbledygook.

Invariant *be* jokes.   The linguistic feature most often picked on by humorists trying to parody Ebonics (see the first three cartoons) was the particular use of the verb *be*. Linguists call it invariant *be*, because, unlike the Standard English *be*, its present-tense form does not change according to its subject (although it sometimes occurs as *be's* or *bees*, especially among older people). In Ebonics, one says "I *be*," "you *be*," "he/she/it *be*," and so on, while in Standard English one says "I *am*," "you/we/they *are*," "he/she/it *is*."

As early as the 1970s and 1980s, invariant *be* had appeared in jokes involving blacks. Bill Cosby recalled a "racist joke" a friend had told him in the early 1980s:

Q: Do you know what Toys 'Я' Us is called in Harlem?

A: We Be Toys.

The following one-liner, a supposedly black version of the airline advertising jingle "Delta is ready when you are," had appeared even earlier:

> Delta be ready when you is.

The use of invariant *be* was not always derogatory, however, and was
often employed playfully by African Americans. Arsenio Hall, for one,
used to begin his 1980s late-night talk show by declaiming:

> Arsenio Hall! We be havin a ball!

Linguists have found that between the 1960s and the 1990s, the
frequency of invariant *be* in the speech of African Americans skyrock-
eted, especially among teenagers. In the late 1960s, William Labov
and his fellow researchers reported that the eighteen teenage members of the Thunderbirds, a gang they recorded in New York City,
used only some five examples each in their interviews. Walt Wolfram,
writing around the same time, found that the four dozen African
Americans from all age groups whom he and his colleagues interviewed in Detroit used even fewer—about two examples each. By contrast, Foxy Boston, a teenager in East Palo Alto, California, whom
Faye McNair-Knox first recorded in 1986, used 385 examples of invariant *be* in her hourlong interview. Guy Bailey and Natalie Maynor
reported in the late 1980s that twelve- and thirteen-year-old African
Americans in Texas were using invariant *be* three times as often as
black Texans over the age of seventy.

It's not surprising, then, that invariant *be* would become *the* icon
of African American vernacular during the Ebonics imbroglio. Unlike
rarer and more complex grammatical patterns of Ebonics, such as
negative inversion ("Didn't nobody leave"), invariant *be* appeared to
be a simple word, a straightforward substitute for Standard English
am, is, or *are.* The story is more complicated, but that didn't stop the
proliferation of *be* quips.

Some of the jokes in this category were clever and creative:

> Q. What do you call an Ebonics transvestite?
> A.   Susan B. Anthony [Susan be Anthony].

Others showed that their creators were hip to the dialect, as does the
cartoon by Jeff Danzinger (see the photo and cartoon insert following page 160), in which he exploits authentic Ebonics lingo—*chillin',
main man, dat's whuzzup,* and *nome sane* (a condensed version of "Know
what I'm saying?") that has become popular in the black community.

But although the cartoonist correctly uses *don't* (rather than *ain't*) as the appropriate negative form of *be* in Ebonics grammar, the appearance of *be* at the end of a clause without an adjective or verb following it ("I be or I don't be") is virtually nonexistent in recordings of everyday Ebonics conversation.

Most of the satirists who aped Black English had no idea how to re-create the dialect accurately. They didn't know (and perhaps didn't care) that the use of invariant *be* and other features is governed by subtle grammatical and semantic rules that most outsiders, white and black, bungle when they try to imitate Spoken Soul.

Consider the following Ebonics joke:

Q. Why were there only forty-nine contestants for the Miss Ebonics USA Pageant?

A. No contestant wanted to wear a banner that said "Idaho" (I da ho').

Cute. But linguistically incorrect. While Ebonics speakers regularly leave out forms of *is* and *are*, they almost never omit *am*. They often contract *am*, as in "I'm da bomb," but they don't delete it. "I da bomb" would be ungrammatical, just as "I da ho" is.

A more fundamental mistake made by cartoonists and columnists who tried to parody invariant *be* was their failure to use the verb form only for actions that occur frequently or habitually, as in this example recorded from the speech of teenager Foxy Boston:

And every day, every day, "Did you go shopping today? What you go buy? You bought this? You bought that? You like it?" And I *be* going, "Yep, Yep, yep."

Most Ebonics satirists used every opportunity to substitute *be* for Standard English's *am, is,* or *are,* whether or not the situations they were referring to occurred regularly. See, for instance, the Scott Willis cartoon in the insert following page 160, where it is clear that the conversation is about what the big guy is doing right then, at the moment of speech ("What you be doin'?" . . . "I be chillin'"). In genuine Ebonics, the exchange would go more like this: "What you doin'?" . . . "I'*m* chillin'."

The mistake was made repeatedly in the popular press. In a *Doonesbury* cartoon dated February 16, 1997 (www.doonesbury.com/flashbacks/pages/1997/oz/db970216.html), a college president is shown reading a headline announcing that "the Oakland School Board is still sticking with Ebonics," while he mutters to himself, "This be perverse." Journalist Patricia Smith opened a syndicated column in the *Oakland Tribune* with the statement, "This don't be no new thang," instead of "This ain't no new thing." And Bill Cosby himself, in the *Wall Street Journal,* wrote, "After all, Ebonics be a complex issue."

Equally off the mark was *Washington Post* columnist William Raspberry, who began a piece entitled "Ebonics Debate: Who Will Benefit?" as follows:

> "'Sup?" the cabbie said.
>
> "No thanks," I said. I was trying to cut back on my caloric intake. "Besides," I pointed out, "it looks to me like you've only got half a filet of fish and what's left of a small order of fries."
>
> "What you be talkin' bout, my man?" he said, "I don't be offerin' you my grub; I be saying hello. You know, like, *what's up?*"

In genuine Ebonics, "What you *be* talkin' bout" would be "What you talkin' bout." "I don't *be* offerin' you my grub" would be "I ain't offerin' you my grub." "I *be* saying hello" would be simply "I'm sayin' hello." But Raspberry's most egregious error comes when he claims, later in the whimsical taxi dialogue, that Ebonics is formed willy-nilly—that it is a language variety without discernible rules or restrictions:

> "I noticed a couple of errors when you tried your French and Spanish on me a while back," I said. "Just out of curiosity, who corrects your Ebonics?"
>
> "That's the beautiful part," the cabbie said. "Ebonics gives you a whole range of options. . . . My brother-in-law tells me that you can say pretty much what you please, as long as you're careful to throw in a lot of 'bes' and leave off final consonants."
>
> As a former proofreader, I couldn't believe my ears.
>
> "They'll have teachers learn a language that has *no right or wrong expressions, no consistent spellings or pronunciations and no discernible rules?* How will that help children learn proper English? What is the point?" [Emphasis added.]

Many of the critics who scripted letters to the editor and Internet tirades insisted that the notion of Ebonics as a systematic form of English was ridiculous. But as any undergraduate college student taking Linguistics 101 knows, all languages and dialects are systematic and rule-governed. The evidence lies both in empirical findings—from studies of thousands of language varieties—and in theoretical assumption. If languages and dialects were not structured, how could speakers communicate reliably with one another, and how could children acquire language or dialect?

Translation jokes. The logical extension of *be* jokes are jokes involving translations of longer stretches of speech or writing. Jokes that translate Ebonics have been around for a number of years. In the 1987 movie *Hollywood Shuffle*, black drama students attending acting school are tutored in crude Ebonics ("You jive turkey mutha-fucka!") so they can more "authentically" play black parts. Even before that, in the 1980 movie *Airplane!*, a white flight attendant finds herself unable to comprehend the speech of a black passenger until a white woman sitting nearby steps in as interpreter:

FLIGHT ATTENDANT *(to black male #1, after he says something indecipherable to her):* I'm sorry, I don't understand.

BLACK MALE #2 *(sitting beside black male #1):* Cutty say he can't hang.

WHITE PASSENGER: Oh, stewardess, I speak Jive!

FLIGHT ATTENDANT: Oh, good!

WHITE PASSENGER: He said that he's in great pain, and he wants to know if you can help him.

FLIGHT ATTENDANT: All right. Would you tell him to just relax, and I'll be back as soon as I can with some medicine?

WHITE PASSENGER: Just hang loose, blood. She gonna catch up on the rebound on the medi-side.

BLACK MALE #1 *(offended):* What it *is,* big momma? My momma didn't raise no dummies! I dug her rap!

WHITE PASSENGER: Cut me some slack, jack!

At least one Internet website (www.AtlantaGA.com), no longer active, included another sample of *Airplane* "Jive" dialogue. This time the conversation was translated from Ebonics into a very formal register:

Person	Ebonics	English Translation
Man 1	Sheeeet. Man, that honky mus' be messin' with my old lady. Got to be runnin' col' upside down his head!	I don't believe this. That white man should stay away from my wife or I will be forced to inflict on him a blunt force trauma to his head with a vengeance, and that is a dish best served cold.
Man 2	Hey Home, I can dig it! You know he ain't gonna lay no mo' big rap upon you, man!	Yes, brother from my home land, I would feel the same way. He is wrong for doing that. He would never have you arrested either, because neither he or anyone else would have you arrested for defending your right.

Another tongue-in-cheek Internet translation from Ebonics to high English was introduced as an entry "turned in by an Oakland High School student who received highest honors at the school district's Ebonics translation competition." The assignment was to render into Standard English the song "One More Chance," by the late rap artist Notorious B.I.G.:

Ebonics	English Translation
So, what's it gonna be? Him or me? We can cruise the world with pearls Gator boots for girls. The envy of all women, crushed linen Cartier wrist-wear with diamonds in 'em. The finest women I love with a passion Ya man's a wimp, I give that ass a good trashin'.	The ultimate decision rests with you. Whom do you choose as your sexual partner? I can take you on cruises around the world. I will dress you in the finest jewelry and footwear. You will be envied by women worldwide in your fine clothes and jewelry. There is a special place in my heart for beautiful women. I will defeat your man in an altercation because he is effeminate.

Sparing neither his rampaging materialism nor his misogynistic ravings, the "translator" lampooned Biggie's lyrics with a keen ear for the nuances of hip-hop's insider lingo. But textbook Ebonics this was not. With a few exceptions, the verbiage of today's rap artist draws more on slang than it does on the grammar of Ebonics.

Most translation jokes involved translations in the other direction, from Standard English into Ebonics. They reveal both what people took Ebonics to be, and what they took its speakers to be like. Several loose versions of Clement Moore's "The Night Before Christmas" (originally entitled "A Visit from St. Nicholas") were striking in this respect. One of the first was circulated via electronic mail in January 1997:

'Twas da Night Befo' Christmas

'Twas da night befo' Christmas and all in the hood
Not a homie was stirring cuz it was all good
The tube socks was hung on the window sill
And we all had smiles up on our grill

Mookie and BeBe was snug in the crib
In the back bedroom cuz that's how we live
And moms in her do-rag and me with my nine
had just gotten busy cuz girlfriend is fine

All of a sudden a lowrider rolled by
Bumpin phat beats cuz the system's fly
I bounced to the window at a quarter pas'
Bout ready to pop a cap in somebody's ——
well anyway

I yelled to my lady, "Yo peep this!"
She said, "Stop frontin', just mind yo' bidness!"
I said, "For real, doe, come check dis out!"
We weren't even buggin, no worries, no doubt

Cuz bumpin an thumpin' from around da way
Was Santa, eight reindeer and a sleigh
Da beats was kickin', da ride was phat
I said, "Yo, red Dawg, you all that!"

He threw up a sign and yelled to his boyz
"Ay yo, give it up, let's make some noise!
To the top of the projects and across the strip mall
We gots ta go, I got a booty call."

He pulled up his ride on the top a da roof
And sippin' on a 40, he busted a move
I yelled up to Santa, "Yo ain't got no stack!"
He said, "Damn homie, dese projects is wack!

"But don't worry, black, cuz I gots da skillz
I learnt back when I hadda pay da billz."
Out from his bag he pulled three small tings
A credit card, a knife, and a bobby pin

He slid down the fire escape smoove as a cat
And busted the window with a b-ball bat
I said, "Whassup, Santa? Why'd ya bust my place?"
He said, "You best get on up out my face!"

His threads was all leatha, his chains was all gold
His sneaks was Puma and they was five years old
He dropped down the duffle, Clippers logo on the side
Santa broke out da loot and my mouf popped open wide.

A wink of his eye and a shine off his gold toof
He cabbage patched his way back onto the roof
He jumped in his hooptie with rims made of chrome
To tap that booty waitin at home

And all I heard as he cruised outta sight
Was a loud and hearty . . .
"WEEESSTSIIIIDE!!!!!!!"

This translation offered an authentic approximation of hip-hop speech, complete with Ebonics pronunciations (*da, befo', smoove, toof*) and slang (*buggin'*, or worrying; *frontin'*, or faking; *40*, for a forty-ounce container of malt liquor; *homie*, or home boy; *hood*, or neighborhood; *hooptie*, or car, usually decrepit, but not in this case; *phat*, or great). But the parody obviously swarms with stereotypes as well.

We have discussed the old-time black-faced minstrel performer and his ludicrous speech. In this recent incarnation, he rides in a "hooptie with rims made of chrome," but he is still grinning. The stereotypes and antics have shifted with the times: handkerchiefs have been swapped for do-rags, worn to protect a hairdo, and straight-razors for nines, nine-millimeter handguns. But the modern stereotypes are as deplorable as ever; the narrator is concerned with superficial externals (gold, leather, designer accessories), obsessed with sex (Santa is hurrying to make a "booty call," and the narrator himself has "just gotten busy"), and poised for violence ("ready to pop a cap in somebody's ——"), while Santa is well practiced in burglary ("I gots da skillz").

Breaking as it did in the Christmas season, the Ebonics controversy spawned many other full-length translations of "The Night Before Christmas," including this less authentic but equally racist one "De Ebonics Crimmus Poem" (from the site www.AtlantaGA.com/crimmus.htm; no longer active):

> I looked out thru de bars;
> What covered my doe;
> 'spectin' de sheriff;
> Wif a warrent fo sho.
>
> And what did I see;
> I said, "Lawd, look at dat!"
> Ther' wuz a huge watermellon;
> Pulled by giant warf rats!!

Such parodies held a hidden irony. In the 1960s, William Stewart argued that stories written in dialect might help some Ebonics-speaking children learn to read because it is easier, theoretically, to "decode" a text that mirrors the way one speaks than to grapple with a text that is foreign. Once the students mastered the dialect stories, they would turn their attention to narratives rendered in Standard English. Stewart said the idea had come to him when he was penning a black-dialect version of Moore's poem for a greeting card. Stewart's version, which followed the wording of the original more closely than the caricatures cited above, began:

> It's the night before Christmas, and here in our house,
> It ain't nothing moving, not even no mouse.
> There go we-all stockings, hanging high up off the floor,
> So Santa can full them up, if he walk in through our door.

This vernacular "Night Before Christmas" was distant from its 1996 counterparts in conception and purpose. (According to Stewart, a twelve-year-old African American student who was having difficulty reading could recite the Ebonics version fluently and accurately. But when she was given the original version, "all the 'problem reader' behaviors returned.")

The "Ebonics Lectric Library of Classical Literature" was the single largest source of Ebonics translation humor on the Internet (www.novusordo.com/indexn.htm; no longer active). It opened with these words:

> Since the recent decision to make Ebonics (Ebony-Phonics) a second
> language in our schools it has become obvious that e-bliterations of the
> classics will be required. We will cover here the greater works of world
> Literature (Litershure) in the hopes of bridging the gap between English and the new Slanguage. The Illuminatus Foundation has come to
> the web to meet that need. . . . Educators are encouraged to study the
> writing style and incorporate it into their daily lesson plans as they will
> be required to teach it under the new laws. Students are encouraged to
> read these works in their own language with a clearer comprehension
> than has ever been possible.

The translated works available on the site included selections from Plato, Milton, Shakespeare, Ovid, and Sophocles. The first few lines of Coleridge's "Rime of the Ancient Mariner" read as follows:

> It be an ancient Marina',
> And he stoppeth one o' three. Sheeeiit.
> "By dy long grey beard and glitterin' eye,
> Now wherefore stoppst dou me?
> The bridegroom's door's be jimmy'd wide,
> And Ah am next o' kin;
> De guests be met, de feast be set, dig dis:
> Mayst hear de merry din."

The translation strategies tended to be simple, and their products were stilted and counterfeit, unlike those of the spoken Ebonics exemplified elsewhere in this book. *Sheeeiit* and *dig dis* were inserted from time to time, "is" and "are" were universally replaced by *be,* in accordance with the misconception about this verb noted previously, and selected words and pronunciations were replaced by their often disparaging "Ebonics" equivalents: "opened" by *jimmy'd,* "I" by *Ah,* "of" by *o',* and so on. The website, in fact, invited visitors to "e-bliterate" any work of literature they wished, using a filter available on-line. The Ebonics Translator (at www.AtlantaGA.com/ebonics.htm; no longer active) offered a similar service.

These translators and others were similar or identical to Jive, a filter posted on the Internet long before the Ebonics controversy. Jive replaced "man" with *dude,* "woman" with *mama,* "something" with *sump'n,* "buy" with *steal,* "did" with *dun did,* "ask" with *ax',* "hi" with *'sup, dude,* and so on. As linguists Maggie Ronkin and Helen Karn noted in 1999, these and other translation devices invariably introduced vulgarities and linguistic derogation. The effect was a mock Ebonics that conveyed the "outgroup ideology that the denigration of English and Western culture in general" would result from Oakland's "having gone too far in respecting and embracing the 'legitimacy and richness of Ebonics.'"

Racial caricatures. The fourth and final category of Ebonics jokes involved racial caricatures or stereotypes. Spoofs along the lines of "Ebonics Homework Assignment" and "Hooked on Ebonics" were by far the most popular of this genre. "Leroy," a fifteen-year-old ninth-grader, was said to have received an "easy homework assignment," requiring him to use fifteen words in as many sentences. In other versions, Leroy was twenty, still in the ninth grade, and an Oakland resident, and the number of words on the assignment had swollen to eighteen or twenty. But these chucklers almost always remained:

> **Catacomb.** Don King was at the fight the other night . . . Man, somebody get dat *catacomb.*

> **Israel.** Alonso tried to sell me a Rolex. I said, Man, that look fake. He said, No, *Israel.*

This strategy of fusing two or more words to resemble another word or phrase also helped "I. B. White" (wordplay on "I be white") compile his 1997 glossary *The Old, Fat, White Guy's Guide to Ebonics.* There were entries for *delight* ("the light, as in, 'Turn off delight, got dammit'") and *splay* ("an expression meaning 'let's start the game'").

This sort of wordplay was benign. Less harmless was the implication in "Ebonics Homework" that Leroy was too stupid to recognize the puns in his slurred interpretations of "cat a comb" and "it's real" and that his teachers were equally clueless ("Leroy got an A!"). Yet these jabs amounted to little more than a lighthearted lampooning of the Oakland proposal.

The list, however, grew ugly. As the fictional homework assignment unfolded, Leroy became much more than just doltish. He was transformed into the image of the Brute Negro (one of the seven black stereotypes of American fiction identified by the late literary scholar Sterling Brown). He became a criminal, an adulterer, and a rapist:

Hotel. I gave my girlfriend da crabs and the *hotel* everybody.

Income. I just got in bed wit dis hoe and *income* my wife.

Fortify. I axed da hoe how much? She said *fortify*.

Disappointment. My parole officer tol me if I miss *disappointment* he gonna kill me.

Honor. At the rape trial, the Judge axed my buddy, "Who be *honor* first?"

When one learns that between 1930 and 1967, 89 percent of the 455 prisoners executed for rape in the United States under civil authority were African American—a proportion far in excess of their representation in the general population—the last joke turns sour in one's mouth. Indeed, many of the same prejudices that fueled that disparity may have contributed during the 1990s to the fact that one in every three black men in the country between the ages of twenty and twenty-nine was either in prison, on parole, or otherwise in the cluthces of the criminal justice system.

Such sobering considerations did not stem the Ebonics satire that rose from the bellies of bigots. There was the "Ebonics Loan Application," for instance:

Approximate Estimate of Income

Thefts $_____, Relief $_____, Unemployment $_____, Welfare $_____
Activities: Gov't Employee _____, Evangelist _____, VD Spreader _____,
Hubcap Salesman _____, Rapist _____

As late as October 1998, nearly two years after the first Ebonics resolution, an undergraduate at a major American university circulated via his dormitory's electronic mailing list a "Gangsta Aptitude

Test," or GAT (hip-hop for "firearm"). Described as "an Ebonics version of the SAT," the test included such multiple choice items as this:

> You just robbed sum jack mo fo with $20 in his wallet. You can buy
>   A. A dime and two 40's.
>   B. A new pair of Fila's.
>   C. Dashiki down the block.
>   D. Yo mama.

And in November 1998, another undergraduate at the same university received an e-mail with this new and even more odious caricature, from which we quote only a few excerpts:

> **Ebonics Meets Windows 98**
>
> Compton City Schools has announced that its special Ebonics version of Windows 98, entitled "Dis be a fresh window," has been leaked to several white suburbs, causing confusion for unsuspecting Caucasian users. . . . On the main screen, My Computer is replaced with "Dis My Shit." The Recycle Bin has been replaced with a Goodwill dumpster, and the Internet Explorer reads, "Titty and Booty Sites." . . .
>
> Users have their choice of three animated screen savers: "Marquee," a li'l G spray-painting dirty words that move across the screen; "Mystify," a 15-year-old crack whore giving birth to 12 children on screen, or "Flying Bullets," a '64 Olds loaded with gangstas doing a desktop drive by. . . .

The "Mystify" screen saver, in particular, gave us the shivers. One has the sense of eavesdropping on a twisted mind, from some earlier century when racist depravity of this type could be expressed more overtly.

What is startling and revealing about such caricatures is that some of them, at least, were created by blacks. Black illustrator Keith Lovett, for instance, threw together a slim paperback in 1997 entitled *Hooked on Ebonics*. It included a twenty-five-item version of the "Ebonics Homework Assignment," as well as a number of innocuous jokes revolving around the theme "Clues That You May Be Hooked on Ebonics" ("You call a girl a 'sister' and she's no kin to you"). Some of the cracks, however, involved insidious stereotypes:

> **Clues That You May Be Hooked on Ebonics**
>
> You see your parole officer more than you see your father.
> You use your ski mask as your ATM card.
> Your gold necklace is thicker than any book you've ever read.

In these and similar "jokes," Ebonics no longer stood for the language variety being debated in Oakland. Instead, it was a cruel proxy for African Americans themselves, an opportunity to resurrect or perpetuate the grossest stereotypes about them. Nowhere is this clearer than in "Ebonic Olympic Games" (novusordo.com/elympic.html; no longer active). In this spoof, the satire is invidious and grotesque, and the creator's fear of or loathing for African Americans, and the clearinghouses of liberalism that he/she sees as sympathetic toward them, crackles like a Roman candle:

Ebonic Olympic Games
(Event List)

Opening Ceremonies
The Torching of the Olympic City
Gang Colors Parade

Track and Field
Rob, Shoot & Run
9MM Pistol Toss
Molotov Cocktail Throw
Barbed Wire Roll
Chain Link Fence Climb
Peoplechase
Monkey Bar Race
100 Yard Dog Dash (100 Yard Dash While Being Chased By Police Dog)
200 Yard Trash Can Hurdles
500 Yard Stolen Car Battery Run
1000 Meter Courtoom Relay (Team of four passing murder weapon—
    not getting caught)
1500 Meter Television Set Relay
Bitch Slapping (Bruises inflicted on wife/girlfriend in three one-minute
    rounds)
Ebo-Decathlon
    Rob Liquor Store
    Guzzle One-Fifth of Fortified Wine
    Drink Six-Pack of Old English 800
    Steal One BMW
    Commit One Car Jacking
    Have Sex With Prostitute
    Pimp Girlfriend to Family Member
    Complete One Drug Deal
    Remove Serial Numbers From One Stolen Gun
    One Additional Felony of Choice

Miscellaneous Events
Graffiti Wall Painting
Name Your Father (Canceled, Considered Too Difficult)
Lying to Police (Canceled, Considered Too Easy)
Welfare Fraud (Canceled, Considered a Lifestyle, Not an Event)

Closing Ceremonies
Grand Finale Firearms Display & Gang War Shoot Out

Sponsors: ACLU, Oakland Board of Education, Congress, and the
Supreme Court

For those behind this most virulent strain of Ebonics "humor,"
Ebonics was never a language. Or a dialect. Or an educational policy.
Or a matter of public outrage. For bigots, Ebonics simply served as a
metaphor for their stereotypes of African Americans—as criminals
and crackheads and welfare defrauders and liars and gangbangers
and sex addicts and objects. Originally intended to stir black consciousness, the term was twisted into the symbol of a degenerate culture and class. Because everyone supposedly agreed that Ebonics was
ludicrous and laughable, one could use this consensus as a cover for
much darker kinds of humor about the stereotypical speakers of
Ebonics, and broadcast over the Internet—and elsewhere—what was
previously uttered only behind cupped hands. And one could implic-
itly invite those who encountered the jokes to share the stereotypes.
In short, "Ebonics" became a new slur, a "nigger" upon whom one
could inflict a Rodney King–style beating while wearing the helmet
of "wit."

Part Five

The Double Self

12

The Crucible of Identity

One ever feels his two-ness—an American, a Negro: Two souls, two
unreconciled strivings; two warring ideals in one dark body . . . The his-
tory of the American Negro is the history of this strife—this longing . . . to
merge his double self into a better and truer self. In this merging, he wishes
neither of the older selves to be lost.

—W. E. B. Du Bois (1903)

I who am poisoned with the blood of both
Where shall I turn, divided to the vein?
I who have cursed the drunken officer of British rule, how choose
Between this Africa and the English tongue I love?
Betray them both, or give back what they give?

—Derek Walcott, 1969

Here is a conversation as ordinary in its context as breathing. It took
place recently in the office of a California elementary school, between
three black people: a second-grade student, or eight-year-old; Miss P.,
the school secretary, in her forties; and a parent in his thirties who
happened to be in the office at the time.

STUDENT: Miss P., my teacher sen' me to the office.

MISS P.: What she sen' you here fuh?

STUDENT: She say I got a rash.

MISS P.: A rash? Where the rash at?

STUDENT: Right here on my chin . . .

MISS P.:   Come over here an' lemme see. [The child walks over to
her, and she examines his chin.] So what you want me to
do? [No answer.] I'ma call yo' dad, boy. [She phones his
father, learns that he can't come for his son right then, and
hangs up.] You know yo' dad got to go to school, boy, he
can't come an' get you. . . .

STUDENT: Where Miss G. at? [Miss G. is a staff member the student
likes.]

MISS P.:   Miss G. in the room nex' to the library. [The child leaves to
look for Miss G.]

PARENT: [To Miss P.] That boy sound jus' like me. He remind me of
me. He remind me of me. Don' seem like that long ago.
Seem like jus' yesterday . . .

These speakers, youth and adults alike, used Spoken Soul because
it is the language in which comfortable informal conversation takes
place daily for them—as is true within vast segments of the African
American community. They drew on it for reasons similar to those
that the novelists, playwrights, poets, preachers, pray-ers, comedians,
actors, screenwriters, singers, toasters, rappers, and ordinary folk
whose extensive and creative use of the vernacular we've documented
in this book drew on it: because it came naturally; because it was authentic; because it resonated for them, touching some timbre within
and capturing a vital core of experience that had to be expressed *just
so;* because it reached the heart and mind and soul of the addressee
or audience in a way no other variety quite did; because to have used
Standard English might have marked the relationships between the
participants as more formal or distant than the speaker wanted. For
these individuals, not to have used Spoken Soul might have meant
they were not who or what or where they were and wanted to be.

The question remains about why Spoken Soul persists despite the
negative attitudes toward it, and its speakers, that have been expressed for centuries. The primary answer is its role as a symbol of identity. This is the driving force behind the maintenance of low-prestige
languages and dialects around the world, including "Schwyzerdeutsch
in Switzerland, Canadian French in Canada, Appalachian English . . .
in the United States, and Catalan Spanish in Spain," all of which, as
psychologist Ellen Bouchard Ryan has noted, have survived despite
"strong pressures to succumb" to the standard languages that domi-
nate them. Pidgin and creole languages worldwide provide additional
examples. Often derided as illegitimate, even degenerate, they are

also exalted and embraced as markers of solidarity; local, national, or ethnic identity; and truth.

For many African Americans, the identity function of Spoken Soul is paramount, and very old. The repressive slave codes enacted in America between the late seventeenth century and the early eighteenth century (including whipping, maiming, branding, ear-nailing and -severing, and castration for various "offenses") may have helped forge an oppositional identity among blacks vis-à-vis whites, expressed in part through a distinctive vernacular. Continued hardships of the nineteenth and twentieth centuries (including lynchings, the denial of equal access to education and employment, segregation, poverty, police persecution, and criminal injustice) not only would have facilitated the development and/or maintenance of distinctive black ways of talking, dressing, dancing, making music, and behaving, but also would have made black Americans reluctant to mimic white ways of talking and behaving.

In the 1980s, anthropologists Signithia Fordham and John Ogbu found black inner-city teenagers in Washington, D.C., hostile to the adoption of a cluster of behaviors defined as "acting white"—at the top of which was "speaking standard English." The opposition is not just to speaking Standard English, which can be done in an identifiably black way, with a black accent and rhetorical style, but also and especially to talking proper or talking white (whether standard or vernacular), with white pronunciation patterns or accents. This attitude remains deeply ingrained today. Working-class teenagers from East Palo Alto and Redwood City, California, recently articulated for us their opposition to talking white and their defiant defense of talking black. For them, Spoken Soul is a litmus test for anyone who claims to be black (although one has to be cautious about the shrinking of Du Bois's consciousness to a one-soul paradigm):

> Then i's these . . . black girls jus' like—ack lak white girls. Ah say, "You wanna be white, go change yo' sk[in] color. Shut up! [Tinky]

> Over at my school . . . first time they catch you talkin white, they'll never let it go. Even if you just quit talkin like that, they'll never let it go! [Reggie]

> It pisses me when the Oreos [black on the outside, white on the inside]—they be trying to correct your language, and I be like, "Get away from me! Did I ask you to—correct me?! No! No! No, I didn't! Nuh-uh!" [Fabiola]

As hip-hop culture and the language, body movements, dress, and music that embody it spread among young Americans of virtually every ethnicity and are adopted by teenagers in countries as distant as Russia and Japan, the status of black language and culture at the popular level is rising, and young African Americans of every class proudly claim it as originally and most authentically theirs.

We shouldn't let this mention of teenagers delude us into thinking, as many do, that Spoken Soul figures in the identities of young people only. Black adults of all ages talk the vernacular, and it functions to express their black identity, too. While it is true that African Americans with less education and earning power use the grammatical features of Spoken Soul more extensively than do those with more education and earning power, the vernacular is often wrongly associated with ignorance. The use, enjoyment, and endorsement of the vernacular by blacks who are well educated and hold good jobs reveal that much more is going on. This category includes not only such writers as June Jordan and such comedians as Steve Harvey, for whom the vernacular is part of their occupational art. It also includes business administrators such as Arch Whitehead (featured on *60 Minutes* and referred to earlier in the book), who eschew Spoken Soul in the world of work and extol it as the language they prefer at home or with friends.

A series of studies conducted since the 1970s reveals that attitudes toward Spoken Soul and Standard English, particularly among blacks, are more complex than what is commonly reported in the press— namely that the former is disdained and the latter extolled. Acknowledging this complexity is one key to understanding the persistence and significance of Spoken Soul.

In the 1970s, education specialist Mary Hoover polled forty-eight parents of elementary students in East Palo Alto and Oakland, California, about their attitudes toward vernacular and standard Black English. (Standard Black English or Black Standard English is a variety in which the speaker uses standard grammar but still sounds black, primarily because of black rhetorical strategies and selected black pronunciations, among them intonation and emphasis.) Hoover also asked about Superstandard, or "talking proper," in which the speaker sheds all traces of black pronunciation and affects a stilted syntax. She found little support for "talking proper," long the butt of humor and deprecation within the black community, but plenty of support for Standard Black English and a distinct preference for it over the vernacular in the classroom and at work, and for reading and writing. However, there was strong support for the vernacular in informal spoken interaction at home and in the community, especially with black family members and friends.

One of the most frequent explanations that the parents gave for wanting to retain the vernacular was its role in the preservation of their distinctive history, worldview, and culture—their soul. The sentiment is not unique to African Americans. As T. S. Eliot observed some fifty years ago: "For the transmission of a culture—a peculiar way of thinking, feeling and behaving—and for its maintenance, there is no safeguard more reliable than a language." Literary critic Cleanth Brooks, noting the maintenance of Welsh in the face of English domination, and other examples, observed that:

> The soul of a people is embodied in the language peculiar to them. . . .
> It is significant that peoples throughout history have often stubbornly
> held on to their native language or dialect because they regarded it
> as a badge of their identity and because they felt that only through it
> could they express their inner beings, their attitudes and emotions,
> and even their own concepts of reality.

Another reason for blacks' accepting and preserving the vernacular is its usefulness in "getting down" with other blacks. A black professor at a midwestern university, interviewed in a study in the early 1990s, explained that she not only used Spoken Soul with her black friends as a release from the stresses of her white-dominated professional life, but also employed it at times to create a positive relationship interaction with black students:

> I think it [black vernacular] can be a unifier in developing a certain
> kind of rapport with them. . . . The personal rapport perhaps gives
> them a greater sense that "I am on your side. . . . There's no barrier
> between us. I can identify with you"—[it's] kind of a signal with the
> language.

We should remember that for many, speaking the vernacular is a source of great pleasure, as well as great utility. As Toni Morrison pointed out, there are some things that soul speakers cannot say, or say as well, "without recourse to my language."

The most recent study of attitudes toward black vernacular and Standard English is an ongoing one being conducted by Jacquelyn Rahman, a linguistics graduate student at Stanford University. In spring 1999, she asked black undergraduates and graduate students there what they thought of the two varieties of English, and found that even among these upwardly bound black academics and pre-professionals, the value of both varieties was endorsed, much as Mary Hoover had found with black parents two decades earlier. On the one hand, Standard English was defended as the variety needed "in a white-dominated world . . . to gain respect and get good jobs," "in formal settings (work, school reports)," and "when I am around the white majority . . . because that is what my audience understands and it's socially more appropriate." On the other hand, Black English was praised for its "spirit, creativity, resilience and soul," for its "character and history," for "being more expressive and vibrant," and because "it keeps me close to my family and friends, as well as serving as a living reminder of my history as a member of a distinctive ethnic group in this country." Virtually all the students said that they were bidialectal, some becoming so after initial school experiences in which they were derided by black classmates for talking white. They draw on one variety or the other as audience and situation demand.

Because we have celebrated Spoken Soul throughout this book, one might be tempted to group us with those who argue that Standard English is unnecessary, and who insist that vernacular speakers need not extend their repertoires. On the contrary, we feel that shunning Standard English too easily lets the power structure and our own would-be spokespeople off the hook, allowing the former more wantonly to disregard the raw voice of protest, and the latter to have one less weapon hopelessly mute in affairs of business and the state.

That mainstream English is essential to our self-preservation is indisputable. Without it, how could we have wrested judgeships and congressional seats and penthouse offices from those who have long enjoyed such privileges almost unchallenged? We have come this far thanks, in part, to a distinguished lineage of race men and women who used elegant Standard English as a template for their struggle against the very oppressor responsible for imposing the language on them. Malcolm X's speeches show his command of Standard English, especially a black Standard English that, like Jesse Jackson's, is non-vernacular in grammar but soulful in its rhetorical style and pronunciation, including intonation and emphasis. (Malcolm himself was quite critical of "ultra-proper-talking Negroes," including "those with their accents so phonied up that if you just heard them and didn't see them you wouldn't even know that they were Negroes.") But in making the transition from the street to the podium, brother Malcolm also had to develop his expertise in speaking and writing Standard English, and his initial discouragement is described in his *Autobiography:*

> I became increasingly frustrated at not being able to express what I
> wanted to convey in letters that I wrote, especially those to Mr. Elijah
> Muhammad. In the street, I had been the most articulate hustler out
> there—I had commanded attention when I said something. But now,
> trying to write simple English, I not only wasn't articulate, I wasn't even
> functional. How would I sound writing in slang, the way I would *say* it,
> something such as "Look, daddy, let me pull your coat about a cat,
> Elijah Muhammad."

Before we even fix our mouths to snub the speech of the marketplace, we must remember Malcolm, and remember also Frederick Douglass's "What to the Slave Is the Fourth of July? An Address delivered in Rochester, New York, on 5 July 1852." Drawing his imposing form upright before the president of the United States and other assembled statesmen, Douglass declared that:

> This Fourth [of] July is yours, not mine. You may rejoice, I must
> mourn. To drag a man in fetters into the grand illuminated temple of
> liberty, and call upon him to join you in joyous anthems, were inhuman
> mockery and sacrilegious irony. Do you mean, citizens, to mock me,
> by asking me to speak to-day? If so, there is a parallel to your conduct.
> And let me warn you that it is dangerous to copy the example of a
> nation whose crimes, towering up to heaven, were thrown down by
> the breath of the Almighty, burying that nation in irrecoverable ruin!
> I can to-day take up the plaintive lament of a peeled and woe-smitten
> people.

By bequeathing to us such eloquence, Douglass commands us not only to master Standard English but also to learn it in its highest form. And we must. For in the academies and courthouses and legislatures and business places where policies are made and implemented, it is as graceful a weapon as can be found against injustice, poverty, and discrimination. Like Douglass and Malcolm X, we must learn to carry Standard English like a lariat, unfurling it with precision. We must learn to use it, too, for enjoyment and mastery of literature, philosophy, science, math, and the wide variety of subjects that are conducted and taught in Standard English, in the United States, and, increasingly, in the world. We must teach our children to do so as well. This, as you know, is no mean feat. It requires time, money and other resources, patience, discipline, and understanding, all of which tend to be in tragically short supply in schools with large black populations. But treating Spoken Soul like a disease is no way to add Standard English to their repertoire. On the contrary, building on Spoken Soul, through contrast and comparison with Standard English, is likely to meet with less resistance from students who are hostile to "acting white." It is also likely to generate greater interest and motivation, and as experiments have shown (see chapter 9), to yield greater success, more quickly.

But if we could wave a magic wand and have all of black America wake up tomorrow talking like television anchorman Bryant Gumbel, shouldn't we do so? Actually, no. Sampling Standard English should not lead us to forget the flavor of Spoken Soul, or vice versa. Just ask yourself: Why would our forefathers and foremothers "sing the Lord's song in a strange land" (Psalm 137:4), if their voices hadn't created a note that was decidedly their own? Without that note, how could they have described to their children their intimate relationships with love and freedom and death, relationships that were dissimilar to those of their masters? In the end, all words (and the rules for pronouncing and combining them) are mighty. As the African concept of *nommo* asserts, spirits are conjured by the saying of words. Ancestors are invoked by the speaking of words. If our enemies can make us forget these words, and then make us forget that we have forgotten, they will have robbed us of our ability to honor and summon our ancestors, whom we so desperately need now more than ever.

True, the vernacular has been abused. (How could we ever forget the prattle of the blackface minstrels?) But we must reclaim it. We must stop importing this shame that is manufactured beyond our communities for something as cellular and spiritual as our language. We must refuse to allow Spoken Soul to remain a stepchild in the family of tongues. We must begin to do for language what we have done historically (in some cases only very recently) for our hair, our clothes, our art, our education, and our religion: that is, to determine for ourselves what's good and what's bad, and even what's *baaad*. The crucial thing is that we hold the yardstick, and finally become sovereign guardians and arbitrators and purveyors of our culture. For all who share this vision, we close with four modest suggestions:

■ Develop a new awareness about the origins, structure, politics, and larger significance of Spoken Soul. We're not suggesting that you case the 'hood thinking about etymology or phonology. Rather, try to keep in mind that all languages and dialects are systematic, rule-governed, and righteous, and that none has ever fallen out of a black hole or been spontaneously conceived.

- Be conscious of our love-hate relationship with Spoken Soul. The next time a brother or sister starts speaking in deep vernacular during a city council meeting and you feel yourself stinging with embarrassment, try to remember the social conditioning and the historical circumstances behind that private shame. We don't promise that you'll overcome your shame, only that you may begin to understand it and, one hopes, reverse it. By the same token, the next time you find yourself submerged in and surrounded by Spoken Soul, acknowledge it silently. Adore it. Taste it as if for the first time. Try to imagine the same scene, the same ethos and ambience, without it.

- Strike such phrases as "broken English," "lazy English," "bad English," and "careless English" from your vocabulary, and teach your friends and family to put little stock in such uninformed and absolutist judgments. You can't speak soul simply by being lazy or careless about speaking Standard English. At the same time, urge youngsters to appreciate and become proficient in Standard English, especially the black Standard English that the Reverend Martin Luther King Jr., Malcolm X, Maxine Waters, Maya Angelou, and other leaders have commanded so well.

- Don't ever shun or jeer a brother or sister because of the way he or she speaks. It is only when we have claimed both Spoken Soul and Standard English as our own, empowering our youth to appreciate and articulate each in their respective forums, that we will have mastered the art of merging our double selves into a better and truer self. Remember: to become an accomplished pianist (jazz *or* classical), you've got to be able to work both the ebonies and the ivories.

We should remember and do these things, because issues of language, class, culture, education, and power will continue to smolder, and will flare up again. As the African American proverb—cast in Spoken Soul—cautions us, "Every shut eye ain't asleep, every goodbye ain't gone."

Notes

Part One
Introduction

1. What's Going On?

The definitions for *soul* are from *The American Heritage Dictionary* (Boston: Houghton Mifflin, 2000). Claude Brown's comments on "Spoken Soul" are from his article "The Language of Soul," *Esquire*, April 1968, pp. 88, 160–161. James Baldwin's remarks are from "If Black English Isn't a Language, Then Tell Me, What Is?" originally published in the *New York Times*, July 29, 1979, and reprinted in Geneva Smitherman, ed., *Black English and the Education of Black Children and Youth* (Detroit: Wayne State University Press, Center for Black Studies, 1981), pp. 390–392, and in Theresa Perry and Lisa Delpit, eds., *The Real Ebonics Debate* (Boston: Beacon Press, 1998), pp. 67–70. Toni Morrison's quotation is from Thomas LeClair, "A Conversation with Toni Morrison: 'The Language Must Not Sweat,'" *New Republic*, March 21, 1981, pp. 25–29. June Jordan is quoted from "Nobody Mean More to Me Than You and the Future Life of Willie Jordan," in her book *On Call: Political Essays* (Boston: South End Press, 1985), pp. 123–139.

Maya Angelou's remarks on the Ebonics resolution were made during a visit to Wichita, Kansas, on December 20, 1996, and were quoted in the Associated Press article "Oakland Decision Spurs Debate over Ebonics," *Wichita Eagle*, December 22, 1996, p. 7A. Kweisi Mfume's denunciation was quoted in John Leland and Nadine Joseph, "Hooked on Ebonics," *Newsweek*, January 13, 1997, p. 78. Jesse Jackson's comment was made on NBC's *Meet the Press* on December 22, 1996, and quoted in Maria Puente, "Calling Black English a Language Prompts Chorus of Criticism," *USA Today*, December 23, 1996, p. 1A. Ward Connerly's critique was quoted in Elliot Diringer and Lori Olszewski, "Critics May Not Understand Oakland's Ebonics Plan," *San Francisco Chronicle*, December 21, 1996, p. A17. Henry Louis Gates Jr.'s comment was quoted by Frank Rich in "The Ebonic Plague," *Wall Street Journal*, January 8, 1997. Bill Cosby's column "Elements of Igno-Ebonics" was published in the *Wall Street Journal*, January 10, 1997. William Bennett's description of the Ebonics resolution and Mario Cuomo's reaction were quoted in Maria Puente, "Calling Black English a Language Prompts Chorus of Criticism," *USA Today*, December 23, 1996, p. 1A. Richard Riley's remarks were quoted in Nanette Asimov, "U.S. Says Ebonics Isn't a Language," *San Francisco Chronicle*, December 25, 1996, p. 1.

Information on legislative efforts to ban Ebonics from use in schools and other official contexts is in Elaine Richardson, "The Anti-Ebonics Movement: 'Standard' English Only," in *Journal of English Linguistics* (Special Issue: Ebonics), vol.

26, no. 2 (June 1998), pp. 156–169. The report of the America Online poll about Ebonics appeared in John Leland and Nadine Joseph, "Hooked on Ebonics," *Newsweek,* January 13, 1997, p. 78. For the America Online quotations cited in this chapter, we are grateful to linguist and school volunteer Lucy Bowen of Menlo Park, California, who printed out hundreds of them and passed them on to us. Full citation information on each America Online comment, including exact time of transmission, is available.

For summaries of Justice Joiner's ruling, see the *New York Times,* July 13, 1979. The ruling itself is reprinted in Geneva Smitherman, ed., *Black English and the Education of Black Children and Youth* (Detroit: Wayne State University Press, Center for Black Studies, 1981). Carl Rowan's comment about the Ann Arbor court case was in a column entitled "Black English," which appeared in the *Philadelphia Bulletin,* July 11, 1979. For information on proposals by Caribbean linguists to consider Creole English in schools, see John R. Rickford, "Using the Vernacular to Teach the Standard," in his book *African American Vernacular English* (Oxford: Basil Blackwell, 1999). One book that exemplifies the 1990s concern with what unites us rather than what separates us as Americans is Arthur M. Schlesinger Jr., *The Disuniting of America: Reflections on a Multicultural Society* (New York: W. W. Norton, 1991, 1998). For more about Propositions 209 and 227 and similar measures in California and other states, see Jewelle Taylor Gibbs's monograph *The California Crucible* (San Francisco: Study Center Press, 1998). The income statistics for African Americans are from Martin Carnoy, *Faded Dreams: The Politics and Economics of Race in America* (Cambridge: Cambridge University Press, 1994). For other income statistics, and for a discussion of the generation gap within the black community, see Faral Chideya, "Money. Power. Respect?" *Emerge,* October 1998, pp. 35–38. For more information on the differences of opinion among African American writers with respect to Ebonics, see chapters 2 and 10, and references there.

Part Two
"This Passion, This Skill, This Incredible Music"

2. *Writers*

We are grateful to Arnold Rampersad, Sonia Sanchez, and Meta Duwa Jones for feedback on an earlier version of this chapter.

The opening epigraph is from Paule Marshall, "From the Poets of the Kitchen," *New York Times Book Review,* January 9, 1983, reprinted in Henry Louis Gates Jr. and Nellie Y. McKay, eds., *The Norton Anthology of African American Literature* (New York: W. W. Norton, 1997), pp. 2072–2079. Marshall attributes the closing quotation to writer Grace Paley. The second is from Henry Louis Gates Jr., *The Signifying Monkey: A Theory of Afro-American Literary Criticism* (New York and Oxford: Oxford University Press, 1988), p. xxii.

John Leacock's play *The Fall of British Tyranny; or, American Liberty Triumphant* was published by Styner and Cist in Philadelphia in 1776. Richard Allsopp's *Dictionary of Caribbean Usage* (Oxford: Oxford University Press, 1997, p. 333) defines *Kojo* or *Cudjoe* as "a name loosely applied to any black man, usually from a rural area, who has a reputation for rough-and-ready force, crude strength, or stubborn resistance," and derives it from "Fante *Kodwo* . . . Ghanaian *Kodzo*," name of a male born on a Monday. The quotations from Stephen E. Henderson are from *Understanding the New Black Poetry: Black Speech and Black Music as Poetic References* (New York: William Morrow, 1973), pp. 31–33. Sterling Brown's "Southern Road" poem, reprinted in part, is from his *Southern Road* (New York: HarperCollins). The quotation about Johnson's reevaluation of dialect use in Brown's poetry comes from *The Norton Anthology of African American Literature*, cited above, p. 121. Arnold Rampersad's comment on "Mother to Son" is from *The Life of Langston Hughes*, vol. 1: 1902–1941. *I, Too, Sing America* (New York and Oxford: Oxford University Press, 1986), p. 43. For the full text of "Queens of the Universe" by Sonia Sanchez, see Woodie King, ed., *BlackSpirits: A Festival of New Black Poets in America* (New York: Random House, 1972), p. 186. Don Lee's poem "Move Un-Noticed to Be Noticed" is in Stephen E. Henderson, *Understanding the New Black Poetry*, cited above, pp. 340–343.

The passage from Claude Brown's *Manchild in the Promised Land* (New York: Macmillan, 1965) is on p. 63. The excerpt from Walter Mosley's *Devil in a Blue Dress* is from chapter 2 (New York: W. W. Norton, 1990). Sherley Anne Williams's "Tell Martha Not to Moan," first published in *Massachusetts Review* in 1967, is anthologized in *The Norton Anthology of African American Literature*, cited above, pp. 2365–2375. The passage from June Jordan's *His Own Where* is from chapter 1 (New York: Thomas Y. Crowell, 1971). Paul Stoller is quoted from his book *Black American English: Its Background and Its Usage in the Schools and in Literature* (New York: Delta, 1975), p. 194. Alice Walker's *The Color Purple* was first published in New York by Harcourt Brace Jovanovich in 1982. The Ntozake Shange excerpt is from *for colored girls who have considered suicide / when the rainbow is enuf* (New York: Simon & Schuster, 1975.)

The Zora Neale Hurston passage is from *Their Eyes Were Watching God* (Philadelphia and London: J. B. Lippincott, 1937). Henry Louis Gates Jr.'s comment about Sterling Brown's and Hurston's reverence for black vernacular is in *The Signifying Monkey*, cited above, p. xii. Daryl Cumber Dance's comment about the ubiquity of dialect in black folklore is in the introduction to *Shuckin' and Jivin': Folklore from Contemporary Black Americans* (Bloomington: Indiana University Press, 1978), p. xx. The quotation from Chapman Milling within the comment is from his foreword to J. Mason Brewer's *Dog Ghosts and Other Texas Negro Folk Tales* (Austin: University of Texas Press, 1958), p. xii. For analyses of black folklore, see Alan Dundes, ed., *Mother Wit from the Laughing Barrel: Readings in the Interpretation of Afro-American Folklore* (Englewood Cliffs, N.J.: Prentice-Hall, 1973). For further analysis of Walter Simmons's watermelon story and other lies, see John R. Rickford, "Riddlin and Lyin: Participation and Performance," in Joshua A. Fishman, ed., *The Fergusonian Impact* (The Hague: Mouton, 1986), vol. 2, pp. 89–106. The "Aunt Dinah Died" jump-rope rhyme is from Linda Goss and Marian Barnes, *Talk That Talk: An Anthology of African-American Storytelling* (New York: Simon & Schuster/Touchstone, 1989), p. 443. The excerpt from James Baldwin's *Blues for Mister Charlie* is from p. 40 of the 1964 edition (New York: Dial Press).

Christopher Hitchens's comments about Baldwin and Black English are in his essay "Hooked on Ebonics," *Vanity Fair*, March 1997, p. 95. The extract from *A Raisin in the Sun* is from pp. 29–30 of the 1966 edition (New York: New American Library; original copyright Robert Nemiroff 1958, unpublished manuscript). John Rickford's interview with August Wilson was conducted on January 14, 1999, at Ujamaa Lounge, Stanford University, and transcribed with the assistance of Akua Searcy. The extract from *Fences* is from pp. 2–3 of the 1986 edition (New York: New American Library/Plume). The *People* magazine article on August Wilson, "Street Talk: Hearing Voices Makes Playwright August Wilson the Talent He Is," by William Plummer and Tony Kahn, appeared in the May 13, 1996, issue, pp. 64–66.

Sylvia Wallace Holton's account of the minstrel show tradition is in her book *Down Home and Uptown* (London: Associated University Presses, 1984), p. 102. Nathan Huggins's remarks about minstrelsy are from *Harlem Renaissance* (New York: Oxford University Press, 1971), p. 251. Three of the best general books on blackface minstrelsy are Robert C. Toll, *Blacking Up: The Minstrel Show in Nineteenth-Century America* (New York: Oxford University Press, 1974); Eric Lott, *Love and Theft: Blackface Minstrelsy and the American Working Class* (New York: Oxford University Press, 1993); and W. T. Lhamon Jr., *Raising Cain: Blackface Performance from Jim Crow to Hip-Hop* (Cambridge, Mass.: Harvard University Press, 1998). The minstrel show dialogue featuring "End" and "Mid" is from Jack Haverly, *Negro Minstrels* (Chicago: Frederic J. Drake, 1902), and was cited in Elizabeth Riles, Phillip Klemmer, Lauren Neefe, and Haresh Kamath, "Minstrelsy: A History and Analysis," in John R. Rickford and Lisa Green, eds., *The AAVE Happenin'* (Stanford, Calif.: Stanford University Department of Linguistics, 1994), pp. 108–124). Zora Neale Hurston's complaint about the inaccuracy of dialect in minstrel shows is from "Characteristics of Negro Expression," a 1934 article reprinted in *The Norton Anthology of African American Literature*, cited above, pp. 1019–1032. James Weldon Johnson's comments on the same topic are in *Along This Way: The Autobiography of James Weldon Johnson* (New York: Viking Press, 1933), pp. 158–159.

The quotation about Joel Chandler Harris playing minstrelsy in his youth is from Eric Lott's *Love and Theft*, cited above, p. 33. The Uncle Remus story is from Joel Chandler Harris, *Uncle Remus: His Songs and Sayings,* ed. Robert Hemenway (New York: Penguin, 1986; orig. pub. D. Appleton, 1880), p. 55. Robert Hemenway's commentary on Uncle Remus is in his introduction to the Penguin Classics edition of Joel Chandler Harris, *Uncle Remus: His Songs and His Sayings* (Middlesex, England, and New York: Penguin, 1982, p. 22). Sylvia Wallace Holton's comments on Thomas Nelson Page are in her book *Down Home and Uptown*, cited above, p. 86. The "Marse Chan" passage is from Thomas Nelson Page, *In Ole Virginia; or, Marse Chan and Other Stories* (New York: Scribner, 1887). Thomas Dixon's *The Clansman: An Historical Romance of the Ku Klux Klan* was first published in 1905 (New York: Doubleday, Page).

Alain Locke's comment about "jingling and juggling" is in his article "Sterling Brown: The New Negro Folk Poet," originally published in *Negro Anthology,* 1934, pp. 111–115, and reprinted in Jeffrey C. Stewart, ed., *The Critical Temper of Alain Locke: A Selection of His Essays on Art and Culture* (New York and London: Garland, 1983), p. 50. The critique of Langston Hughes's *Fine Clothes to the Jew* is quoted from Langston Hughes, *The Big Sea: An Autobiography* (New York: Thunder's Mouth Press, 1986 [1940]), p. 266. Hughes's response to his critics is also in *The Big Sea*, p. 268. "When Malindy Sings" is quoted from *The Complete Poems of Paul Laurence Dunbar* (New York: Dodd, Mead, 1922 [1913]), p. 82. Dunbar's remark about his ability to write in dialect is quoted in James Weldon Johnson, *Along This Way*, cited above, p. 160. Johnson's assessment of Dunbar is in the same book, p. 161. "The Poet" is quoted from *The Complete Poems of Paul Laurence Dunbar,* cited above, p. 191.

The verse of "Sence You Went Away" is quoted from Johnson's *Fifty Years and Other Poems* (New York: AMS Press, 1975), p. 63. (This is a reprint of a 1917 edition published by Cornhill in Boston; individual poems were published elsewhere, 1871–1938.) James Weldon Johnson's remarks about black poets' use of quaint and musical folk speech are from *The Book of American Negro Poetry* (New York: Harcourt, Brace, 1922), pp. xxxix–xl. His subsequent, more critical remarks are from his preface to the revised edition (New York: Harcourt, Brace, 1931), p. 4. The quotation from the preface to Johnson's "Negro folk sermons" is in *God's Trombones: Seven Negro Sermons in Verse* (New York: Viking Press, 1927), p. 7. The lines from "The Pusher" and "The Thirteens (Black)" are reprinted from *The Complete Collected Poems of Maya Angelou* (New York: Random House, 1994), pp. 39, 94.

3. *Preachers and Pray-ers*

The first epigraph is from the sermon "Guidelines for a Constructive Church," delivered by the Reverend King at Ebenezer Baptist Church, Atlanta, June 5, 1966, which is reprinted in Clayborne Carson and Peter Holloran, eds., *A Knock at Midnight: Inspiration from the Great Sermons of Reverend Martin Luther King, Jr.* (New York: Warner Books, 1998), pp. 105–115). The second epigraph is from John R. Rickford's recording of a prayer meeting on Daufuskie Island, South Carolina, on May 24, 1970, presided over by Deacon Walter Simmons.

A more recent study of the African American preaching style is Walter Pitts's *Old Ship of Zion: The Afro-Baptist Ritual in the African Diaspora* (New York and Oxford: Oxford University Press, 1993). Pitts is justifiably critical (see pp. 4–5) of some aspects of an older work on black preaching, William H. Pipes's *Say Amen, Brother! Old-Time Negro Preaching: A Study in American Frustration* (New York: William-Frederick Press, 1951). An excellent article-length study of black preaching is Faye Vaughn-Cooke's "The Black Preaching Style: Historical Development and Characteristics," *Language and Linguistics Working Papers*, 5 (Washington, D.C.: Georgetown University Press, 1972).

As noted above, Deacon Walter Simmons's prayer was recorded on Daufuskie Island, South Carolina, May 24, 1970. The prayer recorded in Austin, Texas, is reprinted from Walter Pitts's *Old Ship of Zion*, cited above, p. 19; and Pitts's comment about the similarities between current prayers and prayers of the 1920s and 1930s is on p. 70 of the same work. Patricia Jones-Jackson's analysis is in *When Roots Die: Endangered Traditions on the Sea Islands* (Athens: University of Georgia Press, 1987), pp. 80–81. The remarks on the religious motif of the train are in the introduction to James Weldon Johnson's *God's Trombones* (New York: Viking Press, 1927). The claim that the Reverend King "delighted in euphony" was made by Richard Lischer in *The Preacher King; Martin Luther King, Jr., and the Word That Moved America* (New York and Oxford: Oxford University Press, 1955), p.120; the passage from Dr. King's sermon is from page 121 of the book.

The Reverend Emil Thomas's remarks are from a service at Jerusalem Baptist Church, Palo Alto, January 3, 1992. Geneva Smitherman is quoted from *Talkin and Testifyin: The Language of Black America* (Detroit: Wayne State University Press, 1986), p. 134. The first passage with the "hunh" expression is from Grace Sims Holt, "Stylin' outta the Black Pulpit," in Thomas Kochman, ed., *Rappin and Stylin Out: Communication in Black America* (Urbana: University of Illinois Press, 1972), p. 193. The second "hunh" passage is from a sermon by Ernestine Cleveland Weems, pastor of a Berkeley Church of God in Christ congregation featured in the documentary *The Performed Word* (Red Taurus Films, The Anthropology Film Center Foundation, 1982, produced by Gerald L. Davis).

Grace Sims Holt's 1972 essay "Stylin' outta the Black Pulpit" is cited above. "The Creation," one of seven "Negro folk-sermons" in *God's Trombones,* by James Weldon Johnson, is cited above. The list of black denominations that exemplify physical possession of the Holy Spirit is from Geneva Smitherman, *Black Talk: Words and Phrases from the Hood to the Amen Corner* (Boston and New York: Houghton Mifflin, 1994), p. 31. The sermon "When You Fail in Your Trying" was presented by the Reverend Jeremiah A. Wright Jr. before Trinity United Church of Christ, Chicago, Father's Day 1998; it can be found in the videotape series *Great Preachers* (Odyssey Productions, 1998, distributed by Vision Video, Worcester, Penn.). Rev. Wright discusses African American language very positively in a sermon entitled "Ain't Nobody Right but Us," in his book *What Makes You So Strong: Sermons of Joy and Strength from Jeremiah A. Wright, Jr.* (Valley Forge, Pa.: Judson Press, 1993: 13–26.

Grace Sims Holt's comment on how black preachers begin their sermons is from "Stylin' outta the Black Pulpit," cited above, p. 191. Henry H. Mitchell is quoted from *Black Preaching* (Philadelphia and New York: J. B. Lippincott, 1970), p. 148. Richard L. Wright's findings are in his Ph.D. dissertation, "Language Standards and Communicative Style in the Black Church" (University of Texas at Austin, 1976). Walter Pitts's less dramatic demonstration of the same point is in *Old Ship of Zion,* cited above, pp. 139–141. The sample of the black vernacular version of the Bible is from *Rappin' with Jesus: The Good News According to the Four Brothers* (New York: African American Family Press, 1994), p. 62. A Gullah version of the Gospel According to Luke (*De Good Nyews Bout Jedus Christ Wa Luke Write*) was made available in 1994 through the American Bible Society. Rev. Green shared the anecdote about his parishioners' enthusiastic reaction to the Gullah version with John Rickford and his students in March 1999.

Minister Louis Farrakhan's "black agenda" speech was presented in Atlanta in 1988. The excerpt from the Reverend Jesse Jackson's 1988 speech is from "Jesse Jackson: The Sermons in His Speeches," a paper by Stanford undergraduates Michael Canul, David Hirning, Heidi Durrow, Matt Langley, and Jervey Tucker, in John Rickford, Bonnie McElhinny, and Arnetha Ball, eds., *The B.E. Happenin* (Stanford, Calif.: Stanford University Department of Linguistics, 1989).

4. *Comedians and Actors*

The Redd Foxx epigraph is from his and Normal Miller's invaluable book for the study of black comedy, *The Redd Foxx Encylopedia of Black Humor* (Pasadena, Calif.: Ward Ritchie Press, 1977), p. 264. The Dance epigraph is from *Shuckin' and Jivin': Folklore from Contemporary Black Americans* (Bloomington: Indiana University Press, 1978), p. xx. Another general study of black comedy is William Schechter, *The History of Negro Humor in America* (New York: Fleet Press, 1979). The most comprehensive and valuable recent book on this topic is Mel Watkins, *On the Real Side: A History of African American Comedy* (Chicago: Lawrence Hill Books, 1999 [1994]).

The lyrics to "Nobody" are by Alex Rogers, and the music by Bert Williams himself; the text appears in *The Redd Foxx Encylopedia of Black Humor,* cited above, p. 47. Sammy Davis Jr. is quoted from the same book, pp. 91 and 92.

Richard Pryor's "Eulogy" is on his audiotape cassette *Is It Something I Said?* (Burbank, Calif.: Warner Bros. Records, 1975, M5 2285). Adele Givens's routine is from an HBO *Comedy Half Hour* that aired on October 8, 1996. Steve Harvey's firing episode is from a live performance broadcast on television on December 23, 1997.

One example of "puttin' on ole massa" is reported in John R. Rickford and Angela E. Rickford, "Cut Eye and Suck Teeth," *Journal of American Folklore*, 89 (1976), pp. 294–309: "The story [was] told to us by Richmond Wiley, a native of the South Carolina Sea Islands, of a slave who used to answer his master's queries and commands with the words 'You ass, sir!' The insult, so obvious to his fellow slaves, was passed off on the master as the slave's slurred pronunciation of 'Yes, sir.' " For three slave narratives that fit into this genre, see Gilbert Osofsky, *Puttin' on Ole Massa* (New York: Harper & Row, 1969). For a description and several examples of "shuckin' and jivin' " to avoid encounters with police and other authority figures, see Thomas Kochman, "Toward an Ethnography of Black American Speech Behavior," *Rappin' and Stylin' Out: Communication in Black America* (Urbana: University of Illinois Press, 1972), pp. 241–264.

Kochman's comment about differences between black and white modes of public debate is from *Black and White Styles in Conflict* (Chicago: University of Chicago Press, 1981), p. 18. Claudia Mitchell-Kernan's description of "marking" is from "Signifying and Marking: Two Afro-American Speech Acts," in John Gumperz and Dell Hymes, eds., *Directions in Sociolinguistics* (New York: Holt, Rinehart & Winston, 1972), pp. 161–179; the marking example involving an Uncle Tom character is from p. 178.

The excerpt from Chris Rock's "My Father" routine is from the cassette recording *Born Suspect* (New York: Atlantic Recording, 1991, 7-82159-4). The excerpt from Bill Cosby's "The Lower Tract" is from the cassette recording *Inside the Mind of Bill Cosby* (Universal City, Calif.: MCA Records, 1972, MCAC-554). Ronald L. Smith's commentary on and quotation from Cosby is from his book *Cosby: The Life of an American Legend* (New York: Prometheus Books, 1997). The segment cited here was part of an excerpt from the first edition of the book (New York: St. Martin's Press, 1986), reprinted in the *Philadelphia Inquirer*, April 15, 1986, p. C03.

Dick Gregory is quoted from *Dick Gregory: From the Back of the Bus*, ed. by Bob Orben (New York: Avon, 1962, p. 16). Moms Mabley is quoted from Jim Lowe, "Jackie 'Moms' Mabley: Star of the Chitlin Circuit," in *Retro*, an on-line magazine (www.retroactive.com/jan98/moms.html), January 1998. Redd Foxx's comments on civil rights marchers are from *The Redd Foxx Encyclopedia of Black Humor*, cited above, p. 239; his observations about black street language and blackface and dialect are from pp. 264 and 234.

House Party, written by Reginald Hudlin, was a Hudlin Brothers film and a New Line Cinema production. The sixth-grade "snaps" from East Palo Alto were recorded by Stanford student Charles Philips in 1989; they appear in an article by F. Charles, R. Haynes, G. Lee, and Philips in John R. Rickford, Arnetha Ball, and Bonnie McElhinny, eds., *The B.E. Happenin: A Mini-Conference on the Expressive Uses of Black English* (Stanford, Calif.: Stanford University Department of Linguistics, 1989). James Percelay, Monteria Ivey, and Stephan Dweck's observations about snaps, and examples, are from *Snaps* (New York: Quill, 1994). See also their *Double Snaps* and *Triple Snaps* (New York: Quill, 1995 and 1996), and James Percelay, *Snaps Four* (New York: Quill, 1998).

Good Times was produced by CBS from 1974 through 1979. *Superfly*, a Sig Shore production, was released in 1972 by Warner Bros. *Hollywood Shuffle*, written by Robert Townsend and Keenen Ivory Wayans, and produced and directed by Robert Townsend, was released in 1989.

Three collections of black humor worth looking at are Philip Sterling, *Laughing on the Outside: The Intelligent White Reader's Guide to Negro Tales and Humor* (New York: Grosset & Dunlap, 1965); Langston Hughes, *The Book of Negro Humor* (New York: Dodd, Mead, 1966); and Dillibe Onyeama, *The Book of Black Man's Humor* (London: Dillibe Onyeama, 1975).

5. *Singers, Toasters, and Rappers*

The first epigraph is from the introduction to Leroi Jones, *Blues People* (New York: Quill, 1963). The second epigraph is from "Street Conscious Rap: Modes of Being," in James Spady, Charles G. Lee, and H. Samy Alim, *Street Conscious Rap* (Philadelphia: Black History Museum Umum/Loh Publishers, 1999), p. xx. Carole Simpson's remarks to the Howard University graduating class were delivered at Commencement, May 1997. James Brown's "Soul Power," originally produced by King Records in 1971, was found on *The CD of JB: Sex Machine and Other Soul Classics* (Polygram Records, 1985).

The lyrics to "You Gotta Move" were attributed to Fred McDowell and the Reverend Gary Davis in the liner notes of the Rolling Stones' 1971 album *Sticky Fingers*. The Georgia Sea Island Singers' version of "I Got to Move," attributed to Mrs. Janie Hunter and the Moving Star Hall congregation, appears in *Ain't You Got a Right to the Tree of Life: The People of Johns Island, South Carolina—Their Faces, Their Words and Their Songs,* recorded by Guy and Candie Carawan (New York: Simon & Schuster, 1966), p. 163.

The lyrics of "Steal Away to Jesus" are from Henry Louis Gates Jr. and Nellie McKay, eds., *The Norton Anthology of African American Literature* (New York: W. W. Norton, 1997), p. 13. "I Will Move On Up a Little Higher" is on *Mahalia Jackson: The World's Greatest Gospel Singer* (Sony Music, 1992). "Mannish Boy" is on *Muddy 'Mississippi' Waters Live* (CBS Records, 1971).

The comments on "signifying" are from Claudia Mitchell-Kernan's "Signifying and Marking: Two Afro-American Speech Acts," in John J. Gumperz and Dell Hymes, eds., *Directions in Sociolinguistics* (New York: Holt, Rinehart & Winston, 1972), pp. 161–179. The definition of toasts by Labov and his colleagues Paul Cohen, Clarence Robins, and John Lewis is from "Toasts," in Alan Dundes, ed., *Mother Wit from the Laughing Barrel* (Englewood Cliffs, N.J.: Prentice-Hall), p. 335. Roger Abrahams's comments on toasts are from *Deep Down in the Jungle . . . Negro Narrative Folklore from the Streets of Philadelphia* (Chicago: Aldine, 1970), p. 97. The "Signifying Monkey" toast is reprinted from p. 153 of that book; the "Great Mac-Daddy" toast, from p. 162; and the *"Titanic"* toast from p. 127. Abrahams's remarks on the kinds of heroes celebrated in toasts are in chapter 3 of his book. The work by Henry Louis Gates Jr. is *The Signifying Monkey: A Theory of Afro-American Literary Criticism* (New York and Oxford: Oxford University Press, 1988). The Dolomite toast is from Bruce Jackson, *Get Your Ass in the Water and Swim Like Me: Narrative Poetry from Black Oral Tradition* (Cambridge, Mass.: Harvard University Press, 1974), pp. 57–59.

LL Cool J's "I'm Bad" is from his *Bigger and Deffer* album (Def Jam Recordings, 1987). Smooth Da Hustler's "Broken Language" is on the *Once Upon a Time in Amerikkka* album (Profile, 1997). Nas's "If I Ruled the World" is from the

Illmatic album (Columbia Records, 1996). For more on freestyling, see the documentary video by Jacquie Jones, *Freestyle* (Department of Communications, Stanford University, 1995). "The Day After" by Goodie Mob is found on the *Soul Food* album (La Face Records, 1995). For information about the ring shout, see Art Rosenbaum, *Shout Because You're Free: The African American Ring Shout Tradition in Coastal Georgia* (Athens: University of Georgia Press, 1998). DMX's "How's It Going Down" is from *It's Dark and Hell Is Hot* (Def Jam Recordings, 1998). "Rapper's Delight," by the Sugarhill Gang, was released as a single in 1979 by Sugar Hill Records, Englewood, N.J., and it was the title rap on the 1996 CD/cassette album *Rapper's Delight: The Best of Sugarhill Gang* (Rhino Records). There are many variant transcripts of the lines we cite from this rap, as a web search for the lyrics of "Rapper's Delight" will confirm. Lauryn Hill's "Lost Ones" appears on the album *The Mis-education of Lauryn Hill* (Columbia Music, 1998). For an older example of *done done* in song, see Ma Rainey's 1924 version of "See, See Rider" ("See, See Rider, see what you done done!") in *The Norton Anthology of African American Literature* (cited above), p. 27. In linguistics circles, the recognized authority on vernacular usage in rap and hip-hop music is Marcyliena Morgan, whose forthcoming books are *Say It Loud: Discourse and Verbal Genres in African American Culture* (Cambridge: Cambridge University Press, 2000) and, with Stephen DeBerry, *Thursday Night at Project Blowed: Underground Hip Hop and Urban Youth Resistance* (Durham, N.C.: Duke University Press, to appear).

Part Three
The Living Language

6. *Vocabulary and Pronunciation*

We are grateful to Thomas Wasow of Stanford University for comments on an earlier version of this chapter.

The epigraphs are from AOL on-line discussions of the Ebonics controversy, December 1996. James Baldwin's article "If Black English Isn't a Language, Then Tell Me, What Is?" was in the *New York Times,* July 29, 1979.

Clarence Major's dictionary is *Juba to Jive: A Dictionary of African-American Slang* (New York: Penguin, 1994). Geneva Smitherman's *Black Talk: Words and Phrases from the Hood to the Amen Corner* was published by Houghton Mifflin, New York, in 1994. A revised and updated version is forthcoming (January 2000). Rudolph Fisher's "Introduction to Contemporary Harlemese" is in *The Walls of Jericho* (New York and London: Alfred A. Knopf, 1928); pp. 295–307. *The New Cab Calloway's Hepster's Dictionary: Language of Jive* was published by Calloway, New York, in 1944. *A 2 Z: The Book of Rap and Hip-Hop Slang,* by Lois Stavsky, I. E. Mozeson, and Dani Reyes Mozeson, was published by Boulevard Books, New York, in 1995. Another recent glossary is Monica Frazier Anderson's *Black English Vernacular: From "Ain't" to "Yo Mama"* (Highland City, Fl.: Rainbow Books, 1994). J. L. Dillard's *Lexicon of Black English* was published by Seabury Press, New York, in 1970. Edith Folb's *runnin' down some lines: the language and culture of black teenagers* was published by Harvard University Press, Cambridge, Massachusetts, in 1980.

Teresa Labov's study, entitled "Social and Language Boundaries Among Adolescents," was published in *American Speech,* 67, 4 (1992), pp. 339–366. Robert

Williams's 1972 Black Intelligence Test of Cultural Homogeneity was copyrighted by him (Black Studies Program, Washington University, St. Louis).

The students who reacted with interest and amazement to the distinctiveness of *ashy* were members of the Society of Black Engineers from various California colleges to whom John Rickford lectured at Stanford in November 1998. The *cut-eye* and *suck-teeth* survey was conducted by John and Angela Rickford in the early 1970s and first reported in their article, "Cut Eye and Suck Teeth: Masked Africanisms in New World Guise," *Journal of American Folklore*, 1976, pp. 294–309; the article has since been reprinted, most recently in John R. Rickford, *African American Vernacular English* (London and New York: Blackwell, 1998). For more on African origins of words in Ebonics, Gullah, and American English, see Joseph E. Holloway and Winifred K. Vass, *The African Heritage of American English* (Bloomington: Indiana University Press, 1993).

The *Dictionary of American Regional English* (Frederic G. Cassidy, chief ed., Joan Houston Hall, associate ed.) is being published by Belknap Press, Cambridge, Massachusetts, in a series of volumes several years apart. The first, A–C, was published in 1985; D–H in 1991; and I–O in 1996. Definitions of *ace-boon-coon, bid whist, bubba, bad-eye, bad-mouth*, and *big-eye* given here are from vol. 1. For a list of all the "black" terms in DARE up to vol. 2, see *An Index by Region, Usage and Etymology to the Dictionary of American Regional English vols. I and II (Publication of the American Dialect Society*, 77) (Tuscaloosa: University of Alabama Press, for the American Dialect Society, 1993). The Mandingo source for *bad-mouth* is from Geneva Smitherman, *Talkin and Testifyin* (Detroit: Wayne State University Press, 1986), and the Hausa and Mandingo sources are from Holloway and Vass's *The African Heritage of American English*, cited above, p. 137. The various African sources for *suck-teeth* are from John and Angela Rickford's "Cut Eye and Suck Teeth," cited above, and from Richard Allsopp's *Dictionary of Caribbean English Usage* (New York: Oxford University Press, 1996).

The domains of black vocabulary use were derived from information in the following sources cited above: J. L. Dillard (1977), Edith Folb (1980), Clarence Major (1994), and Geneva Smitherman (1994). Folb's comment on class differences is from *runnin' down some lines*, cited above, p. 201. Major's notion about black slang as a living, breathing form of expression is from *Juba to Jive*, cited above, p. xxviii. The innovative character and meaning of *shorty* were first noted in an October 1996 assignment by Sterling K. Brown for John Rickford's course "African American Vernacular English" at Stanford; Brown's observations were corroborated by Anakela C. Rickford, a Spelman College student.

Claude Brown's comment on *uptight* is in "The Language of Soul," *Esquire*, April 1968, p. 160. Clarence Major's comment on the same word is in *Juba to Jive*, cited above, p. xxix. Edith Folb provides additional discussion of the evolution of the word in *runnin' down some lines*, cited above, p. 208. James Baldwin's comment on diffusions of black vocabulary is from "If Black English Isn't a Language," cited above, p. 391. Margaret Lee presented her paper "Out of the Hood and into the News: Borrowed Black Verbal Expressions in a Mainstream Newspaper" at the twenty-seventh annual conference on New Ways of Analyzing Variation, University of Georgia, Athens, October 1998. For an excellent discussion of words that cross over from black to white and mainstream usage, see pp. 16–22 of Smitherman's *Black Talk*, cited above. Clarence Major's comment on the inevitability of diffusion is from *Juba to Jive*, cited above, p. xxix.

Claude Brown's comments are from "The Language of Soul," cited above, pp. 88, 160. *How to Speak Southern* by Steve Mitchell was published by Bantam, New York, in 1976. The classic overview of black vernacular pronunciation and grammar, still useful although dated in some respects, is Ralph W. Fasold and Walt Wolfram, "Some Linguistic Features of Negro Dialect," in Ralph W. Fasold and Roger W. Shuy, eds., *Teaching Standard English in the Inner City* (Washington, D.C.: Center for Applied Linguistics, 1970). For a more recent overview, see John R. Rickford, "Phonological and Grammatical Features of African American Vernacular English" in *African American Vernacular English* (Oxford: Blackwell, 1999). For a more technical and detailed recent account of black vernacular pronunciation, see Guy Bailey and Erik Thomas, "Some Aspects of African-American Vernacular English Phonology," in Salikoko S. Mufwene, John R. Rickford, Guy Bailey, and John Baugh, eds., *African American English* (London: Routledge, 1998), pp. 85–109.

Walter Edwards's statistics on the differential use of monophthongal pronunciations like *mah* and *Ah* by blacks and whites in Detroit come from "Sociolinguistic Behavior in a Detroit Inner-City Black Neighborhood," *Language in Society*, 21, pp. 93–115. Erik R. Thomas and Guy Bailey are quoted from "Parallels Between Vowel Subsystems of African American Vernacular English and Caribbean Anglophone Creoles," *Journal of Pidgin and Creole Languages*, 13, 2 (1998), p. 284; for details of pronunciation differences, see pp. 271–281. For data on black pronunciation in the 1930s, see George Dorrill, "A Comparison of Stressed Vowels of Black and White Speakers in the South," in Michael B. Montgomery and Guy Bailey, eds., *Language Variety in the South* (Tuscaloosa: University of Alabama Press, 1986), pp. 149–157.

On Guyanese East Indians and Creole, see Derek Bickerton, *Dynamics of a Creole System* (Cambridge: Cambridge University Press, 1975). For further discussion of past and present relations between black and white speech in the South, see Crawford Feagin, *Variation and Change in Alabama English: A Sociolinguistic Study of the White Community* (Washington, D.C.: Georgetown University Press, 1979), pp. 245–247.

The transcript of Johnnie Cochran's comments was obtained from the following website: http://v90-137.cchono.com/~walraven/simpson/#lists. John McWhorter's comment is from *The Word on the Street: Fact and Fable about American English* (New York: Plenum, 1998), p. 133.

John Rickford's 1972 study was reported in an unpublished term paper, "Sounding Black or Sounding White: A Preliminary Investigation of a Folk Hypothesis," for the course Linguistics 521 at the University of Pennsylvania. A tracing of the spectrograph showing variation in the black male speaker's voice was reprinted in his article, "The Question of Prior Creolization in Black English," in Albert Valdman, ed., *Pidgin and Creole Linguistics* (Bloomington: Indiana University Press, 1977), pp. 190–221. For further discussion of intonation in black speech, see Elaine E. Tarone, "Aspects of Intonation in Black English," *American Speech* 48 (1973), pp. 29–36. The speaker identification study by G. Richard Tucker and Wallace E. Lambert, "White and Negro Listeners' Reactions to Various American-English Dialects," was published in *Social Forces*, 47 (1969), pp. 463–468. Roger Shuy's speaker identification study, "Subjective Judgments in Sociolinguistic Analysis," was published as *Georgetown University Monograph Series on Language and Linguistics*, 22 (1969). The speaker identification study by William

Labov, Paul Cohen, Clarence Robins, and John Lewis is reported in *A Study of the Non-Standard English of Negro and Puerto Rican Speakers in New York City* (1968), vol. 2, sect. 4.7. For more recent speaker identification studies, see Guy Bailey and Natalie Maynor, "The Divergence Controversy," *American Speech*, 64 (1989), pp. 12–39; and John Baugh, "Perceptions Within a Variable Paradigm: Black and White Racial Detection and Identification Based on Speech," Edgar W. Schneider, ed., *Focus on the USA* (Amsterdam: John Benjamins, 1996), pp. 169–182.

The March 1995 segment of the CBS television program *60 Minutes* on black speech was entitled "The Language Factor." For more on the rule deleting initial voiced stops, see John R. Rickford, "The Insights of the Mesolect," in David DeCamp and Ian F. Hancock, eds., *Pidgins and Creoles: Current Trends and Prospects* (Washington, D.C.: Georgetown University Press), 1974.

Walt Wolfram's Detroit study was published as *A Sociolinguistic Description of Detroit Negro Speech* (Washington, D.C.: Center for Applied Linguistics, 1969). Catherine Chappel's study is *A Generational Study of Oakland AAVE [African American Vernacular English]: Linguistic Variation by Class and Age among Oakland Females* (Ph.D. qualifying paper, Department of Linguistics, Stanford University, 1999). Oprah Winfrey's pronunciation is analyzed by Jennifer Hay, Stephanie Hannedy, and Norma Mendoza-Denton in "Oprah and /ay/: Lexical Frequency, Referee Design, and Style," to appear in *Proceedings of the 14th International Conference of Phonetic Sciences* (San Francisco, 1999). The replication by Walter Edwards is reported in his 1992 *Language in Society* article cited above. For another classic study of pronunciation variation by social class, age, and style, see the New York City study by William Labov and others cited above. Quantitative variation in final consonant clusters is reported there and in William Labov, *Language in the Inner City: Studies in the Black English Vernacular* (Philadelphia: University of Pennsylvania Press, 1972; reissued 1998), p. 45.

7. Grammar

We are grateful to Thomas Wasow of Stanford University for feedback on an earlier version of this chapter.

The epigraph from J. L. Dillard is from *Black English: Its History and Usage in the United States* (New York: Random House, 1972). The epigraph from Geneva Smitherman is from *Talkin and Testifyin: The Language of Black America* (Detroit: Wayne State University Press, 1986).

The New York City study, by William Labov, Paul Cohen, Clarence Robins, and John Lewis, was published as *A Study of the Non-Standard English of Negro and Puerto Rican Speakers in New York City* (New York: Columbia University Press, 1968). The Detroit study, by Walt Wolfram, was published as *A Sociolinguistic Description of Detroit Negro Speech* (Washington, D.C.: Center for Applied Linguistics, 1969).

The classic overview of black vernacular pronunciation and grammar is Ralph W. Fasold and Walt Wolfram, "Some Linguistic Features of Negro Dialect," 1970, cited above (p. 242). For a more recent overview, see John R. Rickford, "Phonological and Grammatical Features of African American Vernacular English," 1999, also cited above.

Stefan Martin and Walt Wolfram's comment about similarities in sentence structure between African American Vernacular English and other English dialects is from "The Sentence in African American Vernacular English," in Salikoko S. Mufwene, John R. Rickford, Guy Bailey, and John Baugh, eds., *African American*

English (London: Routledge, 1998), p.11. For more on plural marking and pronoun use in AAVE, see Salikoko S. Mufwene, "The Structure of the Noun Phrase in African American Vernacular English," in the same volume, pp. 69–81.

Data on the frequency with which Foxy Boston and Tinky Gates deleted third-person-singular *s* and possessive *'s* is from John R. Rickford, "Grammatical Variation and Divergence in Vernacular Black English," in *African American Vernacular English,* cited above.

Two of the best sources on invariant *be, done, be done,* and other tense-aspect markers in AAVE are Ph.D. dissertations by Lisa J. Green, "Topics in African American English: The Verb System Analysis" (University of Massachusetts, Amherst, 1993) and Elizabeth Dayton, "Grammatical Categories of the Verb in African American Vernacular English" (University of Pennsylvania, 1996). Both are available from UMI Dissertation Services, Ann Arbor, Michigan (800-521-0600 or 313-761-4700). Green's work is also available in "Aspect and Predicate Phrases in African American Vernacular English," *African American English,* cited above, pp. 37–68. Although our discussion of invariant *be* highlights its most common use as a marker of habituality, several researchers have noted that it is sometimes used to mark events that take place over an extended period at one time, as in the following examples from John Baugh, *Black Street Speech* (Austin: University of Texas Press, 1983), p. 72: ". . . and we be tired from the heat, but he just made everybody keep on working. So they be runnin . . . right . . . really bookin . . . and the police had all the streets blocked off." For further discussion of *steady,* see pp. 85–89 of the same book.

One of the earliest, most comprehensible, and most technical discussions of restrictions on the deletion of the copula in African American English is William Labov, "Contraction, Deletion, and Inherent Variability of the English Copula," in *Language in the Inner City* (Philadelphia: University of Pennsylvania Press, 1972), pp. 65–129. For comparisons of copula absence in African American English with copula absence in Arabic, Hungarian, and other languages, see Charles A. Ferguson, "Absence of the Copula and the Notion of Simplicity," in Dell Hymes, *Pidginization and Creolization of Languages* (Cambridge: Cambridge University Press, 1971), pp. 141–150, and Geoffrey Pullum, "Language That Dare Not Speak Its Name," *Nature,* 386 (March 27, 1997), pp. 321–322. The data on copula deletion frequencies according to grammatical environment is from John R. Rickford, "The Creole Origins of African American Vernacular English: Evidence from Copula Absence," in *African American English,* cited above. The reason some of the copula deletion figures in the chart are given as .25, .12, and so on instead of as 25 percent and 12 percent is that while they are based on observed percentages, they represent deletion probabilities as calculated by a computer program (VARBRUL) that estimates how much various factors contribute to the likelihood that copula deletion will take place. For further information, see John R. Rickford, Arnetha Ball, Renee Blake, Raina Jackson, and Nomi Martin, "Rappin on the Copula Coffin: Theoretical and Methodological Issues in the Analysis of Copula Variation in African American Vernacular English," *Language Variation and Change,* 3 (1991), pp. 103–132.

Irma Cunningham's unstressed *been* sentence from Gullah is quoted from her Ph.D. dissertation, "A Syntactic Analysis of Sea Island Creole" (Ann Arbor: University of Michigan, 1970), p. 65. Beryl Bailey's unstressed *been* sentence is from *Jamaican Creole Syntax* (New York: Cambridge University Press, 1966), p. 46. For more on stressed *BEEN,* see the dissertations by Lisa Green and Elizabeth Dayton, cited above, and John R. Rickford, "Carrying the New Wave into Syntax: The Case of Black English BIN," *African American Vernacular English* (Oxford: Blackwell, 1999). The example of *been like* in Lindsey's play is cited in G. Krapp, *The English Language in America* (New York: Century, 1925), pp. 258–259. The statistics on differences in black/white interpretations of BEEN are in Rickford, "Carrying the New Wave into Syntax," cited above. The "We had BEEN married" example is from Elizabeth Dayton's dissertation, cited above. The "five present tenses" of AAVE were discussed, with the same examples used in this chapter, in John R. Rickford, "Suite for Ebony and Phonics," *Discover,* December 1997, pp. 82–87.

For examples and analysis of *done,* double modals, and other AAVE features in Southern white speech, see Crawford Feagin, *Variation and Change in Alabama English* (Washington, D.C.: Georgetown University Press, 1979). For discussion of the meaning of *fixing to* in Southern white English, see Marvin K. L. Ching, "How Fixed Is *fixin' to?*" *American Speech,* 62, pp. 332–345.

For further discussion of past-tense *had,* see John R. Rickford and Christine Theberge Rafal, "Preterit *had* in the Narratives of African American Preadolescents," *American Speech,* 71, pp. 227–254, reprinted in Rickford, *African American Vernacular English,* cited above; and Patricia Cukor-Avila, "The Evolution of AAVE in a Rural Texas Community: An Ethnolinguistic Study" (Ph.D. dissertation, University of Michigan, 1995). The classic study of indignant *come* is Arthur K. Spears, "The Black English Semi-Auxiliary Come," *Language,* 58 (1982), pp. 850–872.

For a thorough study of *ain't, don't,* and other negative auxiliaries in black speech, see Tracey Weldon, "Variability in Negation in African American Vernacular English," *Language Variation and Change,* 6 (1994), pp. 359–397. The most detailed study of multiple negation is William Labov, "Negative Attraction andNegative Concord," in *Language in the Inner City* (Philadelphia: University of Pennsylvania Press, 1972), pp. 130–196. The negative inversion examples are from William Labov, Paul Cohen, Clarence Robins, and John Lewis, *A Study of the Non-Standard English of Negro and Puerto Rican Speakers in New York City,* cited above, vol. 1. The double-negation example from Chaucer is from *The American Heritage Dictionary of the English Language,* 3rd ed. (Boston: Houghton Mifflin, 1992), p. 555, "double negative." For a more recent discussion of negative inversion, see Peter Sells, John R. Rickford, and Thomas A. Wasow, "Negative Inversion in African American Vernacular English," *Natural Language and Linguistic Theory,* 14, 3 (1996), pp. 591–627.

For discussion of the Harlem repetition experiment with *if,* see William Labov, *Language in the Inner City,* cited above, pp. 61–63. For the Washington, D.C., version of this experiment, see Joan Baratz, "Teaching Reading in an Urban Negro School System," in Joan Baratz and Roger Shuy, eds., *Teaching Black Children to Read* (Washington, D.C.: Center for Applied Linguistics, 1969).

The *Ahma git me a gig* example is from John Gumperz, *Discourse Strategies* (Cambridge: Cambridge University Press, 1982), p. 30. The examples of deleted relative pronouns and double modals from Stefan Martin and Walt Wolfram are "The Sentence in African American Vernacular English," cited above, pp. 31–33. For information on double modals in southern white English and other English varieties, see Crawford Feagin, *Variation and Change in Alabama English,* cited above, pp. 151–174.

For variation by social class, gender, age, and style in the grammar of Spoken Soul, see Walt Wolfram, *A Sociolinguistic Description of Detroit Negro Speech,* cited above. The East Palo Alto data on copula absence and other age-related variations recorded by Faye McNair-Knox are from John R. Rickford, "Grammatical Variation and Divergence in Vernacular Black English," in *African American Vernacular English,* cited above. The study of variation in Foxy Boston's language is John R. Rickford and Faye McNair-Knox, "Addressee and Topic-Influenced Style Shift" (1994), reprinted in John R. Rickford, *African American Vernacular English* (Oxford: Basil Blackwell, 1999).

8. History

The epigraph quoting Carter G. Woodson is from *The Mis-Education of the Negro* (Trenton, N.J.: Africa World Press, 1998; originally published 1933), p. 19. The epigraph quoting John McWhorter is from *The Word on the Street: Fact and Fable about American English* (New York: Plenum, 1998), pp. 174–175.

Information on slaves brought to America by the Spanish in the sixteenth century and on the twenty Africans brought to Jameston in 1619 is from Daniel M. Johnson and Rex R. Campbell, *Black Migration in America: A Social Demographic History* (Durham, N.C.: Duke University Press, 1981), pp. 7–8, and Daniel P. Mannix, *Black Cargoes* (New York: Viking Press, 1962), pp. 54–55. John Hope Franklin and Alfred A. Moss Jr. are quoted from *From Slavery to Freedom: A History of Negro Americans,* 6th ed. (New York: Alfred A. Knopf, 1988), p. 53.

Statistics on black population proportions in Virginia and South Carolina come from Philip S. Foner, *History of Black Americans* (Westport, Conn.: Greenwood Press, 1975), vol. 1, p. 188; Allan Kulikoff, *Tobacco and Slaves: The Development of Southern Culture in the Chesapeake, 1680–1800* (Chapel Hill: University of North Carolina Press, 1986); and Peter Wood, "The Changing Population of the Colonial South: An Overview by Race and Region," in Peter H. Wood, Gregory A. Waselkov, and M. Thomas Hatley, eds., *Powhatan's Mantle* (Lincoln: University of Nebraska Press, 1989), pp. 38, 46. Among those who believe that seventeenth- and early-eighteenth-century African English in the United States outside of Gullah territory was not significantly pidginized or creolized are Peter Wood, *Black Majority* (New York: Alfred A. Knopf, 1975), p. 175; Salikoko S. Mufwene, "The Founder Principle in Creole Genesis," *Diachronica,* 13 (1996), pp. 83–134; and Don Winford, "On the Origins of African American Vernacular English— A Creolist Perspective, Part I: The Sociohistorical Background," *Diachronica,* 14 (1997), pp. 305–344.

Data on Suriname, Jamaica, and colonial America in the seventeenth and early eighteenth centuries come from various sources cited in John R. Rickford, "Prior Creolization of African American Vernacular English? Sociohistorical and Textual Evidence from the 17th and 18th Centuries," *Journal of Sociolinguistics,* 1 (1997), pp. 316–336. Among the most important are: Robert B. Le Page and Andrée Tabouret-Keller, *Acts of Identity: Creole-Based Approaches to Language and Identity* (Cambridge, England: Cambridge University Press, 1985); Bettina M. Migge, "Substrate Influence in Creole Language Formation: The Case of Serial Verb Constructions in Sranan" (M.A. thesis, The Ohio State University, Columbus); and John Hope Franklin and Alfred A. Moss Jr., *From Slavery to Freedom,* cited above. For Derek Bickerton's claim that language learners must constitute 80 percent or more in the contact situation for creoles to emerge, see *Roots of Language* (Ann Arbor, Mich.: Karoma, 1981), p. 4. Data on the proportions of Africans in the first twenty-five years of the founding of Haiti and Martinique are from John Singler, "The Demographics of Creole Genesis in the Caribbean: A Comparison of Martinique and Haiti," in Jacques Arends, ed., *The Early Stages of Creolization* (Amsterdam: John Benjamins, 1995), pp. 203–232.

The Sranan and Ewe versions of "Dogs are walking under the house" are from John McWhorter, *The Word on the Street: Fact and Fable about American English,* cited above, p. 159. For more on Guinea Coast Creole English, see Ian Hancock, "The Domestic Hypothesis, Diffusion, and Componentiality," in Pieter Muysken and Norval Smith, eds., *Substrata versus Universals in Creole Genesis* (Philadelphia: John Benjamins, 1986), pp. 71–102. For more about Tituba's origin and speech, see Samuel G. Drake, *The Witchcraft Delusion in New England* (Roxbury, Mass.: W. Elliot Woodward, 1866), and Elaine G. Breslaw, *Tituba, Reluctant Witch of Salem* (New York: New York University Press, 1996).

Statistics on black-white proportions in various American colonies in 1750 come from John Hope Franklin and Alfred A. Moss Jr., *From Slavery to Freedom,* cited above, p. 61. Table 3 in John Rickford's "Prior Creolization" paper, cited above, reprints and reorganizes the Franklin/Moss data in detail. The quotation from Philip S. Foner about blacks outnumbering whites in parts of Maryland is from *History of Black Americans,* cited above, vol. 1, p. 201. Wood's remark is from *Black Majority,* cited above, p. 187. The quotations from Foner about the 1705 Virginia slave code are from pp. 194–195.

The comments about distinctive black language and culture in eighteenth-century America are adapted from John Rickford's "Prior Creolization" paper, cited above. Marvin L. M. Kay and Lorin L. Cary are quoted from *Slavery in North Carolina 1748–1775* (Chapel Hill: University of North Carolina Press, 1995), pp. 149–150. Allan Kulikoff is quoted from *Tobacco and Slaves,* cited above, pp. 327–328 and 351. The Garden comment about blacks interacting with blacks is cited in Michael Mullin, *Africa in America: Slave Acculturation and Resistance in the American South and the British Caribbean, 1736–1831* (Urbana: University of Illinois Press, 1992), p. 187. The citation from Defoe is from *The History and Remarkable Life of the Truly Honourable Col. Jacque Commonly Called Col. Jack* (London, 1722). Dillard's remarks about language differences between blacks and whites in the novel are in *Black English,* cited above, p. 78.

The Fall of British Tyranny was published in 1776 in Philadelphia by Styner and Cist. The quotations from eighteenth-century newspaper ads about runaway slaves are from Walter M. Brasch, *Black English and the Mass Media* (Lanham, Md.: University Press of America, 1981), pp. 6–8. Dillard's statement about variation in black speech in the eighteenth century is in *Black English,* cited above, p. 85.

For information on slaves landed illegally on Jekyll Island, Georgia, in 1858, see Tom Henderson Wells, *The Slave Ship Wanderer* (Athens: University of Georgia Press, 1968 [1967]). Data on the increase in the U.S. slave population between 1790 and 1860 come from Daniel M. Johnson and Rex R. Campbell, *Black Migration in America,* cited above, p. 25; the estimates of the number of slaves moved by the internal slave trade are from the same source. Josiah Henson's remembrances are narrated in *Father Henson's Story of His Own Life,* ed. Walter Fisher (1962), quoted at some length in Donald R. Wright, *African Americans in the Early Republic, 1789–1831* (Arlington Heights, Ill.: Harlan Davidson, 1993), pp. 40–41.

The Wallace Quarterman transcript is from John R. Rickford, "Representativeness and Reliability of the Ex-Slave Narrative Materials, with Special Reference to Wallace Quarterman's Recordings and Transcript," in Guy Bailey, Natalie Maynor, and Patricia Cukor-Avila, eds., *The Emergence of Black English: Text and Commentary* (Amsterdam: John Benjamins, 1991), pp. 206–208.

Data on post–Civil War black migration come from Daniel M. Johnson and Rex R. Campbell, *Black Migration in America,* cited above, pp. 52–63. Don Winford's remarks about African American dialects are from "On the Origins of African American Vernacular English," cited above, p. 318. For information about African American gains and losses after the war, see chapters 12–14 of John Hope Franklin and Alfred A. Moss Jr., *From Slavery to Freedom,* and chapter 27 of Philip S. Foner's *History of Black Americans,* vol. 3, both cited above.

The list of nineteenth-century sources on black speech essentially follows that presented by Walter M. Brasch, *Black English and the Mass Media,* cited above, pp. 23–58 and 59–145. Brasch's book contains excerpts from and analysis of many sources, including Francis Anne Kemble's *Journal of a Residence on a Georgian Plantation,* written in 1838–1839 and published by Harper and Bros., New York, in 1863.

The estimate of 1.8 million black southerners emigrating comes from Dernoral Davis, "Portrait of Twentieth Century African Americans," in Alferdteen Harrison, ed., *Black Exodus: The Great Migration from the American South* (Jackson: University Press of Mississippi, 1991), p. 11. Other demographic data on the twentieth century come primarily from Daniel M. Johnson and Rex R. Campbell, *Black Migration in America,* cited above; their definition of the index of black segregation, and data on this, are from pp. 149–150. William Labov and Wendell A. Harris outlined the divergence hypothesis in "De Facto Segregation of Black and White Vernaculars," in David Sankoff, ed., *Diversity and Diachrony* (Amsterdam and Philadelphia: John Benjamins, 1986), pp. 1–24. Kennell Jackson's comment on affirmative action is from *America Is Me: The Most Asked and Least Understood Questions about Black American History* (New York: Harper Perennial, 1996), p. 418.

Information on 1993 unemployment rates is from the *Statistical Abstract of the United States,* 115th ed. (Washington, D.C.: Bureau of the Census, 1995), tables 628 and 635. Martin Carnoy's book is *Faded Dreams: The Politics and Economics of Race in America* (Cambridge: Cambridge University Press, 1994); the quotation is from p. 3. The comment about the 1992 riots in Los Angeles is from Kennell Jackson, *America Is Me,* cited above, p. 385. For John Ogbu's concept of "oppositional identity," see "Class Stratification, Racial Stratification and Schooling," in L. Weis, ed., *Race, Class and Schooling. Special Studies in Comparative Education,* 17 (State University of New York at Buffalo, Comparative Education Center, 1986), and Signithia Fordham and John Ogbu, "Black Students' School Success: Coping with the 'Burden of Acting White,'" *The Urban Review,* 18,3 (1986), pp. 176–206.

Molefi Asante's remark on the limited significance of Africanisms is from "African Elements in African-American English," in Joseph E. Holloway, ed., *Africanisms in American Culture* (Bloomington: Indiana University Press, 1990), p. 21. Ernie Smith is quoted from *Ebonics: The Historical Development of African-American Language* (San Francisco: ASPIRE Books, 1997), pp. 7, 9, 21. Ambrose Gonzales is quoted from *The Black Border: Gullah Stories of the Carolina Coast* (Columbia, S.C., 1922), pp. 17–18 and 10. Samuel G. Stoney and Gertrude N. Shelby's assessment of the African words in Gullah is in *Black Genesis* (New York, 1930), p. xv. Mason Crum's is in *Gullah: Negro Life in the Carolina Sea Islands* (Durham, N.C., 1940), pp. 111, 121, 123. The preceding three sources are cited in Lorenzo Dow Turner, *Africanisms in the Gullah Dialect* (Chicago: University of Chicago Press, 1949). For other work on Africanisms in American dialects, see David Dalby, "The African Element in Black English," in Thomas Kochman, ed., *Rappin' and Stylin' Out:*

Communication in Urban Black America (Urbana: University of Illinois Press, 1972); Joseph E. Holloway and Winifred K. Vass, *The African Heritage of American English* (Bloomington: Indiana University Press, 1997 [1993]), and their references. The point about loan translations from African languages was made in John and Angela Rickford, "Cut Eye and Suck Teeth: African Words and Gestures in New World Guise," *Journal of American Folklore,* 89 (1976), pp. 294–309.

Geneva Smitherman's listing of the sound rule in West African languages is in *Talkin and Testifyin: The Language of Black America* (Detroit: Wayne State University Press, 1986), p. 7. John McWhorter's remarks about English sources are in *Word on the Street: Fact and Fable about American English,* cited above, p. 162. Cleanth Brooks's discussion is in *The Language of the American South* (Athens: University of Georgia Press, 1985), pp. 8–13. For more on *th* sounds and their replacement in Nigerian pidgin English, see Anna Barbag-Stoll, *Social and Linguistic History of Nigerian Pidgin English* (Tübingen, Germany: Stauffenberg, 1983), p. 70. Norma A. Niles's remarks about joint African and English influences on Barbadian are in "Provincial English Dialects and Barbadian English" (Ph.D. dissertation, University of Michigan, Ann Arbor, 1980), p. 147. On Jamaican data, see Frederic G. Cassidy, "Multiple Etymologies in Jamaican Creole," *American Speech,* 41 (1966), pp. 211–215.

Ernie Smith's remarks are in *Ebonics: The Historical Development of African-American Language,* cited above, pp. 29–30. William E. Welmers is quoted from *African Language Structures* (Berkeley: University of California Press, 1973), pp. 53 and 71–72. Don Winford's discussion of *r* deletion and other pronunciation features is in "On the Origins of African American Vernacular English—A Creolist Perspective, Part II: Linguistic Features," *Diachronica,* 15 (1998), pp. 102–103. McWhorter's remarks about the deletion of *r* and *l* are in *The Word on the Street,* cited above, p. 173. For more on deleting *b, d,* and *g,* see John R. Rickford, "The Insights of the Mesolect," in David DeCamp and Ian F. Hancock, eds., *Pidgins and Creoles: Current Trends and Prospects* (Washington, D.C.: Georgetown University Press, 1974). The comments about monophthongal [e] and [o] are from Erik R. Thomas and Guy Bailey, "Parallels between Vowel Subsystems of African American Vernacular English and Caribbean Anglophone Creoles," *Journal of Pidgin and Creole Languages,* 13 (1998), pp. 267 and 287.

With respect to British dialect sources, see Gilbert Schneider, *American Earlier Black English: Morphological and Syntactic Variables* (Tuscaloosa: University of Alabama Press, 1989), especially chap. 3, and references. Don Winford synthesizes and extends the work of Schneider and other researchers (including Crawford Feagin and Ralph Fasold) in a judicious manner in "On the Origins of African American Vernacular English—A Creolist Perspective, Part II: Linguistic Features," cited above; the example quoted from William Dunbar is in Winford, p. 131. A newer source, not yet in print as we're writing, is Shana Poplack, ed., *The English History of African American English* (Oxford: Blackwell, 1999), which we were not able to see before going to press. The Philadelphia man's *say* sentence was recorded by John Rickford in September 1972; the Gullah woman's *say* sentence was recorded by John Rickford on Daufuskie Island, South Carolina, in 1970; the Jamaican Creole *say* sentence is from Beryl Bailey, *Jamaican Creole Syntax* (New York: Cambridge University Press, 1966), p. 46. Turner's discussion of *say* is from *Africanisms in the Gullah Dialect,* cited above, p. 211. Asante's discussion of serial verbs and tense-aspect is in "African Elements in African-American English," cited above, pp. 26–31. For habituals, completives, and remote time constructions in African languages, see William Welmers, *African Language Structures,* cited above, pp. 345–352.

The discussion of copula absence here is based on John Rickford, "The Creole Origins of African American Vernacular English: Evidence from Copula Absence," in Salikoko S. Mufwene, John R. Rickford, Guy Bailey, and John Baugh, eds., *African American English* (London: Routledge, 1998), pp. 154–200, which should be consulted for the sources of the data cited and for other details. As we were correcting page proofs, a new study by Danielle Martin and Sali Tagliamante ("Oh, It Beautiful: Copula Variability in Britain"), presented at "New Ways of Analyzing Variation," an October 1999 conference in Toronto, *does* show historical and contemporary evidence of copula absence in Britain, although at lower levels in the one dialect for which frequency data are available (zero *is* = 2 percent, zero *are* = 25 percent) than attested in Spoken Soul or in the Caribbean creoles. For discussion of black-white differences with respect to copula absence and other grammatical features in coastal North Carolina, see Walt Wolfram, Erik R. Thomas, and Elaine W. Green, "The Regional Context of Earlier African-American Speech: Evidence for Reconstructing the Development of AAVE," to appear in *Language in Society,* 29 (2000). The discussion of grammatical differences between an old white man and an old black woman on a South Carolina Sea Island is in John R. Rickford, "Ethnicity as a Sociolinguistic Boundary," *American Speech,* 60 (1985), pp. 90–125. For discussion of black-white working-class similarities in copula absence in a community where class trumps race, see Renee A. Blake, "All o' We Is One? Race, Class, and Language in a Barbados Community" (Ph.D. dissertation, Department of Linguistics, Stanford University, May 1997).

The Ewe sentence without a copula ("Tree the tall") is from Lorenzo Dow Turner, *Africanisms in the Gullah Dialect,* cited above, p. 216. Ewe (or Gbe) is a tone language spoken in parts of Togo, Benin, and Ghana; subscript $_1$ = low tone; subscript $_3$ = high tone. In the table showing frequency of copula absence in creole and African American diaspora languages, the decimal figures represent probability weights calculated from percentages by a variable-rule computer program that takes multiple factors into consideration simultaneously. The ex-slave narrative recordings mentioned are sixteen interviews with former slaves born around the middle of the nineteenth century, recorded mainly between 1935 and 1942 (two in 1971). They are preserved in the Archive of Folk Song at the Library of Congress. Eleven of the recordings are transcribed and discussed by various scholars in Guy Bailey, Natalie Maynor, and Patricia Cukor-Avila, eds., *The Emergence of Black English,* cited above. One new source that uses the ex-slave narrative recordings to argue for creole origins for Black English is David Sutcliffe, "Gone with the Wind? Evidence for Nineteenth-Century African American Speech," *Links and Letters* 5 (1998), pp. 127–145. Darrin Howe's discussion of negation in early Black English is in "Negation and the History of African American English," *Language Variation and Change,* 9 (1997), pp. 267–294.

The divergence hypothesis was first presented in William Labov and Wendell A. Harris, "De Facto Segregation of Black and White Vernaculars," cited above, pp. 1–24. The Texas strand of this research is best summarized in Guy Bailey, "A Perspective on African-American English," in Dennis R. Preston, ed., *American Dialect Research* (Amsterdam and Philadelphia: John Benjamins, 1993), pp. 287– 318, and in Guy Bailey and Natalie Maynor, "The Divergence Controversy,"

American Speech, 64 (1989), pp. 12–39. Critiques of the hypothesis can be found in Ralph W. Fasold, William Labov, Fay Boyd Vaughn-Cooke, Guy Bailey, Walt Wolfram, Arthur K. Spears, and John R. Rickford, "Are Black and White Vernaculars Diverging?" *American Speech,* 62 (1987), pp. 3–80, and in Ron Butters, *The Death of Black English: Divergence and Convergence in Black and White Vernaculars* (Frankfurt: Peter Lang, 1989).

Evidence that Spoken Soul is converging with white vernaculars and Standard English in terms of increasing pronunciation of unstressed initial syllables comes from Fay Boyd Vaughn-Cooke's contribution to "Are Black and White Vernaculars Diverging?", *American Speech,* 62 (1987), pp. 12–32, and in earlier works of hers cited there. Evidence for convergence in terms of the pronunciation of the final vowel in words like *fifty* is presented in Keith Denning, "Convergence with Divergence: A Sound Change in Vernacular Black English," *Language Variation and Change,* 1 (1989), pp. 145–168. For evidence on convergence with respect to the nonmarking of past tense, see John R. Rickford, "Grammatical Variation and Divergence in Vernacular Black English," in Marinel Gerritsen and Dieter Stein, eds., *Internal and External Factors in Syntactic Change* (Berlin and New York: Mouton, 1991), pp. 175–200.

For the latest in the divergence controversy, see William Labov, "Coexistent Systems in African American Vernacular English," in Salikoko S. Mufwene, John R. Rickford, Guy Bailey, and John Baugh, eds., *African American English,* cited above, pp. 110–153. Labov elaborates on the claim that "many important features of the modern dialect [AAVE] are creations of the twentieth century and not an inheritance of the nineteenth." But see John Victor Singler, "What's Not New in AAVE," *American Speech,* 73 (1998), pp. 227–256, for the argument that the presence of supposedly twentieth-century features of Spoken Soul in Liberian Settler English—formed in the nineteenth century—suggests that they are relatively "old" features.

Part Four
The Ebonics Firestorm

9. *Education*

Jesse Jackson's comment in the epigraph was made at a December 30, 1996, meeting with Oakland School District personnel and others before he publicly modified his position on the Ebonics resolution. The Terry Meier epigraph is from "Teaching Teachers About Black Communications," in Theresa Perry and Lisa Delpit, eds., *The Real Ebonics Debate: Power, Language, and the Education of African American Children* (Boston: Beacon Press, 1998), p. 106.

Statistics on the performance of white and black students nationwide in 1992–1994 are from the testimony of Michael Casserly, executive director of the Council of Great City Schools, before Senator Arlen Specter's U.S. Senate panel on Ebonics in January 1997. Casserly's testimony, which included data on the performance of various ethnic groups, covered fifty large urban public school districts, and hundreds and hundreds of schools. Statistics on the performance of African American students in Oakland—released to the media when the Ebonics firestorm arose—are from the December 1996 report of the Task Force on the

Education of African American Students, Oakland Unified School District, p. 5; the recommendations cited here are from pp. 3 and 6. The December 1, 1996, *Sunday Times* (London) report about Oakland's pending resolution was in the article "Parents Force Schools to Halt 'Dumbing of America,' " by James Adams, a Washington correspondent. The account of the December 30, 1996, meetings at Oakland School District headquarters is based on the notes and recollections of John R. Rickford and Angela E. Rickford, who were there along with other linguists and educators. The original wording of the Oakland resolutions is from the minutes of the Oakland school board meeting held on December 18, 1996; the revised wording is from the minutes of the school board meeting held on January 15, 1997. Both versions are reprinted in full in J. David Ramirez, Terrence G. Wiley, Gerda de Klerk, and Enid Lee, eds., *Ebonics in the Urban Education Debate* (Long Beach: Center for Language Minority Education and Research, California State University Long Beach, 1999), pp. 103–106 and 117–118.

Robert D. Twiggs's ideas are detailed in *Pan-African Language in the Western Hemisphere: A Redefinition of Black Dialect as a Language and the Culture of Black Dialect* (North Quincy, Mass.: Christopher, 1973). Robert L. Williams's discussion of Ebonics and the proceedings of the 1973 conference at which the term was developed are in his edited *Ebonics: The True Language of Black Folks* (St. Louis: Robert L. Williams and Associates, 1975). Ernie Smith's 1995 article "Bilingualism and the African American Child" is in Marie A. Ice and Marilyn A. Saunders-Lucas, eds., *Reading: The Blending of Theory and Practice* (Bakersfield: California State University, 1995), vol. 3; quotations here are from pp. 90–91 and 93. Hubert Devonish's comment about the wording "West and Niger-Congo languages" is on page 68 of "Walking Around the Language Barrier: A Carribean View of the Ebonics Controversy," in *Small Axe: A Journal of Criticism* 2, (Sept. 1997): pp. 63–76.

For the full text of California Assembly Bill 1206, introduced by Martinez on February 28, 1997, to prohibit the use of bilingual education funds "for the purpose of recognition of, or instruction in, any dialect, idiom or language derived from English," see: http://www/sen.ca.goc/www/leginfo/SearchText.html. State Superintendent Eastin's remarks are reprinted from the *San Jose Mercury*, December 20, 1996, p. 1A, in an article by Frances Dinkelspiel, "Black Language Policy in Oakland: Talk of the Town."

Coverage of the Oakland Task Force's revised May 1997 recommendations was provided in many newspapers, including the *New York Times* (" 'Ebonics' Omitted in Oakland School Report," by Peter Applebome, May 6, 1997, p. A12); the *Oakland Tribune* ("Positive Response to Proposal for Education without Ebonics," by Jonathan Schorr, May 6, 1997, pp. A1, A9); and the *San Francisco Chronicle* ("Renamed Ebonics Plan Introduced in Oakland Schools," by Lori Olszewski, May 6, 1997, p. A18). The quotations from Sylvester Hodges are from the *Oakland Tribune* report, p. A-9. Etta Hollins's books include *Culture in School Learning* (Mahwah, N.J.: Erlbaum, 1996), *Preparing Teachers for Cultural Diversity*, ed. with Joyce E. King and Warren C. Hayman (New York: Teachers College Press, 1997); and *Racial and Ethnic Identity in School Practices*, ed. with Rosa Hernandez (Mahwah, N.J.: Erlbaum, 1999). For preliminary results from the research on decoding errors, see W. Labov, B. Baker, S. Bullock, L. Ross, and M. Brown, "A Graphemic-Phonemic Analysis of the Reading Errors of Inner-City Children" (http://www.ling.upenn.edu/~labov/home.html); William Labov and Bettina Baker, "Raising Reading Levels of African American Students in Inner-City Schools:

A Progress Report" (manuscript, Linguistics Laboratory, University of Pennsylvania, 1999); and Andrea Kortenhoven, "An Analysis of Reading Errors by African American and Latino Third Graders in East Palo Alto, California" (manuscript, Department of Linguistics, Stanford University, 1999).

For the full text of the Linguistic Society of America's January 1997 resolution on the Ebonics issue, see: http://www.stanford.edu/~rickford/ or http://www.lsadc.org. For a more detailed discussion of the research evidence relating to Ebonics in education, see John R. Rickford, "Using the Vernacular to Teach the Standard," in J. David Ramirez, Terrence G. Wiley, Gerda de Klerk, and Enid Lee, eds., *Ebonics in the Urban Education Debate,* cited above, pp. 23–41. The article is reprinted in John R. Rickford, *African American Vernacular English* (Oxford: Blackwell, 1999), pp. 329–347. Other recent books that deal with African American English and education include John Baugh, *Out of the Mouths of Slaves: African American Language and Educational Malpractice* (Austin: University of Texas Press, 1999); Theresa Perry and Lisa Delpit, eds., *The Real Ebonics Debate: Power, Language, and the Education of African-American Children,* cited above, a revised version of the fall 1997 (vol. 12, no. 1) issue of the journal *Rethinking Schools;* J. David Ramirez, Terrence G. Wiley, Gerda de Klerk, and Enid Lee, eds., *Ebonics in the Urban Education Debate,* cited above; Carolyn Temple Adger, Donna Christian, and Orlando Taylor, eds., *Making the Connection: Language and Academic Achievement among African American Students* (Washington, D.C.: Center for Applied Linguistics, and McHenry, Ill: Delta Systems, 1999); Geneva Smitherman, *Talkin That Talk: Language, Culture and Education in African America* (London and New York: Routledge, 2000); and Walt Wolfram, Carolyn Temple Adger, and Donna Christian, eds., *Dialects in Schools and Communities* (Mahwah, N.J.: Erlbaum, 1999).

Ann McCormick Piestrup's study was published as "Black Dialect Interference and Accommodation of Reading Instruction in First Grade," *Monographs of the Language Behavior Research Laboratory,* no. 4 (University of California, Berkeley, 1973). For a review of the attitudes of teachers to the language of children, including black vernacular, see Frederick Williams, *Explorations of the Linguistic Attitudes of Teachers* (Rowley, Mass.: Newbury House, 1976). For the harmful effects of negative attitudes, see Jacqueline Jordan Irvine, *Black Students and School Failure: Policies, Practices, and Prescriptions* (New York: Greenwood Press, 1990), and Robert T. Tauber, *Self-fulfilling Prophecy: A Practical Guide to Its Use in Education* (Westport, Conn.: Praeger, Tauber, 1996). The contrastive analysis book by H. H. Parker and M. I. Crist is *Teaching Minorities to Play the Corporate Language Game* (Columbia: University of South Carolina, National Resource Center for the Freshman Year Experience and Students in Transition, 1995). For one of the earliest Caribbean proposals to use contrastive analysis with creole to teach Standard English, see Robert B. Le Page's article "Problems to Be Faced in the Use of English as a Medium of Education in Four West Indian Territories," in Joshua A. Fishman, Charles A. Ferguson, and Jyotirindra Das Gupta, eds., *Language Problems of Developing Countries* (New York: John Wiley, 1968), pp. 431–443.

For a good introduction to contrastive analysis with vernacular and Standard English, see Irwin Feigenbaum, "The Use of Nonstandard English in Teaching Standard: Contrast and Comparison," in Ralph W. Fasold and Roger W. Shuy, eds., *Teaching Standard English in the Inner City* (Washington, D.C.: Center for Applied Linguistics, 1970), pp. 87–104. The Los Angeles bidialectal program, directed by Noma LeMoine, and known for years as the "Language Development Program for African American Students," has, in the wake of state propositions

209 and 227, been renamed and reconceptualized as the "Academic English Mastery Program for Speakers of Non-Standard Language Forms." For further information, see Noma LeMoine and the Los Angeles Unified School District, *English for Your Success: A Handbook of Successful Strategies for Educators* (Maywood, N.J.: The People's Publishing, 1999), and the four Curriculum Activity Guides that accompany it. Kelli Harris-Wright discusses the DeKalb County experiment and provides data on its success in her paper "Enhancing Bidialectalism in Urban African American Students" in Carolyn T. Adger, Donna Christian, and Orlando Taylor, eds., *Making the Connection: Language and Academic Achievement among African American Students* (McHenry, Ill.: Delta Systems and Center for Applied Linguistics, 1999). Doug Cummings is quoted from the *Atlanta Constitution,* January 9, 1997, p. B1. For details of the Aurora University experiment with contrastive analysis, see Hanni U. Taylor, *Standard English, Black English, and Bidialectalism* (New York: Peter Lang, 1989).

For a recent overview of dialect-reader approaches, see John R. Rickford and Angela E. Rickford, "Dialect Readers Revisited," *Linguistics and Education,* 7 (1995), pp. 107–128. For the Swedish dialect-reader study, see Tore Österberg, *Bilingualism and the First School Language—An Educational Problem Illustrated by Results from a Swedish Language Area* (Umeå, Sweden: Våsterbottens Tryckeri, 1961). The Norwegian experiment is described in Tove Bull, "Teaching School Beginners to Read and Write in Their Vernacular," in *Tromsø Linguistics in the Eighties,* 11 (1990), pp. 69–84. For discussion of and data on the Bridge experiment, see Gary A. Simpkins and Charlesetta Simpkins, "Cross-Cultural Approach to Curriculum Development," in Geneva Smitherman, ed., *Black English and the Education of Black Children and Youth* (Detroit: Wayne State University Center for Black Studies, 1981), pp. 221–240. Gary Simpkins is working with others on an updated version of the Bridge readers. For a discussion that includes positive remarks about the Bridge readers, but suggests other ways of taking knowledge of black vernacular into account in teaching reading, see William Labov, "Can Reading Failure Be Reversed? A Linguistic Approach to the Question," in *Literacy among African-American Youth: Issues in Learning, Teaching, and Schooling* (Creskill, N.J.: Hampton Press, 1995).

On the rationale for teaching African American children initially in their vernacular, see William Stewart, "On the Use of Negro Dialect in the Teaching of Reading," in Joan C. Baratz and Roger W. Shuy, eds., *Teaching Black Children to Read* (Washington D.C.: Center for Applied Linguistics, 1969), pp. 156–219. Many other articles in this book, and in its companion piece, *Teaching Standard English in the Inner City,* cited above, should be of interest to the inner-city teacher, even today. John McWhorter's critique of dialect-reader and other approaches that make special provisions for dialect speakers is in *Word on the Street: Fact and Fable about American English* (New York: Plenum, 1998), pp. 201–261.

10. *The Media*

The epigraph about language prejudice is from Wayne O'Neil's 1997 article "If Ebonics Isn't a Language, Then Tell Me, What Is?" reprinted in Theresa Perry and Lisa Delpit, eds., *The Real Ebonics Debate: Power, Language, and the Education of African American Children* (Boston: Beacon Press, 1998), p. 42. The epigraph from Theresa Perry is from the same source, p. 13.

The *San Francisco Chronicle* article announcing the landmark policy, "Oakland Schools OK Black English," by L. Olszewski, appeared on December 19, 1996, p. A1. Oprah Winfrey discussed Standard and Black English on a November 19, 1987, broadcast (No. W309), of her television show. For a discussion of Winfrey's stance toward Spoken Soul in this broadcast, see Rosina Lippi-Green, *English with an Accent: Language, Ideology, and Discrimination in the United States* (London: Routledge, 1997), pp. 193–196. "Lingering Conflict in the Schools: Black Dialect vs. Standard Speech," by Felicia R. Lee, was published in the *New York Times,* January 5, 1994. The *60 Minutes* segment on Black English, entitled "The Language Factor," appeared in March 1995. Walter M. Brasch presented his "cyclical theory" in *Black English and the Mass Media* (Lanham, Md.: University Press of America, 1981).

Neil Peirce's piece on Labov's divergence theory, "Bilingual Black English Isn't the Problem," was published in the *Inquirer Magazine* (of the *Philadelphia Inquirer*), May 5, 1985, p. 12. The *Philadelphia Daily News* article "Order to OK 'Black English' in Schools Comes under Fire" was published on August 11, 1969. The quotation outlining the nature of the original lawsuit in the Ann Arbor "King" case is from Geneva Smitherman, "What Go Round Come Round: King in Perspective," in *Harvard Educational Review* (Feb. 1981), pp. 40–56. Reprinted in G. Smitherman, *Talkin That Talk: Language, Culture and Education in African America,* cited above, pp. 132–149. Judge Joiner's quotation is taken from Reginald Stuart, "Help Ordered for Pupils Talking 'Black English,'" *New York Times,* July 13, 1979, p. A8.

Carl Rowan's comments are from "'Black English' Isn't 'Foreign,'" *Philadelphia Bulletin,* July 11, 1979. Vernon E. Jordan Jr.'s comments on the Ann Arbor decision are from "Teacher Preconceptions at Crux of Black English Problem," in *Detroit Free Press* (Dec. 7, 1979), p. 11A. For a full listing of the media's coverage of the King case, see Richard W. Bailey, "Press Coverage of the King Case," in Geneva Smitherman, ed., *Black English and the Education of Black Children and Youth* (Detroit: Center for Black Studies, Wayne State University, 1981), pp. 359–389. Labov's comments on Ebonics as an emotional subject are in "The Ebonics Uproar," *Kansas City Star,* January 9, 1997. Dillard refers to the same pervasive suggestion that Black English has been "made up" in his book *Black English* (New York: Random House, 1972), pp. 11ff. Jesse Jackson's comments on NBC's *Meet the Press* were quoted in *USA Today,* December 23, 1996. The *Rolanda* show featuring Ebonics was recorded on January 17, 1997, and broadcast later in amended form.

For a discussion of the deleterious contributions of headline writers to press coverage of the Ebonics controversy, see Geoffrey Nunberg, "Double Standards," *Natural Language and Linguistic Theory,* 15, 3 (1997). The *Times-Picayune* headline was published December 20, 1996, in the state edition, p. A1. The *Sacramento Bee* headline was published December 20, 1996, p. A24. The *Toronto Star* article "Ebonics' Garbled Message," by K. Kenna, was published on March 3, 1997, p. B5. "Voice of Inner City Streets Is Defended and Criticized," by S. A. Holmes, was published in the *New York Times* on December 30, 1996, p. A7.

The town hall meeting was covered by S. Kleffman in "Ebonics' Town Hall Support," *San Jose Mercury News,* January 9, 1997, p. 1B. The comments of the white accountant and the black welder are from A. Rojas, "Strong Opinions on Ebonics Policy," *San Francisco Chronicle,* December 23, 1996, p. A13.

The Education Trust report that African American and Latino students were losing ground was reported in the *New York Times* article "Report: Minorities Slipping Behind" written by Peter Applebome and published on December 29, 1996, p. A6. The notion of Ebonics as a universal classroom hurdle was explored by R. Sanchez in "Ebonics: A Way to Close the Learning Gap?" *Washington Post,* January 6, 1997, p. A1. The U.S. Department of Education report was cited in S. Kleffman, "Ebonics Furor Draws National Attention to Black Students' Needs," *San Jose Mercury News,* January 5, 1997, p. 1B.

The *Oakland Tribune* reprinted the Oakland School Board's Ebonics resolution on December 29, 1996, p. A9. K. De Witt wrote about Ebonics' pervasiveness in "Not So Separate: Ebonics, Language of Richard Nixon," *New York Times,* December 29, 1996. The insightful *Washington Post* article by R. Weiss was "Among Linguists, Black English Gets Respect," and was published on January 6, 1997, p. A10.

The instructional strategies of the Standard English Proficiency Program were examined by S. Kleffman in "Ebonics Debate Rages," *San Jose Mercury News,* February 14, 1997, p. B1. Peter Applebome's article "Dispute over Ebonics Reflects a Volatile Mix" appeared in *New York Times,* March 1, 1997.

The *International Workers Bulletin* article was "Who Is Promoting Ebonics and Why?" by J. Mackler, published January 13, 1997. *Socialist Action,* 15, 2 (February 1997) published "The Debate on Ebonics: What's Behind the Fury Generated by 'Black English,'" p. 4. Thomas Sowell's column "Black English (Ebonics) Is an Obsolete White Dialect" appeared in the *Detroit News,* January 19, 1997, p. 7B.

Walter Williams's column "'I Be' Talk Has No Ties to Any African Language" appeared in the *Detroit Free Press* on December 26, 1996. Bayard Rustin's "Won't They Ever Learn?" appeared in the *New York Times* on August 1, 1971. George Will's comments on the ABC program *This Week with David Brinkley* were aired on December 29, 1996. Rachel L. Jones's "Not White, Just Right" appeared in *Newsweek,* February 10, 1997, pp. 12–13. Bill Johnson called Ebonics a "linguistic nightmare" in "It's Time to Let Black English Rest in Peace," *Detroit News,* January 3, 1997.

The *New York Times* op-ed column that condemned the "Ebonic plague" was written by Frank Rich and published on January 8, 1997, p. A15. (Others made this invidious implicit comparison with the bubonic plague.) Derrick Z. Jackson suggested that Ebonics was just good business in "Black Slang, White Jive," which the *Boston Globe* published on January 3, 1997, p. A27. Ishmael Reed's *Newsday* piece "The Art of Black English" was in the *San Jose Mercury News,* January 10, 1997. Chauncey Bailey ripped into the Oakland school board on the January 16, 1997, edition of the KQED radio program *Forum.* Nicholas Stix's "Ebonics: Bridge to Illiteracy" appeared in *Liberty* 10, 6 (July 1997), pp. 45–49. To view some of the research on Black English as a bridge to Standard English that Stix distorted in his article, see John Rickford's web page, or www.stanford.edu/~rickford/. See also John Rickford, "Using the Vernacular to Teach the Standard," in his *African American Vernacular English* (Oxford: Blackwell, 1999), pp. 329–347.

Jack E. White's "Ebonics According to Buckwheat" appeared in *Time* on January 13, 1997. *Vanity Fair* contributor Christopher Hitchens wrote "Hooked on Ebonics," which was published in March 1997. Louis Menand wrote "Johnny Be Good: Ebonics and the Language of Cultural Separatism," for the *New Yorker,* January 13, 1997. The *San Diego Union-Tribune* published Rosemary Harris's "The Backlash against Black English Ignores the Beauty of the Words" on January 12, 1997, p. D6.

Leonard Pitts took a more moderate position in "Ebonics Can Be a Bridge to Success," *San Jose Mercury News,* January 9, 1997. *Essence* contributor Khephra Burns wrote "Yakkity Yak, Don't Talk Black!" published in March 1997, p. 150. The *Oakland Tribune* editorial "The First Lessons of a Controversial Idea" appeared on December 29, 1996, p. C8. The *New York Times* op-ed column that maintained everyone was looking down on Ebonics was "The Ebonic Plague," cited above.

The expressed policy against giving away advertising space is from a letter to "Concerned Linguists and Educators" c/o Dr. Geneva Smitherman, written December 18, 1998, by Daniel H. Cohen, senior vice-president of advertising for the *New York Times.* Data on the use of *has* and *have* among black teenagers in New York City is from William Labov, Paul Cohen, Clarence Robins, and John Lewis, *A Study of the Non-Standard English of Negro and Puerto Rican Speakers in New York City* (New York: Columbia University Press, 1968), vol. 1, p. 247. In Labov et al's data, *have* was used for *has* in thirty-five of fifty-two possible cases; *has* was used for *have* in not one of 114 possible cases. For coverage of the flap created by its publication of the "I has a dream" ad, see Lynn Schnaiberg, "Anti-Ebonics Ad Was Mistake, Head Start Group Says," *Education Week,* October 28, 1998.

11. *Ebonics "Humor"*

The epigraph quoting Jerrie C. Scott is from "The Serious Side of Ebonics Humor," *Journal of English Linguistics,* 26, 2 (June 1998), pp. 137–155. The second is from Maggie Ronkin and Helen Karn, "Mock Ebonics: Linguistic Racism in Parodies of Ebonics on the Internet," *Journal of Sociolinguistics,* 3, 3 (1999), pp. 360–380. It should be noted that these two papers and this chapter were written independently of one another, although a few of our examples and sources overlap.

John Leo's column appeared on January 20, 1997. For information on variation between *be* and *be's* or *bees,* see Cynthia Bernstein, "A Variant of 'Invariant' Be," *American Speech* 63, 2 (1988), pp. 119–124. She notes, among other things, that in the *Linguistic Atlas of the Gulf States* samples, speakers under forty-nine years old never used *bees,* while more than half (56 percent) of those forty-nine and over did. Bill Cosby's "We Be Toys" joke was recounted in the *Wall Street Journal,* January 10, 1997.

The data on Thunderbirds' use of *be* came from William Labov, Paul Cohen, Clarence Robins, and John Lewis, *A Study of the Non-Standard English of Negro and Puerto Rican Speakers in New York City* (New York: Columbia University Press, 1968), p. 236. The Detroit data are reported in Walt Wolfram, *A Linguistic Description of Detroit Negro Speech* (Washington, D.C.: Center for Applied Linguistics, 1969), p. 198. Foxy Boston's speech is discussed in John Rickford and Faye McNair-Knox, "Addressee and Topic-Influenced Style Shift," in Douglas Biber and Edward Finegan, eds., *Perspectives on Register* (Oxford: Oxford University Press, 1994), pp. 235–276, and reprinted in Rickford's *African American Vernacular English* (Malden, Mass.: Blackwell, 1999), pp. 112–153. The Texas data on *be* is in Guy Bailey and Natalie Maynor, "Decreolization?", *Language in Society,* 16 (1987), pp. 449–474.

For more information on the discourse marker "Know what I'm saying," see Dawn Hannah, "(Do) (y)(ou) (kn)ow (wha)(t) (I) ('m) sa(y)(i)(n)(g)?: A Case of Phonological Reduction and Pragmatic Expansion" (Stanford University, Department of Linguistics, 1996). Despite the emphasis in this chapter on the habitual meaning of invariant *be,* note that the form is sometimes used for extended duratives, nonhabitual actions drawn out in time. See Guy Bailey and Natalie Maynor, "Decreolization?", cited above. Patricia Smith's *Oakland Tribune* column appeared on December 29, 1996, and Bill Cosby's comment in the *Wall Street Journal* is from January 10, 1997. The William Raspberry excerpt is from the *Knoxville News-Sentinel,* December 26, 1996. *Hollywood Shuffle,* starring and directed by Robert Townsend, was produced in 1987 and distributed by MCEG/ Sterling. *Airplane!,* directed by David Zucker, Jim Abrahams, and Jerry Zucker, was produced in 1980.

William Stewart's version of "The Night Before Christmas" is presented and discussed in "On the Use of Negro Dialect in the Teaching of Reading," in Joan C. Baratz and Roger W. Shuy, eds., *Teaching Black Children to Read* (Washington, D.C.: Center for Applied Linguistics, 1969), pp. 156–219. Moore's poem is a perennial favorite of translators. For a translation into Gullah, see Virginia Geraty, *Gullah Night Before Christmas* (Gretna, La.: Pelican, 1998). The first stanza: " 'E bin de night befo' Chris'mus en' eenside we house, / Eb'ryt'ing settle down, eb'n de mouse. / De cump'ny done lef' f'um de bighouse at las', / En' de fambly all gone tuh Middlenight Mass."

The translation filters used on the www.novusordo.com/indexn.htm and www.AtlantaGA.com/ebonics.htm websites appear to be similar or identical to Jive, from mod.sources.games (Tektronix, Inc., games-request@tekred.TEK.COM). According to Bill Randle, the moderator of mod.sources.games: "Jive and valspeak [a filter for converting English texts to Valley talk] are filters that take an ordinary text file and change selected words into jive (or valspeak). The original author of these programs is not listed in the source code; they were submitted to mod.sources.games by Adams Douglas (adamsd@crash.UUCP)."

Maggie Ronkin and Helen E. Karn are quoted from their paper on "Mock Ebonics," cited above.

I. B. White's *The Old, Fat, White Guy's Guide to Ebonics* (Chatsworth, Calif.: CCC Publications, 1997) was perhaps the first book on Ebonics to be produced in the wake of the controversy. Significantly, it was a comedy piece. For Sterling Brown's discussion of the "brute" and other literary stereotypes, see "Negro Characters As Seen by White Authors," originally published in *Journal of Negro Education,* 2 (January 1933), pp. 180–201, then reprinted in James A. Emanuel and Theodore L. Gross, eds., *Dark Symphony* (New York: The Free Press, 1968).

The statistics about the percentages of African Americans executed for rape between 1930 and 1967 are from the *Statistical Abstract of the United States* (1115th ed., Washington D.C., Bureau of the Census, 1995), p. 220. The criminal justice statistics on African American males between ages twenty and twenty-nine were compiled by the Sentencing Project, and reported by Charisse Jones, "Crime and Punishment: Is Race the Issue?" *New York Times,* October 28, 1995, pp. 1, 9.

The "Ebonics Loan Application" is from Jerrie Scott, "The Serious Side of Ebonics Humor," cited above, p. 142. Keith Lovett's Ebonics joke book *Hooked on Ebonics* was published by St. Simons Press, Atlanta.

. Paradoxically, the same website with the cruel caricature of the "Ebonics Olympic Games" (novusordo.com/elympic.html; no longer active) included a link to a website with a linguistically informed and educationally reasoned discussion of "Black English: Its History and Its Role in the Education of Our Children" (www.princeton.edu/~bclewis/blacktalk.html).

Part Five
The Double Self

12. *The Crucible of Identity*

The W. E. B. Du Bois epigraph is from *The Souls of Black Folk* (Chicago: A. C. Mc-Clurg, 1903). The Derek Walcott epigraph is excerpted from "A Far Cry from Africa," in the collection *In a Green Night: Poems 1948–1960* (London, Cape, 1969). For the California elementary school conversation, we are grateful to Angela E. Rickford.

The quotation from Ellen Bouchard Ryan is from "Why Do Low-Prestige Language Varieties Persist?" in Howard Giles and Robert N. St. Clair, eds., *Language and Social Psychology* (Oxford: Blackwell, 1979), pp. 145–158. For conflicting attitudes to pidgins and creoles, see John R. Rickford and Elizabeth Closs Traugott, "Symbol of Powerlessness and Degeneracy, or Symbol of Solidarity and Truth? Paradoxical Attitudes toward Pidgins and Creoles," in Sidney Greenbaum, ed., *The English Language Today* (Oxford: Pergamon, 1985), pp. 252–261.

The quotations from Signithia Fordham and John Ogbu are from pp. 181–182 and 186 of their article "Black Students' School Success: Coping with the Burden of 'Acting White,'" *Urban Review*, 18, 3 (1986). Ogbu's notion of opposition identity is also explained in this work. The quotations from black teenagers in East Palo Alto and Redwood City, California, are from John R. Rickford, "Grammatical Variation and Divergence in Vernacular Black English," in Marinel Gerritsen and Dieter Stein, eds., *Internal and External Factors in Syntactic Change* (Berlin: Mouton, 1992), pp. 175–200, reprinted in Rickford's *African American Vernacular English*, cited above, pp. 261–280.

A Ph.D. dissertation that deals with the diffusion of African American language to white American youth is Mary Bucholtz, *Borrowed Blackness: Language, Racialization, and White Identity in an Urban High School* (Department of Linguistics, University of California, Berkeley, 1997). Another, covering the diffusion of hip-hop culture to the world beyond America, is Halifu Osumare, *African Aesthetics, American Culture: Dancing towards a Global Culture* (Department of American Studies, University of Hawaii, Manoa, 1999).

Mary Hoover's article is "Community Attitudes toward Black English," *Language in Society*, 7 (1978), pp. 65–87. The Eliot quotation is from *Notes towards the Definition of Culture* (London: Faber & Faber, 1948), p. 57. The Cleanth Brooks quotation is from *The Language of the American South* (Athens: University of Georgia Press, 1985), p. 2. The black professor at a midwestern university is quoted in Barbara L. Speicher and Seane M. McMahon, "Some African American Perspectives on Black English Vernacular," *Language in Society*, 21 (1992), pp. 383–407. Toni Morrison is quoted from p. 27 of Thomas LeClair, "A Conversation with Toni Morrison: 'The Language Must Not Sweat,'" *The New Republic*, March 21, 1981. The study by Jacquelyn Rahman is entitled "Black Attitudes to Black English, Standard and Vernacular" (manuscript, Department of Linguistics, Stanford University, 1999).

The quotations from Malcolm X, which appear in Mary Hoover's "Community Attitudes," cited above, are from *The Autobiography of Malcolm X* by Alex Haley (New York: Grove Press, 1965). The excerpt from Frederick Douglass's address is reprinted from Henry Louis Gates Jr. and Nellie Y. McKay, eds., *The Norton Anthology of African American Literature* (New York: W.W. Norton, 1997), p. 386.

Index

This index does not include material from the Notes section (pages 231–258).

Permissions